CINEMA STUDIES

Cinema Studies: The Key Concepts is essential reading for anyone interested in film. Providing accessible coverage of a comprehensive range of genres, movements, theories and production terms, this is a must-have guide to a fascinating area of study and arguably the greatest art form of modern times.

Now fully revised and updated for its fifth edition, the book includes entries on topics such as:

- Acting
- Audience
- CGI
- Convergence
- Cult cinema
- Digitization and globalization
- Distribution
- Experimental film
- Transnational cinema
- World Cinemas

Susan Hayward is Emeritus Professor of Cinema Studies at the University of Exeter. Her publications include *Luc Besson* (1998), *French National Cinema* (second edition, Routledge, 2005), *Simone Signoret: The Star as Cultural Sign* (2004), *Les Diaboliques* (2005), *Nikita* (2010) and *French Costume Drama of the 1950s: Fashioning Politics* (2010).

CINEMA STUDIES

The Key Concepts

Fifth Edition

Susan Hayward

Routledge
Taylor & Francis Group

LONDON AND NEW YORK

Fifth Edition published 2018
by Routledge
2 Park Square, Milton Park, Abingdon, Oxon OX14 4RN

and by Routledge
711 Third Avenue, New York, NY 10017

Routledge is an imprint of the Taylor & Francis Group, an informa business

First edition published 1996 by Routledge
Second edition published 2000 by Routledge
Third edition published 2006 by Routledge
Fourth edition published 2013 by Routledge

British Library Cataloguing-in-Publication Data
A catalogue record for this book is available from the British Library

Library of Congress Cataloging-in-Publication Data
Names: Hayward, Susan, 1945- author.
Title: Cinema studies : the key concepts / Susan Hayward.
Description: Fifth edition. | London ; New York : Routledge, 2017. | Includes bibliographical references and index.
Identifiers: LCCN 2017004206| ISBN 9781138665767 (hbk) | ISBN 9781138665774 (pbk) | ISBN 9781315619729 (ebk)
Subjects: LCSH: Motion pictures--Encyclopedias. | Cinematography--Encyclopedias.
Classification: LCC PN1993.45 .H36 2017 | DDC 791.4303--dc23
LC record available at https://lccn.loc.gov/2017004206

ISBN: 978-1-138-66576-7 (hbk)
ISBN: 978-1-138-66577-4 (pbk)
ISBN: 978-1-315-61972-9 (ebk)

Typeset in Bembo
by Taylor & Francis Books

For all students of cinema, past, present and future

CONTENTS

Preface, how to use the book and acknowledgements   viii
List of key concepts   x

THE KEY CONCEPTS   1

Bibliography   527
Index of films   564
Name index   580
Subject index   597

PREFACE, HOW TO USE THE BOOK AND ACKNOWLEDGEMENTS

Cinema Studies: The Key Concepts is an in-depth glossary which, it is hoped, will provide students and teachers of film studies and other persons interested in cinema with a useful reference book on key theoretical terms and, where appropriate, the various debates surrounding them. This glossary also gives historical overviews of key genres, film theory and film movements. Naturally, not 'everything' is covered by these entries that are based on my perception of students' needs when embarking on film studies. The intention is also to give teachers synopses for rapid reference purposes. Entries have been written as lucidly and as succinctly as possible, but doubtless there will be some 'dense' areas; I welcome feedback. My own students have been very helpful in this matter.

All cross-references are in bold. Sometimes the actual concept cross-referred may not be the precise form in the entry (for example, *ideological* in bold actually refers to an entry on ideology). Bibliographical citations at the end of certain entries refer to the bibliography at the end of the book. Wherever it is useful to explain the particular relevance or direction of a suggested text, this has been done.

Instead of a table of contents in traditional style, I have supplied a list of all concepts dealt with in this book. Where a particular concept is part of a larger one, the entry is cross-referenced to the main entry where it is discussed; thus '*jouissance*' is entered under the J entries but as a cross-reference to 'psychoanalysis' where it is explained. At the beginning or end of most entries there are signpostings suggesting that you consult other entries – I believe you will find this dipping across useful and that it will help widen the issue at hand.

On the occasion of preparing to revise this latest, fifth edition, I was asked by a couple of readers to provide a separate entry on **Film and Philosophy**, a fairly new trend in academic Film Studies programmes, if not in scholarly theorizing of film. In my view, Film and Philosophy, as a discipline, is rather an advanced practice in Film Studies programmes, appropriate for the most part to MA and PhD levels. And it is for this reason that there is not a separate entry in this volume.

Having said this, philosophy and film have always been co-present, at least since the 1950s (if not before). In the post-war period, Siegfried Kracauer of the Frankfurt School was one of the early thinkers to question film and representations of reality; questions of film and aesthetics were at the core of Rudolf Arnheim's writings; André Bazin of course is another pre-eminent thinker on 'What is cinema?' (with some phenomenological answers!). Coincidentally these authors are where I began my own training in Film Studies, way back in the early 1970s. Thus, I readily acknowledge that philosophical approaches have been incorporated into film theory (some in a lucid way) and that certain philosophers (e.g. Gilles Deleuze) have directly written about film. And so it is that, in this book, philosophical approaches are either touched upon, or referred to in a number of entries, or indeed given a full entry of their own (as in Deleuze's movement image/time image). And to help you navigate, here is a lexicon of the entries where philosophy is at work (either in a fulsome manner or as a gentle undercurrent):

- apparatus
- auteur theory
- deconstruction
- denotation/connotation
- feminist film theory
- film theory
- hegemony
- ideology
- modernism and postmodernism
- movement image/time image
- myth
- postcolonial theory
- psychoanalysis
- semiology/semiotics
- structuralism/post-structuralism
- subject/subjectivity
- voyeurism/fetishism

My thanks for the fifth edition go to my students, colleagues and to others who have communicated to me the usefulness of this book (and pointed out other areas to write about, and mistakes!). On the gritty issue of World Cinemas, my thanks to Gábor Gergely for his careful reading of the entries, and in terms of contents my especial thanks to Josh Gaunt whose depth of input is acknowledged in the separate entries. Finally, I wish to thank Andy Patch for his contributions to this fifth edition (on acting, digitization and globalization, distribution, East Asian Cinema, experimental cinema, and transnational cinema), it was a pleasure to work in such a collaborative fashion.

LIST OF KEY CONCEPTS

acting and performance 3
action movies 5
adaptation 12
agency 17
anamorphic lens 17
animation 18
apparatus 24
art cinema 27
art direction 29
aspect ratio 30
asynchronization/asynchronous
  sound 31
audience 31
auteur/auteur theory/*politique des
  auteurs/Cahiers du cinéma* 32
avant-garde 39

backstage musical *see* musical
Black cinema – UK 42
Black cinema, including
  Blaxploitation movies –
  USA 47
blockbusters 63
B-movies 68
body horror films *see* horror films
Bollywood 68
British New Wave 73
buddy films 75

Cahiers du cinéma group *see*
  auteur/auteur theory, French
  New Wave

cameraman *see* cinematographer
castration/decapitation *see*
  psychoanalysis
censorship 76
CGI 77
cinema nôvo 79
cinemascope 80
cinematographer/director of
  photography 82
cinéma-vérité/cinéma direct/direct
  cinema 82
class 83
classic canons *see* codes and
  conventions
classical Hollywood cinema/
  classical narrative cinema 88
codes and conventions/classic
  canons 91
colour 92
comedy 97
connotation *see* denotation/
  connotation
continuity editing *see*
  editing
convergence 98
costume dramas/heritage
  cinema/historical films 100
counter-cinema/oppositional
  cinema 101
crime thriller, criminal films *see*
  film noir, gangster films,
  thriller

cross-cutting 102
cult cinema 103
cut 103

day for night 106
decapitation *see* psychoanalysis
deconstruction 106
deep focus/depth of field 108
denotation/connotation 110
depth of field *see* deep focus
desire *see* fantasy, flashback narrative, spectator, stars, subjectivity
detective thriller *see* gangster films
diegesis/diegetic/non-diegetic/ extra- and intra-diegetic 111
digital cinema/post-digital cinema 113
digitization and globalization 117
direct cinema *see cinéma-vérité*
director 119
director of photography *see* cinematographer
discourse 120
disruption/resolution *see* classical narrative cinema
dissolve/lap-dissolve 121
distanciation 121
distribution 122
documentary 124
Dogme 95 manifesto/Dogme films 129
dollying shot *see* tracking shot
dominant/mainstream cinema 131

East Asian Cinema 131
editing/Soviet montage 134
epics 138

ethnographic film/gaze 141
European cinema/European film financing 142
experimental film 143
expressionism *see* German expressionism
exploitation movies 145
extra- and intra-diegetic *see* diegesis
eyeline matching 150

fade 150
fantasy/fantasy films 151
female masquerade 154
female spectator *see* spectator
feminist film theory 155
fetishism *see* film noir, voyeurism/ fetishism
film industry *see* Hollywood, studio system
film noir 167
film theory 172
flashback 177
Free Cinema (Britain) 178
French New Wave/*Nouvelle Vague* 181
French Poetic Realism 183

gangster films 185
gaze/look 188
gender 191
genre/sub-genre 197
German expressionism 204
Germany/New German cinema 210
Gothic horror *see* horror

Hammer Horror *see* horror
Hays code 215
hegemony 216
heritage cinema *see* costume drama

historical films/reconstructions
  see costume drama
Hollywood 216
Hollywood blacklist 217
Hollywood majors *see* classic
  Hollywood cinema, studio
  system
horror/Gothic horror/Hammer
  Horror/horror thriller/body
  horror/vampire movies 218

iconography 226
identification *see* distanciation,
  spectator-identification
identity *see* psychoanalysis,
  spectator-identification,
  subjectivity
ideology 227
Imaginary/Symbolic *see*
  psychoanalysis
independent American
  cinema 230
independent cinema 233
intertextuality 233
Italian neo-realism 234

jouissance see psychoanalysis
jump cut 236

lap-dissolve *see* dissolve
lighting 237
look *see* gaze/look, psychoanalysis,
  scopophilia, suture

mainstream cinema *see*
  dominant/mainstream cinema
match cutting *see* cut
melodrama and women's films
  243
method acting 254
mirror stage *see* psychoanalysis
mise-en-abîme 254

mise-en-scène 254
misrecognition *see* psychoanalysis,
  suture
modernism 255
montage *see* editing Soviet cinema
motivation 263
movement-image/time-image
  264
music 266
musical 269
myth 283

narrative/narration 284
naturalizing 288
neo-realism *see* Italian
  neo-realism
New German cinema *see*
  Germany/New German
  cinema
New Wave/*Nouvelle Vague see*
  French New Wave
non-diegetic *see* diegesis

Oedipal trajectory *see*
  psychoanalysis
180-degree rule 289
opposition *see* narrative,
  sequencing
oppositional cinema *see*
  counter-cinema

parallel sequencing *see* editing
patriarchy *see* psychoanalysis
performance *see* acting, star
  system
plot/story *see* classical
  Hollywood cinema, discourse,
  narrative/narration
politique des auteurs see auteur,
  French New Wave,
  mise-en-scène
pornography 289

post-digital cinema *see* digital
 cinema
postcolonial theory 293
postmodernism 300
post-structuralism *see*
 structuralism/post-structuralism
preferred reading 311
private-eye films *see* gangster
 films
producer 311
projection *see* apparatus,
 psychoanalysis
projector *see* apparatus
psychoanalysis 312
psychological thriller *see*
 thriller

Queer cinema 324
quota quickies 329

realism 331
reception theory *see* spectator
reconstructions *see* historical films
repetition/variation/opposition
 see narration, sequencing
representation *see* feminist film
 theory, gender, sexuality,
 subjectivity
resistances *see* avant-garde,
 counter-cinema
resolution *see* classical narrative
 cinema
reverse-angle shot *see* shot/
 reverse-angle shot
road movie 333
rules and rule-breaking *see*
 counter-cinema, jump cut

science-fiction films 333
scopophilia/scopic drive/visual
 pleasure 341
seamlessness *see* editing

semiology/semiotics/sign and
 signification 342
sequence/sequencing 345
setting 346
sexuality 346
shot/reverse-angle shot 350
shots 351
sign/signification *see* semiology/
 semiotics
social realism 354
sound/soundtrack 355
Soviet cinema/school 360
Soviet montage *see* editing
space and time/spatial and
 temporal contiguity 367
spectator/spectator-identification/
 female spectator 368
stars/star system/star as capital
 value/star as construct/star as
 deviant/star as cultural value:
 sign and fetish/stargazing and
 performance 373
structuralism/post-structuralism
 383
studio system 386
sub-genre *see* genre/sub-genre
subject/subjectivity 390
subjective camera 392
surrealism 393
suture 393

Third Cinema 394
30-degree rule 402
3-D cinema/stereoscopic
 imagery 402
thriller/psychological thriller
 404
time-image *see*
 movement-image
time and space *see* space and
 time/spatial and temporal
 contiguity

tracking shot/travelling shot/
    dollying shot 407
transitions *see* cut, dissolves, fade,
    jump cut, unmatched shots,
    wipe
transnational cinema 407
transparency/transparence 410
travelling shot *see* tracking
    shot

underground cinema
    410
unmatched shots 411

vampire movies *see* horror movies
variation *see* repetition
vertical integration 412

violence *see* censorship,
    voyeurism/fetishism
visual pleasure *see* scopophilia
voyeurism/fetishism
    412

war films 414
Westerns 430
widescreen 442
wipe 443
women's films *see* melodrama
    and women's films
World Cinemas/World
    Cinema/Third World
    Cinemas 443

zoom 526

CINEMA STUDIES

The Key Concepts

ACTING AND PERFORMANCE (SEE ALSO ENTRY ON STARS WHERE MANY OF THE POINTS RAISED HERE ARE DISCUSSED IN MORE DETAIL)

Naremore notes that acting 'in its simplest form' is 'nothing more than the transposition of everyday behaviour into a theatrical realm' (1988: 21). But, crucially, the **spectator** is aware that this 'everyday' is simultaneously both present and absent through what Naremore defines as the 'performance frame' (1988: 9). The frame implies the physical limits of film reality, one that demarcates the boundary between the **audience** and the world represented on the screen. As an effect, therefore, cinematic acting (at least in **mainstream cinema**) favours representational over presentational, because in real terms, we, the audience, cannot interact directly with the characters on-screen (the characters are present to us on-screen, but absent to us in that they are not physically present; the image merely represents the body).

Traditionally, film studies has focused on those ancillary components that overlay acting: **stardom, costume, lighting, gender** and **genre**. Routinely, analysis of acting is reduced to notions of believ-ability, realism and the merits of the performance within the reality on-screen. As McDonald asserts, 'judgments about "bad" acting are often formed on the basis that the performer was obviously acting and was therefore unbelievable' (1998: 33). The impact of an actor's per-formance is also affected by the extent to which the actor is fore-grounded (King, 1985: 41). King further considers how an actor, when required to undergo significant transformation for a role, incorporates that of 'impersonation' acting. The actor embodies the character s/he is playing; noted actors who do this are Meryl Streep, Robert De Niro, Al Pacino (even though they never fully disappear within the character). However, those actors whose roles across a series of films are perceived as them performing to 'be themselves' are described by King as 'personification' (1987: 157). Actors in this category who jump to mind include John Wayne, Sylvester Stallone (we know what to expect). King ventures that with a star body the two categories often intersect, a combination that allows us to consider the reality on-screen. As Geraghty argues, the star body needs to discard 'the celebrity trappings' that surrounds it if the 'performance is to be understood' (2000: 192). The actorial embodiment is always poised between the real and unreal, and we know that we are watching a performance because there is always already a gap, however small or large, between imperso-nation and star, or personification and star, between actor and character (for more details on all these points see **Star** entry).

It is important to note that this question of realism is primarily located around **narrative** cinema. Conversely, **Counter-cinema** and non-mainstream films incorporate acting strategies within which the actor deliberately sets out to signify their distance from a character (Higson, 1986). For example, when Godard in *À bout de souffle* (1960) deliberately undermines the casts' 'reality' on-screen by combining, actors, extras and 'non'-acting pedestrians on the Champs-Elysées, and by having characters speak out to the spectator.

A further aspect of narrative cinema is the reinforcement of the notion of performance as continuous. The reality of production is that a performance consists of fragments, a series of 'takes' (of a particular scene), but also, because of logistical necessity, it is mostly a shooting schedule that is out of **sequence** with the actual final narrative that we see on-screen. **Editing** therefore brings together these fragments, creating a sense of continuity, negating the reality of spatial and temporal constraints. As King notes, this fragmentation has led to film acting 'prioritizing a short arc of character representation with an emphasis on moments or epitomizing scenes' (1985: 250). From this production process, we can see how the on-screen actor is a product of various collaborative pressures: camera angles, movement, lighting, editing, **soundtrack**, that accentuate both the actor's body and voice, and draw the spectator to a **preferred reading** of that performance. Also belying this idea of performance as continuous and homogeneous is the fact that, as Maltby points out, the 'constructed nature of a movie emphasizes the extent to which a movie performance is not only the work of the actor.' For example, 'several different bodies may be used to construct a single performance: voices are dubbed, stunt-artists are used for dangerous action sequences, and sometimes hand models and body doubles provide body parts to substitute for the actors' (2003: 371). Whose performance are we observing, therefore?

Acting is as much a product of process as embodiment (personification or impersonation). It incorporates not only the star body, and the surrounding **mythology**, and anticipated gesturality of that star (for example, Chaplin's walk or Nicholson's manic smile), but also the tensions and demands of the creative process for the film production (the numerous takes of a single scene being a prime example). This process is then in turn exhibited on-screen, but edited in such a manner as to hide the flaws and the inconsistencies.

Rozik argues that 'in enacting an action, actors produce a set of signs and sentences, mainly iconic, by imprinting them on their own bodies' (2002: 111). Various approaches have been undertaken to interpret such signs; for example, histrionic versus verisimiliar (Pearson, 1992); integrated versus autonomous (Maltby, 2003); or presentational versus representational (Naremore, 1988). However, Rozik offers a differing model in terms of theatrical acting, arguing that 'instead of the usual dyadic model of actor and character, a triadic model is more appropriate: actor (who produces the signs), text (the set of images inscribed on his [*sic*] body) and character (who exists only in the imagination of the spectator)' (2002: 113). In this model, the actor becomes a bearer of signs, a system of signification on three levels. First, the actor produces **signs** (performing as another, using techniques such as voice, gesture and posture, alongside external influences such as lighting, costume and make-up) which displace or deflect our identification with their star persona. Second, the text is embodied by the actor's performance (so both text and actor, in symbiosis, construct a performance). Third, the spectator also constructs a reading of the composite body (actor, text, performance) to create a third level of meaning with regard to the performance, which in turn is influenced by the style of acting (**method**, for example) and our identification with the traits and expected behaviour of the star body on-screen (for further discussion of these concepts see **Star** entry).

ACTION MOVIES

Action movie is a rather broad and all-encompassing term for a type of film that, generally speaking, will cost a great deal of money to produce, and whose primary aim is to offer the spectator an endless rollercoaster of violent, action-packed images. It is not a genre but a type of film with a look that relies heavily on visual effects to thrill its audiences. Action movies have at their core fast action-packed fight scenes, chase and escape routines. Any top ten list of the 'best-ever' action movies will count amongst its favourites, **science-fiction**, spy thrillers, **fantasy** films, disaster and martial arts movies. As Marshall Julius (1996: 5) puts it so well, action films are 'vengeful cops and car chases, lunatic villains and martial arts masters, male-bonding, gun fights and super secret agents, swords and sorcerers, wartime Nazi-bashing, boys' own adventures, casual destruction and general death-defiance'. In a word, the motivation behind action films is pure escapism. 'Forget the plot ... focus on the mayhem' (1996: 13). Shoot-outs, car chases and crashes galore pack fast-action thrillers; climaxes of fireball explosions and destroyed buildings (even worlds) are the very essence of science-fiction films, disaster and hijack movies;

explosive conventions of all sorts, flying bodies, tanks and planes on fire, torpedo point-of-view shots are all the familiar grist of **war films**. What a feast for the eyes! We thrive on the vicarious fear; enjoy being physically stimulated. Why else would we enjoy a paranoid terrorist action movie such as *Rock* (Michael Bay, 1996) with its threat of spreading the lethal Sarin nerve gas? As King argues (2000: 103), any sense of guilty pleasure we derive from the thrill of it all is compensated for by the fact that we go to these films to escape everyday ordinariness and, moreover, to experience plenitude as a way of making up for the scarcity in our own lives.

Although the action movie is primarily identified with Hollywood, it is worth making a couple of important points in this context. First, that the *nec plus ultra* of the action movie, the Bond movie, is first and foremost a British product (with seventeen Bond movies carrying the GB label from the early 1960s until the early 1990s – albeit with considerable financing from the American producer Albert 'Cubby' Broccoli and, later, his wife Barbara). Bond movies – with their awesome sets by Ken Adam, breathtaking stunts, lavish visuals, extravagant fantasy, to say nothing of Bond's gadgets doing battle against the monster machines of the evil enemy – bespeak an almost overzealous love-affair with technology and design. Indeed, we are invited to sit back and admire the spectacle 'based on lavish plenitude' (King, 2000: 96). Each Bond movie boasts bigger production values than the previous one. As such, the Bond movie has set the tone for many of the subsequent action series or action franchise movies as they are also known (for example, the *Rambos*, begun 1982; *Die Hards*, begun 1987; or the *Lethal Weapons*, begun 1988 – three of the biggest grossing of Hollywood's action spectacular series). However, whereas with Bond we are allowed to get the full picture-show of the action in a big frame (almost in the Bazinian sense of deep focus **editing**), including the special futuristic design of the sets and exotic spaces visited by Bond, the newer action spectaculars offer us a curtailed sense of space in that they are full of rapid editing and discontinuity (a sort of **montage**-style but without the montage-effect). There is an 'unremitting battery of impact effects' (2000: 96). In the end, the speedy cross-cutting editing can destroy any sense of reality because, literally, we get lost. The frenetic editing in the shoot-out in the Korean nightclub in *Collateral* (Michael Mann, 2004) is a good example of this, but so too are the battle scenes in *Troy* (Wolfgang Petersen, 2004) and *King Arthur* (Antoine Fuqua, 2004).

The second important point worth making is that the martial arts action films from Hong Kong, China, Japan, Taiwan and South Korea constitute a very important part of the action-movie heritage – dating back as it does to the early 1970s (if not before; Hong Kong produced quite a number in the 1960s), with the Hong Kong movies by Lo Wei (*The Big Boss*, 1971; *Fist of Fury*, 1972, starring Bruce Lee); followed by Jackie Chan's *Police Story* series (begun 1985) in which Chan also starred; and John Woo's films of the mid-1980s (*A Better Tomorrow*, 1980, starring the Chinese actor Chow Yun-Fat, and one of Hong Kong's top-grossing films ever). Interestingly, there has been a similar shift in film aesthetics to the one described above. According to King (2000: 97), whereas earlier films (of the 1970s and 1980s) favoured the single-shot perspective of a fight sequence allowing us to see the 'real capabilities of the star Bruce Lee' (see *The Big Boss*), now these martial arts/action films have come to rely increasingly on a 'panoply of montage effects'. The integrity of performance shooting (in the dual sense of the word: the wholeness and authenticity of the performance) has been replaced in some instances by the flashing tempo of hyper-violence (as in *Full Contact*, Ringo Lam, 1992, or *Bangkok Dangerous*, Pang brothers, 2001). Alternatively, the special effects of wire-fu action have moved martial arts films into a new realm of the fantastic (see *Crouching Tiger, Hidden Dragon*, Ang Lee, 2000; *Hero*, Zhang Yimou, 2002). Not all films have succumbed to this speed or fantasy effect. Takeshi Kitano has taken this genre somewhere else in his almost poetic rendition of the action thriller (see *Sonatine* 1993).

More recently, South Korea, since the end of dictatorship and the lifting of censorship in 1992, is making it big in the action-movie arena with filmmakers such as Lee Chang-Dong (*Peppermint Candy*, 2000) and Park Chan-Wook (*Old Boy*, 2004, a hyper-violent film about the metaphysics of revenge). This is one of the few countries where indigenous action movies outsell Hollywood products; Hong Kong being another example. Small wonder that Hollywood has stepped in and succeeded in tempting a handful of filmmakers from the East to cross over to the USA by offering them conditions where the industry is more stable and better able to finance big action projects (see especially Hong Kong filmmaker John Woo, for *Face/Off*, 1997; *Mission Impossible II*, 2000). As an interesting side-note, three years after the transfer of Hong Kong's sovereignty to China, co-productions between these two countries began (averaging three films per year to date). Clearly the culture-clash of two entirely distinct governing and economic systems was able to find some resolution, at least within the film industry.

Action movies are not new to Hollywood and can be dated back to as early as the 1930s, at least, and the swashbuckler film, with

Douglas Fairbanks Junior and Errol Flynn being some of the first action heroes as they fought their way out of numerous tight spots. But, even then, studio rivalries ran high, as Hollywood action movies fought to get the punters in. Two Warner Brothers productions starring Errol Flynn, *Captain Blood* (Michael Curtiz, 1935) and *The Adventures of Robin Hood* (Curtiz, 1938), were made as a deliberate ploy to challenge *the* studio major with a reputation for hugely lavish products, MGM (e.g. *Mutiny on the Bounty*, Frank Lloyd, 1935, starring Clark Gable opposite Charles Laughton). Since then this category of movie has moved on technologically and, moreover, come to embrace a broad set of genres – **thrillers**, science-fiction and war films being but the most common. By the 1970s, the levels of violence and destruction on-screen had escalated massively. Lightweight cameras and new special-effects systems were part of the equation. But so too, arguably, were the effects that war technology – as used in the Vietnam war – was having on the Americans in general and film audiences in particular. That war, as indeed subsequent wars (such as the Gulf/Iraq wars), demonstrated that there were seemingly no limits to which war technology could go to root out its enemy (napalm, smart bombs, drones and so on). So, too, it seemed as if there was literally no possible end to the types of explosions that could be created in the cinema world, especially with **digital** technology increasingly entering the frame of action fantasy (see also **CGI**).

Speaking of war and reality, post-11 September 2001 (9/11) one could have expected a crisis in representation where action movies were concerned. Indeed, the spate of epic movies in its aftermath (such as *Troy*) signified a displacement of the action thriller into safer long-ago times, where good and evil can fight it out more clearly. Thus, for a very brief while the terrorist and disaster movie did disappear from American cinema. But not for long. After all, they bring in millions of dollars. And just as a sign of the way in which discourses and technologies of war cross boundaries with ease, let us consider the Arnold Schwarzenegger vehicle *Collateral Damage* (Andrew Davis, 2001). This film was due to come out in October 2001 but was withheld post-9/11 because it was felt it ran too close to reality. It was finally released in 2002. In it, Schwarzenegger plays a firefighter. In the aftermath of 9/11, firefighters had reached an iconic status of courage and bravery, so Schwarzenegger's association with this function would, it was feared, be read as exploitative. This was a first reason to hold back. A second reason was the narrative line: a terrorist bombing. In blowing up the local Colombian consulate, a Colombian terrorist also blows up Schwarzenegger's family and this drives him to attempt to exact revenge. Later, the terrorist tells Schwarzenegger these deaths were collateral damage. No wonder Schwarzenegger is outraged. However, we should pause here. Terrorist bombing and the fact that it causes collateral damage – which here is represented as a very evil thing – should not hide the fact that this term was first coined by the Americans when bombing Baghdad in the first Gulf War in 1991. At that time smart bombs (so-called because they could hit their target and send video proof of this from a camera positioned in the bomb's cone) caused thousands of civilian deaths. In the American case, collateral damage was an inevitability of war; in the case of Schwarzenegger's family, it is the outcome of the actions of an evil and unprincipled terrorist. Despite the similarities with 9/11 and despite a disturbing re-appropriation of war discourses, nonetheless, the film was a success and brought Schwarzenegger back into favour once more as an action hero. In terms of US dominant ideology, this film struck the right note.

In this light of an appropriate post-9/11 tone, the *Bourne* trilogy (2002–2007, starring Matt Damon) adds an interesting dimension. In these three films (*Bourne Identity*, *Bourne Supremacy*, *Bourne Ultimatum*), Bourne, a CIA paramilitary operative and assassin, fails in his mission, suffers a loss of memory, and fights his way out of various agencies' (CIA and Russian FSB) attempts to kill him (he is almost machinic in his abilities) as he tries to establish his true identity. The point, ultimately, is that he is the good guy, although he commits a number of murders and evil acts – much in line with a philosophy (so prevalent under Bush Jnr) that the end justifies the means (as in the fiction surrounding the Weapons of Mass Destruction which allowed Bush to go to war with Iraq).

It is not easy to talk of **codes and conventions** where action movies are concerned. What we can say is that narrative coherence is not an uppermost concern, but that excess is key and there is a great deal of 'male swagger' about (Jones, 2001: 28). Flag-waving can be part of this excess (in war and sci-fi movies especially). Explosions abound as the action hero more often than not stands poised between danger and the dark abyss of annihilation, except that, whatever the threat, death is defied by the hero – no matter how implausible that may be. Perhaps that *is* the only convention, with the cruel exception of Brandon Lee who was shot in the making of *The Crow* (Alex Proyas, 1994) – although digital effects were used to 'bring him back to life' and complete the film. Spatial and temporal incoherence are also a big part of this action cinema. The audience is engulfed in a flurry of images and sounds, and yet – paradoxically – has no sense of direction.

The camera zooms around, fireballs come rushing out filling the screen, and deafening noises come from every which way. With recent developments in **3-D**, action movies bring even more terror and thrills for the spectator to experience (presently 3-D seems to be more oriented towards fantasy films and science-fiction – as with the famous example of James Cameron's epic sci-fi *Avatar*, 2009; or the less successful fantasy film *Clash of the Titans*, Louis Leterrier, 2010).

With the action movie the spectators remain disoriented. They never feel time or space passing as they hurtle from one action to the next. So, ultimately, there is neither spatial nor temporal freedom for us to know where we are or where we might be going. As Kent Jones (2001: 27) states, in his very good study of Michael Bay's films (*Armageddon*, 1998, and *Pearl Harbor*, 2001), despite the fact that these $100 million-plus film extravaganzas are supposedly about speed, bizarrely they are the very opposite of fast and far more about 'hallucinatory confusion and stasis'. In order to feel the speed, he argues, 'you need to know where you are going'. And even if there is no real sense of spatial and temporal dislocation, nonetheless, often there still can be a feeling of stasis. Take, as another example, Michael Mann's *Collateral* where, although the director gives us a sense of a certain Los Angeles, it is a very selective and moody sense of this city, shot as it is by night and in a specific set of districts. We either know these areas or we don't. What we are mostly left with is, first, a dark impenetrable city which we scoot around at speed in a beaten-up taxi; second, a series of violent shoot-outs which are little more than a set of assemblages from Mann's earlier films (furthermore, the film is full of all the old clichés of a hit-man movie); and, finally, even more dispiriting, silly attempts at humour.

Let us pause on 'male swagger' for a moment. For, in this context, our action hero embodies the tradition of its earliest, courtly meaning whereby it referred to the swank of knights and nobles who would carry this swagger into battle (jousting, swordsmanship, etc.). For some of our modern action heroes the swagger begins in the verbal and ends in supremely cool action. Sean Connery as Bond is exemplary. Clint Eastwood, although he is nearly non-verbal, also comes into this category. We are not too perturbed by Connery's violence because the aesthetic value of Ken Adam's fantasy sets and the exotic settings, in which much of the action is located, function in their coolness as perfect foils to Bond's swagger – and the overall effect is hyper-real. Conversely, Eastwood's violence can be very disconcerting because it emanates from such a plausible space. Other heroes can only swank physically – and so are less cool. Charles

Bronson of earlier action-movie years (the *Death Wish* series, begun 1974) comes to mind. In the 1980s to 1990s, Claude Van Damme, Sylvester Stallone and Arnold Schwarzenegger are at one extreme of the swaggering hulk, whereas Mel Gibson (*Lethal Weapon* series) and Bruce Willis (*Die Hard* series), with their lighter frames, are at the other end (and have a few more amusing one-liners to offer). Tom Cruise – who noteworthily does most of his own stunts – and Harrison Ford (*Indiana Jones* series) fall somewhere between the two sets of male swagger. They have the physical strength and display it, but there is that added element that theirs is also a cerebral swagger (as distinct from the wit of Connery and silence of Eastwood). African-American action heroes are also in the frame, especially since the **Blaxploitation** cinema of the 1970s. Wesley Snipes (though by no means confined to this type of film) is a major name (see *New Jack City*, Mario Van Peebles, 1991; *Demolition Man*, Marco Brambilla, 1993; *Drop Zone*, John Badham, 1994); Mario Van Peebles has starred in several (*Posse*, Van Peebles, 1993); and Denzel Washington has also put in a performance or two (*Ricochet*, Russell Mulcahy, 1991). Often, however, the African-American is less the action hero and more the side-kick to the front-running (White) action hero – see, for example, Danny Glover in the *Lethal Weapon* series where he is paired with Mel Gibson. Gibson is the all-risk-taking cop to Glover's more ponderous and careful type. In this role as side-kick, the African-American is contained as safe. By dint of being the voice of reason, he is unlikely to go on the rampage. Casting, then, is a code to watch for when studying these films.

Although action movies are clearly an intensely male category of film, nonetheless, they have spawned a few female action heroes – and they deserve a mention here. Perhaps the only female action hero to become a star is Sigourney Weaver with her *Alien* series (begun 1986). She is the one who daringly stripped off her femininity and allowed a wiry 'musculinity' to emerge in its place. She embodies a certain kind of machisma that few other female action heroes have dared to personify. Nor is this a simple representation, since she also comes to have a very complex relationship with motherhood and reproduction – as one capable of spawning 'monsters'. Other types, however, tend to be both strong and very eroticized (through having big breasts for example). The girlie-women in *Charlie's Angels* (McG, 2000 and 2003) are but one instance of this endeavour to contain the threat of a 'musculinized' female body. Or, the female action-hero's dress-coding can mark her out in a different way as an identifiably safe and fetishized body, such as the dominatrix clothing sported by

Pamela Anderson in *Barb Wire* (David Hogan, 1996). One final type is the completely androgenized body – less common in American films, arguably – as found in Luc Besson's *Nikita* (1990) or the cross-over film *Lara Croft: Tomb Raider* (Simon West, 2001).

see also: **blockbusters, fantasy films, science-fiction**

For further reading see Julius, 1996; King, 2000; Lichtenfeld, 2007; Stringer, 2003; on martial arts films see Meyers, 2001.

ADAPTATION

Literary adaptation to film is a long-established tradition in cinema starting, for example, with early cinema adaptations of the Bible (e.g. the Lumière brothers' thirteen-scene production of *La Vie et passion de Jésus Christ*, 1897, and Alice Guy's *La Vie de Christ*, 1899). By the 1910s, adaptations of the established literary canon had become a marketing ploy by which producers and exhibitors could legitimize cinema-going as a venue of 'taste' and thus attract the middle classes to their theatres. Literary adaptations gave cinema the respectable cachet of entertainment-as-art. In a related way, it is noteworthy that literary adaptations have consistently been seen to have pedagogical value, that is, teaching a nation (through cinema) about its classics, its literary heritage. Note how, in the UK, the BBC releases a film, made for screen and subsequently television viewing, and then issues a teaching package (DVD plus a teacher–student textbook). The choice of novels adapted has to some extent, therefore, to be seen in the light of nationalistic 'value'.

A literary adaptation creates a new story; it is not the same as the original, but takes on a new life, as indeed do the characters. **Narrative** and characters become independent of the original even though both are based – in terms of genesis – on the original. The adaptation can create stars (in the UK context, Colin Firth, *Pride and Prejudice*, 1995; Ewan McGregor and Robert Carlyle, *Trainspotting*, 1995), or stars become associated with that 'type' of role (Emma Thompson, Helena Bonham-Carter, Nicole Kidman, Holly Hunter), whereas the novel creates above all characters we remember and associate with a particular type of behaviour (e.g. Mrs Bennet, Darcy in *Pride and Prejudice*). As André Bazin says (1967: 56), film characterization creates a whole new mythology existing outside the original text.

Essentially there appear to be three types of literary adaptation: first, the more traditionally connoted notion of adaptation, the literary classic; second, adaptations of plays to screen; and, finally, the adaptation of contemporary texts, not yet determined as classics and possibly bound to remain within the canon of popular fiction. Of these three, arguably, it is the second that remains most faithful to the original, although contextually it may be updated into contemporary times, as with several Shakespeare adaptations (e.g. Baz Luhrmann's *Romeo and Juliet*, 1996, which is recast into contemporary Los Angeles). The focus of this entry is primarily on the first type of adaptation, although mention will be made of the third type.

Literary adaptations are, within the Western context, perceived as mostly a European product – almost as if Europe has the established literary canon and northern America has not. It should be pointed out, however, that, while this European **heritage cinema** is the one that predominates and while it represents a deliberate marketing ploy for exports (Europe *sells* its culture to the rest of the world), the United States does have its own literary classics that get adapted – the novels and short stories of Henry James and those of Edith Wharton spring to mind (e.g. *Portrait of a Lady*, Jane Campion, 1996; *The Age of Innocence*, Martin Scorsese, 1993). Jack Clayton's 1974 version of Scott Fitzgerald's *The Great Gatsby* is arguably *the* benchmark movie of lavish literary adaptation Hollywood-style. Modern classics, written by African-American novelists, also rank quite highly (e.g. Alice Walker's *The Color Purple*, Steven Spielberg, 1985, and Toni Morrison's *Beloved*, Jonathan Demme, 1998). Otherwise, Hollywood is more commonly associated with popular fiction adaptations (especially detective fiction).

In relation to other generic types, critical literature on literary adaptations is somewhat thin. There appears to have been a surge of interest during the 1970s (Bluestone, 1971; Marcus, 1971; Wagner, 1975; Horton and Magretta, 1981); then again in the mid-1980s to the 1990s (Morrissette, 1985; Friedman, 1993; Marcus, 1993; McFarlane, 1996; Griffith, 1997); finally, more recently in the new millennium (Geraghty, 2008; Hutcheon, 2006; Lupack, 2002; Stam, 2005). While literary adaptations have not attracted as much analytical attention in the field of film studies as other areas, one could speculate that the first manifestation of critical writing, in the 1970s, is linked to the introduction of film courses into English and foreign languages departments. The fact that the focus of these studies was on questions of fidelity to the original text would tend to support this argument. Furthermore, this interest in literary adaptations could be read as a reaction to the more difficult branch of film theory being practised at that time, namely **structuralism** and, a bit later, **post-structuralism**. The 1990s period of interest appears to correspond to a time when literary adaptations were at their most popular on-screen (particularly in Britain and France). And the most recent spate is broader in its approach, ranging from adaptation theory (Hutcheon and Stam), to recent Hollywood and British successes (Geraghty), to African-American adaptations (Lupack).

Fidelity criticism, which makes up a great deal of literary adaptation criticism (particularly of the 1970s, but still ongoing), focuses on the notion of equivalence. This is a fairly limited approach, however, since it fails to take into account other levels of meaning. Conversely, some studies (Andrew, 1984; Marcus, 1993) have stressed the importance of examining the value of the alterations from text to text. For example, films are more marked by economic considerations than the novel and this constitutes a major reason why the adaptation is not like the novel. Furthermore, it is clear that the choice of **stars** will impact on the way the original text is interpreted; adaptations will cut sections of the novel that are deemed uncinematographic or of no interest to the viewers. In other words, there is always a **motivation** behind the choices made. Marcus (1993) and Monk (1996: 50–51) have pointed to the need for a third-level criticism; that is, to see the adaptation within an historical and semiotic context. Thus, it is not sufficient to show, through fidelity criticism, the difference between the texts, nor does it suffice to do a textual analysis based on a demonstration of how the film renders (or not) the language and style of the original through **mise-en-scène**, **editing** techniques, the symbolic use of images and, finally, the **soundtrack** and **music**. We need to understand the meaning of these differences within a socio-political, economic and historical context. We need to understand the **signs** of difference. Adaptations are a synergy between the desire for sameness and reproduction, on the one hand, and, on the other, the acknowledgement of difference. To a degree, they are based on elision and deliberate lack and at the same time in the privileging, even to excess, of certain **narrative** elements or strategies over others.

Film adaptations are both more and less than the original. More, not just because they are in excess of the written word (through having both image and sound). But, more also, because they are a **mise-en-abîme** of authorial texts and therefore of productions of meaning. To explain: there is the original text (T^1), the adapted text (T^2), the film text (T^3), the director texts (T^{4n}), the star texts (T^{5n}), the production (con)texts (T^{6n}) and finally the various texts' own intertexts (T^{7n}). Such a chain of signifiers makes it clear that the notion of authorship becomes very dispersed. Thus, quite evidentially, the film is less, because the original author is only one among many (we hear complaints from the **audience:** 'it's not what the author wrote'). But, it is also more because of the density of new texts (and textual meanings, purposes and motivations) clustered around the original (again audiences complain: 'it's not at all like the book').

Audiences might complain. And, yet, they go in their droves to see the classics on-screen. Higson (1993: 120) is right to say that the replaying or downplaying of the original material is at least matched, if not superseded, by the 'pleasures of pictorialism'. Our pleasure is deeper than our pained expressions at the end of the film. Strong (1999: 61) usefully invokes the term *neutering*. Although he uses it in a somewhat more specific context – namely, when the adaptive process alters the original's rendering of their own time – essentially this effect of neutering and appropriation of a text is a basic practice of adaptation. To a greater or lesser degree, the adaptation neuters the original interest (or a part of the novelist's intention), thereby appropriating it so that it makes sense within the present context (e.g. Emma Thompson's script for Ang Lee's *Sense and Sensibility*, 1995, provides a feminist re-inscription of the original Austen novel).

Classic adaptations are less than transparent. They materialize the novel into something else and the result is a hybrid affair, a mixture of **genres**. More crucially, a temporal sleight of hand occurs and, thus, intention. By way of illustration of this point, let's take the Austen, Forster and Pagnol novels and their subsequent adaptations. These novels were modern texts of their day and set in their time, yet they were also deeply nostalgic for a lost time in the past (be it for social, economic values or traditions). A major motivation of the narrative, then, is a nostalgia for what is no more. A sense of lack, of loss is redolent within the novel. Over time, however, these once modern texts become classic texts entering the literary canon. By the time they get to the stage of film adaptation, they are no longer of the present time and so become transformed into what we know as **costume** or **heritage** films. What was present is now of the past. A further shift occurs, however, in our reception of the film. It is nostalgic pleasure we are after, not understanding. Thus our focus shifts from a desire to *know* the times the novel is referring to (in socio-economic or political terms), to a desire to *see* the times (in terms of costume and décor). Thus the earlier intention of the narrative – a nostalgia for a past – is neutered. What drives us, the audience, is a nostalgia for the present times of the novel, the lived moment of Austen's heroines, or Pagnol's and Forster's characters – our imagined past, not that of the original text for which that present time represents unwanted change. Both the novel and the film are looking backwards nostalgically, but not at the same past.

Production values tend to match the perceived value of the original text. Thus, literary classics have high production values and the aim is for an authentic re-creation of the past through appropriate **setting**, quality mise-en-scène, minute attention to décor and costume, and for star vehicles to embody the main roles. Audience expectation is such, that demand for authenticity and taste is carefully respected. Conversely, popular-fiction adaptations make no such demands of taste. Sets can be flimsy, actors unknown; the whole purpose here is for cost-effectiveness. A small budget therefore means low production values. It does not necessarily mean, however, a loss of value. Indeed, many of the 1930s and 1940s Hollywood **B-movies** have gained such value that they have entered the Western cinematic canon. Nor have contemporary literary adaptations, while inexpensively produced, been without impact in the evolution of film history. The **British New Wave** of the 1960s, for example, relied heavily on contemporary texts for their source of inspiration and produced a grainy socio-realism (closely aligned with kitchen-sink drama) which mainly focused on the socio-economic crises of young working-class males. The so-called New Scottish cinema also draws on modern literary sources and provides low-budget movies with a raw realism of economic deprivation that mostly, but not exclusively, concerns the young male in crisis and the drug culture of Scottish urban youth (particularly male youth). The adaptation of Irvine Welsh's novel *Trainspotting* (Danny Boyle, 1996) is the benchmark movie in this context (see Petrie, 2005).

Modern adaptations of contemporary novels have national value to the degree that they tell us something of the current political culture that surrounds us; the adaptation of classics has nationalistic value in that they mirror a desire to be identified with values of tradition, culture and taste to which certain elites, especially political elites, and generations aspire. They only refer indirectly to the current socio-political or cultural climate. But it is often possible to uncover traces of the present, nonetheless. As Strong (1999: 286–91) points out, the gay subtext of Forster's *Room with a View* (James Ivory, 1980) comes seeping through even if it does not threaten or challenge the particularly homophobic political culture and legislation of the Thatcher government in Britain at that time. Strong (1999: 63) makes a particularly interesting point about the distinction between contemporary and classical adaptations – one that comes down to gender. Classic literary adaptations with their almost obsessive focus on detail – an effect of miniaturizing – lead to an increased feminization of the original text. If we take this idea further, it is as if the film clothes its male protagonists in such a way as to make them safe, contain them as an ideal male who mirrors in the fanciness and detail of his own costume that of his female counterpart. We may forget the very real power wielded by men as we stand in awe of their prettiness. Viewed in this light, this feminization comes to represent a containment and displacement of our contemporary myth of sexual equality and even unisexuality. The contemporary adaptations such as those of the British New Wave, argues Strong (1999: 62), and to which we could add the Scottish New Wave, are ones that masculinize the original text in their over-investment in the individual youthful male protagonist. These films, that focus on the male, represent him as unruly, potentially threatening, powerful, wild. But given the process of masculinization inscribed into the filmic text, the vicious twist at the end, that he is doomed to fail, die or remain the same, should give us pause for thought.

For background reading on early (1970s–1980s) trends, read texts cited above. But for more recent writing see: Barefoot, 2001; Geraghty, 2008; Hutcheon, 2006; Cartmell and Whelehan, 1999; Lupack, 2002; Marcus, 1993; Monk, 1996; Petrie, 2005; Stam, 2005; Strong, 1999; Washburn, 2001; Wilson, 2002.

AGENCY

Refers essentially to issues of control and operates both within and outside the film. Within the film, agency is often applied to a character in relation to desire. If that character has agency over desire, it means that s/he (though predominantly in **classical narrative cinema** it is he) is able to act upon that desire and fulfil it (a classic example is: boy meets girl, boy wants girl, boy gets girl). Agency also functions at the level of the **narrative** inside and outside the film. Whose narration is it? A character in the film? A character outside the film? The director's? And finally, agency also applies to the **spectator**. In viewing the film, the spectator has agency over the text in that s/he produces a meaning and a reading of the filmic text.

see also: **subjectivity**

ANAMORPHIC LENS

A French invention devised by Henri Chrétien for military use during World War One, this is a wide-angle lens that permits 180-degree vision (see **180-degree rule**). It was not introduced into cinema until 1928 when it was used experimentally by the French filmmaker Claude Autant-Lara. Characteristically, the French film industry did not invest in this new technology, which could have done much to aid its ailing fortunes, and it was the United States which bought the rights to the system in 1952. The following year Fox **studios** was the first to release what was termed a **cinemascope** film, *The Robe* (Henry Koster). The widescreen effect of cinemascope is achieved by a twofold process using the anamorphic lens. First, the lens on the camera squeezes the width of the image down to half its size so that it will fit onto the existing width of the film (traditionally 35mm). Then the film is projected through a projector supplied with an anamorphic lens which produces a widescreen effect with an **aspect ratio** of 2.35:1. Without the anamorphic lens on the projector, the image would be virtually square and its contents hugely distorted – horizontally squashed and vertically stretched as if caught in a concave mirror. The wide-angle effect is now more usually accomplished without the anamorphic lens, through the use of the wide-gauge 70mm film or by printing 35mm onto 70mm film for special releases. And, of course, now that the digital camera is widely in operation, all that is required is a mere flick of the switch to shift from the standard 4:3 to 16:9 widescreen shooting format.

see also: **aspect ratio, cinemascope, widescreen**

For further details see Belton, 1992; Belton, Hall and Neale, 2010.

ANIMATION

Animation is used in cartoons and now also in live-action films. *Cartoons* is the term generally used to describe short animated films, as distinct from the term *animated* or 'animation films' for full-length features. Traditionally, animation has been achieved by shooting inanimate objects, such as drawings, clay or plasticene models, frame by frame in stop-motion photography. In succeeding frames, the object has very slightly shifted positions so that when the stop-motion photos are run at standard speed (twenty-four frames per second), the object seems to move. John Hart (1999: 3) gives a very useful thumbnail sketch of the essential ingredients needed for animation. In cartoons, he explains, artists must make dynamic use of space, compositional devices and colour. They must also use fore, middle and background effectively. Traditionally the main narrative action revolves around the principle of conflict which is mirrored by visual conflict on three levels within the image: size (large and small characters), strong verticals against horizontals, and colours (red against green).

Animation dates back to the early days of cinema. It first appeared in the form of a special effects insert into a live-action film with Georges Méliès' animation of the moon – which he achieved through stop-motion and trick photography – in *Voyage à la lune* (1902). The Frenchman Émile Cohl is credited with having brought the comic strip to film. Unlike printed comic strips, however, he used line drawings, creating stick figures among other objects. His first product *Fantasmagorie* (1908) was a huge success even though it was a spectacle-effects film (to use Richard Abel's term, 1994: 286) and not strictly a narrative text. The film was a series of illogical but seamless transformations of the line drawings (an elephant turning into a house, for example). Cohl's line drawing technique was imitated and adapted by the American Winsor McCay, who was himself originally a comic-strip artist. McCay introduced personality or character-animation through his anthropomorphization of animals. Thus, in 1914, he produced the first animated cartoon, *Gertie the Dinosaur*. In this vein of anthropomorphic stars, Otto Messmer's famous *Felix the Cat* – first conceived of in 1915 – eventually became a series (starting in 1920).

Walt Disney Productions (founded in 1923) continued with this popular tradition of anthropomorphization, providing even greater **realism** to the animated creatures. In 1928, Disney produced the first synch-sound cartoon (*Steamboat Willie*, featuring Mickey Mouse). Disney is also credited with being the first to bring **colour** to **sound** cartoons (by 1932). Full feature-length colour and sound animated films came into their own with his *Snow White and the Seven Dwarfs* (1937) which won a special Oscar. In terms of animated dolls, arguably the most famous is the gorilla doll who is the eponymous hero of *King Kong* (Ernest B. Schoedask, 1933). This also demonstrated clearly that live and cartoon film could be hybridized in a feature-length movie. A slightly more recent and highly successful example of this hybridization *in extenso* is *Who Framed Roger Rabbit* (Robert Zemeckis, 1988).

Disney Productions are not necessarily the pioneers of animation. Prior to the establishment of Disney studios, the Fleischer brothers (Dave and Max), in 1920, launched their *Out of the Inkwell* series. The success of their cartoon character, the clown Koko, allowed them to establish their own studio, Red Seal, in 1921. Although their business was to fail, the brothers went with their studio to work at Paramount and created, most famously, the Betty Boop character and the *Popeye the*

Sailor series. Apart from the importance of their contribution to cartoon style – direct address to the audience, illogical plot developments (reminiscent of Cohl perhaps) – they were also technological pioneers. Dave Fleischer invented the rotoscope process (*circa* 1920) which, simply explained, is a process whereby individual frames of filmed action of live figures are projected onto the back of a glass then traced and rephotographed. Thus, the movements of the animated figures are based on those of live figures and cartoon characters move much like human beings. The Fleischers also introduced, in 1934, the stereo-typical process which gives the illusion of actual depth in the image. Disney Productions would incorporate both these processes into their own cartoon-making practices, either by intuition or by finding a similar process. Imitating human body movement continues as a practice today with some studios – although others spurn this type of hyper-realism, arguing that characters are strictly symbolic representations, not life-like creations. Studios following the imitation of life by transfer nowadays do it digitally with movements being based on motion-capture sensors attached, for example, to the face (see *Polar Express*, DreamWorks, 2004, which uses Tom Hanks' face for the main character).

The Disney style and look have tended to dominate the Western animation tradition. However, the realistic movement for which Disney animated films are so renowned is not the only trend of anima-tion. The United Productions of America (UPA, established in 1941 as a breakaway group from Disney) is perhaps best remembered for its *Mr Magoo* series. UPA was to have an important impact on the evolution of animation style. It used modern art styling which created, in par-ticular, a counter-realistic effect of jerky movements; it also wrote non-violent scenarios – thus again breaking with tradition. Its impact in the late 1940s and early 1950s was felt both on home territory and abroad, particularly in Eastern Europe. Also in the USA, Warner Brothers spawned some of the greatest names in animation. Tex Avery worked for Warner Brothers' cartoon unit (1936–42) and helped them launch, along with Bob Clampett and Chuck Jones, the cartoon character Bugs Bunny, before going on to work for MGM (1942–55). His fast-paced, often violent, surrealist gag-style cartoons which were based on the principle of 'surprise the audience' had, and still have, a great influence (both on animation and on advertising). During this same period, Warners produced a cartoon series entitled *Merrie Melodies* which include two cartoons that warrant a mention given that they seem to contradict, due to their racist content, the reputation Warners enjoyed at the time for producing feature films with social content or criticism at their core. The two cartoons are

Clean Pastures (Fritz Freleng, 1937) and *Coal Black and De Sebben Dwarves* (Bob Clampett, 1942). In the first cartoon, which features an all-Black cast, Saint Peter sends his angels down to Harlem to clean up the night-life. The cast is made up of caricatures of, among others, Cab Calloway (whose music figures in many cartoons of this period), Louis Armstrong, Fats Waller, Stepin Fetchit and Bill 'Bojangles' Robinson. The second is a racist spoof on Disney's *Snow White and the Seven Dwarfs* which, to Warners' credit, it eventually banned from projection (both these shorts are titles held by the British Film Institute's archival collection). Chuck Jones worked for Warners' cartoon unit from the late 1930s until it closed in 1962. He made 300 animated shorts and was perhaps most famous for producing the *Road Runner* series. A central theme to his work was to show how we are driven to follow after things we do not necessarily want (quite an antidote to the American capitalist dream if we stop to think about it – the coyote never gets the road-runner, and may even have forgotten why he chases after him!). After Warners, Jones went to MGM for a while to work on their *Tom and Jerry* series. Finally, in terms of animator greats, mention must be made of Ray Harryhausen who created the stop-motion model animation known as Dynamation (see, for example, the iconic fight with the skeletons in *Jason and the Argonauts*, Don Chaffey, 1963).

Elsewhere, apart from the USA, there were famously several Eastern European Schools of Animation which, starting in the early 1960s, underwent artistic and quantitative growth (Bendazzi, 1994: 333). The Czech School established itself as a major player in the world of animated films. Its worldwide renown begins with its puppet and cartoon animations, many of which cast doubt over reality as a means of subversion. Jiri Trnka's *The Hand* (*Ruka*, 1965) and Jana Marglova's *Genesis* (1966) are exemplary of this allegorical use of animation. The Czech Republic (former Czechoslovakia) enjoyed and still enjoys a wide reputation as makers of children's puppet fables, and Surrealist mixed-medium animated cartoons (toys, puppets, clay figures, drawings, etc.). Its reputation as a significant school is matched in Eastern Europe primarily by Poland, which also has a strong tradition in animation. Walerian Borowczyk and Jan Lenica's use of cut-out graphics (*Dam*, 1957) and Witold Giersz's painting on glass (*Maly Western*, 1960) are just two animation styles introduced by this country into the cartoon milieu. While there is stylistic variety, the Polish School has a definite look which Bendazzi (1994: 341), in his very comprehensive book on world animation, sums up as follows: 'a preference for dark-toned images ... and gloomy themes mostly marked by existential questioning … and heavy pessimism'. Finally (in the former Yugoslavia), the Zagreb School's legacy stems primarily from a group of Croatian animation artists, working in the 1950s and 1960s, whose style (inspired by the modern art styling of UPA) represents a reversal of the Disney realistic tradition.

Animation, although dominated by the American market, is a form of filmmaking that is widely practised in the Western world and the East. Japanese animation is becoming known to us through its presence on television. The industrial expansion of Japanese animation began in 1958 (Bendazzi, 1994: 411). Two major production companies were established around that time: Toei (1958) and Gakken (1959). Gakken, a puppet animation studio, was one of the few companies under the leadership of a woman director, Matsue Jimbo (Bendazzi, 1994: 411). Toei's feature film production tended to focus on two subject areas: legends from the Far East and tales of **science-fiction**. These films, as with many others emanating from Japanese studios, are fast-action, fast-produced cartoons which are often violent in terms of both their subject matter and their fast editing style (Bendazzi, 1994).

One Japanese animation studio that stands out presently is Ghibli (established 1985), which has made eighteen films to date – most famously *Princess Monoke* (1997), *Spirited Away* (2001) and *Ponyo* (2008). It specializes in feature-length animation films and the focus is on children and their perceptions of the world. There is greater moral and thematic complexity to their films, which in turn means that the pace is slower than the typical US or indeed Japanese product. Even more surprising, given the dominant trend of Manga-inspired animation films and their macho fighting culture, is the fact that most Ghibli animations feature a female character for the central role. The key animator is Hayao Miyazaki, with seven of the studio's films to his name, and he is partnered by Isao Takahata. Miyazaki's films are more **fantasy** based than Takahata's, which tend to be more experimental and based in the contemporary. Their work, whether popular or experimental, is marked by their use of realist detail in the backdrops and their skilled draughtmanship – a big attraction to older audiences. *Spirited Away* was an international success and a top-grossing film in Japan. Indeed, on their home territory, Ghibli products habitually outstrip Disney. This may explain why Disney has been a co-funder and, for a while, responsible for distributing Ghibli films in Japan and other countries.

Recent technological advances have seen the introduction of computer-aided graphics (see **CGI**). One might think that this new technology would have reduced production costs. One minute of traditional animation requires on average 1500 drawings and the medium is therefore very costly and labour intensive. But CGI is no cheaper. It is sobering to recall that Steven Spielberg's digitally animated dinosaurs in *Jurassic Park* (1993), made by George Lucas' independent company Industrial Light and Magic (ILM), cost $25 million alone (representing over one-third of the total costs of $66 million).

Digital animation is so sophisticated it can go beyond simply using movement and gestures to convey emotion (as animation has done in the past) and reach into the character's being to give a greater sense of depth. However, the millions of equations it takes to control each character and animate them down to individual frames of film means that it can take days to create a single frame. Often it takes up to two years to make a feature film.

Digital animation has produced greater realism in terms of movement, but can be used without necessarily endeavouring to make the characters more lifelike. Indeed there are two camps on this issue of realism within the US side of the industry: Pixar and DreamWorks. Pixar is considered a pioneer in the computer-animated format (computer-generated image: CGI). Pixar was co-founded in 1986 by Ed Catmull and Steve Jobs (of Apple fame) and, until 2004, was closely linked with Disney before becoming a subsidiary in 2006, when Disney acquired Pixar. They made *Toy Story* (1995) for Disney, the first wholly computer-generated animated film. Since that time, Pixar products have been a huge economic success and grossed seventeen Oscars, the most recent of which was for *Inside Out* (Pete Docter, 2015). Unlike DreamWorks, where greater emphasis is laid on the computer-generated images (e.g. *Antz*, 1998, *Shrek*, 2001) at the expense of the story, Pixar works from the principle that realism is not what is being aimed at and the focus has to be on the story itself. Almost as if taking over Warner Brothers' mantle of making socially committed films, every Pixar film has a message which, as with Ghibli in Japan, is probably why it draws a large demographic audience. Pixar has also understood that, with the advent of computer technology, it is now possible to convey emotional complexity. Pixar uses high-colour reality – and in this context Ed Catmull's big contribution to the media was his invention of texture mapping, which is a system that allows a texture to be poured over the surface of a character in a realistic way without, however, attempting to make them seem real. Conversely, DreamWorks tries to reproduce, through transfer, the movement of live beings at the expense of depth of character. Gags abound in their *Shrek 2* (2003), for example, whereas the characters of Pixar's *The Incredibles* (2004) have a lot to contend with, not least the government's repression of their exceptionalness.

A final mention in this contemporary scenario must go to the British success story, the Aardman Animation group based in Bristol, headed by Nick Park (with David Sproxton and Peter Lord who originated the idea) and best known initially for their *Wallace and Gromit* TV series. A hallmark of their work is their deeply inter-textual play with film **genre** and **classical narratives**. In a sense, this studio uses all the mediums of animation: drawing, modelling, digital animation. Beginning with tracing their animated characters on paper, including each movement, they then shoot a working script of each section of the film, in black and white, based on these tracings before going on to work out each of these rehearsed sections with their plasticene characters and backdrops. All these movements are then painstakingly filmed and encoded into the computer for editing. *Chicken Run* (2000), their first feature film, was a great success; it took two years to make and, unsurprisingly given the huge expense of such an undertaking, was co-funded by DreamWorks.

Animation, because it is not based in the real, has always had inherent within it the potential to problematize representation. So, for example, it can address differently questions of **gender** and race. But, for the more complex takes on the subversive and more fully counter-ideological animated films, we have to look to the experimental work of, amongst others, Oskar Fischinger, Len Lye, Paul Driessen, the Quay brothers and Robert Beer from the West and, from Eastern Europe, the work of Jan Svankmajer and Birovoi Dovnikovi (see Faber and Walters, 2004, for more details).

There is a massive bibliography on animation; what follows is only a sug-gested list: Bendazzi, 1994; Culham, 1988; Faber and Walters, 2004; Furniss, 1998; Ghanian and Phillips, 1996; Grant, 1987, 2001; Hoffer, 1981; Lassiter and Davy, 1995; Lord and Sibley, 1998; Napier, 2005; Pillig, 1992, 1997; Price, 2008; Sandler, 1998; Solomon, 1987, 1994; Taylor, 1996a; Weishar, 2004; Wells, 1998, 2002a, 2002b, 2008.

APPARATUS (CINEMATIC TECHNOLOGY)

As a term, apparatus refers to the technology of the camera and film projector. As a theoretical concept, it refers to the effects of this technology upon the **spectator**. Baudry (1970) was among the first film theorists to suggest that the cinematic apparatus or technology has an **ideological** effect upon the spectator. In the simplest instance, the cinematic apparatus purports to set before the eye and ear realistic images and sounds. However, the technology disguises how that reality is put together frame by frame. It also provides the illusion of perspectival space. This double illusion conceals the work that goes into the production of meaning and, in so doing, presents as natural what in fact is an ideological construction, that is, an idealistic reality. In this respect, Baudry argues, the spectator is positioned as an all-knowing **subject** because he (*sic*) is all-seeing even though he is unaware of the processes whereby he becomes fixed as such. Thus, the omniscient spectator–subject is produced by, is the effect of, the filmic text. A contiguous, simultaneous ideological effect occurs as a result of the way in which the spectator is positioned within a theatre: in a darkened room, the eyes projecting towards the screen with the projection of the film coming from behind the head. Because of this positioning, an identification occurs with the camera (that which has already looked, before the spectator, at what the spectator is now looking at). The spectator is engaged in an exchange *by* the filmic text (via the identification with the apparatus). The film, thereby, constructs the subject; the subject is an effect of the film text (see **ideology**). Thus, the spectator as subject is constructed by the meanings of the filmic text.

By 1975, in order to further clarify the dynamic between screen and **spectator**, film theorists (Baudry, Bellour, Metz) began drawing on Freud's discussions of the libido drives and Lacan's of the **mirror stage** to explain how film works on the unconscious level. In terms of the child's development of his (*sic*) identity, Lacan (developing upon Freud's theory of the **Oedipal complex**) argues that the mirror stage is the moment when the mother holds the child up to the mirror and the child imagines an illusory unity with the mother. This is a first moment of identification, with the mother (as one). This moment is short-lived, however, because the male child subsequently perceives his difference from his mother (in that he has a penis). At this point, the child imagines an illusory identification with the self in the mirror (an ideal image, a unified whole), but then immediately senses the loss of the mother. Lacan refers to this part of the mirror stage as the **Imaginary**. The next phase of the mirror stage is termed the **Symbolic** and can be explained as follows. The child, having sensed the loss of the mother now desires reunification with her. But this desire has become sexualized (because of his awareness of his difference) and at this point the father intervenes. As Lacan puts it, the father enters as the third term into the mirror (reflection), forming a triangle of relationships. He prohibits access to the mother by uttering 'No'. In this way, argues Lacan, language functions as the Symbolic Order. In order for the child to become a fully socialized being/**subject** he must obey the father's injunction; this 'No' is referred to as 'the Law of the Father'. In so doing, the child enters the realm of language (enters the Symbolic Order) — he conforms to the Law of the Father which is based in language (the spoken 'No'). The process of socialization for the male child is complete and eventually fulfilled when he transfers that desire onto a female other (i.e. not the mother but an '(m)other'). (For further clarification see **mirror stage, Oedipal trajectory** under **psychoanalysis** entry; see also **Imaginary/Symbolic** entry; and for a full discussion see Lapsley and Westlake, 1988: 80–90).

By analogy with this psychoanalytic description of the mirror stage, film theorists defined the screen as the site of the Imaginary: making *absence presence* (bringing into the spectator's field of vision images of people/**stars** who are not present in real life; just as the reflection of the child in the mirror is not real, it is not *him*, but an illusory image). The screen also functions to make *presence absence*: the spectator is absent from the screen upon which he gazes. However, the interplay between *presence and absence* does not end here. Although the spectator is absent from the screen, he is present as the hearing seeing feeling subject: without the presence the film would have no meaning. And it is in that respect that the screen is seen as having analogies with the mirror stage. The screen becomes the mirror into which the spectator peers. Thus, the spectator has a momentary identification with that image (for example, of a star body) and sees himself as a unified being (an ideal image). But then he perceives his difference and becomes aware of the lack, absence or loss of the mother. Finally, he recognizes himself as perceiving **subject**. According to this line of analysis, at each film viewing there occurs a re-enactment of the unconscious processes involved in the acquisition of sexual difference (the mirror stage), of language (entry *of* the Symbolic, the Law of the Father), of autonomous selfhood or subjectivity (entry *into* the Symbolic), and, finally, rupture with the mother as object of identification. Not hard to see how **mainstream cinema**, in particular, benefits from this process of identification as a constant lure to return to the movies! It is through the interplay of *absence/presence* that cinema constructs the spectator as subject of the look with all that that connotes in terms of visual pleasure for the spectator (see **gaze**). But, this visual pleasure is also associated with its opposite: the shame of looking; for in this seeing without being seen, cinema makes possible the re-enactment of the primal scene – that is, according to Freud, the moment in the child's psychological development when it, unseen, watches its mother and father copulating (see **scopophilia, voyeurism/fetishism**).

When watching **pornography**, perhaps this shame of looking comes into play, but erotic scenes in films can induce more than visual pleasure, surely, without a sense of shame!

Film as a source for visual pleasure, but which at this stage only addressed the male spectator, is what led the feminist theorist Laura Mulvey to produce, also in 1975, her seminal essay 'Visual Pleasure and Narrative Cinema' which helped, amongst various debates, to move the discussion of the apparatus on from this anti-humanist reading of the spectator as subject-effect, and the presupposition that the spectator is male (for fuller details on these debates see entry on **spectator**). The outcome of these prolonged debates is that the apparatus is less discussed as a theoretical concept, having been replaced by debates around the gaze and spectator theory in which the spectator is now seen as an active producer of meaning who is still positioned as subject, but this time as agent of the filmic text. That is, s/he becomes the one viewing, the one deriving pleasure (or fear, which is another form of pleasure) from what s/he is looking at. S/he also interprets and judges the text. On the negative side of this positioning, it could be said that, in becoming the camera, the apparatus places the spectator voyeuristically as a colluder in the circulation of pleasure which is essential to the financial well-being of the film industry (see Metz, 1975). The economic viability of the latter depends on the desire of the former to be pleasured. Cinema in this respect becomes an exchange commodity based on pleasure and capital gain – pleasure in exchange for money. On the positive side, it could be said that as agent the spectator can resist being fixed as **voyeur**, or indeed as effect, and judge the film critically.

see also: **agency, spectator-identification, suture**

For further discussion see De Lauretis and Heath, 1980; Lapsley and Westlake, 1988: 79–86; Mayne, 1993: 13–76; Metz, 1975; Mulvey, 1975.

ART CINEMA

This term refers predominantly to a certain type of European cinema that is **experimental** in technique and **narrative**. This cinema, which typically produces low to mid-budget films, attempts to address the aesthetics of cinema and cinematic practices and is primarily, but not exclusively, produced outside **dominant cinema** systems. However, it must be pointed out that the **French New Wave** and the new

German cinema, which come under this label, received substantial financing from the state. Other art cinemas, such as the American **underground cinema** tend to be funded by the filmmakers themselves. Art cinema is also produced by individuals – often women filmmakers – who do not come under any particular movement (e.g. Agnès Varda, Liliani Cavani, Nelly Kaplan and Chantal Akerman).

Art cinema has been rightly associated with eroticism since the 1920s when sexual desire and nudity were explicitly put up on-screen. However, for American audiences during the censorship period under the **Hays code** (1934–68), art cinema came to mean sex films. With an eye to the export market, film producers were quick to exploit art cinema's sexual cachet. Perhaps one of the most famous instances of this is the case of Jean-Luc Godard's *Le Mépris* (1963), starring Brigitte Bardot. Upon its completion, two of its producers (Levine and Ponti) insisted that Godard should insert some nude scenes of Bardot. He did this, but not with the anticipated results – far from titillating or sexual, these scenes are moving, tragic.

The term *cinéma d'art* was first coined by the French in 1908 to give cinema – which until then had been a popular medium – a legitimacy that would attract the middle classes to the cinema. This earliest form of art cinema was filmed theatre (mostly actors of the Comédie Française) accompanied by musical scores of renowned composers – making it a quite conservative artefact. During the 1920s, however, owing to the impact of **German expressionism** and the French avant-garde, art cinema became more closely associated with the **avant-garde**. From the 1930s onwards, partly owing to the French and Italian realist movements, its connotations widened to include social and psychological **realism**. And the final legitimation came in the 1950s when the *politique des auteurs* made the term ***auteur*** sacrosanct. This *politique* or polemic argued that certain filmmakers could be identified as auteurs – as generators or creators rather than producers of films. This further widening of its frame of reference has meant that, although art cinema is considered primarily a European cinema, certain Japanese, Indian, Australian, North-American and Latin-American filmmakers are also included in the canon – as well as certain films made by representatives of some minority groups: women, Black people and self-called queers (see **Black cinema**, **queer cinema;** for women's cinema see Kuhn, 1990).

Historically, art cinema was not intentionally devised as a counter-**Hollywood** cinema, even though its production is clearly not associated with Hollywood. It is interesting to note, however, that the 1920s art cinema was a period of great cross-fertilization between

Hollywood and European cinema. Generally speaking, in art cinema narrative **codes and conventions** are disturbed, the **narrative** line is fragmented so that there is no seamless cause-and-effect storyline. Similarly, characters' behaviour appears contingent, hesitant rather than assured and in the know or motivated towards certain ambitions, desires or goals. Although these films are character- rather than plot-led, there are no heroes – in fact this absence of heroes is an important feature of art cinema. Psychological realism takes the form of a character's subjective view of events; **social realism** is represented by the character in relation to those events. The point of view can take the form of an interior monologue, or even several interior monologues (Alain Resnais' and Ingmar Bergman's films are exemplars of this). **Subjectivity** is often made uncertain (whose story is it?) and so too the safe construction of time and space. This cinema, in its rupture with **classic narrative cinema**, intentionally distances **spectators** to create a reflective space for them to assume their own critical space or subjectivity in relation to the screen or film.

see also: **avant-garde, counter-cinema, experimental film, time-image (movement-image)**

ART DIRECTION

This term covers the whole range of labour practices involved in the creation of the visual environment of the film – from the smallest to the largest. Thus, not only costume and set design come under this term of reference, but so too does obtaining the appropriate props. Overall responsibility for art direction lies either with the production designer or art director – the latter is often the designer of the sets or décors. Presently, in film studies' scholarship, costume and set design have become an important topic of research. Clearly, set design, in that it is the visual environment within which characters move about, impacts heavily on the meaning of a **narrative** and as such demands careful analysis when reading a film. Consider for a moment the analysis of **melodrama**'s **mise-en-scène** by Mulvey, Nowell-Smith and Elsaesser (all 1987) – which we now all understand plays an integral part in the meaning of the narrative, referring as it does to the couple's repression of emotion as they struggle to reach a compromise in their complex relationship. But it is also important to study the work of individual art directors since, like **auteur** filmmakers, it is obvious that they too leave authorial marks. For example, late 1930s **French**

poetic realism might well not have come about but for the legacy of the 1920s and 1930s art director Lazare Meerson, whose work heavily influenced the likes of Alexander Trauner and Georges Walkhévitch amongst others of his assistants or disciples. By the same extension, **costume** is an integral part of mise-en-scène and needs to be understood in a variety of ways, starting with an acknowledgement that it is governed by 'complex influences that relate to notions of realism, performance, gender, status and power' (Street, 2001: 2). Costumes tell us a great deal about the body beneath it, either in terms of the body's desire to hide itself, lose its own identity, or, conversely, to project a strong sexuality, a sense of status or class. Costume also has resonances for national cinemas – it displays the cultural pulse of a nation and, if it is France, the nation's undoubted superiority in matters of good taste(!), particularly if the designer is a couturier.

For more reading on costume design and fashion see Bruzzi, 1997; Cook, 1996; Hayward, 2010; Street, 2001.

ASPECT RATIO

This refers to the size of the image on the screen and to the ratio between the width and height. It dates back to the days of silent cinema, when the ratio was fixed at 1.33:1 (width to height) thanks to a standardization of technology brought about by hard-nosed business strategies on the part of the Edison company. Edison contracted its rivals into a cartel that had to use Edison equipment and pay royalties to the company. The cartel dominated the market from 1909 to 1917 when an anti-trust law broke it. Edison went out of business, but the aspect ratio for a standard screen remained the norm internationally until the early 1950s, when the threat posed to film **audiences** by television obliged the film industry to find visual ways to attract or retain audiences.

Although there had been experimentation with other screen sizes, it was not until economic necessity forced the film industry to invest heavily in technology that screens took on different dimensions. The first innovation in size was the 1950s **cinemascope** with a standard aspect ratio of 2.35:1. In the 1970s to the 1990s, widescreen films were more commonly projected either from the wide-gauge 70mm film frame with an aspect ratio of 2.2:1 or from 35mm film with its top and bottom pre-cropped with an aspect ratio of 1.85:1 in the United States and 1.66:1 in European cinemas. Today, however, a great majority of films are digitally mastered and, for cinema theatre projection purposes, the current widescreen cinema standard is 2.39:1.

ASYNCHRONIZATION/ASYNCHRONOUS SOUND

Asynchronization occurs when the sound is either intentionally or unintentionally out of sync with the image. In the latter case, this is the result of faulty editing (e.g. a spoken voice out of sync with the moving lips). In the former, it has an aesthetic and/or **narrative** function. First, asynchronization calls attention to itself; thus, the **spectator** is made aware that s/he is watching a film (so the illusion of identification is temporarily removed or deconstructed). Second, it serves to disrupt time and space and thereby narrative continuity, and as such points to the illusion of reality created by **classical narrative cinema** through its seamless **continuity editing**. Finally, it can be used for humorous effect, as occasionally in the earliest talkies when the advent of sound was met by filmmakers with mixed reactions. There were two camps of thought: those who embraced the new technology and those who feared it would transform cinema into filmed theatre. As an example of this latter camp, the French filmmaker René Clair was concerned that sound would limit visual experimentation and remove the poetic dimension inherent in silent film. His early sound films (mostly comic operettas) play with sound, by confounding the actual source of sound. For example, we see a woman singing framed in a window, then there is a cut and we go into her room and we realize that in fact she is miming to a record player. This draws attention to sound cinema's pretensions at the reality effect (see his *A nous la liberté*, 1931).

see also: **sound, seamlessness (editing), space and time**

AUDIENCE

Always recognized as important by film distributors and exhibitors, the audience has now become an important area of research for film theorists and sociologists (for discussion and references see **spectator**). Considerable work has been done on reception theory (how the audience receives and/or is positioned by the film). More recently, the debate has focused on how the spectator both identifies with the film and becomes an active producer of meaning as subject of the film (see **agency**). The film industry has since its beginnings targeted films to attract large audiences; this has meant that the product is predominantly audience-led. As the audience changes (e.g. from working-class men and women, before World War Two, to women of many classes after the war, to youth from the late 1950s, to home consumption), so too does the type of product. However, with the emergence of the internet as a viable distribution platform, the relationship between audience and product has also altered. Multiple points of access, unencumbered by time, have led to a new wave of on-demand services. Services that also allow the audience to engage with films they want to see, rather than being dictated to by exhibition practices. One aspect is that the hegemony of cinema exhibition is no longer the dominant site of audience consumption. From mobile phones to Netflix, tablets to illegal file sharing, the means of audience consumption has been irrevocably transformed.

The internet has also redefined the relationship between audience and film. Individuals, with a shared passion for a film, are no longer isolated, or reduced to association purely defined by geographical proximity. Fandom has, through the internet, become a viable global, or cyber, community (for example, the Tributes cyber community forged from *Hunger Games* universe, who define themselves via the text). Intriguingly, these imagined communities are, from one perspective, defined by their otherness. Their shared passion, a socially imagined agreement, defines them as being both part and outside of the normative. As Jenkins notes, such fans 'construct their cultural and social identity through borrowing and inflecting mass cultural images, articulating concerns which often go unvoiced within the dominant media' (Jenkins, 1992: 23). The global network, which serves these fan groups, is used to re-engage with the text in a variety of ways. Creating new meaning within the text, applying subversive readings, inflecting alternative meanings or creating new cultural product with the original text as a foundation.

AUTEUR/AUTEUR THEORY/POLITIQUE DES AUTEURS/CAHIERS DU CINÉMA

Although *auteur* is a term that dates back to the 1920s in the theoretical writings of French film critics and directors of the silent era, it is worth pointing out that in Germany, as early as 1913, the term *Autorenfilm* (author's film) had already been coined. The *Autorenfilm* emerged partly as a response to the French *Film d'Art* (with its cachet of art cinema) which began in 1908. The German term *Autorenfilm* is associated with the polemical issue regarding questions of authorship. Writers for the screen campaigned for their rights to these so-called *Autorenfilm* and staked their claim not just to the script, but also to the film itself. In other words, the film was to be judged as the work of the author rather than the person responsible for directing it (Eisner, 1969: 39). In France the concept of auteur (in the 1920s) came from the other direction, namely, that the filmmaker is the auteur – irrespective of the origin of the script. During the 1920s, the debate in France centred on the auteur (often making **art cinema**) versus the scenario-led film (that is, films whose scenarios were commissioned by studios who subsequently appointed the director). This distinction fed into the high-art/low-art debate already set in motion, as early as 1908, in relation to film (the so-called *Film d'Art* versus popular cinema controversy). Thus, by the 1920s, within the domain of film theory, auteur-films had as much value, if not more, than canonical literary **adaptations** which in turn had more value than adaptations of popular fiction.

After 1950, and in the wake of Alexandre Astruc's seminal essay 'Naissance d'une nouvelle avant-garde: la Caméra-stylo/Birth of a New Avant-Garde: the camera-stylo' (*L'Écran français*, 1948), this debate was picked up again and popularized – with the eventual effect, as we shall see, of going some way towards dissolving the high-art/low-art issue. The leader in this renewed auteur-debate was the film review *Cahiers du cinéma* (launched in 1951) and the essay most famously identified with this debate is François Truffaut's 1954 essay 'Une certaine tendance du cinéma/A Certain Tendency of Cinema'. Although it should not be seen as the sole text arguing for auteur cinema, nonetheless, it is considered *the* manifesto for the **French New Wave**.

In the 1950s, the *Cahiers du cinéma* (still in existence today) was headed by André Bazin, a film critic, and was written by a regular group of film critics, known as the *Cahiers* group. This group did not pursue the 1920s theorists' thinking (see **avant-garde**); in fact, they either ignored or totally dismissed it. And it is the later, 1950s debate, that has been carried forward into film theory. Through the *Cahiers* discussions on the *politique des auteurs* (i.e. the polemical debate surrounding the concept of auteurism), the group developed the notion of the auteur by binding it closely with the concept of **mise-en-scène**. This shift in the meaning of the auteur was largely due to the avid attention the *Cahiers* group paid to American/**Hollywood** cinema for the following reasons. During the German occupation of France in World War Two, American films had been proscribed. Suddenly after the war, hundreds of such films, heretofore unseen, flooded the French cinema screens. This cinema, directed by the likes of Alfred Hitchcock, Howard Hawks, John Ford and Samuel Fuller, seemed refreshingly new and led the *Cahiers* group to a reconsideration of Hollywood's production. They argued that just because American directors had little or no say over any of the production process, bar the staging of the **shots**, this did not mean that they could not attain auteur status. Style, as in mise-en-scène, could also demarcate an auteur. Thanks to the *Cahiers* group, the term *auteur* could now refer either to a director's discernible style through mise-en-scène or to filmmaking practices where the director's signature was as much in evidence on the script/scenario as it was on the film product itself. Exemplars of auteurism in this second form (total author) are: Jean Vigo, Jean Renoir, Jean-Luc Godard, Agnès Varda in France; Rainer Werner Fassbinder, Werner Herzog, Wim Wenders, Margarethe von Trotta, Michael Haneke in Germany; Orson Welles, Sydney Lumet, David Lynch, Martin Scorsese, Quentin Tarantino in the United States. Certain filmmakers (mostly of the mise-en-scène form of auteur) have had this label ascribed to them by the *Cahiers* group even though their work may pre-date this use of the term (e.g. Hawks, Ford, Fuller and Hitchcock on the American scene).

The *politique des auteurs* was a polemic initiated by the *Cahiers* group not just to bring favourite American filmmakers into the canon, but also to attack the French cinema of the time which they considered sclerotic, ossified. Dubbing it *le cinéma de papa*/daddy's cinema, they accused it of being script-led, redolent with safe psychology, lacking in social realism and of being produced by the same old scriptwriters and filmmakers whose time was up (François Truffaut was by far the most virulent in his attacks). The effect of this polemic, however, was to establish the primacy of the author-filmmaker/auteur and as such proposed a rather romantic and, therefore, conservative aesthetic (i.e. the auteur as genius, as sole producer of meaning). A further problem with this polemic as it stood at the time was that, by privileging the auteur, it erased context (i.e. history) and therefore side-stepped **ideology**. Equally, because film was being looked at for its formalistic, stylistic and thematic structures, unconscious structures (such as the unspoken dynamics between filmmaker and actor, the economic pressures connected with the industry) were precluded. Interestingly, of two of the writers in the *Cahiers* group who went on to make films, Godard and Truffaut, it is Truffaut's work that is locked in the conservative romantic ideology of the *politique des auteurs* and Godard's that has constantly questioned auteurism (among other things).

This *politique* generated a debate that lasted well into the 1980s, and auteur is a term that still prevails today. Given its innate conservatism one might well ask, why? The first answer is that it helped to shift film theory from what, until the 1950s, had primarily been sociological analysis. The second answer is that the auteur debate made clear that attempts to provide a single film theory just would not work and that, in fact, film is about multiple theories.

What follows is a brief outline of the development of auteur theory through three phases (for more details see Caughie, 1981; Andrew, 1984; Cook, 1985; Lapsley and Westlake, 1988). Figure 1 (overleaf) outlines the three phases of auteur theory and gives a graphic representation of auteurism.

Phase 1

The term *auteur theory* came about, in the 1960s, as a mistranslation by the American film critic Andrew Sarris. What had been a polemic now became a full-blown theory. Sarris used auteurism to nationalistic and chauvinistic ends to elevate American/Hollywood cinema to the status of the only good cinema, with but one or two European art films worthy of mention. As a result of this misuse of the term, cinema became divided into a canon of the good or great directors and the rest. The initial impact of this on film courses and film studies in general was considerable, the tendency being to study only the good or great canon (see Figure 1, phase 1). Thankfully, the impact of cultural studies on film studies, in the late 1970s, and developments in film theory since has served to redress this imbalance.

Phase 2

The auteur debate did not end there. It was picked up in the late 1960s in the light of the impact of **structuralism** (see Figure 1, phase 2). In France, the *Cahiers du cinéma* was obliged to rethink and readjust its thinking around auteurism, and in Britain the film journal *Movie* significantly developed the debate. As a concept, structuralism dates back to the beginning of the twentieth century, primarily in the form of Ferdinand de Saussure's linguistic theories. However, it remained little known until the theories were brought into the limelight by the French philosopher–**semiotician** Roland Barthes in the 1950s – especially in his popularizing essays *Mythologies* (1957). Saussure, in his *Cours de linguistique générale*, sets out the base paradigm by which all language can be ordered and understood. The base paradigm *langue/parole* was intended as a function that could simultaneously address and speak, on the one hand, for the profound universal structures of language or

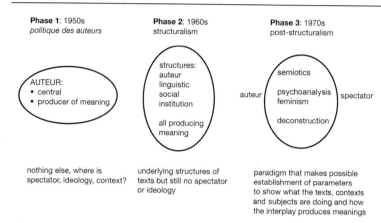

Phase 1: 1950s
politique des auteurs

AUTEUR:
• central
• producer of meaning

nothing else, where is
spectator, ideology, context?

Phase 2: 1960s
structuralism

structures:
auteur
linguistic
social
institution

all producing
meaning

underlying structures of
texts but still no spectator
or ideology

Phase 3: 1970s
post-structuralism

semiotics

auteur   psychoanalysis   spectator
feminism

deconstruction

paradigm that makes possible
establishment of parameters
to show what the texts, contexts
and subjects are doing and how
the interplay produces meanings

Figure 1

language system (*langue*) and, on the other, their manifestations in different cultures (*parole*). Claude Lévi-Strauss' anthropological structuralism of the 1960s (which looked at American Indian myths) continued in a similar vein, although this time it was applied to **narrative** structures. Lévi-Strauss' thesis was that since all cultures are the products of the human brain there must be, somewhere, beneath the surface, features that are common to all.

It is worth labouring this point that this rethinking of film theory, in the 1960s, did not come via film criticism (as it did in the 1950s) but through other disciplines, namely, structural linguistics and semiotics. This pattern would repeat itself, in the 1970s, with **psychoanalysis** and philosophy pushing the debate along, and then history, in the 1980s (see Figure 1, phase 3). The significance of this new trend of essayists and philosophers turning to cinema to apply their theories cannot be underestimated. Not to put too simplistic a reading on their importance, it is unquestionably their work which has legitimated film studies as a discipline and brought cinema firmly into the academic arena.

Structuralism was eagerly seized upon by proponents of auteurism because it was believed that, with its scientific approach, it would facilitate the establishing of an objective basis for the concept and counter the romantic subjectivity of auteur theory. Furthermore, apart from its potential to give a scientific legitimacy to auteurism, the attraction of structuralism for film theory in general lay in the theory's underlying strategy to establish a total structure.

Symptomatic of this desire for order in film theory were Christian Metz's endeavours (in the mid-1960s) to situate cinema within a Saussurian semiology. Metz, a semiotician, was the first to set out, in his *Essais sur la signification au cinéma* (1971, 1972), a total theory approach in the form of his *grande syntagmatique*. He believed that cinema possessed a total structure. To adopt Saussurian terms, he perceived cinema as *langue* and each film as being *parole*. His endeavour – to uncover the rules that governed film language and to establish a framework for a semiotics of the cinema – pointed to a fundamental limitation with such an all-embracing, total approach. The problem became one where theory tended to overtake the text, thus occluding other aspects of the text. What got omitted was the notion of pleasure and **audience** reception, and what occured instead was a crushing of the aesthetic experience through the weight of the theoretical framework.

This is not to say that structuralism did not advance the debate on film theory and auteurism. It did. Auteur-structuralism brought about a major positive change to auteur theory (*à la Sarris*). The British film journal *Movie* pointed out the problems of a resolutely romantic aesthetic in relation to cinema, but saw ways to deal with them. By situating the auteur as one structure among others – such as the notion of **genre** and the film industry – producing meaning, the theory would yield to a greater flexibility. *Cahiers du cinéma* was also critical of the romantic notion of auteurship because the auteur is not a unified and free creative spirit and film, as a text, is a 'play of tensions, silences and regressions' (Caughie, 1981: 128). Thus the auteur was displaced from the centre of the work and was now one structure among several others making up the film text (see Figure 1, phase 2). This displacement allowed other structures to emerge, namely, the linguistic, social and institutional structures and the auteur's relationship to them. And even though, in the late 1960s, the tendency was still to perceive the auteur structure as the major one, it was also recognized that the **studio** and **stars** – amongst others – were equally important contributors to the production of meaning in film. Still absent from the debate, however, were the contextual structures and **discourses** such as the ideological effects of film as practice (how it functions ideologically) and spectator–text relations — these would be part of phase 3 of auteur theory (see Figure 1, phase 3).

After 1968, *Cahiers* made a first attempt to introduce ideology into the debate in its exploration of Hollywood films that either resisted or reflected dominant ideology. For example, in what is referred to as 'the *Young Mr Lincoln* debate', the *Cahiers* group claimed that this film mediated Republican values to counter Roosevelt's Democratic New Deal measures of 1933 to 1941 and to promote a Republican victory in the 1940 Presidential elections. Althusser's discussions on ideology, particularly his concept of *interpellation*/interpolation, made it possible for both *Cahiers* and the British journal *Screen* to start to address the screen–spectator relationship. At this juncture, both journals accepted what, with hindsight, turned out to be a profoundly anti-humanist analysis of spectator positioning. According to Althusser, ideological state apparatuses (ISAs) interpolate individuals as **subjects**. That is, as pre-existing structures, ISAs function to constitute the individual as a subject to the ideology. ISAs manifest themselves as institutions of the state: the police, government, monarchies are ISAs. Just to illustrate: the British are subjects to the monarchy. The individual is, therefore, an effect of ISAs and not an agent. As subject–effects, individuals give meaning to ideology by colluding with and acting according to it. A mirroring process occurs which provides the subject with a reassuring sense of national identity (of belonging). Applied to film this means that cinema, in terms of meaning production, positions the spectator as a subject–effect who takes as real the images emanating from the screen. Thus, meaning is received, but not constructed, by the subject.

Phase 3

Undoubtedly, two seminal essays of the late 1960s, Barthes' 'Death of the Author' (1967) and Michel Foucault's 'What is an Author?' (1969) helped move forward the debates around auteurism and spectator positioning. Barthes argued that a text is a tissue of quotations (suggesting there is no true or single authorial voice), and each text is geological, constructed as it is of multiple layers and meanings. As Foucault explains, the author is a function, amongst others. Texts are products of many other texts and contexts – in our instance of film this means all levels of production ranging from the pro-filmic moment (everything that occurs before filming even begins; so that could be the novel, the novelist, the script and scriptwriter, etc.), all levels of the industrial practice (producers, technicians, stars/actors and so on), to the film itself and, subsequently, distribution, exhibition, audience reception.

This move beyond the concept of a single grand theory or structure heralded the advent of **post-structuralism**, a theoretical approach which embraced a pluralism of theories. In relation to auteur theory, it took the impact, in the 1970s, of post-structuralism (see **structuralism/ post-structuralism**), psychoanalysis, feminism and **deconstruction** to make clear, finally, that a single theory was inadequate and that what was required was a pluralism of theories that cross-fertilized each other (see Figure 1, phase 3). Post-structuralism, which does not find an easy definition, could be said to regroup and, to some extent, cross-fertilize the three other theoretical approaches (psychoanalysis, feminism and deconstruction). As its name implies, it was born out of a profound mistrust for total theory, and started from the position that all texts are a double articulation of discourses and non-discourses (i.e. what is spoken and what is unspoken). In terms of auteur theory, the effect was multiple: 'the intervention of semiotics and psychoanalysis shattering once and for all the unity of the auteur' (Caughie, 1981: 200). Because post-structuralism looks at all relevant discourses (spoken or unspoken) revolving around and within the text, many more areas of meaning production can be identified. Thus, semiotics introduced the theory of the textual subject, that is, subject positions within the textual process, including that of the spectator and the auteur, all producing meanings. Furthermore, semiotics also made clear that the text is a series of **signs** producing meanings.

Having defined the auteur's place within the textual process, auteur theory could now be placed within a theory of textuality. Since there is no such thing as a pure text, the **intertextuality** (effects of different texts upon another text) of any film text must be a major consideration, including auteurial intertextuality. That is, the auteur is a figure constructed out of her or his film: because of specific hallmarks, the film is ostensibly a certain filmmaker's and also influenced by that of others, etc. Psychoanalysis introduced the theory of the sexual, specular, divided subject (divided by the fact of difference, loss of and separation from the mother (see **psycho-analysis**)). Questions of the subject come into play: who is the subject (the text, auteur, spectator)? What are the effects of the enunciating text (i.e. the film as performance) on the spectator and those on the filmic text of the spectator? What are the two-way ideological effects (film on spectator and vice versa) and the pleasures derived by the spectator as s/he moves in and out of the text (see **spectator-identification**)? To speak of text means too that the context must also come into play in terms of meaning production: modes of production, the social, political and historical context. Finally, and simultaneously, one cannot speak of a text as transparent, natural or innocent; therefore it is to be unpicked, deconstructed so that its modes of representation are fully understood.

See Caughie (1981) for a comprehensive review of debates.

AVANT-GARDE

The term *avant-garde* was first used in the modern sense to typify various aesthetic groupings that appeared immediately before and after World War One: cubism and **futurism** (both 1909), Dadaism (1916), constructivism (1920) and **surrealism** (1924). The avant-garde seeks to break with tradition and is intentionally politicized in its attempts to do so. In cinema the avant-garde cachet was first used, in the 1920s, when a group of French film theorists (most famously Louis Delluc, Germaine Dulac and Jean Epstein) turned their hand to filmmaking and sought to create a cinema of the avant-garde. The first point to be made about this loosely banded collective is the pluralism of its members' theoretical approaches to cinema, which clearly inflected their filmmaking practices. Between them, they addressed issues of high and popular art, realist versus naturalist film, the **spectator**–screen relationship, **editing** styles (particularly that of the **Soviet school** and **montage**), simultaneity, **subjectivity**, the unconscious, and the **psychoanalytical** potential of film, **auteur** cinema, cinema as rhythm and as a sign (see **semiology**). Once they turned their hands to making film, experimentation was central to their practice. This experimentation functioned on three overlapping levels: reworking genres, exploring the possibilities of film language and redefining the representation of subjectivity. **Genres** were mixed, intercalated and juxtaposed. Similarly, the popular was fused with the experimental (mainstream cinema with **counter-cinema**), socio-realism with the subjective (**documentary** with **melodrama**). Working within these popular genres allowed these filmmakers to extend, distort, subvert dominant **discourses**. In so doing, these avant-garde filmmakers attacked the precept of filmic **narrative** and spectator omniscience. Their films raised questions about subjectivity and its representation by disrupting **diegetic** time and space. This was achieved in a number of ways: shifts from diegetic continuity to discontinuity, fast editing, disruption of conventional transitional **shots**, disorientating shots through **unmatched shots**, or a simultaneous representation of a multiplicity of perspectives. Thus, the fetishizing **gaze** of the male was also examined, showing an awareness of the underprivileging of female subjectivity. Subjectivity not only became a question of point of view but also included the implicit notion of **voyeurism** and speculation (of the female other – see **gaze**) as well as the issue of desire, and the functioning of the conscious and the unconscious mind (see Abel, 1984: 241–95; Flitterman-Lewis, 1990; Hayward, 2005).

Soviet cinema and **German expressionism** with, respectively, their characteristic editing and **lighting** practices greatly influenced this first avant-garde, as did the surrealist movement and **psychoanalysis**. This avant-garde went through three different stages: subjective cinema (showing the interior life of a character, as in *La Souriante Mme Beudet*, Dulac, 1923); pure cinema (film signifying in and of itself through its plasticity and rhythms, as in *Entr'acte*, René Clair, 1924);

and surrealist cinema (a collision of the first two stages with the intention of giving filmic representation to both the rationality and the irrationality of the unconscious and dream state, as in *La Coquille et le clergyman*, Dulac, 1927 and *Un chien andalou*, Luis Buñuel, 1929).

Since that period, other influences have also come into play. And, interestingly, once again there are three dominant types: first, what Wollen (1982: 92) calls the self-reflexive avant-garde (predominantly American), or what Andrew (1984: 124) terms the American romantic; second, the avowedly political avant-garde (Wollen, 1982: 92) or the European structural materialist film (Andrew, 1984: 125); finally, the narrative avant-garde of the cinema of *écriture* (Andrew, 1984: 126).

Where the American type is concerned, the major influences are the works of what are now called modernist painters but which are in fact those of the avant-garde movements of the early part of the twentieth century (see above). These films have an abstract formalism displaying a self-reflexivity that brings them close in their concerns to the pure cinema of the 1920s avant-garde (as in Maya Deren's *Meshes of the Afternoon*, 1943). As for the second type of avant-garde film, the major influences were Bertolt Brecht and his theory of **distanciation** and Sergei Eisenstein's montage theory. The film practice invoked here is one whereby the film displays its very structures and materiality – that is, it makes an exhibition of its signifying practices, draws attention to the artifice of cinema. Point of view and narrative structure do not exist. So the spectator is under no illusion that what s/he is watching is a two-dimensional projection of the process of filmmaking. This is what Jean-Luc Godard termed making political films politically. This cinema reflects the revolutionary role of the avant-garde, assailing **ideology** by revealing the structures that put it up and keep it in place (as in Godard's *Weekend* and *La Chinoise*, both 1967). The third type more readily recalls the first and last stages of the 1920s avant-garde but also has some parentage with materialist film. Here the narrative avant-garde works with, or on cinematic **codes**, bringing the theory of counter-cinema into practice. This cinema denaturalizes cinema to show that dominant cinematic language is not the only cinematic language and that new modes of subjectivity are possible, including that of the spectator as a producer of the text (see **agency**). Again, this is a predominantly European cinema and, unsurprisingly perhaps, because it addresses issues such as identification, representation, screen–spectator relations and subjectivity as well as production practices (film as work or labour) it is also a cinema associated with feminist filmmakers (e.g. Chantal Akerman, *Jeanne Dielman, 23 Quai*

41

du Commerce, 1080 *Bruxelles*, 1975; Marguerite Duras, *India Song*, 1975; Agnès Varda, *Sans toit ni loi*, 1985).

see also: **art cinema, counter-cinema, experimental film**

For further reading see Andrew, 1984: 119–27; Arthur, 2005; Brakage, 1992; Flitterman-Lewis, 1990; Gidal, 1989; Lapsley and Westlake, 1988: 181–213; MacDonald, 1993; Sitney, 1974, 1978.

BLACK CINEMA – UK

Black cinema is a term used to refer to films made by British Black filmmakers and which extends to British Indian-Asian **directors**. Perhaps because British cinema itself does not have a supremely first-world track record in film production, we should not be too surprised to hear that within UK cinema, Black cinema is, in relation to its counterpart in the USA, quite a small affair. It is, however, a significant cinema although its roots go back only as far as the 1950s and 1960s. If we consider that the major waves of immigration to the UK from either the British colonies or former colonies occurred after World War Two, then it becomes clearer still that, since diasporic communities only came into existence in a significant way at that time, then it is hardly surprising that a diasporic cinema should not begin to emerge until that period. What has to surprise, undoubtedly, is that presently British Black cinema, in terms of feature films, has not grown significantly in numbers since that time, even though there are a number of international successes (see below).

Karen Ross (1996: 53) provides us with some revealing statistics as to the status and availability of Black cinema products. Between 1988 and 1992, the total number of Black films available for hire or archival viewing only grew from 130 to 204 (two-thirds of which are in **documentary** format and therefore are not counted as feature films). Seventy-four films in four years – especially those four years during which Black issues were very much to the fore in British consciousness – is a small output particularly if we consider that only a handful are full feature films. Black cinema certainly became a presence during the 1980s and was born out of a governmental response to the civil disobedience of the late 1970s and early 1980s. The many so-called riots of the early 1980s led to numerous inquiries, the results of which made it abundantly clear that the Black communities felt seriously disenfranchised and without a voice. Public sector financing at a local and governmental level, including grants from the British Film Institute (BFI), was invested into five workshops around the country in major cities where inner-city strife had been at its most vocal. At the same time as the public sector was assisting in financing the workshops, the birth of Channel Four in 1982, with its remit to represent the voices of minorities, meant that there were outlets for the workshops in the form of commissioned work for the channel. Sankofa and the Black Audio Film Collective (established 1983, but now defunct) remain the best known of these workshops. The workshops were concerned as much with film practice as with debates on representation, including historical representation and issues of identity and hybridity. It is perhaps for this reason that much of their production cuts across or is a fusion of documentary and fiction. Given the workshops' ethos, it is not difficult to see how certain film theorists and practitioners have identified this cinematic practice with that of Third Cinema (for a fuller debate of that point see **Third Cinema** entry).

Before the public sector provision of financing for projects came into being (however modest), the output of British Black cinema was very tiny indeed. Among the few filmmakers around, we can list Lloyd Reckord, Horace Ové and Lionel Ngakane (a Black South African in exile who has been claimed by the British as one of their first Black filmmakers). These filmmakers directed a handful of feature and non-feature films, during the period 1960 to 1980, and largely financed their projects themselves. Most of these films are available through the BFI National Film Archive. All, without exception, deal with the question of marginalization and race relations – thereby establishing a tradition that would, to a degree, be perpetuated in the later cinema of the 1980s and 1990s. Reckord's *Ten Bob in Winter* (1963) tells the story of African-Caribbean immigrants newly arrived in the UK. Ngakane's *Jemima and Johnny* (1966) is about an interracial friendship between a Black girl and a White boy that survives the racist hostility of the street upon which they live by being kept secret in the basement of a ruined house. Ové's documentary **cinéma-vérité** style informs his early shorts *Baldwin's Nigger* (1969) and *Reggae* (1970), as well as his first feature film *Pressure* (1975), which is heralded as the first Black British feature film. This film tells the story of an English-born son of Trinidadian parents. Alienated from his White friends and the White values that surround him, this unemployed youth is drawn into the world of thieving and smoking dope. Like other Black youths in his community he becomes the target of police harassment. As a result of all this cumulative pressure, it is not long before he joins his older brother and gets involved with Black Power.

The 1980s to 1990s and a new era of Black cinema

As a BFI production, Menelik Shabazz's *Burning an Illusion* (1981) was the first feature film to come out of the new climate in British Black filmmaking. It is, therefore, a landmark film even though, as we shall see, in some ways it continues the earlier realist tradition that was very much based in the present and not in considerations of history. It is a landmark film in that it sets an agenda – both by what it includes and what it omits – of issues that will concern the politicized Black cinema of the 1980s and 1990s. The film tells the story of a young Black woman, a secretary who, as a result of her Black boyfriend's brutal arrest and subsequent unjust imprisonment, changes from being apolitical into an active participant in Black politics. Her political coming-out is both one of style and politics. As a marker of her new political consciousness, she rejects her White-based dress-codes and straightened hair and adopts an Afrocentric dress and hairstyle. She gives up reading Barbara Cartland and takes on board (at the suggestion of her boyfriend) the writings of Malcolm X. What distinguishes this film from its precedents is the fact that it is a woman-based point of view. What makes it similar is its basis in the contemporary. What makes it ground-breaking is its broader address of race, class and gender and its attempts to show, as Lola Young puts it (1996: 155) 'that relationships are constructed within a racialized social context'. Conflicts of gender are present for a first time in this film even though, as Young (1996: 159) points out, the centrality of this issue disappears towards the end of the film and is subsumed under the question of racial politics.

The debates on and practices of issues of representation were closely interlinked and were a founding ethos of the workshop production of the 1980s and 1990s. It could be argued, therefore, that the nature of the film-work that followed *Burning an Illusion* took up and explored many of the issues raised (either by their presence or absence) in this landmark film. But it also has to be said that, even though outside funding was now available and the Black filmmakers workshops were producing challenging as well as successful films, the amounts were not sufficient to allow for a boom in feature film production and so Black filmmakers still found that, if they were to make films, then for the most part these films would have to be shorts, more precisely documentaries. As a result, there was not a widespread or mass audience knowledge about this new Black cinema (as opposed to what was happening in the United States). Work remained pretty much perceived as independent **art cinema**. John Akomfrah's film career to date best exemplifies this problematic. A member of the Black Audio Collective and subsequent independent filmmaker, his films have been both few and far between and for the most part short docu-art films (seventeen to date). His *Handsworth Songs* (1980) is a 60-minute essay on race and disorder in Britain. The film examines the historical, social and political contexts of racial unrest and seeks, through that broad and historicized optic, to explain why the current anger and dis-illusionment felt within the Black communities are running so high. Akomfrah's *Seven Songs for Malcolm X* (1993) is a 52-minute multi-layered poetic-documentary on the Black leader who was assassinated in 1965 (see also in this context his made-for-TV **documentary** on Martin Luther King, *The March*, 2013). Of his seventeen films to date, Akomfrah has directed only two narrative full feature films: *Speak Like a Child* (1998), an intense story about three friends in a children's home in Northumbria; and *The Nine Muses* (2012), a multilayered film that reflects on diasporic history by weaving documentary footage of Black people and Asians coming to work in the UK with shots of a solitary Black figure in the Alaskan wilderness. Akomfrah's experi-mental work, whether documentary or fiction, pushes the boundaries of filmmaking and consistently questions the way in which we narrate stories. Migration and memory are two key themes that run through-out his films and the way in which they function (for good and ill) to construct Black identity (see his recent documentary on the cultural theorist Stuart Hall, *The Stuart Hall Project*, 2013).

In a different way, Isaac Julien (who was part of the Sankofa Collective for three years) has also been mostly limited to the production of docu-shorts but he has made some features. Perhaps best known for his highly successful feature film *Young Soul Rebels* (1991), for which he won the International Critics' Prize at Cannes, he has also made what might be considered art-style experimental documentaries on important personas in Black history. *Looking for Langston* (1989) is a 45-minute essay on the private world of Langston Hughes, a founding member of the Harlem Renaissance and a homosexual who had to hide his sexuality in a climate of disapproval, within both White society and Black – where Black manhood could not be **queer**. In 1997, Isaac Julien made *Frantz Fanon: Black Skin White Mask* (*sic*), a remarkable composite film made up from documentary footage and re-enacted scenes from the life of this major Black intellectual of the 1950s and 1960s. Julien has continued in this vein of docu-art short films and screen installations, of which his most recent, *Playtime* (2014), is dedicated to the memory of Stuart Hall. He was nominated for the Turner Prize (2001, for *Long Road to Mazatlan* and *Vagabondia*). His films are meditations on the culture of diaspora as well as masculinity, queerness and desire (see his documentary on Derek Jarman, *Derek*, 2008). And his film practice can best be described as that of a **transnational** subject committed to a diasporic cinematic language (as with his docu-fiction art film *Paradiso Omeros*, 2004; or again his installation piece *Ten Thousand Waves*, 2010).

Black women filmmakers are also present in equal numbers, although few have broken through to making a full feature film as yet. Maureen Blackwood's *The Passion of Remembrance* (1986) was made with Isaac Julien and was the first full feature film to come out of a Black workshop, in this instance Sankofa. Elsewhere, Blackwood has mostly made shorts including *Perfect Image?* (1988) and *Home Away from Home* (1993). Other Black women filmmakers to have made shorts include Martine Attile (*Dreaming Rivers*, 1988), Ngozi Onwurah (*The Body Beautiful*, 1990) and Amanda Holiday (*Miss Queencake*, 1991).

Onwurah was the first British Black woman filmmaker to release a feature-length film, *Welcome II the Terrordome* (1995), a hard-hitting political action **thriller**, set in a futuristic city, about the tensions between Blacks and Whites in the wake of a child's death. More recently, three women filmmakers, Amma Asante, Destiny Ekaragha and debbie tucker green, have directed award-winning feature-length films (see Asante's **social-realist** *Way of Life*, 2004, and **costume drama** *Belle*, 2013; Ekaragha's **comedy** *Gone Too Far!*, 2013; tucker green's all-Black cast *Second Coming*, 2014, about marital difficulties).

What unites all the productions in this new wave of Black British cinema is a desire to speak not for the diasporas but from *within* them and to reveal the heterogeneity of Black communities – to undo the **myth** of sameness and at the same time give images that do not show Black people as unmitigated and powerless victims of racism, but as citizens with all the complexities of life before them, including choices of political awareness (in this light, see the hard-hitting urban violence, realist film *Bullet Boy*, Saul Dibb, 2004). The issues addressed involve representation and truth in representation. Thus, the power of these productions is in the frankness of the representation, not in the disguising of bad qualities to enhance only the good. This consciousness about diasporas and identities has led some film critics and filmmakers (e.g. John Akomfrah) to align this film production with **Third Cinema**. Furthermore, history is often a core element to these Black films. Gurinder Chadha's feature film *Bhaji on the Beach* (1993) is exemplary of this tendency. It tells the story of a small community of Asians living in Birmingham. A day trip is organized to Blackpool by a worker at the Saheli's women's centre. These women of all different generations head off to Blackpool. As the day progresses their various tales unfold. One woman is the victim of a wife-beating husband; another is pregnant by her Black boyfriend who only agrees to share the responsibility for the baby right at the end of the film; older women express their weariness at always doing for their family and dream of more fanciful ways of spending their days. Chadha reveals her men and women characters in all their complexities and multiplicity at the same time as she addresses questions of identity and belonging. Chadha remains committed to the above issues (history, identity and belonging), consistently blending them with comedy, a combination which has led her to a number of international successes (*Bend it Like Beckham*, 2002, and *Bride and Prejudice*, 2004). On the whole, however, Black British cinema is still sadly small in terms of production (however, Black acting talent is increasingly coming to the fore and gaining international recognition and fame – even if actors must often travel to Hollywood to find work). To date, therefore, Black British cinema has remained very much an independent cinema that has not managed to merge into **mainstream**. Chadha is one exception, as is the writer-director Asif Kapadia with his first feature film, the award-winning *Warrior* (2001) and his widely acclaimed (and top-grossing) documentaries *Senna* (2010) and *Amy* (2015). Another exception, this time marking a cross-over from art cinema to mainstream, is Steve McQueen (a Turner prize-winner in 1999), the first Black director ever to win an Oscar, for his film *12 Years a Slave*, 2013.

see also: **Black cinema – USA, postcolonial theory, Third Cinema**

For further reading see Attile and Blackwood, 1986; Bourne 2001; Doy 2000; Martin, 1995; Mercer, 1988, 1990; Ross, 1996; Young, 1996. For list of films see Givanni, 1992, and for availability of films see Alexander, 1988; for useful bibliography see Vieler-Portet, 1991. Journals: *Channel Four Black Book, Black Phoenix* now called *Third Text Incorporating Black Phoenix, Black Film Bulletin, Black Filmmaker.*

BLACK CINEMA, INCLUDING BLAXPLOITATION MOVIES – USA

Black cinema is a term that presently appears to refer almost exclusively to African-American film production. However, more recently it has come to encompass Black British cinema and, in future years, it may well extend to include other European diasporic cinema such as French Black or Beur cinemas. Although there is huge debate around the term *Black*, for the purposes of this entry the term *Black cinema* will be primarily used in its more common and traditional conceptualization to refer to a cinema emanating from Black diasporic communities in the USA, to a cinema written from within those communities and which is made by individuals who come from those communities. Diaspora refers to a dispersion of people originally belonging to one nation (country) or having a common culture. Black is generally used to refer to people of African or Caribbean descent/ancestry. However, within the UK (as we saw in the above entry), it is a reference that also extends to Asian-Indians. Within the American context we must not forget that other diasporic communities exist: Native Americans (incorrectly referred to as Indians), Chicanos, and Asian-Americans (of Eastern Indian and Asian origin), and that as far as cinematic production is concerned, it is the latter that have been visibly active in filmmaking (e.g. Wayne Wang and the Indian filmmaker now based in the USA, Mira Nair, whose film *Mississippi Marsala*, is about Indians settled in the USA, 1991). Other Black cinemas, such as African or Indian cinemas tend to come under the overall rubric, **World Cinemas**, newly conceived as a term to counter the more problematic expression Third World Cinema, which until recently had been used to refer to cinemas that are neither of the First World (USA/Hollywood) nor the Second (European cinema) but come from a third space, often a colonized and subsequently postcolonial one. World Cinemas refer, therefore, to indigenous cinemas (primarily those of Latin America, Asia, Africa, and Middle Eastern countries) not to those of the Black diaspora. In this entry I shall use Black except where it is necessary to be specific (i.e. African-American, Indian-Asian, etc.).

In discussing Black cinema, one is also talking about race/racism and cinema's own racism. Daniel Bernardi (1996: 7) makes the useful and valid point that 'cinema's invention and early development coincided with the rise in power and prestige of biological determinism' (i.e. belief in the superiority of certain races over others). As Clyde Taylor (1996b: 17) explains, it is impossible to talk about Black cinema without referring to racism and to Hollywood's 'negrophobia' and equally to Film Studies' 'passive racism'. In defence of film studies and thanks to the impact of cultural studies, as Bernardi (1996: 5–6) points out, since the 1990s there has been a steady growth in scholarship in this area of Black cinema, even though there is a lot more to do (see Bernardi's comprehensive list).

By way of illustrating his remarks about Hollywood's negrophobia, Taylor, using the classic epic file of American film history, Griffith's *The Birth of a Nation* (1915), demonstrates how this film is an **epic** of

White supremacy whose theme of national unity rests on the basis of White values – in particular the hatred of miscegnation (1996b: 19). Ford's **Western** film *The Searchers* (1956) reminds us, lest we believe the mythology of White nationalism has disappeared, that some fifty years later, very similar fears were being expressed. Containment and displacement are at work in this 1950s film, just as it was in Griffith's film forty years earlier. While set in the immediate post-Civil War period with its own set of anxieties over the cultural function of race (post-slavery) – which are expressed through fear of the Native American (Indian) predator on White womanhood – *The Searchers* also reflects America's contemporary late 1950s anxieties about the growth of the Civil Rights Movement's campaign activities. Fear of miscegnation and the genetic determination of race is at the heart of Ford's film, just as it is in Griffith's. If, after Griffith's film, mainstream cinema never again portrayed Black people as a mass menacing White society, then, as Clyde Taylor points out (1996b: 32), this did not prevent Western epic after Western epic from picturing the mass slaughter of Indians (or indeed Mexican bandidos).

Black cinema early days 1890s to 1960s: race films and Black filmmaking pioneers

Both Thomas Cripps (1977, 1982) and Ed Guerrero (1993) have documented the Black presence in early American cinema, not just as figurantes or actors, but also as independent producers and directors in their own right. So, while Edison and others were making their race films using Black artistes (*Pickanninies*, 1894; *Negro Dancers*, 1895; *Dancing Darkies*, 1897; *The Dancing Nig*, 1907; *For Massa's Sake*, 1911), African-Americans were not slow to come forward with images to counter these negative stereotypes of Black people. Thus, first Bill Foster and then Emmett J. Scott, George and Noble Johnson, and Oscar Micheaux formed their own independent production companies to produce realistic images of African-American life for Black audiences.

Before saying more about these early pioneers of Black cinema in America, a brief point needs to be made about *race films*, since some ambiguity surrounds the terminology. Race films specifically targeted Black **audiences** and were mostly made by White directors. These race films, in the early days of cinema (when short films were part of a mass of other visual attractions at fairs and exhibitions), appealed to White audiences as well. The idea of the Black body as object for the **gaze**, as exotic other, came into play very early within cinema history, therefore. Over time, however, race films did not necessarily carry these overly negative connotations. During the years of segregated cinema theatres (starting in the 1900s and lasting in some states as late as the 1960s), Black audiences were the recipients of films 'made for them', but which were not necessarily 'about them'. If race films were all-black films, not all of them typecast their actors. In this context, it is worth mentioning the case of Francine Everett, the Black actress, singer and dancer who, during the 1930s and 1940s, starred in a number of low-budget independent films. Although she could have gone to Hollywood (she was offered but turned down a role in the all Black-cast musical *The Green Pastures*, 1936), Everett refused to accept the stereotyped roles imposed upon Black people. Instead, she made several short musical films and featurettes, which were extremely popular with Black audiences. She made these so-called race films with both White and Black directors (e.g. *Keep Punching*, John Clein, 1939; *Big Timers*, Bud Pollard, 1945, who were White directors, and in 1946, *Dirty Gertie from Harlem USA*, by Spencer D. Williams, an African-American filmmaker).

Returning now to our *Black filmmaking pioneers*: Bill Foster set up his production studios (the Foster Photoplay Company) in Chicago in 1910 and set about producing comedies based on the Hollywood formula but recast in a Black mould. The important point here is that he was the first to turn **genre** inside out, to reverse it (to practise what some Black people term 'grinning'). In his films, Black people are not the unidentified shuffling, obsequious caricature of Black manhood, nor the de-sexed and obedient Black Mama. His films showed a slice of Black community life, including a thriving Black middle class (see *The Railroad Porter*, 1912 and *The Fall Guy*, 1913). Other companies quickly followed: the Lincoln Motion Picture Company (1916, Los Angeles) and Oscar Micheaux's Micheaux Book and Film Company (1918).

Following the outrage felt by Black audiences at the screening of Griffith's *The Birth of a Nation*, Black independent filmmakers retorted with a cinema of their own (most symbolically perhaps with Emmett J. Scott's *Birth of a Race*, 1918). This was not the sole cause for the emergence and quite long duration of a Black independent cinema sector (late 1910s to the 1940s). Other contributory factors were, first, economic and, second, cultural ones. Economic because there was a Black audience out there, in a sense already targeted because of segregation (implicit or actual, depending on the state). Cultural, because the Harlem Renaissance Movement of the 1920s gave a new pride and voice to Black people and tackled head-on the question of Blackness and issues of racism. As we shall see, this phenomenon of cinema-as-resistance to negative or incorrect imaging of Black people re-occurs in the early

1970s and again in the mid-1980s and is equally politically, economically and culturally motivated.

Oscar Micheaux's film-work in this context is perhaps best known and, because his work spanned some thirty years (1918–48), during which he made between twenty-five and thirty feature films, he has left a legacy that acts as an extremely important reference point to historians and makers of Black cinema. Micheaux set up his production company in 1918. Half of his output was produced during the first half of his career (1918–29) and most of his films were based on novels written by him. His early films show the complexities of race, but there is no easy binary opposition. He did not offer a sanitized, idealized image of Black people to counter the Hollywood White image. He attempted to show his personal view of the contemporary Black experience. Thus, his films deal with such difficult questions as concubinage, rape, miscegenation, lynching, gambling, wife-beating, debt, urban graft and passing. For example, in *The Symbol of the Unconquered* (1920), Micheaux exposes the problem of betrayal of one's own race (and Black manhood) when a Black man passes as White. The problem is explored further, since this Black person not only successfully passes but also simultaneously oppresses his own people (this passing-villain collaborates with the Ku Klux Klan to drive home-steaders off valuable oil fields). Inter-marriage is an issue that re-occurs in Micheaux's work and the expressed fear of betraying one's own race if one marries a White woman (*The Homesteader*, 1920, and *The House Behind the Cedars*, 1925). Finally, *The Brute* (1920) was a sharply observed film about gambling and wife-beating which did not please many Black audiences. Micheaux's cinema was based on essentially two environments: the urban and the Western frontier. The frontier held hope for Black people (in Micheaux's view). It was there that they could find a better life freer of the racism and violence of the city.

Micheaux's cinema was a political enterprise – to bring an awareness to Black audiences of the real social and moral difficulties they faced as Black people and also to bring them strong, identifiable images of their own lives. But his representation of Blackness has raised some criticism among more recent historians of Black cinema. As one set of critics puts it, Micheaux's drive for 'racial uplift, which was so important to counter accusations of "inferiority", challenged White definitions of race without changing the terms' (Bowser and Spence, 1996: 67). He did not question those terms and saw himself as 'an empowering interpreter of Black life for the community' (ibid.). This has led to further criticisms that Micheaux reproduced White versions of urban Black people as lazy, unambitious and as wanting something for nothing (ibid.: 72–73). Other critics have remarked how Micheaux's narratives appear to valorize paler-skinned Black people over very dark-skinned Black people (Karen Ross, 1996: 60–61, usefully provides a detailed summary of critics holding this position). But bell hooks (1992: 135) argues convincingly that what Micheaux was really doing was 'calling into question the Western metaphysical dualism which associates Whiteness with purity and blackness with taint'. hooks goes on to argue that by doing so Micheaux provided a subtext by which he 'interrogates internalized racism and the color caste system'. The fact that the baddie in *The Symbol of the Unconquered* was a Black person passing as a White person and was therefore pale-skinned would give credence to this intention. The fact also that passing is an issue in his films from the earliest to the latest (see, for example, *Ten Minutes to Live*, 1932) should lead us to agree with bell hooks (ibid.: 135) that 'Micheaux's work offers an extended cinematic narrative of black sexual politics', including the exploration of 'black heterosexual pleasure within a rigid color caste system that makes the desired object the body most resembling Whiteness'. Micheaux's interest in the expression of desire between Black people within the hetero-sexual context is also extremely modern precisely because he shows the complexities of this desire and, equally significantly, because he makes women in his films the agents of desire as much as the men.

Micheaux's films offer an early form of urban realism; they were some of the earliest Black action genre movies and as such his work represents an important heritage to present filmmakers. However, much of today's African-American cinema seems obsessed with the ghetto, male protagonists are driven by a machismo measured by guns and drugs-dealing and hatred of women and they seem determined that there is no way out except through death. All of which seems to strongly counteract the hopes behind Micheaux's work. However, it is the case that Micheaux's legacy appears to have been followed by the work of the so-called new Black aesthetic – predominantly the work of filmmakers trained at the UCLA film school during the 1970s and early 1980s (see below). And it should also be pointed out that, during the 1960s, there were a few African-American indepen-dents making low-budget films that perpetuated the challenge to the stereotyping of Black people initiated by Micheaux and his con-temporaries (e.g. *The Cool World*, Shirley Clarke, 1963; *One Potato, Two Potato*, Larry Peerce, 1964; and *Still a Brother: Inside the Negro Middle Class*, William Greaves and William Branch, 1968). Further-more, during this same period, Sidney Poitier came to embody the new image of the Black man. A middle-class, highly educated and well-mannered African-American who fought racism by example (and by a few occasional outbursts of well-tuned and supremely controlled anger), Poitier's roles were emblematic of the integrationist politics advocated by Martin Luther King and the films he figured in were about social conscience and the fight against racism. An exemplary film of Poitier as this new Black hero is the inter-racial film and murder melodrama *In the Heat of the Night* (Norman Jewison, 1967) in which he fights Southern bigotry to save the life of a racist White youth from conviction for a murder he did not commit. Despite this positive image, critics have argued that Poitier, as 'the ebony saint', was not afforded in his roles any hint of a sexual life – at least on the surface. Close readings of his performance style would suggest, however, that a strong sense of **sexuality** is present and indeed a great sensuousness.

Black cinema of the 1970s: the authentic Black experience and the new Black aesthetic

By the 1970s the social conscience movies of the 1960s had given way to a new set of images inspired by the new Black militancy and Black pride that emerged as a result of the renewed Civil Rights action of the late 1960s. The Watts riots in Los Angeles in 1965, the assassination of Martin Luther King in 1968, and the galvanizing of the student move-ment of protest as a result of the killing of four White students at Kent State University in 1971 all contributed to this resurgence of a new type of Civil Rights activity. The late 1960s to early 1970s was the time, in America, of the Black Power movement; the mid-1970s, of Black people going to (previously) all-White universities in significant num-bers. In Black history, this time was one of politicized opposition to the dominant **ideology** (not one that sought integration in the way argu-ably Martin Luther King had done and that the 1960s Civil Rights movement had advocated). This oppositional mode also filtered into film schools and, in particular, into the UCLA Film School in the late 1960s and early 1970s. Then, a loosely formed group of Black film-makers, having first made their graduation film, subsequently went on to make films either as real independents or as commercially viable industry-based filmmakers. This loose band of filmmakers were all bound by the same political ethos to challenge Hollywood's monopoly (and its predominantly White capitalist world-view).

Essentially there were two waves of filmmakers: those of the early 1970s and those of the late 1970s. As we shall see (below), those who first broke into the terrain of feature film – Van Peebles, Parks Snr and Jnr – ended up (of all ironies) fuelling the Hollywood cinema machine. During 1971–72, three films rooted in African-American urban culture made by these three filmmakers were big hits, particularly with Black audiences (*Sweet Sweetback's Baadasssss Song*, Melvin Van Peebles, 1971; *Shaft*, Gordon Parks Snr, 1971; and *Superfly*, Gordon Parks Jnr, 1972). The heroes of these films were rough, tough and, most important of all, they were winners. And the films themselves were direct challenges to Hollywood **action films** and Hollywood's representation of Black people. They were sub-genres with a message, therefore. Sadly, however, even though it is clear that Van Peebles never thought that his independently produced film *Sweet Sweetback's Baadasssss Song* (*Song*) would be the cornerstone for some forty Blaxploitation movies to follow in its wake, nonetheless his film, and the two other films mentioned, became the founding stones for a series of very profitable ventures for Hollywood.

As for those UCLA filmmakers who followed later – especially Charles Burnett, Larry Clark, Julie Dash and Hailé Gerima – it was almost as if this second wave of independents had to come in their wake to rectify this cynical appropriation by Hollywood of their earlier compatriots' work. This second wave of filmmakers sought to broaden the frame of reference of Black experiences in America – including that of Black women – and to challenge the stereotypes surrounding their representation. This cinema, a socio-realist/ethnographic cinema, became known as the new Black aesthetic. Unfortunately, it is one that has had a rather small impact on Black cinema and which has struggled financially to survive (see Diawara, 1993 for greater detail). Even though this Black aesthetic cinema lacked a successful business model that would enable it to thrive in the national context, it is one that hits out against stereotypes (including those that Black people produce of themselves) and one that does not conform to the image of Black hero as oppressed but offers images of self-determination for both men and women. This cinema looks at traditions of Black cultures. Equally, it also addresses issues of post-(White)-colonialism and neo-colonialism. Of this category of cinema, the films of Charles Burnett (*Killer of Sheep*, 1977; *To Sleep with Anger*, 1990; *The Glass Shield*, 1995; *Nightjohn*, 1997) and Julie Dash (*Daughters of the Dust*, 1991) are perhaps the best known.

Blaxploitation movies

In the early 1970s, Hollywood was suffering financially (see **studio system**) so, during the period 1971 to 1976, with an eye to profit, it capitalized on the initial success of *Song*, *Shaft* and *Superfly* and made a plethora of what have become known as Blaxploitation films. These films, starring Black actors – but produced by and mostly directed by White people – deliberately targeted Black audiences (a cynical repeat of *race films* in a way). The authentic Black experience had become subsumed into Hollywood capitalism – the very thing it sought to fight. In all three films, *Song*, *Shaft* and *Superfly*, the heroes/anti-heroes succeed against the (White) system. However, it is Van Peebles' film *Song* that remains the clearly politically motivated one, hence the irony of this sub-genre's cooptation by White people. Van Peebles' film reflects the politicization of Black America of the early 1970s. *Song is* about the Black community, more specifically about the law as an enemy of Black people. The eponymous anti-hero, Sweetback, is a pimp (and a stud) who gets elevated to cult hero when he kills two White policemen who have acted abusively within the Black community. He then escapes to Mexico. This film, which was independently produced and cost $500,000 to make, grossed $20 million in the first few months of its release. Similarly *Shaft* and *Superfly*, produced by Hollywood (but directed by African-Americans), made tidy profits. These three films represented a positive moment in Black cultural history. Black people, who hitherto had remained a-sexualized on the screen, now expressed their sexuality for themselves. Black audiences were given strong heroes who did not get dragged down but who actually escaped from the ghetto. Aggressive and rugged individualism was put up on-screen and undoubtedly provided Black audiences with images that both articulated their anger and gave it a positive outcome.

For Hollywood, the success of *Shaft* (which won an Oscar for Isaac Hayes' music score) and *Superfly* meant cheap products bringing in high returns. Now, Black actors became the flavour of the month, provided they were not expensive. However, if they were inexpensive (i.e. not Sidney Poitier), generally speaking, they were not known by the public at large. So, Hollywood turned to musicians and sportsmen (*sic*) to find their stars (thereby guaranteeing further White audience interest as well – what is known as cross-over value). White directors and producers pumped out sequels to these original hits – all much of a muchness (pimp or private-eye beating the system) and simplistically racist (the White person as the fat villain). The success of these mix and match, push-button formulaic films led Hollywood to cast its net a bit wider, generically speaking (e.g. monster movies *Blacula*, William Crain, 1972; **Westerns**, *Boss Nigger* (aka *Black Bounty Killer*), Jack Arnold, 1974; and the series featuring the football star Fred Williamson

The Legend of Nigger Charlie, 1972; *The Soul of Nigger Charlie*, 1973). (For a persuasive counter-reading of *Blacula*, see Leerom Medovoi, 1998.)

For all that the Blaxploitation movies were exploitative of Black audiences, it was surely the first time that a Black presence was so widely visible in movie theatres. Blaxploitation movies had a double-edged result, therefore. On the one hand (and this is particularly true of the earlier Blaxploitation movies – and of course the three pre-blax films), these movies gave a representation of Blackness and Black ghetto life not seen since the Micheaux films (even if, this time, the director is White). They established an African-American identity that was different from the safe-sexed Poitier (or indeed Harry Belafonte). They created new stars, new super-heroes: Jim Brown, Ron O'Neal, Richard Rowntree, Tamara Dobson and Pam Grier (some of whom disappeared during the 1980s only to reappear in the 1990s, as Pam Grier did in Quentin Tarantino's film *Jackie Brown*, 1998). Although the point needs to be made that women heroes in Blaxploitation movies were far from numerous and only two became true stars – Tamara Dobson of *Cleopatra Jones* fame (Jack Starrett, 1973) and Pam Grier – all these women were sexed, armed and potent and fought their own case and cause (e.g. drugs, corrupt White cops). The women-based Blaxploitation movies, while thin on the ground, did nonetheless, as Leerom Medovoi (1998: 15) points out, 'activate feminine narratives concerning racial loyalties and Black pride'. Medovoi notes in particular that Pam Grier's roles in *Coffy* (Jack Hill, 1973) and *Foxy Brown* (Jack Hill, 1974) reveal her as facing anxieties actually felt by Black women viewers between their loyalty to the new African-American way (as exemplified by the Black Power Movement and the new heroic images of Black manhood in Blaxploitation movies) and their longing for an Afrocentrism (a passion for a retrieval of African roots). Finally, on the positive side of Blaxploitation movies we must count the dress-code, language and music that were so firmly Black-encoded.

On the other hand, the down-side of the Blaxploitation movies, particularly the later ones, was the stress Hollywood placed on sex and violence at the expense of the more complex intertwining of identity factors. If sex and violence were a part of this identity, they certainly were not the whole of it in the first three African-American products that Hollywood sought to reproduce in a formulaic and stereotyped fashion. Many Blaxploitation movies deal with the drug plots against the Black community, but these can now be read as attempts by Hollywood to recuperate any articulation of a politicized message such as Black empowerment. The hero may well be a powerful masculine presence; however, the image of militant Black manhood has gone.

In 1976, the Blaxploitation movie craze crashed, for predominantly two reasons: one economic, the other political. On the economic front, although Black people were by far the greatest audiences of these movies, in the 1970s, they only represented 12 per cent of the population. Demographically speaking, they are not then a large target audience, something that Hollywood requires to make profit. So the genre died out, even though, in the late 1980s to early 1990s, cable and syndicated television and video sales upped the demand for all sorts of films and made targeting small audiences a profitable concern. Thus, Hollywood was back making Black-cast movies, this time for TV. The fading of the Blaxploitation boom was also politically motivated. In the late 1970s, as a result of the politicizing effects of the Black Power Movement – at least as far as the representation of Black men was concerned – images of Black people as pimps, junkies, dealers, thieves ran counter to the new images Black men had of themselves. If, however, in the Black cinema of the 1980s and 1990s, Black male images became more diversified, such was not the case for Black women, nor even today. Images of Black women as 'bitch' or 'ho' (whore) still prevail (see below). (For detailed study of Blaxploitation see Lawrence, 2008.)

After 1976 – towards a mainstream Black cinema?

Over the past forty years, two discernible styles of Black cinema have emerged: the populist tradition which comes down to a revival of the Blaxploitation movie (e.g. the Eddie Murphy films of which *Vampire in Brooklyn*, Wes Craven, 1995, merely continues the *Blacula* tradition, comedy-style). At its best, this populist style parodies its antecedents. The second discernible style is the urban African-American ghetto street-life movie, a category which often includes hip-hop-rap and for the most part is male centred. Spike Lee's early films in particular are exemplary of this tradition; but more recently Lee Daniels produced and directed *Precious* (2009), which tells the story, set in Harlem, of an overweight, illiterate teen who suffers abuse from all corners (home and school) and who is pregnant with her second child. Other than these two categories, but to a very minor degree, the more aesthetically-minded Black cinema lives on in a handful of films.

Of the populist/post-Blaxploitation category, Keenan Ivory Wayans' *I'm Gonna Git You Sucka* (1988) was the first and is, arguably, one of the best Blaxploitation parodies. Playfully **intertextual**, it sends up not just the clothes worn during the 1970s (as funny to look at now) but exposes their original parodic/ironic value. That is, the clothes-chic of flares, tight polyester shirts, platform shoes, hot pants so preponderant in the dress-code of White people in the 1970s was none other than a restoration into mainstream culture of the dress-code of double-marginals – Black pimps and prostitutes! Wayans also brought back in the **stars** and the music from the earlier films: we all remember the music of *Shaft* – nostalgia for all, including the stars who were willing to come back and make fun of their previous selves.

If Black cinema became a visible phenomenon in the 1980s, it was thanks partly to the success of the star Eddie Murphy – an exemplar of the populist tradition (and great puller of White audiences). But it was also thanks to the success of early 1980s hip-hop-rap films. This category of Black cinema, though perhaps not ideological, does represent the revival of a specific cultural nationalism: Black urban street life – mainly as it concerns men. Thus, for feminists, Black feminists, it is not an improblematized revival, nor is it an unproblematic representation of Black culture (see below). However, these films are compositions that do run counter to **classical narrative cinema** in their syncopated jazz-like structure and their strong reliance on the rhythm of rap music. They are low-budget products all made for under $10m and grossing up to five times that figure. Lee's *She's Gotta Have It*, 1986, was made for $175,000 and grossed $8.5m; *Do the Right Thing*, 1989, cost $6.5m and grossed over $27.5m. Lee's success opened the door for others, which is a positive outcome. For example, 1991 saw nineteen Black-cast and Black-directed films and that decade became a boom period in terms of African-American cinema products. The 1990s also witnessed a big increase in the number of African-American stars – mostly male stars it is true – and it is difficult not to attribute this greater presence to Hollywood's realization (thanks to the boom in Black cinema) that Black actors are bankable items and should be more widely used.

Spike Lee's story is undoubtedly *the* success story. With twenty-three feature films to his name to date (and a further sixteen documentaries) – most of them made independently or with some funding from the majors (the exception being *Malcolm X*, 1992, see below) – he has become *the* bankable Black filmmaker. While his work is consistently controversial and criticized either for the way he represents women, although to be fair he often makes them into strong characters, or for being sensationalist (but again his restraint in his documentary-fiction *4 little girls*, 1997, should be cited to counter this accusation), or for mis-representing history (in *Malcolm X* for example), he has put Black consciousness on the map and, moreover, he has managed to beat Hollywood by making his films into cross-over films (see *25th Hour*, 2002). He has also brought New York into the frame solidly as a city of reference for his investigations into contemporary American life that is not just limited to the Black experience (see *Summer of Sam*, 1999; *25th Hour*; *Inside Man*, 2006).

Leaving Spike Lee aside, it is the case, however, as Jacquie Jones (1991) says, that Hollywood still holds the purse strings – it chooses the Black directors, actors and the storyline. And these films represent a cinema that does not threaten existing conventions. Citing numerous films, but focusing on Mario Van Peebles' *New Jack City*, 1991, which was independently produced so was perhaps not the best choice to illustrate her otherwise not invalid argument, Jones claims that this cinema proffers a new ghetto aesthetic that magnifies the grim realities of Black urban life, plays on the Black on Black crime **myth** and, finally, serves to illuminate the clichéd image of the Black male for the American audience. At best, then, Black people become sociologically interesting. Ed Guerrero (1994: 30) argues differently that these 'male-focused, "ghettocentric", action-crime-adventure' movies differ from the standard Hollywood studio action-film product and 'implicitly undermine Hollywood's inherent tendency to repress or co-opt resistant or oppositional social perspectives in its films'. Guerrero sees *New Jack City* (among other contemporary ghetto-centric films) as 'caught up in the aspirations and communal problems of the social worlds they depict' and as historicizing 'the cultural, political and economic issues of the resistant communities they represent'.

Undoubtedly, Hollywood co-opted this ghetto-centric/gangster cinema in the same way as it had the early 1970s Black action cinema. And it did so quite swiftly. These cheapies were good value at a cost of between $1.5m and $10m. At that price, returns were guaranteed by Black audiences alone, so any cross-over revenue was pure profit. However, if the budget was in the $30m range, then cross-over became an imperative. While this could seem to compromise Black filmmakers, most African-American filmmakers working within the studio system would argue that they were there 'to expand the definitions and possibilities of being black and to subvert the dominant norm by marketing a "black sensibility" to as broad an audience as possible' (Guerrero, 1994: 30), including of course a White audience.

Leaving that polemic aside, what is interesting in the evolution of Black cinema since its beginnings is the way in which this latest boom – unlike the new Black aesthetic – did not draw on its historical past but was in many ways deeply a-historical. While the ghetto-centric movie draws on the ghetto culture of 1970s Blaxploitation movies, gangster/gangsta-chic has replaced the imagery of Black identity proposed by the earlier movies whose own image is based on the historical and political context of the 1960s Civil Rights Movement and later the Black Power Movement. Gangsta-chic is based on violence and addiction which the 1970s failed to remove (despite the evidence to the contrary in the Blaxploitation films). There is no apparent desire to leave the ghetto – or the 'hood – only to die in it. Guerrero (1994: 30) makes the point that Black people today are worse off economically speaking than they were before the 1960s Civil Rights Movement. The ghetto culture is back but with a difference. The ghetto culture has spiralled down in one long social continuity of governmental neglect. The music is rap and is based on violence and revenge, as is the narrative (the story of the rapper filmmaker Tupac Shakur is but one we can point to). The implicit brotherhood of the Blaxploitation movie has gone and now it is gang warfare. The fight is over drugs and who controls them, not how to get rid of them (this gangster warfare is somewhat reminiscent of the 1930s gangster movies where the fight between gangs was over alcohol).

The film *Menace II Society* (Allen and Albert Hughes, 1993) shows this regressive reality of the 'hood film. The film starts with an evocation by the young protagonist of his father's involvement with the Watts Riots, and then interfaces, through his flashbacks, his parents' life in the 1970s (represented very much in the Blaxploitation movie style) with that of his own current life (represented in the form of the now familiar contemporary hip-hop 'hood film). Ultimately, the present is just a worse manifestation of what was before. Leerom Medovoi (1998: 7) sees the problem in such representations as being located in the fact that they are based on a very narrow historical field, one that is not tied to the destructive legacy of the slave trade but only to the immediate past (see *Juice*, Ernest R. Dickerson, 1992; *Gridlock'd*, Vondie Curtis-Hall, 1997; both Tupac Shakur star vehicles). The broader history behind the current anger, Black rage and destructiveness, is what is missing in these films. Such representations are very few and far between, emanating from the independent films of the new Black aesthetic group (e.g. Barnett and Dash) and which looks at the past – the deep past – as well as to the 'new formulations of identity and subject-hood' (Guerrero, 1994: 28).

In these ghetto-centric films, the reappropriation of Black women by Black male filmmakers has not represented a sign of liberation for women either – a deep disappointment given the positive heritage of their representation in Micheaux's films and some Blaxploitation movies. In the majority of these movies women occupy predominantly two positions: 'bitch', the wilful woman ripe for being brought down, or 'ho', the sexually demanding and not easily satisfied woman. There is, occasionally, the presence of the good woman, the rescuer, the one who utters (however ineffectually) the words of salvation, the one who perhaps represents the missing parent (e.g. *Menace II Society*). For the most part, woman is usually defined in relation to the other male characters, she has no narrative of her own. Misogyny also hits out at the mother, who is often seen as ineffectual, and in return patriarchy is valorized. This is particularly the case in the films of two filmmakers, John Singleton (*Boyz n the Hood*, 1991) and Matty Rich (*Straight Out of Brooklyn*, 1991). In mainstream cinema, Leslie Harris' *Just Another Girl on the IRT* (1993) stands more or less alone as a film that counters this deeply misogynistic view of women in the 'hood.

Since 2000, interestingly and surprisingly, given the current social unease in the USA, with so many shootings of Black citizens, the dominant trend in terms of films made by Black filmmakers has been towards comedy with virtually half of all films falling into this category: some twenty-five films out of fifty-four. Furthermore, the point of view is predominantly male. Of these comedies, twelve are about boys/men on a caper; seven are rom-coms, battle of the sexes-style; six, buddy-films. Not quite what one might expect in this dark climate of real violence. Admittedly, gangsta-action movies are still in evidence (with some fifteen films); but social issues, or biopics, are fairly low down the production list in terms of output (four). And in 2016, only six films were made by Black directors, one of which is a documentary on abortion rights (*Trapped*, Dawn Porter), the other a biopic on Miles Davis (*Miles Ahead*, Don Cheadle). Some film directors have crossed over to TV-series production or direction: John Singleton and Mario Van Peebles, for example (fairly mainstream police or political dramas, some hip-hop and musical dramas). Overall, this suggests that Black cinema is following a more mainstream (if not conservative) route.

Who is the speaking subject?

This new Black cinema (whether populist, urban/ghetto, socio-realist) raises the question of who is the speaking **subject**? Is it 'just' Black? Is it 'just' male and Black? What, in America, is its originating space (i.e. East or West Coast, North or South)? How is it situated in time and space (i.e. in relation to its history)? Speaking the Black subject raises further questions. To whom are these images destined? What about the risks involved in becoming the voice of the Black cause? That is, of speaking about the Black condition rather than from it? Of setting in place a new set of stereotypes (e.g. 'Black as victim')? What, in the final analysis, is to be the relationship with Hollywood? Can Black cinema co-exist with Hollywood in the same time and space?

Black people currently represent 13 per cent of the American population, and they presently make up 25 per cent of the cinema-going audience, which is primarily a youth audience. Black culture permeates American society; particularly the youth class. This should make Black cinema an attractive proposition for Black investment. As yet, however, this has not transpired. The emergence of Black cinema is not thanks to Black financing but is a result of Hollywood's economic policy which has co-opted Black cinema into its industrial monopoly. There are kicks against this, which may herald change. First, there was Spike Lee's much publicized defiance over the financing of *Malcolm X* (1992). Warners produced it but would only put up $28m, Lee needed $34m. He publicly exposed Warners when he named the Black celebrities who helped make up the $6m shortfall. Second, Lee was able (as he had been able to do with the launch of his first film *She's Gotta Have It*) to draw upon the support of an association based in New York: the Black Filmmakers Foundation (BFF, established 1978). The BFF was founded to counter Hollywood's control over film production and distribution and to help finance Black filmmakers' work (founding members include Charles Burnett, Julie Dash, Warrington Hudlin, Charles Lane). This precedent has been followed in recent years (2010) by Ava DuVernay (director of *Selma*, 2014) who launched the independent distribution company and resource collective ARRAY (formerly AFFRM) whose mission is to assist in the 'amplification of independent films by people of color and women filmmakers globally' (arraynow.com). As this book goes to press, DuVernay has just released a timely documentary film, *13ᵗʰ* (2016), that addresses the rough justice meted out to Black citizens in the USA, in violation of the US Constitution's Thirteenth Amendment. Screened at the 2016 London Film Festival, it has been released on Netflix (rather than in cinema theatres), which suggests the determination of the director that this film, which joins the dots from colonial (slavery-ridden) America to the recent movement Black Lives Matter, should be seen by the widest audience possible. Third, Black filmmakers have refused, through their film practices, to be measured by the two key modalities usually imposed by critics on films coming from the margins: authenticity and **realism** (see Kennedy, 1993). Thus, although critics may decry the failure of films which refer to rap-culture, both textually (through their structures) and intertextually (through the presence of rap artists and their songs within the film), to convey the authenticity of the concerns of rap lyrics, they are missing the point that this cinema is not one that is seeking to marginalize itself as **avant-garde** but one that is seeking to deconstruct

hegemonic practices from within. Similarly, why must realism mean one thing only – ghetto Black violence – and not middle-class success? Fourth, in this cinema from the margins, there is another voice getting heard – that of Black female filmmaker (depending on sources, there are between 20 and 40 currently working in the USA, some are documentarists, others feature filmmakers, others still TV directors). This is a voice that gives a different image of Black womanhood to that offered by Black male cinema (see Bobo, 1998; Oshana, 1985). To the misogynistic and at times homophobic images of Lee, Singleton and Mario Van Peebles, Kathleen Collins counters with images of middle-class professional womanhood (*Losing Ground*, 1982), and Heather Foxworth with images that expose Black male sexism within the Black community (*Trouble I've Seen*, 1988). The issue of overweight women is given an interesting twist in Nnegest Likké's *Phat Girlz* (2006), a comedy starring Mo'nique which ends up asserting that size doesn't matter (at least in Nigeria!). Mira Nair's *Mississippi Masala* (1991) comes at inter-racial desire from a new and different perspective that points to the multicultural reality of the United States. In this film, the two young lovers are an African-American man and an Asian-Indian woman – inter-racial marriage in this context reveals itself as having the immense potential of a rich mixture (a Masala) of cultural backgrounds. Finally, African-American women and their sexuality and the way it has been negatively constructed by Black male filmmakers is being addressed in theoretical contexts (see Manatu, 2003).

see also: **Black cinema – UK, postcolonial theory, Third Cinema**

For further reading see authors quoted in above text and see also: Antonio, 2002; Bakari, 1993; Bogle, 1988, 1994; Cripps, 1978, 1993; Diawara, 1993; Donaldson, 2003; Gabbard, 2004; Givanni and Reynaud, 1993; Grant IV, 2004; Guerrero, 1993; Lawrence, 2008; Leonard, 2006; Manatu, 2003; Martin, 1995; Masoud, 2003; Reid, 1993, 2005; Rocchio, 2000; Snead, MacCabe and West, 1994; Taylor, 1986; Watkins, 1998; Wilderson III, 2010; Wilkins, 1989.

BLOCKBUSTERS

The phenomenon of the blockbuster has been around in the West for just over half a century and the term refers to two aspects of the film product: first, its enormous cost and expected financial return; and, second, the array of special attractions and dazzling effects (be it stars, sets, costumes, technical effects) put on-screen to bring audiences in, in their droves. Recent big successes include:

Table 1 Blockbusters

Title	Year	Director	Budget	Box-office
Titanic	1997	Cameron	$200m	$2.185bn
Avatar	2009	Cameron	$237m	$2.782bn
Harry Potter and the Deathly Hallows Pt 2	2011	Yates	$250m	$1.328bn
The Avengers	2012	Whedon	$220m	$1.519bn
Frozen	2013	Buck/Lee	$150m	$1.276bn
Star Wars: The Force Awakens	2015	Abrams	$306m	$2.068bn

Blockbusters are a way for the major production companies to stay on top and dominate competition: because they are so expensive to make, minor production companies cannot afford to compete. They also come with massive financial backing for their publicity campaign to ensure that they attract an audience beyond those who conventionally attend. To this effect an imaginary community is created by the campaign which sells the film on the principle of inclusion – you are either in because you have seen it or out because you have not. Other aspects of selling this inclusion are the spin-off merchandising products (toys, games, etc.). A further vital key factor to their million-dollar success is of course the pre-sale value of the film to TV and DVD, etc.

Blockbusters come in and out of fashion, predominantly for financial reasons. They get dropped, either because the economic climate of the times is unfavourable and studios are suffering financially, or because studios and production companies find themselves over-stretched financially after making losses on a particular blockbuster film that flopped (the most famous case being *Cleopatra*, Mankiewicz, 1963). But it always bounces back. So far, we can trace three cycles of the blockbuster post-1945: the 1950s ending early 1960s; the mid-1970s ending early 1980s (Michael Cimino's *Heaven's Gate*, 1980, is often cited as the flop that put a stop to that period of blockbuster pro-duction); and the 1990s to 2010s (and still ongoing). In each instance, technological advances are exploited with a view to bringing back lost audiences to the cinema theatres. So, in the 1950s, it was **cinema-scope** and **colour**; in the mid-1970s it was the new super-formats of the widescreen (70mm film), use of front projections and motion-control systems for special effects and new sound technology (George Lucas' *Star Wars*, 1977, being an outstanding example); in the 1990s it was the advances in digital technology which made so much more possible in terms of camera work, digital sound and special effects (so much so, it continues to be exploited to its full over a broad set of **genres**); finally, in the 2000–2010s the return of **3-D** technology (first experienced in the 1950s) in a renewed form has enhanced the viewing experience. Special effects, particularly via **CGI**, are now so important that there are several production houses (dotted around the world) devoted entirely to special effects. And indeed, *Avatar*'s $2.8bn worldwide box-office return would seem to indicate this total-digital-effect is welcomed by spectators. The latest super-hero 3-D film, *The Avengers* (Joss Whedon, 2012), with its allegorical reference to the 9/11 disaster in New York, was a massive success ($1.25bn box-office); to say nothing of yet another Star Wars blockbuster (*Star Wars: The Force Awakens*, 2015) with over $2bn to its credit.

Blockbuster is a term, but not a generic type (see **genre**). Blockbuster movies include **action films, crime films, epics, fantasy films, sci-fi films, war films, Westerns**, some **animated films** and of course we must not lose sight of films from Eastern nations – who also have their blockbusters – such as the martial arts films. In blockbusters everything is larger than life, including sound. Take, for example, the outsized beef-cake bodies of the 1980s action films pumping iron to save their nation (Stallone, Schwartzenegger, Van Damme). When purporting to refer to the real – as with war movies – this larger-than-life experience, in order to pass as authentic, can take on the form of the hyper-real (see, for example, the opening sequence of *Saving Private Ryan*, Spielberg, 1998, which re-creates the Allied landing on Omaha beach). Recent developments in computer and video-games have contributed further to this idea of blockbuster films being more than the real and have, as we know, impacted on the use of digital technology in cinema (*Lara Croft: Tomb Raider*, de Bont, 2003, and *Run Lola Run*, Tykwer, 1998, are two examples). So now it is possible and desirable, given target audiences, to invent sets that go beyond the real and yet which have a three-dimensionality that allows them to convince us of a larger-than-life reality – take, for example, the recent *Lord of the Rings* series (Peter Jackson begun 2001); or *Harry Potter* series (begun 2002); or in the animated world, *Frozen* (2013).

What attracts us to blockbusters? The special effects are an essential ingredient, but there is more to it than that. We are there to enjoy the spectacular elements but we are also there because we want to work out the **narrative**. However, there is a tension between narrative and spectacle and often it is quite difficult to find a coherence to the storyline because it is so consistently interrupted by spectacle. King (2000) writes very helpfully about the basic ingredients of the American blockbuster movie and argues that it is not the case that it is all spectacle at the expense of narrative. If we assume that narrative has, as its mission, the production of homogeneity, then the spectacular film is not really going to offer us this. A primary reason, King argues (2000: 4), is that Hollywood's driving mission is to make money and that in its 'desire to appeal to a mass-market [it] is likely to produce a degree of built-in incoherence and conflicting demand'. What the spectacular does have, of course, is **ideological** effects (as does any film for that matter), but they emanate from a particularly narrow frame of reference in that the spectacular offers – merely – a way of reconciling rival or contradictory demands.

The first set of contradictions is based in the **myth** of the frontier. As King explains (2000: 2), the myth of the frontier is a founding-stone of American narrative frameworks (especially the spectacular – we need only think of the Western). The frontier myth is always in opposition with the concept of home (be it domesticity, family, etc.). The frontier within the spectacular broadens in its frame of reference depending on which generic type you are watching. In a war movie, the frontier is clearly represented by troops trying to gain advantage on enemy territory; domesticity, through a longing for home. In action films, the opposition is often murkier – the cause propelling the protagonist into action may not be clear or indeed even honourable (see Michael Mann's *Collateral*, 2004, in this context) and domesticity is represented through the idea of the (heterosexual) couple or family life which, in turn, is often put at risk by all the action going on. The heyday of the 'hulk' action hero, the 1980s, saw men of mighty force and muscle keeping America safe against the threat of Soviet-styled communism (a weird embodiment, if you will, of President Ronald Reagan's 1983 Star Wars policy). These huge iron-fisted bodies were body-built *in extremis* as bulwarks against infiltration – America was impregnable thanks to them (see *Rambo: First Blood Part II*, George P. Cosmatos, 1985 and *Rambo III*, Peter MacDonald, 1988; *Predator*, John McTiernan, 1987; *Cobra*, George P. Cosmatos, 1986).

More recently, in the action thriller, slightly different poles of opposition are set up. Often this generic type takes the form of the individual (the frontier-hero) being pitted against corporate industry, technology that has gone awry, or anonymous government bodies – the anonymity preserving any questioning of America's institutions per se (of course); although, *The Bourne Trilogy*, as a precise example of this type of conflict, does implicate the CIA amongst other covert agencies worldwide. In these action thrillers, the family will be there as the other sphere – once more under threat, as the individual frontier-hero persists in trying to overcome the baddies. Domestic tranquillity is the hoped for outcome, but does not always transpire. The frontier-hero may well lose all that is dear to him in this David and Goliath struggle (see Michael Mann's *The Insider*, 1999). Thus, in terms of reconciling rival demands, we go to see the spectacle with the heightened expectation of an alternative to domesticity – to experience the thrill of the spectacle as opposed to our more humdrum everyday existence. The ideological effect is to bring the concept of the frontier into the civilized sphere (King, 2000: 5), giving us a vicarious but harmless experience of the frontier. Of course, once we read against the grain then we get a sense that the frontier myth with its ideological effects and the institutions they support should be questioned.

The second set of contradictions has to do with the very process of viewing itself. We derive pleasure from the effects bombarding us – what King (2000: 94) refers to as 'in your face' effects. This does not limit itself to action-type movies. **Musicals**, especially more recent ones, also offer this effect. We love this feel of being 'done to' (ibid.: 98); but we also resist it because we would like to linger longer, savour the effects which flash past so quickly. Baz Luhrmann's *Moulin Rouge!* (2001) is a good example of this split response. There is huge enjoyment from the flourish of the cameras and the dazzling sets, costumes, and song and dance routines. However, because the camera never allows us to linger long enough to see everything, so our pleasures are never fully indulged in terms of looking. This 'wanting more' draws us into the erotics of the spectacle (be it musical, action or war movies) – a **scopophilic** process by which we get hooked. However, while we derive pleasure from this bombardment of our senses, we are also engaged in trying to make sense of the narrative – thus there is this further set of contradictions with, this time, spectacle vying with narrative for our attention. At times, a film can come dangerously close to failing to keep us on that knife-edge. Michael Mann's *Collateral* is a good example of this. There is a sense in which this film is a replay of just so many of Mann's visual and thematic obsessions (beginning with *Thief*, 1981). We could ask ourselves does the Tom Cruise character, Vincent, a stone-cold assassin who completely lacks a history, engage us enough to tough-out this action-packed adventure? Is the lack of any real narrative saved for us by the taxi-driver character played by Jamie Foxx – Max Durocher (literally Max of the Rock) – or is he just a conventional (Black) side-kick persona for the central protagonist? Whatever our answers it does not seem to matter as far as box-office records are concerned. Mann's film has been a big commercial success, so clearly audiences are not tired of the formula (yet).

For further discussion of blockbuster films *see* separate entries for **action films**, **crime films**, **epics**, **musicals**, **sci-fi films**, **war films**, **Westerns**.

For further reading see Hall and Neale, 2010; Grant, 2004; King, 2000; Lichtenfeld, 2007; Meyers, 2001; Neale, 2000; Stringer, 2003.

B-MOVIES

Cheap and quickly made, B-movies first came into prominence in the United States during the Depression (early 1930s) when audiences demanded more for their money – a double bill: two films for the price of one. B-movies were screened as a second feature, alongside a major feature film (called an A-movie). Monogram and Republic made B-movies only, mostly **thrillers** and **Westerns**; the major studios also had to turn some of their studios over to B-movie production and some of their productions met with astonishing success (e.g. RKO's *Cat People*, Val Lewton, 1942). Post-war, the Supreme Court decision, in 1948, to end the major studios' cartel over distribution and exhibition opened the screens to independently produced films with a major effect on production practices. The impact of this decision on the Hollywood studios was to re-create fierce competition among the majors. As a result, the cost of making films in and for Hollywood went sky-high. The effect was to put an end to the production of B-movies and to the double bill.

see also: **quota quickies, studio system**

BOLLYWOOD

This term, which is a conflation of Bombay and Hollywood, was coined in the 1980s by the West to refer to the dominant form of Hindi popular cinema produced in Bombay (now Mumbai), namely, the singing–dancing–action films which have now found a place on the world stage. There is a concern that this term has ended up giving a rather limited view of Indian cinema, since there is a far more diverse production than just Bombay commercial cinema (Kabir, 2001: 21). Indeed, there are a dozen regional language cinemas in India and Bollywood production accounts for just 20 per cent of all films released yearly (Dudrah, 2012: 1). However, it has allowed the West to understand that these types of movies represent a large-scale entertainment product that should be viewed in the same way as

Hollywood films are regarded (Kabir, 2001: 21). It has also allowed the West to come to know this cinema rather than being limited to knowing Indian cinema as a small collection of **auteur** films. (See entry on *Indian cinema* in **World Cinemas** entry.)

What is a Bollywood film? First, it is a popular Hindi film with massive audience appeal; helped doubtless by the fact it is presented in a seamless mix of Hindi and Urdu (the two North Indian sister languages understood by about half the population of India). Second, it is a mix of **epic**, romance and **melodrama**. Finally, it is a **musical** love-story based on a set of quite explicitly coded conventions. The story, traditionally about unconditional love, conflict, revenge and redemption, is woven together by a minimum of six songs and two lavish dance routines (with forty-plus people). The average Hindi popular film relies on a conventional **narrative** (boy-meets-girl), and its originality comes down to the musical score and the song and dance routines. In this regard, as with its narrative line, it has quite a lot in common with the Hollywood musical. In terms of cross-fertilization between the two cinemas, however, it is noteworthy that while Bollywood readily borrows plotlines from Hollywood, the reverse is almost impossible because of the complexities of the Bollywood song and dance routines which Hollywood is hard pressed to imitate (Kabir, 2001: 15). Bollywood borrows but, thanks to its own **codes and conventions**, so transforms the initial text that it is hard to detect the original.

Much like the Hollywood musical, the Bollywood musical has its own **ideological** effects. But, whereas the American **genre** sells utopia in the form of harmonious marriage, the Bollywood musical, in its stressing of the importance of honour and self-respect as well as upholding religious and moral values, which include marriage, provides a far broader and more complex image of what it means to be Indian. The *Devdas* story – which has had three iterations (Baraa, 1935; Roy 1955; and Bhansali, 2002) – is a good illustrative example of this obedience-narrative and the consequent ideology at work. It was a narrative that became a popular model for love-triangle films and, in ideological terms, gave a strong warning to those who would attempt to marry against parental authority (Kabir, 2001: 10). The story goes as follows: 'Devdas is a high-caste Brahmin who cannot marry the love of his life, Parvati, his neighbour's daughter, because she is of a lower caste. He later befriends a prostitute who gives up her profession and turns to spirituality. In a downward spiral of self-destruction, the Hamlet-like Devdas becomes an alcoholic and ultimately dies at the gate of Parvati's marital home' (2001: 10).

Bollywood films last between two and a half to three hours, so performance, sets and locations are crucial – especially since the construction of the narrative is formulaic and based in repetition. **Audience** consumption is very different from a Western audience. Audiences interact with the screen (laughing, clapping, hissing), male spectators walk out from time to time (though they readily return for the climatic dance sequences), and so on (Gokulsing and Dissanayake, 2003: 123). But the point is that if these audiences are attracted to these films in their millions, despite their repetitive nature, it is because of the exquisite nature of the sets and exotic locations on the one hand and, on the other, the glamour of their movie **stars**. Love scenes in Bollywood musicals are extremely discreet with little overt **sexuality** (Torgovnik, 2003: 32). Indeed, intimacy of this order is usually confined to the song and dance sequences, hence their enormous importance, and their attraction to male audiences.

Let us now consider the stars since they had such an influence on the genre itself. By the mid-1940s, when the **studio system** collapsed (due to the speculative nature of financing the industry which rendered it unstable), financiers sought safer investment for their (often 'black' economy) money. So they turned to stars and offered them huge fees. The new order had begun: 'from now on stars were to rule the roost' (Joshri, 2001: 26). Raj Kapoor and Dilip Kumar were the first; so, too, was Nargis, the great female star; soon followed by Dev Anand and Guru Dutt. Each generation of stars, in different ways, moved the genre on.

Kapoor and Dutt went on to be filmmakers in their own right. Kapoor set up his own production company (RK Films) and Nargis, his fetish star, was a key factor in the huge success of his productions. Dutt went on to become one of India's leading innovative filmmakers. With his serious take on song to heighten drama, Dutt, along with the likes of Satyajit Ray and Mrinal Sen, was credited with contributing to the Golden Age of Indian cinema (1950s to early 1960s) – primarily a social cinema that dealt with many of the real concerns of India (see entry on *Indian cinema* in **World Cinemas** entry).

In the mid-1960s, thanks to the introduction of **colour**, the Hindi film took a new turning which essentially put an end to the more experimental nature of the Golden Age cinema, returning it to its former formulaic typology. These new films stressed quality in the form of settings and costumes. Production values became all-important at the expense of social drama. By the 1970s, these formulaic films, to keep their attractiveness alive, began to mix genres together and so combined romance, comedy, family drama and **action** (Kabir, 2001: 16).

These became known as the Masala film (so-named after the different spices that make up the Masala curry). It is interesting to think of this labelling in relation to questions of audience consumption; somehow these films were, as it were, good enough to eat (and it is worth remembering that during the 1970s the female star Madhuri Dixit was a cult figure)! In any event, this multi-genre approach is still the dominant film style for the Bollywood musical today (see Dudrah, 2012, for more details).

During the 1970s and through the 1980s, another type of Hindi film was also being made. This was the Bollywood **blockbuster**, angry young man movie with Amitabh Bachchan as *the* superstar. His movies were a defiant challenge to the other more trivial films of Bollywood cinema and had the effect of changing the nature of the Hindi film by bringing violence into the melting pot of this already multi-genre style film. His biggest blockbuster hit was *Sholay/Flames* (Ramesh Sippy, 1975). This shift in mood of the Bollywood film, as embodied by Bachchan and exemplified by *Sholay*, is often associated with the radical shift in the political arena of the time. Indira Gandhi had declared a state of emergency during this period of great civil unrest (Gopalan, 2002: 9). The typical narrative of these more action-based musical films – which are peopled with 'gangsters, avenging women, brutal police, and corrupt politicians' – is stories of revenge and vigilante action (ibid.: 10). *Sholay* gained iconic status itself not just because it had a 'mimetic relationship to reality' (India of the 1970s) but also because, in that it so clearly reconfigured the American **Western** (ibid.), it became 'the legendary source that spurred an entire generation of filmmakers to borrow from globally circulating genres' (ibid.: 11). In its truest sense, *Sholay* was perhaps *the* first Masala movie.

The effect of these action films on the more conventional song and dance Hindi film was to cause a drop in the latter's popularity during the 1980s. However, the action Bollywood film, after a successful run of over fifteen years, subsequently witnessed a 'partial eclipse' by the end of the 1980s – arguably due to the rise to political power of the conservative Bahratiya Janata Party (BJP) with its focus on Indian-ness. In this climate, a reverse trend occurred, with the return of the song and dance family-oriented film which still continue to hold sway (Gokulsing and Dissanayake, 2003: 110) – even though with the coming to power, in 2004, of the more liberal Congress Party there was a greater variety once again (see the amusingly **queer** *Dostana*, Tarum Mansukhani, 2008). And the return to power, in 2014, of the BJP has not yet seriously affected this greater openness. To the West, the popularity of the family-orientated film might seem a curious phenomenon when one considers that, even though the family is still a big cinemagoer, today's audience is, predominantly, a youth audience – especially male, representing about half of India's population. However, as Kabir (2001: 2) makes clear, one of the great advantages that 'Hindi cinema has always enjoyed over the commercial cinemas of other regions is its ability to create a composite world.' Indeed, ever since the Bombay musical films of the 1930s (the first of which was *Alam Ara*, 1931), differences have been glossed over in favour of a composite reality. Thus, this is by no means a new phenomenon. But, this does not mean that the texts lack variety for there is, as Mishra (2002: xviii) rightly points out, an immense complexity to this genre. Today, this composite world is one that successfully combines the global with the local. So, on the one hand, a typical Hindi film will be a product of cultural pickings that appeal to a pan-Indian audience in their reference to global culture, but, on the other hand, it will also always 'revert to tradition', to the status quo that audiences demand when it comes to marriage (Kabir, 2001: 3). This insistence on tradition enables cinema audiences to define what it means to be Indian (ibid.: 3). But it does not detract from their ability to take pleasure in the ideology of consumption that is also put up on-screen in the form of modern fashion and wealthy lifestyles that come from Western influence (Gokulsing and Dissanayake, 2003: 115). This hybrid nature of the new Bollywood film means that it exports well. The presence of the global within the film facilitates identification for the diasporic Indian audiences worldwide but, equally important, the representation of a traditional India offers a mirror of Indian-ness with which they also seek to identify. It is noteworthy in this context that, during the 2000s, diasporic filmmakers turned their hand to making Bollywood musicals and, interestingly, that they have been female directors: Mira Nair, *Monsoon Wedding* (2002); Gurinder Chadha, *Bride and Prejudice* (2004).

From the mid-1990s, the Indian film industry acquired a renewed status with the liberalization of finances. This meant that stars no longer commanded the industry in the same way as they did before and that scripts have increasingly become the starting point for the film before the star (Gokulsing and Dissanayake, 2003: 111). This does not mean, however, the end of megastars. One such superstar is Shahrukh Khan. His film *Devdas* (2002) was an international success even though it was the most expensive Hindi film ever made (an expense that had much to do with the figure he can command). Like earlier stars before him (particularly of the 1950s), Khan has set up his own production company (Dreamz Unlimited), thereby giving himself considerable control over his star image. As for the women who enjoy superstar status as well (though certainly not to the extent of Shahrukh Khan), we can list: Kajol, Karisma Kapoor, Kareena Kapoor, Aishwarya Rai, Preity Zinta.

For further reading see Banaji, 2006; Bose, 2006; Desai, 2004; Dudrah and Desai, 2008; Dudrah, 2012; Gopalan, 2002; Gokulsing and Dissanayake, 2003; Joshri, 2001; Kabir, 2001; Kaur and Sinha, 2005; Mishra, 2002; Rajadhyaksha, 2009; Torgovnik, 2003.

For further discussion *see also* section on Indian cinema in **World Cinemas**.

BRITISH NEW WAVE

The British New Wave, like its French counterpart, was quite short-lived: 1958 to 1964. As a movement, it coincided with the social and cultural changes occurring in Britain largely as a result of the emergence during the 1950s of a youth class. This was a period marked by radical change in music, fashion and sexual mores – this was the era of the 'swinging sixties'. It was also the era of kitchen-sink drama, of a gritty new **realism** on stage starting with John Osborne's play *Look Back in Anger* (1956).

The legacy of the British New Wave is both that particular kitchen-sink theatre of realism and the radicalized **documentary** tradition of the **Free Cinema Britain**. Given that the filmmakers who dominated the New Wave – Lindsay Anderson, Karel Reisz and Tony Richardson – were the same as those of the Free British Cinema group, this part of the heritage is hardly surprising. The Free British Cinema group's work had focused on the youth and working classes at work and in leisure; the New Wave was one that focused on contemporary social issues of youth growing up in a culture of increasing mass communication. Prostitution, abortion, homosexuality alienation caused by mass-communication culture, failures in couples' relationships – these were some of the dominant social problems dealt with. The documentary–realist style is everywhere in evidence in this cinema of the New Wave, with the predilection for location shooting, particularly in northern industrial cities, the use of black and white fast stock film (which gave a grainy newsreel look to the images), and natural **lighting**. **Stars** were not used, although actors who were used, such as Alan Bates, Albert Finney, Richard Burton and Michael Caine, soon found star status thanks to their roles in these films. It is noteworthy that the two women actors most associated with the films of this movement, Rachel Roberts and Rita Tushingham, never gained such status. The majority of the films were based on books or plays written by authors who had first-hand experience of working-class life: Alan Sillitoe, John Braine, David Storey and Shelagh Delaney.

Although some film historians nominate *Room at the Top* (Jack Clayton, 1959) as the first New Wave film, it would be more accurate to say that that film was a precursor to the movement and that Richardson's **adaptation** for the screen (1959) of Osborne's *Look Back in Anger* is in fact the real beginning of this movement. Osborne and Richardson were also flag-bearers in that they were the first to form an independent production company, Woodfall Films, to finance their projects. This was swiftly followed by Joseph Janni's Vic Films, then Bryanston – a subsidiary of British Lion and made up of a consortium of sixteen independent producers – and, finally, Beaver Films, formed by Richard Attenborough and Bryan Forbes. Soon after being established, Woodfall Films sought financial backing from Bryanston to produce Shelagh Delaney's *A Taste of Honey* (Richardson, 1961). This link-up with the British Lion subsidiary would in part seal the fate of this movement, in 1964.

Look Back in Anger with Richard Burton in the protagonist's role as Jimmy Porter was the first of the so-called 'angry young men' films, shortly followed by Albert Finney in *Saturday Night and Sunday Morning* (Reisz, 1960) and Alan Bates in *A Kind of Loving* (John Schlesinger, 1962). The real difficulties of single motherhood and the loneliness that social marginalization imposes on homosexuals are central themes to *A Taste of Honey*. The hypocrisy of authoritarian institutions such as the Borstal comes under fire in *The Loneliness of the Long Distance Runner* (Richardson, 1962). *This Sporting Life* (Anderson, 1963) exposes the corruption and commercialism of the rugby-league business and the brutality to which lovers can be pushed by a lack of communication.

By 1963, over one-third of British film production was New Wave. The movement was riding high and proving that the British film industry could resist **Hollywood** domination. It was, however, this very success, in particular of Woodfall Films which produced the majority of the New Wave films, that brought about the movement's – and thereby the British film industry's – demise. Richardson wanted to make a film adaptation of the novel *Tom Jones*. He wanted to shoot it in **colour** and full costume. This required a considerably larger budget than was typical for a New Wave production. British Lion refused to back the project and so Richardson turned to the American production company United Artists. At this time Hollywood was experiencing severe financial difficulties and was only too pleased to turn its attention to Britain and invest money where overheads and talent were cheap. United Artists' agreement to finance the production of *Tom Jones* (1963) was the thin edge of the wedge that broke the back of the British independent companies and, ultimately, British Lion. Taken by the British success, the major Hollywood **studios** invested in British production projects and, by 1966, 75 per cent of British films were American financed. By 1967, this figure grew to 90 per cent. By the end of the 1960s, when Hollywood began to experience an upswing in its own fortunes, the American companies upped stakes and went home, leaving the British film industry virtually incapable of financing itself. Add to this the selling off, in 1964, of British Lion, which had released the majority of the New Wave films, and the picture of the industry's virtual demise is complete.

see also: **Free Cinema Britain**

For further reading see Hill, 1986.

BUDDY FILMS

Traditionally, buddy films are for the boys. That is, the **narrative** centres on the friendship between two male protagonists. This **genre** was very much in vogue in the 1960s and 1970s, perhaps as a response to the dehumanizing effects of the Vietnam War in which the United States became heavily entangled after 1962. Paul Newman and Robert Redford are the icons of this genre, often appearing together (*Butch Cassidy and the Sundance Kid*, 1969; *The Sting*, 1973, both George Roy Hill). This friendship is totally heterosexualized, there is no possible misreading since the heroes are always doing action-packed things together (shooting themselves out of trouble, primarily) – 'boys will be boys' – and a woman will be 'around' even if very marginal to the narrative (she guarantees the heroes' heterosexuality just in case). Of this era of films, *Easy Rider* and *Midnight Cowboy* (repectively, Dennis Hopper and John Schlesinger, both 1969) are two buddy films that come closest to a more homoerotic friendship (see Eberwein, 2007: 148–153).

The buddy genre developed, in the 1980s and 1990s, to include a proto-father-son friendship, again with the icon Newman but accompanied this time by a younger alter-ego, Tom Cruise (*The Color of Money*, Martin Scorsese, 1986) – signifying a restoration of family values or at least of the value of the father ('every boy needs a man to show him how to be a man'). Though considered a male genre, this phallocentrism has been called into question, in some instances to hilarious effect, as in the film *Thelma and Louise* (Ridley Scott, 1991) in which two women buddies hit the road. Another 'inverted' buddy movie is the very camp and funny Australian-British co-production *The Adventures of Priscilla, Queen of the Desert* (Stephan Elliott, 1994). Buddy films have also, in the light of AIDS, stretched in meaning and produced a sub-genre that addresses gay male friendship (for example *Longtime Companion*, Norman René, 1990). In this particular manifestation, the buddy film has come to represent, in a favourable light, that which it eschewed or feared in its earlier products, a feat reprised in a different way with *Brokeback Mountain* (Ang Lee, 2005) where the Western, that most macho of genres, is hybridized with a buddy film to produce the most poignant of love stories.

CENSORSHIP

In some countries, censorship is quite benign and limited to a rating system to protect minors and to inform audiences of the content of films. Other countries still pursue a very strong line in censorship, banning films in their entirety or insisting on cuts being made. Censorship tends to be imposed in three main areas: sex, violence and politics. The first two have been of primary concern to groups lobbying for the welfare of minors; the third more clearly has been the concern of state institutions and governments. Relaxation of censorship laws began, first, in the late 1960s with the United States; mid-1970s for the United Kingdom, France and Spain – and so on. In some countries, the United States and Germany, for example, it is constitutionally illegal to censor films, even though censorship may be maintained. Generally a country that is more assured in its political culture and does not feel its **hegemony** to be under threat is less inclined to draconian censorship. However, the fact that this is not always the case points to the notion that consensuality is not always a given. Incidents in France around Scorsese's film *The Last Temptation of Christ* (1988) show that the Catholic lobby still has a strong foothold within smaller communities in that it obliged mayors to cancel screenings. Spielberg's *Schindler's List* (1994) was banned in several countries because of the fictionalized nature of the Holocaust. Films that profoundly assault spectator sensibility are still banned to this day: the Russian gore-film *Philosophy of a Knife* (Andrey Iskanov, 2008) and the overtly sexual-horror film *A Serbian Film* (Srdan Spasjevic, 2010) are two recent examples.

Because the United States' film industry is so dominant (at least in the West), the American **Hays** Office/Code is the best-known censoring body. Its official title is the Motion Picture Producers and Distributors of America (MPPDA), popularly renamed the Hays Office after its first president, William H. Hays (serving 1922–45). The Hays Office was established in 1922 in response to public furore over the morality of some of Hollywood's **stars**. However, the point should be made that this office was established by the film industry itself, which thought it in its own interests to set it up as a way of protecting itself against federal intervention. It is curious that sex scandals off-screen should bring about censorship of **narratives** on-screen. But that's what happened – and many careers were broken, even if the scandals were not proved or indeed if a star was acquitted in a trial, as was the case, most notoriously, for Fatty Arbuckle (1921). Hays wanted Hollywood to act as self-censors rather than let state or federal censorship intervene. This meant of course that stars were even more in the pocket of the production companies, thereby finding themselves in the paradoxical position of having simultaneously to be larger than life and yet also totally 'normal' and ordinary – a schizoid existence, the legacy of which still prevails today, that quite possibly led to the untimely death of numerous stars (e.g. James Dean, Marilyn Monroe, Judy Garland, River Phoenix).

While the film industry may have been reasonably successful in watching over its stars, it did not fare so well in self-censoring its own product. Movies privileging the underworld and gangsters, for example, were severely condemned by critics. So in 1934, a production code (based on the Ten Commandments) was published to which all companies had to adhere. In 1968, the code was discarded in favour of a ratings system which still prevails. The office is now the MPAA: Motion Picture Association of America.

For further reading see Kuhn, 1988 (cinema of the silent period); Black, 1994 (Hollywood in the 1930s); Aldgate, 2001, Matthews, 1994 (censorship in the United Kingdom).

CGI

Literally, computer-generated imagery, or computer-animated images, more specifically the application of three-dimensional computer graphics to special effects in film, and is also used, of course, in animation films. As Willis (2005: 10) makes clear, CGI's importance to cinema lies in its ability to 'overcome the representational limits of two-dimensional representational space' (which is the common lot of film). In other words, CGI provides the technology for replicating realistic worlds by giving a three-dimensional feel to a two-dimensional art-form. However, instead of becoming a technology whereby the **narrative** is enhanced, by giving realism an extra edge, overall CGI has been used, by the greatest advocates of the system (with James Cameron in the lead with his company Digital Domain), for the most part as a process of artifice – which is of course the other aspect of CGI, most readily in evidence in its use for animation films. Thus, what tends to dominate CGI-films are dystopian visions of an imaginary world, a world where humans and other humanoids can morph into monstrous creatures.

CGI was first used by George Lucas for the trench-run briefing sequence in his film *Star Wars* (1977) – soldiers are shown what is essentially a simulation computer-graphic. To create this effect, computer-animation wizard Larry Cuba assembled digitized images on a wireframe graphic and then manipulated them through rotation to give a **3-D** effect (for a clear exposition of how this is done for this film and other CGI work of this early period visit http://www.stikkymedia.com/articles/a-history-of-cgi-in-movies). The next major breakthrough came in 1990, with *Total Recall* (Paul Verhoeven), when motion capture for CGI characters was introduced. Motion capture is the process whereby human movement is recorded and then translated into a digital model (CGI characters are then able to simulate human movement). This success was quickly followed by two major hits using CGI. *Terminator 2* (Cameron, 1991) with its shapeshifting terminators morphing into virtually anything; and fully digitally animated dinosaurs in *Jurassic Park* (Spielberg, 1993). Finally, in this pioneering era, Pixar Studios made *Toy Story* (John Lasseter, 1995), the first feature-length **animation** film made entirely with CGI animation.

CGI-inflected films tend, on the whole, to be in the **blockbuster** vein; thus their narrative is often incoherent (even if the ultimate aim is for good to triumph over evil), precisely because, instead of offering heightened reality, this type of film comes close to reality-bending. None of the specific effects (say the various performance capture techniques of the last forty years: rotoscope in *The Lord of the Rings*, Ralph Bakshi, 1978; bullet-time, slowed-down action pieces in *The Matrix*, Larry and Andy Wachowski, 1999; motion capture in *Beowulf*, Robert Zemeckis, 2007), or fantastical sets of *Harry Potter and the Deathly Hallows – Part 2* (David Yates, 2011), or massive humanoid creatures jumping out at us in *Avatar* (James Cameron, 2009) can be read as reality-based. Conversely, they are true to **fantasy** – ours – and as such rejoin the very first era of the cinema of attraction, as Tom Gunning (1986) quite rightly termed early cinema. (For a defence of this CGI-cinema as the new avant-garde cinema of attraction, see Rombes, 2009: 142–47.)

see also: **digital cinema/post-digital cinema**

For further reading see McClean, 2007; Rombes, 2009; Willis, 2005.

CINEMA NÔVO

A cinema that emerged in Brazil in the early 1950s and whose style and critical aesthetic were at first influenced by the **Italian neo-realist** movement – not surprising given that several of the directors active in this cinema had studied film in Rome in the early 1950s, the peak period of Italian neo-realism. Films of this first period were primarily **documentary** in style and portrayed the lives of ordinary people. Later, in the 1960s, this movement became more radicalized and a cinema co-operative was formed that sought to renovate a film aesthetic appropriate to contemporary Brazil where poverty, starvation and violence were the daily diet of most, and concentrated wealth the good fortune of the very few. Filmmakers in this co-operative included Glauber Rocha, Nelson Pereira dos Santos and Ruy Guerra. This cinema was populist and revolutionary: populist because of its blend of history, **myth** and popular culture; revolutionary because, if in its populism it could advocate rights for the disenfranchised and landless peasants (e.g. Rocha's *Antonio das Mortes*, 1969), nonetheless, it made clear that such populist advocacy could do nothing against the harsh conditions in which most Brazilians lived and which dos Santos' film *Vidas Secas* (*Barren Lives*, 1963) so admirably captures.

Although cinema nôvo is more readily associated with its 1960s manifestations, it is important to remember that it pre-dates most of the New Wave movements that occurred in Europe. It is also important to recall that it was far more radical in its purpose than any of its European counterparts. It not only attacked **mainstream cinema** (including Hollywoodized Brazilian cinema), it was also fiercely polemical and based on what Rocha termed an 'aesthetic of hunger' and an 'aesthetics of violence'. Within this context, the films, such as dos Santos' *Vidas Secas* and Rocha's *Terra em Transe* (*Land in Anguish*, 1967) to mention but two, are to be read as 'allegories of underdevelopment' (Stam in Shohat and Stam, 1994: 256) and also as signifiers of impotence not just in the light of poverty but also in the light of the military *coup d'état* of 1964. Nor did this cinema stand still. It evolved from this aesthetic of hunger to an 'aesthetic of garbage' (ibid.: 310), that is, to a syncretic film style that was known as Tropicalist and which was based on Afro-Brazilian culture and **mythology**. In film this manifested itself as an 'aggressive collage' (ibid.: 310) of many simultaneous discourses and speeds of **narration**, much like a palimpsest. As Stam explains in his lucid study of Brazilian cinema (ibid.: 310–12), Tropicalism had moved beyond cinema nôvo's 'opposition between "authentic Brazilian cinema" and "Hollywood alienation"' to a juxta-position of 'the folkloric and the industrial, the native and the foreign'. This garbage style, which also feeds off itself (waste recycling waste) was seen as entirely 'appropriate to a Third World country picking through the leavings of an international system dominated by First world capitalism' (ibid.: 312) (for a magisterial study of this cinema see Stam, 1994: 248–337).

By the early 1970s, the cinema nôvo group's activities had been sup-pressed by the military dictatorship which had come to power in 1964 and whose repressive measures became total by 1968. But this cinema has left an important legacy. It was one of the indigenous film move-ments in Latin America to bring a cinema called Third World Cinema to world attention (see **World Cinemas**). As a protest-cinema it was also an important influence in the thinking behind the **Third Cinema** manifesto published by the Argentinean filmmakers and theorists Fernando Solanas and Octavio Getino in 1969. And as Ismail Xavier argues (1997), although cinema nôvo 'disappeared' it re-emerged in Brazil in a different form. No longer able to make a cinema of direct social critique, former cinema nôvo filmmakers turned to **melodrama** and more specifically to family dramas to make their com-ments obliquely and ironically on Brazil's conservative modernization. This they did with narratives exposing the powerlessness of the patriarch (see Ruy Guerra's *Deuses e os Morios/The Gods and the Dead*, 1970).

For further reading see Chanan, 1983; Johnson and Stam, 1995; Pick, 1993; Shohat and Stam, 1994; *Screen* special issue on Third Cinema, 24: 2, 1983; Solanas and Getino, 1983 .

CINEMASCOPE

Cinemascope and **colour** were introduced in the early 1950s by the American film industry in an attempt to stem the commercial decline of its cinema due to falling audience numbers. Cinemascope is a wide-screen effect made possible through the use of the **anamorphic lens**. The anamorphic lens re-creates before our very eyes the reality of how we look at and perceive the world with 180-degree vision (see **180-degree rule**). In terms of screen effect, the cinemascope creates the sense of greater lateral space, providing the **spectator** with the illusion of a lived space which s/he is (almost) occupying, almost because s/he is on the edge, on the liminal edge of screen space. The other attraction of cinemascope when in a colour-film format was the stereo **soundtrack** (made possible by the space available along the two sides of the film for the soundtracks). The effect was a greater **realism**. Unsurprisingly, considerable theoretical debate ensued.

In **film theory**, cinemascope was welcomed by the *Cahiers du cinéma* group primarily because it extended the possibilities for **mise-en-scène**. For some critics in this group, it also represented the death of **montage**. Montage for the *Cahiers* group, but most especially for Bazin (1967), was an anti-realistic filmmaking practice that manipulated the audience through its juxtapositioning of **shots** and the carving-up of reality. Realism and objectivity could be assured only by the predominance of **depth of field/deep focus** with its long takes and implicit unimpeded vision. Cinemascope, the *Cahiers* group argued, would privilege mise-en-scène and extend the merits of depth of field – meaning would be produced through the framing of shots and movement within the shots. Cinemascope implied a number of things for the *Cahiers* group. First, it gave breadth (that is, space) and thereby created a frieze effect on the screen. In so doing, it recognized the sculptural nature of cinema's **narrative** (*Cahiers du cinéma*, no. 25, 1953). Second, *Cahiers* argued, cinema should not try to create depth but should suggest depth through breadth. Cinema is about lateral movements and space, and cinemascope allows for a freer expression of those two concepts (*Cahiers*, no. 31, 1954). Third, cinemascope implied location shooting and the definitive arrival of colour (*Cahiers*, no. 31, 1954). Finally, because cinemascope provided the **spectator** with almost panoramic vision (that is, virtually consonant with the way human vision functions), it was the perfect solution to the arbitrary divide between audience and screen.

Although, in the 1950s and 1960s, Hollywood perceived cinemascope as appropriate to certain **genres** (such as **Westerns** and **epics**), European cinemas – starting with the **French New Wave** – used it to a subversive effect for intimist films about the failure of human relationships (as for example in Jean-Luc Godard's *Le Mépris*, 1963, or *Pierrot le fou*, 1965).

see also: **anamorphic lens, widescreen**

CINEMATOGRAPHER/DIRECTOR OF PHOTOGRAPHY (DOP)

The person responsible for shooting the film itself, for putting the scene *onto* film. This person is responsible for the general composition of the scene (the **mise-en-scène**, the **lighting** of the set or location, the **colour** balance). The director of photography is also responsible for the choice of cameras, lenses, film stock and filters. Camera positions and movements, the integration of special effects are also the director of photography's responsibility as is the overall style from scene to scene (including balance of light and colour). Finally, they are directly concerned in the process of the actual printing of the film. Digital cameras have removed some of these burdens (light and colour balance, for example, is mostly achieved in camera or at post-production). The cameras are far easier to operate (because so light), thus simplifying much of the DOP's problems (such as camera movement or placement).

For further reading on specifics of the craft see Alton, 1995; Huss and Silverstein, 1968; Petrie, 1996.

*CINÉMA-VÉRITÉ/CINÉMA DIRECT/*DIRECT CINEMA

Initially the title of a Soviet newsreel – *Kino-Pravda* ('film-truth') – which was the filmed edition of the Soviet newspaper *Pravda*, the term was not used to describe a particular **documentary** style until Dziga Vertov (the Russian documentarist who, in the 1920s, shot this newsreel for the paper) coined it in 1940 in reference to his own work. Vertov characterized this cinema as one where there were no actors, no décors, no script and no acting. The French ethnographic documentarist Jean Rouch followed in this tradition, at first quite stringently. His earlier 1950s documentary work was an 'objective' filming of the activities of indigenous people in Francophone Africa – and was termed *cinéma direct*. There was no staging, no **mise-en-scène** and no **editing** – so these documentaries were as close to authentic as they could be. This form of direct capture of reality was picked up on in the late 1950s in Canada (especially Québec) and the USA and was termed Direct Cinema. While it remained strictly non-interventionist, unlike Rouch's *cinéma direct*, editing was often used post-shooting to give structure, and therefore added meaning, leaving this cinema open to criticism as to its authenticity.

Later, in the 1960s, Rouch moved away from this very purist *cinéma direct* to a more sociological investigation where he did intervene in the staging of **shots** and put his footage through the editing process – what has come to be termed *cinema-vérité*. Less objective but no less real, this *cinéma-vérité* attempted to catch reality on film with the intention of provoking its **spectators**. Ordinary people testified to their experiences, answered questions put by Rouch or his colleagues. A handful of French or French-based filmmakers followed in Rouch's tradition (Joris Ivens, Chris Marker, Mario Ruspoli, François Reichenbach, Jacques Panijel and Jean Eustache). *Cinéma-vérité* is unstaged, non-dramatized, non-**narrative** cinema. It puts forward an alternative version to **hegemonic** and institutionalized history by offering a plurality of histories told by non-elites. As such, it is quite a politicized cinema, although Gidal (1989: 129) challenges this reading and sees *cinéma-vérité* as espousing a crude **ideology**. In any event, *cinéma-vérité* impacted on the radical collectives which formed in the immediate aftermath of May 1968 in France – including Godard and Guérin's Dziga-Vertov group. In North America, Direct Cinema was particularly active in the period 1958 to 1962; the Canadian, Québecois Direct Cinema was arguably more provocative than the USA filmmakers who were more inclined towards photojournalism, namely, recording events without intruding. The Canadians focused on the fraught issue of free Québec and the loss of traditions due to modernization.

CLASS

Because film is a system of representation that both produces and reproduces cultural signification, it will ineluctably be tied up with questions of class. Because the film industry is a mode of production in itself, based in capitalism and geared to profit, it is necessarily bound up with considerations of power relations which are also related to issues of class. In both these aspects, clearly, the questions of **gender** and race will also be of significance. Debate around class in **film theory** has been mostly inflected by Karl Marx's definitions of class and by subsequent rethinkings of those definitions first by Antonio Gramsci, Louis Althusser and Herbert Marcuse and then by **post-structuralist** theorists.

The Marxian definition of class and its rethinking

According to Marx, class refers to groups of people who have similar relations to the means of production. That is, they get their living in the same way. Thus, the working classes work the modes of production (mines, factories, etc.), the capitalist classes own the means of production. In between these two distinct classes are others: the middle and lower-middle classes who can be, for example, small business owners or management or trained professionals. Marx also recognized that there can be fractures within each class (e.g. between skilled and unskilled workers or between trained professionals (i.e. diploma-holders) and those who have made it to the same status through work on the ground, and so on). Class is based on objective differences among sets of people and defined, quite negatively, as in opposition to other sets of people: a set of people will forge a class identity to protect its interests against another class. Therefore class is not just about economic relations but also power relations (O'Sullivan *et al.*, 1992: 39–42).

The conflict of ideas is secondary to this first set of conflicts and normally occurs when new material modes of production come into being. However, because new modes of production will cause new ways of thinking about production, the dominant class will endeavour to prevent new thinking by advocating ideas based on the previous order (Burns, 1983). A contiguous way of controlling potential class conflict and maintaining the status quo is through the fracturing of the productive labour force. As a result, the worker is alienated from the total means of production in that s/he is only a part of it (on a production-line doing assembly work). Thus, mass production and technology cause work to be fragmented. The worker is also alienated from the commodity produced which is destined to the market and for profit. Her or his work is built into that profit, s/he pays for it – that is, the exchange value of the commodity is based in part on the repression within the worker's wage of the profit margin (e.g. a worker gets paid the real equivalent of four hours although s/he has worked for eight).

Given that class difference is predominantly based in power relations, it follows that different classes are characterized by divergent **ideologies**. This is the most evident site for the making visible of class conflict. Marx, and Gramsci after him, argues how cultural artefacts manifest these differences (think of Punk as opposed to Vogue dress-codes). They also make the point that culture functions to make sense of those differences (e.g. early **melodrama** explains class difference between the bourgeoisie and the proletariat). Thus, in Marxist thinking, cultural aesthetics is very bound up with the concept of class.

Later Marxists, Marcuse and Althusser, thought that, by the 1960s, it was less a bourgeois/proletariat divide and more an impersonal power that dominated: 'The System' (Marcuse) or 'ideological state apparatuses' (Althusser). This idea, that there was no longer a dominant class, was taken further by French thinkers. On the one hand, it was argued that there was, in the post-industrial society with its new wealth and cheaper products, an emergence of a new middle class and the obliteration of major class differences. On the other hand, some maintained that class differences had become internalized in new kinds of conflict (e.g. around race issues). To Althusser's and Marcuse's anti-humanist position (the human being as a subject-effect of the system/state), Alain Touraine argued that the old class divide had been replaced by different sets of people: those who are in control of the structures of political and economic decision-making, and, conversely, those who are reduced to the condition of dependent participation (Bottomore, 1984).

Although it was grounded in Saussurean structural linguistics and **semiotics**, the **structuralist** and **post-structuralist** debates of the 1960s and 1970s also embraced Marxist thinking. Of particular inter-est and relevance to film studies was Marx's cultural aesthetic, which determined that an art object should not be considered outside or as separate from both its mode and its historical moment of production. Marxist aesthetics insists on the importance of contextual analysis and suggests that textual analysis alone is not sufficient where an evalua-tion of an artefact (i.e. a film) is concerned. What is required is an examination of the underlying structures (labour, finance, manu-facture, etc.) that went into the making of the aesthetic text.

Relevance to film studies and film theory

The Marxist theory of class and cultural aesthetics found its way into film studies and theory in predominantly four ways: analysis of class relations within the text; the historical and cultural contexts of the pro-duction; modes and practices of production; and, finally, the ideological effect of the cinematic apparatus upon spectator–text relations (see **apparatus**, **ideology** and **spectator** for discussion of this last point).

On the first point, it is clear that certain **genres** yield more readily to class analysis than others: **comedy**, melodrama and social problem films (that are a sub-genre of **social realism**) are perhaps the most obvious. To illustrate the point let us take melodrama. One of the earliest traditions in this genre was to pitch the bourgeoisie against the proletariat. Most often, that conflict was also gendered. Here are a few sample scenarios: poor young girl or fallen woman at the mercies of rich fat bourgeois male; poor young man (often an artist) at the mercies of some rich, upper-class vamp or female (often she is married, so it is not her money – but never mind, since she still represents her husband's wealth); wealthy widow falls for proletarian hero; professional woman falls for proletarian criminal (and so on). Melodramas of the 1930s and 1940s centred on social mobility (e.g. the self-sacrificing or scheming mother trying to better her offspring's (usually the daughter's) future).

In Marxist terms, whatever the **narrative** context, clearly the bourgeoisie is the class vested with capital power. Film, in most instances, **naturalizes** capital and power. Only rarely is capital represented as corrupt and therefore to be resisted – and even then, that representation is often caricatural; so, in fact, capital as a bad thing is not being targeted but rather abuse of capital power, for which an individual will be punished. Capital in and of itself, according to the narrative, still remains intact as a good thing. Given Western governments' policies (post-World War Two) to get women out of the factories and back into the kitchen, melodramas from 1945 onwards into the 1950s centred more on the family – particularly the middle-class family. In these melodramas, the family under capitalism comes to be unquestioningly represented. The father is the head of the household and wage-earner, the wife the agreeing consensual woman who will produce children. In Marxist terms, the bourgeois family is a product and thereby a representer of patriarchy and capitalism and of course a reproduction and reproducer of that system. In these melodramas, although class is there, implicitly as an issue, class strug- gle is not. But, because these films deal with family structures, issues of power relations are clearly gendered (see Cook, 1985: 76ff.).

As this starts to make clear, historical and cultural contexts of the production (the second of our four points) yield readings in relation to capital as well as class and gender. The overdetermination or valorization of the family, that is, over-investment in its importance in 1950s melodramas and, incidentally, comedy – the Doris Day factor: the squeaky-clean girl next door – is a case in point. The modes and practices of production (the third point) also yield readings. For example, the film industry functions in exactly the same way as the class system described above. There is the same dynamic of the owning and producing classes, the same principle of alienation through frag- mentation in that each worker does their part of the production process, but is not part of the whole. The traces of manufacture (such as make-up) are elided by the camera-work, the **lighting** and the **editing**. Thus, the mark of the worker is not present in the final commodity which is produced, not for their pleasure, but for profit. The real value, labour, gets lost in the exchange value, the film as a saleable commodity. **Stars** also have an exchange value in much the same way as commodities in any marketplace do – they too must make profit: they are the form of value, not value itself. That is, they are not stars as persons but star images as exchange-value or capital exchange (we pay to see them, agree to the price of the ticket).

Class in cinema is iconographically denoted, is signified by certain referents (clothes, language-register, environment, and so on). Film presents itself as real, places before the spectator the illusion of reality (see **iconography, spectator** and **suture**). So these icons serve to naturalize class, as does the homogeneity of **classical narrative cinema**, structured around the three-act structure of order–disorder–order (similar to the Victorian novel that has a beginning, middle and end, where end means marriage). No matter that there may be new production practices, the film industry will continue to advocate the earlier ideas rather than allow the promotion of new ones. Filmmakers attempting innovative ideas quickly find themselves marginalized by the Hollywood studios – as indeed was the case at different times in their careers for Orson Welles, Francis Ford Coppola and Martin Scorsese. In this respect, **mainstream cinema** represents only the thinkable, that which does not challenge our sense of identity, which, as cinema constantly tells us, however subliminally, is ultimately determined through our gender, and more pervasively our presumed heterosexuality – not through our class or race. In other words, because self-identity or **spectator-identification** is the constant reality-effect of mainstream cinema – we look into the screen-mirror. Our first priority is with whom (not what) we identify. Our first identification is with a person as gender, not a person as class, age or race. In this respect, cinema as a cultural artefact serves hegemonic purposes. The dominant ideology is structured in such a way – at its simplest level because there must be (re)production – that we necessarily think of ourselves as gendered subjects. To think otherwise would be unthinkable (think about the still predominantly negative, even hostile, attitudes to transsexuals, transvestites, same-sex love, etc.). Viewed in this light, representations of class might appear to be a sort of red herring. Far from it, as indeed the continued interest in this issue in film studies makes clear (see the selected bibliography below, with some seven additional titles in the new millennium). As part of the construction of reality or dominant ideology, these representations serve to reinforce the belief that the unthinkable is just that, unthinkable – which is of course what keeps patriarchy, class and hegemonic structures in general in place.

For further reading see Bodnar, 2003; Dave, 2006; Gillett, 2003; Hill, 1986; Powrie, Davies and Babington, 2004; Rowbotham and Benyon, 2001; Shafik, 2007; Stead, 1989; Tarr, 2005.

CLASSICAL HOLLYWOOD CINEMA/CLASSICAL NARRATIVE CINEMA

So-called to refer to a cinema tradition that dominated Hollywood production from the 1930s to the 1960s but which also pervaded mainstream Western cinema. Its heritage goes back to earlier European and American cinema **melodrama** and to theatrical melodrama before that. This tradition is still present in mainstream or **dominant cinema** in some or all of its parts.

Classic narrative cinema is what David Bordwell (in Bordwell *et al.*, 1985: 1) calls an 'excessively obvious cinema' in which cinematic style serves to explain, and not obscure, the narrative. This cinema, then, is one that is made up of motivated **signs** that lead the **spectator** through the story to its inevitable conclusion. The name of the game is verisimilitude, 'reality'. However, an examination of what gets put up on-screen in the name of reality makes clear how contrived and limited it is and yet how ideologically useful that reality nonetheless remains (see **ideology**). The narrative of this cinema reposes upon the triad 'order/disorder/order-restored', also known as disruption/resolution, or in **narrative** terms as the three-act arc. The beginning of the film puts in place an event that disrupts an apparently harmonious order (marriage, small town neighbourliness, etc.) which in turn sets in motion a chain of events that are causally linked. Cause and effect serve to move the narrative along. At the end the disorder is resolved and order once again restored.

The plot is character-led, which means that the narrative is psychologically and, therefore, individually motivated (see **motivation**). Thus, by implication, if the initial event is not individually or psychologically motivated, more than likely it will be left without explanation. Bordwell (Bordwell *et al.*, 1985: 13), citing Sorlin, explains that this is particularly evident when it is an historical event that is supposed to have initiated the narrative line. The event happens 'just like that'. An exemplary film is *Gone With the Wind* (Victor Fleming, 1939). Hyped as 'the greatest love story ever told', it gets told against the backdrop of the American Civil War which gets represented duopolistically as a clash between the southern states' traditions and the northern states' ideological conviction that slavery must be abolished. In this respect, history becomes a-historical (events have no past, no explanation, no cause). As such, history is eternally fixed, **naturalized** (in a not dissimilar manner to the way in which woman in this cinema gets naturalized (see **counter-cinema**)). For example, in a **war movie** we might see that war is bad, but only because of the effects it has on the characters – we do not learn about the causes of the war, nor do they get examined. Think of the Vietnam War films made by Hollywood – even if the representation of that war is harrowing to watch and war, thereby, is not glamorized (as it was in films about World War Two), the complex set of historical circumstances whereby the United States got enmeshed in that war is not touched upon – rather it is the psychological effect of the war on GI Joe that we see. If, in a war-context, a cause is given at all, then it is in the form of an individual (as with Hitler and World War Two).

Classic narrative cinema, no matter what **genre**, must have closure. That is, the narrative must come to a completion (whether a happy ending or not). Any ambiguity within the plot must be resolved. For example, in *Psycho* (Alfred Hitchcock, 1960), Norman Bates may still remain psychotic, but in terms of the narrative or plotline he has been caught for his murderous activities, so there is closure. Whatever form the closure takes, almost without exception, it will offer or enunciate a message that is central to dominant **ideology**: the law successfully apprehending criminals, good gunmen of the Wild West routing the baddies, and so on. What is interesting, however, is which ideological message supersedes all others. In his study of classic Hollywood cinema, Bordwell (Bordwell *et al.*, 1985: 16) notes that of the sample of a hundred randomly chosen films he examined, ninety-five involved heterosexual romance in part of the action and eighty-five had romance as central to the action. Closure mostly means marriage (as with Victorian novels, incidentally), with all that that entails: family, reproduction, property. These representations of a successful completion of the **Oedipal trajectory** are central to the classic narrative cinema. Such a high percentage of romance films points again to the ideological effects of dominant cinema and to its motivated function as myth-maker. However, in its naturalizing heterosexual coupledom and family, it also makes the point that all else must (potentially) be read as deviancy. To return to the example of *Psycho*: Marion Crane is murdered by psychotic Bates, but we know from the narrative that she would never have ended up in his motel and therefore been murdered if she had not stolen money from her male boss in order to buy or lure her lover away from his wife (ex-wife really, but he is paying alimony to her and so cannot afford to 'leave' for Marion). Double-theft. Man as exchange commodity. So Marion is 'punished' for transgressing the patriarchal order: stealing money (from one man) and trying to 'break' up a marriage (by stealing another man and ending his ties with his wife). And, just in case we didn't get the message, at the end of the film her upright sister, who behaves according to the rules, gets her man (the same one her sister failed to secure).

In this cinema, style is subordinate to narrative: **shots**, **lighting**, **colour** must not draw attention to themselves any more than the **editing**, the **mise-en-scène** or **sound**. All must function to manufacture **realism**. Ambiguity must be dissolved through the provision of **spatial and temporal contiguity** – the **spectator** must know where s/he is in time and space and in relation to the logic and chronology of the narrative. Reality is ordered, naturalized: 'life's just like that'. The narrative is goal-orientated and so, naturally, are the characters. This mythico-realistic storyline reflects the other great American myth: that of upward mobility and success. The dream factory makes the American Dream come true.

Let's show how this is done. Bordwell (Bordwell *et al.*, 1985: 5) makes the point that this classic cinema is normative not formulaic (which implies fixity). To achieve the fundamental principle of realism, editing must function to move the narrative on logically and, predominantly but not exclusively, chronologically (even a flashback will, in the main, be narrated chronologically – or the causal chain will be clear). However, editing must not call attention to itself, so continuity is essential. To achieve this, generally speaking, a whole scene is shot in one take – usually in a long **shot** – called a master shot or master scene. After this, parts of the same scene will be reshot, this time in close-ups and medium shots. These are then edited into the master scene and redundant parts of the master scene are cut. To ensure continuity **match cuts** and **eyeline** cuts need to be consistently observed. Match cuts link two shots – one in long the other in medium shot, for example, but related in form, subject or action – creating a seamless continuity (we do not 'see' the cut). The eyeline match allows us to see the direction of the character's **gaze**: we move, unobtrusively from watching the character watching, to watching what she or he is watching (see **continuity editing**).

There are other aspects of editing that might seem not to have reality inherent in them. **Cross-cutting** is an example of how, despite its lack of realism, the reality-effect works. Cross-cutting allows us to see two separate sets of action in different spaces but juxtaposed in time (such as a chase sequence) – normally, with a view to creating suspense. However, since we have been stitched into the narrative as omniscient spectator we do not question our ability to be in two places at once, in fact we expect to 'see it all' (see **suture**). The camera also has a vital role in this reality-effect. The **shot/ reverse-angle shot** used for dialogue establishes a realistic set of exchanging looks – again stitching us into a particular character's point of view. Where necessary, establishing shots are used to orientate the spectator, after which the camera can hone in on the character or part of the setting. Because the plot is character-led, there is an excess of close-ups, not just on the face but on other parts of the body, thus fragmenting the body – which would seem to fly in the face of reality. However, because such shots offer us greater access to the body, they function to reinforce the **myth** of intimacy. We are the **subject** of the gaze and simultaneously identify with the character in the film. The natural effect produced by three-point lighting (see **lighting**) furthers the naturalness of this realism. Colour must suit the emotional or psychological mood of the sequence, setting and/or entire film. Music serves only to reinforce meaning (danger, romance, and so on).

These audio-visual cinematic norms are just as ideologically inflected as the classic narrative norms which they serve. **Feminist film theorists** have pointed out how, with its representations of romantic love, the family and male–female work relations, classic cinema perpetuates and so normalizes patriarchal ideologies which assume the naturalness of unequal relationships – predominantly those of class, race and gender. The reality-effect means 'It is just like life, just like that'.

see also: **movement-image**, **narrative**, **psychoanalysis**

For further reading see Bordwell *et al.*, 1985; Bordwell and Thompson, 1994; Cook, 1985; Dayan, 1974.

CODES AND CONVENTIONS/CLASSIC CANONS

All **genres** have their codes and conventions (rules by which the **narrative** is governed). These are alternatively referred to as classic canons or canonic laws. For example, a **road movie** implies discovery, obtaining some self-knowledge; conventionally the roadster is male and it is his point of view that we see. The narrative follows an ordered sequence of events which lead inexorably either to a bad end (*Easy Rider*, Dennis Hopper, 1969) or to a reasonable outcome (*Paris, Texas*, Wim Wenders, 1984). These canonic laws can of course be subverted as they usually are in **art cinema** or **counter-cinema**. Codes and conventions should not be viewed just within their textual or generic context but also within their social and historical contexts. Codes and conventions change over time and according to the ideological climate of the time – compare any John Wayne **Western** with Clint Eastwood's characterization of the gunman as a problematic hero or anti-hero; or again compare **science-fiction** films of the 1950s with those of the 1980s and 1990s. These shifts may not represent real social change (how many men really question their machismo?), but they reflect, however indirectly, changes in social attitudes (e.g. the effect of the women's movement has rendered unequal power relations between men and women less desirable than before).

see also: **classical Hollywood cinema, narrative**

COLOUR

The history of colour in cinema is a more chequered one than that of **sound**. While, in technological terms, it had been available since almost the very beginnings of cinema, it was not until the full impact of colour television on audience figures was felt (first in the United States, in the 1950s and 1960s; and later in Europe, in the 1970s) that it became fully dominant in cinema practice. It was first introduced on a big scale in the early 1950s in the USA, but even then colour films only accounted for 50 per cent of the production (Cook, 1985: 29).

History

As an idea, colour had been thought of as early as the first days of cinema. By 1896, the American Edison was employing teams of women to hand-paint images in the whole or part of the frame. In France, Méliès was doing much the game thing – single-handedly. A little later, as films got longer and therefore more expensive to paint, Pathé Frères invested in stencil painting – again carried out by women (who incidentally also did the **editing** for these longer films) – a process which the American industry also adopted. By the 1920s, Hollywood had moved on from stencil coloration and was tinting or toning films that were for major release.

The first experimentation with colour film itself came about in 1912 in the United Kingdom when it was used for **documentaries**. Colour film was produced by an additive process; that is, by filming through colour filters and subsequently projecting through the same colour filters. But, this process did not prevail. Instead, modern colour technology was based on the subtractive process (eliminating unwanted colours from the spectrum). This was first done in the 1920s by Technicolor Motion Pictures Corporation (a company set up in 1915).

The principle of technicolour is that of a dye transfer. Technicolor first used two-strip cameras and negatives quite successfully in the 1920s. Then, in 1932, it perfected three-strip cameras and negatives. After shooting, these negatives were processed through an optical printer onto three separate positives through a filter for one of the primary colours. These positives were then individually imbibed with the appropriate complementary colour (also known as the subtractive colour). Thus, the original image, when projected, would have the appropriate colour gradations. Since this colour system could be achieved only through using three-strip cameras and since they had been patented by Technicolor, the company by 1935 had complete control of its product in relation to Hollywood – this monopoly would last nearly twenty years (when Eastman-Kodak colour came on the scene, see below). Technicolor hired out its cameras and its technicians, and processed and printed the film. Technicolor supplied its own colour consultant, Natalie Kalmus (ex-wife of one of the founders of the company), whose job it was to fit the technology to **Hollywood**'s needs – a factor that would considerably affect the **ideology** surrounding colour (see below).

In 1947, the US government's anti-trust law started the process of erosion on Technicolor's monopoly of 35mm colour film. At that time, Eastman-Kodak, in a mutual agreement, was not in competition with Technicolor and had a cross-licensing agreement with the company to use colour for its smaller gauge, 16mm film. In the 1930s to 1940s, colour film was not the dominant factor in film production. Colour was mostly used for **musicals**, **costume dramas** and cartoons – often with great success (*A Star Is Born*, George Cukor, 1937; *Gone With the Wind*, Victor Fleming, 1939). (Incidentally, Walt Disney, who was the first to use technicolour, was so pleased with his short colour-cartoons' success that he acquired exclusive rights for colour cartoons.) However, by the early 1950s the two companies had rescinded their agreement since the anti-trust law had charged both companies with monopolistic practices. Eastman-Kodak continued to improve on its own technology and produced an integral 35mm tri-pack colour film, Eastmancolor (first introduced in 1950 and perfected by 1952) that was easier to use, was suited to any camera, was more light sensitive (faster film stock), cheaper to buy and process than Technicolor. Technicolor's decline in the film industry was further accelerated by the fact that its dye process did not adapt well to **cinemascope**. Although Technicolor finally resolved those problems, it was not before Eastman had garnered most of the market. The Technicolor company (now part of the French conglomerate Thomson) is still involved in feature films but to a small degree and focuses more on research and laboratory processing. With the advent of new camera and digital technologies, Eastman-Kodak found itself struggling with its still-camera film Kodachrome (discontinued in the late 2000s).

Europe and Japan have also produced their own colour systems. Fujicolor (Japan) is by far the most successful of the major non-American colour processes and is noteworthy for its clarity and vibrant colour rendition. Two European colour systems, Agfa and Gevacolor, had some pre-eminence in the 1950s before Eastmancolor more or less garnered the market. Agfacolor, a German product with a huge reputation for colour quality, was the first to introduce the tri-pack system (in the mid-1930s). It ceased production in the 1970s because it was unable to meet demand (its best factory was based in Leverkusen, in former East Germany). Gevacolor (established in 1948, an affiliate of Agfa and based originally in Belgium) had its heyday in the 1950s and was particularly effective for location shooting. It was, however, a rather unstable process, especially in studio shooting where heat affected its colour-saturation. Gevacolor and Agfa consolidated in 1964 (Agfa-Gevaert) but did not survive into the 1980s as producers of motion picture film stock.

The two major manufacturers of the 1970s to the 2000s were Eastmancolor and Fujifilm. Nowadays, nearly all film is shot digitally. Digital cameras have digital image processing chips which convert raw data from the image sensor into a colour-corrected image (what the camera will deem is an optimum choice of colour balance). This digital video is recorded as digital files which are then transferred onto random access media such as hard disc drives or optical discs. Because of the excessive nature of the data stored, these files have to be compressed. And only when compressed can colour be enhanced or adjusted to the filmmaker's desired effect. Thus, in a sense, we can no longer talk about the properties of film colour in the same way as we once could (e.g. Eastman-Kodak was slightly pastel in its rendering; Fujicolor possessed a slight green hue to it).

Colour and theory

Colour film is an ambiguously positioned concept. On the one hand, it can reproduce reality more naturally than black and white film. On the other, it can draw attention to itself and, indeed, have symbolic value. Hollywood had a double response to this. At first, in the 1930s and 1940s, it decreed that colour should be reserved for certain genres that in themselves were not particularly realistic – stylized and spectacle genres (musical, **fantasy**, **epics**). Later, in the 1950s, when colour was more widely used, Hollywood concurred with Natalie Kalmus' dictat that all colour films should endeavour to use colour to underscore mood and meaning. To that effect bright and saturated colours were discouraged (Bordwell, in Bordwell *et al.*, 1985: 356).

But colour also has value and functions in relation to the **scopophilic drive**. Steve Neale's (1985) analysis of the value of colour in film representation makes three essential points. First, colour has a dialectical (i.e. a dual conflictual) function. This came about because colour was initially associated with spectacle and, therefore, was not seen as realist. Subsequently, however, following the advent of colour television – with its documentary and news or current affairs programmes – colour also obtained the cachet of **realism** (thus, incidentally, going back to one of its original meanings in the earliest experiments). Henceforth, the key terms centring the **discourse** about colour became nature/realism on the one hand and, on the other, spectacle/art – two contradictory sets of terms. Simply expressed, if colour is used as spectacle it cannot refer to its realist function, any more than if its aesthetic mode prevails. If the realist mode is invoked, then the film must reflect nature (the colour on-screen is the colour 'out there' in the real world) and, thereby, deny its function as spectacle and/or art.

Neale's second point about colour is possibly the most important (certainly for **feminist film theory**). Referring to the contradiction between the two sets of terms (realism/spectacle), Neale (1985: 152) says that it is at this point that another element enters into consideration: the female body. Women already occupy, within patriarchal ideology, the 'contradictory spaces both of nature and culture' (i.e. nature and artifice) and they are also the 'socially sanctioned objects of erotic looking' (i.e. spectacle). For these reasons, women 'naturally' function as the 'source of the spectacle of colour in practice'. Colour within the film will be determined by the female star's colouring; that is, what colour most complements her (which kind of begs the question: but why so much orange for the two redheads, Rita Hayworth and Deborah Kerr, and so much yellow for the yellowy-blonde Doris Day?). Women also function as 'a reference point for the use and promotion of colour in theory' (the female star is an essential vehicle for colour, she gives pleasure in her look-at-able-ness). Neale concludes, first of all, that 'the female body ... bridges the ideological gap between nature and cultural artifice'; that is, she bridges the gap caused by colour's ambiguity – so she is both realism and spectacle. But the female body simultaneously marks and focuses 'the scopophilic pleasures involved in and engaged by the use of colour in film'. Colour positions her as the site of pleasurable viewing *and* makes the **spectator** want to look at her.

What is significant in this reading is that, in being the embodiment of the dialectical function of colour, the female figure must implicitly be placed in other sets of dialectical functions. Thus, at the same time as the female body bridges the gap between the two sets of terms within the discourse on colour (realism and spectacle), she both *marks* and *contains* 'the erotic component involved in the desire to look at the coloured image' (Neale, 1985: 155). That is, in relation to the erotic, she is simultaneously positioned as **subject** (she contains, she is the holder of the erotic) and as object (she marks, she is the site of the erotic, the 'to be looked-at-ness'). Even though, in mainstream or **dominant cinema**, it is doubtful that this double positioning (subject and object) leads the female body, through its visual treatment, to assume **agency** (to become subject), it is clear that in non-mainstream cinema such agencing could occur. In this respect, colour could be used **counter-cinematically** to subvert the canonical **codes and conventions**.

Neale's third point develops further this potential for colour to subvert. Referring to Kristeva's writings on colour, Neale (1985: 156) argues that, because colour is so closely associated with the psychic and erotic pulsions, it is capable of escaping, subverting and shattering the symbolic organization (i.e. the narrative) to which it is subject. According to Kristeva, colour operates on three levels simultaneously: the objective, the subjective and the cultural. Within the domain of visual perception, the objective level refers to an outside, whereby an instinctual pressure is articulated in relation to external objects. In the case of cinema, this 'outside' would be the images up on-screen at which the spectator looks (instinctual pressure). This same pressure motivates the subjective level and causes the eroticization of the body proper ('seeing is responding'). Finally, the cultural level functions to insert this pressure under the impact of **censorship** as a **sign** in a system of representation. That is, the cultural operates to contain what happens between the objective and the subjective. It is a form of censorship in that the cultural's intentionality is containment of the subjective and erotic processes ('seeing is responding, but watch it does not go too far'). The cultural is not always successful in its purpose of course. Pornographic films are an easy example of this. However, certain scenes in un-X-rated movies can be so erotically charged as to catch the spectator by surprise.

For further reading on colour technology see Bordwell *et al.*, 1985; Dalle-Vache and Price, 2006; Konigsberg, 1993; Misek, 2010; on colour and theory see Brown and Street, 2012; Coates, 2010; Everett, 2007; Neale, 1985; Peacock, 2010.

COMEDY

In film history, comedy is one of the very earliest **genres**. This is not surprising, given that the first actors to come on to the screen were predominantly comedians from vaudeville and music-hall theatres. Early exhibition practices also explain this phenomenon. The first films were short, one-reelers and were included in a mixed-media show presented by a compère in a vaudeville theatre, a music-hall or a tent at a fair. At that time, then, cinema catered for popular taste and the humour on-screen tended to reflect popular comedy – as opposed to comedy of manners or social comedy. The early silent tradition of comedy was gag-based (as indeed was the very first comic film, Louis Lumière's *Arroseur arrosé*, 1895). This developed into routine comedy (Mack Sennett's Keystone Kops comedy series, of the 1910s, with their inevitable chase sequences) and into the emergence of the comic hero (*sic*) as, for example, Charlie Chaplin, Buster Keaton and Fatty Arbuckle. This primarily **gestural** tradition was, in its later manifestations, especially in **sound** cinema, closely allied to farce. Gestural gags now became verbal gags in comedies by the Marx brothers and W. C. Fields. But, as with the earlier tradition, violence was never far from the surface and this comic tradition is noteworthy for its aggressive humour.

As a genre, comedy deliberately goes against the demands of **realism** – hardly surprising given film comedy's heritage. Yet it is a genre that is perceived as serving a useful social and psychological function in that it is an arena, or provides an arena, where repressed tensions can be released in a safe manner. Apart from the gag-based comic tradition, the other dominant style of comedy comes from the more 'polished' comic theatre tradition. The plotline is less anarchic than in the earlier vaudevillesque tradition and therefore less ostensibly aggressive until one examines characterization. Stereotypes are far more foregrounded in this comedy, starting with **gender** (screwball comedies, as we all know, are about 'the battle of the sexes'), but including race, national prejudice, and so on. Some comedy parodies this stereotyping. For example, Marilyn Monroe is much smarter than the dumb blonde she is purported to be in *Gentlemen Prefer Blondes* (Howard Hawks, 1953), *The Seven Year Itch* (Billy Wilder, 1955) and *Some Like it Hot* (Billy Wilder, 1959). Or again, Katharine Hepburn may have to comply with Hollywood's insistence on closure, meaning marriage, but she'll choose her man, she'll whip him into shape before she's at all prepared to consider him as a suitable partner (*Philadelphia Story*, George Cukor, 1940; *The African Queen*, 1951, and the innumerable combinations with Spencer Tracey).

Comedy is still a big tradition in Europe, especially in France where half the film industry's production is comedy. Britain has a strong tradition with its Ealing Comedies and *Carry On* movies. But these are past history (1940–50s and 1958–78 respectively) – as indeed, on the whole, is the British film industry itself. Even good British-made romantic comedy stories (rom-coms) such as *Notting Hill* (Roger Mitchell, 1999) and the *Bridget Jones* (2001–04) series are essentially American productions – although they may star British actors such as the smooth but caddish Hugh Grant and the slightly nicer Colin Firth in the lead male roles, and have a 'made in England' feel to them, the money to make them either comes from Miramax, Universal Pictures or some other American super-conglomerate and, most often, it is an American star for the female lead (for example, Julia Roberts or Renée Zellweger). In the United States, because of demographic shifts in audiences, production tends to target youth audiences, which means action-packed narratives, and much less sassy talk. For this reason, the comedy that is produced tends to be more in the farce and gag tradition than the supposedly more sophisticated talk-humour (note the popularity of the *Wayne's World*, or *Austin Powers* movies of the 1990s). But that is not the total picture for comedy of course. Since the new millennium, rom-coms have seen a big upswing (some 130 just within the US and UK market alone, and France producing some ten rom-coms per year), suggesting a nostalgia for marriage and 'settled-down-ness' which all statistics belie.

see also: **genre**

For further reading see: on silent comedy, Merton, 2007; popular comedy, Brunovska Karnick and Jenkins, 1995; Medhurst, 2007; Rickman, 2001; African-American comedy, Littleton, 2006; rom-coms, Abbott and Jermyn, 2009; Glitre, 2006; Grindon, 2011; Jeffers MacDonald, 2007.

CONTINUITY EDITING – *SEE* EDITING

CONVERGENCE

Refers as a term to the widespread use of all new forms of media both within film production and film exhibition and within **distribution**. Media convergence includes, therefore, all aspects of digital media, social networking media, internet and blogging. These new forms of digital technology provide new film practices, new delivery, distribution and exhibition systems for the desiring consumer(s). Thus, films of all sorts (ranging from products made by independent filmmakers to amateur individuals) can be 'distributed' via these forms of media (see Vimeo as just one example). Previously theatre-released films can be rented online – video on demand.

Production practices have been 'revolutionized' thanks to media convergence. Thus, films can be made for internet or general release; financed, wholly or partly, by credit card donations. There are two outstanding and creative examples of this in recent history. The first was the self-distributed feature length film *Four Eyed Monsters* (Susan Buice and Arin Crumley, 2007) on YouTube – the debt was recouped through online membership. The second was the documentary about climate change starring Pete Postlethwaite, *The Age of Stupid* (Franny Armstrong, 2009), which pioneered the crowd-funding model of distribution (whereby organizations or individuals rent the film for screening and keep the profit for themselves).

Contemporary feature films with cinema-theatre release will also incorporate many aspects of the diversity of new media within their narrative as much as within their actual production practices (see entry on **digital**). In the former instance, mobile phones, use of laptops, tablets, etc. move the story on (see, for example, the widespread presence of this new media in *Redacted*, Brian De Palma, 2007; or the presence of US aerial drones in *Body of Lies*, Ridley Scott, 2008). In the latter instance, the entire process of filming is entirely digital (filming and **editing** and projection) and can of course include **CGI** (see *Avatar*, James Cameron, 2009).

Convergence also refers to the 'chatter' surrounding films. Thus, debates are held about a specific film on the internet, blogs and other forms of social networking, by mobile phone, etc. This latter form can have a huge impact on the success or failure of a film (we are no longer in the world of word of mouth, a very slow process of information flow; now the chatter is very fast indeed, a matter of seconds in fact). Thus, the world of film criticism has changed, because the new media makes meta-commentary possible – all consumers can air their views on films (new and old releases alike). It is no longer the critic's choice that prevails, as an opinion at least.

Lastly, in this new interactive age of digital media convergence, it is now possible for any individual to remix pre-existing movies (or trailers) – what is referred to as 'movie mash-ups' (Tryon, 2009: 14). While this practice can be considered pure bricolage and entirely playful, unfortunately, media convergence also includes the vexed issue of piracy (see Tryon, 2009, on the famous case of Michael Moore's *Sicko*, 2007).

see also: **digital cinema**

For further reading see Rombes, 2009; Tryon, 2009.

COSTUME DRAMAS/HERITAGE CINEMA/ HISTORICAL FILMS

Costume dramas are often literary **adaptations**, although original scripts are also in the mix, as are films based in historical fact. The term is still in use today, but another, looser term has been in use since the 1980s to refer to costume films: heritage cinema. The 1980s saw an exponential rise in production of costume/heritage films, mostly emanating from European cinemas. Although by the 1990s, the US also joined in this profitable new trend (Martin Scorsese's *The Age of Innocence*, 1993, being a prime example); as did pan-European productions (*Orlando*, Potter, 1992; *Sense and Sensibility*, Lee, 1995).

The Merchant-Ivory adaptations of E. M. Forster's novels (beginning 1985 with *Maurice*) are perhaps the best known of the first wave of heritage cinema, but we should recall that *Chariots of Fire* (Hudson, 1981) initiated heritage cinema – a cinema which celebrates the past and has been criticized for its nostalgic, even conservative aesthetics (a view reinforced by the associations made, in the UK, with the ideology of Mrs Thatcher's government). If we look at history, in general, it is probably safe to say that costume dramas tend to be more in evidence during periods where a nation's political culture is less stable (France of the 1950s, for example). But it should also be said that this cinema is popular with audiences as much because of the attention to detail as because of the enjoyment of the actual **narrative**. Thus, while it is retro and promotes an idealistic image of the past, and in many instances reinforces bourgeois sentimentality, nonetheless, it is still possible to read these dramas as more than just theme-park museum aesthetics. Within the narratives, issues such as **gender** relations, **class** and **sexualities** come to the fore; critiques of **ideological** positionings can be uncovered (especially when reading against the grain).

Costume, heritage and historical films are set in a historical period and refer in general terms to the time in history through the costumes and décor which, by convention, should be in keeping with the time. Authenticity is the key term where costume dramas are concerned, at least in terms of the production practices. From **setting**, costumes, objects, to use of **colour** (especially once it was fully introduced in 1952), every detail must appear authentic. Hence the very high costs of producing such films. The narrative focuses on a fictional story set in the past, or the life of a real person or event. Where the historical film is concerned, it is often highly fictionalized, invests the moment or person with 'greatness'. 'Authenticity' serves a different purpose in this context. In this respect, historical films have an ideological function: they are serving up the country's national history before the eyes of the indigenous people, teaching us our history according to the 'great moments' and 'great men or women' in our collective past – our heritage on-screen. Costume dramas and heritage cinema, when serving up literary adaptations, function in a not dissimilar, ideological way; this time feeding us the 'classics' of our nation's culture (e.g. for the UK, Shakespeare, Dickens, Forster; for France, Dumas, Hugo, Zola; for the USA, Fitzgerald, James, Wharton).

see also: **adaptations, genre**

For further reading see Bruzzi, 1997; Cook, 1996; Harper, 1987, 1994; Hayward, 2010; Street, 2001; Vincendeau, 2001.

COUNTER-CINEMA/OPPOSITIONAL CINEMA

This type of cinema can be found in a variety of cinemas: **experimental, avant-garde** and **art cinema**. At its simplest it is a cinema that, through its own cinematic practices, questions and subverts existing cinematic **codes and conventions**. In its aesthetic and often political concerns with the how and the why of filmmaking, it is a cinema that can be quite formalist and materialist – that is, both the structure and texture of the film will be visible on the screen (for example, through **jump cuts**, a play with perspectival space, a stripping down of colour to its primaries, and so on). The effect is that the film becomes very discontinuous in its look. In this cinema **spatial and temporal contiguity** will be deconstructed, the security of the **setting** offered by a logical **mise-en-scène** will be decomposed and all other elements of **seamlessness** and compositional continuity will be exposed (see **editing**). This is a cinema that draws attention to itself, its manufacture and the production of meaning. There is no safe **narrative**, no beginning, middle and end, no closure or resolution. Needless to say, **spectators** are not stitched or **sutured** into counter-cinematic films, but are intentionally

distanced by these practices so they 'can see what is really there', and reflect upon it rather than be seduced into a false illusionism.

Although as a practice this questioning and, potentially, self-reflexive cinema goes back to the 1920s, it was in the early 1970s that the term *counter-cinema* was coined – largely because film theorists and some filmmakers (notably Jean-Luc Godard and Agnès Varda in France and the **underground film** movement in the United States) began to question Hollywood's **hegemony** and **dominant cinema**'s system of representation. It is in this latter respect that **feminist film theorists** first took an interest in the possibilities of counter-cinema to do more than just retransmit women's issues by doing it politically – by exposing the way in which dominant cinema has represented as **natural** woman's position as object and not **subject** of the **gaze**, as object and not agent of desire (see **agency**). Women filmmakers, in subverting cinematic codes, not only denaturalized dominant film hegemony insofar as verisimilitude is concerned. Through their films, they also made visible the meaning of phallocentric fetishization of women as spectacle and receptacle. By denormalizing dominant practices, they made visible what was made invisible: woman's subjectivity and difference – which fetishism denies (see **subjectivity**). An example is Sally Potter's *Thriller* (1979), which rejects the male gaze and seeks to find and assert woman's right to her own subjectivity.

Counter-cinema, then, is oppositional, exposes hegemonic practices, unfixes – renders unstable – stereotypes, makes visible what has been normalized or invisibilized.

see also: **deconstruction, feminist film theory, naturalizing, time-image**

For further reading see Gidal, 1989; Johnston, 1976; Kaplan, 1983: 142ff.

CROSS-CUTTING

Literally, cutting between different sets of action that can be occurring simultaneously or at different times. This term is used synonymously but somewhat incorrectly with *parallel editing*. Cross-cutting is used to build suspense, or to show the relationship between the different sets of action that are occurring at the same time. Parallel editing in its truest sense refers to paralleling two related actions that are occurring at different times, but which are in some way connected (for example, bringing an earlier memory into a present event).

For further discussion *see* **cut, editing**.

CULT CINEMA

Cult cinema is now an established part of film studies. What makes a film a cult is primarily down to audience celebration, it enjoys a devoted following, small or large (irrespective of its quality). We could say that there are two fundamental types of cult films, both having in common that, often, they may not have succeeded at the box-office, and, most significantly, that they, in some way, subvert **mainstream cinema**, challenge conformity, cross boundaries (including good taste!) – either through being transgressive (*The Rocky Horror Picture Show*, Jim Sharman, 1975, which is still in limited release) or **experimental** (*Eraserhead*, David Lynch, 1977). A first type, labelled 'cult classics', are those films that fail initially, but which have enough of a popular following that, over a period of time, they obtain cult status and finally become listed amongst the world's classics (a sample range goes from *La Grande illusion/The Grand Illusion*, Renoir, 1938, to *Casablanca*, Michael Curtiz, 1942, to *The Big Lebowski*, Coen Brothers, 1998). Second, 'midnight movies' (so-called, originally, because of their midnight screening), are those films which 'play at the margins of cinematic illusion' (Telotte, 1991: 10), are non-conformist, often crudely fashioned, and are 'so bad, they are good' (the *Living Dead* series, 1968–2010, is a prime example). Given their often limited release, these films obtain an original small fanbase that then grows to a larger or smaller degree. Nowadays, cult following is rendered considerably easier thanks to DVD releases.

Because cult films are not a **genre**, they tend to be of all categories: **horror, science-fiction**, and **fantasy** may be the dominant types; but some **pornographic** films have obtained this status – the 1970s *Emmanuelle* series from France, *Deep Throat*, Gerard Damiano, 1972 from the US. All develop a knowing audience (hence the term 'cult'), all respond to the audience's desire for the unfamiliar (no matter how horrible!).

For further reading: on definitions of cult cinema see Telotte, 1991; Mathijs and Mendik, 2008; and for a good overview of the top 100 cult films worldwide see Mathijs and Mendik, 2011; for Asian cult cinema see Weisser, 1997.

CUT

The splicing of two shots together. This cut is made by the film editor at the **editing** stage of a film. Between sequences the cut marks a rapid transition between one time and space and another, but depending on the nature of the cut it will have different meanings.

Jump cuts, continuity cuts, match cuts and cross-cuts

These are the four types of cut typically used for cutting between one sequence or scene and another, although jump cuts and match cuts are also used within a sequence or scene.

Jump cuts Cuts where there is no match between the two spliced **shots**. Within a sequence, or more particularly a scene, jump cuts give the effect of bad editing because they do not obey the **30-degree rule**. The camera, literally, jumps about without any intention to orientate the **spectator**, with the effect of jolting the spectator along. Spatially, therefore, the jump cut has a confusing effect. The jump cut disorientates not only spatially but also temporally (especially between sequences). The lack of spatial and visual logic serves (see **distanciation**) to distance or alienate the spectator. The most quoted film which exemplifies all of these uses of the jump cut is Jean-Luc Godard's *À bout de souffle* (1959). The prime example, in terms of shock-effect, occurs between sequences 1 and 2: in a countryside lane the protagonist shoots a motorcycle cop dead, runs across a field – cut – to the protagonist in a Paris telephone booth. The result is a lack of coherence in terms of time and space. Within sequences, jump cuts around enclosed spaces make those spaces unfamiliar. Most unusual of all is the use of jump cuts within dialogue. In the same film, the two protagonists (Michel and Patricia) at one point are sitting talking in a car as they drive around Paris. However, we never fully decipher what they are saying because of the numerous jump cuts inserted into the dialogue. The effect is a jerky, one-sided conversation that serves to alienate the spectator. Godard (1982) claimed he inserted these jump cuts because his film (his first) was far too long, by an hour; thus he opted to keep Michel's words only. He may be pulling our leg. However, it does go to show how economies of scale force decisions that eventually become canonized as art.

Continuity cuts These are cuts that take us seamlessly and logically from one sequence or scene to another. This is an unobtrusive cut that serves to move the **narrative** along.

Match cuts A cut from one shot to another where the two shots are matched by the action or subject and subject matter. This cut is the exact opposite to jump cuts within a scene. These cuts make sure that there is a spatial–visual logic between the differently positioned shots within a scene. Thus, where the camera moves to and the angle of the camera make visual sense to the spectator. For example, in a duel, a shot can go from a long shot on both contestants via a cut to a medium close-up shot of one of the duellists. The cut matches the two shots, is consistent with the logic of the action. This is a standard practice in **Hollywood** filmmaking, to produce a **seamless** reality-effect. **Eyeline matching** is part of the same visual logic: the first shot shows a character looking at something off-screen, the second shot shows what is being looked at. Match cuts then are also part of the seamlessness, the reality-effect, so much favoured by Hollywood.

Cross-cuts These are cuts used to alternate between two sequences or scenes that are occurring in the same time but in different spaces. Generally they are used to create suspense, so they are quite commonly found in **Westerns, thrillers** and **gangster** movies. These cuts also serve to speed up the narrative.

Montage cuts, compilation shots and cutaways

These are all used within sequences or scenes, although montage cuts can in fact compose a whole film (see **editing**).

Montage cuts A rapid succession of cuts splicing different shots together to make a particular meaning or indeed create a feeling (such as vertigo, fear, etc.). First employed by the **Soviet school**, they became incorporated into **avant-garde** or **art cinema**. They can be used to deconstruct one set of meanings and put in place another (e.g. the slow pomp of a funeral procession can be deconstructed and reconstructed by a rapid montage of shots into an indictment against the bourgeoisie, as in René Clair's *Entr'acte*, 1924).

Compilation shots A series of shots spliced together to give a quick impression of a place (shots of Paris, London or New York to establish the city) or a quick explanation of a situation (police arriving at a murder scene: shots of the crowd, journalists, police, detectives, finally the corpse) or a character's impression of an event (watching the highlights of a sporting event, or a performance of some sort).

Cutaways Shots that take the spectator away from the main action or scene. Often used as a transition before cutting into the next sequence or scene. For example, inside a court scene the day's proceedings are coming to an end, cutaway shot to the outside of the courthouse then cut to the next day in the lawyer's or solicitor's office.

Cuts give rhythm to the film; so getting that tempo right is essential. A film, therefore, goes through several cuts before the editor – usually working in tandem with the director – comes up with what is known as the rough-cut (within Hollywood this cut is sometimes referred to as the director's cut, but it is not the final cut). Adjustments and changes are then made to produce a fine-cut before the final-cut is made and the film is ready for the post-synchronized **sound** mix to be transferred on to its optical/digital soundtrack.

see also: **editing, sequencing**

DAY FOR NIGHT

A form of shooting in daylight with the intention of creating a night effect either by underexposure of the film stock or through using filters on the camera. Either way the purpose is to save on production costs. François Truffaut pays homage to this effect in his 1972 film *La Nuit américaine/Day for Night*.

DECONSTRUCTION

Originally a term used by the German philosopher Martin Heidegger (in his major study, *Being and Time*, 1927) in relation to language, more precisely the word, which the French philosopher Jacques Derrida (in his work *Of Grammatology*, 1967) later extended to textual reading, and which **film theory** has taken on board (see **post-structuralism** entry). Heidegger's term, *destruktion*/destruction, is a process whereby categories and concepts that tradition has imposed upon a word can be investigated (including cultural and historical contexts). A word cannot have meaning in isolation; we understand it in relation first to its opposite (think of black/white); then in relation to its context (including **denotation/connotation**); then history; and so on. Derrida's analysis went further, investigating the relationship between text and meaning. Derrida argued that meaning can only be interpellated in relation to other **signs**. That is, a concept can only be understood in relation to its opposite. Let us take as an illustrative example, **mainstream cinema** and **counter-cinema**. We understand the **codes and conventions** of the former through bringing it in relation to the latter, thereby having an understanding of the codes and conventions (the system of signs) that pertain to the one practice as opposed to the other. It then follows, as indeed Derrida argues, that rather than just having knowledge of a text as a system of signs, we understand the parts of the whole and in turn the structures and processes of meaning production (such as cultural, political, industrial, economic and historical contexts and of course, ultimately, **ideological**).

In relation to film history, it is clear that deconstruction was being practised and deconstructive films were being made as early as the 1920s. Noël Burch (1973) argues that the first deconstructive film was the **German expressionist** film *The Cabinet of Dr Caligari* (Robert Wiene, 1919), an interesting thought given that the codes and conventions of **dominant cinema**, which this film contested, were barely in place. But this claim also suggests that any new cultural **discourse**, once it assumes a dominant status, will bring in its wake an oppositional cultural discourse. Thus, discourses constantly renew themselves. In film theory the term *deconstruction* is largely associated with counter-cinema, although, as we shall explain below, it had important implications for the development of film theory. Deconstructive film does what the term implies: it deconstructs and makes visible through that deconstruction the codes and conventions of dominant cinema; it exposes the function of the cinematic **apparatus** as an instrument of illusionist representation and attacks the ideological values inherent in that representation. It refuses the logic of a homogeneous filmic space and **narrative** closure. Deconstructive films are counter-cinematic in both aesthetic and political terms. However, politics and aesthetics until recently have rarely meant sexual politics. With the exception of Germaine Dulac's and Maya Deren's **surrealist** films of, respectively, the 1920s and the 1940s, feminine **subjectivity** had hardly been addressed at all until the impact of the women's movement of the 1970s brought in its wake **feminist theory** and feminist films. Feminist film theory was the first to seize upon the usefulness of deconstruction. We think of Claire Johnston's important 1976 essay, 'Women's Cinema as Counter-cinema', in which she argues for an understanding of the processes of meaning construction. Through a deconstruction of the modes of production, cinematic codes and conventions would be exposed as well as their ideological function. The introduction of deconstruction into film theory opened the door to a much broader approach to film studies; and of course, as the paragraph above makes clear, it allowed for a clearer understanding of what was at work in films that opposed mainstream cinema.

Derrida's notion that 'no meaning can be determined out of context' (1979: 81) set the tone. And, from the 1980s on, film studies dealt with texts and contexts as a matter of courses. Interestingly, in the 1980s, the publishers Routledge picked up on this trend with its series of books on national cinemas (e.g. *German Film: Texts and Contexts, French Film: Texts and Contexts*, and so on). Furthermore, and just as significantly, by making clear the importance of text to context, Derrida signalled that the meaning of any given text is determined by the actual reader. Moreover, that reader, given his or her awareness of other texts, will produce further, new meanings still (both in relation to the first text and the subsequent ones; see **inter-textuality**). In relation to film theory, this brought to light the importance of spectator–text relations as more than a one-way system. Spectators were now considered just as much producers of meaning as the filmic texts. Thus, since the late 1990s and through the 2000s, spectatorship and reception theory have become integral parts of film theory.

For further reading see Derrida, 1979; Gidal, 1989; Kuhn, 1982.

DEEP FOCUS/DEPTH OF FIELD

These two terms are not interchangeable but they are deeply inter-connected because the technique of deep focus is dependent on a wide depth of field. Depth of field is a cinematographic practice whereas deep focus is both a technique and a film style with theoretical and **ideolo-gical** implications. Depth of field refers to the focal length any particular lens can provide. Greater depth of field is achieved by a wide-angle lens and it is this type of lens that achieves deep focus. With deep focus, all planes within the lens' focus are in sharp focus – thus background and foreground are both in focus. Deep focus then is a technique which uses fast wide-angle lenses and fast film to preserve as much depth of field as possible. Although some critics have credited the filmmaker Jean Renoir with first using this type of focus so that he could make long takes and not have to edit to create movement (movement of course occurring within the frame), it is traditionally Orson Welles who is credited as the first to use the effect in *Citizen Kane* (1941). Because deep focus requires a small aperture, it also requires fast-film stock and this was not available until the late 1930s. Renoir created the illusion of deep focus by creating depth of space through staging in-depth and adjusting the focus according to what was of main interest. Staging in-depth is a perspectival strategy that dates back to the 1910s in cinema history. It is a system whereby the illusion of depth is created by characters moving from the back to the foreground or by the **mise-en-scène** privileging the background or middleground characters. The background could be brought ('pulled') into sharp focus and the foreground would be slightly out of focus (Salt, 1983: 269). However, as David Bordwell (in Bordwell *et al.*, 1985: 344) makes clear, neither Renoir nor Welles were in fact the first to achieve deep focus. Bordwell *et al.* (1985: 344–46) list several examples of its use in 1940s films and point also to the work of the US cinematographer Gregg Toland (who, incidentally, shot *Citizen Kane*), where it is already in evidence as early as 1937, in *Dead End* (William Wyler). In fact, Toland had already experimented with deep focus in his silent cinema work, the earliest example of which is Arthur Edeson's *The Bat* (1926).

The theoretical and ideological debate over the merits of deep focus over **montage** was first launched, in the 1950s, by André Bazin in his essay 'The Evolution of the Language of Cinema' (Bazin, 1967: 23–40). When speaking of montage, Bazin does not mean it entirely in the more limited way in which we now tend to refer to it (as the **Soviet cinema style** of editing), but to an 'ordering of images in time' (ibid.: 24) used by many cinemas in the pre-sound era. Bazin offers a definition of montage as 'the creation of a sense of meaning not proper to the images themselves but derived exclusively from their juxtaposition' (ibid.: 25). Pre-war classics of the American screen, Bazin tells us, used montage just as much as any of the more experimental schools (Soviet or **German expressionism**), it just did so in an invisible way (ibid.: 24). He goes on to explain that montage, however used, imposes its interpretation on the **spectator** and takes away from realism (ibid.: 26). To formulate his debate, Bazin distinguishes between two trends in cinema, the one pre-sound that is much invested in the image and which has major recourse to the use of montage; the other, the cinema of the 1940s and which is primarily invested in reality (ibid.: 24). His first point is not to dismiss montage as a cinematic style appropriate only to silent cinema, but to state that the spatial unity of a film should dictate the dropping of montage in favour of what he terms 'depth of focus' but which we now refer to as deep focus.

For Bazin, deep focus made a greater objective **realism** possible. Since deep focus, contrary to the fast editing style of montage, usually implies long takes and less editing from shot to shot, this style of shooting is one that draws least attention to itself and, therefore, allows for a more open reading. As Bazin says (ibid.: 36), 'depth of focus reintroduced ambiguity into the structure of the image if not of necessity ... at least as a possibility'. Certain films, according to Bazin (thinking specifically of *Citizen Kane*), are unthinkable if not shot in depth. Deep focus' great virtue for Bazin was that the spectator was not subjected to the ideological nature of montage which rests as it does on a priori knowledge (i.e. that montage will produce a specific meaning). Rather, deep focus presents the spectator with a naturalism of the image that refuses all a priori analysis of the world (see **ideology**). But we would argue that montage and deep focus editing, while seemingly ideologically opposed, are about two different ways of reading film. In both instances, the spectator is 'responsible' for creatively reading what s/he sees. Montage creates a third meaning through the collision of two images. A meaning that is produced outside the image, in point of fact. The sequence of images in conflict (what Eisenstein termed a montage of attractions) provokes a creative reaction within the spectator who produces for him/herself a third meaning, whereas deep-focus editing produces meaning within the image, and the spectator takes his/her own reading from the image before him/her.

see also: **editing**

DENOTATION/CONNOTATION

Two key terms in **semiotics**. Following on from Ferdinand de Saussure's work on signification (see **semiology/semiotics**), Roland Barthes coined these two terms to give greater clarity to the way in which **signs** work in any given culture. They are what Barthes termed the two orders of signification. Thus, there is a first order of signification (denotation) and a second order (connotation). These in turn produce a third order: **myth**. Denotation means the literal relationship between sign and referent; thus, *tree* denotes the object referred to. In film terms, this first order of meaning would refer to what is on the screen, that is, the mechanical (re)production of an image; for example, three people in a frame (a three-**shot**), two men and a woman. The second order of meaning, connotation, adds values that are culturally encoded to that first order of meaning. And it is at this second order of signification that we can see how signs operate as myth-makers. That is, they function as crystallizers of abstract concepts or concepts that are difficult to conceptualize – they make sense of the culture (e.g. institutional, social) in which individuals or communities find themselves.

Returning, by way of illustration, to this three-shot. At the denotative level, the two men are standing either side of the woman. The main source of **lighting** is coming from the side, casting one of the men into the shadows. The camera is at a slight low angle, thereby slightly distorting the features of the characters. At the connotative level of meaning, the reading produced is as follows: this image is signifying the dangers of a triangular relationship. In **classical narrative cinema** – which reposes on the triad order/disorder/order-restored – convention has it that a triangular relationship must end with the demise of one character (in our example, the man in the shadows), so that order can be re-established. Within that cultural convention we can also see how the third order of signification, myth, gets produced and feeds into **ideology**. The myth that triangular relationships are doomed, and cause disruption to order, implicitly makes clear that heterosexual coupledom is the only ideologically acceptable face of sexuality.

For further reading see Barthes, 1957, 1973.

DIEGESIS/DIEGETIC/NON-DIEGETIC/ EXTRA- AND INTRA-DIEGETIC

Diegesis refers to **narration**, the content of the narrative, the fictional world as described inside the story. In film, it refers to all that is really going on on-screen, that is, to fictional reality. Characters' words and gestures, all action as enacted within the screen constitute the diegesis. Hence the term *diegetic sound*, which is **sound** that 'naturally' occurs within the screen space (such as an actor speaking, singing or playing an instrument on-screen). The term *non-diegetic sound* refers to sound that clearly is not being produced within the on-screen space (such as voice-over or added music). Of course film is about the illusion of reality into which the **spectator** gets comfortably stitched (see **suture**). And to a degree even diegetic sound and space are totally illusory and falsely constructed: the sound because with most films it is post-synchronized; the space because the actual images and **shots** we see are the result of countless takes – so neither is ultimately 'naturally' there (see **naturalizing**). Certain film-makers will play on or with this illusory nature of cinema through the use of extra-diegetic sounds. Extra-diegetic sounds or shots apply to sounds or shots that come into screen space but have no logical reason for being there. They are inserted as a form of **counter-cinematic** practice or **deconstruction** to draw the **spectator**'s attention to the fact that s/he is watching a film. Jean-Luc Godard is a famed practitioner of this.

The term *diegetic* also refers to **audiences**, so that there are diegetic audiences: audiences within the film. These are often used to draw attention to the **star** in the film or to act as a backdrop to display the star. These diegetic audiences also serve to draw us, the *extra-diegetic* audience, into the screen and thereby into the illusion that we too are part of the diegetic audience. **Musicals** very commonly use diegetic audiences, dancing and singing around the main protagonists – usually a couple – just to show off how brilliant the couple is in performing their song and dance. **Westerns** also use the diegetic audience to show off the bravery of the hero in contrast with their own cowardice (see, for example, Gary Cooper in *High Noon*, Fred Zinnemann, 1952).

Finally, *intra-diegetic* sound. This refers to sound whose source we do not see but whose presence we 'know' to exist within the story; for example, the voice-over of a narrator whose story we are being told and who is also portrayed in the film, that is, who exists on the same level of reality as the story and characters in the film. Michael Curtiz's *Mildred Pierce* (1945) is a classic in this domain. At times we only hear the heroine's disembodied voice recalling moments of her past in voice-over as we **flashback** to images of her in the frame, but we know the voice belongs to her and that she is a character in the story. She recalls in voice-over in the first flashback: 'I felt all alone ... lonely' after her husband, Bert, had left her. Another classic example of this use of intra-diegetic sound is *Rebecca* (Alfred Hitchcock, 1940). At the very beginning we hear the disembodied voice of a woman say: 'Last night I dreamt I went to Manderley.' A little later in the film, we realize that that 'I' and the 'I' of the female protagonist are one and the same. At that moment, we realize the earlier sound was intra-diegetic – an interesting way of creating suspense. The voice-over of a protagonist who is announcing a flashback in her or his life, then, is intra-diegetic. Most typically the protagonist's face will dissolve into an image of an earlier time as we hear the voice-over say, 'and yet it was only yesterday' (as in *Le Jour se lève*, Marcel Carné, 1939). In fact flashbacks themselves could be seen as intra-diegetic because although they are part of the **narrative**, they nonetheless interrupt the narrative flow in the present. Interior monologue is also intra-diegetic and is quite distinct from the non-diegetic voice-over of an omniscient narrator who gives information about the story but is not personally part of the story. Intra-diegetic sound, then, at its simplest refers to the inner thoughts or voices of a narrator whose story we are witnessing. It also creates a different order of audience **identification**. During those intra-diegetic moments the character's **subjectivity** becomes ours: there is a double privileging – we are positioned not only physically but also psychically as the **subject**.

DIGITAL CINEMA/POST-DIGITAL CINEMA

In terms of cinematic release, *the* digital first was in 1999 with the successful digital cinema screening of *Star Wars Episode I: The Phantom Menace* (George Lucas). But the phenomenon did not really take off fully until 2008, after a series of profitable 3-D films made it seem a going concern. Now, virtually all cinema theatres project in digital.

It may seem strange, therefore, to be talking already of the post-digital in the same entry as digital when the full impact of the digital technological 'revolution' has not yet been fully felt. However, almost as we have now come to consider **modernism/postmodernism** as co-existing entities albeit to different degrees of relevance and importance depending on the era (i.e. one is in the shadow of the other, but always co-present), so too we have to see digital and post-digital as co-existing entities today in the film world (as I shall develop below).

The first, obvious point to make is that digital technologies have impacted not just in the domains of production and post-production, but also in the area of **distribution** and exhibition of film. Celluloid film is gradually disappearing from our cinema screens; the projected image now comes to us through a delivery point in the form of a hard drive. The economics of such a delivery system are self-evident. Not only can screening quality be guaranteed (the film does not have to suffer the wear and tear of running through sprockets, getting torn, becoming scratched at the beginning of each reel, and so on), but also the costs of multiple print runs are avoided (no small consideration if a film has a 400-theatre release). Because a film is now a digital product, its mode of delivery is easier, faster and of course multiform and not limited to the cinema theatres: internet downloads on computers, mobile phones or tablets; television films on demand (e.g. via Netflix) are also part of the story (see **convergence**).

The second self-evidence is the great democratization brought about by this technology. Anyone can set themselves up both as filmmaker (in terms of **producing**, **directing**, soundtracking, **editing**, an individual can be a complete '**auteur**') and distributor/exhibitor (the film, once edited on the personal computer, can then be uploaded onto any number of internet sites, such as Vimeo or YouTube) – without incurring crippling expense. Even hi-spec HD cameras are 'affordable' (e.g. the 4K Red Camera, known also as the Red One); the full-frame sensor DSLR technology means images are of a professional standard and are indistinguishable from 35mm film (e.g. *Social Network*, David Fincher, 2010, was shot on the Red One).

Film-formatting (from 35mm to widescreen) are at the touch of a switch on the camera (and so on).

The third and final (obvious) point to be made in terms of the impact of this technology concerns the expressed fear (by some) that the digital age marks the end of cinema. This chestnut comes round with each new technological advance in cinema (e.g. **sound**, video, now digital). As a technology, the capturing of images is still a matter of light coming through the camera lens – this fundamental principle of photography remains a constant, therefore. What differs are solutions produced to meet the same (always existing) problems, all of which can now be fixed digitally: weather changes impacting on **lighting** continuity, blue-screening to save on location shooting, etc. A related issue regards film's purported ability to represent reality. The long take, because it is shot in real time, has been long-associated with cinematic **realism** (Bazin, 2011). Because it offers an open-ended reading for the spectator, it is the closest film can come to guaranteeing spectator **subjectivity**. With digital film, the potential for the long take has doubled in length (from 20 to 40 minutes; see David Lynch's *Inland Empire*, 2006). Although this extended single-shot is a digital first, we should not forget that Hitchcock (for one) had already experimented in this way with *Rope* (1948) – in blocks of ten-minute takes (the length of a 35mm film camera magazine at that time). Moreover, in the 1960s, Andy Warhol made several real-time films; his most famous being the eight-hour long *Empire* (1964). While it has the appearance of being a single-shot, it is, rather, a single-framed shot of the Empire State building in New York shot on a huge number of 16mm 100-foot film reels at 24 frames per second for six and a half hours (each reel is 100 feet and lasts about four minutes). To accentuate the sensation of watching time go by, the film was then screened at 16 frames per second to give it a longer duration. So it is not necessarily true that this long-take shift, which digital technology allows for, would particularly alter our way of perceiving time and receiving film. What it does do, however, is offer choice. Always available before, conceptually at least, now the choice is of a different order. The length of the shot can extend the duration of our **gaze**, our point of view (an entire film could be made up of two long takes of 40 minutes; a total of 80 minutes, two slices of real time); it also makes it possible for the actor to offer fuller, more complex **performances** in a single shot (because there is no stopping and starting again by having to change the film magazine); thus, it widens the **spectator**'s ability to perceive actors' shifts in performance; finally, it allows for what Rombes (2009: 40) refers to as an 'uncontrolled emergence of the real into the frame' itself, a capturing of mistakes as well as the randomness of life, warts and all.

It is also true that special effects, the direct opposite of cinematic realism, can abound in digital cinema. Thus, in terms of special effects, the most recent – in relation to performance capture technology – is Mocap/Motion Capture (but by the time this book is in print, a new form will probably have replaced it!). We are familiar with examples of this in the *Lord of the Rings* series (Peter Jackson, 2001–03) and *Avatar* (James Cameron, 2009). Then there is the virtual camera's real-time playback system (SimulCam) which now makes it possible to see the actors in performance-capture clothing (Mocap suits), projected by the virtual camera as the imaginary computer-generated characters they are playing (Gaunt, 2011: 87). The entire (pre-recorded) CGI environment can be seen through the SimulCam's viewfinder and on live monitors on the set. This allows the human actors to interact directly with the CGI creations and for the director to frame the image exactly as s/he wants.

Thus, the change brought about by digital is one of degree where cinema is concerned. The point is, also, that cinema must, as with all art (popular and **avant-garde**), evolve both to survive and to engage those who wish to consume it. Just as the film practices have evolved so too have consumption practices. But, again, these are more a matter of degree and ergonomics than a threat to cinema theatres. So multiplexes have made their seating more comfortable and provided drink and popcorn holders on the arms. Some cinemas have introduced sofas into sections of their theatres. Indeed, if we consider theatres for a moment, at its simplest, of all the principal roles in terms of exhibition (which is after all the consumer-spectator end of things), the most profoundly affected by this new technology is surely the projectionist – a role that is considerably diminished and now requires no specialist training: just slot in the hard drive or optical disks or streaming or downloading and press 'play' (that is, until something breaks down!).

All of this makes the digital technology interesting, but it does not necessarily mark a huge shift in cinematic ontology. What the digital does offer, however, without question, and what demarcates it from previous technologies is what can be referred to as its purity, its 'cleanliness'. Clean sound, clean images, and so on (for a good example of this clean, cold, clinical sterility of the digital see Michael Haneke's *White Ribbon*, 2009). In its search for purity, cinema has finally found its technological *nec plus ultra*. And it is at this precise point that the concept of the *post-digital* comes into being. In the digital age, it is almost as if the drive behind the technology is to reproduce the immateriality of the digital itself (an interesting kind of self-reflexivity in perfection – who says Narcissus is dead?). There is, however, something undeniably cold about the binary 'one/zero' logic of the digital whereby the precision of digital signals (that are transmitted as a sequence of '1' and '0') ensures noise-immunity and image-perfectibility. Moreover, this digitally stored information (always already retrievable) will not age, nor wear and tear. Such immateriality is, however, in denial of the human touch, the notion of flawed perfection. There is, within the creative human spirit, a desire, always, to resist or challenge this 'inhumanity'. Thus, we could argue that there is in-built in this technology, almost ineluctably, a need to re-introduce humanity back into the cold sterility of the digital technology (Gaunt, 2011: 5) – hence the concept, post-digital.

This trend began as early as the 1990s in the domain of music – popular and avant-garde – when musicians deliberately introduced intentional mistakes into their compositions or practices (Gaunt, 2011: 6). Scratching, smudging, glitching, distorting – all these became methods whereby the pure aesthetics of the digital were roughed up, given a human-error factor. This humanization of digital technologies, what Kim Cascone was first to coin as the post-digital aesthetic (2000: 12), soon made its way into film practice. If the digital can produce pure-cinema, then the post-digital recognizes the possibility of digital decay, affirms that memory and its artefacts are not pure durables. To signal the human failure element, post-digital cinema produces data-moshing, glitch-art anti-aesthetics – humanizing aesthetics which, paradoxically, were first introduced in theoretical and practical terms by the **Dogme 95** movement (established by Lars Von Trier and Thomas Vinterberg's *Dogme Manifesto*) with its shaky, degraded images and disorderly imperfection. Indeed, its first official film *Festen* (Vintenberg, 1998) was digitally shot (on mini-DV) – almost as if the technology had arrived just in time for Von Trier and Vintenberg to pare filmmaking back to its essentials (Willis, 2005: 14).

The other significant aspect of post-digital cinema aesthetics and practice concerns its production methods. Because of the lightweight nature of the technology (camera and edit), it has become much easier to develop a collaborative, democratic approach to filmmaking whereby cast and crew can be more directly involved in the process. Mike Figgis' *Time-Code* (2000) is the first to maximize on this concept of filmmaking. In this film, four stories are shot in real time over the period of two weeks; each day's four-screen 90-minute shoot is subsequently reviewed by cast and crew and discussed as to how to improve or adjust performances and technical logistics (Gaunt, 2011: 85).

In summation, both the digital and the post-digital eras bring to the world of cinema and its technology principles of democratization, interactivity and media convergence. In practice, the former appears – at its most extreme, through its pursuit of pure immateriality – cold and lacking in humanity; much as modernism (in its extreme manifestations) did before it. The latter is more playful, more reflective of the human touch and condition in its flawed aesthetics. It uses bricolage, pastiche, parody and intertextuality, and pleasures itself in the potential of the new technologies – a very postmodern ethos if you will.

For a much fuller discussion of all these issues see: Alexenberg, 2011; Ascher and Pincus, 2007; Cascone, 2000; Figgis, 2007; Gaunt, 2011; Le Grice, 2006; Manovich, 2001, 2005; McClean, 2007; Mulvey, 2006; Pepperell and Punt, 2000; Rombes, 2009; Tryon, 2009; Willis, 2005.

DIGITIZATION AND GLOBALIZATION

Since cinema's inception (1895), this medium has experienced significant technological and industrial change: from silent cinema to the talkies of the late 1920s, through to **cinemascope** and **colour** of the 1950s and, most recently, the CGI effects in the late twentieth century, and **digital filmmaking**. However, the rapid transformation in the twenty-first century of our society into a digital one, with the advent of the internet, demarcates the next technological transition, and challenge, for the cinema industry.

Digital devices and new **distribution** channels have overturned traditional, analogue technology and media. As Palfrey and Gasser note, 'the digital era has transformed how people live their lives and relate to one another and to the world around them' (2008: 3). For cinema this has seen a transition away from celluloid towards digital within **mainstream cinema**, with the productions of *Star Wars Episode I: The Phantom Menace* (George Lucas, 1999) and *Star Wars Episode II: Attack of the Clones* and *Avatar* (Cameron, 2009) being early exemplars of digital's potential. Non-mainstream cinema has also been at the vanguard of digital filmmaking. **Dogme films** were using digital cameras as early as 1998 (*Festen*, Vintenberg).

The effect of digital technology is both one of democratization but also one of malleability. For the consumer there is a new relationship to creation. As McKernan argues, 'today's digital technology has democratized this most powerful form of storytelling, making it affordable enough for practically anyone to use' (2005: xi).

Furthermore, cinema, which traditionally captured a 'reality' in front of the lens, is now as malleable as plastic. With the advent of the digital age, the moving image is now a fluidic point as 'shot footage is no longer the final point but just raw material to be manipulated in a computer where the real construction of a scene will take place' (Manovich, 2002: 255).

It should be pointed out that this shift towards digital takes us back, conceptually at least, to the advent of cinema! Manovich argues that 'cinematic realism is being displaced from being its dominant mode to become only one option among many' (1999: 14). Much as in early cinema, paint was added directly to film or stencilling was used, so now the image is once again easily manipulated, re-created. Thanks to the digital nature of 'film', computers can create an 'elastic reality' (Manovich, 1999: 47). The reality is that, for filmmakers and **audience** alike, new technologies offer many alternatives for storytelling, and further ways to consume the product, a far cry from the **studio system** model of before.

The major implications for a globalized digital market mean that the traditional models of **distribution** and exhibition are being displaced. As McKernan notes, 'instead of having to be physically transported to theatres in large, heavy film cans by fleets of trucks, digital movies can be distributed to theatres via satellite' (2005: 185). Furthermore, with the shift towards a transmedia model, the impact of a film is as a part of a greater whole (somewhat like the early cinema traditions, which was part of a panoply of attractions at the fair). This model is one within which the consumer becomes active rather than passive. As Jenkins proposes, 'to fully experience any fictional world, consumers must assume the role of hunters and gatherers, chasing down bits of the story across media channels, comparing notes with each other via online discussion group, and collaboration to ensure that everyone who invests time and effort will come away with a richer entertainment experience' (2006: 21). For example, The Matrix trilogy of films (1999–2003) inspired a series of Japanese animation videos called *Animatrix* (2003) and the video game *Enter the Matrix* (2003). As Jenkins says, 'if *Casablanca* exemplifies the classical cult movie, one might see *The Matrix* as emblematic of the cult movie in **convergence** culture' (2006: 10).

Moreover, the way we consume such film-media has changed dramatically. With a shift away from traditional models of production, distribution and exhibition, so has emerged, digitally, a new relationship between art and consumer. In 'Parallax Historiography: The Flâneuse as Cyberfeminist', Catherine Russell discusses the fluidity of contemporary **spectatorship**, drawing parallels between early cinema and contemporary visual culture, with spectatorship 'conceived as more fluid, mobile, unstable, and heterogeneous' (2000: 2). Similarly, in 'Click This: From Analog Dreams to Digital Realities', Anna Everett describes the rapid shift into 'a consumer-driven on-demand media services environment few could have predicted [in 1999]' (2004: 93). Such fluidity of consumption is typified by Soderbergh's *Bubble* (2005), which was released on the same day in theatres, on DVD and via cable television, subverting the traditional six-month window that protected the aura of theatrical release.

Consumption is now on demand and online. The question of what this means for exhibition still remains unanswered. As Grant comments, 'when we no longer need to go to the cinema because the cinema comes to us, then cinema loses whatever "aura" it may have had' (2004: 89). Thus, on the one hand, we have the rise of home entertainment as an alternative distribution trend. But, on the other, we have access to the new technological advances in portability. We are no longer bound to a singular viewing space. Instead we can engage with a text at any point. Selecting from a vast library of titles, **genres** and decades. The shrinking screen, which many in the new media ominously refer to as the third screen, transforms our relationship to/with visual entertainment. As a result, contemporary mediamakers (one suspects) will be compelled to produce content appropriate to our tiny, portable screens.

DIRECT CINEMA – *SEE CINÉMA-VÉRITÉ*

DIRECTOR

The person responsible for putting a scenario or script onto film. Sometimes, but not always (particularly in **Hollywood**) the director has complete responsibility for the final version of the file (known as the director's cut). In the early days of cinema, the director typically had complete control over the whole product. With the coming of **sound**, as products became more expensive to make, that control diminished (to varying degrees depending on the film industry) and the director worked in closer collaboration (or disharmony) with the **producer** and **stars**. By the 1950s, thanks to the effect of **auteur theory**, the role of the director was once again elevated to the status of creative artist on the basis that some could be said to have a discernible style. Since the 1970s, in the West, film has become so expensive and the **audience** primarily a youth audience that studios or producers have had to target audience demand. This has meant that, with the exception of a few directors who are well known on the international circuit (e.g. Cameron, Jackson, Nolan, Scorsese, Spielberg, Tarantino), stars are once again in the ascendancy and films are **genre**-led (mostly **action movies**, grand spectaculars, **blockbusters** and romance). The role of the director remains, however, as the one responsible for seeing the film as a whole and seeing it through to completion. In film studies the term more commonly used for director is filmmaker, since it refers very clearly to their function.

see also: **cinematographer, producer, studio system, vertical integration**

DISCOURSE

Discourse replaces the more imprecise word *language*. Discourse refers to the way in which texts are enunciated (brought into being). For example, cinematic discourse differs from that of a novel or a play, since it tells the story through image and **sound**. Discourse also refers to the social process of making sense of and reproducing reality and thereby of fixing meanings. Cinematic discourse reproduces 'reality' and tells stories about love and marriage, war and peace, and so on.

In that discourses are simultaneously the product and the constituter of reality (they speak for and speak as the **hegemonic** voice), they both reflect and reinforce **ideology** and in this respect they reflect power relations – that is, there will be dominant and marginal discourses. In cinema, for example, there is **mainstream/dominant cinema** which is the dominant discourse and then the marginal discourses of, say, Black, gay and lesbian or women's cinemas.

Discourses 'differ with the kinds of institutions and social practices in which they take shape, and with the positions of those who speak and those whom they address' (Macdonell, 1986: 1). Thus, there are different types of discourses: institutionalized discourses (law, medicine, science); media discourses (television, newspapers); popular discourses (pop music, rap, comic strips, slang). These discourses, although they fix meaning, do not fix them as eternal. Thus, discourses cannot be separated from history any more than they can be disassociated from ideology since they serve to make sense of the culture in which we live. For example, legal or medicinal discourses fix the way in which the treatment of crimes or illnesses are dealt with at a particular time in history. It is clear that seventeenth- and eighteenth-century legal and medicinal practices are not the same as today (we do not use the stocks for punishment of petty crime or leeches for curing ailments).

Discourses, then, are social productions of meaning and as such are wide-ranging: political, institutional, cultural, and so on. Although film is predominantly perceived as a cultural discourse, social and political discourses are, of course, equally present. And dominant film discourse both reflects and reinforces dominant ideology (starting with heterosexuality and marriage). Furthermore, as with other discursive texts, there are discourses not just within film but also around it. Discourses around cinema attempt to fix its meaning, and these can range from theoretical discourses on cinema (**auteurism**, **spectator–film** relations, **sexuality**, etc.) to more popular discourses such as film reviews, trade journals and articles in fanzines. Or these discourses can be based in other discourses not necessarily related to cinema (such as **psychoanalysis** and feminism). Or, finally they can be either critical discourses (e.g. film reviews, students' essays) or populist ones (as in fanzines, popular press, blogs).

To illustrate how film discourses within a film operate in relation to history, ideology and reality construction, see the discussion of the shift in meanings in the entries on **horror** and **science-fiction** movies.

DISSOLVE/LAP-DISSOLVE

These terms are used interchangeably to refer to a transition between two **sequences** or scenes, generally associated with earlier cinema (until the late 1940s) but still used on occasion. In a dissolve a first image gradually dissolves and is replaced by another. This type of transition, which is known also as a soft transition (as opposed to the cut), suggests a longer passage of time than a cut and is often used to signal a forthcoming **flashback**. If it is not used for a flashback but as a transition between two sequences or scenes, then it usually connotes a similarity between the two spaces or events – even though that similarity may not at first be apparent.

DISTANCIATION

A term first coined in relation to theatre, specifically by Bertolt Brecht in relation to his own theatre production in the 1920s and

1930s, although the principle on which it is based, alienation, comes from the **Soviet cinema/school** of the 1920s. Brecht's purpose was to distance the **audience**, through numerous strategies, so that it could adopt a critical stance and perceive how theatre practices and characterization serve to reproduce society as it is ideologically and institutionally constructed (see **ideology**). By denormalizing theatre, by showing its artifice (staging and **acting**), he wanted to politicize his audience into thinking that society itself could be denormalized and therefore changed. Distanciation in film is an integral part of **avant-garde** films and **counter-cinema**, and is achieved in a number of ways. First, on a visual level, fast **editing, jump cuts, unmatched** shots, characters speaking out of the screen to the audience, unexplained inter-titles (written or printed words on a blank screen between shots to explain the action or supply dialogue, common in silent films but distracting in sound films because they are unnecessary), **non-diegetic** inserts – all serve to distance and indeed disorientate the **spectator** (as in Jean-Luc Godard's films). Second, on the **narrative** level, distanciation is achieved by either over-filling or under-filling the narrative with meaning (Chantal Akerman's films are exemplary of the latter, Godard's of the former). Finally, characterization: distanciation occurs here through the anonymity of the character, her or his two-dimensionality and inscrutable physiognomy (Robert Bresson's and Alain Resnais' films are good illustrations of this practice).

see also: **naturalizing**, and **spectator-identification**

DISTRIBUTION

There is limited writing on the topic of distribution which is habitually referred to 'as a purely logistical space of transportation, warehousing, inventory, stocktaking and market research' (Lobarto and Ryan, 2010: 188). It is often positioned as a 'neutral technology of trans-mission linking production and exhibition', an area that within film studies is 'a relatively unpopular topic of research' (ibid.). However, as Lobarto and Ryan persuasively argue, distribution 'is not an afterthought in contemporary film industries. Decisions made by distributors, often before the cameras start rolling, work to shape texts in the most pro-found ways' (ibid.). Central to its gatekeeper function, it is distribution that decides which texts are circulated and, equally importantly, those that should not be distributed (Cubitt, 2005). Just as significantly, dis-tributors decide the extent of distribution both in terms of exhibition and which channels to serve (from cinema to television, DVD to the internet).

The emergence of digital equipment, supplanting traditional 35mm, and digital projectors has totally redefined distribution. Due to the non-physical nature of digital, as Lehman and Lurr argue, important films can open on 'over 3,000 screens in the US' (2003: 362). Whereas traditional 35mm distribution would require an individual print for each screen, incurring storage, transportation and logistical costs. Lehman and Lurr correctly point out that at a rough cost of $1,800 per print, the average spent on 35mm per year is $800m.

Though digital distribution has spelled the end for 35mm exhibition in the majority of cinemas (some regions like India are an exception), it has offered an opportunity for alternative channels. Netflix, for example, has recently moved into producing and distributing its own films, completely bypassing both theatrical and DVD distribution streams.

The landscape of distribution has dramatically changed since the late twentieth century. The emergence of digital distribution platforms (YouTube, Netflix) is only one part of the story. Ancillary markets are equally crucial in that they form a majority of the revenue. As Gomery (2009: 105) explains, cinema exhibition accounts for only one-sixth of the revenues generated by the average Hollywood release. For example, *Star Wars: The Force Awakens* (Abrams, 2015) set box-office records for ticket sales with over $2bn globally. However, the film is estimated to deliver $9bn over the next two years via various ancillary ventures including: toys, DVDs, television rights, cosmetics, video games – the list is endless. Thus, all films compete in a distribution arena that has the potential to support, or prevent the reach of an individual film. Alongside this, a standard **blockbuster** has to succeed not only within the theatre exhibition loop, but further deliver results in other markets.

Finally, with the advent of digital platforms, distributors are no longer shackled to the physical object. We no longer need to leave home to watch the latest blockbuster. Aside from illegal channels (such as file sharing), the 'long-tail' strategy, derived from technological advances, has implications for distribution and the availability of films. Whereas, in the past, a film would have a theatrical release, then be sold on DVD, followed by a subsequent television broadcast, before finally being removed from print, the advent of the internet provides an accessible and near infinite space within which films can be accessed. An unlimited supply, alongside cheaper costs and the development of niche markets unfixed from geographical constraints, is redefining the model of distribution as we journey through the twenty-first century.

DOCUMENTARY

Theoretical debate surrounding documentary practice tends to focus around two major axes: first, that of truth; second, that of who is the speaking subject, that is, who is the purveyor of this truth – the filmed subject, or the filmmaker, or both? Whose authenticity is it? Can representational work (as film is) ever provide truth? A classic illustration concerns the very first documentarist Flaherty. Originally, it was believed that his film *Nanook of the North* (1922) merely documented the everyday life of the Eskimo, with no interference from the filmmaker. However, it then transpired that some of the sequences in the film were staged, thereby distorting the truth about the Eskimo's life (nowadays, we might typify Flaherty's work as documentary reconstruction). Rouch's anthropological films of the 1950s to 1960s were later upheld as the exemplar of documentary realism because he recorded events as they unravelled in front of an unmoving camera (see **cinéma-vérité**). In the final analysis, it is safest to say that documentary is not based in fiction; but this does not mean that it does not have fictional elements. As Jane Chapman (2009: 4) so clearly puts it: 'a documentary will never be wholly true to reality; but neither will it eliminate reality altogether simply because it is representational.' (For a full array of debates read, in this order: Nichols, 1991, 2001; Renov, 1993; Bruzzi, 2000, 2006; Chapman, 2009.)

The first filmmakers to make what they called *documentaires* were the Lumière brothers in the 1890s. These documentaries took two essential forms. First, the recording of social life (family and friends, workers at the factory, etc). Second, travelogues from all over the world (including coronations). Thirty years later, the British filmmaker and critic John Grierson reappropriated the word to apply to Robert Flaherty's *Moana* (1920). Grierson was the founder of the 1930s documentary group in Britain and was one of the theorists influential in determining the nature of documentary. According to Grierson, documentary should be an instrument of information, education and propaganda as well as a creative treatment of reality. In the late 1940s, the academicism of Grierson's position was severely criticized by Lindsay Anderson and other founder members of **Free Cinema**. According to these critics, the use of the documentary as a means of social propaganda took away the aesthetic value of documentary film and, on an ideological level, normalized intellectual condescension and social elitism (see **naturalizing** and **ideology**). Although Grierson's position, with hindsight, does appear elitist, if we examine the climate of the times in the late 1920s, the reasons for that position do at least become clear. In the United Kingdom (as in the United States), after 1918, there began a progressive development in popular democracy. By 1928, both men and women in the United Kingdom had equal rights to vote. Grierson, who had worked in the United States during the period 1924 to 1927, was struck by the intellectual concerns about mass democracy – such as lack of education among the electorate, which made the ordinary voter uninformed when making choices – and was determined to do something about it. This feeling of the need to educate was held by other members of the British establishment who, like Grierson, saw cinema as an excellent means of education. So he worked between 1930 and 1939, first with the Empire Marketing Board and subsequently with the GPO, as producer of some forty-two documentaries on aspects of British life, institutions, governmental agencies and social problems – all with the intention of involving citizens in their society. *Coalface* (1935), about the miners and their labour, and *Night Mail* (1936), about the Post-Office workers are exemplary films in this regard.

An alternative voice in documentary work emerged a little later, in the late 1930s, primarily in the films of Humphrey Jennings. Jennings was a poet and a painter, interested in **surrealism** and Marxism, in literature and science. Unlike Grierson's liberal elitism, which focused on the dignity of labour (albeit as divorced from the social context), Jennings' films focused on the everyday life and sounds of ordinary men and women (as in *Spare Time*, 1939). He was the first documentarist to go outside London into the northern parts of the UK and to make films about industrial workers. A great concern of his was the Industrial Revolution and its effects on Britain and British people. Many of Jennings' films were made, appropriately, for the Mass Observation Unit – a unit set up by left-wing thinkers to observe ordinary people through registering accounts of their lives and feelings. Jennings' intimate observation of the ordinary also had a poetic, surreal quality to it, shown in the way he framed his images of industrial Britain and juxtaposed images of the ordinary with those out of the ordinary.

Although the tradition of recording other cultures dates back to the travelogues made by the Lumière brothers, it is Robert Flaherty who is acclaimed as the first documentarist in that tradition. The first so-called documentary is his *Nanook of the North* (1922), about Eskimo life. Flaherty also directed a film for Grierson, *Industrial Britain* (1931–32) – surprisingly given Flaherty's romantic world-view. In the Soviet Union, during the 1920s, Dziga Vertov recorded Soviet progress in his documentaries made for *Kino-Pravda*/Film-Truth. Interestingly, in his work, we can trace the possible heritage of the two British tendencies mentioned above. Vertov, like Grierson, saw documentary as an educative tool, but his style – an **avant-garde** formalism, achieved by **montage**, to the point of **deconstruction** – showed an aesthetic preoccupation with the image that we also find in Jennings' work. During the 1930s, the Soviet filmmaker Medvedkin took the possibilities of documentary onto a new stage: he shot, developed and projected filmed documentation (all done on the spot) to workers as he travelled around the Soviet Union by train – this work became known as *ciné-train*.

Owing to lack of financial resources following World War Two, many aspiring filmmakers in Europe had to turn to documentary work before they could go on to make feature films (Alain Resnais, Georges Franju and Agnès Varda in France, and Ken Russell in the United Kingdom spring to mind). Although some of these directors, especially those just mentioned, made important politicized documentaries, they hardly constituted a movement. The next important development to occur was in the 1960s, with the rise of the *cinéma-vérité* group in France and the **direct cinema** in the United States. Two new technological developments contributed to this documentary style – television and the lightweight camera. Television news had the appearance of live images. The lightweight camera made it possible to be unobtrusive and mobile and to catch reality on film. Certain earlier documentary traditions also inflected their work: ordinary people testified to their experiences whether, for example, it was the everyday experience of Parisians in the summer of 1961 (Jean Rouch and Edgar Morin's *Chronique d'un été*, 1961); the French people's experience of the German Occupation (*Le Chagrin et la pitié*, Marcel Ophuls, 1970); or the miners' strike in the United States (Barbara Kopple's *Harlan County USA*, 1976).

The late 1960s represents a true watershed for the documentary in that it became politicized, if not universally, then in some major continents and Eastern nations (Africa, Latin America, Japan, North Vietnam). Part of this politicization of the documentary can be imputed to the growing disquiet felt at the USA's role in Vietnam, to say nothing of America's power-mongering (neo-colonialism) in other nation-states (especially Latin America where, in the name of combating communism, it attempted to establish puppet military governments). The Argentinian filmmakers Getino and Solanas' *La hora de los hornos/ The Hour of the Furnaces* (1968) is one of the best known (see entry on **Third Cinema**). Many filmmaking collectives and independent filmmakers made documentaries challenging the establishment. By the 1970s, feminist films were also much in evidence and were about individual women's lives, motherhood, prostitution. Black women and women of colour also got their first foothold in the filmmaking process. Lesbian and gay filmmakers found a voice through the documentary and dealt with their lifestyles as well as gay politics. During this period some of the major themes tackled were abortion (even in France, where it was then still illegal: see *Histoire d'A*, Charles Belmont and Marielle Issartel, 1973), sexual identity, civil rights, racism and economic exploitation.

Developments in video technology (1980s) and, more recently, digital technology (1990s onwards) have led to the emergence of numerous collectives and workshops in Europe and the United States. It has also led to a further and a still greater democratization of the camera and to more voices from the margins finding a mode of expression. It has also led, particularly in the new millennium, to the vocalization of dissent on the one hand and, on the other, to a proliferation of autobiographical texts (see *Supersize Me*, Spurlock, 2004, as an example of both types). In the 1980s, two documentary filmmakers stand out for spearheading new approaches: Nick Broomfield and Errol Morris. Broomfield's self-reflexive style (in which he lays bare the process of filmmaking, including the difficulties in getting to the interview subject: see *Tracking down Maggie*, 1994) and his neutral, observational stance, align him with the *cinéma-vérité* tradition (see *Chicken Ranch*, 1988, about prostitution in Nevada). Morris' approach of using re-enactments was, at the time, quite radical. His documentary, *The Thin Blue Line* (1988), investigates the conviction of a man sentenced to death for the murder of a policeman that he did not commit. Morris' film juxtaposes a series of interviews with re-enactments of the fatal shooting of the police officer to show how judicial expediency and perjury led to the wrong man being accused (in the event he was released).

Documentaries as a social record of 'difficult' issues have been a fairly consistent trend since at least the 1960s. More recently, however, the legal system, in particular in the USA (more precisely in Florida and Texas where the death penalty is readily practised), has been the focus of a few notable documentaries. The impact of Broomfield's *Aileen Wuornos: The Selling of a Serial Killer* (1993), which revealed the incompetence of her original lawyer, assisted in Wuornos' retrial (even if it did not spare her from Death Row and execution). In the follow-up documentary, *Aileen Wuornos: Life and Death of a Serial Killer* (2003), Broomfield's film questioned the legality of her execution given that Wuornos was clearly of unsound mind. Herzog's *Into the Abyss: A Tale of Death, a Tale of Life* (2012) exposes the moral squalor of state-sanctioned murder. Finally, Thet Sambath, a leading Cambodian journalist, has put this own life at risk through his courageous documentary film about the Kmer Rouge killing fields: *Enemies of the People* (co-directed with Rob Lemkin, 2010) and he is under considerable pressure from the government not to complete his follow-up film, *Suspicious Minds*, which exposes current politicians for their involvement in the killing fields (still not completed/released as of this book going to print in 2017).

Since the 2000s, the documentary has become a major cinematographic attraction with, almost yearly, at least one '**blockbusting**' film (in terms of audience figures). Michael Moore's film-essays on capitalism, globalization and their corrupt practices have led the way (*Roger and Me*, 1989; *Sicko*, 2007; *Capitalism: A Love Story*, 2009); as have his exposures of the failures of American policies at home and abroad (gun laws, see *Bowling for Columbine*, 2002; the second Iraq war, *Fahrenheit 9/11*, 2004). Climate change documentaries (such as Oscar-winning *An Inconvenient Truth*, Davis Guggenheim and Al Gore, 2006) are as popular with audiences as films on animal life (*March of the Penguins*, Luc Jacquet, 2005), or an individual's remarkable bravery, or folly, or artistic talent (see, respectively, *Touching the Void*, Kevin MacDonald, 2004; *Man on Wire*, James March, 2008; *Pina*, Wim Wenders, 2011 – shot in **3-D**), or prehistoric caves (*Cave of Forgotten Dreams*, Herzog, 2010, also shot in 3-D).

In the 2010s, in the light of the Arab Spring, a new radical form of political documentary practice evolved thanks to the new technologies, the internet and social networking. Primarily, these take the form of mobile or satellite phone-shot documentaries of conditions in the various North African and Middle Eastern nations in the light of their various struggles to democracy. Often, these films are smuggled out on memory sticks and subsequently uploaded onto websites. Reality-driven representations are, therefore, becoming more and more immediate. Further details on this and specific filmmakers can be found in the individual nations' entries under **World Cinemas**.

see also: *cinéma-vérité*, **ethnographic film**, **World Cinemas (North Africa, Middle East)**

For further reading see: for a general history and/or politics of documentary, Aitken, 2005; Baker, 2006; Barsam, 1992; Chanan, 2007; Chapman, 2009; Ellis, 2011; Ellis and McLane, 2005; Geiger, 2011; for theory on the documentary see: Bruzzi, 2000, 2006; Grimshaw, 2002; Hogarth, 2006; Nichols, 1991, 2001; Renov, 1993, 2004; for the British documentary see: Lovell and Hillier, 1972; Winston, 1995.

DOGME *95*/DOGME *95* MANIFESTO/ DOGME FILMS

The Dogme *95* manifesto, written by the Danish filmmakers Lars von Trier and Thomas Vintenberg, was first made public a full century after the 'birth' of cinema (1895) and forty years on from the polemical **auteur** manifesto of the *Cahiers du cinéma* group (1954). As with the *Cahiers* group before it, this new manifesto was borne out of these filmmakers' weariness with old formulas for film **narrative** and practice and a desire to hit out against the economies of production in the era of globalization. As with the earlier *Cahiers* manifesto, Dogme *95* produced a new radical film practice greatly assisted, it has to be said, by the advent of yet another new democratizing and lightweight cinematic technology. Thus, where in the 1950s and 1960s the New Wave Cinemas took advantage of the lightweight Camflex cameras and produced a new style and practice, so by the mid-1990s Dogme film had early digital technology to hand to help implement their manifesto.

Dogme *95*, drawn up in a spirit as much of seriousness as irony and playfulness, made a vow of chastity and a commitment to abide by the ten commandments set out in its manifesto. Its bare bones are as follows:

1 Location shooting; no special props
2 **Sound** produced as part of image; **diegetic** music only
3 Camera hand-held
4 Film in **colour**; no special **lighting**
5 No optical work or filters
6 No superficial action
7 Film must take place in the here and now
8 No **genre** movies
9 Film format Academy 35mm
10 **Director** cannot be credited

Rules 1, 4 and 9 were almost immediately broken (and 10, since we can source all the Dogme films to their director). For instance, the very first feature film to be produced by the Dogme movement, *Festen* (Vintenberg, 1998), used props and special lighting for one scene and the film was shot on mini-DV (as opposed to Academy 35mm). Von Trier also broke the rules with the second Dogme film, *The Idiots* (1998), using non-diegetic **music**. But maybe the intent was to break the rules, as if to point to the filmmakers' natural instinct to subvert any such laying down of 'laws'. As such, these 'transgressions' stand as a playful ironizing of the very rigidity of their own rules.

Dogme 95 represents an important moment in non-mainstream cinema, and its impact has been felt in **mainstream** as much as in **avant-garde** and **art cinema**. The intention behind the manifesto, and the subsequent Dogme films, was to strip film of bourgeois illusion (a similar principle invoked by the founders of auteur theory, incidentally), to position the films as an alternative to **Hollywood** and for filmmakers to find an authenticity in their work (Gaunt, 2011: 82). The Dogme manifesto called for more collective filmmaking as a response to the failure of individualism within film – in this regard, Dogme film practice goes in the opposite direction from that of the auteur-filmmakers of the 1950s and early 1960s, as does, moreover, Dogme's vow of chastity involving 'all aspects of film production' and its calls 'for more collective responsibility on the part of directors, camera operators, actors and editors' (ibid.).

Dogme 95 gained in international popularity amongst independent filmmakers almost immediately. This was not just because of the startling nature of the declaration of the manifesto at a conference celebrating cinema's centenary in Paris, but also because of the critical success of the first three Dogme films: *Festen*, *Mifune* (Soren Kragh-Jacobsen, 1999), *The Idiots*. So, it has become something of a **transnational** movement (Hjort and MacKenzie, 2003: 31). And the first non-Danish Dogme films to receive the official Dogme stamp of approval were France's *The Lovers* (Jean-Marc Barr, 1999) and USA's *Julien Donkey-Boy* (Harmony Korine, 1999). In all, some 260 Dogme-seal-of-approval films to date have been made; however, only forty-odd have achieved any notable success or attention. Again this ratio (1:15) is quite similar to that of the **French New Wave**.

Independent filmmakers whose work gives evidence of many of the Dogme rules include Daniel Myrick and Eduardo Sánchez (*Blair Witch Project*, 1999), Mike Figgis (*Time-Code*, 2000; *Hotel*, 2001), David Lynch (*Inland Empire*, 2006) – although, of course, the advent of new **digital** technology made many of these filmmakers' experimentation along these lines an inevitable pursuit.

But there has also been a recuperation of the Dogme 'style' into mainstream cinema – even by Von Trier and Vintenberg themselves (both using major **stars** and budgets of around $10 million in *Dogville* and *It's All About Love*, respectively, both 2003). A new kind of minimalist aesthetics and improvisation is in evidence in European and Hollywood products of the last decade or so (e.g. the improvised feel of *Wonderland*, Michael Winterbottom, 1999; *Bamboozled*, Spike Lee, 2000, shot on mini-DV). Of all things, the Dogme-look is also present in Danish and Swedish television crime series – almost taking

Von Trier back to where he started (*The Kingdom* TV-miniseries, 1994–97).

For further reading see Gaunt, 2011; Hjort and MacKenzie, 2003; Kelly, 2000; Stevenson, 2003.

DOMINANT/MAINSTREAM CINEMA

Dominant cinema is generally associated with Hollywood, but its characteristics are not restricted to Hollywood. As Annette Kuhn says (1982: 22), it is in the relationship between 'the economic and the ideological [that] dominant cinema takes its concrete form'. Thus all countries with a film industry have their own dominant cinema and this cinema constantly evolves depending on the economic and **ideological** relations in which it finds itself. Given the economic situation, the film industry of a particular country will favour certain production practices over others. For example, the assembly-line system and vertical integration of Hollywood's **studios** in the 1930s and 1940s have now given way to a fragmentation of the industry and to the rise of independent filmmakers whom Hollywood studio companies now commission to make films. On the ideological front, the dominant filmic text in Western society revolves round the standardized plot of order/disorder/order-restored. The action focuses on central characters and so the plot is character-driven. **Narrative** closure occurs with the completion of the **Oedipal trajectory** through either marriage or a refusal of coupledom. In any event, closure means a resolution of the heterosexual courtship (Kuhn, 1982: 34). This resolution often takes the form of the recuperation of a transgressive female into the (social) order (Kuhn, 1982: 34). Visually this ideological relation is represented through the 'reality' effect – the illusion of reality. The **continuity** of the film is **seamless, editing** does not draw attention to itself. The **mise-en-scène, lighting** and **colour** are appropriate to the **genre**. **Shots** conform to the **codes and conventions** dictated by the generic type.

For further reading see Bordwell *et al.*, 1985.

EAST ASIAN CINEMA

Feedback regarding the fourth edition highlighted the absence of a consideration of East Asian Cinema. I am very clear that the remit of this book isn't to lay out a comprehensive discussion of East Asian Cinema (an impossible task); however, this section will give a brief overview of what is meant by, and associated with, the term East Asian Cinema. Moreover, I stress that it is more a *term* than a *concept*. A useful homogenizing term used (in the singular, paradoxically) by the West to incorporate several pan-East Asian cinemas (or parts of cinemas, as is the case, say, for some of the more contemporaneous Japanese cinema) which have come to prominence over the past three decades or so. Therefore, if East Asian Cinema is being given a separate entry to **World Cinemas** (where it also could be argued it belongs), it is partly because of its hybrid identity but, primarily, because it emanates from countries that are primarily identified as advanced economies. It does not belong, then, under the *cinemas of China* which are produced by emerging economies and which are discussed in the **World Cinemas** entry.

At one level we can define East Asian Cinema as typified by various national cinema associations, principally Japan, Hong Kong, Taiwan and South Korea, and China (although, for reasons explained above, I see China as a separate cinema). Each, in turn, is associated with a particular style or **genre**: Japanese manga, 'modern romance TV drams, *anime* and horror films; Hong Kong action films; Chinese martial arts and costume drama films; Korean blockbusters and the so-called *Hallyu* or Korean Wave; an emerging Asian "Auteur Cinema" ... and regional co-productions' (Lee, 2011: 3). These genre traditions also evoke the cross-over sensibilities implicit within East Asian Cinema; for example, *manga*'s hyper-kinetic violence and strong aesthetics that in turn influence, and are influenced by, video games and *anime*.

However, such a positioning, which as you will notice is extremely narrow-band at least in terms of genre, ignores the complexity behind the term East Asian Cinema, which should be perceived far more readily as what Milner and Johnson define as a 'free floating signifier ... the exact meaning of which is not yet settled' (2002: 1). Indeed. For example, should not the cinema of Thailand, in particular due to the emergence of arthouse auteurs (Pen-ek Ratanaruang, Apichatpong Weerasethakul) and cult films such as *Ong-Bak* (2003), be situated within East Asian Cinema? Such mutability situates East Asian Cinema as, what Lim and Dissanayake argue, 'an idea in process' rather than a 'geographical given' (1999: 3). In a sense what we are dealing with here, in regard to terminology, is the muddling of two approaches. The one, applied in something of a simplified manner, pertains to the question how to deliver film courses in the West on such a broad remit as East Asia (who, what, where is to be included?). The other, more appropriate question in my view, is how to address the complex nature of cinematic practices in the East Asian region (how does it function?) which can be seen as primarily **transnational**.

This latter is a key concept to consider within one's understanding of East Asian Cinema (see entry on **transnational cinema**). Central to this discussion is Japan, which has influenced the production and consumption of cultural products (since the 1950s), but whose economic and cultural hegemony over the East Asian region has been contested, starting in the late 1990s, by Chinese-speaking nations (e.g. Hong Kong, Taiwan) and South Korea. As Chaudhuri notes, a 'converging pattern of rapid and drastic societal change' (2005: 93) has been a defining influence on East Asian Cinema, with each nation interpreting pan-East Asian events through their own national cinema and, thereby, providing differing perspectives on events such as Japan's colonization of the region before and after World War Two, the victory of the Communist Party in China in 1949, and the economic turmoil that brought uncertainty and malaise to the East Asian region at the end of the twentieth century.

Conversely, however, such regional turmoil has also led to regional cooperation between these nations (including Hong Kong and China, to which it is now affiliated). As Lee notes, 'a key arena of cultural production ... involving multiple localities of production and consumption is cinema' (2011: 3). Co-production has become a predominant characteristic of East Asian Cinema since the 1990s. In this light, as Lee explains, East Asian Cinema denotes a regional (by which he means pan-East Asian) configuration of 'film art and practices' (2011: 1). And as Teo remarks, successful pan-East Asian films have been based on a sense of 'universality', primarily through **mise-en-scène**, **setting** and character (2008: 355). These have made for ready exportation to the West: action movies, and films which might be mainstream releases in the East Asian market, but which the West have labelled as **art cinema**, what Hunt and Leung refer to as the 'mutating currencies of transnationality' (2008: 5). In turn, the co-production model can also bring together varied cultural, financial and artistic resources primed, not for the West, but for the 'China market', a model that has led to **blockbusters** (Lee, 2001: 5).

In the context of transnationalism, since the 1950s, Japan has consistently been at the forefront of the intersection of East and West. In the 1950s, Akira Kurosawa became the first transnational Asian filmmaker, and Ishiro Honda's *Godzilla* (1954) the first East Asian global icon (this astonishing film deals with the horrific aftermath of the atomic bombings of Japan in World War Two). Further, it has been Japan that, as Chaudhuri argues, has 'mediated' the 'influence of American consumerism and Western modernization' (2005: 93).

Transnationalism, quite naturally, functions in both directions, as is the case with **Hollywood**. The remaking of East Asian Cinema films such as *Ringu* (Hideo Nakata, Japan, 1998) under the title *The Ring* (Gore Verbinksi, 2002; with two sequels 2005 and 2017); and, of course, Kurosawa's *The Seven Samurai* (1954) remade as a western, *The Magnificent Seven* (John Sturges, 1960; with three sequels at least), or Honda's *Godzilla* which has subsequently been remade by Hollywood in differing periods (1956, 1963, 1970, 1985, 1998, 2014; and still to come 2019 and 2020!).

EDITING/SOVIET MONTAGE

Editing refers literally to how **shots** are put together to make up a film. Traditionally a film is made up of sequences or in some cases, as with **avant-garde** or **art cinema**, episodes, or, again, of successive shots that are assembled in what is known as collision editing or montage. At its simplest there are four categories of editing: continuity editing; **cross-cutting** or **parallel** editing; **deep focus**; and montage.

A film can be constructed entirely using one category (as, for example, Sergei Eisenstein's montage films of the 1920s); generally speaking, however, it tends to be made up out of two if not all categories. Each category has different implications in terms of temporal relations. Time can seem long or short. Time can have an interior or an exterior reality. Interior temporality is suggested by the sequence and is fictional. Exterior temporality occurs when there is a direct correspondence between sequence time and time within the **narrative** (i.e. reel time equals real time – in its most extreme manifestation see Andy Warhol's 1960s films). Again, generally speaking, a film will use both kinds of temporality.

Continuity editing

As the term implies, this type of editing follows the logic of a chronological narrative. One event follows 'naturally' on from another. Time and space are therefore logically and unproblematically represented. Beginnings and endings of sequences are clearly demarcated, shots throughout the sequence orientate the spectator in time and space and the end of a sequence safely indicates where and when the narrative will get picked up in the following sequence. This is a strategy in film practice that ensures narrative continuity. The film does not draw attention to the way in which the story gets told. The editing is invisible, and as such offers a seamless, spatially and temporally coherent narrative. Spatial continuity is maintained by strict adherence to the **180-degree rule**, temporal continuity by observing the chronology of the narrative. The only disruption of this temporal continuity in mainstream cinema comes in the form of a **flashback**.

Continuity editing is the one most readily associated with **classical Hollywood cinema** and is one which produces a very linear text. This linearity or chronological order gets broken only when there is a **flashback** or a cross-cutting to a parallel sequence. In both instances, however, this break with linearity is signalled. The logic of the narrative is maintained. For example, a fade or dissolve with a voice-over ('and yet it was only yesterday') is used to signify that a flashback is coming; a quick series of cuts between two locales at the beginning of a parallel sequence to link them up logically for the spectator. (For detailed discussion, see Bordwell *et al.*, 1985: 60–69.)

However, theoreticians have made the point that this seamlessness masks the labour that goes into manufacturing the film and as such has an **ideological** effect. This cinema gives the **spectator** the impression that reality presents as **natural** what is in fact an idealistic reality (no fault-lines can be perceived). The spectator has a sense of unitary vision ('it's all there, before me') over which s/he believes s/he has supremacy ('it's all there, so I know everything that's going on'). In this respect, the spectator colludes with the idealism of the cinematic reality-effect.

Seamlessness

Seamlessness (see also **suture**) is a key effect of continuity editing and is used to refer to the **Hollywood** film style where – in the name of **realism** – the editing does not draw attention to itself. The spectator is presented with a **narrative** that is edited in such a way that it appears to have no breaks, no disconcerting unexplained transitions in time and space. Hence its seamlessness (with which **lighting**, **sound** and **colour** collude). It is the opposite of an editing style that draws attention to itself (e.g. through **jump cuts** and **unmatched shots**), mostly found in oppositional, non-mainstream, **counter-cinema**.

For further discussion of continuity editing, see **apparatus**, **spatial and temporal contiguity**, and **spectator**. Bordwell and Thompson (1980) provide a very full and useful introduction to the concepts and strategies of continuity editing, and also to alternatives. For more detail on the continuity system within classical Hollywood cinema see Bordwell *et al.* (1985: chapter 16).

Cross-cutting editing versus parallel editing

Cross-cutting is limited as a term to the linking-up of two sets of action that are running concurrently and which are interdependent within the narrative. The term *parallel editing* has been used incorrectly to refer to the same effect, probably because it is a literal way of explaining the effect of cross-cutting: putting in parallel two contiguous events that are occurring at the same time but which are occurring in two different spaces. However, as a term, parallel editing actually refers to the paralleling of two related actions that are occurring at different times (a classic example is Alain Resnais' *Hiroshima mon amour*, 1959, which brings into parallel a wartime memory and a present love-affair). Both styles of editing are used for reasons of narrative economy (they speed it up) and of course suspense. They also assume that there will be a resolution in one space and time of these two sets of action. Unsurprisingly, Hollywood, with its love of linearity and safe chronology makes little use of real parallel editing and primarily uses cross-cutting. Commonly cross-cutting is used in **Westerns** (John Wayne or Clint Eastwood on the way to rescue some damsel or town in distress) and **gangster** or **thriller** movies (cuts between the goodies and the baddies, victim and killer, for example).

Deep focus editing

André Bazin was the first to qualify this style of editing as objective **realism**, although the United States cinematographer Gregg Toland was arguing as early as the mid-1930s for the realism of **deep focus**. Shooting in deep focus means that less cutting within a sequence is necessary so the spectator is less manipulated, less stitched into the narrative and freer to read the set of shots before them. Ideologically then, as an editing style it can be considered counter-Hollywood, or at least counter to seamlessness (see **ideology** and **suture**). Certainly Hollywood, at different times in its history, used deep focus photography, that is, shots staged in depth; it did not, however, use deep focus editing – clearly, with its emphasis on stardom, cuts to the close-up are inevitable. (For detailed analysis see Bordwell, in Bordwell *et al.*, 1985: 341–52.)

(Soviet) montage

Montage editing came out of the Soviet experimental cinema of the 1920s and, although it was Lev Kuleshov who first thought of the concept of montage, it is primarily associated with Sergei Eisenstein (director of *Strike*, *Battleship Potemkin*, both 1925, and *October*, 1928). In his films of the 1920s, Eisenstein adapted Kuleshov's fundamental theory that collision or conflict must be inherent to all visual **signs** (see **semiology**) in film. Juxtaposing shots makes them collide or conflict and it is from the collision that meaning is produced. Here is a simple illustrative example, provided by Eisenstein: the first set of shots depicts a poor woman and her undernourished child seated at a table upon which there is an empty bowl; cut to the second set of shots depicting an overweight man with a golden watch and chain stretched over his fat belly; he is seated at a table groaning with food – the rapid juxtaposition of these two sets of images through fast editing causes a collision that in turn creates a third set of images (construed in the **spectator**'s mind), that of the oppression of the proletariat by the bourgeoisie. A first principle of **montage** editing, then, is a rapid alternation between sets of shots whose signification occurs at the point of their collision. Fast editing and unusual camera angles serve also to denaturalize **classical narrative cinema**, and this is a second principle of montage editing. In fact, as far as narration goes, given Einsenstein's revolutionary task (to present the proletarian story), it is unsurprising that his editing style indicated a privileging of the image over narrative and characterization (i.e. there is no single hero, only the proletariat as hero). Montage is largely used by art and avant-garde cinemas, but mainstream cinema has also incorporated it to spectacular effect (as in *Jaws*, Steven Spielberg, 1975). Perhaps the most ironic of all recuperations of montage editing, though, must be the use of these principles in film and television advertisements.

see also: **Soviet cinema**

Montage versus deep focus editing

Montage and deep focus editing are seemingly ideologically opposed. Yet in both instances, the spectator is 'responsible' for creatively reading what they see. Montage creates a third meaning through the collision of two images. A meaning that is produced outside the image in point of fact. The sequence of images in conflict (what Eisenstein termed a montage of attractions) provokes a creative reaction within the spectator who produces for them a third meaning. Conversely, deep focus editing produces meaning within the image; the spectator takes their own reading from the image before them. Montage is also a style of editing that works towards **deconstruction** because it draws attention to itself, and that is certainly a major way in which it has been used by art and avant-garde filmmakers. A good illustration is Luis Buñuel's surrealist film *Un chien andalou* (1929). First, the montage editing of this film gives an aesthetic plasticity to it, drawing our attention to the film form. Second, the juxtaposition of images clearly produces anti-clerical and anti-bourgeois meanings.

It is also evident that these two editing styles create opposite rhythms through their visual impact. Montage editing is fast, jerky and abrupt; deep focus is quite slow and uniformly even. An alternation of these two styles in a film would create two very distinct times, either juxtaposed or contradictory. In other words, the temporal exteriority (i.e. real time) and objectivity of deep focus editing would juxtapose or indeed be contradicted by the temporal interiority and subjectivity of montage editing. Perhaps one of the most extreme examples of this incorporation of both styles into film is Alain Resnais' *L'Année dernière à Marienbad* (1961), where time is completely destroyed by the juxtaposition, particularly within sequences, of these two styles.

see also: **sequencing, spatial and temporal contiguity**

For further reading see Salt, 1977.

EPICS

In the beginning there were *The Ten Commandments* (1923) and *Ben Hur* (1920), and they were so successful they went forth and multiplied and, born anew in **sound**, there were *The Ten Commandments* (1956) and *Ben Hur* (1959). But then there was *Cleopatra* (1963), and she was so wilful and costly that she ruined **Hollywood** and did the epic in. ... So one official version of this **genre**'s rise and fall might have it. And of course, because epics cost so much to make, it is a case of economies of scale. Epics not only cost a monumental amount of money, they require huge sets, casts of thousands and, above all, a monumental hero played – at least since the advent of sound – by a monumental **star**. And as for topic, it is usually taken from history: biblical or 'factual';

certainly most preferably from a distant past so that the **ideological** message of national greatness would pass unremittingly. Generally speaking, in Western society *the* nation is the United States because the epic is predominantly an American genre, Hollywood having the resources necessary to produce it.

It must not be overlooked, however, that Italian cinema also had a strong tradition in epics from the 1920s to the 1960s. Enrico Guazzoni's 1913 *Quo Vadis* (about Nero's persecution of the Christians) clearly inspired the American epics of D. W. Griffith and Cecil B. de Mille. Moreover, at one point, in the 1950s, Italy's film industry (in the primary form of producer Dino De Lauretis) tried to counter Hollywood's domination by producing its own Italian product: *Attila* (Pietro Francisci, 1954); *Hercules* (Francisci, 1958); *Colossus of Rhodes* (Sergio Leone, 1961). For the most part, though, Italian epics post-war did not measure up to the American product and were largely dismissed as *peplums* (sword and sandal films, mostly produced in series: Hercules, Samson, Goliath, etc.).

Arguably, D. W Griffith's *The Birth of a Nation* (1915) was the first great epic and David Lean's *Lawrence of Arabia* (1962) the last. The heyday of the sound epic was the 1950s, starting with *The Robe* (Henry Koster) in 1953, the first **colour** film to be made in **cinemascope**. The major reason for a resurgence in production of this genre was of course economic but there were also ideological reasons for its re-activation. Hollywood's popularity was on the decline. Home leisure, especially television, was keeping **audiences** away from the movies. To attract them, film studios were having to produce big spectacles that no television set could muster. So, on the economic front, colour, cinemascope and epics seemed a surefire cocktail to seduce audiences back in. The other factor in their appeal was the grandeur of the themes – biblical or historical – based in heroic action and moral values which of course fed into the dominant cultural climate of the time: the Cold War conflict between Western capitalism and Eastern/Soviet communism. The ideological function of these epics became one of reaffirming the image of the United States as a superpower; of asserting the need of its citizens to be cleaner than clean in the face of the threat of communism that McCarthy and the House of Un-American Activities (HUAC) were determined to cleanse its nation of and, finally, of the socio-economic need for clearly defined **gender** roles in the economic restructuring of the nation's post-war job market (i.e. that women should relinquish jobs they had taken up during the war period and go back into the domestic sphere and become consumers of the new technology that had been domesticated for their purpose).

From this, it might seem easy to see why an epic based on Cleopatra might sound the death-knell for the genre. After all, it was about a woman, a leader, a queen (even) who picked and chose her men and spat them out when she had had enough of them. Strong, self-assertive women were not the norm on-screen and the feminist movement had yet to come to the United States. In any case this brand of 'Hollywood feminism', to use Thomas Elsaesser's term (1987: 69), was far removed from any feminist ideology. So that was not the reason why this film was the swan-song for Hollywood and its epic tradition. This was the period of John F. Kennedy (the youngest president of the United States), of optimism, change and collectivism (of Camelot, as the period was known). As a topic, Cleopatra was out of date – even though in terms of fashion the creations designed for Elizabeth Taylor's Cleopatra had a profound influence on women's garments, hairstyle and make-up well into the late 1960s. Nonetheless, the cost and the epic grandeur on- and off-screen, the numerous changes of directors, locations, scripts, Taylor's illness, her affair with Burton, represented a type of excess that was out of touch with the spirit of the age. And so it was that Cleopatra marked the end of Hollywood's movie imperialism, old-style.

Interestingly in the early years of the new millennium, epics in the Western world made a bit of a comeback. The reason for this cannot entirely be put down to a perceived need to stay away from **blockbuster** action-packed contemporary spectaculars in the wake of the New York Twin Towers disaster of 11 September 2001 (9/11), since the first big success in this run was Ridley Scott's *Gladiator* (2000). It is, however, a part reason doubtless. The year 2004 saw a literal 'plethora' of epics with three big-cast movies: *Troy* (Peterson), *King Arthur* (Fuqua) and *Alexander* (Stone). These films are about imperial grandeur. But they are also more disconcerting than that, particularly if read a bit more closely. In each instance, greed for more, or a determination to 'take back' what is deemed rightfully 'theirs', propels the spectacular blood-letting narratives. Deceit and cunning are used, so too is lying about the real cause for the engagement in warfare, slain or dying heroes are brutally treated – all very contemporary in the light of the Iraq war. We have come a long way from the slave underdog hero of *Spartacus* (Kubrick, 1960). So ideological readings come into play. If these post-9/11 epics are to be believed, then they play into the nation's belief that America remains the only super-power. Peculiarly, it is as if the **myth** of David and Goliath is reversed. A righteous giant Goliath is fighting a weak but treacherous David in the form of faceless enemies, because it is his nation that is under attack; and, as these films make clear, the enemy must be overcome by any means necessary. This narrative certainly reflects President Bush's rhetoric of that time (early 2000s). Since the end of the Bush era, however, epics have once again been on the wane.

see also: **genre**

For further reading see: on Hollywood epics, Burgoyne, 1990, 2009; on Hollywood and Italian epics, Elley, 1984; Hall and Neale, 2010; on the return of the epic, Elliot, 2014; on music in the epic, Meyer, 2017.

ETHNOGRAPHIC FILM/GAZE

Ethnographic film is one which provides an anthropological study of a given society or culture (a first, albeit problematic, example being Flaherty's *Nanook of the North*, 1922; see **documentary**). In so doing it aims to be as objective as possible in its scientificness. Thus, the ethnographic gaze is one that attempts neither to interpret for the viewer, nor to cheat in what it shows. In this way it is reminiscent of the *cinéma-vérité* work done by Dziga Vertov and Jean Rouch. However, only rarely can the ethnographic **gaze** be neutral or at least come from within the culture in question. Typically, the documentarists/ethnographers are Eurocentric in their provenance. Inevitably, therefore, the cinematic eye will be predominantly that of an outsider, not an insider with an inner/indigenous knowledge of that culture (see Minh-ha, 1989). Two interesting examples to contrast in terms of outsider/insider ethnographic gaze are the American **avant-garde** filmmaker Maya Deren's *The Divine Horsemen*, a film about Haïtian voodoo practices, which she was invited to film during the 1950s (it was edited, 1973–77, a decade after her premature death), and the indigenous Australian artist Tracey Moffatt's *Night Cries: A Rural Tragedy* (1990), a re-negotiation of Charles Chauvel's *Jedda* (1955), which dwells on the social problem of Aboriginal children who were taken away from their natural parents to be raised by White families. The first example is that of an outsider invited inside because of her recognized gifts as an artist and her sympathies with voodoo practices, but significantly she could never bring herself to edit her footage into a final film form – the footage *was* the experience. The latter example is that of an insider formalistically redressing the White ethnographic gaze and showing how that experience felt from an indigenous point of view.

For further reading see Grimshaw, 2002.

EUROPEAN CINEMA/EUROPEAN FILM FINANCING

Entries in this book have been made on various individual European cinemas when, at a point in history, they could be said to constitute either a movement or a school (for a list, see the end of this entry). When talking about European cinema it must be borne in mind that political **ideologies** have meant that Europe has never been a stable unified entity. For example, from World War Two until 1990, there were two Europes, as is best exemplified by the former division of Germany into two Germanies (East and West). So clearly it is impossible to talk about *a* European cinema – at least from this side of the Atlantic. Viewed from the United States, more particularly **Hollywood**, European cinema, since 1920, has been construed as a global concept and perceived as meaning two distinct things (at least). First, European cinema is predominantly **art cinema** and is often more sexually explicit than the home product (see **Hays code**). Second, it is the only true rival to Hollywood and must at all costs be infiltrated and dominated. The most recent trade agreements (GATT) between the United States and Europe are but the latest in a series of attempts by the American film industry to secure favourable deals for the export of its products into Europe – an attempt which France, as one of the few European countries still to possess a viable film industry, has steadily resisted.

Because Hollywood is still so dominant in Western culture, it continues to be *the* point of reference. Thus, in Western Europe a nation's cinema is defined, in part, in relation to what it is not (i.e. 'not-Hollywood'), in relation, therefore, to an 'other'. This in turn produces two strategies. First, European countries produce films with the intention of intruding into that other's territory. France and the United Kingdom, in particular, have done this with some degree of success with their **heritage** films (such as *Manon des sources*, Claude Berri, 1985; *Cyrano de Bergerac*, Jean-Paul Rappeneau, 1990; *A Room with a View*, 1985 and *Howards End*, 1992, both Merchant-Ivory). Second, with a view to protecting its own financial interests, an indigenous industry makes products specifically for the national **audience**, thereby drawing on its nation's cultural specificities, something which Hollywood of course cannot do. France, Germany and Spain in particular follow this practice.

European film production is largely dependent on three sources: state-aid mechanisms, tax incentives, television finance. There is also co-financing with the USA (often this is the case with UK productions).

Since the late 1980s, when European film industries were in a fairly parlous state (including France), a series of programmes were created: the European Community's MEDIA (I and II), and the Council of Europe's pan-European Eurimages. The MEDIA programmes supported European Union film industries in terms of training, development and production, and **distribution** and exhibition. Eurimages' purpose was (and still is) to foster, between European partners (EU and non-EU), the co-production and distribution of fiction and **documentary** films (Jäckel, 2003: 75). Eurimages also supports along with MEDIA the exhibition of European films with a network of film theatres: EUROPA CINEMAS (Jäckel, 2003: 82). These various measures mean that Europe has a vital film industry (especially in terms of the variety of productions which still manage to maintain the concept of cultural diversity between nations) even if the USA still dominates the market at the same levels as in the 1980s (around 70 per cent).

see also (listed chronologically): **German expressionism, Soviet cinema, French poetic realism, Italian neo-realism, Free Cinema (British), French New Wave, British New Wave, Germany/New German cinema, Dogme films**.

For further reading on European cinema see Sorlin, 1991; Vincendeau, 1995; Forbes and Street, 2000; Ezra, 2004; Galt, 2006. On European film financing see Finney, 1996; Jäckel, 2003.

EXPERIMENTAL FILM

Though a convenient collective categorizing, the films that embody 'experimental' are incredibly varied in both **motivation** and style and, typically, are interconnected only by a perceived 'otherness' to that of mainstream **narrative cinema**. It is important to note that when discussing experimental, as well as the **avant-garde**, I am not including **art cinema**. As Smith notes, the latter is 'often supported by government policies designed to promote distinctive national cinemas' (1998: 396).

From cinema's earliest advances, experimental cinema has existed as both provocateur and interrogator. Re-evaluating, countering and dismissing the hegemonic structures of film narrative, commercialization and identity that **spectators** accept as normative (see **normalizing** and **preferred reading**). At its most radical, experimental cinema challenges our understanding of cinema and our preconceptions.

Experimental films tend to be low-budget productions because they are often self-financed, or supported by private patronage or grants. In the post-World War Two era, the majority of filmmakers adopted the relatively inexpensive 16mm equipment to shoot and exhibit their work. With variable lenses and shooting speeds, such equipment 'could be found on the war surplus and amateur film markets', putting 'the means of production in the film maker's hands' (Rees, 1997: 538). Some filmmakers transitioned to Super-8 in the mid-1960s, the format offering a larger, brighter (usually colour) image when projected. Now, in the era of **digital** technology, the capability to shoot HD quality is an available option to all filmmakers, both amateur and professional. With the emergence of digital platforms such as Vimeo and YouTube, the capability to distribute work is now one with a global reach.

However, pre-digital **distribution** was confined to specific geographical locations, restricted by budget and logistics. Cinema 16, 1947, became a primary exhibitor and distributor of experimental films in the USA. Supporting the art of various pioneering university film programmes, the model of self-financed and film society screenings became a dominant means of production and distribution over the next two decades. In Britain, the workshops of Cinema Action toured screenings aimed at a 'working-class audience' (Nelmes, 2007: 274) with the aim of making filmmaking available to all and not simply the province of the elite. With the emergence of digital platforms (e.g. YouTube, Kickstarter, Vimeo), the capability of independent filmmakers to reach an audience has moved beyond geographical and temporal limitations.

Experimental film is preternaturally diverse in its approach. Thus, while all tend to foreground aesthetic function over **narrative** coherence, filmmakers approach these concerns through an array of differing modes. Maya Deren's Freudian psychodrama *Meshes of the Afternoon* (1943) took a **surrealist** approach to depicting personal reality using slow-motion, an absence of a score and a circular narrative structure to provide an unending, non-temporal dream-like quality to the experience. Duration can be a preoccupation in other modalities, from Warhol's *Eat* (1963) with each shot lasting the length of the film in the camera, to Breer's *Fist Fight* (1964) whose frenzied shots last a matter of frames. Or Oshima's *Nihon no Yoru to Kiri/Night and Fog* (1960) that developed an intricate **flashback** structure within which to articulate concerns such as political memory and the conflict between generations. As Deren has argued, 'narrative pattern has come to completely dominate cinematic expression in spite of the fact that it is, basically, a visual form' (1946: 59). Warhol's films such as *Sleep* (1963) and *Empire* (1964) take Deren's point to an artistic conclusion, denying narrative or drama.

A further, crucial aspect of experimental cinema is that it functions as a formative space within which minority voices gain space to express themselves. The work of Kenneth Anger, synonymous with the cult film *Scorpio Rising* (1964), adopted **underground** aesthetics to explore representations of homosexuality and gay culture within a climate of criminalization.

To this day, experimental cinema still pulls at and teases the sanctity of film. For example, Les LeVeques' *Backwards Birth of a Nation* (2000), as the title implies, subverts D. W. Griffiths' *Birth of a Nation* (1915), a film synonymous with narrative cinema and questions of representation (including racist stereotyping). LeVeques compresses the 187-minute film into 13 minutes, inverts the black and white images in each frame, and screens the film backwards.

Finally, as much as experimental cinema seeks to subvert and question the aesthetic concerns of narrative cinema, as with all things, the **mainstream** goes on to appropriate and incorporate this 'otherness' into its own production practices. Moreover, it is also the case that cross-fertilization can occur in another (more unexpected) way with the transition of experimental filmmakers such as Lars Von Trier, Steven Soderbergh, Gus Van Sant and Sally Potter into mainstream productions.

EXPLOITATION MOVIES

A term that has gained critical currency and which refers to films which are generally low in production values but which target specific **audiences** through exploiting specific topical themes or **narratives** about specific social groups. In a sense, exploitation movies have always been around (in the form of **pornography**, for example). But in the West, especially **Hollywood** cinema, we can determine several key moments: the 1950s 'teen pics'; the 1970s **Blaxploitation** movies; the mid-1970s European sexploitation movies, mostly emanating from France after the lifting of censorship; and the more recent (mostly American) teen comedies and nasties. Since there are already entries on blaxploitation and pornography, I will focus in this entry only on the first and last categories.

Teen pics

The 1950s saw the major launch by Hollywood of what are termed 'teen pics' – a form of exploitation films that deliberately targeted teenagers who had become a new exploitable consumer market (although arguably there were earlier forms in the 1930s with the Mickey Rooney and Judy Garland films). The mid-1950s was a period of conspicuous consumerism amongst middle-class teenagers. Youth was associated with a hedonistic commitment to pleasure and leisure unrelated to adult concerns. Their generation's aggressive rock-'n-roll **music** filtered into their behaviour and hep-talk slang, which also excluded adults, of course. The teenage cult was something Hollywood needed to exploit in the light of competition it was experiencing from television. Product-placing in these films was part of what made them exploitation films. But it was primarily the nature of their narrative that capitalized on what was perceived as the teenage problem which earned them this label. Arguably and ironically, it was the success of Nicholas Ray's *Rebel without a Cause* (1955), starring James Dean as the angry rebel teenager, whose parents do not understand him, that set the ball rolling for teen pics. Hollywood was keen to capitalize on this tale of youthful alienation. But what Hollywood failed to understand (hence the irony) was the novelty of Ray's approach, which was to tell the story from the teenager's point of view. The whole motivation of the film was that the audience comes to feel the truth of the adolescent's anguish at the end of the film (and that the problem also lies with the parents). However, this was not picked up on by Hollywood, which went on to produce either teenage problem movies or teenage sweetheart stories.

The distinction between a 'teen pic', whose audience-address is clearly the youth classes, versus a movie that proselytizes about the problem (and so really targets more of an adult audience) can perhaps be best summed up by comparing the reception of Ray's film to that of another teen pic of the same year, Richard Brooks' *The Blackboard Jungle*, which achieved almost the opposite effect. Though well intentioned as a film that attempts to understand the teenage problem, its point of view is that of the teacher, in a tough New York inner-city school, who has to contain the hoodlums in his class. As opposed to Ray's film, the moralizing tone of the adult is never far away.

As far as teen exploitation movies are concerned, perhaps the first film of this type was Don Siegel's *Crime in the Streets* (1956), which takes this teenage problem a stage further, bringing teenage gangs into the city streets and portraying them as perpetrators of ugly gratuitous delinquent violence. Thus, a first type of exploitation 'teen pics' – of deviant, alienated youth – was spawned. By the late 1950s, American International Pictures took the lead in making this type of exploitation movie and produced teen-gang movies (*Dragstrip Girl* and *Motorcycle Gang*, both Edward Calm, 1957; *Dragstrip Riot*, David Bradley, 1959) or drug-related 'teen pics' (*High School Confidential,* Jack Arnold, and *The Cool and the Crazy,* William Witney, both 1958), where warring gangs, drag-car/hot-rod chases, high-speed motorbiking, and drugs send the protagonists on a downward spiral (often to death).

But teenage delinquency or trauma was not the only side of the exploitation business. Hollywood also tried to sell a more wholesome image, which tended to break down into two types: either the nice boy and nice girl next-door narrative or a rock-'n-roll musical starring (budget permitting) a marketable rock star. Of the first kind, A *Summer Place* (Delmer Daves, 1959) and *Blue Denim* (Philip Dunne, 1959) are exemplary. The teenagers mimic adult behaviour as they conduct their sexual awakenings. In the latter category, the first to make a breakthrough was *Rock around the Clock,* starring Bill Haley (Fred Sears, 1956). This was sanitized wholesome rock-'n-roll, with youngsters jiving and going through early teenage love struggles. The films acted as vehicles for selling the music and a certain idea of teenage culture which could not upset the parents. In this same typology of films, because of his huge popularity, obviously the Elvis movies stand out – but even here his image was sanitized and his notorious pelvic movements kept under wraps. Typically, he got to play either the misunderstood rock star who gets thrown into jail (*Jailhouse Rock,* Richard Thorpe, 1957) or the tender crooning lover (see *Love Me Tender,* 1956; *GI Blues,* Norman Taurog, 1960).

Teen-exploitation pics

More recently a new wave of 'teen-exploitation pics' has come to the screen. These can be broken down into two broad categories: the teen comedies and the teen nasties. The recent teen comedies have moved away from their earlier prototype of the 1960s beach-party, surfing or biker teen movies that sold glamour and music (see *Gidget,* Paul Wendkos, 1959, starring Sandra Dee, and *The Wild Angels,* Roger Corman, 1966, starring Peter Fonda and Nancy Sinatra). Nor do today's teen nasties conveniently fall under the 'trash' label that was so easily conferred upon the 1950s teen problem pics. Interestingly in the 1950s, their very schlock nature allowed teen audiences to make them into cult films (see the example of *I Was a Teenage Werewolf,* Gene Flower, 1957). The more contemporary teen comedies follow zany implausible plots: *Wayne's World 1* (Penelope Spheeris, 1992) and *Wayne's World 2* (Stephen Surjik, 1993) are good examples. Even though Wayne and Garth are not strictly speaking teens themselves, they are, however, proto-teens and their off-beat humour (and nasty sexist epithets) appealed hugely to youth audiences. The slightly less zany *The School of Rock* (Richard Linklater, 2003), with its take on the anarchic youthful teacher who leads his teenage class to moderate success, is another illustrative example of the implausible tale – despite its narrative proximity to the American Dream that everyone can be a winner. Other teen comedies mix the serious with the comedic in an attempt to dramatize the way in which the youth class has been unable to overcome the beastliness and egocentrism of its parents and so is doomed to live either on the periphery of society or as a genius drop-out (see *Garden State*, Zach Braff, 2003, for example). Nor are these teen comedies without their nastiness. *Ghost World* (Terry Zwigoff, 2001) exemplifies this trend with its two bored female teenagers, Enid and Rebecca. Living in suburbia, they are driven by the emptiness of their alienation to get up to numerous unpleasant tricks at the expense of others. Even the comedy-drama *Juno* (Jason Reitman, 2007), about teenage pregnancy, is not without an egotistical tone: after all, having renounced her first impulse to have an abortion, Juno's decision to go through with the birth is, nonetheless, predicated on the fact that her child will be adopted by a comfortably-off middle-class woman, Vanessa. Even 'better', in the end, Juno gets her boyfriend back (Paulie, the father of her child); baby meantime has gone off with Vanessa to its fancy nursery.

The second category, teen nasties, is not really a true continuation of the teenage problem films of the 1950s, although it does owe something to it, insofar as we are presented with alienated youth. The difference comes in the form that their anomie takes as a result of their sense of alienation. Instead of taking it out on themselves as individuals, or being the victims of a cruel mishap, or gangs beating up on each other, now (in their often drug-induced state and intrinsic sense of boredom) they plan sadistic murders, or get into power-play relations that are heavily sado-masochistic in their nature. In the teen nasties category there has been a spate of films which, despite their directors' pleas that they are only showing the truth, have been accused of teensploitation. Thus, in terms of power-play relations, illustrative examples include *Thirteen* (Catherine Hardwicke, 2003), about a teenage girl's depression and addiction, and *Ken Park* (Larry Clark, 2002), about the dysfunctional and abusive home-lives of a group of teenage friends. *Hard Candy* (David Slade, 2005) goes a step further (and is partly inspired by a true story) and reverses the power relations. This time a male sexual predator is pursued by a 14-year-old female vigilante, tortured and forced to commit suicide. The question is: are these films timely looks at teenage problems (including internet grooming) or merely prurient narratives to disquieten its audiences? The same questions arise in terms of murder narratives. Two films clearly come to mind: *Bully* (Larry Clark, 2001) and *Elephant* (Gus Van Sant, 2003). Both are based on true events and both are starkly different in their representation. In *Bully*, Clark comes close to a prurience with youth that leaves one uneasy – lingering as he does particularly on the female teenager body. Clark claims that he made this film about the murderous revenge upon a bully by his gang as an attempt to wake us up to the way many kids are living today (2002: 25). All eight of the teens in this film are portrayed as pretty unlikeable: the (eventually) murdered bully; three of the gang who are drugged out of their minds; the teen slut; a best-but-bullied friend and his manipulative girlfriend; and, finally, a teenage hoodlum human. The film falls into so many clichés, starting with the moral bankruptcy of contemporary America. But it also ends up saying, more or less, that all the central characters in the film were bullies of one sort or another – which, in anybody's world-view, is a pretty sweeping generalization on today's youth. Less prurient in its representation, Van Sant's *Elephant* is based very unloosely on the Columbine high-school massacre (1999). Van Sant wanted to remain dispassionate, to offer no answers and so chose not to give the bigger picture, but aimed rather to give us 'a clean portrait of an event', shot in an unobtrusive **documentary** style, in order to show the day's incidents as a part of the 'messy complexities of reality' (2004: 18). But, as with *Bully*, hints of a confused **sexuality** haunt our reading of the two main male protagonists. Is it because of their homo-erotic relationship that the girlfriend in *Bully* wants her boyfriend's best friend murdered, to get her rival out of the way? Does the fact that the two high-school killers in *Elephant* get bullied at school and have a homo-erotic relationship cloud our ability to read the messy complexities of real life that Van Sant wants to portray for us? The point is that these teen nasties show a very unpleasant side to young people between the ages of 13 and 18, and we have to wonder about adult prurience and an unhealthy preoccupation on their part with the 'problem' with youth, which in turn all too easily leads to a demonization of youth culture. And the question becomes: why? Why are these films being made? Is it in our interests to see youth as abject? Of course, some of these stories are based on truth. But the point is, surely, if these stories must be represented at all, to try to give them the necessary development that will allow the spectator to move away from simplistic snap judgements. Do we want these films to help create an environment for change? Or do we simply go and see them to have our worst prejudices confirmed and feel helpless to make change happen?

For further reading see Doherty, 1988, 2002; Gidal, 1989; Harper and Mendik, 2000; Schaefer, 1999; Schofield Clark, 2003; Shary, 2005.

EYELINE MATCHING

A term used to point to the **continuity editing** practice ensuring the logic of the look (see **gaze**). In other words, eyeline matching is based on the belief in **mainstream** cinema that when a character looks into off-screen space the **spectator** expects to see what s/he is looking at. Thus, there will be a cut to show what is being looked at: object, view or another character. Eyeline then refers to the trajectory of the looking eye. The eyeline match creates order and meaning in cinematic space. For example, character *A* will look off-screen at character *B*. Cut to character *B*, who – if s/he is in the same room and engaged in an exchange either of glances or words with character *A* – will return that look and so 'certify' that character *A* is indeed in the space from which we first saw her or him look. This 'stabilizing' (Bordwell and Thompson, 1980: 167) is true in the other primary use of the eyeline match which is the **shot/reverse-angle shot**, also known as the reverse angle shot or shot/countershot, commonly used in close-up dialogue scenes. The camera adopts the eyeline trajectory of the interlocutor looking at the other person as s/he speaks, then switches to the other person's position and does the same.

see also: **editing, 180-degree rule, shots**

FADE

A transition between sequences or scenes generally associated with earlier cinema – up until the late 1940s – but still used on occasion. In this transition an image fades out and then another image fades in. In use from 1899, the fade was one of the first forms of transition that could be edited within the camera, so its historical importance resides in the fact that earliest filmmakers realized they could henceforth make films that were composed of more than just a single action taken in one take. The cut as a transition came a little later, in 1901. The use of the fade suggests a lapse of time and possibly a change of space (e.g. if a character gets knocked out s/he may go out with a fade and come back 'some time later' through a fade-in in the same room).

FANTASY/FANTASY FILMS

Generically speaking, fantasy films englobe four basic categories: **horror**, **science-fiction**, fairy tales and a certain type of adventure movie (journeys to improbable places and meetings with implausible creatures, such as *Planet of the Apes*, Franklin Schaffner, 1967). Fantasy films are about areas 'we don't really know about' and, therefore, areas we do not see as real. However, fantasy is the expression of our unconscious, and it is these films in particular that most readily reflect areas we repress or suppress – namely, the realms of our unconscious and the world of our dreams. It is also true that these films, as indeed with other **genres**, act metonymically as enunciators of dominant **ideology** and social **myths**. As we know, mainstream **Hollywood** cinema's great subject is not **sexual** identity but heterosexuality and more precisely the family. When this dream is threatened, the 'threat' must be removed. The doubly deviant woman in *Fatal Attraction* (Adrian Lyne, 1987) – she is not a mother but a career woman and she is sexually voracious – must be removed so that family life can go on. Norman Bates' victim in *Psycho* (Alfred Hitchcock, 1960) was a deserving one because she was a double thief stealing her boss's money *and* stealing another woman's husband. Cyborg movies (the artificial reproduction of humans), as Kaplan (1992: 211) argues, are clearly related to the issue of reproduction rights and who controls them. (It is noteworthy that probably *the* first cyborg novel was written by a woman, Mary Wollstonecraft Shelley, *Frankenstein*, 1818.) It is also noteworthy that the number of these films has increased since the legalization of abortion in many countries in the Western world. Men want either to have control over reproduction, as in *The Fly* (David Cronenberg, 1986) and *Alien 3* (David Fincher, 1992) or to destroy the reproductive organism, as in *Dead Ringers* (Cronenberg, 1988).

    Fantasy is inextricably linked with desire, which, according to Lacan, is located in the Imaginary (see **psychoanalysis**) – that is, the unconscious. Fantasy, then, is the conscious articulation of desire, through either images or stories – it is the **mise-en-scène** of desire. In this context, film puts desire up on-screen. The film industry is the industry of desire, Hollywood is the dream factory. But film is not just film; it is also a nexus of text relations which function as fantasy structures enunciating unconscious desire.

There is no single set or level of fantasy (just as there is no one desire). Just to illustrate: the fantasy created by the filmmaker is in relation to, but distinct from, the fantasy perceived by the **spectator** as constituted subject; and, as constituting subject the spectator creates yet another fantasy; but, given that fantasy structures are multiple, spectator identification is equally multiplicitous. For example (but of course by way of fantasy!), with *Rebel Without a Cause* (1955) the filmmaker Nicholas Ray could have fantasized that his film was about teenage malaise and alienation in 1950s America and that James Dean was an archetypal anti-hero. Given Ray's own background – as a loner, something of a drifter and misfit – he could also have fantasized Dean as his alter-ego. A male teenage spectator, seeing the film when it was released, would identify with Dean which, as constituted subject, he is supposed to do, but in this context he would fantasize Dean as his alter ego. As constituting subject, his reading of the film and the character portrayed by Dean could concur with the **documentary** realism created by Ray but not necessarily read the film as a 'problem film' per se in which, as Dean exclaims, 'we are all involved'. He could read it instead as a realistic portrayal of youth culture and, too, its embattlement against uncomprehending adults or parents. The film becomes appropriated, encultured – a **cult film** of the spectator's life (as he fantasizes it). Finally, given the multiplicity of identificatory positions, this spectator can identify with both Sal Mineo and Natalie Wood (Dean's friends) as Dean's **diegetically** adoring audience – thus satisfying both homo-erotic and hetero-erotic desire.

The second point to make in relation to these structures of fantasy is that, since fantasy is the mise-en-scène of desire and since desire is located in the unconscious, it follows that cinema, in creating images that we as spectators wish to look at, calls upon the structures of our own unconscious and makes us privy to them. The cinematic **apparatus** functions in this respect to position us as voyeurs to our own fantasies. According to Freud, storytelling is a child's way of dealing with its anxiety around sexual differences and dependencies, most particularly on its mother. Storytelling, then, is creating fantasies that emerge from our unconscious desires and fears. Cinema **narratives** relay these fantasies before our eyes, the primary ones being as follows: the fear of abandonment by and desire for unity with the mother/([m]other); the fear of castration (Freud) or the fear of being devoured by the mother (Melanie Klein); the bastard and foundling fantasies; the desire for illicit viewing (of parental coitus) – the primal scene (see **psychoanalysis** for more details).

Let's take *Jurassic Park* (Steven Spielberg, 1993) to explore this set of fantastic mise-en-scènes. The devouring mothers are of course the re-created dinosaurs – all female (at least at birth) and the result of genetic engineering (men tinkering with reproductive rights). These dinosaurs that become sexually ambiguous after birth – they are able to change sex – are also the attacking father and terrifying parents illicitly viewed/fantasized as copulating. The children, Lex and Tim, fear abandonment, and this is fulfilled when they are separated from their 'parents', the two palaeontologists Ellie Sattler and Alan Grant, in whose care they have been placed. Incidentally, it is this same 'father' (Grant) who poses the threat of castration in the opening sequence when he draws the talon of a dinosaur over a young boy's stomach in reply to his persistent questions about dinosaurs – no child-liker he! Father as life-giver and life-destroyer is also exemplified in the role of this reluctant 'father': when Lex and Tim are being attacked in the Land-Rover, Grant eventually has to try to rescue the life-threatened children.

In this film, the foundling fantasy, whereby the child can reject the family because the parents are not hers or his and are too lowly, is inverted. The foundlings, Lex and Tim, are eventually accepted by Grant when, at the end of the film, he fulfils the **Oedipal trajectory** by saving his 'family'. He even feels protective to the point that the boy ends up cradled asleep in his arms. The only 'bastards' in this movie are the illegitimate dinosaurs. They are the illegitimate children of the billionaire entrepreneur John Hammond – their 'mother'. Again an inversion, this time sexual. In the bastard fantasy, the mother is perceived by the child as not being possessed by the father – because of her illicit liaisons with other men. She is also perceived as lowly and immoral – a prostitute. This fantasy then breaks up the notion of the family unit: the child sides with the real mother against the father and, moreover, because of her status, the child can even possess her. In the film, as a result of Hammond's illicit reproductive practices, the dinosaurs do break up the 'family' unit; and they unite with Hammond as mother against the father (all the people they kill are men); they also leave Isla Nublar(!) with Hammond in the form of the blood in the amber on his stick – but now Hammond is a fallen (wo)man, exposed for his immorality, a potential prey to be possessed by his dinosauric children.

For further reading see Bellin, 2005; Bourgault du Coudray, 2006; Butler, 2009; Donald, 1989; Furby and Hines, 2012; Von Gunden, 2001; Walters, 2011; Worley, 2005.

FEMALE MASQUERADE

In its basic sense, female masquerade means a display of ultra-femininity. How it comes about and how it is used against the grain, as it were, needs to be understood because it is particularly useful as a concept when investigating **genres** that strongly forefront female protagonists, such as **film noir**. Indeed, female masquerade often comes into play in relation to the femme fatale – although that is not the only genre of course (it occurs in **melodramas** and **musicals** too). Masquerade functions, first, as a disavowal of difference. According to Freudian and Lacanian **psychoanalysis** the male's fear of castration by the female leads him to two major strategies of containment of the female body: **voyeurism** and **fetishism**. The male desire to repress the feminine leads to an overinvestment in the female parts. This allows the male to fetishize the female form more easily. The exaggerated female parts of the body draw attention to themselves and can, thereby, become over-endowed with meaning. And it is in those very parts that the male can seek out the hidden phallus and perceive, for example, in the stiletto heels and long slinky black dress (or gloves, or cigarette holder) a projection of his own phallic being. This fetishizing process works to render the female body safe. So, in the end, by masquerading as ultra-feminine, the female form in this fetishistic relationship ultimately masquerades as phallic.

But, the masquerade also functions as a colluding assertion of difference and disavowal. For, in order for this containment to fully work, the female has to collude with this positioning. And she colludes in order to survive within patriarchal society. Thus, female masquerade is a key tool to this collusion. That is, the female colludes with the male by overstressing her feminine traits – primarily through her dress-code but also gestures. In a sense, though, she is knowingly putting on a mask (Doane, 1982). Consider two recent films, *My Week with Marilyn* (Simon Curtis, 2011) and *The Iron Lady* (Phyllida Lloyd, 2011), which expose how female masquerade is precisely what these two women have to perform in order to both give the men what they want and get what they, Marilyn and Mrs Thatcher in this instance, want. Performing femininity becomes a strategy for winning (as Mrs Thatcher/Meryl Streep says with equal amounts of irony and self-deprecation: 'the hat can go; but the pearls are non-negotiable').

And it is here that the masquerade function starts to open up into a subversive space. For not all women will accept this positioning as fetish. However, they might use the practice of the predominant structure of the masculine, fetishizing **gaze** to their advantage and masquerade for their own purpose. For example, a woman who wants to occupy a masculine place (be it for power or sexual reasons) would need to disguise this ambition, or suffer immediate retribution. And we know only too well how many femme fatales seek (through an illicit obtaining of wealth) this place of power or empowerment. How better to disguise this ambition than by donning the mask of femininity; thus hiding her transgressive desires (namely, to get rich in the capitalist flow, or to follow sexual desires that are proscribed to her). The female masquerade in this context functions to help the woman get what she wants (or nearly; most often she gets caught out at the end and 'punished'). The disguise through masquerade is so complete the man falls for it. He is seeing her one way, but she, fully knowingly, is perceiving herself in completely the other way. Linda Fiorentino in *The Last Seduction* (John Dahl, 1994) offers a strong reminder to all men (who don't understand) that a masquerade is at play and that she intends and does win in the end!

This putting on a mask has a second subversive effect, however. The knowledge of putting it on means also that there is knowledge of what lies beneath – that in fact the mask can be taken off. This suggests that there is a gap between the masquerading woman and the real woman underneath. So here the woman who knowingly masquerades, is showing precisely through her ultra-feminine traits (be it through clothing or gestures) how patriarchy functions to position her. In this context the excess of femininity in its parodic and ironic value ends up destabilizing the desired-for image, defamiliarizes female iconography and ultimately threatens the male gaze (Doane, 1982). Modleski (1988) analyses Hitchcock's ultra-feminine women protagonists in this light and shows just how powerful their (ironic) return of the look can be.

FEMINIST FILM THEORY

Although there were women filmmakers back in the 1920s and even earlier (see Hayward, 1992) making statements about the suitability of the camera to a woman's expression of her own **subjectivity**, feminist film theory did not come about fully until the late 1960s as a result of the second wave of feminism – the first wave being the Suffragists and Suffragette movement of the early 1900s. This second wave took the world of academia and journalism in the Western world and Australia by storm and very quickly began to generate texts related to women's issues and, just as importantly, to disciplines taught within academia – including film studies. Indeed, no discussion of film (or television for that matter) can ignore feminist film theory which, since the early

1970s, has so strongly impacted on film studies – starting with the issue of **gender** representation. Essentially, to date, we can distinguish three periods in the evolution of this theory: the early 1970s; the mid-1970s to the early 1980s; the mid-1980s to the present.

Although we use the term *feminist film theory*, Annette Kuhn (1982: 72) rightly points out that there does not exist one single theory, rather a series of 'perspectives' (making these debates very much part of the **postmodern** era, therefore). Thus, the following three sections set out the history and the debates of those periods and look at the impact of each period as well as the problems and outcomes each generated, which, in turn, served to push the debate along.

Feminist film theory 1968 to 1974

The effect of this first period of feminist film theory was to shift the debate from **class** to gender. Feminist film critics examined the question of feminine identity and the representation of women in film images as the site/sight or object of exchange between men. At this point the focus of these analyses was exclusively **Hollywood** cinema. Exemplary of this approach was Molly Haskell's book *From Reverence to Rape: The Treatment of Women in the Movies* (1974). In her book, American journalist Haskell made two very important points. First, she suggested that film reflects society and vice versa and in so doing reflects the **ideological** and social construction of women who are either to be revered (as the virgin) or reviled (as the whore). Woman is, according to Haskell, a fixed construction, her feminine essence repressed by patriarchy. Second, in her analyses of the 1930s and 1940s Hollywood cinema, she made the important distinction between **melodrama** and women's films – the latter, as she pointed out, being made specifically to address women. This second point, that of the central role of the female protagonist *and* female **spectator**, led to a renewed and different focus on **genre** and the possible aesthetic and political consequences of gender difference.

Meantime in Europe (especially in the United Kingdom), Haskell's reading of a presumed feminine essence represented three major problems for feminist film theorists, who included Claire Johnston, Laura Mulvey, Pam Cook and Annette Kuhn. They pointed out that a belief in a fixed feminine essence meant legitimating patriarchy through the back door. By accepting the fixed essence of woman as a predetermined 'given order of things', implicitly, what was also being accepted was the 'naturalness' of the patriarchal order (Lapsley and Westlake, 1988: 25). The British feminists, arguing along Althusserian lines, also pointed out that film was as much productive of as it was a product of ideology and, furthermore, that – in the same way that Althusser theorized that the **subject** was a construct of material structures – so too was the spectator a constituted subject when watching the film. The time was ripe for a moving on from a causal and reductionist debate. Historical materialism (an analysis of the material conditions within historical contexts that placed women where they were), **semiotics** and **psychoanalysis** were the tools invoked to investigate beyond the reflectionist statements produced by the American authors.

Feminist film theory 1975 to 1983

In 1972, Claire Johnston, Laura Mulvey and Linda Myles organized the Women's Event at the Edinburgh Film Festival. To accompany the Event, Johnston edited a pamphlet, *Notes on Women's Cinema*, published in 1973, which contained her own ground-breaking essay: 'Women's Cinema as **Counter-cinema**'. This text was one of the first to make clear that cinematic textual operations could not be ignored. To change cinema, to make women's cinema, Johnston argued, you had first to understand the ideological operations present in actual **mainstream** film practices. The task was to determine both the 'how' of female representation and the 'effect' of female positioning in the process of meaning construction. Under the 'how', of first importance was a reading of the **iconography** of the image. How was the female framed, lit, dressed, and so on? Under the 'effect', of primary significance was the female's positioning within the structure of the **narrative**. In the first instance, what was required was a reading of the image as **sign**, a need to understand the **denotation and connotations** of the image. In the second instance, the psychology of the narrative had to come under scrutiny and question why, repeatedly, do so many narratives in mainstream cinema depict the woman as the object of desire of the male character who has embarked upon his **Oedipal trajectory**? Camera-work and **lighting** make it clear that she is a figure upon whom he can fix his fantasies. These, then, are the textual operations constructing ideology which, argues Johnston, we must come to understand through a **deconstruction** of the modes of production, which in turn leads to an exposing of the cinematic and narrative codes at work. Only then can an oppositional counter-cinema become a possibility (Johnston, 1976: 217). This formidable recipe of foregrounding film practices and female subjectivity would, Johnston believed, effect a break between ideology and text – a dislocation that would create a space for women's cinema to emerge.

The other ground-breaking essay of this period was Laura Mulvey's 'Visual Pleasure and Narrative Cinema' (1975). Mulvey's focus was less on textual operations within the film and more on the textual relations between screen and spectator. This important text is perceived as *the* key founding document of psychoanalytic feminist film theory. Since this issue is discussed in much greater detail under **spectator**, I will confine myself to a brief summary here. In this essay, Mulvey seeks to address the issue of female spectatorship within the cinematic **apparatus**. She examines the way in which cinema functions, through its **codes and conventions**, to construct the way in which woman is to be looked at, starting with the male point of view within the film and subsequently the spectator who identifies with the male protagonist. She describes this process of viewing as **scopophilia** – pleasure in viewing. However, she also asks what happens to the female spectator, given that the narrative of **classical narrative cinema** is predominantly that of the Oedipal trajectory and since that trajectory is tightly bound up with male perceptions and fantasies about women? How does woman derive visual pleasure? Mulvey can conclude, only, that she must either identify with the passive position of the female character on screen, or, if she is to derive pleasure, she must assume a male positioning. This deliberately polemical essay met with strong response by feminist critics. The next section details the development of that debate. For now let's examine the third aspect of theoretical work during this period: textual analysis.

In the United States, particularly, feminists turned their attention to analyses of the textual operations in film and their role in constructing ideology. Essays in the influential journal *Camera Obscura* – launched in 1976 by a breakaway group from the earlier *Women and Film* collective – were instrumental in revealing the ideological operations of patriarchy; and through applications of structural-psychoanalytic theories they demonstrated how narrative codes and conventions sustain patriarchal ideology in its conditioning and control of women. Textual analysis focused on narrative strategies and, in particular, picked up the question of genre and its role in structuring subjectivity – a point which, as we have seen, Molly Haskell had raised in drawing the distinction between melodrama and women's films.

The intervention of psychoanalysis and feminism now brought melodrama and women's films into the critical limelight, focusing on the **discourses** that construct the symbolic place of 'woman and the maternal'. The **Western** too was investigated. The dominance of male-defined problematics within the narrative, the role of women as mere triggers (*sic*) to male action and choice and, finally, the counter-

Oedipal trajectory of so many of its heroes – all these narrative strategies are exposed. Why indeed do so many gunmen ride off into the sunset leaving 'the woman' behind? **Film noir** was another genre which under scrutiny could not hide the dominance of a male subjectivity whose gaze, motivated by the fear of castration, either **fetishizes** the 'threatening', dangerous woman into the phallic and, therefore, unthreatening other or seeks to control and punish the perceived source of this fear. (See **female masquerade, melodrama, Western** and **film noir** for a full discussion; and for more detail on these points see **psychoanalysis**.)

Another part of the feminists' strategy in their textual analyses was to read against the grain and, in particular, to foreground sexual difference. **Horror** and film noir, because of their voyeuristic 'essentialising' practice, were prime targets of investigation, but so too were melodrama and women's film because of their focus on the family and the so-called 'woman's space'. Thus, for example, in a film noir or horror film a woman's annihilation, which on the surface might appear as a result of her own actions, may in fact be read as the male repressing the feminine side of his self by projecting it onto the woman and then killing her. Alfred Hitchcock's *Psycho* (1960), for example, plays on this sexual identity in crisis in a number of very complex ways. Norman Bates adopts numerous positions: that of his castrating, phallic mother who constantly reminds him that women are filth; so, in disguising or dressing himself up as her, he becomes that filth – which, of course he must eradicate; he is also the voyeuristic gaze of mainstream cinema looking through numerous holes (peeping Tom) at the woman's body and, finally, the male gaze that must annihilate that which he must not become – woman and filth.

Melodrama is historically perceived as a theatre form that reflects nineteenth-century bourgeois values whereby the family at all costs will prevail, remain united and in order. When the genre was taken up by early cinema, this reflection continued. Superficially by the 1930s and 1940s, melodrama and women's films appeared not to challenge the patriarchal order. However, in their narrative construction these films gave space for a woman's point of view. And it was in this respect that a reading against the grain was possible. Closure for these films meant that order and, if possible, harmony in the family had to be restored. But what caused the initial disorder? Most often conflict between the two sexes. Unlike the Western or **gangster** movie and the dominance of male-defined problematics which only the hero's action can resolve, here we are confronted with 'the way in which sexual difference under patriarchy is fraught, explosive and erupts dramatically into violence within its own private stamping ground, the family' (Mulvey, 1977: 39). There is something tantalizing in the implications of this reading against the grain that goes something like this: if melodrama and women's films are the only sites where narrative strategies expose the contradictions in patriarchal ideology and if the domestic sphere is the private stamping-ground of patriarchy in all its contradictions, then how much indeed the rest of mainstream cinema must work to assert in public spaces that patriarchal ideology is without contradiction. And how dangerous it would be if female subjectivity crept out of the private domestic sphere and exposed those contradictions. If melodrama did not exist, Hollywood would have had to invent it.

Feminist film theory 1984 to 2010s

The revalorizing of certain genres that previously had been dismissed, scorned even, was an important accomplishment, as was the opening up of the debate around female spectatorship. However, by the mid-1980s feminists felt that the focus on the textual operations of films was too narrow and that a film needed to be examined within its various contexts – that is, the historical and social contexts of its production and reception. Clearly, this move broadens the debate around spectatorship and reintroduces the question of **class**, which had been superseded during the last two periods by questions of gender. Since Mulvey's 1975 essay on female spectator-positioning as male, the debate had moved on to consider that positioning as masochistic (Silberman, 1981), or as either masochistic or transvestite (Doane, 1984). But the significant breakthrough came in De Lauretis' (1984: 152) rereading of an earlier essay by Modleski (1982) from which she deduced that the female spectator enjoyed a double-desiring position. As a result of the mother/daughter relationship, in which the daughter never fully relinquishes her desire for her mother, the female spectator is positioned bi-sexually. And it is her constant shifting back and forth between the two positions (within film narrative) that creates woman's enigma (Modleski, 1988: 99). This shifting means also that women can never become fully socialized into patriarchy – which in turn causes men to fear women and leads them, on the one hand, to establish very strict boundaries between their own sex and the female sex and, on the other, to the need to 'kill off' the woman, either literally or by subjugation.

Explicit within Modleski and De Lauretis' arguments is that there is a female Oedipal trajectory and that the notion of lack and penis-envy is a patriarchal construct designed to preserve the status quo of male dominance and to side-step the issue of sexual difference. The fact that texts have been constructed around the castration **myth** does not, argue these feminists, make it any more real but merely points to the lengths to which patriarchal ideology will go out of its fear of the (m)other. Modleski and De Lauretis single out women's films as rare exceptions to this neglect or disavowal of a female Oedipal trajectory in cinema. But this does not necessarily make them a 'good thing'. In this genre, that is deliberately woman-centred to attract female audiences (the story is apparently told from the woman's point of view), the narrative often plays on the two positionalities of desire (female and male) that define the female's Oedipal situation (De Lauretis, 1984: 153). By the end of the film, however, this shifting back and forth will and must be brought to an end for the female protagonist (and, presumably, the female spectator). The female protagonist's desire for the female is suppressed in favour of desire for the male. This suppression is rendered even more explicit when the mother or surrogate mother is represented as quite monstrous, as the phallic mother. The Oedipal trajectory is still there and is completed. Hitchcock's *Rebecca* (1940) is one such film where the heroine eventually turns away from her evil set of surrogate mothers (especially Mrs Danvers) and enters into maturity (i.e. a full relationship with her father-figure husband).

This revelation of a female Oedipal trajectory, according to De Lauretis (1984), is not where feminist film theory must stop. After all 'the cinema works for Oedipus', which means that the heroine's double-desiring within the film narrative is eventually resolved along Oedipal lines. She will 'kill off' the mother and marry her father. The ideological operations of patriarchy cannot tolerate women sustaining their double desire. Why else in both *Now Voyager* (Irving Rapper, 1942) and (although a thriller and not a women's film per se) *Marnie* (Alfred Hitchcock, 1964) is it a male – more specifically with *Now Voyager* a psychiatrist – who rescues the heroine from the (phallic) mother? (For discussion of *Rebecca* see Modleski, 1988; for *Now Voyager* and *Marnie*, Kaplan, 1990.)

So far so good. However, feminist thinking by now was also perceiving the limitations of psychoanalysis. Although Lacan's notion of the construction of the subject through language/discourse opened up the debate on sexual difference, there still remained the problem that femininity was still defined in relation to masculinity – the feminine other to the masculine subject. Power relations were also seen in that light. There was a need to move on from questions of gender and to broaden the debate to include questions of class and power relations between women, of differences among the spectating female subjects, of the film industry as more than just an ideological institution or apparatus of patriarchy that renders women (in their multiplicity) invisible and constructs an essentialized Woman – and also to see these questions in relation to history. Only after this broadening of the debate could gender be reintroduced – because, as we shall explain, it had been relocated.

In the United Kingdom, feminists began to incorporate the historical–materialist approach of work done in cultural studies – which examined popular culture within the sphere of class, gender and race and in relation to power and resistances to that power. In the United States, feminists more specifically turned their attention to the French philosopher Michel Foucault and his theory of power as well as his 'notion of the social as a practical field in which technologies and discourses are deployed' (De Lauretis, 1984: 84). By technologies Foucault meant the conjuncture of power (*technos*) and knowledge (*logos*). *Logos* also means *discourse*. Thus *technologies* means *discourses of power*. This last point will be discussed more fully when we examine the effect of another of Foucault's theories, the technology of sex, on feminist theory. But first to power theory.

There are certainly problems with adapting Foucauldian theory to film theory (see De Lauretis, 1984: 84–102); but, in the sense that he more or less evacuates gendered subjectivity, it makes it easier to see what else is there. In arguing, in relation to power, that 'discourses produce domains of objects and there are modes of subjection' (Lapsley and Westlake, 1988: 101), Foucault points to a multiplicity of positionings; there are some where individuals have power, others where they do not. Foucault's statement (1977: 194) that 'power produces; in fact it produces reality' means that the individual, as a product and producer of power, is both a producer and a product of reality. But it also means that reality is produced from a multiplicity of positions within the power network. It is for this reason that Foucault argues that power comes from below. It is useful, he states, to see power *not* as hierarchized from the top down, but rather as being omnipresent (1978: 93), since all social relations are power relations. Domination evolves from a complex set of power strategies or investments, so it is possible to pinpoint not one source but, rather, several. Foucault also makes the point that, at all stratifications of power, there are resistances to those power relations and that these resistances, far from being in a position of 'exteriority in relation to power', coexist alongside the nexus of power relations (1978: 94–96). Finally, within the context of this synopsis, Foucault insists that power, in and of itself, is neither negative nor positive and that what does matter is how it gets exercised (1977: 194). That is, power in its exercise is a 'silent, secret civil war that re-inscribes conflict in various "social institutions, in economic inequalities, in language, in the bodies themselves of each and everyone of us"' (Merquior, 1985: 110–11).

In terms of feminist film theory, there are two main points of application of Foucault's thinking on power. First, the notion of cinema or the film industry (particularly Hollywood) as unique producer of the reality-effect no longer holds. The multiplicity of positions that produce the reality-effect include not just the textual operations of the film products themselves, but also the conditions or (im)positions of production and reception. Thus, the social relations of power between the different parts of the industry (i.e. scriptwriters, continuity and location assistants, camera and lighting crew, editors, **directors**, **producers**, **distributors**, exhibitors, and so on) are as much parts of the reality-effect as the spectators. (The use of the plural here draws attention to the fact that several scriptwriters, directors, etc. may be involved in the making of a single film, thus increasing the notion of a plurality of producers of meaning.) How that reality is produced is as much an effect of the power relations and resistances within the industry as it is within the **audiences**. The spectator can no longer be seen as the single construct of an ideological apparatus. Audiences are multiplicitous. There is not *a* 'female' or 'male' spectator but different socio-cultural individuals all busy producing reality as the film rolls by. Instead, age, gender, race, class and sexuality affect reception and meaning production. This broadening of the context in which a film is analysed has enabled feminist film theorists to move away from the male-centred effects of psychoanalytic readings, but without necessarily having to throw out psychoanalysis itself, which could be refocused within this context. In other words, femininity no longer needs to be defined in relation to masculinity; nor does it have to be perceived as a single construct: Woman. As Doane (1982: 87) says, femininity can now be seen as a position constructed 'within a network of power relations'. So, femininity becomes more than just a male construct. Femininity can be viewed as multiform and pluralistically positioned: *women*. By implication, femininity can be viewed, as De Lauretis says (1989: 25), from 'elsewhere' – from women's points of view.

This point leads on to the second, which concerns resistances. Resistances, as Foucault says, exist alongside the nexus of power relations. As always present, they filter through social and institutional strata – they leave their traces. This means also that they get caught up at some point within power relations, even though as resistances themselves they have moved on. I am talking here about counter-cinema. Interestingly, Foucault talks about resistances as counter-investments (1978: 97) – that is, counter-investments are the opposite of what occurs with power (whereby individuals have vested interests in adopting one discursive practice over another). In this light, counter-cinema counters the workings of power relations in mainstream cinema, but does not stand as exterior to them. It gives voice to a multiplicity of **discourses** that are in contradiction or counterpoint, thus simultaneously exposing the complex set of stratifications and power strategies that lead to domination (i.e. **hegemony**) and proposing a making visible of what is so palpably dissimulated by hegemonic investment (i.e. the discourses that get dropped). This means that patriarchal hegemony is revealed as no more of a fixed essence or totality than femininity. Rather, what this counter-cinema discloses is that patriarchy has come about as a result of investments in certain discourses over others (including psychoanalysis). By extension, these counter-cinematic practices expose the 'silent civil war' mentioned earlier that reinscribes conflict into institutions, language and individuals. In this respect, women's counter-cinema is about discursive disclosure, that is, the expression of other knowledges normally passed over in silence. Moreover, because counter-cinema is not exterior to power relations, those practices of exposure and disclosure get recuperated to some degree into dominant cinema. In the meantime, new resistances are in formation. Although recuperation into the mainstream does serve to normalize resistance, recuperation in Foucauldian terms means also to choose to invest in a discourse until now ignored and unpractised. Vested interests change as we know; so too, then, must the present hegemony, however slowly. As Claire Johnston (1976: 217) said several decades ago: 'we should seek to operate at all levels: within male-dominated cinema and outside of it.' The fact that women currently do this, although the numbers are still quite small, attests to that possibility for change.

If we bear this in mind, it should become clear why gender could be reintroduced into the debate. In his first volume of *The History of Sexuality* (1978), Foucault talks of the technologies of sex, by which he means the way in which sexuality is constructed by discourses that are in the culture's vested interests. In her brilliant and groundbreaking essay 'Technology of Gender', Teresa De Lauretis (1989: 2) argues that gender is also a product of various social technologies, including cinema. Foucault's discussion of the technology of sex, just like his theory of power, evacuates the idea of gendered subjectivity. But to do this, De Lauretis asserts, is to ignore the 'differential solicitation of male and female

subjects' and 'the conflicting investments of men and women in the discourses and practices of sexuality' (1989: 3), which is why she insists
on a technology of gender. In the first instance, De Lauretis is referring to
the ways in which the technologies of gender construct gender in terms of
sexual difference – in this respect institutional discourses, which are
'implemented through pedagogy, medicine, demography and economics' (ibid.: 12), are the power/knowledge investments producing 'meanings, values, knowledges and practices' as they concern or
interpolate or solicit the male and female subject differently (ibid.: 16).
Division of 'labour' is a prime example: Man as producer, Woman as
reproducer. As far as cinema is concerned, we have seen (above) how
feminist theory was already focusing on how discourses construct the
symbolic place of Woman. So the institutional representation of femininity was, as De Lauretis acknowledges, already under scrutiny. What is
different about this way of looking is that male and female subjects are
viewed not in relation to masculinity but in relation to different power
strategies.

In the second instance, De Lauretis is signalling that men and
women do not have the same investments in terms of discourses and
practices of sexuality. How could they, given their different histories?
Women 'have historically made different investments and thus have
taken up different positions in gender and sexual practices and identities'
(ibid.: 16). And it is at this point that De Lauretis starts to 'rough-map'
(her term) the possibilities for changes or dislocations in the social –
that is, power-relations of gender. She goes on to argue that
the 'female-gendered subject [is] one that is at once inside and outside
the ideology of gender' (ibid.: ix). We saw earlier how the ideology
of gender fixes Woman (as feminine, maternal or eternal); that is,
Woman fixed on-screen inside the ideology of gender – not woman as a
multiplicity of discourses, nor the multiplicity of women as this
Foucauldian approach makes possible to discuss. This multiplicitous
woman is the female-gendered subject outside the ideology of gender,
the one who, currently, is not represented on-screen; but the one that
is off-screen and, yet, by being off-screen, as off-screen space implies,
is inferred on-screen:

> [T]he movement in and out of gender as ideological representa-
> tion, which I propose characterizes the subject of feminism, is a
> movement back and forth between the representation of gender
> (in its male-centred frame of reference) and what that repre-
> sentation leaves out, or, more pointedly makes unrepresen-
> table. ... These two kinds of spaces are neither in opposition to one

another nor strung along a chain of signification, but they co-exist concurrently and in contradiction.

(De Lauretis, 1989: 26)

Even if mainstream cinema through its textual operations and industrial practices tries to conceal the on-screen space that the multiplicitous woman occupies, it no longer can, says De Lauretis, because the 'practices of feminism have shown them to be separate and heteronomous spaces' (1989: 26).

Feminist film theory over the past three decades or so has exercised considerable influence over film theory in general – and it continues (as indeed the ongoing publications make clear, see below). But the debates have to broaden further still. It has not yet, as Black feminists have said, dealt with the social and cultural experiences of all women. And the feminist voices have been predominantly White and middle class. The effects of cultural studies in the United Kingdom since the early 1980s have caused some change in this respect. The study of popular culture has not been a White-only area of investigation. Blacks and Asians are writing about and creating their own experiences. Increasingly, Black women are entering into the academy, particularly in the United States. The voices of Latin-American women, Asian women and Asiatic women as well as those of Black and White women are being heard and seen on the screen – and in growing numbers. Finally, the extension of feminist film theories to the area of world cinemas, as Soshin Chaudhuri (2006: 124) points out, 'offers further opportunities for these theories to be interrogated and refined through encounters with different cultural contexts'. Indeed, cross-cultural film criticism 'has emerged as one of the most exciting of feminist theory's current impact' (ibid.: 125). Rey Chow has investigated Chinese cinema through the feminist optic of the gaze and female voice (1995); Kyung Hyun Kim has used feminist readings of masculinity in crisis to discuss South Korean post-war cinema (2004).

The debates move on, as the reading list makes clear.

see also: **film theory**

For readings on feminist film theory see Brunsdon, 1986; Chaudhuri, 2006; Chow, 1995; De Lauretis, 1984, 1985, 1989, 2005; Doane *et al.*, 1984; Haskell, 1974; Johnston, 1973; Kaplan, 1983, 1990, 1997; Kuhn, 1982; Lesage, 1974; McCabe, 2004; Mellencamp, 1995; Moi, 1985; Mulvey, 1989; Penley, 1985, 1988; Whelelan, 2000. For readings against the grain see Creed, 1993; Doane, 1992; Kaplan, 1980; Kuhn, 1985; Mayne, 1984; Modleski, 1988; Penley, 1989; Williams, 1984. For profiles on women filmmakers see Kuhn and Radstone, 1990; Ramanathan, 2006. On female spectatorship see Pribham, 1988; Mayne, 1993; Hull *et al.*, 1982; Stacey, 1993. On Black feminism see Attile and Blackwood, 1986; Davis, 1981; Davies *et al.*, 1987; hooks, 1981; Hull *et al.*, 1982; Moraga and Anzaldua, 1981.

FILM NOIR

This is a term coined by French film critics in 1946 to designate a particular type of American **thriller** film. After the liberation of France in 1944, which saw the lifting of the ban (imposed by the occupying Germans) on the importation of American films, French screens were inundated with **Hollywood** products, including a new type of thriller. By analogy with the label given by the French to categorize hard-boiled detective novels – *roman noir* – the term *film noir* was coined to define this new-looking film. The film noir, predominantly a **B-movie**, is often referred to as a sub-genre of the crime **thriller** or **gangster** movie – although as a style it can also be found in other genres (e.g. **melodrama**, **Western**). This is why other critics see film noir as a movement rather than a **genre**. These critics point to the fact that, like all other film movements, film noir emerged from a period of political instability: 1941 to 1958, the time of World War Two and the Cold War. In the United States, this was a time of repressed insecurity and paranoia: the American Dream seemed in tatters and American national identity under severe strain. During the war, women had moved into the workforce and had expanded their horizons beyond the domestic sphere; at the same time men were removed from that sphere – which they had controlled – to go to fight. The men's return to peacetime was a period of maladjustment: what had 'their' women been up to? Where was their role at work and in the political culture generally? And what had they fought the war for, only to find the United States involved in a new kind of hostility based in suspicion and paranoia? So the question of national identity was also bound up with the question of masculine identity. But it is also the case that many of these early noirs (e.g. *The Maltese Falcon*, John Huston, 1941) were based on detective thrillers written in the inter-war years (called pulp-fiction, with hard-boiled private eyes such as Sam Spade/Humphrey Bogart). For example, Dashiel Hammett's *The Maltese Falcon* was published in 1930. So this dark mood is as much a response to the Great War and the economic disaster of the late 1920s, the Great Depression (1929-38) as it is to the effects of World War Two.

Rather than a genre or movement it might be safer to say that film noir is above all a visual style which came about as a result of political circumstance and cross-fertilization. Film noir has a style of cinematography that emphasizes the impression of night-time photography with high-contrast lighting, occasional low-key lighting, deep shadows and oblique angles to create a sense of dread and anxiety. The various claims, therefore, to a single heritage are not really in order. The French claimed a first with Marcel Carné's *Le Jour se lève* (1939) – a very dark film; the Americans believed they had strong claims to the honour with their thriller films of the 1940s (e.g. arguably the first one, John Huston's *The Maltese Falcon*, 1941). Certainly the visual **codes** given to express the deep pessimism of the **French poetic realist** films of the latter part of the 1930s (exemplified by the work of Carné, Julien Duvivier and Jean Renoir) were in part antecedents to the film noir. But so too was the 1920s **German expressionist** style insofar as the distorted effects created by **lighting**, **setting** and use of shadows reflected inner turmoil and alienation so associated with film noir. However, it would be political events that would complete the cross-fertilization. In the late 1930s and early 1940s, as the threat of war increased and anti-Semitic pogroms continued, a considerable number of European filmmakers and technicians fled to America, more particularly Hollywood. The most significant impact was made by the émigré filmmakers who had worked in Germany and who were associated in one way or another with German expressionism. Fritz Lang, Josef von Sternberg, Billy Wilder, Robert Siodmak, Otto Preminger, Douglas Sirk, Max Ophuls are but the most famous names.

There are three main characteristics of film noir which emanate from its primary founding on the principle of contrastive lighting: chiaroscuro (*clair-obscur*/light-dark) – the highly stylized visual style which is matched by the stylized **narrative** which is matched, in turn, by the stylized stereotypes – particularly of women. The essential ingredients of a film noir are its specific location or setting, its high-contrast lighting as well as its low-key lighting, a particular kind of psychology associated with the protagonist, and a sense of social malaise, pessimism, suspicion and gloom (not surprising given the political conjuncture of the time). The setting is city-bound and generally a composite of rain-washed streets and interiors (both dimly lit), tightly framed shots often with extreme camera angles – all reminiscent of German expressionism. The cityscape is fraught with danger and corruption, the shadowy ill-lit streets reflecting the blurred moral and intellectual values as well as the difficulty in discerning truth. Characters are similarly unclear, as is evidenced by the way their bodies are lit and framed: half in the shadows, fragmented. The net effect is one of claustrophobia, underscoring the sense of malaise and tension. The protagonist (according to classic canons the 'hero' is a male) is often side-lighted to enhance the profile from one side and leaving the other half of the face in the dark, thus pointing to the moral ambiguity of this main character who is neither a knight in shining armour nor completely bad (interestingly the prototype for this characterization goes back at least as far as Edward G. Robinson's gangster portrayal in *Little Caesar*, Mervyn LeRoy, 1930). He usually mistreats or ignores his 'woman' (either the wife, very much tucked away out of the city, or the moll with the golden heart who invariably sees the 'truth') and gets hooked on a *femme fatale* who, more often than not according to the **preferred reading**, is the perpetrator of all his troubles (see *Double Indemnity*, Billy Wilder, and *Murder My Sweet*, Edward Dmytryk, both 1944). This 'hero' is often obsessive and neurotic and equally capable of betrayal of his *femme fatale*. The ambiguity of his character is paralleled by the contortions of the plot, whose complexities seem unresolvable, particularly by the hero, who, until the very end, seems confused and unclear about what is happening. In this respect, film noir is about power relations and sexual identity. The power the *femme fatale* exerts over the hero is his own doing, because he has over-invested in his construction of her **sexuality** at the expense of his own **subjectivity**. He has allowed her to be on top because of his own insecurities about who he is. (For a full discussion of this crisis in masculinity see Krutnik, 1991.)

But that's only half the story, because film noir is not so clear-cut in its misogyny. Film noir gives a very central role to the *femme fatale* and privileges her as active, intelligent, powerful, dominant and in charge of her own sexuality – at least until the end of the film when she pays for it (through death or submission to the patriarchal system). In this respect, she constitutes a break with **classical Hollywood cinema**'s representation of woman (as mother/whore, wife/mistress – passive). These women are interested only in themselves (as the frequent reflections of them in mirrors attest) and in getting enough money by all means foul, to guarantee their independence. By being in contradiction with the ideological construct of women, such an image construction makes readings against the grain eminently possible. As Janey Place (1980: 37) says, as far as these women are concerned, 'It is not their inevitable demise we remember but rather their strong, dangerous and above all, exciting sexuality.' These women are symbols of 'unnatural' phallic power: toting guns and cigarette holders like the best of the men – to get what they want. They move about easily in traditionally male spaces, bars, etc. They might even dress like men with their very tailored suits with broad shoulder-pads; or they might slink out of the shadows, thigh-first, dressed in clinging sequinned evening gowns – playing the **female masquerade** to the hilt. Either way, they are mysterious, ambiguous and deadly (guns and looks can kill). In both instances, they are empowered by their sexuality. (Examples are *Woman in the Window*, Fritz Lang, 1944; *Gilda*, Charles Vidor, 1946; *Kiss Me Deadly*, Robert Aldrich, 1955.)

Ultimately, film noir is not about investigating a murder, although it might at first appear to be. Generally speaking, in the film noir the woman is central to the intrigue and it is, therefore, she who becomes the object of the male's investigation. But, as you will have guessed, it is less her role in the intrigue that is under investigation, much more her sexuality because it is that which threatens the male quest for resolution. The **ideological** contradiction she opens up by being a strong, active, sexually expressive female must be closed off, contained. For that is the **diegetic** logic and visual strategy of film noir. However, there are obvious difficulties in containing this woman. And this is reflected by the narrative strategies inherent in film noir. There is, as Gledhill (1980: 14) points out, a proliferation of points of view. Whose voice do we hear through these multiple **discourses** each telling a story? Who has the voice of author/ity? The devices used in film noir – voice-over and **flashback**s (which primarily privilege the male point of view), diegetic narratives issued by different characters (the woman, the police, the private eye) – are just so many discourses vying for dominance. In the end, film noir is about which voice is going to gain control over the storytelling and – in the end – control over the image of the woman (ibid.: 17). This struggle occurs both between men and between the man and the woman, but, more importantly, what this struggle foregrounds is the fact that the woman's image is just that: a male construct – which 'suggests another place behind the image where woman might be' (ibid.: 17) – the female masquerade at its most potent. Food for feminist thought, but not the director's cut! There has to be closure – which means implicitly a closing-off of the ideological contradictions that such a suggestion makes plain. And in the end, closure does occur, but at a price. It is the male voice (that of the Symbolic Order, the Law of the Father) that completes the investigation (see **psychoanalysis: Imaginary/Symbolic**). However, as the multiplicity of points of view that prevailed until the closing moments show, guilt is not easily ascribed to only one person. Because of the lack of clarity, it is not quite so easy to 'Put the blame on Mame, boys'. (For an interesting play on female/male subjectivities see *Mildred Pierce*, Michael Curtiz, 1945. Of the three flashbacks, the first two are hers, the last and 'truthful' one is that of the male and representative of the law, the police detective.)

There are contextual reasons for this struggle for dominance. As Janey Place (1980: 36) says, **myths** do not only mediate dominant ideology, they are also 'responsive to the *repressed* needs of culture'. Thus, in film noir, this construction and subsequent destruction of the sexually assertive woman must be viewed within the economic and political climate of the 1940s and 1950s. I have already mentioned the repressed insecurity and paranoia respective to the political climate of those two decades. On the economic front, thanks to World War Two, women went into work in the 1940s in huge numbers to help the war effort – and in many cases did so by replacing 'their' men who were at war. By the end of the war, these formerly independent women were being pushed back into the family and the domestic sphere. Thus, as social text, film noir challenges the family by its absence, as does the film noir woman who, as sexually independent, contributes to the instability of the world in which the male protagonist finds himself. The 1940s film noir can be read, then, as an expression of male concern at women's growing economic and sexual independence and a fear of the men's own place in society once they returned from war. The 1950s film noir functioned to reassert the value of family life, not just so that the men could get their jobs back, but so that national identity, so much under siege in post-war United States, could be reasserted. We see here how film noir articulated the repressed needs of American culture. Furthermore, the masochistic sexual fantasies implicit in the threat the *femme fatale* poses for the male protagonist are, in this respect, tied up with questions of (male) identity. But they are 'nothing' really in relation to the sadistic closures designed for the woman: death, being outcast, or being reintegrated into the family.

A sign that film noir has grabbed the imagination in a deep sense as a generic or sub-generic type is not just that it continues to be *re*-produced (despite the fact that intrinsically it is associated with a particular period in social history, early 1940s to late 1950s), but that so much continues to be written about it (to date, 2017, this new millennium has seen the publication of at least 100 new books on the subject). In terms of film production, therefore, we get nostalgic remakes of noir movies (*The Man Who Wasn't There*, Joel Coen, 2001), nostalgic homages to the earlier format (Rian Johnson's hard-boiled homage to Dashiel Hammet and Billy Wilder, *Brick*, 2005; Ryan Gosling as a sort of Humphrey Bogart in *Drive*, Nicolas Winding Refn, 2011), or alternatively neo-noirs which hark back to that period of Hollywood film history (*LA Confidential*, Hanson, 1997). In terms of the continued critical writing, we can only surmise that the troubling nature of noir-ness has created a mystique all its own and, thereby, an endless desire to be revisiting and unravelling the nostalgic territories of the uncanny.

see also: **genre** and **female masquerade**

For further reading see Cameron, 1992; Conard, 2006; Copjec, 1993; Fay and Nielan, 2010; Flory, 2008; Kaplan, 1980; Krutnik, 1991; Luhr, 2012; Modleski, 1988; Stephens, 1995. Of this millennium: Dickos, 2002; Dimendberg, 2004; Hare, 2003, 2004; Mason, 2002; Pettey and Palmer, 2014a, 2014b, 2014c; Phillips, 2000; Porfirio *et al.*, 2002; Spicer, 2002; Schwartz, 2001; Slocum, 2001.

FILM THEORY

This entry limits itself to a reasonably brief history of the development of theory since the beginning of the twentieth century. Specific details of major developments are given in other entries.

Although there is no attempt to be deterministic here, there does appear to be a quite convenient way of carving up film theory into epochs of theory-pluralism and theory-monism. Indeed, we can determine three epochs: 1910s to 1930s, a period of pluralism; 1940s to 1960s, a period of serially monistic theories; 1970s to 2010s, pluralism once more.

1910s to 1930s – theory-pluralism

Cinema was very quickly perceived to be an art form. Arguably the genesis of film theory was in France. The earliest reference to film as art occurred with the start, in 1908, of Film d'Art's productions (the first of which was *L'Assassinat du duc de Guise*, set to the music of Saint-Saëns). However, one of the earliest attempts to align cinema with other arts can be found in the filmmaker Louis Feuillade's advance publicity sheet *Le Film esthétique* (1910) for his film series. In his manifesto he begged the question: since film appeals to our sight and, therefore, has as its natural origins painting and the theatre, surely cinema can provide those same aesthetic sensations? He also perceived cinema as a popular art and as an economic art (a synergy between technology and the aesthetic) and as an artistic economy (art closely allied with capital). A year later, Ricciotto Canudo published in France his manifesto 'The Birth of a Sixth Art', in which he established the two main lines of debate that would preoccupy theorists well into the 1920s and in some respects into the 1930s: the debate around cinema's **realism**, on the one hand and, on the other, around a pure non-representational cinema based on form and rhythm.

A few years later a German psychologist, Hugo Münsterberg, introduced the idea that cinema was not filmed reality, but a psychological and aesthetic process that revealed our mental experiences. After World War One, the debate widened further, mainly among French critics and filmmakers, and addressed issues of high and popular art, realist versus naturalist film, the **spectator**–screen relationship, **editing** styles (a debate much influenced by the **Soviet cinema** of the 1920s), simultaneity, **subjectivity**, the unconscious and the **psychoanalytical** potential of film, **auteur** cinema versus script-led cinema, cinema as rhythm and as **sign**. In the 1930s, following the advent of **sound**, the ground shifted and the debate centred on the very polemical issue of whether sound was a good or bad thing for the aesthetics of cinema. Certain critics claimed that it was the death-knell for **experimental** cinema; others thought that it brought with it the chance of a new radicalization of cinema. By the advent of World War Two, film theory could be said to fall into two general camps: the realist, ontological theorists (Balász, Bazin and Kracauer) who argued that film was linked with social praxis, that is, it acted as a **transparence** on society and its interactions with individuals, but was also revelatory of mental states; the formalists (Eisenstein and Pudovkin), for their part, looked to the compositional aesthetics of film and advocated film's artificiality as key to meaning-production.

1940s to 1960s – theory-monism

This was predominantly the period where the search was on, particularly after 1946, for a total theory. Speculatively, we could say that this desire for total theory is easily understandable in the light, postwar, of the Jewish and atomic holocausts – to such irrational acts of inhumanity, surely, only a single unified vision could provide security and stability. The two main theories to mention here are, first, the **auteur theory** (1950s) and, second, **structuralism** (1960s), although we should also point out that these two were preceded by Alexandre Astruc's (1948) concept of cinema as language (*caméra-stylo* as he defined it).

Both single-theory concepts were soon discovered to be too limiting. As explained in the auteur entry, the effect of seeing film as a matter of authorial signs (whether stylistic or thematic) was too limiting, denying the other structures and production practices that go into making a film. It was also a conservative romantic aesthetic insofar as the filmmaker was singled out as the aesthetic genius. Finally it was fraught because it introduced the idea of 'great' directors.

Similarly, structuralism and auteur-structuralism, which 'replaced' auteur theory in the 1960s, ran into difficulties, this time of total theory crushing the aesthetic. Structuralism was a theory which, it was believed, could be applied to all aspects of society and culture. However, it ended up in rigid formalism which removed any discussion of pleasure in the viewing. Although this theory purported to reveal all hidden structures behind filmmaking (modes of production, impact of **stars** on choices, socio-historical context of production and so on), nonetheless it still continued to focus on the filmmaker and her or his product – hence the term *auteur-structuralism*. The key theorist in this debate as it concerned cinema was the semiotician Christian Metz (1971, 1972), who devised a linguistic paradigm that could account for all elements of a film's composition – almost a grammar of film (see **semiotics**). Analysing film this way meant that a critic could scientifically and objectively evaluate a film and at the same time determine the style of a particular auteur or filmmaker and indeed determine also if a particular film was consistent with that filmmaker's style. The focus, therefore, was on the hidden structures and codes in the text and in this respect it answered the question of how the text comes to be. It did not, however, determine how it comes to have meaning. Thus, ultimately the limitation of this total theory was its formalism (for fuller discussion see **auteur theory**, **structuralism**).

1970s to 2010s – theory-pluralism

Total theory made it evident that a single theory would never be sufficient to explain and analyse film. Where in this total theory, for example, could one talk about the **spectator**–text relationship? However, there was no need to throw the baby out with the bathwater, hence the term *post-structuralism*. Psychoanalysis and semiotics, in their structuralist phase, had started to shatter the concept of the unity of the auteur. The effects of **deconstruction** theory, introduced by Jacques Derrida around 1967, would help to do the rest. Deconstruction helped to recentre the theory debate in a pluralistic context. In essence, deconstruction stipulates that a text is not transparent, natural or innocent and therefore must be unpicked, deconstructed. The non-transparency must be investigated to show just how many texts there are – all producing meaning. There is no longer any single reading of a text, nor indeed is there any final reading.

Post-structuralism, then, did several things. It defined the auteur's place within the textual process – the auteur was now a figure constructed out of her or his films (a far less authoritative position). It established the importance of **intertextuality** – the effects of different texts upon one another. There is no such thing as a 'pure' text, all texts have intertextual relations with others. As far as film is concerned, this means relations with other films and of course with the 'invisible' texts such as the modes of production, the dynamics between actors, crew and filmmaker (and so on). Post-structuralism also established the fact that film has **ideological** effects, therefore the question of the **subject** comes into play (who is the subject: the text, the auteur, the spectator? All three, as it transpires). What also comes into play is the question of the effects of the enunciating text (the film as performance) upon the spectator. In the final analysis, post-structuralism opened up textual analysis to a pluralism of approaches which did not reduce the text to the status of object of investigation but as much a subject as those reading, writing or producing it.

During the 1970s and 1980s, in Anglo-Saxon countries, the impact on film studies of cultural studies (dealing amongst other issues with questions of **class**) and subsequently (in the 1980s–90s) of **postcolonial theory** also helped to push the pluralistic nature of film theory forward. As indeed did another significant area of theory, **feminist film theory**. Beginning in the mid-1970s (with the writings of Johnston, Mulvey), and still ongoing, feminist film theory reopened the whole question of gendered **subjectivity** and **agency**, not addressed since the 1920s. Who held the gaze, within and without the screen, was a fundamental issue raised in this area. **Genre** and **gender** also generated questions: if certain film-genres were gender specific (e.g. **Westerns** for men, **melodrama** for women), what were the ideological operations at work and what were the spectator–text relationships depending on what sort of genre was being viewed? Further, given the ostensible gendered subjectivity of the viewer, what could be said about pleasure in viewing?

Gender studies, implicit in the above, led to debates surrounding performance (see Butler, 1990) and this in turn led, in the mid-1990s, onto a new swathe of theoretical debates surrounding the body. Steven Shaviro's seminal and polemical 1993 study *The Cinematic Body* (*Theory out of Bounds*) set the ball rolling. Shaviro challenged the primacy of the psychoanalytical route adopted in film studies of the 1970s to 1980s. He advocated an approach to film that focused on bodies and their affects (including the body of the film text itself and its ability to create physical–visceral responses). Laura Marks pursued the logic of body theory in her discussion of the film as skin (*The Skin of the Film: Intercultural Cinema, Embodiment, and the Senses*, 2000) – which examined the way in which cinema transmits the physical sense of space and memory (which itself is based in our senses: smell, touch, hearing, sight and taste). Marks discussed the concept of haptic visuality (the ability of film to make us feel – have a tactile, as well as other sensory responses) to show how film enables an experience of cinema as a multi-sensory affect and an embodiment of culture.

This focus on the body has led, unsurprisingly perhaps, to an opening up of film theory to the fields of science and philosophy as a means of discussing the relationship between cinema, perception and the body. Thus, some theorists have turned to the phenomenology (the philosophy of experience) of Merleau-Ponty and investigated its relevance to film spectatorship and film practice. As Frampton explains (2006: 40), in terms of spectatorship, film 'shows us the expression of mind in the world'; it allows us a strange, distanced possession of the world. But, in terms of film practice, cinema also owns the objects and characters that it manifests in its images. Thus, the experience in cinema is double: 'the filmgoer's experience of the film, and the film's experience of its characters and objects' (Frampton, 2006: 41). According to this approach, film is a mechanistic assemblage that brings itself into being (as if a body, a textual body) and in so doing allows for social meaning (a body-text that has meaning and can be read). In its being-ness, time and space are brought together as synthesized in its experience; and as such we can talk about the film-body (see Sobchack, 1993). Other theorists look to Deleuze and his vision of cinema as time and movement (see entry on **movement-image/time-image**). Others, still, have sought an alliance with cognitivism as a way of explaining how we see, feel and understand film, arguing that perceptions and sensations are processed by the brain. The introduction into film theory of evolutionary theory, which seeks to reveal how human biology as well as human culture determine how films are made and experienced, was the next step along this more cognitive approach. Torben Grodal, in his polemical study (*Embodied Visions: Evolution, Emotion, Culture and Film*, 2009), provides the first really detailed model of an evolutionary theory of film. Grodal uses the breakthroughs of modern brain-science to explain central features of film aesthetics and to construct a general model of aesthetic experience – what he terms the PECMA flow model (perception, emotion, cognition, motor action) – that demonstrates the movement of information and emotions in the brain when viewing film. Grodal also reflects on social issues at the intersection of film theory and neuropsychology. These include moral problems in film viewing, how we experience realism and character identification, and the value of the subjective forms that cinema uniquely elaborates. Finally, in this domain of analytical approaches emanating from science and philosophy, some theorists argue, most convincingly of all, that the relation between cinema, perception and the spectator is both a visual and an embodied one and 'is inherently linked to the body and the senses' (Elsaesser and Hagener, 2009: 169 and 173).

Thus, we are in the land of a pluralism of theories – they are to be used as a crafted set of tools to investigate the complex artefact that is film. Clearly there is no single theory, no unified theory; nor should we really seek for such a constraining uniformity.

For further reading see: Downing and Saxton, 2010; Heath, 1978; Schweinitz, 2011; Shaviro, 1993; Sobchack, 1992; for clear discussions of theories up until the early 1990s see Andrew, 1984; Lapsley and Westlake, 1988 reprinted 1992; for overviews see Furstenau, 2010; Trifonova, 2009; for new holistic approaches see Elsaesser and Hagener, 2009; Grodal, 2009; for film and philosophy see Frampton, 2006; Marks, 2000; Rodowick, 2010; Shaviro, 1993; Sobchack, 1993.

FLASHBACK

A **narrative** device used in film (as in literature) to go back in time to an earlier moment in a character's life and/or history and to narrate that moment. Flashbacks, then, are most clearly marked as **subjective** moments within that narrative. Flashbacks are a cinematic representation of memory and of history and, ultimately of subjective truth. Interestingly, flashbacks date back to the very beginnings of film history – at least as early as 1901 with Ferdinand Zecca's *Histoire d'un crime* – thus coinciding with the birth and burgeoning of **psychoanalysis**. In this respect flashbacks are closely aligned therefore with the workings of the psyche and an individual's interpretation of history. Furthermore, because flashbacks almost always serve to resolve an enigma (a murder, a state of mental disorder, etc.), they are by nature investigative or confessional, which again brings them close to the process of psychoanalysis. Finally, because they also reconstruct history, flashbacks can serve nationalistic purposes or conversely can be used to question certain social values.

Maureen Turim's excellent and thorough analysis, *Flashbacks in Film: Memory and History* (1989), is still the only major study on this cinematic trope (for a synopsis I refer you to this entry in the fourth edition of *Cinema Studies: The Key Concepts*).

FREE CINEMA (BRITAIN)

According to Lindsay Anderson, one of the founders of Free Cinema, this movement coincided with the explosion onto the theatre boards of John Osborne's *Look Back in Anger* (1956). Free Cinema was a term Anderson coined, in 1956, to designate a series of documentaries and shorts he was putting together for screenings at the National Film Theatre. The first programme (February 1956), which launched the manifesto 'Free Cinema', contained three films: *O Dreamland* (Anderson, 1953), *Momma Don't Allow* (Reisz and Richardson, 1955) and *Together* (Mazzetti, 1956). In the manifesto, Anderson and a small group of filmmakers called for a change in the way British cinema was being made and committed themselves to innovation on both a technical and **narrative** level. There were six programmes in all (from 1956 to 1959) and the basic ethos linking the films, which included the work of French, Italian and Polish filmmakers, was that the films were free because they were made outside the framework of the film industry and because their statements, which were commentaries on contemporary society, were entirely personal. Although these films were personal statements, nonetheless, there was a strong emphasis on the relationship between art and society (including an openness to representations of the working **class**) and an insistence that the filmmakers were committed to the values expressed in their work. Thus, in the context of the first programme, Anderson's film was about ordinary people enjoying a fair at Margate, Reisz and Richardson's about youth dance culture (the jive) and Lorenza Mazzetti's about two deaf men working as East End dockers. Although distinct as narratives, nonetheless, the unifying theme was the representation of the working classes and, in terms of look, the use of lightweight cameras giving a granular socio-realist appearance to the **documentary**. Mazzetti's film, which was the longest at fifty-two minutes, was arguably the one that most closely resembled a feature film (it shows how these two men survive not just the bleakness of London's East End but also finally turn the tables on those who continuously abuse their deafness).

Rather than a movement, however, we should speak of a tendency in cinema. First, because the Free Cinema programme itself was international and made up of an eclectic grouping of films made by young contemporary filmmakers – and as such represented the deep-felt need for new voices to be heard: this constitutes an appeal, not a movement. Second, because, on a national scale, Free Cinema films were produced by only a handful of filmmakers, and while they may have shared common ideals, they had no style in common with the exception of the work of the three filmmakers who founded this so-called movement: Lindsay Anderson, Karel Reisz and Tony Richardson. As Richardson himself stated, in an interview in *The Listener* (2 May 1968), Free Cinema was a label invented to designate a number of documentary films made by the three filmmakers during the 1950s; it was not a case of a movement but a sharing of common ideals where cinema was concerned. In any event, the legacy of Free Cinema is closely related to the work of these three filmmakers and it is on this that the rest of this entry will focus. (For a wider debate see Lovell and Hillier, 1972.)

Among the common ideals held by these filmmakers, two stand out as most significant: first, documentary films should be made free from all commercial pressures and, second, they need to be inflected with a more humanist and poetic approach. In this respect, Free Cinema was born out of the 1930s documentary tradition of Humphrey Jennings rather than John Grierson whom this group of filmmakers criticized (see **documentary** entry). A third important point in relation to the emergence of this cinema is that both Anderson and Reisz were critics for the film review *Sequence* (launched by Anderson in 1946), and that it is out of writings for this review that the ethos of Free Cinema was born. This review criticized the British documentary for its conformity and apathy and feature film for its conventionality and lack of aesthetic experimentation. *Sequence* was a new departure in film criticism. In their articles, Anderson and Reisz examined the style rather than the content of a film and deplored British cinema's adherence to **classical narrative cinema**. They denounced the bourgeois, suburban tradition inherent in this cinema and accused it, through its lack of **transparence** on the working class, of avoiding reality.

These three Free Cinema filmmakers were unanimous in their condemnation of the monopolizing practices of the British film industry. In the 1950s, full feature films were produced by only two companies: Rank Organisation and ABC (a branch of Warner Brothers). And the films that predominated were, according to Anderson *et al.*, insipid **comedies** or **war films** that glorified the British fighters, trivialized the horrors of war and perpetuated the tradition of the class system (*The Dam Busters*, Michael Anderson,

1955, being exemplary of this second type of film). Needless to say, financing for their own film projects was not forthcoming from Rank or ABC! On the whole they had to self-finance, which is why their first films were shorts or documentaries. They did, however, manage to obtain some resourcing from the British Film Institute's Experimental Film Fund and the giant industrial company Ford of Dagenham. Ford commissioned a series of documentaries – entitled *Look at Britain* – of which Free Cinema were responsible for two: Anderson's *Every Day Except Christmas*, 1957, and Reisz's *We are the Lambeth Boys*, 1959. The BFI Experimental Fund produced five films: *Momma Don't Allow* (Richardson and Reisz, 1956), *Together* (Lorenza Mazzetti, 1956), *Nice Time* (Alain Tanner and Claude Goretta, 1957), *Refuge England* (Robert Vas, 1959) and *Enginemen* (Michael Grisby, 1959).

The primary characteristic of these filmmakers' documentaries and shorts was their belief in the importance of everyday life and people. They were committed to representing working-class life as it was lived, not as it was imagined. In their images nothing is forced, giving an authenticity that makes their films close in spirit to the humanism of Jennings' documentaries (what Anderson (1954) terms 'public poetry'). What links the three filmmakers is the fact that their work focuses on the individual and the collective; that, in terms of **editing**, they use juxtaposing rhythms (slow or fast). Indeed, their rhythmic editing had strong connotations with jazz – deliberately since jazz was part of the working-class subculture (*Momma Don't Allow* deals explicitly with jazz and dancing as a social and sexual liberation for the working-class youth). The other important link between the three is the continuity in the style of their films, undoubtedly due to the presence on four out of their six Free Cinema films of the cameraman Walter Lassally. Finally, a contributing factor to the continuity in their style was the homage their films paid to those filmmakers they considered constituted their own heritage: John Ford, Marcel Carné, Jean Cocteau, Robert Flaherty Jean Grémillon, Humphrey Jennings, Jean Renoir, Vittorio De Sica, Arne Sucksdorff and Jean Vigo.

What of the legacy of the Free Cinema? Certain critics claim that it left very little trace at all, and that the **British New Wave Cinema** of the late 1950s (of which *Look Back in Anger*, Richardson, 1959, was the first film) was not, as other critics claimed, a direct outcome of Free Cinema but of the literature and theatre of the time. The 'truth' of course lies somewhere in between: the New Wave movement came out of the conjuncture of literary trends and the Free Cinema documentary tendency. This argument is sustained by the fact that the names of these three filmmakers reappear as directors of these

New Wave films. In 1959, Tony Richardson founded a production company with John Osborne, Woodfall Films (with financial support from Bryanston Films, a subsidiary of British Lion). This company produced most of the New Wave films. Richardson, who had earlier directed the stage performance of *Look Back in Anger*, now made it into a film. Reisz made *Saturday Night and Sunday Morning* (1960) and Anderson *This Sporting Life* (1963). All these were key films for British cinema.

For more details of this legacy see **British New Wave**.

FRENCH NEW WAVE/*NOUVELLE VAGUE*

Not really a movement, but certainly an important moment in film history, the French New Wave came about in the late 1950s, although, as we shall see, it did have precursors. The term refers to films made, on the whole, by a new generation of French filmmakers which were low-budget and, most importantly, went against the prevailing trends in 1950s cinema of literary **adaptations, costume dramas** and massive co-productions – a cinema which had been labelled by the *Cahiers du cinéma* group as the *'cinéma de papa'* (daddy's cinema; see **auteur**).

The term *Nouvelle Vague* was not in the first instance associated with filmmaking. Indeed, it was originally coined in the late 1950s by Françoise Giroud, editor of the then centre-left weekly *L'Express*, to refer to the new socially active youth **class**. However, the term very quickly became associated with current trends in cinema because of the appeal of the youthful actor Gérard Philipe and, more especially, the tremendous success of twenty-eight-year-old Roger Vadim's *Et Dieu créa la femme* (1956) and the mythologizing effect it had on Brigitte Bardot. This meant that producers in the late 1950s wanted work made by 'young ones' – both on-screen and behind the camera. This demand helped to propel a new wave of filmmakers onto the screen. This was not the exclusive reason, however, for this 'new' cinema. In demographic terms, the older guard of filmmakers, who had held the reins from the 1930s through to the 1950s, were ageing fast or dying off. This created a gap for a new wave of filmmakers (some 170 in the period 1959–63) who in turn became associated in people's minds with the *Nouvelle Vague*. In the collective memory, all that remains of the *Nouvelle Vague* today is this group of filmmakers – not the new youth class. A misnomer made **myth**.

Misnomer or not, an important effect of this demand for a *jeune cinéma* was that it created the myth that those making it were all young. There was also a commonly held belief that, because some of the more notorious first films of the New Wave to hit the screens were made by critics from the influential *Cahiers du cinéma* group (Claude Chabrol, Jean-Luc Godard, Jacques Rivette, Eric Rohmer, François Truffaut), all of this cinema came from filmmakers who had not been through the normal circuit of assistantship to established **directors**. The facts attest differently. The filmmakers loosely grouped into this so-called *jeune cinéma* were in their early thirties. During the period 1959 to 1960, of the sixty-seven filmmakers making their first feature film, only 55 per cent came from backgrounds not directly attached to filmmaking, and the remaining 45 per cent was made up of film assistants and short-film directors (such as Alain Resnais and Agnès Varda).

Another myth perpetuated was that this cinema coincided with the birth, in 1958, of the Fifth Republic. Two films, *Le Beau Serge* (Chabrol, 1958) and *Les 400 Coups* (Truffaut, 1959), were seen as the trail-blazers of this New Wave, shortly followed by Godard's *À bout de souffle* (1959) and Resnais' *Hiroshima mon amour* (1959). History is not so convenient. There were of course precursors. On the one hand, there was the influence on filmmaking practices of the theoretical writing, primarily emanating from the *Cahiers du cinéma* journals of the 1950s, which advocated the primacy of the **auteur** and **mise-en-scène**. And, on the other, there were filmmakers who were already making low-budget, non-studio films that went counter to **dominant cinematic** practices of the 1950s. They were just not associated with any group. In fact Agnès Varda's 1954 film *La Pointe courte* is often cited as the herald of this movement. A first set of hallmarks of Varda's style that are recognizable in the New Wave films are the modes of production and the **counter-cinema** practices she put in place such as location shooting, use of non-professional actors (or unknown ones from the theatre, such as the young Philippe Noiret), a deliberate **distanciation** so that **spectator-identification** cannot occur, no necessary sense of chronology or **classical narrative**. Her subversion of **genres**, her use of counterpoint, of juxtaposing two stories – one based in the personal, the other in the social – and her deliberately disorienting **editing** style are other important features of her cinematic style, which Resnais for one has acknowledged as influencing his own filmmaking practices.

Another last myth that needs examining is the belief that because this cinema was controversial or different in style it was also a radical and political cinema. This is predominantly not true: the New Wave filmmakers were largely non-politicized. If their films had any political aura, it came down to the fact that some filmmakers carried on the 1930s tradition of criticizing the bourgeoisie, but now placed their narratives in contemporary **discourses** – that is, viewing the bourgeoisie from the youth point of view. The other reason why the New Wave might have been perceived as political, or a reason *post facto*, is that there were in fact two New Waves. The first occurred in the period 1958 to 1962, the other during 1966 to 1968. The first New Wave was anarchic, but only in relation to what preceded it: the *cinéma de papa*. The second New Wave was more clearly a politicized cinema. Hindsight may have conflated the two moments into one and perceived it as political. Politicized or not, both were to inform and have an impact on future cinemas (for more details, see Hayward 2005: 205–37).

Although this cinema was criticized for its focus on the individual – with its emphasis on the auteur and the confessional style of the films – beyond its impact on narrative and aesthetics, it left one other very important legacy. Thanks to the huge influx of filmmakers into the industry (around 170), production practices had to be reconsidered. For money to be spread around, films had to be low-budget. Given the number of filmmakers, the cheaper, lightweight camera came into its own. As a result there was a democratization of the camera. This pioneering effect was to make the camera more accessible to voices formerly marginalized. Thus, by the 1970s and 1980s, women, Blacks and Beurs (the Arab community in France) were entering filmmaking.

see also: **auteur/auteur theory**

For further reading see Godard, 1980; Hayward, 2005; Kline, 1992; Marie, 2003.

FRENCH POETIC REALISM

In the mid-1930s, the liquidation of the two major film trusts in France, Pathé and Gaumont, meant that the small independent **producer** could take up pole position. Whereas, before 1935, the two majors had dominated production, after 1935 and until 1939 on average 90 per cent of the French films produced were by small independent film companies. This had a fortunate effect on the French film industry. The collapse of the major commercial **studios** facilitated France's **art cinema**. Independent producer-**directors** were, for a while, free to make their films, and moreover could access the majors' studios and technical services, as well as their cinema circuits. A small faction of these independents, most famously Yves Allégret, Marcel Carné, Julien Duvivier, Jean Grémillon and Jean Renoir, became loosely banded under the label of the poetic realist school. But, despite their small number, they nonetheless re-established France's ailing international cinematic reputation which had been on the decline ever since World War One, by which time the **Hollywood** majors had completely cornered the international market.

Poetic realism has been seen in relation to its historical context as shadowing the rise and fall of the Popular Front in France – a consolidated party of the left which eventually came to power in 1936. The party was voted in on a wave of optimism for its platform of social reforms. However, because of the economic climate and the threat of war these were never fully implemented. The party was in power for a thousand days, but, after only six months in office, it was obvious that little or no change was going to be possible given the political and economic climate. The optimism of this movement is echoed in the representation of working-**class** solidarity as exemplified in Renoir's *Le Crime de M. Lange* (1935) and the optimistic title of his *La Vie est à nous* (1936). As markers of the decline of the Popular Front and of the desperation felt at the ineluctability of war come deeply pessimistic films such as Marcel Carné's *Quai des brumes* (1935), *Le Jour se lève* (1939) and Renoir's *La Règle du jeu* (1939).

This simplistic reflection needs nuancing, however, since not all the films in this grouping necessarily gave this straightforward early optimism/later pessimism message. Furthermore, not all the filmmakers in this group were sympathetic to the left. At the height of the popularity of the Popular Front government, at least two 1936 films are undyingly pessimistic in their message. These are Duvivier's *Pépé le Moko* and *La Belle équipe* (both starring the poetic realist fetish star Jean Gabin). In the first, Pépé dies at his own hands. Wanted by the police, he holes up in the Casbah in Algiers where he is surrounded by an adoring gang and mistress, but all he can dream of is returning to Paris – the price for fulfilling that desire is death. In *La Belle équipe*, male working-class solidarity is exposed for its weakness as it swiftly becomes eroded by the alluring presence of a woman. Duvivier was not a man of the left, which might explain his dark films in this euphoric period of the early Popular Front. However, another filmmaker, Jean Grémillon, this time of the left, was making similarly bleak films around the same time. His *Gueule d'amour* (1937) portrays the destruction of a man who forgoes his duties (as a soldier) for his passion for a 'heartless' woman (whom he eventually murders).

In poetic realist films there is a strong emphasis on **mise-en-scène**: décor, **setting** and **lighting** receive minute attention and owe not a little to the influence of **German expressionism**. Poetic realism is a re-created **realism**, not the socio-realism of the **documentary**. In this respect the realism is very studio-bound and stylized. For example, parts of Paris are studiously reproduced in the studio – an almost inauthentic realism (or hyper-realism). This stylized realism of the mise-en-scène is matched by the poetic symbolism within the **narrative**. The narrative is heavily imbued with the notion of fatalism. The male protagonist is generally doomed and the film's **diegesis** is so constructed as to put the deterioration in his psyche on display. This is the mise-en-scène of male-suffering par excellence. Setting, gestures, movement (or lack of it), verbal and non-verbal communication are all markers for this decline and so too are the lighting effects. To this effect, side-lighting is frequently used on the protagonist's face, or part-lighting of the space in which he finds himself, or highlighting objects that are of symbolic value to him. Indeed, objects are endowed with symbolism to quite a degree of abstraction and resonate throughout the film, measuring the state of the protagonist's degeneration as he responds to their recurrence in the film.

A major reason why all aspects of the film-process function so intensely to create this aura of poetic realism is that these films are, in the final analysis, the result of team work. There is the director, but there are also – of major importance – the scriptwriter, the designer for the sets, the lighting expert and the composer of the **music** soundtrack. Carné, for example, worked with the poet Jacques Prévert who scripted several of his films, he had Alexander Trauner as his set designer and Joseph Kosma was a frequent composer to his films.

For further reading see Andrew, 1995, Crisp, 1993.

GANGSTER FILMS

The gangster film is the one most readily identified as an American **genre** even though the French filmmaker Louis Feuillade's *Fantômas* (1913–14) is one of the earliest prototypes. It is in the contemporaneity of its **discourses** that the gangster film has been so widely perceived as an American genre. This genre, which dates from the late 1920s, came into its own with the introduction of **sound** and fully blossomed with three classics in the early 1930s: *Little Caesar* (Melvyn LeRoy, 1930), *The Public Enemy* (William A. Wellman, 1931) and *Scarface* (Howard Hawks, 1932). In the United States this was the period of Prohibition (1919–33), during which the manufacture, sale and transportation of alcoholic drinks was forbidden, and the Depression

(1929–34), when worldwide economic collapse precipitated commercial failure and mass unemployment.

These two major events in the United States' socio-economic history helped to frame the mythical value of the gangster in movies. Prohibition proved impossible to enforce because gangsters far outnumbered the law enforcers. Prohibition, however, brought gangsters and their lifestyle into the limelight as never before. Gang warfare and criminal acts became part of the popular press's daily diet and soon became transferred onto film. In fact, many of the gangster films of that period were based on real life. Gangsterism viewed from this standpoint was about greed and brutal acts of violence – in summary about aggression in urban society. But, the gangster movies were not as straightforwardly black and white as that. The male protagonist embodied numerous contradictions, which in turn facilitated **spectator–identification**.

If we consider the second socio-economic factor mentioned above, we can find a possible reason for the complex and nuanced characterization of the gangster-hero. The Depression exposed the **myth** of the American Dream – which said that success, in the democratic and classless society guaranteed by the American Constitution, was within the reach of everyone. How could this be so when the society was so evidently hierarchized into the haves and have-nots – as the effects of the Depression made so blatantly clear? According to the American Dream, success meant material wealth and, implicit within that, the assertion of the individual. The gangster was associated with the proletarian **class**, not the rich and moneyed classes of the United States. Therefore, the only way the gangster could access wealth and thereby self-assertion – that is, success, the American Dream – was by stealing it. Accruing capital meant accruing power over others. In this respect, the gangster embodies the contradictions inherent in the American Dream: success, when it comes, can only do so at the expense of others. And because the gangster points up these contradictions, his death at the end of the film is an **ideological** necessity. He must ultimately fail because the American Dream cannot be fulfilled in this cynical way, and he must also fail because he cannot be allowed to show up the Dream's contradictions.

The classic gangster film came into its own with the advent of sound, which reinforced the **realism** of this genre. Warner Brothers (see **studio system**) was the first studio to launch this genre in a big way with *Little Caesar* and *The Public Enemy*, and their films are seen as the precursors to **film noir**. Warners had finally become vertically integrated by 1928, and entered into full competition with the other majors. Warners were also very much associated with social-content films, and indeed, after the launch of Roosevelt's New Deal (1933–34), became identified with the new president's politics of social and economic reform. **Social realism** and political relevance, combined with a downbeat image, endowed Warners' films with a populism that made their products particularly attractive to working-class **audiences**, a major source of revenue for film companies.

The gangster movie, in its naked exposure of male heroics, has been likened to an urban **Western**. But unlike the Western, where rules are observed, the gangster movie knows no rules, other than death. Central to the gangster film is the antagonism between the desire for success and social constraint. The gangster will choose to live a shorter life rather than submit to constraints. Hence the aura of fatalism that runs through the film. But, as far as the spectator is concerned, for the duration of the film, where violence is countered with violence, where there are no rules, the spectator witnesses an urban nightmare as the **narrative** brings the plot to the brink of a social breakdown.

The gangster film is highly stylized with its recurrent **iconography** of urban **settings**, clothes, cars, gun technology and violence. (In more recent film history, the film that most fulsomely parodies and yet pays homage to this genre and its iconicity is Quentin Tarantino's *Reservoir Dogs*, 1992.) The narrative follows the rise and fall of a gangster; as such it provides a learning curve that of course has ideological resonances for the spectator (beware of the temptation to turn to the bad) – but not before there has been a first pleasure in identifying with the lawlessness of the hero. During his (fated) trajectory towards death, the protagonist's coming to self-awareness – rather than self-assertion, which is what he initially sought through success – functions cathartically for the spectator: we 'learn' from the gangster's mistakes. Furthermore, the use of the woman who is romantically involved with the protagonist and in whose arms he (often) dies – as the law enforcers stand menacingly around the prostrate couple, armed to the teeth – positions the spectator like her and therefore as sympathetic, understanding even, to the gangster. And thus, although the message of the film – 'the gangster must die for his violent endangering of American society' – intends to provide the spectator with a sense of moral justification, there is a counter-reading on offer that critiques American society which says that ultimately the 'little guy' must fail.

The classic age of the gangster movie (1930–34) was brought to a swift halt in an ambience of moral panic. Pressure was put on the **Hays** office to do more than ask the film industry to apply self-**censorship**. In 1934, the Production Code (see **Hays code**), which condemned, among other things, films glorifying gangsters, became mandatory.

Given the popularity of the genre, film companies were not going to give up such a lucrative scenario. Forced to water down the violence, they produced a set of sub-genres: private-eye films and detective thrillers. That is, without dropping much of the violence, they now foregrounded the side of law and order resolving disorder. Told to put a stop to the heroization of gangsters and violence, they simply shifted the role of hero from gangster to cop or private eye. Thanks to the Hays code intervention, the seeds for the film noir were sown. The sadism of the gangster became transformed into the guilt and angst of masculinity in crisis of the film noir protagonist. Against the ambiguous urban landscape of some modern American city, the hardboiled detective seeks justice. The ambiguity of the city reflects the ambiguity and complexity of a society where corruption reigns and law cannot easily bring the guilty to justice. Thus the detective is often a private eye, outside 'official' law, a law unto himself. As a marginal, by being outside he can solve the crime and bring the perpetrators to justice (Cawelti, 1992).

see **film noir** and the separate entry for **thriller**; see also **psychoanalysis**

GAZE/LOOK

This term refers to the exchange of looks that takes place in cinema. But it was not until the 1970s that it was written about and theorized. In the early 1970s, first French and then British and American film theorists began applying **psychoanalysis** to film in an attempt to discuss the **spectator**–screen relationship as well as the textual relationships within the film. Drawing in particular on Freud's theory of libido drives and Lacan's theory of the mirror stage, they sought to explain how cinema works at the level of the unconscious. Indeed, they maintained that the processes of the cinema mimic the workings of the unconscious. The spectator sits in a darkened room, desiring to look at the screen and deriving visual pleasure from what s/he sees. Part of that pleasure is also derived from the narcissistic identification s/he feels with the person on-screen. But there is more; the spectator also has the illusion of controlling that image. First, because the perspectival illusion, which the cinematic image provides, ensures that the spectator is **subject** of the gaze. And, second, given that the projector is positioned behind the spectator's head, this means that it is as if those images are the spectator's own imaginings on-screen. Let's see what the theorists have to say about all of this.

Christian Metz (1975) draws on the analogy of the screen with the mirror as a way of talking about spectator positioning and the **voyeuristic** aspect of film viewing, whereby the spectator is identified with the gaze (since the gaze cannot be returned, the spectator is voyeuristically positioned). However, Metz argues, because he (*sic*) is identified with the gaze, this also means that he is looking at the mirror. In other words, through the look, the spectator is re-enacting the mirror stage. In this respect, this identification is a regression to childhood. Raymond Bellour (1975), for his part, talks about the cinema as functioning simultaneously for the **Imaginary** (i.e. as the reflection, the mirror) *and* as the **Symbolic** (i.e. as language, through its film **discourses**; see also **psychoanalysis**). In both instances, these two theorists assert, the spectator is at the mirror stage and about to acquire sexual difference (in looking into the mirror the boy child sees his sexual difference from his mother). You will note that the female spectator got left out of this debate. It would take the work of the British feminists Laura Mulvey (1975) and Claire Johnston (1976) to take this debate further, closely followed by American feminists (see **feminist film theory**). But, by the early 1970s, the debate around the gaze had got as far as saying that, at every film viewing, there occurs a re-enactment of the boy child's unconscious processes involved in the acquisition of sexual difference (mirror stage), of language (entry *of* the Symbolic) and of autonomous selfhood or **subjectivity** (entry *into* the Symbolic order and, thereby, the Law of the Father, and, consequently, rupture with the mother as object of identification).

Thus, the spectator is constructed as subject, derives visual pleasure from seeing his self as having an identity separate from his mother, and – aligned with his father whose patriarchal law he has entered – he can now derive sexual pleasure in looking at the (m)other; that is, woman – the female (m)other.

It is not difficult to see that Oedipal desire is indeed a male reality (as opposed to **fantasy**). In fact, Bellour (1975) particularly draws attention to the notion of male representation or characterization in cinema as a reiteration of the Oedipus story (see **psychoanalysis: Oedipal trajectory**). Cinema actively encourages Oedipal desire. **Hollywood**'s great subject is heterosexuality, the plot resolution 'requires' the heterosexual couple formation. Cinematic practices, then, are a perfect simile for Oedipal desire in that their looking-relations structure woman as object and man as **subject** of desire. Insofar as the exchange of looks is concerned, in **dominant cinema**, it comes from three directions – all of which are 'naturally' assumed as male. First, there is the pro-filmic event – the look of the camera, with behind it the cameraman (*sic*). Second, the **diegetic** gaze: within the film the man gazes at the woman, a gaze she may return but is not able to act upon (see **agency**). Finally, there is the spectator's gaze which imitates the other two looks. The spectator is positioned as the camera's eye and also as the eye of the beholding male on-screen, because as spectator he is subject of the gaze. A nice **naturalizing** of Oedipal desire if ever there was one!

Small wonder that feminists took up this concept of the gaze and submitted it to some more rigour. As E. Ann Kaplan (1983: 30) says: 'Dominant Hollywood cinema ... is constructed according to the unconscious of patriarchy; film **narratives** are organized by means of a male-based language and discourse which parallels the language of the unconscious.' And it is for this reason that she makes such a strong plea for feminists not to reject psychoanalysis as a male construct, which it is, but to examine it and by exploring it learn how to counter its effects. The first step was to expose the naturalization of the triple position of the look. Laura Mulvey's vital and deliberately polemical article 'Visual Pleasure and Narrative Cinema' (1975) started the debate by demonstrating the domination of the male gaze, within and without the screen, at the expense of the woman's; so much so that the female spectator had little to gaze upon or identify with. The exchange or relay of looks within film reproduces the **voyeuristic** pleasure of the cinematic **apparatus**, with all that that connotes of the male child viewing, unseen, his parents copulating (what in psychoanalytic terms is called the primal scene). Visual pleasure equals sexual pleasure, yes, but for the male.

Kaplan (1983) asks 'Is the gaze male?' She comes up with an answer that opens a door for readings against the grain, for readings that do not necessarily show the woman as object of the gaze. While conceding that in **mainstream** Hollywood cinema it is men on the whole who can act on the desiring gaze, she nonetheless makes the point that to own and activate the gaze is to be in the 'masculine' position, that is, to be dominant. She then goes on to argue that both men and women can adopt dominant or submissive roles. But of course this does not mean any real change, the same binary opposition, masculine/feminine, is still in place. And as Linda Williams cautions 'When the Woman Looks' (i.e. becomes 'dominant') she usually pays for it, often with her life: 'The woman's gaze is punished ... by narrative processes that transform curiosity and desire into masochistic fantasy' (1984: 85). So this ability to switch roles is not necessarily fortunate – it is even potentially dangerous. (See entry on **spectator**, stage three, for further discussion on this point).

Having recognized the existence of the dominance/submission structure, the next stage, Kaplan (1983) argues, is to question why it is there. What need, whose need does it fulfil? If cinema does mimic the unconscious, then it must reflect what is repressed – latent fears around **sexuality** and sexual difference. It is for this reason that she advocates investigating film through psychoanalytic methodology as a first step towards 'understanding our socialization in patriarchy' (1983: 34). It is here that the readings against the grain become possible. By exposing how woman is constructed cinematically, this reading refuses to accept the normalizing or naturalizing process of patriarchal socialization.

see also: **apparatus, psychoanalysis, scopophilia, spectator**

For further detail *see* **feminist film theory**.

For further reading see Kaplan, 1997; Mulvey, 1975, 1989.

GENDER

Gender has a socio-cultural origin that is **ideological** in purpose and must be seen as quite distinct from the notions of biological sex and **sexuality**. Part of the ideological function of gender has been to dissimulate this difference and to see sex and gender as the same. This in turn, as we shall see, makes possible numerous slippages, including the notion of a fixed sexuality. The ideological function of gender 'has been to set up a heterogeneous and determinate set of biological, physical, social, psychological and psychic constructs as a unitary *fixed* and unproblematic attribute of human subjectivity' (Kuhn, 1985: 52, my emphasis). The ideological function of gender is to fix us as either male or female and is the first in a series of binary oppositions that serve to construct us as male or female. As Kuhn points out, these binary oppositions are socially, psychologically, physically and biologically grounded. Thus, within this ideological functioning of gender, the female is positioned as economically inferior to the male, is associated more with the domestic than the public sphere, is more emotional, less strong than the male. She is the site of reproduction and not production, which is the male domain, and so on. It is clear how this essentialist approach (woman is this/man is that) fixes gender and leads to a **naturalizing** of gender difference (which we accept as 'natural').

During the 1980s, feminist critics marshalled gender relations into the centre of the debate around sexuality. In so doing they sought to problematize gender relations which up until then had not been considered as problematic. In Western culture, masculinity had not been seen by men as determined by gender relations. It was free from such considerations, natural and therefore unproblematic. In language, the masculine is the linguistic norm and the female is defined in relation to it (e.g. actor/actress). During the 1970s, the focus of feminist thinking had been on issues of femininity. But it became clear that, in order to challenge any essentialist reading of the female, gender relations would have to come under scrutiny. Femininity could not be seen in isolation, but as part of other categories of difference, starting with the vexed issue of gender difference. This, in turn, would finally place scrutiny of masculinity on the agenda.

There are, arguably, two dominant debates surrounding gender relations, both of which found a voice first within feminist theory, and subsequently within cultural studies, gay studies, literary and **film theory**. These debates are rooted in **psychoanalysis** and Marxist materialism. Both debates have contributed significantly in moving the whole question of gender relations into wider arenas and in so doing have helped, rather than hindered, an understanding of how gender is not a simple case of sexual difference, as ideology would have us believe, but a series of hierarchical power relations cleverly disguised so as to hide the way in which gender is imposed by force. Furthermore, these debates have shown the importance of historical and social processes with regard to gender relations and have stressed the way in which they can occlude other forms of social determination such as race, **class** and sexuality. These debates have examined how cultural practices reproduce gender ideology and have also demonstrated the importance of understanding how the inscription of gender and renditions of sexual difference operate in dominant culture. To understand the construction of gender and how gender ideology functions are vital first steps to countering them, to the uncovering of alternative readings.

The psychoanalytic debate draws largely on Jacques Lacan's rooting of subjectivity in language (see **psychoanalysis: Imaginary/ Symbolic**). The child, in order to complete its socio-sexual trajectory, must move from the Imaginary illusion of unity with the self and desire of the mother into the Symbolic Order. This order is the patriarchal order and represents social stability and is governed by the Law of the Father. This approach shows how patriarchal language serves to perpetuate gendered subjectivity and how it is hierarchically deterministic. The male is fixed in language as 'he', but he is also subject of that language since, in entering the Symbolic Order, he joins ranks with his father to perpetuate the Law of the Father. Conversely, the female in entering the Symbolic Order is fixed by language as 'she'. But, because she is not *of* the patriarchal language, she is not subject but object. This approach, then, makes it possible to see how sexual relations are rooted in power relations that are linguistically based. Through this approach, the ideological functions of gender relations are exposed. It does not go far enough, however, for two reasons. First, it smacks of a self-fulfilling essentialism: 'it will always be like this'. Thus, psychoanalysis explains subject-construction and so, to a degree, sanctions it. Second, if it does show a way to challenge gender ideology it assumes that it will take place at the level of language. But this is to ignore the other forms of social determination such as history, class and race.

This was the objection of the Marxist materialists. And it is their debate that has served both to balance the psychoanalytical approach and to broaden further the frame of investigation. They see gender-ideology as a social and cultural construction that attempts to construct gender upon purely binary lines. The notion of a fixed and gendered subjectivity becomes impossible as a concept, they argue, since it assumes that only one category of difference exists: masculinity and femininity. The impossibility of such an ideological stance becomes clear if one considers that power relations also affect gender relations. Because masculine is the linguistic norm, a first hierarchy imposes itself. In the Western world we live not only in a patriarchal world but also in a homo-social world. Power is invested in the masculine and, in order for it to stay there, men bond (the political and economic establishment, military forces, just to mention two obvious instances). Yet, here already, problematics arise. For how far removed is the homo-social relation from the homo-erotic one? Why is there such a prevalence of homophobia in society if it does not bespeak this desire to conceal that we live in a homo-social environment? Racial and class difference are other categories that gender-ideology seeks to dissimulate. Why otherwise the prurience with the potency of the Black male or the working-class hero? They are perceived first as their sex and sexuality.

This fixing of a gendered subjectivity attempts to disguise the fact that gender is not as stable as ideology would have it. And it is here that we understand why gender ideology seems so necessary to the safe functioning of a patriarchal world. Gender is constructed not just through language, but through social ascriptions and cultural practice. Thus, gender-ideology is represented in a variety of cultural practices: literature, mass media, cinema, and so on. However, it is the examination of the inscriptions of gender into cultural practices that allows not only for a **deconstruction** of gender-ideology to take place but also for other differences to emerge. Where to situate cross-dressing, transsexualism and transvestism if gender is so fixed? What to do with lesbians and gay men? What about masquerade and metaphorical transvestism? The sexual subject or subjectivity here is 'defined' in terms of either otherness (transvestism, etc.) or sameness (homosexuality, etc.) but not difference. Clearly the binary oppositions start to collapse under such questions.

A film which poses these questions and remarkably exposes the problems inherent in gender-ideology is Neil Jordan's *The Crying Game* (1992). Here no sexual identity is fixed. A Black soldier, Jody, posted in Northern Ireland, falls into an IRA trap by letting a woman seduce him. Taken captive, he shows a photograph of his lover, Dil, to his captor, Fergus, with whom he has established a rapport. His lover, also Black, lives in London and works as a hairdresser. After Jody dies, Fergus, who is on the run from his IRA masters, goes to London and seeks her out. He goes to the salon where she works and has her cut his hair. He has already changed his name to Jimmy so the haircut completes the disguise. He is immediately attracted to Dil. However, Dil is a transvestite. But her/his cross-dressing is so successful that she/he dupes all, including Fergus/Jimmy. Only when their relationship gets to the point of making love does Jimmy 'discover the truth'. At first he is horrified and runs away. But Dil seeks him out and their relationship resumes. The IRA masters are closing in on Jimmy but they also 'know' about his relationship with Dil so her life is in danger. In order to save her, Jimmy disguises Dil into a slimmer version of her/his dead lover Jody by cutting her hair and making her/him dress in Jody's cricket whites.

The point here is that no sexuality, no gender-identity is fixed. Jody, it now transpires, was bisexual – the name Jody itself is sexually unidentifiable. Dil (an equally ungendered name) can assume any gender and so is completely unfixable. All is in a fair state of flux. Indeed, the mirroring of the double disguise of Fergus/Jimmy and Dil/Jody makes this point clear. Fergus, until meeting Dil, thought of himself as heterosexual. His attraction to Dil changes his perceptions of his identity. When he transforms Dil into Jody he assumes Dil's earlier role when she completed his disguise as Jimmy. All sorts of levels of play around Fergus/Jimmy's sexuality are encoded into this: metaphorical transvestism (becoming 'Dil'), homo-eroticism (fabricating 'Jody'), homosexuality (loving Dil).

Mainstream cinema does not function, however, to undermine dominant ideology. Quite the reverse. But this does not mean that its own functioning as an ideological **apparatus** cannot be unpicked or that alternative readings to the **preferred reading** cannot be given. Conventional signs of gender fixity can come under scrutiny. **Lighting** and **colour** are but two primary and evident areas for this scrutiny. Lighting, particularly with black and white films, was used differently for male and female stars to point to their gender difference and to a set of binary oppositions. The use of back-lighting to give the heroine a halo effect and front-lighting to bring out the whiteness of her skin was intended to point to the virginal and pure nature of American womanhood. It was used also to point to her fragility when contrasted with the deliberately contrastive lighting used for the hero. This lighting brought out his handsome dark looks, pointing to his strength and manliness. Colour is also used to point to gender difference. Indeed, since the introduction of colour it is noteworthy how the female and male protagonists are shot differently. As Neale (1985: 152) makes clear, colour is used to signify woman's look-at-able-ness, woman as the 'source of the spectacle of colour'. And, since the advent of colour, there has been an even greater emphasis on the fragmentation of the female body (Turner, 1988: 81). Other conventions play into this strategy of gender differentiation. Thus **mise-en-scène**, the **iconography** of the image, gesturality in performance styles, the function of the **gaze**, just as much as lighting and colour, are also conventions at the service of gender-ideology that can be questioned. Clearly, if these can be questioned then so too can the idea of a fixed gendered spectator (see **spectator**).

By way of illustrating this notion of questioning, let us take a fairly extreme example, that of cross-dressing. As we shall see, the function of cross-dressing in **mainstream cinema** can be critically examined in the light of the debates around gender. For a start, why is it that we must not be allowed to be completely duped by cross-dressing? Why in the film *Tootsie* (Sydney Pollack, 1982) must we always be aware of the phallus under Tootsie's dress? How come neither Jack Lemmon nor Tony Curtis are allowed to convince fully as a woman in *Some Like it Hot* (Billy Wilder, 1959)? In other words, why is it that male sexuality must not be completely repressed? What occurs to women who cross-dress? Annette Kuhn's brilliant essay on cross-dressing (1985: 48–73) addresses these questions and provides some illuminating answers. Cross-dressing, she argues, foregrounds the performance aspect of dress and problematizes gender identity and sexual difference (ibid.: 49). Clothing as performance threatens to undermine the ideological fixity of the human subject: change your clothes and you change your sex (ibid.: 53). Cross-dressing plays with the distance between the outer-clothed self (gendered clothing) and the self underneath (the gendered body). Thus, sexual disguise plays on gender fixity, makes it possible to think about it as fluid (ibid.: 56). With its potential to denaturalize sexual difference (ibid.: 55), it is small wonder that cross-dressing is so contained in mainstream cinema. Thus, we are always in the know. We derive pleasure from knowing/not-knowing: *we* know it is a masquerade but we do not know if or how it will be found out (see **naturalizing**).

It is probably because of its potential to threaten ideological fixity that for the most part cross-dressing occurs in **comedies** or **musicals** (**genres** that operate in fairly asexual and unrealistic spaces). Given that Hollywood is obsessed with selling gender difference and particularly heterosexuality, it is naturally wary of destabilizing cultural stability. Not surprisingly then, cross-dressed women for the most part have to suppress desire, or suspend it until their 'true identity' comes out. Not so the male cross-dresser. He can make clear his desire for the woman – indeed it is an essential ingredient to the comedy. What this tells us is that 'lesbianism', as evinced by a male cross-dresser attracted to a woman, is safe. The joke is at the lesbian's expense – because the cross-dresser is so evidently straight. If, however, he is not straight, he threatens the status quo – and for this reason is unlikely to be seen in mainstream cinema (compare, for example, *Tootsie* with *The Kiss of the Spiderwoman*, Hector Babenco, 1985). A female cross-dresser must suppress her sexuality if she wants to occupy a central position. No other comportment can be countenanced, otherwise she implicitly masquerades as homosexual – which as we have already discussed is one of the greatest taboos of all, and is no position for a woman to play with. To make this cross-dressing completely safe, even though she is cross-dressed, the male protagonist continues to probe and seek to assure himself of her sex (see *Victor/Victoria*, Blake Edwards, 1982). Unlike the male cross-dresser whose disguise within the **diegesis** is taken as a given, the female cross-dresser's disguise then is not. In either case, male or female cross-dresser, it is not gender-bending but gender-pastiche that is on offer.

see also: **feminist film theory, Oedipal trajectory (psychoanalysis), sexuality, subject/subjectivity**

For further reading see Butler, 1990, 1993; Codell, 2007; De Lauretis, 1989; Dines and Humez, 1995; Gabbard and Luhr, 2008; Kirkham and Thumin, 1995; Phillips, 2006; Radner and Stringer, 2011; Showalter, 1989; Tasker, 1993; Tasker and Negra, 2007.

GENRE/SUB-GENRE

As a term, genre goes back to earliest cinema and was seen as a way of organizing films according to type. But it was not until the late 1960s that genre was introduced as a key concept into Anglo-Saxon **film theory** even though the French critic André Bazin was already talking of it in the 1950s with reference to the **Western**. The debate around genre in the 1970s served to displace the earlier debate around **auteur theory** – even though, in more recent times, genre and auteur theory have become reconciled.

Genre is more than mere generic cataloguing. As Neale (1990: 46 and 48) points out, genre does not refer just to film type but to **spectator** expectation and hypothesis (speculation as to how the film will end). It also refers to the role of specific institutional **discourses** that feed into and form generic structures. In other words, genre must be seen also as part of a tripartite process of production, marketing (including distribution and exhibition) and consumption. Generic marketing includes posters, souvenirs, film press releases, hyperbolic statements: 'the greatest war movie ever!' – all the different discourses of 'hype' that surround the launching of a film product onto the market. Consumption refers not only to audience practices but also to practices of critics and reviewers. Clearly, genres are not static, they evolve with the times, even disappear. Generic conventions as much as genres themselves 'evolve', become transformed for economic, technological and consumption reasons. Thus, genres are simultaneously conservative and innovative insofar as they respond to expectations that are industry- and **audience**-based. In terms of the industry, they repeat generic formulas that 'work' and yet introduce new technologies that shift and modernize generic conventions. This same paradox holds true for audiences with their expectations of familiarity as well as change and innovation.

Some general principles

Neale (1990: 63) remarks that the term *genre* is a fairly recent one, at least in its reference to popular mass entertainment. Prior to the nineteenth century, it was literature or high art that was generic. But, with the impact, in the late nineteenth century of new technologies which made popular entertainment more accessible, the position has reversed. The need to commodify mass culture and target different sectors of the public has meant that it is now popular culture that is generic.

Genre is seemingly an unproblematic concept, but this is not the case. And this is particularly evident with film. First, because generally speaking a film is rarely generically pure. This is not surprising if we consider film's heritage which is derivative of other forms of entertainment (vaudeville, music-hall, theatre, photography, the novel, and so on). As Neale says (1990: 62), film constantly refers to itself as a cross-media generic formation. Thus, a clear generic definition cannot immediately be imposed on a film even if a genre can be defined by a set of **codes and conventions** (as in, say our expectations of a **road movie** or a **musical**). But, because genres themselves are not static and because, as we have just mentioned, they are composed of several intertexts, they are, of course, mutable (see **intertextuality**). They rework, extend and transform the norms that codify them (ibid.: 58). As we shall see, attempts at straitjacketing a genre are virtually impossible. Neale (ibid.: 58) offers a term that helps to clarify this problem when he refers to 'genre texts' which could be seen as distinct from genre itself. Genre would stand for the generic norms, and genre texts for the actual film products. In a similar drive for clarity, Alan Williams (quoted in Neale, 1990: 62) speaks of 'principal genres' to refer to what he sees as the three main categories of film: **narrative** film, **avant-garde** film and **documentary**. He reserves the term *sub-genres* to refer to what we term *film genres*.

A second problematizing factor is that genres also produce sub-genres, so again clarity is proscribed. For example, sub-genres of the **war movie** are Resistance films, certain colonial films, prisoner-of-war films, spy films (most of which cross boundaries with the **thriller** film genre) and so on. A third factor is that a genre cannot be seen as discrete and ideologically pure (see **ideology**). As Robin Wood (1992: 478) makes clear, genres are not 'safe' but are ideologically inflected. Ideological inflections within film genre find representation through a series of binary oppositions which, among other hegemonic 'realities', reinforce **gender** distinctions. For example, constructs of **sexuality** are based around images of the active male versus the passive female, independence versus entrapment (i.e. marriage and family). **Sexuality** is constructed also as good/bad, pure/perverse. Furthermore, these are attributes which are most commonly attached to women – thus reinforcing the virgin/whore **myth** of woman. Constructs of society beyond heterosexuality and the 'desirability' of marriage and reproduction posit the evils of city versus rural or small-town life, the work ethic and capitalism versus fraudulent attempts to get rich quick (i.e. good capitalism versus bad capitalism).

Although it is important to be aware of the ideological function of a genre, it is equally important to be aware of the dangers of reductionism inherent in an ideological approach to genre. As we shall make clear in the next section, genres are inflected as much by the capitalist imperatives of the film industry as they are by audience preference and the socio-historical realities of any given period. And, as we have already mentioned, genres evolve and change over the years, some even disappear only to reappear decades later. This would indicate, as Leo Braudy (1992: 431) believes, that genre serves as a barometer of the social and cultural concerns of cinema-going audiences. A good illustrative example is what has happened to the Hollywood **epic**. We saw how it had strong appeal until *Cleopatra*, in the 1960s. Thereafter it was all but extinct until the terrorist attack on the Twin Towers in New York – an event known as 9/11 (11 September 2001), after which the epic had a brief resurgence. Presently, it appears to be on the wane again.

Genres have codes and conventions with which the audience is as familiar as the **director** (if not more so). Therefore, some genre films 'fail' because the audience feels that they have not adhered to their generic conventions sufficiently, or because they are out of touch with contemporary times. Alternatively, the non-conformity of a film to its generic conventions can lead an audience to make it into a **cult film**. Film genre, therefore, is not as conservative a concept as might at first appear: it can switch, change, be imbricated (an overlapping of genres), subverted. Indeed, in terms of product, genre films do get parodied, bent and broken. And this is part of the process of generic change, but also a way of cinema challenging dominant ideological discourses. Thus, for example, in the early to mid-1950s the earlier sense of a secure national identity established by **Westerns** (pre-war) which gave a strong representation of America's pioneering spirit started to be challenged by certain films beginning with Delmer Daves' *Broken Arrow* (1950) which suggested there were doubts as to how the West was truly won.

This type of challenging does not limit itself to the level of narrative alone. It can also find parodic form by taking the codes and conventions to task as, for example, with Mel Brooks' *Blazing Saddles* (1974, which mocks the Western) or Robert Altman's spoof on the private-eye genre *The Long Goodbye* (1973). Interestingly, the 1970s marked a period in Hollywood cinema where parody was quite extensive and genres got so bent they forced spectators to question what they had just seen. *Chinatown* (Roman Polanski, 1974) and *The French Connection* (William Friedkin, 1971) are very good examples of this practice. In both of these films the bending of the generic codes is such that we, the spectator, are constantly held at a distance – both because we don't quite understand what we are seeing and because we have no entry in by way of identification with the central protagonist. In these two films, the upholders of the law are shown as both effective and ineffective, as blind in their determination to win at all costs and eventually (while they may have solved the crime or mystery) being completely unable to make the arrest or bring the story to a positive conclusion.

Finally, in this context of the unfixity of genres, we the audience also participate in the process of change. Because genres are simultaneously bound by certain conventions and expectations and are intertextual, we carry a wealth of knowledge ourselves which means that we too, in a parodic and iconoclastic fashion, can make readings of the films against the grain.

Some approaches: structuralism, economies of desire and history

Mention was made at the beginning of this entry of the genre debate displacing the **auteur** debate. You will note from the auteur entry, however, that the auteur debate did not disappear. Indeed, it has gone through several phases, much like the genre debate itself. Gledhill (in Cook, 1985: 58–68) gives a superb synopsis of the debates, so I will make only brief mention of the impact of the structuralist debate on genre theory (see **structuralism**). This debate made two things possible. First, it relocated genre in a much wider set of structures (after it had been through the 'total structure' rites of passage in the 1970s). Second, it reconciled the auteur/genre debates and dissipated the misconception that the two concepts are mutually exclusive.

Until the late 1960s genre had been considered only in terms of codes and conventions and as a system for codifying films. However, it is easy to perceive why such a reading of genre made it a prime site for **structuralist** practice. Metz argued that genres go through a cycle of changes: 'a classic stage, to a self-parody of the classics, to a period where films contest the proposition that they are part of a genre, and finally to a critique of the genre itself' (Metz, 1975, quoted in Turner, 1988: 86). Although not all genres necessarily follow this dynamic, some do seem to (e.g. the Western). Most helpful in examining the dynamic nature of genre, however, was the application to genre of Vladimir Propp's description of the narrative as a set of oppositions. An analysis, over a period of time, of the structure of a genre through a set of oppositions made it possible to see where change had taken place – even to the point of being able to discern where inversion occurred. The classic example of this Proppian approach is Wright's (1975) investigation of the Western. Wright demonstrates how a first set of oppositions established in the classic Western evolves over time so that in more recent Westerns there is a completely inverted set of oppositions. For example, what was valued in the earlier Western was civilization and strong socialization. It was the hero's function to ensure that those outside society – the bad, weak-willed villains – remained out in the wilderness. Having saved a situation, the hero might well move on, but society and order had been made secure and were seen to be good – so the hero has upheld the values of civil society. In later Westerns, the hero is no longer inside society as an upholder of civilization. Rather, civilization is now seen as corrupt and weak. And it is the villains who now live inside society, the hero outside, in the wilderness.

Wright makes the point also that these changes reflect social change and audience expectations. Thus, for example, *Butch Cassidy and the Sundance Kid* (George Roy Hill, 1969) says much about the young generation of that time and their desire to be free and on the road. Wright's analysis serves, usefully, to make the point that genres are less about ritual than we might at first believe. As Neale (1990: 58) puts it, conventions of a genre 'are always in play rather than being, simply; re-played'. Moreover, since genres are about **spectator**–text relations as well as socio-historic relations, it becomes evident that genre must be discussed in relation to the numerous structures that serve not to fix it but to sustain it. The value of structuralism in relation to genre history is, then, that it broke the hold auteurism had on critical thinking about film and showed how structures other than that of the auteur had to be taken into consideration insofar as the production of meaning was concerned.

In an earlier informative essay on genre, Neale (1980: 19) argues that genres are a fundamental part of cinema's machinery. The cinema machinery or **apparatus** regulates the different orders of **subjectivity** including that of the spectator (ibid.: 19). This means that a genre, just like the apparatus of which it is a part, becomes part of a system that regulates desire, memory and expectation (ibid.: 55). Neale draws a useful conclusion on the strategies that genres fulfil in relation to the economies of desire (ibid.: 55). First, genres operate over a series of textual typologies (**war movies**, **Westerns**, etc.), what Neale calls 'instances', and so offer the possibility of regulating desire over a determined number of genre texts (i.e. there are only so many textual instances possible). In this way, they help the industry to control demand and, therefore, production. Second, genres contain the possibilities of reading. That is, generic codes and conventions give a **preferred reading**, thus regulating memory and expectation. This provides the industry with the wherewithal to control 'the effects that its products produce' (ibid.: 55).

The idea of generic limitation is clear enough: we can actually see how that worked during the heyday of the **studio system** when studios specialized in the production of certain genres and not others – in other words, economies of scale dictated that their production machine was geared to specific output. The second point needs further clarification and can best be explained in relation to four essential component parts of genre: technology, narrative, **iconography** and **stars**. Genres exhibit the technology of cinema. Depending on the genre, different aspects of cinema's technology are put on display. For example, colour and **cinemascope** or **wide-screen** are important technological devices for the Western; **science-fiction** requires special effects. Not to use them could be to frustrate spectator expectations and therefore not to regulate desire. Indeed, the voyeuristic and fetishistic (see **voyeurism/fetishism**) nature of film technology – the camera as probe and as container of the image – makes possible the fusion of desire and technology into an eroticization of technology (e.g. Stanley Kubrick's *2001: A Space Odyssey*, 1968; David Cronenberg's *Dead Ringers*, 1988). Arguably, today's Computer Graphic Imaging (**CGI**) has brought us to the point where digital practice has fetishized the image itself. We look to the thrill that special effects can now create for us. They are as important as the film narrative itself (think, for example, of the marvellous CGI effects in the Harry Potter series or Martin Scorsese's *The Aviator*, 2004).

Genres also act as vehicles for stars. But stars, too, act as vehicles for genres. As we know, narrative structures and iconography are two functions whereby the audience recognizes the genre. Thus, the star becomes a vehicle for the genre. In this light, genres are the discursive or narrative site in which the star can exhibit her/his potential to fulfil the demands, codes and conventions of a particular genre and perhaps even surpass them (take any Robert De Niro film as an example). Genres are also the iconographic site in which the star (male or female) can display the body or have it displayed (obvious examples include Marilyn Monroe, James Dean, Marlon Brando, Brad Pitt). On these two counts (narrative and iconography), memory expectation and desire are all activated within the spectator and regulated by the strategies of performance: we recall the genre and the star and we expect certain things of them and are gratified.

Genres refer to others of their own type and so are both inter-referential and intertextual. This means also that they are inscribed in history. The latest Western refers back generically to the other Westerns made since the very first one. But there are also social motivations behind the making of a genre: why do Westerns or **gangster** movies exist? What needs do they fulfil? So genres are therefore motivated by history and society even though they are not simple reflectors of society (Neale, 1980: 16). For example, the Cold War films of the 1950s made on both sides of the 'Iron Curtain' were an attempt to allay fears of insecurity in the face of technological advancement (atomic bombs, space exploration), and to vindicate the merits of either Western or Eastern bloc ideologies (capitalism and communism). **Film noir**, as a sub-genre of the thriller, had its heyday in the 1940s and 1950s, a time when the United States was at war and immediately afterwards. During that time, the role of women had fundamentally changed. They were now at work, part of the social and public sphere. But what of 'their men' over 'there' fighting? What could they expect to find once they got 'home'? Home, the United States, was no longer the safe patriarchal regime they had left behind them. Nor did peace hold much promise given the apparent threat of communism. Film noir, viewed in this light, has been seen as an expression of male insecurity in the face of social change and a growing disillusionment with the lasting efficacy of peace. Genre speaks to its times (as well as its nation) – think, for example, of the **Blaxploitation** movies of the 1970s in the USA and how it tried to undermine the rise of the African-American's Black consciousness movement of that same period. More recently should we feel concern at the appeal of the retro-genres that are so successful presently? Neo-noirs and neo-melodramas are having considerable success. Are they reappearing in parodic mode or in slavish repetition? If we think in terms of the following titles – *Road to Perdition* (Mendes, 2002), *Mulholland Drive* (Lynch, 2001), *The Man Who Wasn't There* (Coen Brothers, 2001), *Far from Heaven* (Haynes, 2002) – perhaps we are justified in thinking that these few examples alone give us room to say with confidence that genre is once again re-examining itself and challenging its spectator.

In conclusion, genre can be identified by the iconography and conventions operating within it. But genre is also a shifting and slippery term so it is never fixed and, either through economic and historical exigencies, or through intentional parodic practice, is in a constant process of change.

see also: specific genres

For further reading see Altman, 1999; Grant, 1986, 1995, 2003, 2007; Grodal, 1997; Langford, 2005; Neale 1980, 1990, 2000; Schatz, 1981.

GERMAN EXPRESSIONISM

A term used to refer within cinema studies to a particular filmic style which emerged in Germany during the years 1919 to 1924 and which is associated with a period in world cinema history – that of Weimar Germany's cinema of the 1920s (for full discussion of Weimar cinema, see Elsaesser, 2000). German expressionism has been applied to cinema by analogy with the preoccupations of the expressionist movement in modern art of the early part of the twentieth century whose aim was to convey the force of human emotion and **sexuality**. The word *expressionism* means 'squeezing out', thus making the true essence of things and people emerge into a visible form. Its themes are revolt, self-analysis, madness, and primitive, sexual savagery (Courthion, 1968: 7–9). A deliberately anti-bourgeois aesthetic movement, its precursors number, among others, Edward Munch (*The Scream* being arguably *the* emblematic painting of expressionism) and Vincent Van Gogh. The expressionist movement was famous for its crudely painted forms and vibrant colours (landscapes, figures and still lives). Expressionism (whose history loosely spans some thirty years, 1900–30) was primarily the work of artists from northern and central Europe (Austria, Germany, Scandinavia and Switzerland) and its exponents came primarily from two main groups of artists: the Blaue Reiter (based in Munich) and the Brücke group (based in Dresden) which was founded in 1905 and disbanded in 1913. Many, indeed some of the greatest, exponents of expressionism were not part of these groups but solitary painters. Artists of that movement who are most renowned today include Wassily Kandinsky, Gustav Klimt, Egon Schiele and Chaïm Soutine.

In its reaction to bourgeois aesthetics, through its rejection of **realist** modes of representation, expressionism can be qualified as a modernist movement. In its preoccupation with sexuality and emotional uncertainty it stands as a movement that does not necessarily embrace the optimism of **modernism**, but looks rather at the psychological effects of this new age of technology on the individual. The impact of Freud and **psychoanalysis** – particularly his work on hysteria – must not be ignored in this discussion of expressionism. Expressionism, in its attempts to display a metaphysics of the soul, mirrors to a degree the efforts in psychoanalysis to bring the workings of the unconscious to the fore, to the level of consciousness where the malaise or hysteria can be expressed. Expressionism was not limited to painting but was manifest in the literature, theatre and architecture (again primarily) of Scandinavian and German-speaking countries and spread from these domains into cinema in terms of **narrative**, set and **mise-en-scène**. Indeed, expressionistic architecture with its strange and distorted structures found its major outlet in theatre and film sets – the economics of the time were not in a position to permit experimentation on real buildings (Silberman, 1996: 307). The impact on cinema of the famed Max Reinhardt theatre in Berlin – especially Reinhardt's theatre work of the period 1907 to 1919 – can be read as emblematic of this cross-fertilization process between different cultural arenas. Several of the main film actors associated with German expressionistic film came from his troupe (Conrad Veidt, Werner Krauss and Emil Jannings, to name the most remembered today). Furthermore, Reinhardt's use of expressionist sets and high-contrast chiaroscuro **lighting** were later to become two of the major mise-en-scène strategies of German expressionist film. It should be added, of course, that German expressionism's famed predilection for chiaroscuro (the use of highly contrastive lighting, literally light and dark), which is already in evidence in German films of the 1910s, was undoubtedly due in part to the influence of Danish cinema lighting practices of that time.

The German expressionist film movement emerged for several conjunctural reasons. Critics of different generations have read different things into this movement. Some have seen it as reflecting a German mentality on the brink of madness, obsessed with death and fatality and ready to encompass fascism (Kracauer, 1992, and to some extent Eisner, 1969). Others have seen these films as an attempt to escape, even into horror, from the dreadful effects of the economic crisis and inflation (Manuell and Fraenkel, 1971). More recently, this movement has been relativized within a broader context of German film production and seen as more of a continuation of pre-war film traditions than a new departure (Elsaesser, 1996: 143; although Eisner also hints at this, 1969: 17).

In terms of context, post-World War One Germany was facing a period of terrible poverty and constant insecurity. The reprisals taken on the vanquished Germany by the implementation of the Versailles Treaty, in the form of heavy reparation payments, were such that the period 1918 to 1924 was one of civil strife and staggering inflation. Thus, this nation, which had (like its enemies) suffered terrible losses on the battlefields, lost its empire (its colonies became mandates of the League of Nations) and, in the early post-war year of 1919, faced civilian deaths of three-quarters of a million from malnutrition. Insecurity took the form of political instability as well as fears on the part of the Weimar Republic and its ruling government (1919–33) of what was perceived as the communist threat. Nor was Weimar Germany itself exempt from accusations of corruption and decadence, despite the fact that the 1920s was a period associated with 'Expressionism, Weimar culture and a time when Berlin was the cultural centre of Europe' (Elsaesser, 1996: 136).

Berlin might well have become the cultural capital of Europe in the 1920s, but it was also perceived as the capital of decadence primarily because the pre-war 'strictures in morality and social convention were thrown aside by the young' (Manuell and Fraenkel, 1971: 13), **censorship** was abolished (albeit briefly: 1918–20); politically, there were pockets of communist activity and, finally, sexualities of all types had emerged onto the civic scene. Berlin was red and it was hot. But, economically speaking it was a city of crashed markets and rampant poverty. It was, then, a city of huge contrasts and paradoxes. To this effect, German expressionist film could be said to reflect the mood of the times.

The thematic preoccupations of pre-war cinema – which had shown such a fascination with the trappings of modernity through its representation of the modern city and its technologies, mostly associated with speed and the motor car, trains and telephones (particularly in crime and detective films) – were not replaced by post-war cinema as such, but were given a darker treatment in films associated with German expressionism. Fascination with modernity was replaced with a representation of its dehumanizing effects (e.g. industrialization is to be feared; see Lang's *Metropolis*, 1926). And the effects of the economic conditions on the metropolitan realities of Berlin are reflected in Lang's *Dr Mabuse, the Gambler* (1922), a sinister tale in which Mabuse acts as a cypher for the corruption and social chaos so much in evidence not just in Berlin but more generally, according to Lang, in Weimar Germany.

There is considerable debate as to whether German expressionism was in fact a film movement. For example, Thomas Elsaesser argues (1996: 141) that thematically and stylistically there were precedents in pre-war German cinema, particularly in the form of the **fantastic** films which exploited, among other literary trends, German Gothic-Romantic legend and fairy tales. The fantastic film was an important tradition in pre-war cinema associated primarily with the filmmaker Paul Wegener (ibid.: 141). It was a tradition which married conservative content with experimental style. For Elsaesser, therefore, the German expressionist film movement was not a new departure but a tail end of the fantastic film tradition (ibid.: 141). Manuell and Fraenkel (1971: 33) make the point that legendary costume films and **costume dramas** were far more prolific at the time than German expressionist films. What is clear is that German expressionism cannot be seen as standing for all of the so-called Golden Age of German cinema (1920–29), although its impact on the evolution or development of film style was quite significant (especially its impact on mise-en-scène as **semiotically** charged; see **melodrama**). In real terms, German expressionist films were very much in the minority of film production during the 1920s (only ten or so have survived into the canon) and their existence has perhaps more to do with film industry practices than with necessarily a conscious aesthetic or film movement per se.

In the post-war years, the move was to consolidate the German film industry and to rationalize it much along the lines of the **Hollywood** vertically integrated **studio system**. A major merger operation took place in 1917, combining larger production firms with smaller ones. This merger brought about the foundation of UFA (the Universum-Film Aktiengesellschaft). The German film industry became largely identified with UFA although some production companies managed to remain – albeit only for a short while – independent from UFA. One such company was Decla, headed by Erich Pommer. And, in a sense, it is thanks to him and his willingness to take a risk on something new that the 'first' so-called expressionist film, *The Cabinet of Dr Caligari* (1919), saw the light of day (although its Berlin première, according to Silberman (1996: 307), was 26 February 1920). It appeared to herald a new cinema. However, this film was part of a broader strategy put in place by Pommer at Decla. Namely, a production programme that was aimed more particularly at producing a cinema that was based, as Thomas Elsaesser (1996: 143) puts it, on 'a concept of product differentiation'. In any event, this new cinema was one which was to last in reality for a short five-year period (1919–24). Thus, the expressionist film was one film style amongst others. For its part, in this age of consolidation, Decla merged with Bioskop in 1920 (becoming Decla-Bioskop) and subsequently with UFA in 1921 (although some film historians quote 1920) – Decla-Bioskop remained under the tutelage of Pommer who continued to produce expressionist films.

The German expressionist film is a highly stylized type of film. Hallmarks of this style are oblique camera angles, distorted bodies and shapes, bizarre and incongruous **settings** that are almost Gothic in their look and framing. Lighting is similarly highly stylized in its use of heavy contrast between light and dark (known as chiaroscuro or high-contrast lighting) creating dramatic shadows. The subject matter is equally surreal and Gothic and about unnatural acts or realities – a projection on-screen of a character's subjective and often mad world. Marc Silberman (1996: 308–10) makes some interesting points in relation to the dynamic tension between setting and actorly style. The expressionist film focused on the formal issues of the image, mise-en-scène was abstract and primarily two-dimensional. The lack of depth of the image contrasted with the 'obsessive interiority' of the acting – at least the **acting** of the central male protagonists. The actor's body, Silberman explains (ibid.: 309), was a 'formal element within the mise-en-scène that could be coupled with or set off against other elements like set design'. At times, then, the body 'conforms to architectural lines' (ibid.: 309) – as in the case of Cesare, the somnambulist in *The Cabinet of Dr Caligari*, and his movement along the walls, or Nosferatu's shadow ascending the stairs in Murnau's 1921 film of the same name. As such, set design, lighting and the body are all interrelated squeezings-out of a psychology. At other times, the actor's gestures can be mechanical and abrupt, 'creating a mechanical, artificial rhythm' (ibid.: 309) – the evil Mephistopheles (played by Emil Jannings) of Murnau's *Faust* (1926) is the embodiment of this type of deliberately contrastive dramatic and explosive acting.

In German expressionist films, then, the actor's body is as much a producer of meaning as the mise-en-scène. But, as Silberman argues (1996: 310), the centrality of the body as 'the focus for the metaphysics of the image' was not a new tendency, but one which owed its heritage to the *Autorenfilm* (the art film) of the early 1910s. What is also striking in these expressionist films is the contrast between the intensity and interiority of the angle and the limited camera action and sparse editing style. The camera is quite static, and editing is quite standard and basic. Silberman is right to make the point (ibid.: 310) that as far as the concept of the modernity of the cinematic **apparatus** is concerned, expressionism effectively denied, or missed the opportunity of, experimentation with the technology of the apparatus – at least until the process of editing known as **montage** (see **editing**) impacted on German cinema (by the mid-1920s). The later expressionist films (e.g. Murnau's *The Last Laugh*, 1924, and Lang's *Metropolis*, 1926) show a new approach to camera and editing practices. The camera is 'unchained' and has 'replaced the actor as producer of meaning' (ibid.: 312) and fast, at times montage-style of editing reflects the modernity of the apparatus as a twentieth-century technological instrument of speed (ibid.: 312).

The emblematic film of this movement was the film that 'launched' it, the Austrian filmmaker Robert Wiene's *The Cabinet of Dr Caligari*. This horror film tells the story of the delusions of a young lunatic, Francis, whose perception of reality we are treated to until the very final twist at the end of the film when we discover that *he* is the madman not Dr Caligari. According to Francis' version of reality, Dr Caligari is a mad and sinister doctor who wants to display his somnambulist Cesare (played by Conrad Veidt, *the* fetish **star** of this movement) at the local fair. Display, however, is not his real motive, or so Francis would have us believe. The doctor's secret, hidden motive is to exploit the sleepwalking Cesare to carry out the murders of people who thwart his, the doctor's, desires. The film ends with us discovering that Francis is the true lunatic and that what we have just witnessed is no more than his delusions for which he is now receiving treatment from the doctor he believed to be Doctor Caligari.

Although the look of the film is definitely expressionistic (the sets were painted and designed by the expressionist artists Hermann Warm, Walter Reiman and Walter Röhrig), in terms of the narrative, with its themes of death, tyranny, fate and disorder, this film continues the long line of German romanticism (as exemplified by the Brothers Grimm and Friedrich Schiller) and can also be seen as a film following in the fantastic tradition established by Paul Wegener before the 1914 to 1918 war (Elsaesser, 1996: 141). As we recall, the expressionist movement itself was deliberately anti-romantic and anti-naturalist in its focus. So it could be argued that while the film is stylistically expressionistic, it is not so thematically. The final outcome of the film is fairly estranged from the expressionist ideal as well. The submission by the youth (the son) to the all-knowing paternalistic doctor suggests a quite conservative reading, one which advocates obedience (rather than rebellion) to a strong authoritarian figure (Murray, 1990: 26–27). However, in that the film appears to be a psychological outpouring of Francis' sexual regressions and transgressions (through his expression of an imagined and distorted world-view), it is close to the expressionistic practice of squeezing-out the inner self. It is worth reading Kracauer's (1992: 21–33) account of the making of this film and that of Manuell and Fraenkel (1971: 17–18), since the original script, by Carl Mayer and Hans Janowitz, was far more radical and politicized.

Whatever our reading of it now, at the time of its release *The Cabinet of Dr Caligari* met with huge international success particularly in France and the USA. The German film industry imagined that it could impose itself on the international scene by capitalizing on this success. Decla-Bioskop was absorbed into UFA by 1920/1921 and this major conglomerate, with the help of Erich Pommer as Head of Production, set about producing expressionist films that would export well. Fritz Lang's *Destiny* (1921) and *Dr Mabuse, the Gambler* as well as Friedrich Murnau's *Nosferatu* (1921) were hugely successful and allowed Germany to enter foreign markets in a way unknown before (the sale of just one of these films to one foreign country would finance the production of a new film). Added to this financial success story was the cultural respect these films obtained for a country that had lost a world war and with it a considerable international prestige. In this regard it is not possible to dissociate the German expressionist film from nationalistic values. Viewed in this light, this movement strikes us as more conservative than perhaps its **avant-garde** experimental style would lead us to believe.

For a number of different reasons the fortunes of this movement soon waned and, by 1924, it more or less came to an end although the style lived on for a while in a handful of films: Lang's *Metropolis* (1926) – which was a box-office failure – *M* (Lang, 1931) and Georg Pabst's *Kameradschaft* (1931). There were two major reasons for this movement's decline. The first was economic. The deutsche-mark had regained strength by 1923 and its stabilization meant that the former export trading advantage disappeared (Elsaesser, 1996: 144). The second had to do with the emigration of personnel, primarily to the United States who – either for political or professional reasons – went to Hollywood to work. Thus, Leni, Lubitsch, Murnau and Lang – to name but the most renowned – left Germany and took with them their own filmmaking practices which had considerable influence on Hollywood production styles particularly in relation to the horror film and **film noir**.

see also: **French poetic realism**, **mise-en-scène**, **modernism** and **horror**

For further reading other than authors mentioned in the text see also Coates, 1991; Roberts, 2008; Scheunemann, 2003.

GERMANY/NEW GERMAN CINEMA

A movement that came into forceful being by the early 1970s although its roots go back to the early 1960s when, inspired by the **French New Wave** and the **Free Cinema** (**Britain**), twenty-six young filmmakers and film critics signed the Oberhausen Manifesto in 1962. The manifesto declared its intention to create the new German feature film. It swore a death to the established film industry (*Papas Kino*, daddy's cinema) and promised the birth of a new cinema that would be international. The first outcome of this Manifesto, which drew the government's attention to the lack of provision for new potential talent, was the foundation of the Board for the New German Cinema (1964).

However, this new wave cinema was quite distinctly marked from its two sources of inspiration in that it was directly politically motivated as a movement. Indeed, this film movement needs to be understood within its historical, political, economic and geographical moment. Officially, the movement had two generations: Young German Cinema of the 1960s and New German Cinema of the 1970s and early 1980s. The generational shift had more to do with **ideological** changes than with two distinct groups of filmmakers. The major shift was away from the auteurist approach (*autorenfilm*) which led to an emphasis on individual creativity at the expense of a politicized cinema (see **auteur** entry). The New German Cinema focused on establishing a new aesthetics and a corpus of social critical films which at the same time recognized the needs of the industry, and as such its cinema products were less rarefied than the 1960s outputs. This new wave of German cinema spans twenty years (1962–82), its 'death' being marked by the suicide of one of its major proponents, the filmmaker Rainer Werner Fassbinder. However, such a date would exclude many films made during the 1980s that are clearly part of the New German Cinema ethos. Thus, it might be better to say that, by the mid-1980s, three conjunctural moments did, in some respects, serve a semi-death knell to this cinema. These were: the effect of television and, equally importantly, the conservative Kohl government, which withdrew much of its financial support from this radical cinema, plus the departure of a number of the original and more renowned filmmakers to work on the international production scene.

If we regard the movement as beginning in 1962, then in political terms we must recall that in 1961 the Berlin Wall was erected, splitting this great city into two ideological realities (capitalist and communist) and thus effectively signifying the already very real division of Germany into two parts: the West (FRG) and East (GDR). Post-war in the West, interestingly, the film industry had been dispersed by the allies with centres in Munich, Hamburg and West Berlin as a deliberate strategy to counter a re-formation of the film industry into one oligarchy (as it had been during the Third Reich in the form of UFA). No such thing occurred in East Germany which, post-war, inherited the former Weimar studios at Babelsberg (near Potsdam), thus keeping its film industry, DEFA, very much as a centralized affair.

This New German cinema emanated, then, from West Germany and, unlike films produced by the industry in East Germany, it was a cinema which attempted to come to terms with its nation's recent past, namely the Nazi era. The cinema it was rejecting was that of the National Socialist film industry of the 1930s and 1940s, a cinema which still prevailed in the 1950s in the **mainstream** production with its highly popular provincial films (the so-called *Heimat* films – a **genre** which Edgar Reitz, in his sixteen-hour TV series *Heimat,* 1984, would subvert and reinscribe into a completely new meaning: a German political history told through the chronicle of provincial family life from the end of World War One to 1982). The motivation of the New German cinema was to give a renewed credibility to the cinematic **apparatus** and industry after the abuse it had received under Nazi rule (as a propaganda tool). The government saw the merit of this motivation and wanted to exploit the non-conformist practices of this new wave cinema to give a new image to the new Germany.

In economic terms, this new and resisting cinema emerged at the very moment when the industry was itself in decline due to a major drop in **audience** numbers thanks to the increased consumption of television sets. With the industry under threat it was easier for spaces to open up for a new type of cinema. This same phenomenon occurred in Britain and France with their new waves, although it was a much slower process. Moreover, with West Germany, audience reception of this new wave German cinema was by no means as enthusiastic as the initial reception of the French and British new waves in the two other countries. Indeed, German audiences showed very little interest in this new indigenous product. It was left to the French and American audiences to appreciate this new and strongly politicized cinema.

The names most famously associated with this movement, or perhaps it would be more appropriate to call it a collective of young, independent filmmakers much in the **auteur** tradition, are those of Rainer Werner Fassbinder, Wim Wenders, Werner Herzog, Volker Schlöndorff, Hans Jürgen Syberberg, Alexander Kluge and Jean-Marie Straub (a Frenchman living in Munich and who worked in close collaboration with Danièle Huillet, also French). And the fetish **stars** most commonly linked with these filmmakers are Hanna Schygulla and Klaus Kinski. Kaes (1996: 616) distinguishes two phases in this cinema: the Young German Cinema of the 1960s and the New German Cinema of the 1970s. During the first phase, Alexander Kluge, a legalist by profession, was an effectual negotiator with the German government and successfully brought about the establishment of the Board for the New German Cinema with an official fund (of five million deutsche-marks) for the young German filmmakers. But the established film industry took a dim view of this and lobbied the government to pass a Film Subsidy Law whereby films borrowing from the government would have to commit themselves to a return of at least half a million deutsche-marks, effectively closing the door on this new movement's access to that form of state funding. The government appeared eager, however, to fund a national cultural product and the collective was only too ready to accept state subsidies. So other forms of funding, at a federal level, came into play. So too did grants, prizes and awards which went part of the way to helping this new cinema. Two film schools were established: the German Film and Television Academy in West Berlin (DFFB, 1966) and the Film and Television School in Munich (HFF, 1967). By 1971, after several years of making short films and a few feature films under considerable hardship, some of the filmmakers decided to take on board the **distribution** and international sales of their films. They formed the Authors' Film Publishers and were particularly successful in selling films outside West Germany (as it then was) but less so within the country.

Perhaps it was the subject matter of their films that deterred home audiences, because as Kaes (1996: 617) points out, the Young German Film 'was a cinema of resistance – against the mass-produced entertainment industry of the Nazi period and the 1950s, against the visual pleasure of lavish productions, and against the ideology of the economic miracle'. This new cinema strove for authentic **documentary** and its style was one of grainy **realism**. The films of the first phase, in the main, explored the fraught relationship of Germany to its past (Straub and Huillet's *Machorka-Muff*, 1962; Kluge's *Yesterday Girl*, 1966; Schlöndorff's *Young Törless*, 1966). Respectively, the themes dealt with in these films range from the continuing power wielded by the German military during the 1950s, the inescapability of one's past, and the conformity of intellectuals during the Nazi era (for further details see Kaes, 1996: 616–17). Films of the second phase continued to be socially and politically motivated and examined not just the German-speaking countries' recent past but also the contemporary scene. Fassbinder's *Fear Eats the Soul* (1974), Kluge's *Strongman Ferdinand* (1976) and the collectively directed *Germany in Autumn* (1978) take a hard look at contemporary Germany from the point of view, respectively, of racism, fascism and the state of the nation in general including political **censorship**. Herzog's films stand out as different within this movement in that they tend to be in the romantic tradition and historical in their settings (as with *Aguirre, Wrath of God*, 1972). In most of his films, Herzog blends documentary, **ethnographic** authenticity with a surrealistic vision to narrate the story of an individual who is either driven mad by his own aspirations to fulfil an impossible ambition or alienated by the society in which he finds himself. His films, often based on the real lives of historical personages, treat the extremes of colonialism – that is, racism and the total disregard for otherness.

But that is not the whole story of this cinema. If the most famous filmmakers were male and Munich-based, there was also a radical

West Berlin film culture, an important part of which was the group of women filmmakers (*Frauenfilme*), but which has been mostly overlooked by histories of cinema – the exceptions being Thomas Elsaesser's book (*New German Cinema: A History*, 1989), a special *Jump Cut* issue (no. 2, 1982), Julia Knight's book (*Women and the New German Cinema*, 1992), the two-volume edited *Gender and German Cinema* (Frieden *et al.*, 1993), and Sabine Hake's study (*German National Cinema*, 2002). Some fifty-six women directors have contributed films (shorts, **experimental** video or feature length) to this movement. They, like their male counterparts, were mostly born after World War Two and were, in the 1960s, part of the new generation of filmmakers. If the male filmmakers encountered difficulties with the establishment, at least not so many doors were closed to them as to the women. In the 1960s, it was difficult for women to get into film schools and mostly, if they did get in, they received very little by way of technical training. Unlike their male counterparts, they did not 'burst onto the scene' in the 1960s. Perhaps it is their late start that has made them less 'noticeable' to film historians.

Primarily their output started in the 1970s – a significant date, since their emergence coincided with the feminist movement in Germany (as elsewhere in the Western world) – a movement to which many were firmly committed. Exemplary of this commitment was the founding in 1974 by Helke Sander of the first and only European feminist film journal *Frauen and Film* (*Women and Film*). The journal's major objectives were to analyse the workings of patriarchal culture in cinema and to develop a woman's cinema and a feminist aesthetics. Among the women filmmakers, the best known abroad are Jutta Bruckner, Margarethe von Trotta, Doris Dörrie, Helke Sander and Helma Sanders-Brahms, although obviously there are many others. Their 1970s films tended to focus on real-life issues such as abortion (illegal in West Germany), domestic violence, the **myth** of the economic miracle of the Adenauer era of the 1950s, working conditions and the possibilities of social change. Sabine Eckhard's *Paragraph 218* and *What We Have Against It* (1976–77), Cristina Perincioli's *The Power of Men is the Patience of Women* (1978), Jutta Bruckner's *Years of Hunger* (1980) and Barbara Kasper's *Equal Wages for Men and Women* (1971) are, respectively, examples of these tendencies in the women's cinema in the 1970s. Later, in the 1980s, the tendency was to explore the issue of whether there is a feminine aesthetic and a different, even disruptive, way of viewing the world (as in Ulrike Ottinger's *The Mirror Image of Dorian Gray in the Yellow Press*, 1984, or Helke Sander's *The Trouble with Love*, 1984). In any event, by the 1980s, West

Germany, as Knight (1992: 13) points out, 'boasted a highly acclaimed women's cinema and a vibrant feminist film culture as part of its new cinema', a point that negates the assumption made by film historians that the New German cinema died in 1982.

Women filmmakers associated with New German cinema continue to practise their art within Germany. Many of their male counterparts have, however, left and relocated in the USA (either in Hollywood or New York). This contestatory cinema of resistance has not therefore died as such, but has become very much a minority production within an already minority national cinema. Amongst the women of that generation, Dorris Dörrie's *Happy Birthday Türke!* (1991) serves to remind us that there are still issues on the political agenda – such as the question of marginality and difference – that need voicing and constant vigilance. But so too amongst the younger generation of filmmakers does the work of Wolfgang Becker, *Life is All You Get* (1996) and Andreas Dresen, *Night Shapes* (1998). Thus the legacy of New German cinema lives on.

For further reading see Corrigan, 1983, Elsaesser, 1989; Hake, 2002; Kaes, 1996; Knight, 1992; Rentschler, 1988.

HAYS CODE

In 1922, the Motion Picture Producers and Distributors of America (MPPDA) was established. It quickly became more popularly known as the Hays Office – after the MPPDA's first president, William H. Hays (1922–45). The MPPDA (later to become the Motion Picture Association of America) was established in response to public outrage at the sex scandals in **Hollywood** and the sexual contents of films. The MPPDA was a bulwark between state and federal governments on the one hand and the film industry on the other. Hays was politically powerful and had a strong moral reputation and his job was to prevent intervention and **censorship** being governmentally imposed. The MPPDA applied pressure on the film companies to control their **stars** and the content of their films – a form of self-censorship which more or less worked until 1930. In 1934, under renewed pressure from the general public (and the moral brigades), the MPPDA produced the Motion Picture Production Code which was to act as a guideline for the industry on taste and decency. However, by 1934, public reaction to the industry's products again became vociferous, particularly at the violence portrayed in **gangster** films, and so the production code became mandatory. In 1968, the code was replaced by a ratings system, still in place today (MPAA: Motion Picture Association of America).

HEGEMONY

A concept devised by the Italian political thinker Antonio Gramsci to describe the winning of consent to unequal **class** relations. It is a more succinct term for the expression often used in its place: dominant **ideology**, which, within the Western world, is taken to be a white, middle-class male construct. This particular socio-economic group exercises leadership in such a way that the subordinate groups see that it is in the general interest to collude with that construct. The dominant groups (elites) make sense of the institutions through which they govern those not in power, by showing that they (as elites) are but representatives of those institutions that govern us all. Thus, they use consensual terms such as *our government, our economy, our educational system*. Those who are subordinate to it, then, are not 'coerced', but their consent and collusion in being so dominated emanates from a desire to belong to a social–political–cultural system, to a nation – to have a sense of nationhood. Mainstream or **dominant cinema** functions consensually in its mediation of hegemonic values (the family, social mobility, etc.) and as such is inscribed within that hegemony. In its **transparency** on the class interests of the dominant group, cinema reveals them as 'natural', therefore unquestionable and desirable.

see also: **ideology, naturalizing**

HISTORICAL FILMS/RECONSTRUCTIONS *SEE* COSTUME DRAMAS/HERITAGE CINEMA

HOLLYWOOD

Known as the 'dream factory', Hollywood was originally an escape route from the controlling powers over film companies of the Eastern Trust (1909). The climate, the mountains and plains and low land prices of California made Hollywood an ideal and profitable place to set up film **studios**. Huge studios were built in the Hollywood neighbourhood as well as extravagant mansions for the **stars** in nearby Beverly Hills. Production techniques were unique. By the

1920s, Hollywood was producing 90 per cent of the American film product, and exporting massively abroad so that it was the most important film industry worldwide. By the 1930s, the Hollywood studios were totally **vertically integrated** (controlling production, **distribution** and exhibition). In the same period, Hollywood was making around six hundred films a year (six times the number of most Western nations at that time) and exercised a major influence over American **audiences**. All changed in 1948, when a Supreme Court decision put an end to the vertical integration of the Hollywood studios. Then came television, destined to be Hollywood's major rival. Thought of as an intrinsically American phenomenon, Hollywood, however, is no longer an all-American industry. Since the 1990s, it has progressively been bought up by multinational companies.

see also: **classical Hollywood cinema, studio system, stars, vertical integration**

For details on all these issues see **studio system**.

For further reading see Bordwell *et al.*, 1985; Higson and Maltby, 1999; Maltby, 2003; Neale and Smith, 1998; Vasey, 1997. For an interesting, sideways look at Hollywood see Robe, 2010. For contemporary Hollywood see Elsaesser, Horwath and King, 2004; King, 2002.

HOLLYWOOD BLACKLIST

As a reaction to the Cold War, the United States was extremely preoccupied with the Red Scare ('Reds under the beds'), and the fear that its institutions were in grave danger of infiltration from communists or subversives. To track down subversives, the House of UnAmerican Activities Committee (HUAC) was established in 1947 and, under the leadership of Senator McCarthy, a witch-hunt was led to unearth people who had associations in any way with communism or subversive activities. People denounced people; people tried to protect people. And **Hollywood** was no different. It too came under HUAC's scrutiny and Hollywood, to protect itself against government intervention, blacklisted numerous people in the industry who had been accused or denounced as communists or subversives. Hollywood wanted to show that it was patriotic, but many careers were destroyed. Only ten members of the industry (known as the Hollywood Ten) refused to testify before HUAC and were sent to prison for their courage.

HORROR/GOTHIC HORROR/HAMMER HORROR/HORROR THRILLER/BODY HORROR/ VAMPIRE MOVIES

This **genre** is not always easy to distinguish from **science-fiction** films; indeed, some critics see sci-fi films as a sub-genre of horror – but that is arguably too limiting. And perhaps Bruce Kawin's definitions, separating the two, are amongst the most helpful (1995: 313). While acknowledging that both promote growth and understanding, he argues they do it in different ways – a first difference being that the sci-fi movie addresses our conscious state more than the horror movie, which first addresses our unconscious. Naturally, sci-fi can be a projection of our worst fears – but generally speaking these fears have their first articulation in the conscious state, only secondarily in the unconscious. The tendency of sci-fi, Kawin tells us, is to 'extend into some hypothetical time and place the unexamined assumptions of the present culture' (ibid.: 321); in other words, sci-fi speaks to our relentless pursuit of technology. We learn from experience that technology (our own invention) can bring us great harm as well as good. Whereas the 'direction in which the horror film leads its audience – into the unconscious and through the implications of evil and of dream – can prove beneficial to the audience' because it allows us to examine our unconscious (ibid.: 322). In horror movies the monstrous is visited upon us for us to deal with, whereas in sci-fi we explore our evolution or our monstrous potential – and it is here that overlap between the two genres occurs of course.

The horror movie has its origins in the late nineteenth-century Victorian Gothic novel, although it does have earlier antecedents, most famously Mary Shelley's *Frankenstein* (1818), and also Dr Polidori's lesser-known *The Vampyre* (1819). It is for reasons of its English and European heritage that this genre is not necessarily solely a Holly-woodian one (unlike the **Westerns** which are based on and in US history). Indeed, in terms of the American horror products, many were made outside the official walls of **Hollywood** (e.g. the Miami-made gore movies of H. G. Lewis in the 1960s – see *Blood Feast*, 1963; Tobe Hooper's *The Texas Chainsaw Massacre*, 1974; Abel Ferrara's *The Driller Killer*, 1979). Furthermore, British cinema also had its heyday with this genre in the form of the Hammer Horror series (1950s to 1970s). Even so, Hollywood has a long track record with this genre dating back to 1931 (in terms of **sound** movies) with films such as *Dracula* (Tod Browning, 1931) and *Frankenstein* (James Whale, 1931) and the numerous sequels these two icons of horror have spawned.

As Neale (2000: 93–94) makes clear, other **intertexts** beyond the Gothic novel also influenced the **codes and conventions** and **mise-en-scène** of this genre. First, theatrical performances of the Gothic novels established an initial tradition and frame of reference for the sets and décors; second, circus and freak-shows were used as a source of inspiration for characterization; third, early 1900s cinema **adaptations** of the Gothic novel and 1920s **German expressionism** both contributed to the systems of **narration** as well as to the principles of **lighting** and décor.

The earliest type of horror movie is the hidden monster – whether it lies within our own beings (as with *Dr Jekyll and Mr Hyde*, 1908) or an unsubstantiable being such as the vampire. In this context we think of the myriad Count Dracula movies, but interestingly the first prototype was a female vampire made famous in Feuillade's *Les Vampires* series (1915–16), starring the music-hall actress Musidora as the notorious Irma Vep (anagram of Vampire). Feuillade's series picked up on the earliest tradition of vampire stories which had women as the predatory beasts. Lesbian desire is foregrounded in this series (women/virgins swoon under Vep's advances before succumbing to her) rather than the more stereotypical representation of woman as vamp, the bloodsucking killer of men. This is not, however, the dominant tendency of the vampire film, which tends to centre on the male. There are literary reasons for this male predominance, since the earlier vampire stories themselves underwent a regendering. The vampire was last 'seen' as a woman in Sheridan Le Fanu's novel *Carmilla* (1871) and was superseded some twenty years later by Bram Stoker's *Dracula* (1897). The rest is history. With one or two rare exceptions, the agent of vampirism is male (see Kuhn and Radstone, 1990: 243).

The vampire film had its heyday in Hollywood during the 1930s (mostly at Universal). The mise-en-scène at that time was influenced by German expressionism – more particularly by the lighting and sets of two German silent horror movies, Robert Wiene's *The Cabinet of Dr Caligari* (1919) and Friedrich Murnau's *Nosferatu: A Symphony of Terror* (1922). After World War Two, the vampire film tended to disappear – being replaced by other sorts of alien 'unnaturalness'. However, it made a brilliant and vigorous comeback in the United Kingdom under the name of Hammer Horror films (produced by Hammer Production Limited). These were made from the late 1950s to the late 1970s and starred Christopher Lee and Peter Cushing (for Hammer's policy and strategy see Cook, 1985: 44–47). During the 1970s, the acid-cold dinner-suited vampire, hitherto so much in evidence, gave way to a slightly more romantic version – almost to the point of deserving love (the impact of flower-power perhaps; see John Badham's *Dracula*, 1979). With the relaxing of **censorship**, the erotic-lesbian female vampire made a brief reappearance (as in *Vampire Lovers*, Roy Ward Baker, 1970; *Le Rouge aux lèvres*, Harry Kumel, 1971; *Vampyres*, José Larraz, 1974; and as late as Tony Scott's *The Hunger*, 1983). By the early to mid-1980s, vampire films had all but disappeared, doubtless due to their unsuitability in the face of AIDS. But Francis Ford Coppola came back with a *Dracula* (1992) supposedly faithfully based on Bram Stoker's original. And in 1994 Neil Jordan's *Interview with the Vampire* transformed vampirism into a sexual aesthetic not without homo-social/sexual overtones. And it is noteworthy that, since the 2000s, some eighty-five vampire films have been released (including series such as *Underworld* and *Twilight Saga*), a remarkable resurgence of the generic type on an international scale, indicating a renewed fascination with the concept of blood-lust and a fearful apprehension of the exchange of bodily fluids.

Vampire films are not, however, the whole or even the main canon of horror movies. As indicated, they dominated 1930s horror, but it should also be acknowledged that there were other monster-type horror movies during that decade such as *Frankenstein* and its sequels. These were about man-made monsters returning to haunt us and as such can be considered cross-generic (horror and sci-fi).

Essentially, horror is composed of three major categories: the 'unnatural' (which includes vampires, ghosts, demonology, witchcraft, body-horror); **psychological** horror (e.g. *Peeping Tom*, Michael Powell, 1959; *Psycho*, Alfred Hitchcock, 1960); and massacre movies (e.g. *The Texas Chainsaw Massacre*, Tobe Hooper, 1974). All three categories are a distinctly post-World War Two phenomenon. Having said this, it is important, as always, to note that there were precedents (as well, of course, as overlaps within the categories), and in this context, because they are the precursor to the psychological horror movie, it is worth recalling the series of **B-movies** produced during the 1940s for RKO by Val Lewton beginning with Tourneur's *Cat People* (1942). Lewton's films mix the unnatural with the psychological but they also brought horror more into the realm of the 'real' by locating the narratives within the domestic sphere and playing on the notion that horror is more imagined than seen. Just to cite three of his most famous productions: in *Cat People* the central female protagonist (Simone Simon), a newly wed, is haunted by her sexual frigidity and imagines that she is turning into a panther; in *I Walked with a Zombie* (Tourneur, 1943), an updating of *Jane Eyre* and set in the Caribbean, Rochester's wife is no longer mad, but the victim of a voodoo spell – the aura is one of unremitting psychological fear and ambiguity; finally, in *The Seventh*

Victim (Robson, 1943), Satanism penetrates Greenwich Village (New York) as a young woman searches for her suicidal sister.

As proof that our fascination with horror is a constant, it is worth reminding ourselves that, on an annual basis, around forty horror films are produced worldwide. It is also worthy of note that since the last two editions of this book (2006 and 2013), over thirty academic books have been written on the genre (an average of three a year at least). Moreover, focus has widened in these studies to embrace European and East Asian horror (on British horror, see Walker, 2015; Italian, Baschiera and Hunter, 2016; Japanese, Balmain, 2008; Korean, Peirse and Martin 2013; Spanish, Làzaro-Reboll, 2012).

The 'unnatural' horror type

This pre-eminently takes the form of the body-horror movie that by and large has become associated in the first instance with the 1950s era and the double fear of the Cold War and the post-nuclear world in which people found themselves. The sci-fi movie is where much of the paranoia of the Cold War comes into play, with aliens attacking from Mars and the like. But that was not its exclusive location. Thus, Hitchcock's **thriller**/horror *Vertigo* (1958) clearly has Cold War resonances (the whole question of identity – are people who they say they really are – links into the 'red-scare' mentality of America in the 1950s).

Bodily mutation movies were very much a central preoccupation of the unnatural horror type movie. Of course, their message, that monsters can either appear out of normal bodies or can be introduced into society, equally links them into representations of the Cold War fear. A classic is *The Blob* (Irvin Yeaworth Jnr, 1958) in which a nasty (red) blob of snot invades a small American town and proceeds to suck the life-blood out of every American institution (including a diner). But see also Eugene Lourié's series of beast-monster horror movies, *The Beast from 20,000 Fathoms*, 1953, *The Colossus of New York*, 1958, or the British-produced *Gorgo*, 1961. In each of these films a monster is resurrected (often within an urban context, New York or London) and creates fear and destruction. But what is interesting is that, much like their earlier body-monster prototypes, to whom they (however indirectly) refer, *King Kong* (1933) or *Frankenstein*, they also draw our sympathy – sending a contradictory message: if only we can know our enemy we might see 'him' as less monstrous. Fear expressed in these bodily mutation films was also a reflection of the post-nuclear society. Bodily mutation from man to beast and back again had a forerunner in the 1920 film *Dr Jekyll and Mr Hyde* (John Robertson) and was then, as in the 1950s, concerned with the psychological effects upon the human being of advances in science. But, by the 1950s, the concerns had moved on because of the very real reference point of the atom bomb. Mutilation, destruction or disintegration of the body, that was at the core of these horror films, emanated from a consciousness of the effects on the human body of real science (the dropping of the atom bomb on Hiroshima and Nagasaki). The Japanese produced holocaust films of these effects (e.g. *Godzilla*, Ishiro Honda, 1954), and the Americans did not neglect them either (as with *Them*, Gordon Douglas, 1954).

During the 1970s, this incursion into horror-realism was dropped in favour of a re-entry into the realms of fiction. This did not necessarily mean that films lost their political edge, particularly, starting with *The Night of the Living Dead* (George Romero, 1968) and culminating in David Cronenberg's 'body-as-host-to-mutants' films of the mid- to late 1970s (*Shivers*, 1974; *Rabid*, 1976; *The Brood*, 1979). In these films, evil is seen to triumph over good. The zombies of the *Night of the Living Dead* attack and eat the 'normal' inhabitants of a small 'normal' farm town in 'normal' America and the community's reaction is everyone for themselves. Set against America's political context of the time, of racism and civil unrest, Romero's message is a strong one: individual self-preservation and cowardice have made us corrupt – we are the living dead. Meantime, Cronenberg's films focus on the body in a different way as the centre of evil. His bodies become invaded by alien organisms that act to bring out our worst compulsions and expose our repressed nastiness. In his films, bodies are subjected to physical plagues that act metaphorically for the socio-sexual and political morass we have created. These plagues take the form, respectively, of slug-like parasites turning humans into sex-mad zombies, a strain of rabies transforming its victims into a murderous community and, finally, an Institute of Psychoplasmatics letting its psychotic patients out on the loose, including an avenging mother on the rampage. Located in between these two types of politically motivated horror movies, but still in the realm of evil, stands the controversial film *The Exorcist* (William Friedkin, 1973) and its story about the possession of a 12-year-old girl. It left audiences traumatized in the cinema theatres (literally being sick, going mad and so on). While it can also be classified as a psychological horror film, it is perhaps more readily identifiable as an unnatural horror type because of the way in which the girl's body is overtaken and invaded by the devil. The representation of dark powers in respectable upper-middle-class Georgetown (Washington,

DC) gives the film a slight politicized edge, though not as strongly as Cronenberg's and Romero's work. It is more ostensibly about religious faith and the influence that evil (in the form of the devil) can exert on individuals. It makes evil visible, but it also shows the heroic good (in the form of the two exorcists who are willing to give their lives to save the girl). As such, then, it is very much a battle between good and evil within the realm of religion. But this is not a stand-alone Satanist horror film. Roman Polanski's *Rosemary's Baby* (1965) pre-dates it by some five years and has a more complex contemporary message that reflects the unease America was feeling as the 1960s drew to a close. The narrative is as much based in sexual politics and urban paranoia as it is in one person's belief that her husband may be the devil incarnate who has impregnated her with an alien satanic child.

During the 1980s and 1990s, the unnatural horror film continued to express anxiety of the body (often, but not always, male) as a dis-eased space (*The Thing*, John Carpenter, 1981; *Alien³*, David Fincher, 1992). And it is not difficult to read into these films of those two decades a preoccupation with the politics of health, a fear of invasion of un(fore)seeable substances (cancer, AIDS). This represents quite a shift from the earlier 'unnatural' category of films – especially the vampire films that were so clearly about **sexuality** and bourgeois conformity.

In the 2000s to 2010s, for the most part it has been a case of remakes of earlier horror movies, or a return to the concept of earlier series (George Romero with various Living Dead films: *Land of the Dead*, 2005; *Diary of the Dead*, 2007; *Survival of the Dead*, 2010). Claire Denis' *Trouble every Day* (2001) and Danny Boyle's *28 Days Later* (2002) take up more contemporary fears; in both instances, the outbreak of a viral infection (set loose from a science laboratory). In Denis' film, scientific experimentation with 'exotic' carnivorous and vampire-like plants brought back from Africa, coupled with experiments into human sexuality, leaves two of the characters with a carnivorous bloodlust. Both are driven, henceforth, when in a state of lust, to sexual cannibalism. In Boyle's film, the experimentation is on chim-panzees. The virus, known as the Rage (i.e. rabies-like), spreads like wildfire and turns people into psychotic killers. Unsurprisingly, society as we know it collapses and only the good few stand a chance of saving humanity. In both these films, the message, however, is the same as with the earlier horror films: our unnatural dark uncanny side can very swiftly, it seems, be unleashed (albeit by the flick of an invisible switch!). I leave the implications of the choice of 'initial' source (Africa; chimpanzees) for others to consider – but White man's fear of the 'dark continent' springs very readily to my mind.

Currently, in the West, amongst the younger exponents of the unnatural horror category, James Wan is a stand-out with his series: *Insidious* (2011 and 2013), *Conjuring* (2013 and 2016); and his function as executive producer of the *Annabelle* and *Saw* series.

The psychological horror film and the massacre movies

The psychological horror film and the massacre movies (also known as slasher movies) reveal, albeit in very different ways, a particularly vicious normalizing of misogyny (see **naturalizing** and **psycho-analysis**). Hitchcock is often credited, with his film *Psycho*, as the filmmaker who perceived the idea of locating horror within the human psyche – thus melding the psychological thriller with the horror genre. One can always find antecedents to be sure, but it is certainly the case that this very disturbing film with its cutting knives and graphic scenes of murder (hinted at rather than seen, recalling Lewton) helped to bring about the slasher movie of the 1970s.

Very few of these movies fall short of being 'hate-women-movies' (the slasher movies in particular can arguably be interpreted as a backlash on the early 1970s feminist movements). By way of understanding this quite dominant trend in this cinema, it is useful to look at what Richard Dyer has to say, in an article on Coppola's *Dracula* (1992), about vampirism. He makes the point that nineteenth-century vampirism originates in a bourgeois society that has become aware that its concealed dependency on the working **class** (which came about as a result of the industrial capitalist democracy) is now being uncovered. In other words, dependence of the stronger on the weaker, as it is about to be exposed, breeds an almost irrational fear which is registered through the body. The vampire assails bourgeois morality by seducing its virgins and drinking their life-blood (what chance the bourgeoise surviving the attacks of the mob?). Class issues are sexualized: the brute force of the working class (bestiality) will undo (deflower or destroy) the future of middle-class capitalism. Similarly, in the psychological horror films and massacre movies, male dependence on the female for his **subjectivity** (sense of identity derived from his difference from the female) again becomes registered through the body. Female presence exposes the dependency. Thus penile instruments (phallus replacements or substitutes) such as knives or chainsaws are used to re-castrate the phallic woman. Although the woman is hier-archically positioned as weaker, as is the working class, nonetheless, she is finally stronger, since she holds the key to male identity through her difference. The killing is therefore an irrational response to the fear of exposure. *He* must kill *her* before the dependency is exposed.

Interestingly, as Mark Kermode points out (2003), much of the slasher-movie output since the 1970s heydays has been one of remakes – suggesting a form of self-cannibalization that would be funny if the films were not so horrid. Thus, the 1980s and 1990s slasher movies (perhaps first triggered by the populist *Psycho*-imitated slasher *Halloween*, Carpenter, 1978) have emptied the radical political edge of gore cinema and replaced it with **postmodern** horror pastiche – classic examples of which are *Friday the 13th* (Cunningham, 1980, and its sequels), *A Nightmare on Elm Street* (Craven, 1984, and its sequels) and *Scream* (Craven, 1996, and its sequels). These are remakes (incessantly pointing back to their earlier prototypes) whose only claim to renewal can be imputed to the special effects which lift them beyond the creaky effects of the 1970s or even 1950s masters. The current slew of remakes in the 2000s (e.g. *The Exorcist: The Version You've Never Seen*, Friedkin (remaking himself almost!), 2000; *The Texas Chainsaw Massacre*, Nispel, 2003; *Texas Chainsaw 3D*, Luessenhop, 2013) still suggests that, apart from the growth in effects offered by **CGI** which allow for the virtualization of even more implausible action, the genre is stuck.

This is not to say that we should be dismissive of the horror genre. Robin Wood, writing on the horror genre, is probably right in saying that, because horror films are linked to the unconscious, they can represent that which other genres repress (1979: 13). Thus, the horror genre occupies a revelatory rather than a complacently reflective relationship to **ideology**, the forms and meanings of which can be summed up as follows: the horror film represents all that our society represses (including the Id drives); our anxieties about modern consumer culture, including our reliance on technology; our anxieties about the **Oedipal trajectory**, including man's fear of castration and 'horror' or fear of reproduction; society's fears of otherness (the female reproductive body, **queer** sexuality, ethnic otherness).

Cook (1985: 99) explains that, despite its popularity as a genre, the horror film did not achieve respectability in critics' circles until the 1970s. She attributes this change to the impact of psychoanalysis on **film theory**. To have taken the genre seriously prior to this time would have meant dealing with the suppression of the Id, a repression of certain unspeakable desires (sexual and psychological). It is instructive that until the psychological thriller of the 1960s, which suggested that the monster is repressed in us and not external to us (although Cocteau's

La Belle et la Bête, 1946, certainly made this point thirty years earlier), our Id, our own other, took the form of an alien or monster outside of us – as if the genre itself could not face up to the suppression of the inner Id either. This would suggest that the **spectator**, beyond the thrill of being frightened by the terror and violence made visible before them, is also attracted by the implicit ambivalence inherent in the genre as to where it should locate sexual and psychological 'abnormalities'. In this context what do we make of *The Silence of the Lambs* (Jonathan Demme, 1990) in which we almost come to like the charismatic Hannibal Lecter, the cannibalistic and cultured serial killer?

see also: **genre, science-fiction films**

For further reading see Baschiera and Hunter, 2016; Carolyn, 2008; Chibnall and Petley, 2002; Creed, 1993; Harper, 2004; Hardy *et al.*, 1986; Hopkins, 2005; Humphries, 2002; Jancovich, 1992, 2002; Kuhn, 1990; Neale, 2000; Paul, 1994; Powell, 2005; Schneider, 2004; Tudor, 1989. On the Hammer Horror industry see Kinsey, 2007, 2010; Rose, 2009. For a taste of horror worldwide see Schneider, 2003. On Asian horror, Galloway, 2006; McRoy, 2005.

ICONOGRAPHY

A means whereby visual motifs and style in films can be categorized and analysed. Iconography can study the smallest unit of meaning of a film (the image), as well as the largest (the generic qualities of the whole film). Iconography then stresses both **mise-en-scène** and **genre**. Iconography also refers to the dress-codes of characters in the film. Iconography is, therefore, historically marked – the icons of one period will not be icons for another – and so it points to the shift over time of the look of a particular genre. It also points to social and sexual changes. If there appears to be no change, that too merits investigation.

For illustrative purposes let's take the iconography of the **Western** and the **gangster** film. Both genres have their dress-codes and their 'tools of the trade' (Cook, 1985: 60). The horse, the six-shooter, the spurs, boots, waistcoat, neckerchief (etc.) for the Western; fast cars, automatic rifles, flashy suits for the gangster film. The Western's hero smokes a cheroot, the gangster a cigar. The gangster lives in urban spaces, mostly in dark enclosed environments – at least in the gangster movies of the 1930s and 1940s. Action takes place at night. In more contemporary gangster films, action takes place day or night. In the Western, the hero is mostly moving across vast plains or desert land, arriving in small towns, tying his horse up to the inevitable cross-bar in front of the saloon (or wherever else he is headed). What differentiates these genres primarily is that the Western almost 'never changes' – the iconography remains almost the same, even in Clint Eastwood's Western films, despite their challenge to the **ideological** message of Westerns (as in *Pale Rider*, 1985; *Unforgiven*, 1992 – both directed by and starring Eastwood). Gangster movies' iconography, however, does shift with the times. The special **lighting** effects of the 1930s and then 1940s **films noir** are no longer a prerequisite in more contemporary gangster films. Even the iconography of violence has 'evolved' – nothing is spared in its mise-en-scène.

Part of the reason for this absence of change for Westerns has to do with **audience** expectation. The Western refers to a time gone by, but it is still part of the United States' cultural history and, as part of the currency for the society for which it works, it must perpetuate the existing iconography. If it does not, it disturbs. Such is not the case for the gangster film. Audience expectation is quite the opposite. Urban violence is very much an everyday preoccupation in the United States, as is gang warfare. This might explain the advent, in the 1990s, of a new type of gangster movie: Black gangster films. This became a popular genre – speaking, as it did, to both the reality and the myth of Black urban violence (e.g. *New Jack City*, Mario Van Peebles; *Boyz n the Hood*, John Singleton, both 1991).

Iconography has connotative powers beyond the visual imagery. For example, dress-codes reflect more than just the historical period. Gangsters in 1930s films wear very flashy suits as opposed to the detective in his sober suit, connoting excess versus order. Women, in particular, 'say' a lot through their clothes: the power-dressing woman, almost masculinized in her shoulder-padded tailored suit (as in 1940 movies); the untrustworthy *femme fatale* in a long slinky gown – preferably with a slit thigh-high – and so on.

IDEOLOGY

Ideology as a theoretical term comes from Marxism. Ideology is the **discourse** that invests a nation or society with meaning. And, since it reflects the way in which a nation is signified, it is closely aligned to **myth**. Ideology, then, is at the interface of language and political organization (*logos*, the discourse of, or on ideas). It is a system of ideas that explains, makes sense of, society. But the 'making sense', as Karl Marx points out, is predominantly the domain of the ruling **classes**, who assume their right to rule as natural. Thus, according to Marx, ideology is the practice of reproducing social relations of inequality.

The ruling classes not only rule, but they also rule as thinkers and producers of ideas and so control the way the nation perceives itself and, just as importantly, they regulate the way other classes are perceived or represented. From this 'misrepresentation' (i.e. the ruling classes' assumption of their natural right to govern and to determine the status of other classes) comes Marx's idea of ideology as false consciousness. But the subordinate classes also act with false consciousness, says Marx, if they accept that their position is natural, that is, if they accept the prevailing ideology as it makes sense of their subordination (see **naturalizing**).

Louis Althusser (1984: 37) takes issue with Marx's notion of false consciousness and makes the point that ideology is not just a case of a controlling few imposing an interpretation of the nation upon the subjects of the state. He suggests that, in ideology, the subjects also represent to themselves 'their relation to those conditions of existence which is represented to them there' (ibid.: 37). In other words, they make ideology have meaning by colluding with and acting according to it. Why this consensuality? Because of the reassuring nature of national identity. The nation-state gives people a sense of identity: status and pride. The state is *their* state, the governing body is *their* indigenous governing body, not some foreign ruler's, and so on. Ideology, then, is a necessity and it is produced 'by the **subject** for the subjects' (ibid.: 44). Thus, society renders ideology material (gives it a reality) and so, too, do the subjects. Individuals recognize and identify themselves as subjects of ideology. Althusser's central thesis that 'ideology interpolates individuals as subjects' (ibid.: 44) – that is, that ideology constructs the subject, that the subject is an effect of ideology – has had profound implications for the theorizing of **spectator–text** relations. As we shall see, this recognition and identification process by which ideology functions is one that film readily re-enacts.

Ideology infiltrates everyday life and serves the ruling classes, collusion notwithstanding. The rulers are after all those who have produced and control the institutions in which we as subjects function and by which we understand our society. School, the family, the media, are obvious institutions that are permeated by ideology. However, even though dominant ideology serves the ruling classes (who put it there in the first place), ideology is not a static thing nor is it immutable. Within dominant ideology, because it is composed of so many diverse institutions and institutional practices, there are bound to be contradictions. So, while ideology is dominant (and despite its 'naturalness'), it is also contradictory, therefore fragmented, inconsistent and incoherent. Moreover, it is constantly being challenged by resistances from those it purports to govern: groups such as the Black Power movement in the United States, the feminist movement in the Western world and some parts of the Eastern world, subculture groups such as the punk movement, the recent Arab Spring revolutions – these are just some of the most obvious examples.

Where does ideology fit into a discussion of cinema? Cinema is an ideological **apparatus** by nature of its very **seamlessness**. We do not see how it produces meaning – it renders it invisible, **naturalizes** it. Mainstream or **dominant cinema**, in **Hollywood** and elsewhere, puts ideology up on-screen. Hollywood's great subject, heterosexuality, is inscribed into almost every **genre**. So genre is a first place to examine the workings of ideology. The other area is, of course, that of representation (class, race, **gender**, age and so on). Genres function ideologically to reproduce the capitalist system. They are hermeneutically determined; that is, there will always be closure, a resolution at the end. In this respect, they provide simple common-sense answers to very complex issues, the difficulties of which get repressed. Already, however, we can see how generic convention is opening itself up as ideologically contradictory. Even though it is seemingly producing meanings that support the status quo, nonetheless, generic convention is quite distinct from the social reality that it purports to reflect. Social reality does not present easy solutions, life is not 'order/disorder/order restored' as the **classical narrative** system would have us believe. But, because of the reality-effect which seamlessness produces, the spectator is easily stitched into the narrative (see **suture**), the process of recognition and identification is underway and so, too, the ideological function of film – which is why generic repetition works so well and we go back again and again to the movies.

However, because ideology is contradictory, some films unintentionally show 'disjunctures in their relation to ideology' (Kuhn, 1982: 86), what Kuhn calls structuring absences (ibid.: 87). In other words, what gets repressed, left out, draws attention to itself by its absence. The much-quoted example is the **historical** biopic film *Young Mr Lincoln* (John Ford, 1939) which the *Cahiers du cinéma* group subjected to a detailed textual analysis (*Screen*, vol. 15, no. 3, 1972). Although supposedly a historical film about a man of enormous political importance, it is precisely history and politics that are the structuring absences of that film. The question then becomes why? To 'imbue the figure of Lincoln with qualities of universalism – precisely to represent the man as outside history, and thus to elevate him to the ahistorical status of myth' (Kuhn, 1982: 87). Another reason could be the historical context. At the time of its release (1939), the United States was maintaining an isolationist policy as

Germany began its war on Europe. It was choosing to stand outside of history. So this was not the time for political history lessons, nor for statements (good or bad) about the nation-state. As a-historically positioned, the United States could not 'show' history, that is, the 'reality' of Lincoln's time. Thus, it could not proselytize about the abolition of slavery or show the nation as politically divided (the Civil War). The need for a man of mythic status also points to a nation facing a contradiction or dilemma which it seeks to resolve through the very creation of that **myth**. Universalism implies being above all conflict. Finally, still within the historical context, the *Cahiers*' reading examined the film within its domestic political sphere and claimed that it mediated Republican values to counter Roosevelt's Democratic New Deal measures (1933–41) and to promote a Republican victory in the presidential election of 1940 in which it failed on both counts (see Cook, 1985: 189).

There are, then, films which show the contradictions inherent in ideology. Two of the earliest advocates of applying symptomatic readings to expose the ideological operations in film, Comolli and Narboni, put it succinctly when they say that such films contain an 'internal criticism ... which cracks the film apart at the seams. If one reads the film obliquely looking for symptoms, if one looks beyond its apparent formal coherence, one can see that it is riddled with cracks: it is splitting under an internal tension which is simply not there in ideologically innocuous film' (1969/1977: 7). **Melodrama** and **women's films** would seem to be just such innocuous films with their ideologies of romantic love, the family and maternity. But, feminist readings against the grain have rendered visible the patriarchal ideology upon which these films feed and exposed the ideological contradictions inherent in that ideology (see **feminist film theory** and **melodrama**).

see also: **hegemony** and **class**

IMAGINARY/SYMBOLIC – *SEE UNDER* PSYCHOANALYSIS

INDEPENDENT AMERICAN CINEMA

A term that refers to a film practice that began in the 1970s and is still in place. The first wave of so-called independent American filmmakers were directors such as Francis Ford Coppola, Martin Scorsese, Dennis Hopper and Paul Schrader, although of course they had antecedents in the form of the late 1950s director John Cassavetes – often referred to as the forefather of today's US indie cinema (see *Shadows*, 1959). This group emerged from what is known as the post-classical era of **Hollywood** and as such either set up their own production companies (Coppola's Zoetrope in California) or got their work produced by independent producers and friends (Scorsese, Hopper). Scorsese is, of course, also famous for bringing East Coast film production to the fore (e.g. Taplin-Perry-Scorsese Productions for *Mean Streets*, 1973) and for foregrounding in particular an unglamorous edgy New York in full spin with the various political crises of the 1970s (starting with Vietnam; see *Taxi Driver*, 1976). Schrader, in a different way, investigates other aspects of political corruption in the form of working-**class** exploitation and union bosses' alliances with the mob. The raw-edge political nature of the 1970s films (Hopper's *Easy Rider*, 1969, *The Last Movie*, 1971; Scorsese's *Mean Streets*, *Taxi Driver*; Coppola's *The Conversation*, 1974, *Apocalypse Now*, 1979; Schrader's *Blue Collar*, 1978) is a legacy that remains with subsequent waves of independent filmmakers in that their films continue to address social and contemporary issues. For example, David Lynch's work closely examines the moral squalor of small-town communities. From his earliest *Eraserhead* (1979) via *Blue Velvet* (1986) and *Lost Highway* (1996) to *Mulholland Dr.* (2000) and *Inland Empire* (2006) he explores the limits of decadence and human morbidity. The dreams of nightmares are his world, becoming morality plays that are almost familiar to us based as they are in a middle-America topography known to us all.

Independent cinema, as it devolves from the Cassavetes heritage into the present, is one that does not strive for perfection or the **seamlessness** of Hollywood; it is not the production values that count but the vision of the filmmaker – indeed, a good indie film will often show the poverty of its means of production, producing what could be termed a guerrilla or grunge cinema (reminiscent of some of the Latin American **Third Cinema** of the 1970s). Grainy images, jerky **editing**, improvised dialogue, sprawling **narratives**, long takes and flawed images go hand in hand with this kind of product – associated with some aspects of Hal Hartley's work (*Trust*, 1990, *Amateur*, *Flirt*, both 1995), Paul Thomas Anderson (*Boogie Nights*, 1997, *Magnolia*, 2000) or the one-offs (to date), Kevin Smith's *Clerks* (1994) or Darren Aronofsky's *Pi* (1998). But there is also the more polished indie product – one whose heritage is less Cassavetes and more Scorsese and Coppola and which also speaks to yet another cinema, that of the European arthouse cinema. This is the one we associate with the work of Jim Jarmusch (*Mystery Train*, 1989); Steven Soderbergh, who once said about his *The Limey*, 1999, 'it's *Get Carter* made by Alain Resnais' (1999, 12); Quentin Tarantino; and Sofia Coppola. As another type there is the work of a number of filmmakers (which includes the above category of filmmakers), also very polished, which takes the myths of America and also the **myths** propagated by American cinema itself and turns them on their head. The Coen brothers (*Fargo*, 1995, *The Man Who Wasn't There*, 2001), John Sayles' films (*City of Hope*, 1991, *Lone Star*, 1995, *Sunshine State*, 2002) and Jim Jarmusch's *Dead Man* (1995) come to mind, as do two other filmmakers who come more readily into this category of production but who also cross boundaries into **queer cinema**: Gus Van Sant (*Drugstore Cowboy*, 1989, *My Own Private Idaho*, 1991) and Todd Haynes (*Velvet Goldmine*, 1998).

What is interesting is that quite a number of these contemporary indie filmmakers – like some of their 1970s antecedents (Scorsese for one, although he has had a tumultuous relationship with Hollywood) – have successfully crossed over into **mainstream**, most famously the Coen brothers, Haynes, Soderbergh and Tarantino. (Perhaps it is also worth mentioning that many indies of this period have been financed by Hollywood offshoots.) Their motivations are either to cash in on their cachet and finance their independent personal projects or to try to work at change within the system. Some filmmakers step in and out of Hollywood – like Van Sant who has successfully mixed this practice although he has only made two films with Hollywood: *Good Will Hunting* (1997, with Miramax), which won him two Oscars; and *Finding Forrester* (2000, with Columbia). This has not prevented some critics from accusing him of selling out. However, he had already announced through his film *Psycho* (1998) – which had the appearance on paper of being a remake of Hitchcock that Universal were only too pleased to finance, but which was a **shot**-by-shot **deconstruction** of the masterpiece – that he was on his way back to his independent ways. *Gerry* (2001), the style of which was inspired by the Hungarian auteur Belá Tarr, and the **documentary** feel of *Elephant* (2003) confirmed this return (see also *Last Days*, 2005, *Paranoid Park*, 2007 and *Milk*, 2008).

Predominantly, the work of these contemporary indie filmmakers reveals to us the world of losers, nobodies, displaced people, confused and dysfunctional loners. *The Royal Tenenbaums* (2001) and *Moonrise Kingdom* (2012) by indie filmmaker Wes Anderson are some of the latest in this long line of ironic studies of America – the America

Hollywood seeks to disguise if not hide. But what is of course remarkably absent from the above list of filmmakers is, first, the presence of women indie filmmakers – Sofia Coppola (*Virgin Suicides*, 1999, *Lost in Translation*, 2003, *Marie-Antoinette*, 2006, *Somewhere*, 2010) stands out virtually alone (Kathryn Bigelow struggles in mainstream) – and, second, African-American/Black filmmakers (men and women). With regard to the latter group, an entry has been made under **Black cinema USA**. With regard to the former, that, regrettably, has yet to come.

For further reading see Backman-Rogers, 2015; Hillier, 2001; Holmlund and Wyatt, 2005; Tzioumakis, 2006, 2013.

INDEPENDENT CINEMA

This term refers to films made by filmmakers independently of the dominant, established film industry. Because they are made outside **mainstream** cinema practices they tend to be **avant-garde** or **counter-cinematic**, and, even if not **experimental**, they all tend to give an alternative voice to dominant **ideology**. They are mostly low-budget films either privately financed or in certain countries partly subsidized by government.

The entry above focuses on one well-known form of independent cinema: **independent American cinema** (which is more of a practice than a specific movement). Of course there are many others, some of which are discussed under separate entries in this book, such as **cinema nôvo**, the various European **New Wave cinemas** (Britain, France, Germany), **Dogme 95 films** and, finally, some of the independent cinemas discussed under **Third Cinema**.

see also: **avant-garde, counter-cinema, underground film**

INTERTEXTUALITY

Literally this expression means texts referring to texts, or texts citing past texts. Intertextuality is a relation between two or more texts that influences the reading of the intertext. This latter term refers to the present existing text, which, in some part, is made up by reference to other texts. Most films are intertextual to some degree – a text referring to other texts, an intertext in whose presence other texts reside. For example, a film may be based on an original text, a novel or play. The shooting style of the film may be painterly, suggesting painted texts to which it might be referring. **Shots** or combinations of shots might refer back to earlier films (by way of a homage to earlier directors). Songs within a film are an intertext. Thus, if the **star** playing the central protagonist is also a well-known singer, the audience will expect a song. That performance refers to another part of the star persona that has been developed outside of filmmaking and so refers to another text: the star as singer.

ITALIAN NEO-REALISM

A film movement that lasted from 1942 to 1952. Although critics credit Roberto Rossellini's 1945 *Roma città aperta/Rome Open City* as being the first truly neo-realist film, Luchino Visconti's *Ossessione/ Obsession* (1942) was really the herald of this movement. In fact the scriptwriter of Visconti's film, Antonio Pietrangeli, coined the term *neo-realism* in 1943 when talking about *Ossessione*. The main exponents of this movement are Visconti, Rossellini and Vittorio De Sica.

Rossellini called neo-realism both a moral and an aesthetic cinema, and, in order to understand what he meant we need to look at the historical context in which this cinema emerged. During the period of fascist rule under Mussolini, the type of cinema that was being produced was divorced from reality and concerned, only, with promoting a good image of Italy. The government had decreed that crime and immorality should not be put on-screen. The films primarily produced were slick middle-class **melodramas**, disparagingly called (after fascism) 'white telephone movies'. During the fascist government's control of the film industry some 'good' did come about: the famous Cinecittà studios (Italy's answer to **Hollywood**) were built and the Italian Film School was established, as was the first film festival: the Venice Film Festival (1932). And, perhaps more significantly, some filmmakers took a moral and aesthetic stance against fascism.

Neo-realism, then, owes its existence in part to these filmmakers' displeasure at the restrictions placed on their freedom of expression. And it is in this light that Visconti's 1942 film can be seen as the harbinger of neo-realism. But he too had precedents to his own film style. During the 1930s, Visconti worked as an assistant with the French filmmaker Jean Renoir: a significant apprenticeship, first, because of Renoir's association with the **French poetic realist** movement and, second, because he worked with Renoir on a film that historians perceive as the precursor to the Italian neo-realist movement, *Toni* (1934). Undoubtedly, the social and pessimistic realism of poetic realism did cross-fertilize into neo-realism, but the point to make about *Toni* is that it was a film based on a true story of an Italian immigrant worker in France whose passion for a woman led him to murder. Renoir used non-professional actors, shot the film on location and kept to the original **soundtrack**. The film has a grainy, realistic look, which the crackling soundtrack reinforces in its **documentary** verisimilitude. Visconti's *Ossessione*, while not a true story, was loosely based on an American pulp fiction novel, James M. Cain's *The Postman Always Rings Twice*. The film was shot on location in northern Italy and tells the story of a labourer who becomes obsessed by a woman and agrees to her plan to murder her husband. Having accomplished the deed, she gets killed in a car crash (gets 'her just deserts'). With this tale of sordid obsessions and shots redolent with lust and sensuality, Visconti was deliberately defying governmental decrees of cleanliness and propriety on-screen. The film was released, but in a heavily censored cut, and Visconti did not make another film until 1948, *La Terra trema/ The Earth Trembles*. However, the seeds for neo-realism were sown.

By 1943, fascist rule in Italy was coming to an end and, in 1944, Italy was occupied by the Allies. The fall of fascism allowed for the truth to be told about the impoverished conditions of the working **classes** and of urban life. And this is precisely what a small group of filmmakers did. They rejected the old cinema and its **codes and conventions** and went for the gritty reality. The basic tenets of this movement were that cinema should focus on its own nature and its role in society and that it should confront **audiences** with their own reality. These principles had implications for the style and content of this cinema. First, it should project a slice of life, it should appear to enter and then leave everyday life. As 'reality' it should not use literary adaptations but go for the real. Second, it should focus on social reality: on the poverty and unemployment so rampant in post-war Italy. Third, in order to guarantee this **realism**, dialogue and language should be natural – even to the point of keeping to the regional dialects. To this effect also, preferably non-professional actors should be used. Fourth, location shooting rather than studio should prevail. And, finally, the shooting should be documentary in style, shot in natural light, with a hand-held camera and using observation and analysis. These are very exacting demands, and in fact only one film meets with all these tenets: De Sica's *Ladri di bicicletti* (1948, *Bicycle Thieves*), although Visconti's *Terra trema* comes very close (it falls short, because it is a literary adaptation) as does *Roma città aperta* (which used a mixture of professional and non-professional actors, including *the* fetish **star** Anna Magnani, and used three small studio sets).

Roma città aperta was based on real events that Romans lived through during the period 1943 to 1944. This was before the Allied forces had arrived in the city and the Germans were still in control. The **narrative** is focused on the goings-on of the Italian Resistance during a three-day period. Resistance fighters die during these three days, but the impression given is that we have picked up on their story and that of others in the film and that these people's lives go on once the film has ended. However, it is the difficulties of the production that also give this film its feel of authenticity. Rossellini had to use newsreel stock, which gave the images their grainy realistic look. Money and film stock were extremely difficult to come by. Virtually the whole film was shot in Rome.

As film movements go, neo-realism was not particularly short-lived. It lasted ten years, even fourteen if we take into consideration that the last neo-realist film was De Sica's *Il tetto/The Roof* (1956). In a sense, neo-realism was officially 'demised' in the early 1950s by the government when it appointed Giulio Andreotti as Director of Performing Arts and gave him extensive powers. Any films giving a bad image of Italy were denied screening rights in Italy and, because he controlled bank loans, Andreotti could go so far as to withhold money from films he considered too neo-realist in **motivation**. The Cold War mood of the early 1950s also contributed to governmental dislike of the **social realism** inherent in these films, which they perceived as politicized and of the left – even though, of the filmmakers concerned, only Visconti was avowedly a Marxist.

Despite its demise, neo-realism had a huge impact on future film-making practices in Europe, the United States and India. The **French New Wave** widely acknowledged its debt to this movement, and resonances of its style are clearly in evidence in the **British New Wave**. A younger generation of Italian filmmakers was also much influenced by the neo-realists' work, in particular Emmanuel Olmi, Michelangelo Antonioni and Federico Fellini. And in India, Satyajit Ray's films of the late 1950s are strongly marked with the tenets of neo-realism.

For further reading see Bazin, 2011; Brunette, 1987; Haaland, 2014; Marcus, 1987; Millicent, 1987; Schoonover, 2012; Shiel, 2006; Wagstaff, 2007.

JUMP CUT

The opposite of a match cut, the jump cut is an abrupt cut between two **shots** that calls attention to itself because it does not match the shots **seamlessly**. It marks a transition in time and space but is called a jump cut because it jars the sensibilities; it makes the **spectator** jump and wonder where the **narrative** has got to. Within a sequence, the jump cut splices two shots of the same person together, but neither the **30-degree rule** nor the **reverse-angle shot** is observed. Thus, the impression of fragmentation is even more strongly felt, to the point where the brutality of this transition can suggest madness or, at the least, a state of extreme instability. Between sequences, the jump cut has quite the reverse effect of the standard cut. The narrative is transposed from one time and space to another without any explanation such as a shot or voice-over. This fragmentation of time and space can either produce a disorientation effect (within the **diegesis** and for the spectator) or put in question the idea that all lived experience can be explained by the comforting cause–effect theory. Jean-Luc Godard is undoubtedly one of the best exponents of this use of the jump cut (especially in his 1960s films; see *À bout de souffle*, 1959). His characters appear disoriented in a world where reason seems incapable of imposing a logical order on events. Equally, the spectator is disoriented and troubled by the non-causality of the images and the narrative.

see also: **cut, match cutting, spatial and temporal contiguity**

LIGHTING

This entry is in three parts: technology, practice, **ideology**.

Technology

In the earliest cinema, only natural lighting was used; most of the shooting was done in exteriors or in **studios** that had glass roofs or roofs that could open to the sunlight. As **narratives** became more complex (early 1900s) and as increased demand for products meant working to tight shooting schedules, using ordinary sunlight was not satisfactory enough since it was not easily controllable. Thus, artificial lighting was introduced to supplement existing light. The first type of lighting was the mercury-vapour lamp (invented in 1901 by Peter Cooper-Hewitt). These lights (known as Cooper-Hewitts) look much like neon strip-lights – they were packed into units of nine strip-lights. These units were then fixed in pairs one on top of the other onto wheeled, goose-necked units (so as to create wall and overhead lighting) and placed along the three walls of the studio (some twelve units in all). This lighting was based on blue and green wavelengths which suited the then orthochromatic film stock. Orthochromatic stock was sensitive to the blue and green end of the spectrum, but not to yellow and red. Used in studios, this lighting gave a gentle and soft effect to the image which then had to be matched, for consistency's sake, by any outside or real sunlight shooting through the use of light diffusers (where orthochromatic film would be more highly contrasted). While enormously efficient, the mercury-vapour lighting system had one main drawback. It could not provide directional light and therefore could not achieve contrast or highlighting effects. Thus, while maintaining the diffused lighting effect provided by vapour lamps, other systems of lighting had to be developed for effects lighting and to give a greater **realism** to the filmed image. To achieve contrast and a greater naturalism, non-incandescent arc spot-lights (which gave a blueish light) – known as Klieg lights (named after the Kliegl brothers who designed them) – were introduced (perhaps as early as 1905, but certainly by the early 1910s). It was at this point that **Hollywood** developed its three-point lighting system (key, fill and back-lighting).

After World War One, another type of arc-light was introduced into the panoply of lighting devices: the sun-arc. Originally, the sun-arc had been a high-powered arc-searchlight used during the war to spot (among other things) enemy aircraft. This powerful carbon-arc lighting was as bright as sunlight – the range of these floodlights varied from 650 to 10,000 watts. It gave much more flexibility to shooting schedules; shooting at night became possible, for example. While most of these carbon-arc lights have been replaced over time, first by tungsten-filament lighting and later by tungsten-halogen lamps, the so-called Brute, a 225-amp carbon-arc spotlight, is still used today for colour films and especially for creating sunlight. Carbon-arc lighting disappeared slowly, beginning in the late 1920s. Carbon-arc lighting was expensive to run, in terms of both electricity costs and maintenance. When **sound** was introduced and, with it, panchromatic film, incandescent lighting had to become the chief source of lighting – carbon-arc lamps on their own produced too much blue light and were very noisy. Panchromatic film was a black and white film sensitive to all colours of the spectrum and so could provide more subtle shades of 'colour' in gradations of greys unlike the orthochromatic film which was sensitive only to blue and green and so produced, in the main, highly contrasted black and white images. (For more details on this period see Bordwell *et al.*, 1985: 270–75, 294–97; Dyer, 1997: 84–96.)

Colour film has worked with an association of tungsten and carbon-arc lighting. Whether black and white or colour, there are two basic systems for lighting: floodlight and spotlight. Floodlight gives diffuse illumination, while spotlight, as the name implies, focuses on a specific area or subject. As colour stock and lighting systems improve so a more natural image can be obtained for those filmmakers whose drive is for realism. A more recent development in lighting technology is the HMI lamp. Originally introduced by Osram of Germany in the 1970s, this is a metal hydrargium medium arc-length iodide lamp. These lamps, though expensive and heavy to transport, yield three to four times more light than that produced by incandescent lights. HMIs were originally used for exterior key and filler lighting but are now being used for studio work. (For useful reference books on lighting terminology and use see John Alton, 1995; Richard Ferncase, 1995.) With **digital cinema**, the lighting principles remain pretty much the same; and of course there is the added advantage that lighting can be immediately checked and amended thanks to the calibrated monitor that allows the technical crew to see the effects straightaway.

Practice

As far as Hollywood was concerned (and still is in the main), lighting should not draw attention to itself, although it should be used for dramatic and realistic effect. In other countries' cinemas, however, lighting was used to aesthetic effect quite early in cinema history. For example, the low-angle and low-key lighting effects so closely identified with **German expressionist** cinema of the 1920s and the high-contrast lighting (called chiaroscuro) for signalling the mood and workings of the unconscious had already been used for emotional effect in Danish films as early as 1910.

These exceptions aside, lighting for dramatic effect became quite standardized by 1915, for probably two reasons: the predominance of studio shooting and the advent of the **star** system (in both Europe and the USA). As mentioned above, lighting became a three-point affair. It is one that is still in practice today, albeit with the variations one would expect with technological progress. There are three primary positions for lighting: key lighting (hard lighting focused on a particular subject), fill lighting (extra lights) to illuminate the overall framed space fully, and back-lighting (normally used to distinguish the figure in the foreground from the background, and so known also as a separation light). This is the basic system of lighting and one of its first effects is to eliminate or greatly reduce shadows. The key light is placed to the front and side of the subject who is looking between the key light and the camera; the fill light is a soft light normally placed near the camera on the opposite side of the key, it is a soft light that fills in areas of shadow cast by the key light and thus decreases the image-contrast. The fill light can also be placed on top of the camera – this is known as an Obie, so-named after Merle Oberon for whom the light was designed to give maximum effect to her face in close-up (curiously this light fitting is also known as a basher). The rover fill is – as the name suggests – a fill light mounted onto a dolly so that it can follow the subject. The back-light highlights the edges of the subject, it is aimed towards the camera from above and behind the subject; when in this position this form of lighting is known also as a hair light because it creates a halo effect on the head. Hair lighting was very much a feature of **classical Hollywood cinema** (1930s–60s), but it was already in use as early as the 1910s. Back-lighting that comes from behind but to the side of the subject is known as a kicker or kick-light.

There are two types of lighting for a scene: high-key and low-key. High-key lighting refers to a brightly lit scene with very few (if any) shadows – and is often used in **musicals** and **comedies**. Low-key lighting refers to a scene where the lighting is predominantly dark and shadowy, the key light does not dominate. Low-key lighting often includes the concept of high-contrast lighting effects (also known as chiaroscuro) – a use of contrasting tones of highlight and shadow which is predominantly associated with **film noir**, **horror**, psychodramas and **thrillers**. Some film analysts are adamant that low-key lighting and high-contrast lighting must not be confused (Konigsberg, 1993: 191), precisely because they are not the same. High-contrast lighting means what it says – there is a strong contrast between light and shadow. Thus, a film noir may have moments when the shooting is done with low-key lighting and, at others, with high-contrast – and it is perhaps worth keeping the distinction clear.

Day-for-night and night-for-night shooting are the last two elements of lighting practice that need mentioning (there are of course many more variations and fine details to lighting and Ferncase's book on lighting, mentioned above, is an invaluable reference tool). Day-for-night shooting is when night-time is simulated while shooting exterior scenes during the day. François Truffaut famously made a film entitled *La Nuit Américaine/Day for Night* (1973) which shows you exactly how this conceit is achieved. Essentially the day-for-night effect is achieved by shooting late in the afternoon, and most importantly through the use of underexposure (small tense aperture) and filters. Night-for-night means shooting exterior night scenes at night – often using very fast film stock.

With all this detail on lighting to bear in mind, it is quite helpful to embrace Bordwell and Thompson's (1980: 82–84) useful identification of the three major features of lighting: quality, direction and source – since this little triumvirate neatly encompasses film lighting practice. Thus, the quality of light can be hard or soft, the direction can be front, side, back, and occasionally under (the light comes from below the subject), the source will be key and/or fill.

Lighting and ideology

As we have seen, classic Hollywood cinema frowns upon lighting that is not subordinate to the demands of the narrative, and adheres therefore to quite strict rules of dramatic lighting: the lighting should fit the situation but never supersede it to the point of artificiality or extreme abstraction which, it was believed, would create unease in the **audience**. The idea that cinema-going and watching must be safe, unchallenging and non-disruptive is a key **ideological** aspect of what we call the **seamlessness** of Hollywood and mainstream cinema. Lighting, in this context, colludes with an **editing** style that does not call attention to itself. The desired effect, **realism**, is of course totally artificial given that the cinematic **apparatus** is not presenting real life to us – either through its images or its narrative. Use of lighting that does draw attention to itself is in some way challenging to this effect of realism and is, therefore, crucial in considerations of **mise-en-scène** precisely because it disrupts and distorts the reality effect. Thus, for example, frontal lighting on its own flattens the image and removes the illusion of three-dimensionality; it draws to our attention the fact that film is two-dimensional and that perspectival space is an illusion (indeed, to some **avant-garde** filmmakers, perspective is a bourgeois aesthetic that comes to film from painting). Side-lighting on its own highlights objects or people in a distorting and denaturalizing way, catching only one side of their volume. Similarly, backlighting on its own disorients and distorts, bringing out menacing silhouettes, for example. In each and every case we are made aware that lighting is at work.

Richard Dyer in his book *White* (1997: 82–142) makes some extremely valuable points about the ideological effects of lighting as it is practised in the Western world. Dyer points out how, from very early cinema, lighting, along with film stock and make-up, has always assumed the construction of whiteness as its touchstone (ibid.: 90–91).

He speaks of the white-centricity of the aesthetics of lighting that still prevails today (ibid.: 97). And he goes on to discuss what this implies in the filming of blackness and black faces. The history of light technology is one that has always privileged the white face. It has also been a device for highlighting **gender** differentiation. For the woman, light reveals her glowing whiteness and blondness (in all her purity). Differently marked by light, the dark-haired, dark-suited white male finds his face illuminated by a source of light (sidelight for example) that exposes his intelligence, virility or whatever – or indeed, at times, his own white face will be illuminated in a reflective way by the woman whose face is the 'source of all light'. Back-lighting, while it is used to suggest depth to the different planes in the image, has ideological effects when it is used as a hair light which was very much the case of classic Holly-wood cinema. It brings out the blondness of the white woman's hair, signalling her great virtue. Dyer (91–92) explains how, in early cinema when orthochromatic film stock was used, fair hair became black or looked dark unless special lighting in the form of back-lighting was used. Similarly, female stars had to wear extremely heavy white make-up so that their skin would show as white (almost pasty-white to our contemporary eyes) on the screen. These white faces had to be arc-lit because tungsten lighting (with its red and yellow wave-lengths) would have brought out those same colours in white faces, thus making them look dark or black on the film stock. Under these fierce lights, not only did make-up frequently melt and run, but the eyes also suffered terribly from burning under the Klieg lights (the so-called 'Klieg eyes').

Neither film stock nor lighting has been significantly altered or evolved to take on board the representation of blackness on-screen. Even when film directors speak of their attempts to shoot black actors correctly, the process is represented as a problem (as Mike Figgis did in speaking about shooting *One Night Stand*, 1997). The assumption is hardly ever made that the technology might be the problem.

Dyer (1997: 102) argues carefully to show how 'movie lighting discriminates on the basis of race' and confines the Black person to the shadows. Moreover, because movie lighting practice 'focuses on the individual' and 'hierarchizes' (it signals who or what is important and who or what is not), it is clear that in its inability to show blackness and therefore the Black person as important and as an individual it 'expresses a view of humanity pioneered by white culture' (103). However, with advances in digital technology, the question of appropriate lighting can at last be properly addressed – either through light-balance technics in the camera or in post-production. There is no longer any excuse for black skins to be incorrectly illuminated (as is evidenced by Steve McQueen's *12 Years a Slave*, 2013, and Ava DuVernay's *Selma*, 2014).

There are plenty of 'how to' manuals on lighting (see Viera and Viera, 2005; Malkiewicz, 1986); but for best reading on the practice see Alton, 1995.

MELODRAMA AND WOMEN'S FILMS

Melodrama's earliest roots are in medieval morality plays and the oral tradition. Subsequently, the tradition found renewed favour in the French romantic drama of the eighteenth and nineteenth centuries and the English and French sentimental novel of the same period. These dramas and novels based in codes of morality and good conscience were about familial relations, thwarted love and forced marriages (Elsaesser, 1987: 45). The melodrama coincides, in historical terms, with the rise of **modernism** and can be seen as a response to the French Revolution, the Industrial Revolution and modernization. In the early 1800s, the post-Revolutionary bourgeoisie sought to defend its newly acquired rights against the autocratic aristocracy – including the *droits de seigneur*. According to Peter Brooks (quoted in Kaplan, 1992: 60), with the emergence of the bourgeoisie as a propertied **class** 'the ethical imperative replaces the tragic vision'. The melodrama focus, then, is essentially on the family and moral values and not the dynastic and mythic deities (as it was in Greek tragedy). Thus, the melodrama – at least in these earliest stages – pitted bourgeoisie against feudalism. Many a tale related the ravishment of the middle-class maiden by the villainous rich aristocrat. In this respect, class conflict was repressed into the sexual, manifesting itself via sexual exploitation or rape. This concept of repression is key to an understanding of melodrama.

It is important to remember that, as a **genre**, melodrama also developed alongside nineteenth-century capitalism – and that capitalism gave rise to the *need* of the family to protect, through the inheritance system, the bourgeoisie's newly acquired possessions (including property). The family becomes the site of patriarchy and capitalism – and, therefore, reproduces it. The Industrial Revolution, for its part, placed the family under new and different kinds of pressures. It brought about the separation of the work from the home environment. Middle-class women withdrew from the labour market and working-class women and children entered the factories – leading to an increased urbanization of the proletariat (Gledhill, 1987: 20–21). This in turn led to the fear of the mob. The middle class felt assailed on both sides, by the aristocracy and the working class. In Europe, in particular, classes became increasingly polarized as opposed to hierarchized as they had formerly been (since the United States denies, constitutionally, that it has a class structure, it would be fairer to say that its citizens were socio-economically constituted into different groupings). The early theatre melodrama reflects these preoccupations. However, it is noteworthy that the cinematic melodrama, until World War Two and in some isolated cases until the 1950s, also reflected class concerns.

The end of the nineteenth century marked the birth of the consumer culture. It should be recalled that, prior to the existence of cinema theatres (the first appearing in 1900), one of the venues for cinema was the department store (in both Europe and the United States). The idea was that the film screenings would attract not just **audiences** but also customers. Film, then, was very early identified with consumerism. Because it was seen as an integral part of selling consumer culture, it quickly became evident that it was necessary to address a female audience as much as a male one, since the woman is supposedly the arbiter of taste in the home – as opposed to the male who is the arbiter of justice outside the home (as in **Westerns**, for example). A legacy of this targeting of a female audience, through the melodrama, is the high investment, if not over-investment, in **mise-en-scène** – a surplus of objects and interior décor. But this is not the only reason for excessive mise-en-scène (see below).

It is in its relationship to social change and upheaval that melodrama is such an interesting genre to investigate, particularly since it does not marginalize the woman (as do so many other genres). Having been derided for years, in the early 1970s, melodrama finally became recognized, in terms of cultural history alone, as an important generic type to examine. Peter Brooks and Thomas Elsaesser, closely followed by Geoffrey Nowell-Smith, were pioneers, examining the genre from both a Marxist and a **psychoanalytic** point of view. By the late 1970s, given that it primarily foregrounded the female character, it was also taken on as a genre for investigation by feminist film critics (see **feminist film theory**). Laura Mulvey and Mary Ann Doane led the way, followed shortly by a host of feminist theorists (Kaplan, Mellencamp, Williams, Cook, Gledhill, LeSage, Kuhn, Brunsdon to name just a few).

Melodrama does two things in relation to the social changes and advent of modernization. It attempts to make sense of modernism in its practice of mass production (e.g. the factory) and of the family. To take the first point, mass production, modernism exposed the reality of the decentred **subject** caused by alienation under capitalism and technological depersonalization (see **modernism**). Melodrama becomes an attempt to counter anxieties produced by this decentring and the massive scale of urban change – hence the 'moral polarization and dramatic reversals' that structure this genre (Gledhill, 1987: 30). Bourgeois values are felt to be under threat – perhaps because they never had time to become fully established (unlike feudalism) – and, viewed in this light, the melodrama is quite paranoid. Thus, for the bourgeoisie the social, which to them means Victorian morality and what assails it, must be expressed through the personal (Elsaesser, 1987: 29). The everyday life of the individual must be invested with significance and justification (ibid.: 29). The melodrama as a popular cultural form takes this notion of social crisis and mediates it within a private context, the home (ibid.: 47). Melodrama, then, reflects the bourgeois desire for social order to be expressed through the personal. In this respect, we can also see how there is an over-investment in the family, how its starting point is in excess (Gledhill, 1987: 38). Because the social is internalized, there follows an externalization of the psychic states (Gledhill, 1991: 210). In the process of internalizing the former, the latter are pushed out into the open. And because the melodrama is focused on the family (its conflicts and related issues of duty and love), characters adopt primary psychic roles. More ciphers than developed personalities, they lack depth. As Gledhill (quoting Brooks) puts it, 'melodrama of psychology' is what you get (1987: 210). Dramatic action takes place between and not within the characters (ibid.).

Melodrama serves to make sense of the family and in so doing perpetuates it, including the continuation of the subordination of the woman. However, there is a twist. In the melodrama, the male finds himself in the domestic sphere (home). So he is in the site no longer of production but of reproduction. The home represents metonymically the site for the **ideological** confrontation between production and reproduction. The alienation of the labour process becomes displaced (the man brings the experience of alienation home with him) and the family – especially the woman and children – is supposed to fulfil what capitalist relations of production cannot (Cook, 1985: 77). The cost of this displacement is repression (sexual) and woman's self-sacrifice. If, for the bourgeoisie of the nineteenth century, melodrama's ideological function was to disguise the socio-economic contradictions of capitalism, then, in the final analysis it failed. Because it reproduces the family and within it the displaced sense of alienation, the melodrama makes visible, in the form of familial tensions, the exploitation and oppression differingly experienced by members of the family. Laura Mulvey (1987: 75) argues that 'ideological contradiction is the overt mainspring and specific content of melodrama ... its excitement comes from conflict not between enemies, but between people tied by blood or love'. Mulvey goes on to say, 'there is a dizzy satisfaction in witnessing the way that sexual difference under patriarchy is fraught, explosive and erupts dramatically into violence within its own private stomping ground, the family'. Finally, on this point Mulvey (1987: 76) states that for 'family life to survive, a compromise has to be reached, sexual difference softened, and the male brought to see the value of domestic life'. The male is not in his typically ascribed space, in the work sphere, the sphere of action. He is in the domestic, female sphere, which is the non-active, even passive sphere. In order to achieve a successful resolution to the conflict, the male has to function on terms that are appropriate to the domestic sphere. In this way, he becomes less male and in the process more feminized. And this is undoubtedly one of the reasons why the melodrama appeals to the female **spectator**. The female spectator also derives pleasure from seeing the ideological contradictions exposed on-screen – they provide her with a mise-en-scène of her own experience. As for the male spectator, pleasure is derived from seeing the contradictions 'resolved'.

In this same essay, Mulvey develops these points by relocating melodrama in relation to sexual difference. She distinguishes between the masculine melodrama and its function of reconciliation and the female melodrama and its function of excess and unresolved contradictions. Because patriarchal culture in its over-evaluation of virility is in contradiction with the ideology of the family, the male in the masculine melodrama has to achieve a compromise between the male and the female sphere. For an exemplary film of this order, see *The Giant* (George Stevens, 1956) where one man 'does' – Rock Hudson – and one man doesn't – James Dean. In female melodramas there is not necessarily a resolution or reconciliation. Indeed, it is 'as though the fact of having a female point of view dominating the **narrative** produces an excess that precludes satisfaction' (Mulvey, 1987). What Mulvey is arguing is that the female point of view often projects a **fantasy** that is, in patriarchal terms, transgressive – and so cannot be fulfilled. Despite the fact that in the end the female protagonist loses out, the female spectator identifies with and gains pleasure from her behaviour during the unfolding of the narrative. The example Mulvey quotes is *All that Heaven Allows* (Douglas Sirk, 1955). A middle-class widowed mother ('past' the age of child-bearing, we are informed) falls in love with her younger male employee, a gardener.

But she is only allowed to 'unite' with him once he has been rendered 'impotent' (and bedridden) by a car accident. For fantasizing too far, she gets only half her man.

Codes, conventions and structures

A first point is that while there are arguably two dominant categories of melodrama (masculine and feminine), nonetheless, as a genre it remains remarkably unfixed in that traces of its generic make-up can be found in many other genres or sub-genres (such as the **musical**, the **thriller** – especially the **film noir** where the hero is pushed to wish his own death – and the Gothic thriller of which Hitchcock's work is exemplary). Given that melodrama is quite unfixed and that it is also a fairly global phenomenon (not purely an American genre), it is perhaps surprising that until recently not a great deal has yet been made in theoretical film analysis about genre and questions of national identity (though, on Mexican melodramas, see Dever, 2003). This section makes some general points about melodrama; the next deals specifically with the woman's film and female melodrama.

The melodrama focuses on the victim. The earliest scenarios staged persecuted innocence and the drive to identify the good and the evil. Alternatively, the melodrama offers a triangular setup, with the male tempted away from his family and all that is 'good' (and usually rural) by an 'evil' temptress or vamp living in a sumptuous city apartment. Variations include the 'fallen' woman, the single or abandoned mother, the innocent orphan, the male head of household as ineluctable victim of modernization. The two main driving forces behind the genre are Victorian morality and modern psychology (Gledhill, 1987: 33). For the most part, melodrama is nostalgic: it looks back at what is dreamt of as an ideal time of respectability and no antisocial behaviour. It dreams of the unobtainable. Emotions, including hope, rise only to be dashed, and for this reason the melodrama is ultimately masochistic. Melodrama plays out forbidden longings, symptomatic illness and renunciation (*Imitation of Life*, John Stahl, 1934, has all of these). In the late 1940s, masochism was displayed in the form of inner violence, the self-sacrificing mother or wife (*Stella Dallas*, King Vidor, 1937; *Mildred Pierce*, Michael Curtiz, 1945). In male melodramas, the focus was less on masochism – unless the film was in the **gangster** and subsequently film noir tradition. In the 1930s, they focused on the protagonist's unwillingness or inability to fulfil the **Oedipal trajectory** (see under **psychoanlysis**). French male melodramas of that period exemplify this, especially the films starring Jean

Gabin. The characters played by James Dean in his films of the 1950s certainly reflect an unwillingness to fulfil society's expectations of male adulthood (for an unusual twist on this, see him in *The Giant*).

The heyday of the melodrama as far as **sound** cinema and **Hollywood** are concerned is from 1930 to 1960. In the period after World War Two, the genre became revitalized, thanks to the introduction of a popularized reading of Sigmund Freud. Interestingly, by the early 1950s, the male melodrama really came into its own and the focus now became either the father–son relationship as conflict, or the middle-class husband or lover or father who has succumbed to social pressures. Nicholas Ray's *Rebel Without a Cause* (1955), and *Bigger than Life* (1956), respectively illustrate these representations. Male melodramas, through a portrayal of masculinity in crisis, expose masculinity's contradictions. The male either suffers from the inadequacies of his father (*Rebel Without a Cause*), or is in danger of extinction from his murderous or castrating father (as in *Home from the Hill*, Vincente Minnelli, 1959), or, finally he fails in his duty to reproduce (the family), or simply fails his family (*Bigger than Life*; *The Cobweb*, Minnelli, 1955). (For more detail on male melodrama see Grant, 1986; Schatz, 1981.) Numerous readings can be offered for this development. First, the change in women's lives that resulted from their entry into the workforce during the war gave them an unprecedented economic independence and created great unease for the returning men-folk after the war. Second, the feeling of paranoia generated by the Cold War, and the failure of post-war American ideology to deliver promises, left veterans wondering why they had fought the war after all. And, finally, the fairly dominant presence in the production of this genre of European immigrant filmmakers (Sirk, Max Ophuls, George Cukor, Minnelli) and those outside the Hollywood system (Ray) meant that a more detached eye was able to observe the contemporary United States and American masculinity in crisis; or that the European émigrés had rekindled the melodrama post-war.

Ideas about **psychoanalysis** were introduced into film melodrama, where they made women 'safe': women's behaviour was easily explained away through psychology so their psychosis was not a threat. Psychoanalysis explained the newly emerging youth culture and revealed the male as victim, trapped in late capitalism. It did not vastly alter the narratives of this genre (so earlier prototypes can always be found), it simply provided open psychological interpretations and **discourses** to explain why clashes, conflicts and ruptures occur in the family. Thus, the father-figure is marked as more dysfunctional than in the earlier melodrama, he becomes transgressive as in madness (*Home from the*

Hill) or completely ineffectual and unable to uphold authority (*Rebel Without a Cause*). The female is also represented as transgressive, but mostly quite different from her male counterpart. She puts on display the conflicts at the heart of feminine identity between female desire and socially sanctioned femininity (Kuhn, 1990: 426). Socially sanctioned femininity – that is, motherhood, and integration into the family – means that she has in the end to resume that position or disappear (*All that Heaven Allows*; *Imitation of Life*, Sirk's 1959 remake of Stahl's 1934 film; and, as an earlier example of the disappearing woman, *Christopher Strong*, Dorothy Arzner, 1932). The female rejoins her male counterpart in the melodramas that position her as suffering from some psychotic malaise: the major difference being that only a doctor – or at least a man – can help her resolve it (as in *Marnie*, Alfred Hitchcock, 1956 – or an earlier prototype, *Now Voyager*, Irving Rapper, 1942). However, for an interesting reversal of this plotline (e.g. woman doctor treats male neurotic) see Hitchcock's *Spellbound* (1945).

The melodrama is an oxymoronic product in that it has to produce dramatic action while staying firmly in place; this gives it an inherently circular thematic structure, hence often the recourse to **flashbacks** (Cook, 1985: 80). This circularity also signals claustrophobia. The melodrama is played out in the home or in small-town environments. Time is made to stand still, suffocating the child, teenager, young adult – especially women. Windows and objects function similarly to suffocate, entrap and oppress. The décor or mise-en-scène becomes an outer symbolization of inner emotions, fragility or torment (Elsaesser, 1987: 59). And the desire for the unobtainable object or other is just one final nail in the coffin of this claustrophobic atmosphere. The melodrama as a genre turns inwards for drama. So too do the characters, in the form of inner violence which can take the form of substitute acts (ibid.: 56). Aggressiveness by proxy or behaving in a way that is completely at odds with what is desired are forms of displacement-by-substitution (ibid.: 56). Elsaesser demonstrates how this principle of substitute-acts is Hollywood's way of portraying the dynamics of alienation. And he cites (ibid.: 64) the pattern of *Written on the Wind* (Sirk, 1956) as exemplary: 'Dorothy Malone wants Rock Hudson who wants Lauren Bacall who wants Robert Stack who just wants to die.'

Melodramas are often highly stylized. Elsaesser (1987: 53) points out that this is to do with the effects of **censorship** and morality codes – very much in effect until the 1960s (see **Hays code**). In this regard, style becomes used as meaning. In order to convey what could not be said (primarily on the level of sex and repressed desire), décor and mise-en-scène had to stand in for meaning. Curiously here, as Elsaesser (ibid.: 54) makes clear, the popular cultural form of melodrama has a modernist function (style standing in for meaning). Given that the melodrama seeks to be grounded in realism and modernism does not, but wishes to signify through process and form and not content, melodrama, by signifying meaning (repressed desire) through style or form, finds itself making sense of modernism in a most unexpected way (see entry on **modernism**). On this issue of realism and stylization, Nowell-Smith (1987: 73–74) talks about the syphoning off of unrepresentable material into excessive mise-en-scène and refers to it via Freud's concept of conversion hysteria – the return of the repressed (i.e. 'if I can't have a phallus, I'll have a doric column'). According to Nowell-Smith, the repressed for the woman may well be female desire, but for the male it is the fear of castration. Acceptance of that fear or possibility is repressed in melodrama at the level of the story but reappears, returns through music or mise-en-scène (ibid.: 73–74). Gledhill (1987: 9) summarizes Nowell-Smith in the following succinct terms: 'if the family melodrama's speciality is generational and **gender** conflict, verisimilitude demands that the central issues of sexual difference and identity be "realistically" presented. But these are precisely the issues realism is designed to repress.'

The female melodrama and the woman's film

These two obviously overlapping categories of film have been sub-divided by various feminists into different types. Doane (1987) defines four: the female patient, the maternal, the impossible love and the paranoid melodrama. Kaplan (1992), focusing primarily on the mother melodrama, has three typologies: the sacrifice paradigm, the phallic mother paradigm, and the resisting paradigm. Modleski (1992) speaks of hysteria, desire and muteness as behavioural comportments of women in melodrama. Masochism is everywhere, except in the resisting paradigm – and even there it comes close.

Before going into further detail on these matters, it is useful first of all to consider that most of these melodramas were adaptations of female fiction – particularly those films produced during the 1930s and 1940s. This fiction embraces stories in women's weeklies, women's romance novels and women's historical romances. Second, apart from Dorothy Arzner in the United States, most filmmakers making these films were men. Given that the novels at least were often very long, scriptwriters and filmmakers went for stage adaptations of the fiction if they existed, or reduced the text to a narrative that held together and lasted around ninety minutes. The point here is that this leads to a density of **motivation** which in turns feeds into this notion of melodrama and excess (Elsaesser, 1987: 52). The gender shift from female author to male filmmaker or *auteur* also poses some interesting questions. Traditionally, the male is used to working in the non-domestic sphere. Here, however, the filmmaker finds himself in the very sphere in which he is expected to reach compromise. Thus, not only is he reproducing the site of reproduction by the very act of filming, he is also functioning on terms that are appropriate to the domestic sphere. This potential feminization of the filmmaker makes possible an unintentional opening up of gaps for moments of subversion within the filmic text and subversiveness in terms of spectator pleasure – including, of course, readings against the grain (see Modleski, 1988, and her readings of Hitchcock).

In the female melodramas, also known as weepies or tearjerkers, the central character is female and what is privileged is a female per-spective. We are in the world of emotions not action. The appeal of the woman's film for the spectator (primarily female, but also male) is the mise-en-scène of female desire. It thematizes female desire, it produces, therefore, female **subjectivity**. It puts woman's *jouissance* (unspeakable pleasure) up on-screen. Of course, the genre also destroys her for this, in the end. One way or another she is reinscribed into her 'Lawful' place as (m)other (see **psychoanalysis**). In this respect, it comes as no surprise that women's films function ideologically as repression of female desire and reassertion of the woman's role as reproducer and nurturer. Or, if she is incapable of resuming or assuming that role, then she must stand aside, disappear, not be. The tears come because of the ultimate unfulfillability of desire – the spectator sees only the dream. The dream-fantasy stands for the real (Fischer, 1989: 101).

Women's films then reproduce the scenarios of female masochism (Doane, 1984: 80). As Doane explains, female masochistic fantasies are de-eroticized. This is particularly evident in the impossible love melodrama. Lucy Fischer (1989: 101) examines Max Ophuls' *Letter from an Unknown Woman* (1948) as an example of masochistic fantasy functioning not as a vehicle 'for sexuality but *instead* of it'. The woman in the film, Lisa, is seduced as a young woman by a 'brilliant' pianist. He abandons her, she bears his child. Even though she never meets him again, at least not until it is too late, she devotes her life to him. She lives her life through her fanciful desire for him. An entire life for one night. She survives on imaginary images of her lover, thereby substituting fantasy for eroticism (ibid.). Melodrama reproduces here, unquestioningly, the assumption that a woman's main concern in life is love. The woman in love is the one who waits and as she waits she fantasizes *he* who is absent (ibid.: 95). Desertion of the man is a frequent trope in this type of melodrama and until recently this meant being left with nothing, including no financial support.

A similar de-eroticization takes place within the paranoid woman's film, often also referred to as the Gothic woman's film. This latter typology includes *Rebecca* (Hitchcock, 1940) and *Gaslight* (Cukor, 1944). In both films the woman is entrapped in the house. Doane (1984) talks of these films as 'horror-in-the-home' melodramas where marriage and murder are brought together in the female protagonist's mind. After an often hasty marriage (why, one wonders?), the wife fears that her husband has murderous intentions – she even hallucinates them. However, because the actual narrative assumes that this fear is based in female frigidity fear of sex or even rape, it is evidently a male fantasy that is up on-screen. As Doane says (ibid.: 79), this has consequences for the **gaze** and **subject** positioning. She argues that a despecularization and hence de-eroticization takes place because it is supposedly the woman's point of view but it is, in fact, a male fantasy. This two-way 'gazing' cancels out real **agency**: the first gaze, female, is undermined by the second, all-knowing male gaze. A first point, then, is that what gets taken away is female desire. But the question arises: does not the female spectator identify with the female protagonist and get commodified up on-screen? Thus, do we too get positioned masochistically? Further, if as sometimes appears to be the case, the 'investigating' gaze is seemingly represented as female, then, since we too (as spectator) are positioned within it, there occurs a doubling of the fear factor (good suspense tactics if you are Hitchcock). The twist of course, as we have just noted, is that even though she appears to agence the gaze, she does not really understand what she sees. She misreads the information, often because part of the picture is proscribed her. In these films, the home becomes the body (ibid.: 72–73) which the female investigates (remember that in film noir it is usually the male who gets to investigate the female body). This is far too dangerous for patriarchy to countenance. Thus, the male contains a secret space of his own, a final space the woman is not allowed to see (ibid.: 80). This space is either within the house (usually a room in the attic) or mentioned by name (so contained within patriarchal law) – as by De Winter in *Rebecca* when he talks of the boathouse. In the end, although she sees, the woman understands nothing. What she sees will only have meaning once the male re-specularizes it for her – as De Winter does at the end of the film.

Women's films point to Hollywood's capacity to produce a female **subjectivity** and then destroy it. This occurs even more strikingly in patient melodramas. Here, female subjectivity, female desire, is re-articulated onto the body as a site of symptoms and illness. Conversion hysteria functions to transfer desire not onto objects or mise-en-scène, but onto the body itself. Women suffer from some sort of psychosis (see, for example, *The Snake Pit*, Anatole Litvak, 1948). This is induced either by their own sense of guilt, unfulfilled love or transgressive behaviour, *or* by the effects on the psyche of a dominating, aggressive 'phallic' mother. In the first instance, this illness is a 'punishment'. In the second, the illness so cripples the daughter that she cannot entertain 'normal' relations with men. In these films, the gaze shifts away from the woman and becomes relocated in the eyes of the male, usually a medical expert who investigates the problem and, naturally, resolves it. Hysteria can cause muteness as in Joan Crawford's case in *Possessed* (Curtis Bernhardt, 1947) and she can be brought to speak only by the administration of a special drug injected into her body by the doctor. We come to understand what traumatized her through the flashbacks which only the all-knowing doctor can induce. (See Doane's excellent analysis of muteness (1984: 76–77) and Modleski, 1992: 536–48.)

In phallic mother scenarios, as, for example, in *Now Voyager*, again it is the male, a psychiatrist this time, who releases the victimized daughter and 'castigates' the bad, possessive mother for oppressing her daughter. Even untrained psychiatrists can dabble in the art, as does the rich businessman Sean Connery in *Marnie*, or the detective in *Mildred Pierce*. The point is that they represent the all-seeing, all-knowing male. The point is also that, under the medical or pseudo-medical gaze, the female body is de-eroticized. But, as Doane says (1984: 80), in patriarchal society 'to desexualize the female body is ultimately to deny its very existence'. It is, of course, also to deny the woman the epistemological gaze; effectively 'a body-less woman cannot see' (ibid.). The point is, finally, that in this way any threat to male dominance is safely contained.

see also: **genre**

Major references for this entry include Elsaesser, Mulvey, Nowell-Smith, Harper and Gledhill, all in: Gledhill, 1987; Cook, 1985; Feuer, 1982; Doane, 1982, 1984, 1987; Kaplan, 1983, 1992; Modleski, 1988, 1992.

For further reading see also Bratton *et al.*, 1994; Brooks, 1976; Cook and Dodd, 1993; Dever, 2003; Harper, 1994; Kuhn, 1982; Mayne, 1984; Mercer and Shingler, 2001; Rheudan, 1993; Rosen, 1973; Singer, 2001; Thomas, 2000; Williams, 2002. For discussion of the revival of women's films since the 1990s see Campbell, 2005; Garrett, 2007.

METHOD ACTING

A style of acting that was adopted by the Actors Studio, founded in 1947 in the United States and which was derived from the Soviet actor and director Konstantin Stanislavsky. The method was to act completely naturally, to so infuse one's own self with the thoughts, emotions and personality of the character that one became that character. Simultaneously, the actors must draw on their own experiences to understand what motivates the characters they play. Often the performance is understated – certainly never in excess. The method is seen as totally realistic and is best exemplified by the actors Marlon Brando (although apparently he only went once to the Studio and did not like it), Montgomery Clift, James Dean, Rod Steiger and Julie Harris (see, for example, *A Streetcar Named Desire*, Elia Kazan, 1951; *From Here to Eternity*, Fred Zinnemann, 1953; *On the Waterfront*, Kazan, 1954).

MISE-EN-ABÎME

This occurs within a text when there is a reduplication of images or concepts referring to the textual whole. Chinese boxes or Russian dolls are concrete examples of mise-en-abîme – the outer shell being *the* full-size *real* thing, those within a constant referral to the original. Mise-en-abîme is a play of signifiers within a text, of sub-texts mirroring each other. This mirroring can get to the point where meaning can be rendered unstable and in this respect can be seen as part of the process of **deconstruction**. Some examples taken from films will make these points clear.

The film within a film is a prime example of mise-en-abîme. The film being made within the film refers through its **mise-en-scène** to the 'real' film being made. The **spectator** sees film equipment, **stars** getting ready for the take, crew sorting out the various directorial needs, etc. (as in Stanley Donen's *Singin' in the Rain*, 1952; or François Truffaut's *La Nuit Américaine/Day for Night*, 1973). The **narrative** of the film within the film may directly reflect the one in the 'real' film (as in Karel Reisz's *The French Lieutenant's Woman*, 1981). **Voyeurism** gets ruthlessly mise-en-abîme in Michael Powell's *Peeping Tom*, 1960 – at the same time as it is a mise-en-abîme of cinema itself.

MISE-EN-SCÈNE

Originally a theatre term meaning staging, it crossed over to signify the film production practices involved in the framing of shots. Thus, first, it connotes **setting**, **costume** and **lighting**; second, movement within the frame. The concept became endowed with a more specific meaning by the *Cahiers du cinéma* group (established in 1951) who used it to justify their appellation of certain American filmmakers as auteurs (for further clarification see **auteur**). Given that these directors were working under the aegis of **Hollywood**, they had no control over the script but they could stage their shots and so be deemed to have a discernible style. Mise-en-scène is the expressive tool at the filmmaker's disposal which a critic can read to determine the specificity of the cinematographic work. That is, the critic can identify the particular style of a specific filmmaker and thereby point to it as an authorial sign.

In more general terms, however, mise-en-scène refers to what is visible in the frame (décor/setting, lighting, costume, the actors) and how the interaction of these elements provides meaning which the **spectator** interprets. For example, in **melodrama**, interiors are often very richly textured (huge rooms, ornate staircases, marbled pillars, rich velvet and silk furnishings, imposing furniture, and so on). Characters can seem dwarfed or overwhelmed (even half hidden, lost) in these environs. It is as if emotions are stifled by the décor which in itself is highly sexualized, what with soft textures and phallic pillars. This all suggests that human relationships, at least sexualized ones, are unable to express themselves fully, if at all (see, for example, *All that Heaven Allows*, Sirk, 1955); or, alternatively, that manifestations of wealth supersede manifestations of love (see *The Giant*, Stevens, 1956). For more extreme use of mise-en-scène (as a rendition of psychic states) then surely **German Expressionism** is a classic exemplar, as in its different way are **Horror** and **Sci-fi** films.

For more detail see Gibbs, 2002.

MODERNISM

Modernism is most easily understood as an art movement, although it does have socio-political resonances as explained below. You will note from the entry on **postmodernism** that it is difficult to pinpoint where modernism ends and postmodernism begins. It is better to think in terms of an overlap between the two – an overlap that occurs, first, because not all aspects of art became postmodern simultaneously and, second, because there is not often full agreement, among critics and theorists, on the categorizing of a particular cultural artefact. Thus a novel, say, might find itself being termed a modernist text by one critic, but a postmodern text by another. This happens with the novels of Samuel Beckett. This inability to insert a dividing line points to the fact that, to a certain – if not considerable – extent, post-modernism reacts less against the conventions of modernism than we might believe, even though we are aware that it must in some way be different, because it comes after ('post' modernism).

Modernism finds its roots in the Enlightenment period of the eighteenth century and man's (*sic*) belief in the supremacy of human reason over all other considerations. It was a period that marked the end, or rather decline in Western society of a theocratic (God-centred) interpretation of the world. As evidence of this belief in the power of human reasoning to understand the world, this age was also termed the Age of Reason. This belief in human reason meant that 'man' could achieve clarity or enlightenment in scientific thought and natural philosophy (i.e. natural science – maths, astronomy and physics); he would come to understand the way things really are in the universe and, thereby, be able to have control over nature and make the world a better place. Jeremy Bentham's enlightened prison reforms came from this spirit – including his concept of the panopticon as an alternative to cell emprisonment and the cruelty of prison treatment. The panopticon was conceived as a circular prison-building wherein the observer (the guard in the centre) could observe everyone else without the prisoners knowing they are being watched. It was intended as a system of benign total surveillance. But, as we shall see, the outcome of total surveillance is far from benign.

As such, then, the Enlightenment represented an optimistic belief in progress. Science and technology were man's tools whereby he could implement change. Science, or scientific thought, was the only valid thought, and facts the only possible objects of knowledge. In philosophy, the task was to discover the general principles common to all the sciences and to use these principles as guides to human conduct and as the basis of social organization. Man controlled nature, and all procedures of investigation had to be reducible to scientific method.

Not all was optimism, however. Even during that period some philosophers expressed disquiet at the totalizing effect of this positivist philosophy of science. Thus, a strain of pessimism exists alongside the waves of optimism; a pessimism with which we have to concur if we look at the end of the eighteenth century in France and its bloody Revolution, particularly during the Reign of Terror. Writers of that time pointed to the ends to which man could go. The Marquis de Sade's writings are but one extreme. But consider also the 'humane' invention devised to kill off all those who fell victim to the Revolution: the guillotine. Designed by Dr Guillotine to make death more swift and efficacious and therefore more humane, in the end it allowed for the acceleration of executions because it was so swift. In other words, it became an instrument for mass execution.

The industrial age of the nineteenth century was a logical continuance of the Enlightenment's belief in science and technology, and represents the optimistic strain of belief in progress. Art, however, echoed the other, pessimistic, strain of the Age of Reason and signified as a counter-culture to scientific thought, producing, first, romanticism (a nostalgia for what was lost) and, second, **realism** (a desire to show the mostly negative effects of technological progress). The Enlightenment, then, produced two strains; and modernism, as its natural heir, continued in the same vein. Modernism perpetuates the belief in scientific research and the pursuit of knowledge. It believes in the positing of universal truths, such as progress, of which science and technology were its major proponents. However, it also expresses profound disquiet at those beliefs which it perpetuates. This fear of mechanization found ready expression in the Frankfurt School of Thought (first established in 1923). Their first objection was that the mechanical reproduction of art (posters of great artists' work, music recordings of the great composers, and so on) moved art towards a standardization (of look or **sound**, depending on the artefact), which in turn led to a trivialization of the original. Thus, for example, the recording of **music** becomes sanitized because it is pure sound (homogenized into a perfect clean sound, devoid of human traces). Their second objection concerned the cultural industry in general (in our instance the film industry) in that it produces and circulates cultural commodities which manipulate the consumers *en masse* (e.g. **audiences** in the case of film). Mass culture, in the view of the Frankfurt School, renders people docile and passive, receptive to the **ideological** messages inherent in the cultural product.

As a movement, we could loosely say that modernism begins at the end of the nineteenth century and 'ends' at the end of the 1960s, when **post-structuralism** heralded the arrival, if not the existence already, of postmodernism. Modernism was born as a reaction against realism and the tradition of romanticism. As a movement, it is often also termed the **avant-garde**. However, it is truer to say that the avant-garde is part of the modernist aesthetic – not all modernist art is avant-garde, but avant-garde art is modernist. In its vanguardism and perception of itself as an adversary culture, modernism is 'relentless in its hostility to mass culture' (Huyssen, 1986: 241). It believes that only high art can sustain the role of social and aesthetic criticism. In this context, modernism's belief in progress means also a belief in modernization – including belief in the 'perpetual modernization of art' (ibid.: 238) – a constant renewal of that role of art as critique, therefore.

Modernism eschewed the **seamless** verisimilitude of realism and sought to reveal the process of meaning-construction in art. Formal concerns were, therefore, paramount. To give a couple of examples: with the realist novel, plot and character construction lead us through a **narrative** where the process of narration does not directly draw attention to itself – we are stitched into the narrative (see **suture**); a modernist novel, however, deliberately draws attention to its process of meaning-construction from the very first reading – compare a Jane Austen novel with one by Virginia Woolf, for example. In painting, the realist aesthetic seeks to create the illusion of 'truth' before your eyes, as in a Constable painting, say. This illusion starts with the principle of perspective which gives a sense of three-dimensionality. A modernist cubist painting removes perspectival space and transposes the three-dimensions 'truthfully' onto a flat two-dimensional surface. So, in a Picasso portrait, the eyes are flattened out onto the canvas and the nose is placed to the side of the face and not between the eyes. Similarly, just as the novelist draws attention to their own mode of meaning production, modernist painters draw attention to the materials they use (e.g. Georges Braque, Jackson Pollock). In that respect, modernism is highly self-reflexive (art referring to itself).

As we know, the modernist movement and the avant-garde are closely associated with modernization and as such espoused a belief in its tools and an investment in self-reflexivity that was deliberately counter-illusionist. Nonetheless, not all its proponents were of the optimistic vein. Indeed, many expressed a mistrust of science and technology – even though, as we have already noted, they were inextricably part of it. This mistrust was characterized by a deep pessimism about the modern world and came about as a result of the brutal effects of science and technology on human life in the two World Wars. The wanton destruction of human lives through chemical warfare, bombs of mass extinction, the using of technology and architecture to create a final solution – as in the case of the Holocaust – all these were products of man's reason. It may not be possible to see fascism purely as a formidable crisis of modernist culture (Huyssen, 1986: 268). However, it is not impossible to see it as a logical end to the principles of modernism taken to their extremes of anti-humanism. In this respect, then, modernism embraces the two strains evoked in the case of the Enlightenment. The tragedy, and thereby the paradox, for the modernist artist is being part of the culture and age that s/he in some regards despises: 'I am part of this age of self-reflexive formalism that can also build the technology for mass destruction.'

It is here that we can see a first set of paradoxes inherent in this movement (as we would in any movement of course). The paradox is this: in its self-reflexivity and focus on the individual, modernism seems quite anti-humanist. Yet, in its mistrust of science and technology, it has all the appearances of a relative humanism. This is further compounded when we consider that the modernist age evolved alongside, and in certain domains was part of, modern industrial technology. If we consider architecture we can make this point succinctly. Modernist architecture believed in drawing on all materials possible – especially modern materials, such as reinforced concrete – to construct buildings heretofore unimaginable. And yet – and here is the anti-humanist aspect of this movement – in its belief in the functionality of cheaply produced materials and their being put to use in the building of community spaces in a rationalized and standardized fashion (as with Le Corbusier's ideal concrete village – which he called living machines/*machines à habiter*), it has left many countries with a legacy of concrete jungles and towers which, though inhabited, are essentially uninhabitable. Belief in the unending potential of its materials led modernist architecture to profoundly anti-humanist practices.

Another, related and important, aspect of modernism that needs explaining is the mood of alienation and existential angst that pervades this movement and which comes about as a result of the climate of pessimism generated by the two World Wars. This mood of alienation emanates from a sense of fragmentation of the self in the social sphere and a concomitant inability to communicate effectively with others. This fragmentation of the self, in turn, raises the question of identity: 'who am I in all of this?' In terms of its manifestation in modernist art, this tendency can best be illustrated by the novel. In the modernist novel, there is no traditional narrative of beginning, middle or end, nor is there an omniscient protagonist. Character definition is mostly, if not totally, absent. In its place, an interior monologue or stream of consciousness explores the subjective experience of an individual. In this context, the coincidence of the beginning of this movement with the emerging importance of **psychoanalysis** – especially in the work of Freud – cannot be sufficiently stressed. It is clear that it had a significant impact on modernism and made possible the exploration of the inner self as a way of, if not responding to, then at least describing the effects of alienation on human individuality. In this regard, then, modernism is again very self-reflexive.

Lastly, in its belief in a unified underlying reality, modernism once more shows its debt to the Enlightenment. However, as we have already made clear, this leads to conceptual strategies that end up having **ideological** implications in that modernism can help to legitimate structures of domination and oppression – as in the use of technology in wartime mentioned above. In this regard, we can perceive other structures that it has served to legitimate – structures of **class**, binary structures around sex and race, and so on. Modernism's belief in a rationalistic interpretation of the world found its acme in the 1950s within critical theory and philosophy. The whole concept of **structuralism** can be seen as an attempt to provide a reassuring set of underlying structures that are common to all: be it in the domain of the human brain, language, cultural artefacts, social organization, and so on. Structuralism was to have an important impact on film theory and, albeit to a much lesser degree, on film itself. (For further details on this last point see Gidal, 1989.)

Modernism and cinema

If we now consider cinema's place in the modernist period we come up against a first apparent contradiction. Technologically speaking, the camera, although a modernist artefact, is seen as an instrument for reproducing reality and, as such, it is more readily associated with realism than modernism. The entire cinematic **apparatus** is geared towards creating the illusion of reality and it achieves this primarily through the very seamlessness of its production practices. Second, as John Orr (1993: 60) points out, the camera as a technological instrument has grown up as part of the culture of surveillance. It is also part of war technology – for example, the wide-angle lens, which made **cinemascope** possible, is a product of World War One technology, produced as it was for tanks' periscopes to give a 180-degree view. War technology turns the weapon, the camera, into a **gaze**. 'Knowledge of the image becomes a form of potential capture of the symbolic, seizure of the image, and as we know the human gaze is part of this quest for knowledge, including self knowledge, a form of mirroring' (ibid.: 60). The camera is also extremely self-conscious, not just because it reflects itself but also because someone (filmmaker, **spectator**) has to watch what the camera is watching for it to have any 'meaning'. In its self-reflexivity, the camera has, built into it, the very essence of modernism which it could exercise, provided production practices do not render its operations invisible. But, of course, this is precisely what **mainstream narrative cinema** does.

However, as with all other art forms, cinema also has its avant-garde – although, unlike other modernist art forms, it is not explicitly hostile to mass or popular culture. In fact, many avant-garde filmmakers wanted their work to reach mass audiences. Modernist cinema should be seen, therefore, as a global term that includes the work of filmmakers of the avant-garde – which, depending on the period in history, can mean **surrealist** cinema, **counter-cinema** and **underground cinema** (to name but the most obvious). The work of these filmmakers explores and exposes the formal qualities of film. Modernist cinema, in privileging formal concerns, is one that both makes visible and questions its meaning-production practices. In this regard, modernist cinema questions the technology it uses, questions its power of the gaze, questions its power to represent (among other things **reality**, **sexuality**, and, just occasionally, the female body). It questions *how* it represents and *what* it represents. Modernist cinema turns the gaze into a critical weapon, turns the camera as an instrument of surveillance upon itself, starting with the fragmentation, destruction or **deconstruction** even of **classical narrative** structures.

Modernism focuses on questions of aesthetics and artistic construction. And much of modernist cinema follows that trend. Formal concerns are foregrounded over content. Certainly, the **Soviet cinema** of the mid- to late 1920s espoused the modernist principles of meaning being produced from style – principally from **editing** styles. And the **montage** effects, produced by fast editing, of Sergei Eisenstein's films (such as *Strike* and *Battleship Potemkin*, both 1925) influenced other European cinemas of the avant-garde. The avant-garde and surrealist cinema in France of the 1920s is another early manifestation of this modernist trend. Filmmakers of this generation in the early 1920s were interested in the visual representation of the interior life of a character, that is, a formal rather than narrativized projection onto screen of the character's subjective imaginings and fantasies – dreams even (as in *Fièvre*, Louis Delluc, 1921, about female **subjectivity**, hallucination and desire). This subjective cinema gave way, by the mid-1920s, to a concern with the plasticity of the medium and its temporal and spatial qualities. The intention was to create a pure cinema where film signified in and of itself through its rhythms and plasticity (e.g. Jean Epstein's *Photogénies*, 1924; René Clair's *Entr'acte*, 1924). Later in the 1920s, a third avant-garde was conceived out of the earlier two modes. Under the influence of surrealism, this avant-garde cinema became interested in how the temporal and spatial properties of film as well as its plasticity could be employed to reflect the workings of the unconscious – especially its suppression of sexual obsessions or desires. Germaine Dulac was, arguably, the first to combine surrealist and avant-garde preoccupations in her film *La Coquille et le clergyman* (1927).

The various American avant-garde movements of the 1930s and 1940s pursued the French avant-garde tradition, particularly in its latest manifestation. Maya Deren's haunting *Meshes of the Afternoon* (1943) is an exemplary film in this respect. Deren stars in this film of paranoid dream fantasies. Her experimental play with time and space is just one way by which she achieves this sense of paranoia. By using a loop system (a single piece of film that is continuously repeated) with a sequence of a young woman fearfully coming down an anonymous street, traditional notions of time and space are eroded – instead we feel the urgency and inescapability of the woman's fear as well as the timelessness in which it is felt.

The American avant-garde of the 1960s to the mid-1970s, when it more or less died out (see also **underground cinema**), tends to echo the middle period of the French avant-garde with its notion of pure cinema. It produced, among other cinemas, a minimalist cinema – where the pro-filmic event (that which the camera is aimed at) is reproduced on-screen and becomes, simultaneously, the filmic event (Gidal, 1989: 16). These films were either performed events involving the filmmaker or a static camera standing outside a building for hours on end. In each case, time itself is being filmed. Andy Warhol's film *Empire* (1964) is an extreme case. His eight-hour film shot in static frame outside the Empire State building on innumerable reels of 16mm film watched time go by. Generally speaking, Warhol was more contained, making single-frame shoots of thirty minutes (e.g. *Kitchen*, 1965). The plasticity of the film was also explored by either painting onto it or scratching it and by the use of tight compositional editing (as in Carolee Schneeman's *Fuses*, 1964, which uses all three modalities to provide an intimate portrait of a couple's sexual relationship).

As we indicated above, some modernist cinema, within its formal probings and experimentation, also addressed questions of subjectivity and sexuality. However, it is not a cinema that is readily associated with politics per se. That being said, at certain points in history, aesthetics and politics do combine to produce a political cinema, particularly in Europe. Jean-Luc Godard, in the mid- to late 1960s talked about making a political cinema politically. By that he meant making political films through a political aesthetics of film. As with the other, primarily aesthetic modernist cinema, the process of meaning-production is exposed. The difference here lies with the non-subjective intentionality of this political cinema and the greater degree of fragmentation of meaning production. In the first instance, we are privy no longer to the inner workings of the mind but, rather, as to how ideology constructs us. In the second instance, fragmentation, the gaps between signifier (the meanings produced) and the signified (the modes and means of production) are opened up and the relationship between the two is exposed. The illusion of realism and its ideological resonances are made transparent. The film as **sign** and as **myth** is deconstructed before our eyes. Godard, Agnès Varda and Margarethe von Trotta are exemplary filmmakers of this second tendency of modernist cinema – a political aesthetic cinema, what is also known as counter-cinema.

see also: **postmodernism**

MONTAGE – *SEE* EDITING/SOVIET MONTAGE

MOTIVATION

Motivation functions on a number of levels within a film to give the **diegesis** verisimilitude; it is a cinematic convention designed to create **naturalism**. David Bordwell (in Bordwell *et al.*, 1985: 19) defines four types of motivation which serve to give a film unity and make the film's causality seem natural (see **naturalizing**). These four types are: compositional, realistic, **intertextual** or generic, and artistic. Compositional motivation means the arrangements of props and specific use of **lighting** (if necessary) as well as the establishment of a cause for impending actions so that the story can proceed. For example, a dimly lit room in which only one object, the telephone, is highlighted suggests that the phone will ring and the protagonist will answer it and take action as a result. Realistic motivation concerns **setting**. The décor must be motivated realistically. So, in a **historical reconstruction** attention goes into every detail (**costumes**, sets, objects, etc.) to ensure that verisimilitude prevails. Realistic motivation also includes **narrative** plausibility. Motivation for actions must appear realistic. Generic motivation means that all **genres** have **codes and conventions** which they follow. Thus, although a **musical** is not compositionally or realistically motivated, within its own specificity the singing and dancing are entirely justified. Intertextual motivation, the complement to generic motivation, refers to the justification of the story as it relates to the conventions of other similar texts. Bordwell (in Bordwell *et al.*, 1985: 19) quotes the **Hollywood** film narrative: 'we often assume that a Hollywood film will end happily simply because it is a Hollywood film.' Or the **star** can be the source of intertextual motivation: if s/he is a singer as well, the audience will expect a song. If s/he leads in real life the life s/he is portraying on-screen, that again is a form of intertextual motivation (guaranteeing authenticity as well as **realism**). Finally, artistic motivation appears when the film calls attention to its own aesthetics. With Hollywood this happens, particularly when the technical virtuosity of filmmaking practices is highlighted, as in the studio spectacular.

For more detail see Bordwell in Bordwell *et al.*, 1985: 12–23 and 70–84.

MOVEMENT-IMAGE/TIME-IMAGE

These two concepts were forwarded, in the 1980s, by French philosopher Gilles Deleuze in his two seminal books on cinema (1986 and 1989). They are useful, in a theoretical context, when we come to discuss the way in which we experience film in terms of either narrative-time or duration. At its most fundamental, cinema is about the projection of movement in time and its simultaneous perception by the spectator. Deleuze, in his consideration of time in cinema, determined two types of image: the movement-image, by which he meant, essentially, unbroken, linear **narrative** (see below for further discussion); time-image, referring to non-linear narrative unfurling in discontinuous time (often found in **auteur**-based or New Wave European cinemas). Both concepts are useful to **film theory** when considering issues of narrative time and **spectator** perception, as I shall now explain.

According to Deleuze, the shot is the *movement-image*. As a concept, it refers, therefore, to the actual movement in time that we perceive on-screen. The duration of the movement is the duration of the image or sequences of images. The movement-image is, then, the mobile section of a duration; it reproduces time as a 'homogenous form that links one action to another' (Colebrook, 2002: 153). As such, it renders all points of view, not a single one. Because it is the mobile section of duration, it represents the action of that time, whichever character's it is. Viewed in this light, cinema frees point of view, which means that the spectator can experience the different points of view. His/her perception is not immobilized. According to Deleuze, both early cinema and **classical narrative cinema**, which are primarily based in a system of cause and effect (an event sets in motion a series of actions which are eventually resolved), are governed by the movement-image; 'in standard cinema we are given the actions and events, with time or history providing the unity or field within which they are located' (ibid.). In terms of perception, the movement-image is our linear experience of the film's narrative. But, as we can also gather, this experience is not a passive one; the spectator enjoys multiple points of view; perception is thereby multiple, even though we have followed an essentially straightforward narrative (based on the principle of 'what happens next?').

Time-image refers to a more complex perception of the cinema. Time is no longer derived from movement (as above). Indeed, time now becomes a question of duration – a depth of time, if you will, which allow us to sense time itself. According to Deleuze, modern cinema is governed by the time-image – he is referring primarily to post-war auteur cinema. Movement is folded into time. Whereas in **mainstream cinema** movement is subjected to action, now it is subjected to duration. Duration allows us to sense things not within chronological time, but to come to perceive the nature of cinema as a layered, complex, interior experience of the materiality of film (be it **colour, sound**, events, time itself) in which time is a lived time, a time that endures and flows. Imagine a spiral – think of that as durational time. On that spiral, place events in a story, dotted here and there. Now, stretch that spiral: events are in a completely different relation to time than they were when the spiral was compressed. Further, because events are thus aligned and can be compressed or extended, we can understand how they are no longer mapped within linear time; and we understand, also, how we can perceive events differently at all times – at one moment (say, a compressed moment) event 'a' and 'b' are touching each other; at another moment (when the spiral is stretched) these two same moments are no longer in the same relation. This is how we can understand how movement is folded into time. This is the time-image, durational time.

Alain Resnais' *L'Année dernière à Marienbad/Last Year at Marienbad* (1961) provides an excellent illustration of time-image versus movement-image cinema. As the narrator of the story struggles to impose a cause and effect narrative to explain how he met the woman he claims to love, images and events defy his attempts. He represents linear narrative (movement-image cinema); however, the unfurling narrative – despite his voice-over – completely belies his reading of events, last year at Marienbad. Indeed, the film footage and the **editing** of the woman's trajectory through the film's duration create a non-linear discontinuous, labyrinthine narrative that provides a completely different, totally unstable reading of the events. This is time-image cinema that stretches and compresses events.

For further reading see Colebrook, 2002; Colman, 2011; Kennedy, 2002; Martin-Jones, 2006.

MUSIC

Curiously, music (as distinct from the **musical** genre) has only recently become an area of interest to film theorists. Precursors, such as Chion (1994) and Gorbman (1987) notwithstanding, it is only now, in the new millennium, that it has become theoretical territory within film studies. What follows is a general outline of the functions of music (for theory see suggested further reading below). First, music is, generally speaking, specially scored for a film. This is not to say that music scoring for films is not **intertextual** – clearly it will be. Obviously, early **sound** music borrowed from theatre **melodrama** as a prototype (to imitate), and also from light orchestra music and of course theatre musicals. In this arena of intertextuality, part of a film's music score may take as a deliberate quotation the music of others. Think, for example, of Mahler's Fifth Symphony for *Death in Venice* (Visconti, 1971); or popular songs already familiar to audiences – for a spectacular and anachronistic use, Baz Luhrmann's *Moulin Rouge!* (2001) is hard to surpass. On the whole, however, original scores are what predominate. Second, the musical score must have a form. Very much like a building, music acts as one of the **narrative** frameworks of the film. For example, certain musical themes will return throughout the film – each appearance refers back to the earlier one and recalls for us the emotions we experienced at that time (think, for example, of the screeching violins in *Psycho*, Hitchcock, 1960). Third, the score has to fit the film – but not slavishly – for its purpose is to bring the film alive and to help seal the **spectator**–screen relationship. When at its best, in this context, the score works with the image in a delicate tension. If the music is too slavish, then it takes the mystery out of the film itself and encodes the **preferred reading**; it becomes too descriptive and thereby too prescriptive emotionally (the swelling of chords as someone is left heartbroken is a good example). What has been overlooked is that the image is not the music and vice versa, and so needs to hold itself in counterpoint to the image. As such, music becomes some-thing more than just a reflection of a character or an action or mood. In this regard, music comes in one of three ways: it is composed beforehand (the composer has a certain idea of the script and works from that), or it is composed alongside the shooting of the film (the composer watches the rushes and adapts the musical score to what is seen), or, finally, it is composed afterwards. It is in the second instance that we can see how a composer is the most likely to influence the nature of what the filmmaker is trying to achieve. But, it is also the case that a score composed to the film once it is cut can greatly influence the feel of a film. One of the most intriguing cases is Miles Davis' spontaneous scoring of Louis Malle's *Ascenseur pour l'échafaud/Lift to the Scaffold* (1956). Davis improvised as the edited film rolled by; Malle for his part said that, thanks to Davis, his rather banal film was transformed into an interesting one. Fourth and finally, many aspects of a film score respond to fashion and taste, or more interestingly can be the initiators of fashion and taste. In this latter regard it is worth recalling Bernard Herrmann's scores for Hitchcock's movies, most famously *Psycho* and *Vertigo* (1958). In these two films (as in others), Herrmann brought **modernist** music to lay **audiences** (he is not alone of course, Dmitri Shostakovitch is another composer we could cite). Herrmann, like many of the most famous music score composers for film, was classically trained. The modernist music of Schoenberg and Berg deeply influenced his own compositional practice, and elements of this can be found in his work for Hitchcock amongst others. So watching these films entailed listening to quite **avant-garde** music if the audiences did but know it. In this context, we are reminded that early silent cinema (of the 1910s and 1920s) used classical composers' music to legitimate their products for middle-class consumers. Thus, the music of Saint-Saëns, Hindemith and Schoenberg gave cinema its authentic cachet as a seventh art – assuring its spectators that they were indeed conforming to good taste. This practice of using classical composers still prevails today; a good example being Michael Nyman's work for Peter Greenaway's films of the 1980s.

In terms of effects, music can tell us about a character, reflecting deep, even unconscious human qualities. There are many composers we could cite in the European context. Georges Auric is a prime example of this ability to reveal the state of the unconscious. Auric composed 125 scores for cinema. During the 1930s, along with several other important composers (Darius Milhaud, Maurice Jaubert, Arthur Honegger), he was part of the wave of composers who served to bring an aura of quality to French cinema in the light of the advent of sound. Moreover, along with Jaubert in particular, Auric was a significant contributor to the pessimistic and introspective feel of the late 1930s **French poetic realist cinema**. He was also a significant composer to Jean Cocteau's films (*La Belle et la Bête*, 1946, and *Orphée*, 1950) – and no one could go more into the unconscious than in his work. This notion of film composers working with particular film directors gives us a number of famous duos within Western cinema. We have already mentioned a few, to which we must add Nino Rota who worked with Fellini and Coppola. Amongst his huge output (around 150) of inventive but derivative (often self-plagiarized) scores, he gave us the music for *The Godfather* (1972) and *The Godfather: Part II* (1974). His music is often used to ironic effect (e.g. the waltz in *The Godfather*) and draws on a huge range of styles. Often he scores films without seeing the script or film, thus creating a feeling of detachment between music and image (Dyer, 2004: 44). In this way the music can 'argue' against the image, creating dissonances or contradictory signs which of course opens up gaps and challenges us to understand what we are hearing and seeing with greater depth. It is noteworthy, especially in his scoring for Fellini, that a queer **sexuality** often emanated. Fellini was fascinated by homosexuality (see especially, *Satyricon*, 1969 and *Casanova*, 1976) and Rota supplied the essentially **queer** music to match (Dyer, 2004: 45). Howard Shore and David Cronenberg have worked together for over forty years (from *The Brood*, 1979 to *A Dangerous Method*, 2011) – and the range of music created goes from aggressive terror to more suggestive and ambiguous tonalities, often pointing to an unclear **subjectivity** (think of the twins in *Dead Ringers*, 1988; or the cross-dressing in *M. Butterfly*, 1993). Another famous duo is Ennio Morricone and Sergio Leone of spaghetti **Western** fame. Moreover, Morricone used an eclectic tonal palette ranging from harmonica to whips, electric guitars to trumpets and full orchestra. The music becomes almost a character – perhaps the alter-ego of Leone with its plaintive effect that is nostalgic and revelatory of an obsession with death. A final note in this context: despite the fact that they scored for other filmmakers, composers such as Morricone tended to become associated with a particular **genre**. In this vein, mention should also be made of John Barry who became associated with a particular film type – namely the Bond movies (ten of which he scored, from the 1960s to the 1980s).

Music also can tell us about **gender**. In its stylized form it can fix gender (soft romantic score-lines for the woman, harder ones for the male). But just as it can fix, so too it can unfix. If we compare the Western's music, with its huge optimistic sweeping landscape-type music (à la Aaron Copland), with that of the nervy edgy urban (sometimes jazz-like) music of **film noir** we can easily see how the former speaks to virile (fixed) masculinity and the latter to a masculinity in crisis (unfixed). In this regard, we can see how music also relates to **sexuality**. We have already mentioned Shore's music for Cronenberg. But see how sexual obsession and uncertainty abounds in the scores of Herrmann's music for Hitchcock. Just consider this in relation to *Psycho*. Originally, Hitchcock wanted the shower scene without music, but was eventually persuaded by Herrmann that it needed the music score to give it the vicious relentlessness and sexually pathological edge. Brian Easdale's music for Powell's films works well to evoke the **psychological** edge of sexual repression that drives its protagonists (female and male alike) to pathological behaviour. We need only mention three of his most famous films – *Black Narcissus* (1946), *The Red Shoes* (1948) and *Peeping Tom* (1960) – to get the idea. What is worth noting, too, in the case of these three films alone, is the queer sub-text that also prevails. In the first film, the nuns, unnaturally isolated, either scream out for male congruence or, it is suggested, find relief with each other. In the second, the young dancer is driven delirious by her ambition to succeed at the expense of a sexual life, but more significantly the impresario/male dancer homosexual relationship remains only just hidden. Finally, the repressed photographer of *Peeping Tom* displaces onto the women he kills his own sexual neurosis brought about by his father, with whom he can never find sublimation. As a last example let us consider David Raksin's music for Preminger's *Laura* (1944) – especially Laura's theme which is used to reveal the detective Mark's progressive falling in love with the dead woman (namely Laura). The music allows us to witness Mark becoming increasingly uncomfortable with his feelings about her as he struggles to regain control. The overriding feeling is of his inner conflict: how can he desire a dead woman who lives on only as a portrait? (See Burt (1994: 168–85) for a detailed analysis.)

see also: **musical, sound/soundtrack**

For further reading on music and theory see Buchanan and Swiboda, 2004; Burt, 1994; Chion, 1994; Cooke, 2008; Coyle, 2010; Davison, 2004; Dickinson, 2003; Donnelly, 2001, 2005; Gorbman, 1987; Inglis, 2003; Kalinak, 1992; Kassabian, 2000; Powrie and Stilwell, 2005; Reay, 2004; Redner, 2010; Slobin, 2008; Wojcik and Knight, 2001.

MUSICAL

This entry is in two parts: a schematic history of the **genre** and an overview of its structures and strategies.

History

The musical is seen as a quintessentially American or **Hollywood** genre, in much the same way as the **Western**. Unlike the Western, however, it is a hybrid genre given its descent from the European operetta (particularly Austrian) and American vaudeville and the music-hall. Although Alan Crosland's *The Jazz Singer* (1927) is generally accepted as the first **sound** film. In fact the first all-talking, all-singing, all-dancing musical was the *The Broadway Melody* (Harry Beaumont, 1929). It is a noteworthy musical for a number of reasons, not least its title, which generated three further *Broadway Melodies* in the 1930s alone. Noteworthy, too, because its title refers topographically to a major source of Hollywood musicals, New York's Broadway. Furthermore, it established the tradition of the backstage story as an integral part of the musical. This tradition developed also into the sub-genre of the backstage musical (generally speaking a less expensive model to produce) – of which *Singin' in the Rain* (Stanley Donen, 1952) is arguably the best exemplar. *The Broadway Melody* also brought the lyricist Arthur Freed to the attention of the MGM mogul Louis B. Mayer, who by the mid-1930s had finally agreed to give him a relatively free rein as producer. Freed was responsible for a major shift in the **codes and conventions** of the musical, which during the late 1920s and early 1930s had been fairly conservative. He was also responsible for convincing MGM of the need for a stable of musical **stars**.

MGM is the **studio** most readily associated with this genre. However, one of the first all-time great musical pairings – Fred Astaire and Ginger Rogers – was with RKO. In 1933, Astaire and Rogers were paired up as a supporting team to the main story in *Flying Down to Rio* (1933). **Audience** response was such that they became an overnight success, and, during the 1930s, they were regularly RKO's best box-office hit and the ideal romance couple (at least on-screen). Traditionally, they played the roles of the man-about-town sophisticate and the girl next-door, and their story was set in contemporary times. The other famous romance pair of that period, Jeannette MacDonald and Nelson Eddy, figured for the first time together in 1935, in an MGM production, *Naughty Marietta* (Woody Van Dyke). This romantic couple appeared mostly in **costume** operettas and often the roles were reversed, MacDonald being the woman with **class** and Eddy the penniless prisoner (as in their first film) or in the role of some kind of out-of-society type (as in *New Moon*, 1940).

Musicals at this time had a fairly naive plot and were primarily perceived as vehicles for song and dance. However, it is worth considering just what this means. First of all, the **narrative** did incline towards simplicity – and was based on the Cinderella/Prince Charming **myth**. Often it was a case of 'boy meets girl/boy hates girl/girl hates boy', but because there was such an undoubted attraction they come together in the end: 'boy gets girl'. It is in this respect that, as Richard Dyer (*The Movie 75*, 1981: 1484) says, the musical points to its generic and **ideological** function as a 'gospel of happiness'. But, as far as the singing and dancing were concerned, routines and performance were a far more complex affair. Some of the greatest names from Broadway – lyricists and composers – were brought in by Hollywood: Cole Porter, Irving Berlin, Ira and George Gershwin, Jerome Kern, Rodgers and Hart, a bit later Oscar Hammerstein. The reason for bringing such talent in was twofold. In the early 1930s, the musical genre was experiencing a slump, much like the rest of Hollywood, because of the Depression. To bring some excitement and panache into the musical and thereby attract audiences, Hollywood decided to buy in Broadway hits. By referring to Broadway, Hollywood also sought to bring artistic clout to its own productions.

These great names of American popular **music** did much, in the 1930s, to shape the look of the musical. At first, because they were commissioned to package songs for the films, the song and dance routines were worked through more like items in a review show. The songs paid little attention to plot and characterization. Indeed, characters seemed to burst into song and dance in an artificial and arbitrary way. Alternatively, the breaking into song and dance was given a rational explanation – for example, tapping a rhythm or something tapping a rhythm, or using a specific word or expression that necessarily introduces a song. However, once Fred Astaire had broken into the big time this changed and, because of his meticulous planning of his dance routines, composers were brought into closer alliance with the actual production practices, including, of course, the storyline. Astaire's work in collaboration with Irving Berlin and Jerome Kern certainly produced some of the best musicals of the late 1930s. Astaire insisted on full **shot** photography with no cutting away for his dance routines, whether solo or with Ginger Rogers (with whom he made nine films during the period 1933 to 1939). This meant that music and choreography had to be worked out in the minutest detail. Music and dance informed each other (as, for example, in *Top Hat*, 1935; *Follow the Fleet*, 1936; *Carefree*, 1938).

The other move in the 1930s to counter the slump brought on by the Depression came with the highly stylized films of Busby Berkeley – the master of drill precision with his fanciful and abstract approach to dance routines using hundreds of chorus 'girls' to create geometrical patterns through their movements under the eye of the camera. His 1930s films (made for Warner Brothers) were almost pure spectacle, with little attention to narrative, but full focus on the capacity of the human form to exude an erotic sensuality. To this effect, he used a single camera that roved over the human formations either through tracking or crane shots. Berkeley was the first to put female nudity into the musical (*Roman Scandals*, 1933); he is equally famous for his 'crotch shots' (*Gold Diggers of 1933*). As Altman (1989: 257) puts it, Berkeley offered sex through the **gaze** – with the camera acting as the eye; in his spectacles 'the show's power (was mainly) identified with the woman's lure'.

By the end of the 1930s, the musical was on the wane again. Ginger Rogers had split from Fred Astaire; MacDonald and Eddy were very faded stars indeed. Several strategies were adopted. At MGM, thanks to Freed's insistence that talent should be nurtured amongst the contract actors and thanks too to his success in producing *The Wizard of Oz* (Victor Fleming, 1939), a new musical formula was introduced. This combined youth and music in the form of the 'kids putting on a show' musical. The star vehicles were Judy Garland (launched by *The Wizard of Oz*) and Mickey Rooney (already a star for his Andy Hardy series). Together, they made four musicals in this vein (*Babes in Arms*, 1939; *Strike Up the Band*, 1940; *Babes on Broadway*, 1941; *Girl Crazy*, 1943). At Universal, child actors were used as well, but this time as a vehicle for bringing popular classics into the musical arena. Thus Deanna Durbin sang her way through *One Hundred Men and a Girl* (1937) and managed to persuade the great conductor Stokowski to conduct an out-of-work orchestra. By the 1940s, other, new formulas were introduced. To the classic musicals and putting-on-a-show musicals were added composer biographies (*Yankee Doodle Dandy*, 1942; *Rhapsody in Blue*, 1945; *Till the Clouds Roll By,* 1946; *Night and Day*, 1946; *Words and Music*, 1948) and biographical musicals of 'stars' with a showbiz background (*Lillian Russell*, 1940; *Incendiary Blonde*, *The Dolly Sisters*, both 1945).

Of these three traditions, it is the last, the 'life-stories' of performers that fared best in terms of continuation. They went on well into the 1950s and indeed into the 1970s as with *A Star is Born* (1954); *I'll Cry Tomorrow* (1955); *Lady Sings the Blues* (1972); *The Rose* (1979). What is interesting is that it is mostly the biography of female performers that 'fascinates'. Generally speaking, their story is one of an unprecedented rise to success followed by a slow decline through drugs, alcohol and self-neglect – even though they carry on singing. Implicitly, fame is too hard or hot for them to handle. Ironically (since it was the opposite of the real-life situation), of the four films quoted above only *A Star is Born* is an exception – with the husband (played by James Mason) of the emerging star (played by Judy Garland) being the one to fall into alcoholic decline.

It was, however, Freed's conception of the musical that was greatly responsible for revitalizing the genre and marking it out as an MGM product, particularly during the 1940s and 1950s. His idea was that song and dance should move the narrative on, that there should be nothing arbitrary about the introduction of song and dance – indeed that the progression from speech to song to dance should be a natural one (see **naturalizing**). Apart from Judy Garland, Gene Kelly (who had been signed up from Broadway in 1940) was another star vehicle of this period to carry out Freed's conception of a greater naturalism. To this effect, Kelly was instrumental in introducing the contemporary urban musical such as *On the Town* (1949), which closely integrated song, dance and story and which was partly shot on location. Similarly *An American in Paris* (made in 1951, but for which the music had been written in 1937 by George Gershwin shortly before his untimely death) portrayed the vitality of the musical scene in Paris in the late 1930s with the heavy influence of jazz and contemporary music. By the mid- to late 1940s, contemporary music in musicals, under the influence of Glenn Miller and Duke Ellington (to name but two), also included Big Band Swing (see *The Glenn Miller Story*, 1953).

Freed's other smart move was to bring the Broadway director Vincente Minnelli to MGM. With a reputation for lavish and stylish musicals on stage, Minnelli was, nonetheless, also a firm believer in the integrated type of musical Freed advocated. His first film musical was with an all-Black cast, *Cabin in the Sky* (1943). He then went on to work with Judy Garland and together they produced some of their best work: *Meet Me in St Louis* (1944), *Till the Clouds Roll By* (1946) and *The Pirate* (1948).

By the late 1940s, Astaire was persuaded out of early retirement by MGM and enjoyed felicitous dance pairings with Judy Garland and Cyd Charisse. He also joined the studio that housed his only 'real' rival, Gene Kelly. Their styles are so different, however, that rather than considering them as rivals – at least with hindsight – we might better see them as exemplary of the two dominant tendencies of the musical as it relates to the American cultural system; that is, to selling marriage (Altman, 1989: 27). On the one hand, there is the stylized inventive elegance of Fred Astaire; on the other, the brash energetic experimentation of Gene Kelly. Astaire is the witty, cool, man about town who gets his woman. Kelly with his edgy over-insistence on his virility remains a man child who is not too convinced about marriage. In terms of a legacy, it is fair to say that between them and with Garland and Charisse they helped to revitalize the musical and became part of the heyday of the 1950s **colour** musical that also included other great musical stars such as Frank Sinatra and Bing Crosby.

The period 1930 to 1960, despite some severe dips, marked the great era of the Hollywood musical. By the 1950s, the studio system was on the decline and there was an increasing need to target audiences more systematically. Popular Broadway hits still made it onto the screen (e.g. *Oklahoma*, 1955; *The King and I*, 1956; *South Pacific*, 1958; and – imported from Britain – *My Fair Lady*, 1964). But dwindling audiences meant that new strategies had to be developed. Thus, Hollywood linked up with the record industry as a means of targeting a new audience: the youth class. So, a spate of teenager musicals was produced, mostly starring Elvis Presley – who, if he could not act, could certainly sing and dance. Presley literally sold sex through his song-and-dance routines (arguably his most famous rock musical is *Jailhouse Rock*, 1957). Britain briefly imitated this trend, primarily in the Cliff Richard series of musicals (such as *Expresso Bongo*, 1959; *Summer Holiday*, 1963). However, these solo star performances – at least in the United Kingdom – were soon superseded by pop group musicals in the form of the Beatles (*A Hard Day's Night*, 1964; *Help!*, 1965).

The trend, in the so-called 'hip sixties', was also for a greater **realism** in the musical and non-musical stars. *West Side Story* (1961) *is* exemplary in this respect. Set in Manhattan, it tells the story of rival gangs (White Americans versus Puerto Ricans). A modern *Romeo and Juliet* narrative, the film treats racism, juvenile delinquency and young love in a serious fashion. It is also one of the first musicals to create a more believable world and to end in tragedy. This greater realism in the musical gets carried into the 1970s with the disco-dance musicals of *Saturday Night Fever* (1977) and *Grease* (1978), both with John Travolta (the former film made him into a star).

The 1970s saw a profusion of rock musicals that ranged from **documentary** types (*Woodstock*, 1970) to realism (the Jamaican film *The Harder They Come*, 1972) to **fantasy**-cum-flower-power (*Godspell*, 1973; *Jesus Christ Superstar*, 1973; *Hair*, 1979). But, the early tradition of the 1930s did not disappear – *the* exemplary star vehicle for the traditional musical was Barbra Streisand. Just a few of her films serve to show not just how prolific she was, but how her range goes from **comedy** to tragedy to performer-biography and so incorporates the heritage of the traditional musical from 1930 to 1960: *Funny Girl* (1968),

Hello Dolly! (1969), *Funny Lady* (1975) (all performer-biographies); *On a Clear Day You Can See Forever* (1970) (comedy); *The Way We Were* (1974) (tragedy) – and so on. Indeed, even after its heyday, the musical (albeit on the decline) never fully abandoned its traditional values. For example, Robert Wise, who directed *West Side Story*, went on to direct *The Sound of Music* (1965) – a sweetly sugary musical that in the final analysis sells marriage. And in France, Jacques Demy had a brief stab at the genre, combining realism with sweet sugariness, with *Les Parapluies de Cherbourg* (1964) and *Les Demoiselles de Rochefort* (1967).

The musical was very much on the wane in the 1980s, only occasionally reappearing in fairly unextravagant forms such as the backstage musical, for example, *Fame* (1980). Dancing or **road movie** musicals that use contemporary songs for their musical soundtrack represent another inexpensively produced form of musical. John Travolta resurfaces in *Staying Alive* (1983) to dazzle us with his disco-dancing technique. The 1990s witnessed something of a mini-revival, thanks, arguably, to the high-impact effect of *Evita* (Alan Parker, 1996) which set a trend of cross-overs (taking stage musicals to screen – as, for example, *Chicago*, Rob Marshall, 2002; *Phantom of the Opera*, Joel Schumacher, 2004; *Mamma Mia!*, Phyllida Lloyd, 2008). What is interesting, however, is that the genre, since the 1990s, has in some ways moved out of its Hollywood orbit and gone **transnational** – each product seeking to challenge the pre-existing codes and conventions (see below). The Australian filmmaker Baz Luhrmann looks like he has been itching to make a full-on musical ever since his *Strictly Ballroom* (1992) which sets a teenage love story within a ballroom dancing contest. His *Moulin Rouge!* (2001) is a tour de force. Another Australian filmmaker, Stephan Elliott, brings camp to the musical in explicit style with the very gay and very funny *Adventures of Priscilla, Queen of the Desert* (1994). In the European context, Lars Von Trier offers his own macabre idea of a musical with *Dancer in the Dark* (2000). For further discussion of the impact of this transnational revival see the end of the next section.

Structures and strategies – codes and conventions

(In this section I refer, primarily, to the American musical; I also refer to several useful and important studies on the genre: Dyer, 1977a, 1986; Feuer, 1982; Altman, 1989.) The musical is extremely self-referential: it spends most of its time justifying its existence – as, for example, with the putting-on-a-show musical (one of the most common generic types) – 'the show must go on!' In this type of musical there is a double referentiality pointing to the narcissistic and exhibitionist nature of the genre. Apart from the sombre-ending musicals, the general strategy of the genre is to provide the **spectator** with a utopia through the form of entertainment. The entertainment is the utopia. So again self-referentiality is at work.

According to Dyer (1977a: 3) there are five categories functioning within this utopian sensibility: abundance, energy, intensity, **transparency** and community. All are related to the ideological strategies of the genre: selling marriage, **gender** fixity, communal stability and the merits of capitalism. Abundance starts with the décor and the costumes – it insists on the United States' wealth and well-being. Energy is the dance-and-song routine, but also the camera-work – it is also the hallmark of (White) America's pioneering spirit. Intensity derives from the sense of intimacy that the spectator takes pleasure in when watching the body perform – literally, the body 'putting-itself-on-show'. Transparency refers to the reflection the musical purports to give on the American way of life of which the folk community is an essential ingredient. Altman (1989: 25), for his part, talks of the musical as an 'ode to marriage' and the marrying of riches (as exemplified by the male) to beauty (in the form of the female). The musical must also be seen in the light of its contextual relationship with social moments (such as the Depression) and structures of pleasure – especially since it is not always the female form that we enjoy watching dance. For example, Gene Kelly and John Travolta provide, albeit in somewhat different ways, visual pleasures that have more in common with each other – starting with the insistence on virile **sexuality** – than the visual pleasure offered by Astaire.

Altman (1989: 27) makes the point that cause and effect are fairly tenuous in the musical and that it is less a case of chronology or psychological **motivation** than one of paralleling stories in a comparative mode. He is of course referring to the classic period of the American musical (1930–60) – although his reading still holds true for the reprise classic musical (the happy-love musical) that persists after 1960. In that it reconciles terms that seem irreconcilable (starting with sexual difference), the musical 'fashions a myth out of the American courtship ritual' (ibid.: 27). The musical then is based on the principle of duality or pairings, of male/female oppositions, which it ultimately resolves. Thus, the paralleling serves to set up a series of binary oppositions, starting with the one based in gender. Each of the two characters embodies the opposite of the other and it is those oppositions that must be resolved for marriage to occur (ibid.: 24). These oppositions are what

Altman calls dual-focus structures (ibid.: 19). They generate a chain of oppositions: sexual, background, national origin, temperament, age, colour of hair. Thus, for example, in *Gigi* (Vincente Minnelli, 1958) characters are paired: Gigi with Gaston, and Gigi's grandmother with Gaston's uncle. **Settings**, locations, trips and songs are paired. Roles and activities are paired: Gigi is the girl child about to emerge into woman-hood, Gaston is an established businessman; she is frivolous, he serious. However, as their story develops he takes to fun and she to being more serious. Their marriage then becomes a merging of adult and child qualities as well as a containment of the generational problematic and its potential incestual value. Gaston is after all a generation older than Gigi – a gap mirrored, in reverse, in the uncle/grandmother love affair (see Altman, 1989: 22–27).

Opposites eventually attract and can be melded. Even Gene Kelly, who is an interesting exception to the dual-sexuality focus, is eventually brought into the community: which means marriage, children and so on. We mostly remember Kelly dancing alone, the childlike clown and self-centred show-off who in the end has to grow up. In this way, says Altman (1989: 57), Kelly embodies an American dream – he keeps the 'good' of his childlikeness and also matures. In this respect only, he is also in the vein of the female child role rather than the serious mature male role. Opposites are, then, finally reconcilable, and this applies to all the binary oppositions that the musical generates. This includes the work/entertainment opposition, which is often a strategy of the backstage musical. This type of musical opposes the 'real' with 'art'. The real world of work is drab and ordinary; that of the stage is ideal and one of beauty. In *Silk Stockings* (Rouben Mamoulian, 1957) – a remake of *Ninotchka* – Cyd Charisse is the serious (i.e. dull) business-like Soviet representative and Astaire the happy-go-lucky (i.e. fun-loving) Hollywood director. Charisse comes to learn that entertainment is in fact good business. This type of opposition can generate a slightly different one if both characters represent different types of 'art'. Thus, in a musical one character can be a musician or ballet dancer, the other a music-hall entertainer or tap-dancer. The former sees her or his 'art' as high art and therefore serious work and, conversely, sees the other's work as entertainment, not serious – therefore hardly work at all, and certainly low art. In reverse, the entertainer sees the other as a snob who has not lived. By the end of the musical, both come to see the merit of the other's work (see *An American in Paris*, or, on a slightly different tangent of opposing theatre worlds, *The Barkleys of Broadway*, Charles Walters, 1949).

The musical therefore functions ideologically to resolve the fear of difference. In this way, it functions as a text which disguises one of society's paradoxes. By extension, of course, this means that it makes invisible the other sets of paradoxes that are inherent in society thereby ensuring society's stability. Thus, the musical also makes safe the notion of the community as *the* place to be. Musicals that fall into this category are typically called 'folk musicals', and implicitly deal with the American folk. Small-town or agricultural communities are common in this type of musical (as in *Oklahoma*, Fred Zinnemann, 1955; or *Seven Brides for Seven Brothers*, Stanley Donen, 1954). Central to these musicals are home and the family. Family groupings, the extended family – all work towards the well-being of the community. To this effect, this joyous folk musical nearly always gets threatened by a baddie or gang warfare – the 'other' outside who threatens the stability of the community. Although they are less present, even large cities are represented as a coherent community. For example, St Louis in *Meet Me in St Louis* is humanized to the level of a small-town community (Altman, 1989: 275).

This same levelling also occurred for all-Black-cast musicals (with White directors and composers) – of which in the heyday of the musical genre there were only a few. Apart from the first all-Black-cast musical, *Hallelujah* (Vidor/Berlin, 1929), *Cabin in the Sky* (Minnelli/Duke, 1943) and *Porgy and Bess* (Preminger/Gershwin, 1959) are the two most often quoted. These latter two films contain the Black characters within a safely boundaried community (Catfish Row and Kittiwah Island for *Porgy and Bess*) and give a White-eyed version of the Black folklore. Similarly *Hallelujah* contains the Black characters within the family household consisting of shanty houses and the cotton fields. This film, however, is based not on the traditional oppositions evoked above for all-White musicals but on the opposition chain of religion/sexuality virtue/sin. In terms of Black folklore, it includes a further opposition, this time in relation to 'Black' music – or rather the White person's perception of it: church music and jazz, where the former is associated with virtue and goodness, the latter with sin and woman-temptress. Other than these full-blown White-eyed visions of Blackness (to which we can add the minstrelsy plantation musical *The Green Pastures*, William Keighley and Marc Connelly, 1936), there is the isolated presence of Paul Robeson playing a slave on a cotton farm in *Show Boat* (Whale/Kern, 1936), in which he sings *Old Man (sic) River*, or an ennobled African helping the White man (*Sanders of the River*, Alexander Korda, 1935; *King Solomon's Mines*, Stevenson, 1937, in both of which he sings African songs). In all cases,

he is contained within a White colonialist environment. As a last measure of this levelling and normalizing, tap-dancing, which is a Black
tradition, is totally recuperated into White musicals with no
acknowledgement of its Black origins until the 1970s when tribute is
finally paid to that heritage in the British-made *Black Joy* (Anthony
Simmons, 1977) and the Motown-produced *Thank God it's Friday*
(Robert Klane, 1978).

Altman (1989: 32ff.) isolates four key functions of the cinematic
apparatus in the musical construction: settings, **iconography**, music,
dance. A key technique for settings was to use repetition for comparative
purposes, to underscore the duality of the sexual oppositions. Therefore,
work and home spaces have similar settings or décor; or, alternatively, the
two spaces in which the protagonists move (and dance) – be they work
or home – mirror each other. Similarly, the proliferation of other
couples serves as mirrors to the main couple or pair. In terms of iconography, what dominates is the duet and the solo shot. But even in
the presence of the solo shot the spectator fills it in because s/he
knows that the coupling is pre-ordained (ibid.: 39). Similarly with the
music. The duet is there for the maximum tension and climax of the
narrative. However, the solo carries most of the musical and, as with the
solo shot, the spectator fills it in with the missing other (ibid.: 40). Finally,
dance: the camera dances with the characters. It either adopts the
position of a watching audience and is, therefore, static and panning
left to right; or it is fluid, using tracking or crane shots (as we saw
with Busby Berkeley). As with the other key functions, the camera
catches solo, duet or group dancing. In order to invest these shots with
energy – particularly when the camera is static – the tendency is to cut
up the shooting with close-ups on feet, hands and faces. The exception
to this rule is, as we have seen, Astaire, who insisted on full shots for his
routines – whether solo, duet or ensemble.

Dyer (*The Movie 75*, 1981: 1584) speaks of a standard model for a
genre as having three periods: primitive, mature, decadent. We have
seen how the musical has had a chequered career, reflecting partly
audience taste, partly finance (the musical is a very expensive genre to
produce), partly due to social conditions (emergence of a youth class,
greater choice of leisure pursuits, periods of economic recession). This
entry has mostly talked about the first two periods, so a brief word is
necessary on the last. By the decadent phase Dyer means that the time
in the genre's development has come when its codes and conventions
can be questioned. Until the 1960s and 1970s the musical did not
question itself – as we have seen it indulged in narcissistic auto-satisfaction.
Arguably, the rock musical of the 1960s started the questioning of the

codes and conventions of the genre. It is interesting to note that some critics qualify *Easy Rider* (Dennis Hopper, 1969) as a rock musical – even though there is no on-screen singing and dancing, just a soundtrack of rock music – whereas most see it as a **road movie**. The point in this debate is not really what genre it is but rather that it typified, for some, a definite change in the orientation of the musical because the message of the film was politicized in its counter-cultural aspirations and because the use of contemporary songs on the soundtrack was a break with copyright law. Similarly, African-Americans started putting their own culture and music up on-screen in films such as *Shaft* (1971) and *Superfly* (1972) – which in some ways backfired because Hollywood co-opted their work in a series of **Blaxploitation** movies (see **Black cinema USA**).

A filmmaker often quoted in the context of the decadent period of the musical is Bob Fosse. *Sweet Charity* (1969) and *Cabaret* (1972) are exemplary of his challenge to Hollywood. He mixes elements of art cinema with movie entertainment – the influences of Federico Fellini and Bertolt Brecht respectively are felt in these films. High and low art are therefore reconciled from the beginning. Dance style goes from the fluid to the ugly and brash. The camera-work similarly goes from the fluid to the vertiginous. And there is 'no such thing as happiness'. Nor, incidentally is there any such thing as the good all-American folk community, or the merits of capitalism. All is either a bit seedy, decadent or just plain vulgar. No 'Nice, nice Miss American Pie' here. But, perhaps the musical to end all musicals is Robert Altman's *Nashville* (1975). Nashville, the so-called heart of country and Western music and all-American folk, literally disintegrates before the specta-tor's eyes. Altman's musical goes nowhere, comes from nowhere, it tells you nothing, it is not about country and Western music, no one mirrors anyone, and, finally, what pairing there is remains dysfunctional from beginning to end. Nothing is reconciled and the film ends in a solo performance.

As we mentioned at the end of the history section, since the 1980s, the musical re-manifested itself under new guises – often cross-overs – but, in terms of numbers, production was on a much smaller scale. The Australian Baz Luhrmann has taken the musical by the scruff of its neck and shaken it into something new, highly entertaining and zestful at the same time as offering new challenges though his own interpretation of the musical. First, he brings the musical back to spectacle and makes it an attraction that directly addresses youth audi-ences. He began this with *Strictly Ballroom*, continued it with *William Shakespeare's Romeo and Juliet* (1996) – a fabulous modernization of

Shakespeare's story about the thwarted and doomed lovers told in a pop-video style – and brings this effort to renovate to full-blown excess in *Moulin Rouge!* Second, he is completely unafraid to use music in a **postmodern** fashion: picking out songs of any period to match the mood he wants to convey, despite the fact that, as for example with *Moulin Rouge!*, his film is set in the past (Paris of the Belle Epoque in this instance). As Luhrmann rightly comments (2001: 16) this anachronistic use of song is not new: 'it's very common for musicals to utilize music that people have a previous relationship to'. In *Moulin Rouge!* there is only one new song – all the rest are borrowed and/but it is their clever placing that alters them, at the same time as we sense them as familiar. Indeed, this whole film is an essay on the intrinsically 'borrowed' nature of genre in general and the musical in particular – and of course its starting point is the earlier film versions of *Moulin Rouge!* themselves (E. A. Dupont, 1928; Sidney Lanfield, 1934; John Huston, 1952). Yet, in his **mise-en-abîme** of **intertexts** (musicals, melodramas, classical era cinema and early primitive cinema), Luhrmann makes something new happen. He takes the backstage/putting-on-a-show musical and fills it with excess. The plush, rich mise-en-scène is everywhere, even the tacky artificiality of the city-scape backdrops is self-consciously excessive, as too is the play with gender and sexuality in the secondary or chorus roles. Thus, on the one hand, everything points to the non-natural effects of the musical genre – especially the richness of décor being brought into a backstage musical (which generally speaking is about the poverty of the means of production) – and to the pleasure we receive in viewing this excess. But, on the other hand, Luhrmann also takes our pleasure away. The camera-work is full of energy, dashing all over the place during the song and dance routines – almost as if on a trapeze wire itself. Yet, just as soon as a routine begins (in both the show routines and the backstage ones), the camera cuts away. We know that in a musical the camera can mingle in with the dancers, follow them around (it is one of the conventions) or stay at a distance and follow the movement as would a spectator watching a stage performance. Luhrmann's camera-work does both but neither – it begins, then pulls away. So we never get to see our main protagonists (or indeed much of the rest of the cast) in a protracted sense dancing for us, the camera consistently cuts away. And this is Luhrmann's other big challenge to the genre: his camera-work functions to undermine the very concept of the musical. Rather than show it all and give us the pleasure of bodies moving in full view, it frustrates our pleasure by what it conceals: Nicole Kidman is never on the trapeze long enough for us to look; she never does a proper dance routine with Ewan McGregor (and so on). In essence the film is chaotic. It is also painterly (just like the source it draws on, Toulouse-Lautrec's Belle Epoque Paris) and as such the space is cut up in unusual ways. It has something for everyone: songs for all generations, it rocks like a pop-video and – for the younger ones – there are special effects dotted throughout (courtesy of the Australian company Animal Logic). A truly postmodern, transnational high-concept, high-camp spectacle, it appeals to young audiences as much as to older generations – do we seriously mind not getting it all?

With Luhrmann, then, there is still pleasure in the withdrawal of pleasure – we cannot have it all but we can have some. Such could not be said of Lars Von Trier's revival of the genre with *Dancer in the Dark* which is so unremittingly about loss and lack of plenitude – the bleak narrative of the sacrificial good mother who ends up going to the gallows brings it closer to a Janáček opera than a musical. And yet, in its daring, it too makes some important contributions to our thinking about this genre. While Luhrmann asks us to ponder the self-reflexivity of the genre by excessively layering its inherent rich-ness (colour, music, décor, etc.), Von Trier goes in the completely opposite direction. Colour is filtered down to a dowdy green and brown; narrative is stripped down to a bare sketch-line, and a sense of improvisation overrides any notion of strong choreography or actor direction. In all these ways, including the hand-held camera work for the acting scenes, we can see how Von Trier has brought the **Dogme** manifesto, with its vow of chastity in cinema practice, into the musical genre as a way of creating a new kind of realist musical (not seen since *West Side Story* perhaps). Significantly also, working against the genre's predominant trope of selling the idea of community, in Von Trier's film there is no sense of community. The mother, Selma (played by Björk), is loved by one other person only (a factory worker, Kathy, played by Catherine Deneuve). But, Selma loves only her son whom she will do everything to protect (including commit murder). The musical in effect is hers alone, and in her head. As an escape-mechanism from the terrible existence she is subjected to, she sings herself into a space of fantasy, making excursions into song and dance where no one and no thing, including her advancing congenital blindness (hence the title of the film), can assail her. Perhaps this is why for these 'musical' scenes, Von Trier reserved his one moment of excess. He positioned one hundred cameras around the set to capture, from every angle, Selma's song-and-dance routines. The idea was to keep away from anything artificial (such as the camera weaving in and out or holding a 180-degree perspective on the performance as with theatre). By recording these performances of Selma's mind in this way, Von Trier lets Björk reveal the deep authenticity of this beleaguered woman. Deep inner processes are not something we normally associate with the musical; therein lies the challenge of Von Trier's film. We are no longer in the realm of music and dance functioning to build a character or story (the traditional functions of a musical), but of a character building her own inner self before us, formulating her identity through her own song and dance (appropriate in a way since Björk composed the music and wrote all but one of the songs). By dancing in the dark, she asserts her self. Almost as if – to recall the title of Dick Hebdige's famous 1988 study about sub-cultural practices of resistance to dominant ideology – she is hiding in the light.

For Bombay musicals *see* **Bollywood**; *see also* **genre**, **studio system**

For further reading, beyond authors mentioned in the text, see Cohan, 2002; Grant, 2012; Knight, 2002; Marshall and Stilwell, 2000; Muir, 2005; Smith, 2005. For a special study on MGM see Cohan, 2005.

MYTH

Myth is a key concept in semiotics to refer to the way in which reality is represented. Roland Barthes is the main philosopher associated with this concept, the principles of which he set out in his book *Mythologies* (1957). Having shown how myth operates to produce meaning (see **denotation/connotation**), he proceeds to analyse certain aspects of popular culture and explain how these cultural artefacts (like cinema) produce meaning. Cultural artefacts have a mythic function, they are just so many ways by which we understand the culture in which we find ourselves. Myth mediates reality. Myth is a concept that primarily refers to a process of signification by which any given society 'explains' its history and culture. For example, classical **Hollywood** cinema sells its **audiences** the two greatest myths of all times: the American Dream (in the form of capitalism and the self-made man, *sic*) and the Family.

Myths are part of everyday life and change across time. History and culture inform myth but, equally, myth serves as a way by which history and culture are 'explained' as a natural process (for example, good versus evil in **war films** or **Westerns**). Myth, then, is part of the **ideological** process of **naturalization**. The **structuralist** and anthropologist

Claude Lévi-Strauss argued that 'a dilemma or contradiction stands at the heart of every living myth. The impulse to construct the myth arises from the desire to resolve the dilemma' (quoted in Cook, 1985, 90). We can see how this concept of myth is at the heart of **classical narrative cinema**'s three-act discursive strategy of order/disorder/order-restored. **Dominant cinema** seeks always to resolve a dilemma: to assert a 'truth', be it good triumphant over evil, family values, etc. In terms of film as a cultural artefact, Barthes asserts that film is a sign system that functions mainly on the level of myth (how many after all achieve the American Dream?). As such, mainstream cinema loses all tangible reference to the real world – even as it seeks to locate the 'reality-effect' (see **apparatus**). Mainstream cinema spends a lot of effort disguising the fact that what it is showing is pure illusionism (for example, despite what war movies tell us, of good triumphing over evil, war itself is less about winning than it is about killing).

For more detailed discussion *see* **denotation/connotation**, **semiology/semiotics**

For further reading see Barthes, 1957, 1973.

NARRATIVE/NARRATION

Narrative involves the recounting of real or fictitious events. Narrative cinema's function is storytelling not description, which is, supposedly, a part function of the **documentary**. Narrative refers to the strategies, **codes and conventions** (including **mise-en-scène** and **lighting**) employed to organize a story. Primarily, narrative cinema is one that uses these strategies as a means of reproducing the 'real' world, one which the **spectator** can either identify with or consider to be within the realms of possibility. Even **science-fiction** films have a narrative with which the spectator can identify (e.g. forces of good fighting it out with those of evil). The **motivation** of the characters moves the story along to make a 'realist' narrative. In mainstream cinema, it is traditionally the male who is the prime motivator of the narrative – that is, it is his actions that set the narrative in motion. However, female characters can also act as prime motivators of the narrative even though they mostly remain as object. For example, when the woman is at the centre of the enigma around which the film revolves, as is often the case in **film noir**, she is still, usually, the object not **subject** of the narrative. She is the object of investigation, since it is her 'enigma' or story that must be probed, investigated and finally resolved by the male protagonist (for a classic in this mode, see *Laura*, Otto Preminger, 1944).

Narrative is one aspect of film. Indeed, storytelling is not all of the film. It is the spine of the film, if you will, but it is not its aesthetics. Images, mise-en-scène, **sound**, lighting, **colour**, décor, etc., these are the technics and base elements of film, its style. And it is these that, in combination with the actors' performance and the narrative (whether in the traditional three-act mode or deconstructive art mode), make the meaning of film. With this caveat in place, let us now consider the theoretical discourses used to analyse and discuss narrative.

Because narrative exists in so many cultural forms (novel, film, theatre, mythology, painting, etc.) it appears 'as natural as life itself' (Lapsley and Westlake, 1988: 129). And it is this naturalness, or **naturalizing** process that film theorists have sought to contest, at least since **structuralism**. Narrative structures and narrative analysis of film first became an area of theoretical investigation as part of the structuralist debates on cinema. The study of the spheres of action and narrative functions in fairy tales, by Vladimir Propp (1920s), and the structure of folk narratives by Claude Lévi-Strauss (1950s) were systems applied by film theorists to film narrative (see Metz, 1972; Heath, 1981). Structuralist narratology looked for common structures underlying the diversity of narratives – as if seeking a grammar of narrative. Theorists later turned to the work of Gérard Genette (1980) because he makes clear and useful distinctions between three types of narration: first, film as a narrative function; second, the narration going on within the film; third, the narrating of the film itself. Thus, he distinguishes between narrative, **diegesis** and narrating: three terms which allow us to determine the textual effects of narrative. He uses *narrative* to refer to the undertaking to tell an event. Where film is concerned, narrative would refer then to film as a narrative statement, to its function as a narrative text – what often gets referred to nowadays as film text. His second term, *diegesis*, refers to the succession of events and their varied relations that make up the particular story. Thus, with film, diegesis refers to the story we see projected up on-screen and refers, therefore, to both the storyline and the visual mise-en-scène. His third term, *narrating*, refers to the act of enunciation. In film this third term refers, in the first instance, to the acts of utterance within the film, the 'act of producing a form of words which involves a human subject' (Hawthorn, 1992: 57). It refers, therefore, to the characters whose utterances motivate the narrative – bringing the film text into being-ness. In the second instance, enunciation refers to the **spectator**–text relations.

In other words, as the narrative is being narrated to us, we are witnessing the act of narrating. But, crucially, in the act of watching it, we too are creating a narrative – that is, we give a meaning to what we see, which is a different narrative to the one up on the screen (because it is ours). (In the simplest of terms, think, for example, how each time you revisit a film you have a slightly different take on it).

The three-act arc of **classic narrative cinema** as exemplified by **Hollywood** (especially the cinema of the 1930s to the 1950s) still remains a focus of Anglo-Saxon film theorists. Studies examine how this narrative format, for the most part, negates the female point of view and is predominantly based on male **sexuality**; thus films tend to be Oedipally over-determined (i.e. there is a dominance of Oedipal narratives). Thus, narrative in cinema tends to follow a fairly standard set of patterns which can be defined by the triads: order/disorder/order, or order/enigma/resolution – often referred to as disruption/resolution. These triads often, but not exclusively, trace the successful or unsuccessful completion by the male protagonist of the **Oedipal trajectory** (see under **psychoanalysis**) – that is, simply put, to enter successfully into the social conventions of patriarchy, find a wife and settle down. In this way, the narrative achieves closure. In order for these triads to have a cohesive structure, the film narrative is structured on the principle of another strategic triad: repetition/variation/opposition. To keep the film diegesis tight, visual or **discursive** elements get picked up again during the unravelling of the narrative (repetition) and/or altered somewhat (variation) and/or, finally, shown in a completely contradistinctual way (opposition). A good example of this strategy, which all films use to varying degrees, can be found in the various car sequences that punctuate *Thelma and Louise* (Ridley Scott, 1991). Compare the first car sequence, where the characters escape from the drudgery of their humdrum existence (one form of a life sentence), with the final one, which represents an exhilarating assertion of their right to an alternative resolution to their predicament than that of a life sentence in prison.

Currently, ecological, cognitive and evolutionary theories are relatively recent avenues being introduced into film studies and appear to bear some relevance to the narrative debates. This theoretical cluster of interlinked theoretical approaches was initially created for studying human nature as part of the natural sciences; subsequently, there have been attempts to integrate the natural science with the social sciences and humanities. As the following makes clear, some of the implications of these approaches for **film theory** in relation to narrative are useful – especially in terms of **spectator**–text relations – but there are caveats that need putting in place also.

Cognitivist theorists, as most readily embodied by David Bordwell (1986, 2008), examine narrative style. They argue that, in terms of comprehension, the spectator is guided by the generic codes and conventions of the narrative structure; in this way, the film is a text from which the spectator derives meaning. Viewed in this light, plot clearly supersedes image; images exist solely to communicate meaning, which the spectator interprets and relates to the plot. This, in turn, implies that images are not there in and of themselves and moreover that they can be rationalized. While it is true that images convey meaning, that is not all they do. They have, much like painting, a plasticity all of their own, and in that resides meaning also. If anything, the cognitivist approach can serve to open up spectator–text relations, but we should be wary of its over-privileging narrative-plot over the filmic experience; namely, aesthetics, performance, and so on – what Frampton refers to as the 'event of all film' and a 'concept of film-being' (2006: 112).

Evolutionary and ecology study in literature and film has emerged as a distinct approach to narrative (see Grodal, 2009; Boyd *et al.*, 2010). This approach examines how constructing narratives is a natural human process that assists individuals in adapting to their environment(s) and in understanding the human condition. Yet, while this paradigm adds to our understanding of the arts, it is only one more approach to the spectrum of critical theories, and, moreover, it does appear to have antecedents. Arguably, we could point out that Lévi-Strauss' structuralist paradigms, or indeed Propp's narrative functions, already suggested this shared processual practice well over half a century ago (see also **structuralism**). In this same vein of antecedents, cognitive and evolutionary theorists argue that language is based in metaphors; so, incidentally, did Barthes (see **myth**). Moreover, they claim that metaphors are themselves rooted in biology or the body; body theory, already in vogue since the 1990s and 2000s would concur.

These new theoretical avenues argue that the arts, in this instance film, help organize the human mind by giving emotionally and aesthetically modulated models of reality. By participating in the simulated life of other people (via film, in this context) one gains a greater understanding of the **motivations** of oneself and other people (incidentally, the humanist philosopher Montaigne held these views back in the seventeenth century). The idea that the arts and, in our case here, film narratives function as a means of psychological organization subsumes the precept that the arts provide adaptively relevant information, but they may also resist rationalization, a practice which these theoretical models cannot embrace. According to these theoretical models, the arts enable us to consider alternative behavioural scenarios, enhance pattern recognition, and serve as a means for creating shared social identity. While this is certainly true, none-theless, it is only part of the story. For one, not all of filmic repre-sentation can be read this way (as explained above). Moreover, this approach is Lévi-Strauss' structuralism under another name. Accord-ing to theorists in this field, this precept allows a theory of film to evolve which is naturalistic; one in which cognitive psychology, evolutionary and ecology theories, and brain science can tell us about movies – how films are made and experienced. While the implica-tions for our understanding of spectator–text relations (namely, reception theory) are clear, what it leaves to one side is the whole aesthetic experience; namely, how films are.

see also: **classical narrative cinema, diegesis, dominant cinema, Oedipal trajectory** (under **psychoanalysis**)

For further reading see Altman, 2008; Bordwell *et al.*, 1985; Bordwell, 1986; Boyd *et al.*, 2010; Branigan, 1992; Garwood, 2015; Grodal, 2009; McMahon and Quin, 1986; Martin-Jones, 2006.

NATURALIZING

A process whereby social, cultural and historical constructions are shown to be evidently natural. As such, naturalizing has an **ideological** function. Thus, the world is 'naturally' shown in film (and in television in much the same way) as White, bourgeois, patriarchal and heterosexual. These images of Western society are accepted as natural. Naturalizing, then, functions to reinforce dominant ideology. Naturalizing **discourses** operate in such a way that **class**, race and **gender** inequalities are represented as normal. Images construct woman as inferior and object of the male **gaze**. Black **sexuality** is represented as potent and, therefore, dangerous and to be contained. The working class gets fixed as naturally subordinate (intellectually and economically) to the middle classes. And so on. Very slowly, resistances to this naturalizing process are emerging through the work of a handful of filmmakers. An exemplary film which takes on board the naturalizing of inequalities and exposes the ideological function of such a process is Ken Loach's *Ladybird, Ladybird!* (1994).

see also: **ideology**

For further reading see Bordwell *et al.*, 1985; Lapsley and Westlake, 1988: chapter 5; Neupert, 1995.

OEDIPAL TRAJECTORY – *SEE UNDER* PSYCHOANALYSIS

180-DEGREE RULE

Also known as the imaginary line, this is a 'rule' that ensures consistency of the **spectator**'s perspective. Essentially, when shooting a scene, cameras should stay on one side of this imaginary line, otherwise the spectator would get disorientated. As the diagram below illustrates, the three cameras (C1, C2, C3) are on one side of the line and pointing at the object on the line (e.g. character A or B). As the film unravels on-screen, the spectator takes up any one of those three camera positions depending on which shot-position (camera 1, 2 or 3) has been chosen at any given time and **edited** into the final **cut**. There is a perfect logic *to* and *in* this perspectival space and **gaze** for the spectator.

But what if, in a sequence, all of a sudden the camera (say, C1) was on the other side of the line without obeying any continuity rule such as the 30-degree rule, or a narrative clue which provided a logic to the switch in places? The spectator's perspective would be reversed: s/he would be seeing things the wrong way round. This would be most evident in a **shot/reverse-angle-shot** sequence in which two people are having a conversation and in which the camera has crossed the line. Their positions would be reversed: character A would be in character B's position. The 180-degree rule would be broken, causing disorientation. (See **shot/reverse-angle-shot** for the correct procedure to follow.)

see also: **30-degree rule**

PORNOGRAPHY

There is general agreement on the view that pornography in film can be described as any set of images that exist solely for the purpose of sexual arousal and feature nudity and explicit sexual acts. Originally the word, coming from Greek antiquity, meant the writing of harlots – which suggests that women as much as men did the writings or made the images to stimulate sexual excitement. Now, of course, it is seen very much as the domain of the male author or filmmaker intent on exploiting our need for arousal.

In terms of pornographic film, while it is known to have been around since at least the 1920s (which suggests it was there beforehand), it is only with the lifting of **censorship** in the West (late 1960s to mid-1970s) that it has become more 'out there'. The lifting of censorship in the USA in the late 1960s meant that, very quickly, porn movies could now come out (obtain general release) – albeit with an X-rating. Although *Deep Throat* (Damanio, 1972), starring Linda Lovelace, is *the* notorious porn film, the first important porn film in USA film history is *Behind the Green Door* (Mitchell Bros, 1971). Apart from the USA, where the porn industry was big business during the 1970s, France is worth a mention because of the extraordinary situation the lifting of censorship created for the film industry in the mid- to late 1970s. For a period of four years (1975–79), the X-certificate French pornographic movie constituted nearly half of the nation's total film production – which meant that, in terms of levies and taxes to which this cinema was subjected, the porn movie was supporting the French film industry to the tune of 14 per cent of its total budget. No mean feat as far as money-shots go!

By the late 1970s, however, the expansion of video meant that the porn industry once more went underground (so to speak). Video-porn films cut away from the expense of film productions as well as the draconian taxes and levies imposed by various governments on this particular category of film. It is in this light of porn's disappearance as a film form proper that we can understand P. T. Anderson's *Boogie Nights* (1997) and its nostalgic evocation of the permissive 1970s, including its porn industry. As Howard Hampton (2001: 40) points out, however, Anderson's film – with its film-within-a-film structure – reflects a nostalgia for a cinema that never got made: high porn. The closest anything got to high porn was porn chic with, in the European context, Bernardo Bertolucci's *Last Tango in Paris* (1972, an Italian-French co-production), and, within the US context, Paul Schrader's *Hardcore* (1978). But, because video-porn is a multi-billion industry, **Hollywood** has had to find strategies to compete, and this it has done through its stretching of the R-certificate (which only means restricted viewing) to cover films that come very close to porn in their sexual graphicness – but many of which are distributed as part of Hollywood's A-list. By the mid-1980s, in response to the challenge represented by the video-porn industry, Hollywood had created its own erotic thriller, a hybrid genre of **film noir** and porn – its first most famous prototype being *Fatal Attraction* (Lyne, 1987). It begs the question: did Veronica Rocket's 1983 *Smoker* – a porn film that answered back with ball-breaking sexual terrorism – send Hollywood down this path of film production where women seemingly have **agency** and fight back? Films in this category include *Final Analysis* (Joanou, 1992), *Basic Instinct, Body of Evidence* (respectively, Verhoeven and Edel, both 1993). Although these erotic-thriller-females may have more power than their passive sisters in the porn world, this is hardly an argument for a progressive view of women. Giving women the power to fight back, and even kill, is still a male **fantasy** and a projection of their flirtation with the death drive (and thereby also a way of controlling it – since the man mostly wins in the end). It is hard to see in these narratives a 'taking hold of the patriarchal fantasy apparatus', as Douglas Keesey argues (2001: 47). Giving agency does not mean having agency.

Since the late 1990s, however, hard-core sex scenes have made it into the mainstream in a different way – generally with critical value – and once again it is to the French context that we must turn. Arguably, Catherine Breillat's work, which has consistently dealt with female **sexuality** (dating back from the mid-1970s incidentally), is one that has pioneered this development. Her *Romance* (1999), a young woman's journey into and investigation of her sexual self, figures hard-core porn star Rocco Siffredi and includes real intercourse. Her *Anatomy of Hell* (2004), again starring Siffredi, is an artful take on sado-masochistic liaisons where the woman controls the **narrative** that will eventually bring the male protagonist to leave his brutally macho posturing and find his emotional self. These films challenge the effects of porn. In a sense Breillat's work, because it shows us what ultimately is the 'unwatchable' (remember that censors outside France have consistently cut the rape scene from her film *A ma soeur*, 2001), obliges us to recognize that, conversely, adult porn is about showing the watchable. It is in this regard – as Breillat's critique demonstrates – that porn becomes, bizarrely, normalized with the effect that it is written on every woman's body ('porno'-'graphy'). Breillat's work then does take hold of the patriarchal fantasy **apparatus** and turn it around. And this is perhaps why she defended the right to mainstream screening of Virginie Despentes and Coralie Trinh Thi's controversial revenge road movie *Baise-moi* (2000). It is nasty in its hard core as it is nasty in its revenge killings – but it is correct in that it turns around the mirror to men to face themselves in all their pornocratic imaginings around women (that women are flesh to be penetrated and objects to be discarded at will).

Sadly, this kind of critical take on pornography is not one that looks like diminishing its exploitative practice. Nowadays porn is everywhere. We can obtain it on video and bring it home to watch. We can download it from the web. We can even have interactive porn on the internet if we so wish – all within the safe walls of our own domestic sphere. Is mediated sex, bliss? Steve McQueen's film *Shame* (2010) would suggest not.

Debates over pornography in terms of its definition and its supposed effects diverge into two radically opposed critical camps. A first, perhaps liberal view holds that pornography gives greater visibility to more and varied sexualities and helps towards a greater tolerance and understanding. As Brian McNair says (1996: 49), it permits 'the affirmation or strengthening of minority or subordinated sexual identities'. Conversely, a conservative view, and indeed one held by many feminists (albeit for different reasons), asserts that pornography is a 'fundamentally amoral/immoral category of representation, deeply implicated in negative social phenomena' (ibid.).

Whereas the 'anti-pornography' camp (led by Andrea Dworkin) dismisses all pornography as 'bad', the 'pro-pornography' camp takes care to establish differences between various forms of pornography (primarily: hard, soft, child) and, in that distinction, to make clear that while some versions are unacceptable (particularly child pornography), other forms can be liberating. Pornography aimed at women, lesbians and homosexuals can serve to assert their respective sexualities as meaningful, as **subjectivized** not objectified. Female or marginalized sexualities can also appropriate the dominant form of heterosexual pornography and adapt it to their own readings (i.e. read it against the grain). As McNair says (ibid.: 129), 'in the private worlds of fantasy and sexual relationships ... women have increasingly used pornography – subversively decoding male-orientated material on the one hand, consuming material produced by women for women on the other'.

Two views dominate in the 'anti-pornography' camp. First, certain feminist groups who see pornography as degrading to the female and as reinforcing patriarchal **ideology** (for detailed discussion see Dworkin, 1991; Griffin, 1988; Itzin, 1992). Pornographic films, the claim goes, lead to violence against women. The second category, the conservative (moral majority view), condemns pornography for entirely different reasons. Not as a protest against the degradation of women, but as a protest against what this group perceives as an attack on family values and marital sex (McNair, 1996: 49).

For further reading see authors cited in the text; *see also*: Baird and Rosen-baum, 1991; Church-Gibson, 2004; Dines *et al.* 1998; Easton, 1994; Ho, 2002; Lehman, 2006; McNair, 2002; Rodgerson and Wilson, 1991; Segal and McIntosh, 1992; Stevenson, 2000; L. Williams, 2004; L.R. Williams, 2005.

POSTCOLONIAL THEORY

The following outline sets out the basic concepts of postcolonial theory. References for further reading are supplied at the end of this entry but a useful starter reader is Padmini Mongia's *Contemporary Post-colonial Theory: A Reader* (1996) and Ashcroft *et al.*'s *The Post-Colonial Studies Reader* (1995) and *Key Concepts in Post-Colonial Studies* (1998). There are two ways of spelling 'post-colonial', one with the hyphen and one without, and considerable debate surrounds how it should be spelt. One way of distinguishing the usage is to say that the spelling *post-colonial* refers to the historical concept of the post-colonial state (it refers then to the period after official decolonization). The spelling *postcolonial* refers to varying practices that in some way are influenced by or relate to the postcolonial moment. Thus, postcolonial refers to theory, literature, cultural practices in general, to ways of reading these different cultural practices. It refers, too, to the postcolonial **subject**. But clearly one type of post-coloniality does not exist without the other; thus, some authors/critics use both spellings simultaneously. Bearing this in mind, the spelling *postcolonial* is opted for here except where it is clear that the reference is to the historical moment of post-colonialism. Where both concepts are implicitly co-present, both terms will be used.

Edward Saïd's book *Orientalism* (1978) is one of the key texts in postcolonial theory. In fact, it launched many of the debates in the West that have subsequently come to dominate postcolonial theory. The postcolonial debate is not limited to the West, however. Indigenous African and Asian intellectuals have been part of this (after all) global debate. And it is important to remember that the first major writer on the question of colonialism and post-colonialism was Frantz Fanon, whose texts of the 1950s and early 1960s form the foundation of this theory. Fanon was a psychiatrist working in Algeria during the years of the struggle for independence (1950s). His writings on colonialism and racism, *Black Skin, White Masks* (1967) and *The Wretched of the Earth* (1968), studied the effects of colonialism on the psyche of the colonized people. In *Black Skin, White Masks*, Fanon argues (through his famous neo-Freudian question 'What does the Black man want?')

that the colonized seeks only to occupy the place of the colonizer. Thus, once the country has obtained independence, the colonized elite **class** (the intellectual class) will only mimic what the White colonizer has already done. Later, in *The Wretched of the Earth*, he explores more fully what this means and what the real function of the colonized elites must be once independence is achieved. He goes into great detail about the role of the native poet (the educated intellectual) who must give over his being to both reviving the past – the bleached-out history of the colonized, the memories of traditions whose importance and signification colonialism has attempted to belittle, demean and wipe out – and to helping his people towards a national consciousness. In this process of freeing the wretched of the earth, the native poet helps them build the nation anew. In other words, the poet must draw from the past (pre-colonial times) to help make the future, a new national culture. He must help in the forging of a third way that is neither stuck in old traditions that cannot now be reinstituted, nor in the colonialist/post-colonialist moment since that would merely represent a new form of oppression and enslavement.

Fanon's writing held enormous sway in the USA during the forming of its own Black consciousness (1960s and 1970s). And by the 1980s issues of race, identity, colonialism and nationhood, and the problem of representation had been brought very much to the foreground of theoretical thinking in the West thanks to the works of Saïd, Stuart Hall, Gayatri Spivak and Homi Bhabha. During the 1980s, the question of post-colonialism/postcolonialism was also being debated in Africa – particularly in the works of Kwame Appiah and V. Y. Mudimbe. Debates here focus on the transition of African societies through colonialism. Questions of the following order arise. Where is the space of post-coloniality – the 'imagined' cleared after-space that 'post' implies – in African nations and cultures to be found? What does postcoloniality/post-coloniality mean to the nations the West so easily describes as post-colonial? Who are the practitioners of this postcoloniality/post-coloniality (politicians? ordinary Africans in their respective nations?) and what does it mean to be a postcolonial/post-colonial subject? In fact, what is being raised here is the whole problematic of the term postcolonial/post-colonial and the concept of postcolonial theory. Whose term is it? As Mongia asserts (1996: 6), 'postcolonial theory's provenance is greatest … in First World academies'. Who voices it? Not just 'authentic' voices from the developing world now working in Western academic institutions, although they are, arguably the major agencies of this **discourse**. Finally, what are the dangers inherent in the use of this word and the application of this theory? A new kind of totalizing theory that places all 'post-colonial' nations and their cultures on a par? Clearly, there is no stable, fixed definition even if the West were to try to establish one – and certainly not from within the nations themselves. The identities of the nations (and thus the postcolonial subject) are diverse and not to be seen as a homogeneous whole.

Saïd's analysis in *Orientalism* begins to raise some of the above questions. He shows how the Orient was and still is simultaneously a construction (as an imaginary exotic other) of the West and constructed (discursively fixed as a homogeneous real geographical space) by the West. In both instances, the West is able to exert power over the Orient. Orientalism is a Eurocentric/Occidental view that dominates the Orient through its exercise of knowledge over and about the Orient. It interprets the Orient through its Western applied sciences of anthropology and philology/linguistics and in so doing it achieves 'knowledge' of the other which endows it with authority over the other. That knowledge is the source of the West's power over the Orient. And of course it is this relationship of power that has been evidenced, in the past, by Occidental imperialism/colonialism.

Although colonialism of a geographical kind may be over for the West, nonetheless this relationship of power is still one that is practised in cultural (and indeed we could add **ideological**) terms. Saïd makes the point that the study of the Orient (through anthropology linguistics, etc.) permits a fixing – in homogenizing 'scientist' discourses – of the already constructed other. This erasure of identity (through homogenization) again makes the practice of imperialism a very 'untroubled' one for the West. This practice of Orientalism is not limited to the 'Orient' but occurs in all territories colonized by the West (Africa, New Zealand, Australia). And this practice still prevails today in Western studies of the former colonies. It is in this context of 'knowledge of the other imposed from outside' that we can measure the enormous significance of the theory of negritude put forward, in the 1930s and 1950s, by the native poets Léopold Sédar Senghor (from Senegal) and Aimé Césaire (from the former French West Indies) in which they argued for an African subjecthood and aesthetic in their own right. This was the first important movement along with that of the Harlem Renaissance – the African-American diasporic movement (of the 1920s in the USA) – to assert African claims to cultural distinctiveness. Later, in the 1950s, Latin America, particularly in its literature of magic realism (which later became transposed into its cinema), would lay equal claim to its right to be understood from within.

Postcolonial theory seeks, in a dialogic process (coming from many points of view), to expose this 'natural' linking of Western knowledge with oppression (i.e. imperialism/colonialism) and to re-think the very way in which knowledge has been constructed. Western **modernist** thinking, emanating from the Enlightenment of the eighteenth century, has created closely aligned terms which are perceived as interrelated on a one-to-one basis. These terms are democracy, nationalism, citizen-subject. However, this perception of the relationship between the citizen-subject and the nation-state is far too narrow and it suggests a homogeneity that certainly does not prevail today. There is not a unified (single) citizen-subject any more than there is a unified (single) nation-state and there is not a one-to-one relationship between the two concepts. For a start such a conceptualization of the relation excludes issues of race, ethnicity, **gender** and **sexuality** – in other words, it excludes all 'othernesses' or multicultures. Postcolonial theory seeks, then, to question and critique the historicism of the West which has posited Europe as its theoretical subject. This European historicism is what is known as Eurocentrism (see Shohat and Stam, 1994). It is a position that 'naturally' assumes that 'history is the West' and that all the rest is 'subaltern' (Spivak, 1985). *Subaltern* is a term which Gramsci coined to mean the silenced history of those subjected to the ruling classes. It was adopted by South Asian Studies to refer to the 'lost' history of the subaltern cultures of the Asian peoples. In other words, colonial study and, indeed, some forms of post-colonial study, in their focusing only on the elite cultures of the colonized, have neglected – or reduced to silence – other subaltern voices (peasants, workers, women, and so on).

Postcolonial theory is not a single theory any more than the colonization before it was one homogeneous event with single char-acteristics. Colonialism is not one and the same and does not produce equal effects. And that is part of what postcolonial theory tries to unravel. It does not seek to impose a grand narrative (obviously that would be to fall into the same trap, or snake-pit, as the histor-icized, Eurocentric approach before it). Thus, care must be taken not to impose the Eurocentric concept of 'history-as-chronological "progress"' onto the three key concepts that postcolonial theory investigates: pre-colonialism, colonialism and postcolonialism. These are syncretic terms. They always already co-exist. When we speak of the subaltern's history, we cannot speak of a history that is linear. This is possibly why the concept of 'transvergence' is becoming an increasingly attractive term within postcolonial theory. The term is Novak's (2002) and originates in architecture. As a concept it is associated with instability or fracture, and so is a means of challenging the nature of knowledge based in continuity and consistency (ranging from politics of consensus to denial of difference and exclusion of otherness). Thus, to quote Higbee (2007: 85), 'transvergence, in a very postmodern way, aims to expose and foreground (celebrate even) such differences'. Because transvergence allows for 'a myriad of possibilities', it challenges fixed notions of nation; insider/outsider; centre/margin, etc. (ibid.: 86). It dissolves the concept of binaries (so dear to **hegemony**), allowing for 'shifting and multiple positionings' (ibid.: 86). And, because it is always already in a state of flux and becoming, it challenges fixity, celebrates discontinuity, fragmentation, and in so doing 'foregrounds the experiences of the alienated marginalized other' (ibid.: 87). Marginality is no longer a space of otherness; nor is it just a point of resistance; it is a voiced, agenced, unpredetermined space.

Locating the postcolonial subject

The most difficult area to date (in terms of agreement between theoreticians) is how to locate the postcolonial subject. One of the main proposals forthcoming is that the postcolonial subject is hybrid, that s/he occupies a space between – or in between – two cultures. This term avoids being limited to the use of binary terms of opposition self/other or centre/marginal and allows for a subject position that is not defined in relation to a hierarchical notion of subjectivity (such as the speaking subject and the silent/silenced native). This in-between space is one of contradictions and ambivalences – in the first instance because the two cultures do not match, they are distinct. This in turn makes clear that there is no unified culture per se. And that the location occupied by the postcolonial subject is also by its very nature hybrid. This in-between space is, then, a third space (it is neither the first nor the second of the two interdependent cultures whose hybridization makes up the postcolonial subject). Thus, the postcolonial subject occupies a third space from which his/her identity is enunciated. However, and this is the crucial point, by occupying this third space, the postcolonial subject is occupying a place of potential resistance. And this is why. By the very nature of his or her location, the postcolonial subject *embodies* the contradictions and ambivalences of the two cultures; thus, s/he makes possible the exposure of those very same contradictions and ambivalences inherent in and between each culture. By so doing, the postcolonial subject 'invalidates' the rhetoric of imperialism and colonialism. Namely, at the same time as s/he shows how Western historicism and discursive fixity function, the postcolonial subject exposes the fact that there is no discursive fixity, and that Western knowledge cannot fix the 'other' and thereby exercise power and authority over it.

The hybrid nature of postcolonial culture is, then, the conceptual tool that can prise open rational **modernist** discourses that make secure an a priori knowledge of the world of the 'other'. Hybrid identity is not fixed but is 'an unstable constellation of discourses' (Shohat and Stam, 1994: 42). Thus syncretism and transculturalism are manifestations of hybrid culture. Syncretism refers to the bringing together of many diverse cultural traditions into one performative text (film, theatre, whatever) (see **World Cinemas** where this concept is explained in more detail). Transculturalism or transculturation refers to a cross-fertilization effect between two cultures whereby cultural traditions 'migrate' from one culture into another culture. The contact between the two cultures is mediated by the hybrid culture and refashioned to produce a third text (an easy illustration of this process is the re-appropriation of oil drums to make steel-band drums, the band in turn produces a performance – the music of that performance in its turn will most likely be syncretic, drawing on many musical traditions).

The notion of hybridity is not without its own set of problems. And it has been criticized for emanating from **post-structuralist** discourses of fragmented subjectivities. The problem becomes that the hybrid subject (as described by Bhabha and others) is such a scattered and fragmented entity that it runs the risk of lacking specificity, of being uprooted in history or space (what is the imagined third space after all?). Furthermore, critics have argued that the cultural hybridity occupied by this subject is specific to the migrant intellectual living in the West from where he (*sic*) 'comes to signify a universal condition of hybridity' that is superior in understanding to both cultures 'he' represents (Ahmad, 1996: 286). The major criticism levelled at such migrant intellectuals is that they become 'Truth-Subjects' (ibid.: 286). Furthermore, or perhaps worse still, in that this play with identities de-centres the subject (through its a-specificity and a-history), it also detaches it from any attachment to nation, class or gender (ibid.: 287). This does not mean, however, that we should lose sight of the term *hybridity*; for reasons explained above, it has great subversive value. What this criticism makes clear, though, is that as a concept it is not 'enough'. It, too, excludes and therein also lies its usefulness. Through its very exclusion it makes visible what also needs to be addressed. Such is the case for the position of women in these debates as well as questions of class and caste. Feminism has made clear that there is not a single category of colonized (see Spivak, 1985; Suleri, 1992). Indeed, women are subjected to a double colonization or oppression, nor does that oppression evaporate post-colonially (as indeed some Third World women and men filmmakers have made evident – see, for example, the Palestinian Michel Kleifi's *Marriage in Galilee*, 1987, and the Tunisian Moufida Tlatli's *The Silences of the Palace*, 1994).

The issue of the speaking subject and his/her location remains an ongoing debate in critical postcolonial theory. However, a part answer to the question of **agency** – of who is the speaking postcolonial subject – has been to invoke Gramsci's notion of the subaltern (see above). Again it is not an unproblematic term – it runs the risk of essentialism and of creating a binary between elite/subaltern within the concept of the other (i.e. the 'other' is made up of 'elite/subaltern' subjects). This in turn risks continuing the modernist train of binarism around subjectivity (self/other). Subaltern is a useful term though. It can and does refer to the voices – especially oral voices and cultural traditions – of those who are seemingly even more disempowered than the elite post-colonial subjects (Guha, 1982). It reminds us that there are other multiple voices to be thought about, listened to. It also reminds us that their discourses of representation are not necessarily grounded in colonial or post-colonial discourses – even though, if they are to be heard as resistant voices, the subalterns' speaking position can only be defined by its difference from the elite. Finally, in this context, transvergent theory is also helpful because it can negotiate a subject positioning (or cultural identity) not based in binaried differences, but in process of becoming, unfixed and always under negotiation.

Postcolonial theory of film

Postcolonial theory when applied to cinema studies helps us to read (through a non-Eurocentric eye, hopefully) films emanating from postcolonial/post-colonial countries as well as films from the diaspora. These films, which explore questions of representation, identity and location politics (i.e. who is the speaking subject and where is s/he speaking from?), also question the centre/margin binaries imposed by Western thought. Models of colonialist discourse are exposed, as are the practices of dependency theory (the way in which global capitalism functions to maintain the impoverishment of the economically colonized developing world). The legacy of the exploitation of the colonized body is explained through a demonstration of how the diasporic movements, generated by slavery, are later matched by the ecological imperialism of the formerly colonizing nations. That is, for example, how Europe's need for immigrant labour replaced the earlier 'transportation' of slave labour to various colonies (see Gilroy, 1993). The colonized raced body was a commodity through which colonialism operated its power, and yet, without that body, colonialism could not have remained propped up – therein lies the paradox of colonialism (its major contradiction). But, this is not the only cinema that postcolonial theory examines. It is used also to analyse films made by the West – both during the colonialist era and in the postcolonial moment – which either directly or indirectly display their Eurocentrism.

see also: **Black cinema – USA, Black cinema – UK, cinema nôvo, Third Cinema, World Cinemas**

For further reading see texts referred to in entry and see also: Ahmad, 1996; Appiah, 1992; Bernstein and Studlar, 1997; Bhabha, 1994; Chambers and Curti, 1996; Childs and Williams, 1997; Fanon, 1967, 1968; Gilroy, 1993; Guha, 1982; Hall, 1996; Heffelfinger, 2011; Higbee, 2007; Low, 1996; McClintock, 1995; Malik, 1996; Martin, 2007, 2011; Mudimbe, 1988, 1992, 1994; Naficy and Gabriel, 1993; Saïd, 1978; Shohat and Stam, 1994; Shohat, 1996; 2003; Spivak, 1985, 1987.

POSTMODERNISM

This term entered into critical **discourse** in the late 1960s. As a concept it was seen as exemplifying a counter-position to **modernism**, especially modernism in its latest manifestation as total theory: **structuralism**. And for this reason it is a term often associated with **post-structuralism**, to which, arguably, it is connected. Although the two concepts do indeed co-exist, some critics feel that postmodernism (also known as 'the postmodern') refers more to an age – particularly the 1980s and 1990s, although it is still ongoing – rather than to a theoretical movement to which, of course, post-structuralism belongs. There appears to be no easy definition of postmodernism. Indeed, there are many different ways in which it is perceived. These are never totally contradictory readings but, depending on the positioning of a particular thinker, writer or theorist, it can be given a different interpretation. This of course points to its pluralism as a concept and is something to be welcomed after the strictures of modernism and structuralism. It is also a reason why postmodernism gets aligned with post-structuralism, which is similarly pluralistic in its approach. Post-structuralism is more readily concerned with opening up the problematics in modernism and as such constitutes a critical theory of modernism. Postmodernism is perceived more as an historical condition within which are contained social, political and cultural agendas and resonances. These are interpreted either as reflective of a mentality of 'anything goes', therefore nothing works, or of a questioning of the modernist ideals of progress, reason and science. In the first instance, theorists claim that the postmodern condition signals the death of **ideology**. In the second, it heralds a new scepticism about the modernist belief in the supremacy of the Western world, the legitimacy of science as the source of knowledge, and technology as the marker of human progress – and, in the world of aesthetics, the advocacy of high art over popular culture.

Ultimately, then, postmodernism is a vague term. However, in its eclecticism lies its power to be non- or anti-essentialist; it neither has nor provides a fixed meaning; in its pluralism lies its ability to be read either positively or negatively.

A first set of readings – mainstream postmodern culture and oppositional postmodern culture

Some critics see the postmodern as an effect that is a reaction against the established forms and canons of modernism. In this regard, it takes issue with modernism's positive belief in progress and a unified underlying reality. Postmodernism reacts against modernism's optimistic belief in the benefits of science and technology to human kind. But, as the entry on modernism makes clear, this optimism is only part of the picture: certain modernists did not share this optimism, but mistrusted science and technology. Viewed in this light, then, postmodernism continues the pessimistic vein that already prevailed in modernism. According to Fredric Jameson (1983), postmodernism, as an effect, also represents the erosion of the distinction between high art and popular culture. The postmodern does not really refer to style but to a periodizing concept 'whose function is to correlate the emergence of new formal features in culture with the emergence of a new type of social life and a new economic order' (Jameson, 1983: 113). In other words, it is a conjunctural term at the interface between artefact and the new moment of capitalism. This new moment of capitalism is varyingly called post-industrial or post-colonial, society modernization, consumer society, media society, neo-liberal even. More recently it has come to mean globalization. The artefact is what is produced by and within that moment in capitalism. What is significant is that the term *postmodern* is consistent with the way in which Western contemporary society defines itself – that is, in relation to the past (post-colonial), but also in relation to social practice (modernization, consumer) and technology (media). In its consistency with Western definitions, these critics argue, the postmodern looks back, is retrospective, is not defined as other, but as *post*modern, as coming after. In its lack of history (defined only in relation to the past), it rejects history, and because it has none of its own – only that of others – the postmodern stands eternally fixed in a series of presents. This reading places postmodernist culture as a-historical.

According to this view, the postmodern era has little of the optimism of post-structuralism. It is more akin to a cult than to a movement. Although Anglo-Saxon theorists refer to this concept as post-modernism or postmodernity, it is instructive to note that the country whence the term emanated, France, deliberately omits the 'ism': *le postmoderne*. This very omission warns us that this is a non-collective phenomenon and that, by implication, it focuses on the cult of the individual (a position not all critics agree with; see below). Curiously, this hedonism recalls the aesthetic culture of the symbolists at the end of the nineteenth century – particularly in France. The *fin-de-siècle* mood of that time – a direct reaction to the political, intellectual and moral crises taking place – manifested itself in a neo-romantic nihilism wherein the individual artist became a cult figure. The death of ideology at that time left the artist in the presence of a spiritual void. How to fill the abyss of nothingness? The response was aestheticism, art for art's sake, as an end in and of itself which led to a self-sufficient formalism. In other words, only form, not content, could fill the void.

It is this pessimistic vein which finds its heritage, first, in the tragic modernist and later in the a-historical postmodernist cultures. Both are traumatized by a technology that has created ideological structures of suppression and domination never seen before. Modern technology allowed images of this technology at work to be recorded (by the camera) and be brought to our attention. If there was not much footage of World War One shown publicly, archival film shows enough of the horrors of trench warfare. World War Two images of the apocalyptic events of the Holocaust and the dropping of the atomic bomb have left modernist and postmodernist alike with seemingly unanswerable questions. How to invent, comes the cry, when invention can lead to such wholesale destruction of humanity? In answer to this daunting set of questions, modernism in its pessimistic mode presents a world as fragmented and decayed and one in which communication is a virtual impossibility. In its response to these same questions, according to theorists providing the a-historic reading of postmodernity, post-modern culture, which can see itself only in relation to the past, bifurcates. The majority tendency is unoppositional, a unidirectional reflection towards the past, providing a conservative cultural production – that is, mainstream culture. The minority is **avant-garde** and oppositional. (See Dyer (2007) for more on this.)

In relation to the contemporary cultural aesthetic, then, the post-modern adopts two modes. In its mainstream mode, it manifests itself through mannerism and stylization, through *pastiche* – imitation of what is past. In its oppositional mode – that is, in its despair at the nothingness of the abyss – it turns to *parody*, an ironization of style, form and content (as in Samuel Beckett's plays and novels). Whether mainstream or oppositional, the postmodern aesthetic relies on four tightly interrelated sets of concepts: simulation, which is either parody or pastiche; pre-fabrication; **intertextuality** and bricolage. What separates the two tendencies is that the oppositional postmodern aesthetic experiments with these concepts and innovates, through subverting their **codes**; whereas, the mainstream postmodern aesthetic merely replicates them. Hence the need for two distinguishing terms – parody and pastiche – for the first concept, simulation. Parody is the domain of oppositional art. Pastiche pertains to the symptomatic, in that it imitates previous **genres** and styles, but, unlike parody, its imitation is not ironic and is therefore not subversive. In its uninventiveness, pastiche is but a shadow of its former thing. Postmodern art culls from already existing images and objects and either repeats or reinvents them as the same. To make the distinction clear, we could turn to the world of fashion and say that punk is parody, chic-designer-punk is pastiche.

The three remaining concepts, then, are either played out in a parodic or pastiche modality. As you will see, there is considerable overlap between the concepts. In postmodern cinema, images or parts of sequences which were fabricated in earlier films are reselected (the latest Star Wars film is a case in point: *Star Wars: The Force Awakens*, Abrams, 2015). In much the same way that pre-fabricated houses are made up of complete units of pre-existing meaning; so the visual arts see the past as a supermarket source that the artist raids for whatever s/he wants. A film could be completely constructed out of pre-fabricated images (and even sounds). This is particularly true for **mainstream** postmodern cinema. For example, a filmmaker wanting to insert a song-and-dance routine could select Gene Kelly's dance of the title song in *Singin' in the Rain* (1952), for a **flashback** she or he could clip in the beginning of *Sunset Boulevard* (Billy Wilder, 1950); and so on. Robert Altman's *The Player* (1992) makes reference to this pastiche culture of pre-fabrication (two studio scriptwriters discuss a possible script which they describe as *Out of Africa* meets *Pretty Woman*).

In this context of pre-fabrication, note how clever Quentin Tarantino's films are. While they appear to be a **mise-en-abîme** of filmic quotes, the orchestration of the quotes is so brilliantly achieved that what appears pastiche is in fact parody. He selects the quotes and then brutally overturns them. Take, for example, *Reservoir Dogs* (1991). The ten-minute torture scene in the empty warehouse, which is horrendous in its horror, is also excessively comic because the torturer, the psycho-pathic Mr Blonde, dances to a 1970s song, 'Stuck in the Middle with You' – a song that relates to a paranoid, if not drugged perception of 'reality'. Meantime, as he slices up his victim, he asks, in time with the song, 'was that as good for you as it was for me?' According to Tarantino, the filmic quotes are Abbott and Costello monster movies which combine the comic with the horror (*Sight and Sound*, vol. 2, no. 8, 1992). They also, in their seemingly gratuitous violence, recall many a Scorsese scene of violence (for example, *Taxi Driver*, 1970). This scene, as with other quotes in the film, also pulls from the **B-movies**. Again, they are pushed to their limits. This particular torture scene derides the false bravura of cops and gangsters who 'shoot it out' – here ears are cut off, faces are slashed (before even a gun is shot!), and people torched – all to the sound of music and dancing. Not even *The St. Valentine's Day Massacre* (Roger Corman, 1967) nor *The Godfather* (Francis Ford Coppola, 1972) could match these extremes of violence-in-excess. It is precisely in scenes such as this one that the film achieves the parodic. Through this use of violence, Tarantino exposes the **spectator**–film relationship as one of sado-masochism. We might bleed with Mr Orange as he lies in the warehouse dying, but we also find ourselves dancing with Mr Blonde. Compounding the parodic is Tarantino's expressed intention of making us brutally aware of the manipulative hand of the **director** – 'he can shoot scenes like this' – and our collusion with him 'we choose to watch'. In this respect, Tarantino's work must be seen as oppositional. This makes the point that opposi-tional culture, postmodern or otherwise, can reach mass **audiences**. Tarantino is one of today's successful postmodern filmmakers who can dissolve the divide between high art and low art without reducing his film to pulp, that is, to a mere series of good images.

Intertextuality, which in many respects can be seen as closely aligned with mise-en-abîme and as overlapping with pre-fabrication, is a term that refers to the relation between two or more texts. All texts are necessarily intertextual; that is, they refer to other texts. This relation has an effect on the way in which the presently constructed text is read. All films are, to some degree, always already intertextual. Within mainstream pastiche cinema, the most obvious intertextual film is the remake. Within the parodic mode and of the more contemporary and popular filmmakers, Tarantino's films are exemplary in the way that they refer to other texts. *Pulp Fiction* (1994), for example, refers in many of its décors to the paintings of Edward Hopper – so in part the intertext is composed of painterly texts. Tarantino readily acknowledges his references to the film texts of Jean-Luc Godard. And certainly *Bande à part* (1964) with its own references to the American **musical** – which Godard reinscribes in a parodic mode – is a text to which *Pulp Fiction* refers. Tarantino talks about his film being based on three storylines that are the oldest chestnuts in the world, filmic **narratives** based on pulp fiction: a member of the gang taking out the mobster's wife whom he must not touch; the boxer who is supposed to throw the fight; gangsters on a 'mission' to kill (*Sight and Sound*, vol. 4, vo. 5, 1994, 10). Characters within film can also be intertextual of course. Again to cite Tarantino's film: Butch, the boxer, is an intertext of the character of Mike Hammer in *Kiss Me Deadly* (Robert Aldrich, 1955) and the look of the actor Aldo Ray in *Nightfall* (Jacques Tourneur, 1956).

Finally, among these concepts, comes bricolage. This is an assembling of different styles, textures, **genres** or **discourses**. In oppositional postmodern art, this takes the form of replicating within one discourse the innovations of another. For example, the **deconstruction** of time and space that occurs in the *nouveau roman*/new novel is replicated in the films of Marguerite Duras, Alain Resnais and Alain Robbe-Grillet through a use of **montage** that disorientates. The most common replication in cinema of other textural mediums is the plasticity of video and painting which can be found in many of the 1980s filmmakers' work – both mainstream and oppositional.

In mainstream postmodern cinema, genres are mimicked and not renewed. In terms of subjects, themes and style, the spectator of today is reviewing either images of modernist cinema or mediatic images of its own age. With a few exceptions there are no social or political films made in this context of mainstream postmodern (exceptions being perhaps Sofia Coppola's *Lost in Translation*, 2003, and *Marie-Antoinette*, 2006; or again Steve McQueen's *Hunger*, 2008, and *Shame*, 2011; if indeed they are mainstream). This dearth of subjects coincides with a cinematographic mannerism which manifests itself in at least three ways. First, by a prurient (necrophiliac?) fixation with genres and images of a bygone cinema – nostalgia at its worst. Second, by a servile simulation of television visual discourses. And, finally, by manipulating and elevating virtual reality and computer graphics (**CGI**) to the status of real. It is in this sense that mainstream postmodern filmmakers of today display a disdain for culture with a capital 'C'. All culture, 'high' and 'low', is assimilable or quotable within their texts, so that the binary divide is erased. The dissolution of the divide would be a good thing, but the result still has to have meaning. Instead, in their formalism and mannerism they aim purely and simply for the well-made image – 120 minutes of good publicity clips. They invent nothing. John Orr (1993: 12) points out that this cinema of pastiche, in its emptiness, lends itself to a double reading or, rather, contradictory readings. This cinema will appeal to right and left, Black and White. *Forrest Gump* (Robert Zemeckis, 1994) is an excellent example, since both the left and the right have found it consonant with their own ideologies. As Orr says (1993: 12), this cinema, while so patently empty, is also potentially dangerous – schizoid, as Orr puts it.

A second set of readings – negative versus positive readings of the postmodern

(Here I am drawing on the useful and illuminating analyses to be found in Bruno, 1987; Hawthorn, 1992; Huyssen, 1990; Kuhn, 1990; Nicholson, 1990.) In terms of current writing about postmodernism, there are at least as many positions as there are areas of concern. What follows is a summary of those positions as they affect readings of post-modern cinema. There is of course some overlapping or cross-fertilization but it is worth spelling them out if only to reiterate the pluralism of postmodernism. Postmodern discourses have been elaborated with refer-ence to architecture, human sciences and literature, the visual arts, technology, cultural theory, social, economic and political practices, feminism and **gender**. As has already been mentioned, these dis-courses generate either positive or negative readings of the post-modern.

Negative readings tend to focus on what is perceived to be the essential schizophrenia of postmodernism: a schizophrenia which can, for example, be detected in contemporary architecture's random histor-ical citations which have been pasted or pastiched onto so many postmodern façades (Huyssen, 1990: 237). Roman colonnades are mixed with Georgian windows, and so on. Jameson believes that this schizophrenia comes about as a result of a refusal to think historically (Kuhn, 1990: 321). Baudrillard sees this post-industrial society as the society of spectacle that lives in the ecstasy of communication (Bruno, 1987: 67). This society, he believes, is dominated by electronic mass media and is characterized by simulation (Kuhn, 1990: 321). Baudrillard explains that this post-industrial society is one of reproduction and recycling, so rather than producing the real it reproduces the hyper-real (Bruno, 1987: 67). By this he means the real is not the real, is not what can be reproduced; but, rather, that which is always already reproduced which is essentially a simulation (ibid.: 67). The hyper-real, then, is a simulacrum of the real. Perfect simulation is the goal of postmodernism; thereby no original is invoked as a point of comparison and no distinction between the real and the copy remains (ibid.: 68). In this implicit loss of distinction between representation and the real, Baudrillard perceives the death of the individual (note how this is the 'direct' opposite of other postmodern critics' readings of the individual as central; see above).

In order to make this point clearer, it is useful to compare the effects of the industrial machine on the individual (the **subject**) versus those of the post-industrial machine. Whereas the industrial machine was one of production, the post-industrial one is one of reproduction (Bruno, 1987: 69). In the former case, the industrial machine led to the alienation of the subject – the subject no longer commanded the modes of production. In the latter, the post-industrial machine leads to the fragmentation of the subject, to its dispersal in representation (ibid.). It has no history, is stuck in the ever-present. It is in effect without memory. According to Lacan, the experience of temporality and its representation are an effect of language (1977: 70). If, therefore, the subject has no experience of temporality, has no link with the past or the future, then it is without language – that is, it lacks the means of representing the 'I'. This creates a schizophrenic condition in which the subject fails to assert its **subjectivity** and fails also to enter the **Symbolic** Order. Therefore it is stuck in the **Imaginary**, perhaps even in the pre-Imaginary (see **psychoanalysis**). The question becomes 'who am I?' – even, 'who made me?' It is remarkable that the 1990s produced a spate of monster films on-screen where the question of reproduction has been central to the narrative (e.g. *Jurassic Park*, Steven Spielberg, 1993; *Mary Shelley's Frankenstein*, Kenneth Branagh, 1994) and identity (*Interview with the Vampire*, Neil Jordan, 1994). An analysis of these films would doubtless produce the missing link between past, present and future – that is, the figure of the mother who is so pre-eminently absent from these films as site of reproduction, the reproduction machine of post-industrialization (male technology) having reproduced her (genetic engineering).

Postmodernism, as we know, refers to a general human condition in the late capitalist world (post-1950s) that impacts on society at large, including ideology, as much as it does on art and culture. Certain theorists, amongst them so-called neoconservatives, see postmodernism as a dangerous thing both aesthetically and politically (Huyssen, 1990:

255). In terms of aesthetics, the danger resides in the popularization of the modernist aesthetic which, through the dissolution of the divide between high art and low art, promotes hedonism and anarchy. It promotes anarchy because it removes the function of modernist art as critique – and as such makes possible the maxim 'anything goes' – and hedonism in that it takes the subjective idealism of modernism to the point of solipsism (Hawthorn, 1992: 110). That is, the individual subject becomes the only knowable thing. Politically speaking, because it reacts against modernism's belief in knowledge and progress, postmodernism rejects meaning (in the sense of believing that the world exists as something to be understood and that there is some unified underlying reality). Ideology becomes distinctly unstable in this environment.

However, postmodernism is not necessarily perceived negatively, particularly by those living in it – primarily the youth generation, but also other groupings (as I will explain). Postmodernism in its positive mode celebrates the present and is far more accepting of late capitalism and technology. It also celebrates the fact that mass communication and electronics have revolutionized the world (Hawthorn, 1992: 111). Postmodernism delights in and is fascinated by technology. The internet represents the height of communication in the present through mass technology. Virtual reality can 'let me be there' without moving. Late capitalism means a disposal of the productive base: commodities are produced where it is most advantageous, the labour market has become internationalized and fragmented. But, it has also produced multinational corporations, which means that capital itself is concentrated in the hands of the few. For example, the world is so small that Reebok or Nike can have their central office in New Jersey or Eugene, Oregon yet not have a factory outlet anywhere in the United States. The factories are placed in parts of the world where labour is cheapest (the worst form of globalization, surely).

To the criticism that postmodernism has lost the edge of art as critique and that, in its art-for-art's sake positioning, it resembles the *fin-de-siècle* mood of the nineteenth century, we could argue that postmodern art appears – within its celebratory and playfully transgressive (of modernism) mode – to reject this function of art, or proposes that popular culture is just as capable of offering a critique as high art. In this latter respect, the populist trend of postmodernism (as exemplified by pop art and its reference to comic-strip culture, and by pop music: rock, punk, acid, grunge, garage, etc.) – in its deliberate counter-culture positioning – challenges modernism's hostility towards mass culture as exemplified by the Frankfurt School (Huyssen,

1990: 241). It also rejects modernist belief in the 'perpetual modernization of art' (ibid.: 238) and questions the exploitation of modernism for capital greed and political need. To explain: during the 1940s and the Cold War of the 1950s, modernism, in the form of abstract expressionism (as seen in the paintings of Willem de Kooning or Jackson Pollock), was a school virtually 'invented' and subsequently institutionalized as canonical high art by the United States (read: the CIA and art critics). This was done for propagandistic and political ends. The intent, successfully carried out, was to move the centre of the art world out of Europe (and the threat or taint of communism) and to make New York the world capital (in both senses of that word) of art.

Postmodernism's effect of dissolving the binary divide between high and low art has, domino-style, generated others. The positive side of 'anything goes' is that dichotomies no longer function tyrannically as exclusionary. Modernism had represented a masculinization of culture, due in part to a bohemian lifestyle that excluded most women at least at first (Hawthorn, 1992: 109), but due also to the primary areas of modernism: architecture, painting, film, theatre (the modernist novel coming, arguably, later in the 1930s). Thanks to its creative relationship between high and low art, postmodernism has made space for minority cultures, has brought about a fragmentation of culture that is positive. Thus, where gender and race are concerned, this dissolution of binary divides and de-privileging of a meritocracy within dichotomies have led, first, to a pluralism within the question of subjectivity and, second, to a questioning of defining people in relation to the concept of 'otherness'. In its rejection of universal norms, postmodernism refutes generalizations that exclude, and advocates a plurality of individualized agency (Nicholson, 1990: 13). In this respect, therefore, gender and race are no longer dichotomized. Postmodernism represents, then, a cultural liberation.

Small surprise that for some groupings – particularly those who had previously been excluded by the high principles of modernism – postmodernism is seen as liberating and celebratory. Voices from the margins, minority cultures, are finding spaces within contemporary culture. In the Western world, this has meant hearing, among others and in differing degrees of volume, the voices of Black people, women, women of colour, gays, lesbians, ecologists, animal rights supporters, disabled people and so on. Some of these voices have found their way onto film. Since the 1980s, there has been an emergence of Black men and women filmmakers (see **Black cinema** entries), Black **stars**, gay and lesbian filmmakers all of whom have also managed to come into the mainstream – marking the beginnings of a pluralism therefore in this highly competitive arena.

This pluralism has extended into **film theory** perhaps with greater speed than into the filmmaking practices themselves. And this is due in part to postmodernism's impact upon, or coincidence with, developments in cultural studies towards a mapping of our cultures – seeing culture as pluralistic (starting in the 1960s with Raymond Williams *et al.*). It is also due to its conjuncture with feminism. Feminist criticism exposed the masculine determinations of modernist art and culture and as such, albeit through a differing optic, echoed the postmodern position. In its critique of the normalizing function of patriarchy, feminism joined up with postmodernism's critique of the modernist belief in knowledge and its use of 'master narratives' to legitimate scientific research and the pursuit of knowledge (Kuhn, 1990: 321). In the name of knowledge, modernism has presented a very dislocated and partisan view of the world – one that excludes more than it includes, one that belongs to a particular gender, class, race and culture (Nicholson, 1990: 5). Feminism rejects modernism's belief in reason and objectivity and its concomitant belief in total theory. Feminism opposes, therefore, all generalizations because they exclude (see **feminist film theory**).

Because feminism raises the questions of identity identification and, ultimately history (or lack of it where woman's place is concerned), postmodernism seems, then, a natural ally to feminism (although not all feminists agree; see Nicholson, 1990). Counter to modernism's construction of the individual as a single subjectivity in relation to the 'other', postmodernism and feminism make possible the notion of a 'plurality of individual agents' (Nicholson, 1990: 13). For example, there is no longer a single standard norm wherein gender, identity and sexual orientation are fixed as heterosexual (ibid.: 15). Furthermore, it becomes possible to talk in terms of gender- and race-based subjectivities (Huyssen, 1990: 250).

The importance of this concept of pluralism for film theory is clear. The construction of subjectivity through the cinematic **apparatus** can be examined. This in turn generates questions around the **gaze** and leads to its investigation: who owns it, is it exclusively male? The whole debate around **sexuality** on-screen gets opened up. The issue of spectator–text relations now becomes yet another way by which the filmic text can be understood as an ideological operation. Thus, gender issues are no longer reduced to an 'either/or', but are discussed within frameworks of gender fluidity, resistance to gender fixing, whether on-screen or in connection with the spectator and the text.

More recently still (since the 2000s), body theory has entered into the mix of theories postmodernism so readily embraces.

see also: **modernism, structuralism/post-structuralism, film theory**

For further reading on the postmodern and cinema see Boggs, 2003; Booker, 2007; Denzin, 1991; Dyer, 2007; Hebdige, 1988; Natoli, 2001.

PREFERRED READING

In mainstream cinema, images and films, as a whole, are encoded in such a way as they are given a preferred reading. They are meant to mean what they say. The **narrative** triad ('order/disorder/order'), the filmic **codes and conventions** germane to a particular **genre** (e.g. the **lighting** and décor in **film noir**), characterization (e.g. heroic active male, scheming female, passive female victim), the **iconography** of the image – all these become just so many ideological operations of the cinematic **apparatus**, the internal workings of the film text which create a closed text, one where the meaning is encoded from the outset. Of course, the **spectator** may not necessarily accept that preferred reading. Indeed, feminist critics have made readings against the grain (or oppositional readings) – particularly of the film noir and the **melodrama** (see **feminist film theory**).

see also: **classical narrative cinema, dominant cinema, ideology**

PRODUCER

The individual responsible for the financial and administrative aspects of a film production (through all the stages from production through to **distribution**, including advertising). In the **studio** days of **Hollywood** and film industries in the West (up until the late 1950s and early 1960s), the producer was, generally speaking, attached to a studio. Since that time, producers have mostly functioned as independents and so are responsible for attracting money to a film project. Typically, the producer will be presented with an idea for a film project and will then set about trying to find finance for it (by submitting it to a studio or going to various groups and individuals to obtain financing). The producer manages the entire production and works in close collaboration with the **director**/filmmaker. The producer sorts out locations, studios, schedule of production, controls the management of budgets, the hiring of stars, **cinematographer**, screenwriter, and special effects studios.

see also: **director, studio system, vertical integration**

PSYCHOANALYSIS

What follows is a mapping of the major debates in psychoanalysis as they have been introduced into and developed in **film theory**. Psychoanalysis did not fully enter into film theory until as late as the early 1970s. This might surprise, given that cinema is a contemporary of Freudian psychoanalysis (both emerging at the end of the nineteenth century) and that film **narratives** (whether **realist** or **surrealist**) are projections of our imaginings and therefore deeply linked to both our consciousness and our unconscious. It would take the coincidence in the late 1960s of two occurrences in theoretical thinking to bring about the entry of psychoanalysis. On the one hand, the late 1960s witnessed a reaction against the effects of **structuralism** and its 'total theory' strategy. On the other hand, this period saw a widening of the debates in Freudian psychoanalysis thanks to the impact of the writings of Jacques Lacan. These were subsequently taken up in critical theory in general and film theory in particular.

There are predominantly two strands of psychoanalysis, particularly on the question of **subjectivity**, that have found their way into film theory: Freudian and Lacanian. And they have so far been applied in three main areas of investigation: the film texts themselves; the **apparatus**–spectator relation which later evolved into **spectator**–text relations; and **fantasy**. Psychoanalytic theory has developed significantly in film theory since its earliest applications. Despite the conviction with which some theorists have taken up psychoanalysis, it is noteworthy that not all film theorists are confirmed adherents to the merits of psychoanalysis – so the debate remains an active, not to say controversial, one. It is worth noting that, for all that some critics and theorists claim that psychoanalytic film theory is 'dead', nonetheless, since 2006, there have been thirty-five books in English alone published on the subject.

Freud's theory of the subject, including his account of the Oedipal complex

Freud's psychoanalytic approach was to investigate, to probe the psychological functioning of our human psyche and the relations we form with the outside world. Freud believed that we strive to fulfil our needs and desires (including, especially, sexual ones) and suffer pain if we are unable to do so. We also feel guilt for our desires, particularly if they cannot be fulfilled, and become self-critical, even self-hating. Freud maintained that, generally speaking, we repress these feelings of frustration and self-disgust into the unconscious. The unconscious does not remain perpetually buried, but can resurface in dreams or through projection. In the former case, dreams represent a return of the repressed so they are the vehicle for that which re-emerges from the unconscious. In the latter case, we impose, project, our frustrations onto something or someone external to us.

Freud determined three parts to our psyche: the id, ego and super-ego. The id is the uncontrolled, repressed part of the psyche which the ego, as the consciousness, attempts to control. The super-ego, as the term suggests, attempts to act as a higher-order authority over the id and the ego by trying to gain a greater critical conscience in relation to the workings of the psyche and to understand them. The super-ego is also identified with the parental voice within the psyche. Where the boy child is concerned, the super-ego represents an inter-nalizing of patriarchal authority – that is, he accepts the suppression of desire (for the mother) in order to gain access to the same rights as his father. Thus, patriarchy regenerates itself.

Freud's account of subjectivity is important in at least one further significant way and concerns his notion of the Oedipal complex. In referring to the Oedipal **myth**, Freud sought a means whereby he could explain a child's acquisition of 'normal' adult **sexuality**. Freud was primarily concerned with the male child's Oedipal phase (in a later section I discuss the female subject). The Oedipal phase is also, in Lacanian terms, the latter phase of the **mirror stage** (see next sec-tion). For Freud and Lacan, the male child, who at first is bonded to his mother (through the breast), imagines that he is a united whole with her. However, once he is held up to the mirror by his mother (she who shows him to himself), he perceives his difference from her (in that he has a penis). He becomes aware of the illusory nature of his unity with his mother and yet still desires unification. Thus, the desire for the mother is now sexualized.

The dyadic mother/child relationship, although a precursor to entry into the social, is nonetheless narcissistic in its mutual identifi-cation and desiring. For growth to take place into a plurality of rela-tions and into the order of civilization and culture, the child must be removed or severed from its imaginary unity with the mother. This dyadic structure must give way to a third term: the father. This moment is what Freud terms the Oedipal complex or crisis. The father intervenes, forming a triangular structure, forbidding the child sexual access to the mother. The male child renounces his desire for his mother for fear of castration. He notes that his father has the phallus and his mother does not. He assumes that his mother is castrated and that, therefore, his father – he who possesses the phallus – has the power to castrate him. Both mother and father carry the threat of castration for the male child: he could become 'she who is without' if he disobeys either parent's prohibition (in this respect Alfred Hitchcock's *Psycho*, 1960, at first sight appears to offer a classic scenario of the castrating mother). The male child obeys the father, enters into a pact with him in that he renounces his mother momentarily, until it is time for him to find his own female and accede, in his turn, to paternal status which is the reward for renouncing the mother. The question of the female child gets less attention in Freud (and for that matter Lacan). The Oedipal crisis for the male child, then, manifests itself by this renouncement of the mother, what Freud terms primal repression. This moment of primal repression marks the founding moment of the unconscious. In other words, those unspoken sexual drives and desire for narcissistic union with the mother are repressed. The male child must repudiate his mother and become like his father, in terms of masculinity, but not like his father in terms of his love object – it cannot be the mother (although, as Freud points out, ultimately, it always is the mother). And it is here that we have the basis for the so-called Oedipal trajectory (see below) that has been associated with **classical narrative cinema**. The protagonist must successfully complete his trajectory through first resolving a crisis, usually of a triangular nature (rivalry for a woman, for example), and then attaining social stability. (See section below: ***psychoanalysis and film theory*** for an application of the Oedipal complex to cinema narrative.)

For further reading see Freud, 1931.

Lacan's theory of the subject – including his linked concepts of Imaginary/Symbolic, the mirror stage, misrecognition, and 'jouissance'

What of Lacan and his development and rethinking of Freud's theory of the subject? First of all, it is important to stress here that Lacan focused only on the male child. I will come to the case for the female child when we get to the discussion of the *female subject*.

Lacan shifted the frame of reference away from Freud's pre-occupations with the sexual drives and looked to language as the site for the construction of the subject, of subjectivity. This shift is justifiable in a number of ways, starting with the fact that Freud himself posits the Oedipal complex at an age when the child can talk. In other words, the speaking subject comes into being at the moment of the primal repression (of the desire for the mother). At the same time as the male child enters into the Oedipal complex, Freud notes that he turns his attention to objects other than his mother in order to compensate for the fear of her loss. Freud talks about the child's *fort/da* game (gone/there). The child throws a reel of cotton on a piece of string away ('*fort*/gone') and, in retrieving it, emits the sound '*da*/there'. The cotton reel, according to Freud's reading, is a substitute for the mother; the game a way of coming to terms with the loss of the mother (i.e. of being separate from her, abandoned by her). The game and the word become a way of mastering her absence. That absence and control of absence is marked in language: 'da'. For Lacan, the game represents the child's entry into language and the reel functions as a symbol standing in for what is missing. It signifies lack. According to Lacan, the child is born into the experience of lack and spends the rest of his life trying to recapture an imagined entity which is the moment he associates with pre-lack – the imagined unity with the mother.

A second reason for Lacan turning to a linguistic model follows closely on from the above and concerns the child's shift, thanks to the *mirror stage*, from the *Imaginary into the Symbolic*. The mirror stage is a kind of 'half-way house' between the Imaginary and the Symbolic. It belongs to the Imaginary domain, but moves the child from the dyad with the mother into an identification with its own specular image. Prior to the mirror stage, the child has no sense of separateness from the mother and, therefore, imagines itself as one (what Lacan refers to as the Imaginary). It is only after the mirror stage that it knows its difference and/or separateness from the mother. By this time, however, it has entered the Symbolic Order, which is based in language – that is, the 'Law' of the Father (accepting the verbal warning of the father: 'No'). Until this mirror phase, the child is pre-lack and pre-linguistic. Entry into the Symbolic is entry into language. But, it is also entry into lack. Language, therefore, becomes indissolubly based in and bound up with the concept of lack. Born into the experience of lack, the child as-speaking-subject is lack. What does this mean?

Primal repression for Freud is, as we have seen, the founding moment of the unconscious. Lacan, referring to this repression as primary, perceives this moment as an opening up of the unconscious, by which he means that the unconscious emerges as a result of the repression of desire. Lacan explains this occurrence in the following manner: the speaking subject comes into existence only because of the repression of the desire for the mother who is now lost. The boy child has relinquished its illusory/Imaginary identity with the mother and entered the Symbolic. Thus, every time the child enunciates 'I am' he also enunciates 'I am lack'.

Entry into language signifies both the birth of desire (the boy child recognizes it) and the repression of desire. Entry into language means entry into the social order, but it also means experiencing lack even further because desire can never be fully satisfied (no return to unity with the mother). Thus starts the unfulfillable search for the eternally lost object, what Lacan calls *l'objet petit-a* ('little "o"', *autre* meaning other, the [m]other).

According to Lacan, there are three determining moments concerning the boy child's development as he moves from the *Imaginary to the Symbolic* – which is the necessary progression for development into the social order. The three moments are: the *mirror phase, accession to language* and the *Oedipus complex*. First, let's examine the mirror stage, which the child goes through around the age of 6 to 18 months. When the mother holds the child up to the mirror, it assumes that the reflection it sees in the mirror is itself. In this respect, it begins to develop a sense of identity separate from the mother. This is the moment in which the child sees itself as a unified being at the centre of the world. It experiences a moment of pure *jouissance* (jubilation) in this narcissistic identification. The body is taken for the love-object. The child *sees* itself as whole, whereas in actual terms, until now, it has sensed itself as fragmented and uncoordinated. It sees in the mirror image the ideal image, the unified/whole. This narcissistic moment of self-idealization produces *misrecognition* in identification. It also produces alienation. This imaginary mastery over the body anticipates what is not yet there, actual mastery of the body. This ideal image is also the one the (m)other is holding up to be seen – she holds up the ideal image. So the child also identifies with what it assumes is the mother's perception of it. The child moves from the utterance of misrecognition, 'that's me', to that of alienation, 'I am another'. That alienation has a double edge. That is, the child senses it is not that unified coordinated image in the mirror ('I am another') and because the perception with which the child identifies in the mirror is that of the mother's (she holds up the ideal image), the image is conditioned by the mother's look ('I am who my mother desires me to be').

Alienation occurs, then, because the image can signify as real *only* because of the presence of the (m)other – what Lacan, as we have seen, terms little 'o' – and identification is possible only in relation to another. This need of the other to sustain one's identity exposes the gap between the idealized image and the subject. This means there can never be a unified self, only a *divided subject*. The child is a divided self between, on the one hand, the false sense of unity with the self, the ideal image (the ego-ideal), and, on the other, the need for its subjectivity to be confirmed by another.

In order to obtain a social identity the boy child has to suppress its desire of the mother. Again, Lacan's version of the child's *Oedipal phase* has much in common with Freud's, but the difference is the use of a linguistic model rather than a purely bio-sexual one. This is what Lacan defines as the *Symbolic Order*. At the moment that the male child recognizes his desire for his mother, the father intercedes and imposes the patriarchal law. The father is the third member to enter the reflecting mirror. It is he who represents, to the child, the authoritative figure in the family. So, the child imagines what the authoritative figurehead would say – the father is, therefore, a symbolic father. The father proscribes incest. This taboo is imposed linguistically and is defined by Lacan as the Law of the Father. Because it is based in language, patriarchal law is a Symbolic Order. In the Oedipal phase, then, the male child imagines himself to be what the mother lacks and therefore desires – that is, the phallus. However, this is proscribed by the Law of the Father, the patriarchal 'No'. Prohibition of fulfilling the incestual drive is marked in language. And the child will comply, for fear of castration by the father. The male child enters into the Symbolic and adopts a speaking position that marks him as independent from the mother. When the child enters into the Symbolic, it enters language, but it also succumbs to the Law of the Father, laws of society, laws that are determined by the Other (with a capital 'O'). The Other is a term which is coterminous with the Symbolic Order, language and the Law of the Father. Lacan's use of the term Other allows him to formulate clearly the distinction between the Imaginary and the Symbolic orders. Thus, in shorthand form he can refer to the capital 'O' as distinct from the little 'o', which refers to the imaginary relations with the other that take place within the Imaginary (the mirror-image, the mother). The capital 'O' represents, then, the Law of the Father and the danger of castration – in these terms decapitation (being decapitalized from 'O' to 'o').

The male child conforms to the patriarchal law, upholds it and thus perpetuates it for generations to come. He follows in the 'name-of-the-father', so that when he says 'I' it comes from the same authorized speaking position as the language of the father, the Other. He becomes the subject of the Symbolic. However, as we know, his desire for the mother does not disappear, it gets repressed and enters into the unconscious. This means that his identification with the mother's object of desire, the phallus, does not disappear either, not altogether. For example, Lacan notes how the **fetishist** articulates this relation to desire around fetishistic objects such as women's shoes and bits of clothing. These are symbols of the mother's/woman's phallus insofar as it is absent and with which the fetishist identifies. We are reminded that in **film noir** the *femme fatale is* commodified in a fetishistic way (slinky black dress, high-heeled shoes, painted fingernails). The transvestite similarly articulates this desire for the phallus in that he identifies with the phallus-as-hidden under the mother's dress. In other words, he identifies with a woman who has a hidden phallus. Fetishism, as we also know, is a strategy of disavowal faced by the fear of castration: the fetishist 'completes' the female body and in so doing denies difference, denies the lack. A reading of *Psycho* in this light shows not only to what degree Norman Bates had fetishized his mother for fear of castration but also how unable (unwilling) he was to forgo his desire to become or identify with his mother's object of desire, the phallus. In his disguising/cross-dressing himself as his (dead) mother, he becomes both fetishist and transvestite.

For a more extended version of this part of the entry (including a discussion of Lacan's third term 'The Real') see Hayward, 2006: 311–29.

Psychoanalysis and the female subject

So far in this entry, little or nothing has been said about the female subject. Freud devotes two essays to the matter, but Lacan does not examine it in much detail. Indeed, for Lacan the woman does not exist as subject, she is 'not being', 'not all', she is the 'other' of the phallic function (*'l'objet petit-a'*). Lacanian feminists and feminist theorists do, however, investigate female subjectivity and argue that there is such a thing as a female Oedipal trajectory (see **Oedipal trajectory**, below, and **feminist film theory**).

As far as Freud is concerned, the female child enjoys a pre-Oedipal relationship with the mother that is similar to the male child. Freud sees the Oedipal complex for the girl as dynamically different from the boy (see Freud's essay: 'Female Sexuality', 1931). According to Freud, the girl sees herself as born in lack, so she rejects the mother and turns to the father to get herself a penis (in the form of a baby).

That desire for the father gets transferred onto a male other (who is ultimately the father, albeit a substitute). Successful completion of the trajectory for the female, then, is motherhood (getting a penis in the substitute form of a baby). However, Freud argues that because there is no castration fear, the female child never fully gives up the Oedipal complex and that she is thus always bisexually poised.

When the girl child perceives her sameness with her mother, she experiences her lack as being non-phallic. Her sexual drives impel her towards the truly phallic, the father, who in turn imposes the Law of the Father and forbids her access. For Lacan, as we have seen, sexual difference is inscribed in language only in relation to the phallus (the Symbolic Order). Thus, when the girl child says 'I', the question becomes whose 'I' is it? She cannot be subject of the Symbolic in the same way as the boy child can, because the authorized speaking position is that of the father, and language is marked by the phallus. If she cannot be subject, then she must be object of the Symbolic (that is, language); and if she is object of the Symbolic, then she must also be the object of desire rather than the subject of desire (she is fixed, constructed by language since it is not hers).

And yet, here's the paradox: the female child will never fully relinquish her desire for her mother (because there is no recognition of it within the Law of the Father); however, she will never fully enter the Symbolic Order (because the Law of the Father as language does not, in the final analysis, apply to her but to the male child). And it is here that questions surrounding female subjectivity become of real interest, because, as such, the female child is doubly poised both sexually and in relation to language. With regard to the first point, she is doubly desiring both of her own sex (through her sameness to her mother who is not forbidden to her) and also of the male sex (a desire she must fulfil by finding a male other than her father). In terms of language she is also doubly positioned. She is not subject of language, but object *of* the Symbolic Order. But, she is also (obliged by patriarchy to be) *in* the Symbolic. As we have seen, she must be there in the patriarchal constructs of sexual identity because her reflection has to be in the mirror for the male to recognize his difference. In other words, she must be present as the 'other' to affirm masculine identity.

Here's the rub. Unlike the male child who has a vested interest in obeying the father and entering the Symbolic Order (for fear of castration), the female child does not have the same interest. She can, therefore, resist/withhold confirming male subjectivity. To do so, however, risks being punished. After all, in order to fulfil her Oedipal trajectory and enter the social order of things she must function as the (m)other in affirming the male Other. Thus, as we note, in **film noir** where the female (the *femme fatale*) does not return the ideal image to the male, she most often perishes. But, as you have probably guessed, even if the female does return it, that is not without its problems either. Whose perception of the subject is she confirming (hers, the mother's)? The male child identifies not just with his own image but with what he assumes is the mother's perception of him. His subjectivity is, to his mind, conditioned by the (m)other's look and of course (however subconsciously) by his desire of the mother. How can the female other hope to replicate that?

Psychoanalysis and film theory

The key concepts we need to bear in mind when considering the impact of psychoanalysis on **film theory**, then, are: the Oedipal trajectory, the unconscious and the repression of desire; the construction of subjectivity and the notion of the divided self; the Imaginary and the Symbolic. (For greater detail, see Benvenuto and Kennedy, 1986; Grosz, 1990; Lapsley and Westlake, 1988).

Oedipal trajectory

The term 'Oedipal trajectory' is a concept used in film psychoanalytic theory to refer to a convention of **classical Hollywood cinema** whereby the male protagonist either successfully or unsuccessfully fulfils the trajectory through the resolution of a crisis and a movement towards social stability. In other words, after much difficulty (depending on the film **genre**), he finds a woman and 'settles down'. In terms of cinema narrative, the male protagonist moves, through the resolution of a crisis, towards social stability. In **mainstream cinema**, the female is a stationary site (i.e. passive object) to which the male hero travels and upon which he acts (i.e. he is the active **subject**). If he fails to achieve this trajectory, as is the case, say, in **film noir**, then it is possible to talk about masculinity in crisis. He fails to find social stability by failing to marry the female other (in a film noir, for example, either he or she dies). It is interesting to note that the other genre in which the male hero often does not 'settle down' is the **Western**. But, in this instance, the failure to complete the trajectory is mostly read positively. Implicit in the Western, with its assertion of the **myth** of the West (frontiersmanship, etc.), lies the notion that the cowboy or gunslinger or Western hero cannot yet settle down: the West is still to be won.

From a psychoanalytical perspective, cinematic **narratives** that embrace the Oedipal trajectory articulate how the threat of castration (as represented by the woman who lacks the phallus) is dispelled and the masculine role of the patriarch is assumed. Two strategies are employed to contain the threat: **voyeurism** and **fetishism**. These strategies form part of the narrative. Thus, with the first strategy the woman is objectified through the **gaze**, is voyeuristically placed as object of surveillance and, thereby, made containable, safe. The male gaze probes and investigates her. She cannot return the gaze because she is not subject. She is the object (the mother) in the mirror who reinforces or confirms the male's subjectivity (this is the role of the mother in the mirror stage, according to Freud and Lacan). And the male, in recognizing his difference (his subjectivity), asserts his superiority over the female (m)other. The alternative strategy is to fetishize the female, to construct her as a fetishized object, to deny her sexual difference. This he does by a fragmentation of her body and an over-investment in parts of the body (breast, legs, etc.). In this way, the woman becomes commodified as a whole and unified body – and therefore of course unthreatening to the male because she is the same as he. The body is rendered phallic, a masculinized female image (tight, slinky black dresses, pointy high heels and long painted fingernails are good examples of this). In fetishizing the body, it is denied its difference. Both strategies reinforce the notion of a naturally stable male subjectivity and reaffirm the naturalness of the patriarchal order to which the female must comply through her passivity and, of course, to which the male complies through his activity (see **naturalizing**).

The female Oedipal trajectory is particularly relevant in relation to women's films and **melodrama** in terms, partly of mother/daughter relations but also, subliminally, lesbian relations. Clearly, the female child is never completely free from desiring her mother. Because of their sameness, there is unity in identification. As with the male child, the mother is her first love-object. But, there is no perceived difference, so there is no fear of castration. What then will motivate her to turn away from her mother and desire the father? Freudians argue that she turns away through penis envy. The mother cannot provide her with a penis so she will turn to the father for him to provide her with it in the form of a child. Lacanians, at least feminist Lacanians, argue that since she must enter into the social order of things – that is, patri-archy – she will be obliged to turn from the mother even though she will never fully relinquish her desire of the mother. To fulfil her Oedipal trajectory and enter into the social order of things, the female child must function to confirm male subjectivity. To withhold such confirmation means punishment – either through conforming to the norm, marginalization or death. In classical narrative cinema, independent women eventually 'come to their senses' and marry the man (if it's **comedy**), or are 'brought to their senses' (if it's a film noir or **thriller**). (For further reading see Kaplan, 1992; Krutnik, 1991; Modleski, 1988: 42–55; Penley, 1989.)

Construction of subjectivity and the divided self

In the 1970s, film theorists (primarily French: Metz, Bellour, Baudry all 1975), recognizing the limitations of a 'total theory' structuralist approach, turned to psychoanalysis as a way of broadening the theoretical framework. Drawing on Freud's account of the libido drives and Lacan's of the mirror stage, they sought to explain how film works at the unconscious level. By establishing an analogy of the screen with the mirror, they discovered a way of talking about **spectator**–screen relations (see **apparatus**). They argued that at each viewing there is an enactment for the spectator of the move from the Imaginary to the Symbolic Order; that is, an enactment of the unconscious processes involved in the acquisition of sexual difference, language and subjectivity. In other words, each viewing represents a repetition of the mirror and the Oedipal stages. Bellour makes the point that cinema functions simultaneously for the Imaginary (as mirror) and as the Symbolic (through the film discourses). And the spectator is in a constant state of flux between the two. We have already noted how, in terms of subjectivity, the two Orders (Imaginary/Symbolic) are always co-present (to clarify this point further see **apparatus** and **suture**).

According to these theorists, in that cinema functions simultaneously for the Imaginary and the Symbolic, it follows that the cinema constructs the spectator as subject. Insofar as the spectator is positioned voyeuristically by the filmic apparatus, the spectator is also identified with the look, with all that that connotes in terms of visual pleasure. The projector functions as the eye, and that eye is all-seeing. Thus, visual pleasure is also bound up with the principle of lawless seeing (unwatched by those on-screen, the viewer watches). Going to the cinema implies the desire to repeat pleasure in viewing. But, because viewing also involves a re-enactment of the Imaginary narcissistic identification with the image and with lawless seeing, it implies that there is a desire to repeat the experience of *jouissance*/jubilation. Given this identificatory process, it is not difficult to see why Metz would speak of cinema-going and viewing as a regression to childhood, to that moment where the subject is a unified whole and not divided.

Metz argues that it is not just the process of voyeurism that is involved in film-viewing, but also that of fetishism. Fetishism and voyeurism are, as we explained, the two strategies adopted to disavow difference. Fetishism occurs on-screen within the image, as in the case of the fetishizing of the body of the *femme fatale* in film noir. But, says Metz, fetishism operates also at a far more basic level. The image as image and the cinematic apparatus as apparatus are both fetish, because they stand in for, make present, what is absent. As such, they disavow what is lacking, they disavow difference. Similarly, the spectator, in watching cinema, is disavowing lack, difference. The spectator knows that presence is absence, that what is there is not there, that what is being seen is lack (absence). Yet, the spectator, says Metz, disavows it and the apparatus in its **seamlessness** disguises this absence, it sutures the spectator into that disavowal (see **suture**). Again the subject asserts its whole, rather than divided self.

It is in these investigations into cinema's relation to voyeurism and fetishism and its relation to the Imaginary and Symbolic Orders that these early years of psychoanalytic film theory made their greatest inroads into the advancing of film theory. Cinema was seen to embody psychic desire. The screen became the site for the projection of our fantasies and desires, that is, for our unconscious. In this way, it was presumed that the cinema positioned the spectator as desiring subject, therefore, as subject of the apparatus – starting with the camera, with which the spectator identifies. These first theorizings were not entirely unproblematic, however. Indeed, they presented at least three problems, not least of which was the exclusively phallocratic reading of cinematic practices. These issues were picked up by **feminist film theorists** – starting with Laura Mulvey (1975). The identified problems were, first, that in this reading it is assumed that the spectator–screen relation is only one-way; second, that the subject is male in its positioning; and third, that film texts are organized in such a way as to give a **preferred reading**.

Feminist film theorists, while acknowledging that psychoanalysis, as a discourse, oppresses women, nonetheless insisted that it was for that very reason that it was important to investigate it seriously, not simply to understand it, but to be able to expose the phallocentric construction of subjectivity – starting with Freud's notion of penis envy and Lacan's assertion that our subjectivity is determined in relation to language and its signifier, the phallus. To understand how women have become positioned as they have, the argument goes, is to make possible a **deconstruction** of that construction. In terms of **film theory**, the film text in this context stands as a dream, a **fantasy** or the analysand, and the critic or theorist takes on the role of the analyst. Thus, for instance, feminist critics have managed to look at 'themes (such as mother/daughter bonding or Oedipal triangles) in order to understand how *patriarchal signifying systems have represented such systems*' (Kaplan, 1990: 15, her stress). Furthermore, through this deconstructionist approach they have been able to give readings against the grain; that is, readings that are not the encoded, preferred reading. (See entry on **feminist film theory**.)

During the 1980s and 1990s, therefore, problems brought about by a phallic-centred reading of cinema have been largely debated and that reading has been contested. As a result, psychoanalytic film theory has developed considerably in the areas of spectator viewing and textual analysis. Spectator positioning is now seen as more heterogeneous or pluralistic (across **gender**, **class**, race, age, sexuality nationality and creed). The spectator-subject is as much constituting of as constituted by the filmic text (see **ideology**). So the spectator–screen relation is at least two-way. Finally, the Oedipal trajectory of the classical narrative is no longer perceived as exclusively male – particularly within film genres that are not evidently all-male, such as melodrama and film noir. The female Oedipal trajectory is now being investigated in terms, first, of mother/daughter relations and, second, of lesbian relations (even if subliminal).

For a sample reading of applications of psychoanalysis to film see Aaron, 2007; Doane *et al.*, 1984; Doane, 1992; Fuery, 2004; Indick, 2004; Kaplan, 1980, 1983, 1990, 1992; Krutnik, 1991; Kuhn, 1982, 1985; Lebeau, 1994, 2001; Lurie, 1980; McGowan, 2004; Modleski, 1982, 1988; Mulvey 1989; Rose, 1986; Zizek, 1999, 2010.

QUEER CINEMA

Queer cinema has been in existence for decades although it lacked a label. Films of Jean Cocteau and Jean Genet in France in the 1930s and 1950s (such as *Le Sang d'un poète*, Cocteau, 1934, and *Le Chant d'amour*, Genet, 1950) are cited as the forefathers (*sic*). It is a cinema that is identified with **avant-garde** or **underground** movements (e.g. Anger and Warhol 1960s films in the USA). In the avant-garde world of cinema, lesbian filmmakers' presence is quite strong too (e.g. Ulrike Ottinger, Chantal Akerman, Pratibha Parmar). Although we could go on listing names for this heritage of Queer cinema, another of the greats has to be Rainer Werner Fassbinder (working in the 1970s and early 1980s) – even in his seemingly mainstream (European art) films he was taking **genres** to task and reinterpreting them through a gay and queer sensibility (see *Fear Eats the Soul*, 1974; *The Marriage of Maria Braun*, 1979). And it is fitting perhaps that his last film, *Querelle* (1982) – based on Genet's 1947 novel – is fully about gay and queer desire. And, finally on this list, what could be queerer and braver than the Brazilian filmmaker Hector Babenco's 1985 film *The Kiss of the Spiderwoman* in which the macho arch-revolutionary succumbs to the charms of the flamboyant queen in his prison cell?

Queer cinema itself was introduced as a concept, in 1991 at the Toronto Festival of Festivals, to refer to a spate of films (beginning in the late 1980s) that re-examined and reviewed histories of the image of gays. These films proposed renegotiated subjectivities, men looking at men, **gazes** exchanged, and so on. They also took over genres previously considered **mainstream**, subverting them by bringing the question of pleasure onto screen and the celebration of excess. In certain cases, these films reinscribed the homosexual text where previously it had been elided. See, for example, Derek Jarman's historical film *Edward II* (1991), or Tom Kalin's murder/crime **thriller** *Swoon* (1992). The latter is a remake/retake, setting the record straight(!) of two earlier versions of the true story of a murder committed by two young men of a 14-year-old boy in Chicago in 1924. The first version was the Hitchcock film, *Rope* (1948), and the second a Richard Fleischer film, *Compulsion* (1959). Both films completely elide the homosexual dimension of the two killers' relationship.

Always a cinema of the margins, only in the 1990s, in the light of the tragedy of AIDS, has Queer cinema become a more visible cinema. Indeed, the New Queer Cinema, as this cinema is also labelled, has presently become a marketable commodity if not an identifiable movement. One of the leaders of the American Queer cinema is Gus Van Sant (with his two films *My Own Private Idaho*, 1991, *Even Cowgirls Get the Blues*, 1993). New Queer Cinema was a term coined in a 1992 *Sight and Sound* article by B. Ruby Rich to describe the renaissance in gay and lesbian filmmaking represented by the Americans Todd Haynes, Jennie Livingstone, Gus Van Sant, Gregg Araki, Laurie Lynd, Tom Kalin and the British filmmakers Derek Jarman and Isaac Julien. Queer cinema is not a single aesthetic but a collection of different aesthetics – what Rich delightfully refers to as 'Homo-Pomo'. It is a cinema that takes pride in difference. Queer cinema is above all a male homosexual cinema and focuses on the construction of male desire. Some lesbian filmmakers have made films that come under this label and it is instructive that they have made films that address not just their **sexuality** (as in *Go Fish!*, Rose

Troche, 1994) but also that of their male counterparts (*Paris is Burning*, Jennie Livingstone, 1991).

Queer as a politics has not resolved lesbian invisibility. There exists still (as within the heterosexual world of the film industry) an inequality of funding for lesbian filmmakers as opposed to gay filmmakers. Gay is perhaps more cool than lesbian at present. One does wonder – cynically perhaps – whether *Philadelphia* (Demme, 1993) would ever have been financed by Hollywood if the New Queer Cinema had not come along at the beginning of the 1990s and enjoyed the success it did with mainstream as well as gay audiences. It is also worth considering that *Philadelphia* was the top-grossing 'gay-themed' film ever in both the USA and the UK, until the huge success of *Brokeback Mountain* (Ang Lee, 2006) (respectively $77m versus $83m; £10m versus £11m). Having said that, there are some lesbian feature films, although for the most part they pre-date New Queer Cinema – an exception being Patricia Rozema's beguiling *When Night is Falling* (1995). Of the 1980s films, we can count *Born in Flames* (Lizzie Borden, 1983), *Desert Hearts* (Donna Deitch, 1985), *I've Heard the Mermaids Singing* (Rozema, 1987). Due to lack of financing, most lesbian filmmakers have opted for video to develop their **counter-cinema** in an unfettered way much as other marginal cinemas before them have done – such as women's cinema, and **cinema nôvo** as it developed into garbage cinema (see Sadie Benning, *Jollies*, 1990; Pratibha Parmar, *Khush*, 1991; Shu Lea Cheang, *Fresh Kill*, 1994).

Queer theory

It is quite probable that Queer cinema as a term came about by identification with trends in critical theory begun in the mid-1980s, namely Queer theory. Queer theory can be seen as a desire to challenge and push further debates on **gender** and **sexuality** put in place by **feminist film theory** (amongst others) and also as a critical response to the numerous **discourses** surrounding AIDS and homosexuality. Queer theory is, arguably one of the first truly postmodern theories to be born in the age of **postmodernism**. In its practice it is extremely broad. It is a concept that embraces all non-straight approaches to living practice – including, within our context, film and popular culture. As a politics, it seeks to confuse binary essentialisms around gender and sexual identity, expose their limitations and suggest that things are far more blurred (e.g. think of the **spectator** pleasure derived from watching Robbie Williams wearing a dress and singing one of his many hit songs – as he did in one of his video promos). It is more than a subversion of straightness; it is also more than an exposing of the fact of **hegemonic** homo-sociality and the hypocrisy of denial. It is in fact far more celebrative than that. In a sense it challenges everyone's assumptions about gender and sexuality. It shows how you can queer-read ('queried') virtually everything as just one other, equal not subordinate, way of reading the texts. Queer readings go 'against the groin' (Verhoeven, 1997: 25). Queer theory examines queer at work, that is, the making or writing about gayness by authors and filmmakers. Doing queer work can be done by all sexualities. Thus, straights, bisexuals, transsexuals, transgenders, gays and lesbians who are writing or making texts about gayness are performing, enacting Queer(ly). Queer theory can open up texts and lead us to read texts that seem straight, differently – or view them from a new and different angle. Thus, a queer reading can reveal that you are watching (reading) something far more complex than you originally thought you were (think of **buddy films**, for example). The actor or filmmaker does not have to be queer, but the text or performance may offer itself up for a queer reading (Joan Crawford as the cross-dressing gun-toting but butchly feminine Vienna in *Johnny Guitar*, Nicholas Ray, 1954).

New Queer Cinema is unconcerned with positive images of queerness, gayness or lesbianism, but is very clearly assertive about its politics – starting with the expression of sexuality as multiplicity and not as fixed or essentialized. Thus, stereotypes of queerness get reappropriated and played with. True camp (not the appropriated camp of straight cinema) privileges form over content but with a purpose. Queer camp is about trashing stereotypes with flash and flounce and dress in excess. It is about ridiculing consumer passivity through deliberate vulgarity. It is about (as in the original French sense of the word *camper:* to play one's role) assuming fully and properly one's performative role. In terms of stereotypes, camp itself and narcissism get some royal send-ups in *The Adventures of Priscilla, Queen of the Desert*, Stephan Elliott (1994) and in *Go Fish!* Queer cinema challenges the view that homosexuality and lesbianism must have value ascribed to it (as good or bad) – it just is. There are political implications about homosexuality and lesbianism, but so too are there about race – as indeed Black gay and lesbian filmmakers make clear (*Looking for Langston*, Isaac Julien, 1988). And, although it pre-dates New Queer cinema and is made by a White director, Stephen Frears' *My Beautiful Launderette* (1985), was a breakthrough film in this context (detailing the love relationship between a British Pakistani youth and his former schoolfriend, a White working-class street punk). In Queer cinema and theory, the gaze, as well as questions of visual pleasure, come under scrutiny. Since the relays of looking are different within the screen, so too must they be outside the screen and in the spectator's eyes. More pleasures can be experienced by the spectator as s/he adopts different positionalities within the **narrative**. In some ways this is not so new if we think of **pornography** and the pleasure in viewing for the spectator (male or female) of the typical triad set-up, which includes a lesbian scene or two to get things warmed/hotted up. But it may be that Queer theory makes us feel more comfortable speaking about it. Interestingly, pornography as a critical debate within film studies has only truly emerged in the 1990s – perhaps coming on the heels of the effects of Queer theory.

Queer cinema has crossed over into mainstream and not all of it is made by gay or lesbian filmmakers. And this, in a way, is the point. It is not that it has been co-opted, although some critics' responses to the Wachowski brother's lesbian neo-noir *Bound* (1990) warn us how difficult it is to be clear on this; as indeed does Peter Jackson's *Heavenly Creatures* (1994) and, more recently, Abdellatif Kechiche's *La vie d'Adèle* (*Blue is the Warmest Colour*, 2013). However, I would argue that this cross-over is more a case of queerness being a recognized state-of-being, amongst others. In 1998/1999 alone, there were six very ostensibly queer films (at the very least), two of which were made by women and all of which were box-office successes: *Being John Malkovich* (Jonze, 1999), *Boys Don't Cry* (Peirce, 1999), *Gods and Monsters* (Condon, 1999), *High Art* (Cholodenko, 1998), *Love is the Devil (Study for a Portrait of Francis Bacon)* (Maybury, 1998), *The Talented Mr Ripley* (Minghella, 1999). None of these films gloss over on what it means to have a queer identity, nor indeed the difficulties this can represent in terms of social acceptability. Only the first film has a light outcome with a lesbian relationship asserting itself after a series of fun-filled adventures entering into the mind and eyes of John Malkovich. *Gods and Monsters'* study of the career of the gay film-maker James Whale (he directed the 1930s *Frankenstein* movies) gives us a sense of what it was like to be queer in Hollywood at a time when hetero-normativity was de rigueur. The other four films, it has to be said, however, are quite dark, either because death is the outcome of the intolerance of others (*Boys Don't Cry*; *The Talented Mr Ripley*), or because they unflinchingly show the harder side of lesbian and gay society (*High Art*; *Love is the Devil*).

Queer cinema advocates multiplicity: of voices and of sexualities – a good example is the exploration of lesbian sexuality in Pawel Pawlikowksi's *My Summer of Love* (2004). Multiplicity in a generic sense also: vampire films and **comedy**, **thrillers** and **musicals**. These narratives unstick the queer from the moribund representation to which much of mainstream cinema has confined it. Queers are neither the depressed anomics nor the serial killers some filmmakers would have us believe (see Winterbottom's offensive *Butterfly Kiss*, 1994). To rewrite Foucault: 'Queer is everywhere.' Queer is being nominated for and winning Oscars. There have been three award winners in the past twenty years – Jonathan Demme's *Philadelphia* (1993); Ang Lee's *Brokeback Mountain* (2005); Gus Van Sant's *Milk* (2008) – and two nominations – Duncan Tucker's *Transamerica* (2005) and Tom Ford's *A Single Man* (2009). The signs of queer globalization are there to see. Almodovar's work is an obvious first citation in terms of Europe. But Asian queer is also on the scene (Chen Kaige's *Farewell · My Concubine*, 1993; Zhang Yuan's *East Palace/West Palace*, 1996; Wong Kar-wai's *Happy Together*, 1997). It is no longer a case of having to find it, but 'to connect'.

For further reading see Aaron, 2004; Bad Object-Choices, 1991; Benshoff and Griffin, 2004; Bristow, 1997; Burston and Richardson, 1995; Creekmur and Dory, 1995; Dorenkamp and Henke, 1995; Dyer, 1977b, 1990, 2002; Fuss, 1992; Gever *et al.*, 1993; Gill, 1995; Grossman, 2000; Hanson, 1999; Horne and Lewis, 1996; Jackson and Tapp, 1997; Kuzniar, 2000; Mell-Metereau, 1993; Rich, 1992; Russo, 1981, 1987; Schoonover and Galt, 2016; Stacey and Street, 2007; Weiss, 1990; Whisman, 1995. For a documentary film of Queer, see *The Celluloid Closet*, Rob Epstein and Jeffrey Friedman, 1995.

QUOTA QUICKIES

Quota quickies was a term used in the late 1920s through the 1930s to refer to British films made in less than a month and costing £1 per film foot. They were low-budget films specifically intended to meet quota demands established by the government and were screened as part of the value-for-money double-bill fare on offer in cinemas during the difficult economic years following the financial crash of the late 1920s (known as the Great Depression). The 'King' of quota quickies (at least in terms of numbers produced and directed) was George William King, with fifty to his name (see, for example, *Sweeney Todd: The Demon Barber of Fleet Street*, 1936).

Steve Chibnall (2007) has written an extremely full and clear study of the quota-quickies phenomenon. In it, he makes a plea for the cultural–historical relevance of this too readily dismissed (and often derided), low production-value film artefact. In his book, Chibnall puts to rest many of the misconceptions about this second-order, B-rated type of British film that was produced in its masses during the period

1928 to 1937. Consider, for a start, that 50 per cent of all British films produced during those ten years were quota quickies (ibid.: 13). They were, therefore, in more than just numerical terms, an important phenomenon in British film history. It is also worth considering that Michael Powell began his career making quota quickies (e.g. *Red Ensign*, 1934). Moreover, the enforced increase in production helped 'unlock American finance' for the British film industry (ibid.: 2). The number of stages in studio quadrupled; production underwent a six-fold increase; and British cinema (which, thanks to investment, quickly adapted to **sound** technology) became the largest industry outside America (ibid.: 2–3). This effect brought the renowned silent cinema filmmaker George Pearson back from **Hollywood** to work in British film – even though he remained very critical of the impact of quota quickies on the global reputation of Britain's film industry (ibid.: 5).

Quota quickies came about as the result of protectionist legislation put in place by the British government: the 1927 Cinematograph Films Act. The aim was to redress the imbalance currently experienced by the British film industry in the face of competition from Hollywood. The Act established a minimum quota of British films for distributors and exhibitors (to rise from 5 to 20 per cent in a ten-year period). A double-bill generally meant the screening of a quota quickie followed by a full-length American feature film. These quota quickies had to be films made by a British subject, made in Britain, or by a company based in the (then) British Empire, with all studio scenes shot within the Empire (Chibnall, 2007: 2). This did not, however, prevent American studios and 'renters' (those responsible for **distribution** and exhibition) from quickly taking over the market. American **studios** set up their own 'satellite studios' in the UK (ibid.: 4); and renters commissioned films or acquired them to fulfil the quota requirements (ibid.: 3). As Chibnall explains: 'the early days of quota production were volatile and confused. As City investors burned their fingers and looked for businesses with more secure prospects, the ground was largely cleared for the American distribution companies to finance British production on their own terms' (ibid.: 4). Only British International Pictures held their own against the likes of MGM, Universal and Paramount.

Clearly, production values were not going to be high, nor, on the whole, was content. Films were just barely feature-length (averaging 40–70 minutes); and their B-movie status was not particularly improved either by the fact that projectionists often had to cut the film length to meet the demands of the exhibition programme. The films tended to be **comedies**, **documentary** shorts, or live variety performances such as those of George Formby and Max Miller (thanks of course to the advent of **sound**). As Chibnall rightly points out (2007: 8), audiences must have gained some pleasure from viewing them, because if their screening had adversely affected the box-office, the practice would have been brought to a grinding halt a lot earlier than it was.

The Quota Act was modified, by the Cinematograph Films Act, in 1938 when it came up for reconsideration after its ten-year first cycle; and was finally repealed in 1960 by the Films Act.

For full details see Chibnall, 2007.

REALISM

The term *realism* comes from a literary and art movement of the nineteenth century which went against the grand tradition of classical idealism and sought to portray 'life as it really was'. The focus was on ordinary life – indeed, the lives of the socially deprived and the conditions they had to bear. As far as the film camera is concerned, it is not difficult to see why it is perceived as a 'natural' tool for realism, since it reproduces 'what is there' (i.e. the physical environment). Film as cinema makes absence presence; it puts reality up onto the screen. It purports to give a direct and 'truthful' view of the 'real world' through the presentation it provides of the characters and their environment. Realism functions in film on both the **narrative** level and the figurative (i.e. pictorial/photographic). In this regard, physical realism marries into **psychological** realism via the narrative structures. Generally speaking, realist films address social issues. However, because the narrative closure of these films tends to provide easy solutions, this form of realism on the whole serves only to **naturalize** social problems and divisions and not provide any deep insight into causes.

There are, arguably, two types of realism with regard to film. First, **seamless** realism, whose **ideological** function is to disguise the illusion of realism. Second, aesthetically **motivated** realism, which attempts to use the camera in a non-manipulative fashion and considers the purpose of realism to be its ability to convey a reading of reality, or several readings even. As far as the seamless type of realism is concerned, film technique – supported by narrative structures – erases the idea of illusion, creates the 'reality effect' and provides a **preferred reading**. It hides its mythical and **naturalizing** function and does not question itself – obviously because to do so would be to destroy the authenticity of its realism (see **myth**). Nothing in the camera-work, the use of **lighting**, **colour**, **sound** or **editing** draws attention to the illusionist nature of the reality effect. The whole purpose is to stitch the spectator into the illusion – keeping reality safe (see **suture**).

Conversely the realist aesthetic, first strongly advocated by French filmmakers in the 1930s and subsequently by André Bazin in the 1950s, is one that recognizes from the start that realist **discourses** not only suppress certain truths, they also produce others. In other words, realism produces realisms. And, although due caution must be exercised when making a realist film, this multiplicity of realisms means that a film cannot be fixed to mean what it shows – as occurs in seamless realism. The realist aesthetic recognizes the reality-effect produced by cinematic mediation and strives, therefore, to use film technique in such a way that, although it does not draw attention to itself, it nonetheless provides the **spectator** with space to read the text for herself or himself; in other words, technique functions in this instance so as not to provide an encoded preferred reading. Rather, it seeks to offer as objectively as possible a form of realism. So this type of realism uses location shooting and natural lighting. Most of its cast is composed of non-professional actors. It employs long **shots** using **deep focus** cinematography (to counter manipulation of the reading of the image), long takes (to prevent the controlling effects of editing practices) and the 90-degree horizontally angled shot which, because it is at eye level, stands as an objective shot.

After World War Two, the American public wanted a more realist view of the country, which it found in the spate of **films noir**. In Italy, economic necessity as much as a desire for a non-manipulative realism produced **Italian neo-realism**, which picked up on realist traditions already in place in French and Italian cinema of the 1930s. Indeed, Jean Renoir – one of the major advocates of a politically motivated **socio-realist** cinema – is credited with making the first film of this kind, *Toni* (1934). In the 1960s, France, for its part, pursued its interest in politically motivated realist films, albeit on a small scale, with the **cinéma-vérité** and **documentary** works of such filmmakers as Jean Rouch; North America with its **Direct Cinema**. Finally, from the late 1950s into the 1960s, New Wave cinemas emerged from Britain, France and Germany and provided the slice-of-life realist cinema (see **British New Wave**, **French New Wave**, **New German Cinema**).

see also: **documentary, naturalizing, social realism, suture**

For a full discussion of the debates around realism see Aitken, 2006; Armstrong, 2005; Hallam and Marshment, 2000; Hill, 1986; Lapsley and Westlake, 1988: 157–80; Nagib, 2011; Williams, 1980.

RECEPTION THEORY – *SEE* SPECTATOR

ROAD MOVIE

Road movies, as the term makes clear, are movies in which protagonists are on the move. Generally speaking, such a movie is **iconographically** marked through such things as a car, the tracking **shot**, wide and wild open spaces. In this respect, as a **genre** it has some similarities with the **Western**. The road movie is about a frontiersmanship of sorts given that one of its codes is discovery – usually self-discovery. The **codes and conventions** of a road movie have meant that until fairly recently this genre has predominantly been a **gendered** one as masculine. Generically speaking, the road movie goes from A to B in a finite and chronological time. Normally, the **narration** of a road movie follows an ordered sequence of events which lead inexorably to a good or bad end. Compare the bad ending for the travellers in *Easy Rider* (Dennis Hopper, 1969) or again the teen hoodlums on the run in *Badlands* (Terrence Malick, 1973) with the reasonable solution for the protagonist in *Paris, Texas* (Wim Wenders, 1984). Generically speaking, the traveller is male and the purpose of the trajectory is to obtain self-knowledge (even in old age: see *The Straight Story*, David Lynch, 1999). However, women have occasionally been portrayed as the travellers (as in *Thelma and Louise*, Ridley Scott, 1991) – and in this we can perceive a readiness to subvert or parody the genre. *The Adventures of Priscilla, Queen of the Desert* (Stephan Elliott, 1994) ironizes the macho-masculinity of the genre in a different way – this time a dancing troupe of drag-queens sets off across the Australian desert and all find fulfilment in one way or another. *Transamerica* (Duncan Tucker, 2005) gives an interesting transsexual twist to the road movie, with a happy ending, in the form of a father–son reconciliation, when Bee (a transsexual woman) goes on the road with her long-lost son.

see also: **genre**

For further reading see Cohan and Hark, 1997.

SCIENCE-FICTION FILMS

These are considered by some critics to be a sub-genre of the **horror** movie (see Cook, 1985: 99); by others as a **genre** distinct from horror films (see Kuhn and Radstone, 1990: 355); by others yet again as a sub-genre (along with horror movies) of **fantasy** films (Konigsberg, 1993: 303). These varied critical positions point to the difficulties in demarcating and categorizing genres in general and this one in particular. Interestingly, the French use all three categories, *fantastique*, *horreur* and *science fiction* to distinguish between films which other countries might be satisfied to lump under one label, namely horror. The genre's enduring popularity is surely underscored by the fact that from the 1990s to 2001, on average, some twenty sci-fi films were released yearly, but that, since 2002, on average some thirty sci-fi films are released yearly, most of which (66 per cent) are made in the USA. This figure shows how, post-9/11, sci-fi films are up by one-third which suggests a response to those calamitous events. This trend continues, albeit on a slightly diminished scale. The USA alone has produced some forty sci-fi films over the period 2013 to 2016, with a preponderance towards dystopian narratives (17 films), monster/alien/invading germ narratives (16 titles), but with a lesser drive towards space narratives (7).

Science fiction as a literary genre came about in the mid- to late nineteenth century in response to advances in science and technology. Two exemplary authors of the genre, Jules Verne and H. G. Wells, from opposing positions, described science's prowess in making possible what up until the turn of the century had seemed impossible (e.g. submarines and space craft). Film, insofar as it can make visible what is invisible, seems a natural medium for this kind of **narrative**. However, science-fiction films have been more erratic in their appearances on-screen than most other genres. For example, there were only a few produced during the silent era and it could be said, as a genre, it came into its own only after 1950 (for reasons that become clear below).

The earliest examples of science-fiction movies date back to Georges Méliès with his *films fantastiques* that portrayed voyages to the moon and to the centre of the earth (1902). These, however, were benign comic narratives of humans encountering a series of adventures with strange phenomena which nonetheless ended 'happily' – marked by a return to safety (i.e. the earth's surface). Apart from Méliès' work, which was very loosely based on Verne's writing, films in this genre have tended to be grounded more in the Wells-ian fear of science outstripping our understanding and taking us over. Science-fiction films produce a futuristic vision where we are no longer in control of what we have created (this curiously assumes that we currently do control science). This genre relies on the **audience**'s willingness to suspend disbelief and does so by playing on our fears of science. The few science-fiction films made before 1950 tended to focus on technology as the science-demon that would destroy humanity.

After 1950, the trend was for humanity to be at risk from alien intruders that either invaded the earth or caught up with humans in outer space in a spacecraft or on an alien planet (upon which the humans unquestioningly had the greater right to be, it would appear). It was not until this period that this genre or sub-genre became identified as a **Hollywood** genre. Up until then, apart from the *Flash Gordon* serials (1936–40), what little science-fiction had been produced in Western culture was of European origin – the most remarkable example being Fritz Lang's *Metropolis* (1926) with its futuristic city, and William Menzies' space fantasy *Things to Come* (1936, story and script by H. G. Wells). However, the 1950s was *the* period of the Cold War at its highest. 'Reds under the bed', McCarthyism and the House Un-American Activities Committee's witch-hunt of supposed communists, the threat of the nuclear deterrent (albeit only the Americans ever used it, in World War Two against Japan: Hiroshima and Nagasaki), the threat or fear of totalitarian regimes – all of these elements fed into the American political culture of the 1950s and found a steady reflection in contemporary film production. Aliens came in their droves from outer space onto the American screen (*Invaders from Mars*, *War of the Worlds*, *It Came from Outer Space*, all 1953 films, and *It Conquered the World*, 1956, etc.).

The American paranoia and neurosis at alien threats (real or imagined) was differently expressed in Britain during the 1960s – probably because, like the rest of Western Europe, the country found itself uneasily and weakly positioned between the two superpowers (USA and former USSR). The dominant fear in the British sci-fi context was the ability (to say nothing of the capacity) of these two giant nations' nuclear weapons of mass destruction to blow the world apart. The first of these films was Val Guest's *The Day the Earth Caught Fire* (1961) in which nuclear-bomb testing causes the earth to tilt on its axis and heat up. Kubrick's *Dr Strangelove: or, How I Learned to Stop Worrying and Love the Bomb* (1964) is of course better known and portrays the levels of insanity to which power (especially total power in the form of the bomb) can push leaders.

The next watershed year in Hollywood terms is 1968, producing two strands of science-fiction movies – the one slightly more optimistic than the other but where technology and aliens are far more ambitiously portrayed in terms of their threat to humankind. During this period of the less 'black-and-white' take on technology and aliens, issues of conscience were raised. We need to recall that the political mood in

Europe and the USA was one where authority was being challenged and questions being asked (e.g. about America's presence in Vietnam). In the European context – as part of these films of contestation – we could mention Tarkovsky's *Solaris*, 1972. But British-produced Kubrick's *2001: A Space Odyssey* most clearly posits the question of man's responsibility as the maker of the technology – as indeed Hal, the computer aboard the 2001 spaceship, reminds us. Although Hal is destroyed because of his severe, life-threatening malfunctioning, it is never resolved whether he is friend or foe. This ambiguity surrounding Hal is mirrored in the representation of the alien in science-fiction films of late 1970s and early 1980s (*The Man Who Fell to Earth*, Roeg, 1976; Spielberg's *Close Encounters of the Third Kind*, 1977 and *E.T.*, 1982). This type of alien is generally unthreatening (once you get to know 'him') and often offers us a lesson in humility before departing (presumably back to whence it came).

However, in terms of narrative, the above was not always the outcome. Films also revealed how intolerance, chauvinism and racism continued to reign. This is much of the tenor of the *Planet of the Apes* series, begun in the late 1960s to the early 1970s: mankind seems doomed, not because of technology so much, but because of his inability to embrace tolerance. In Schaffner's 1967 *Planet of the Apes*, astronauts crash onto what appears to be an unknown planet only to discover that they have crash-landed, back in time, into the world at a more primitive stage along the evolutionary scale – or maybe not, because it is mankind who is now subjected to laboratory experiments by the apes. In the sequel, Ted Post's *Beneath the Planet of the Apes* (1970), a tribe of human mutants (buried beneath a post-apocalypse New York) worship the atom bomb. Humankind fails to improve with knowledge it would appear. Later in the series, the apes become mankind's slaves – *Conquest of the Planet of the Apes* (Thompson, 1972) – and eventually they all slug it out in *Battle for the Planet of the Apes* (Thompson, 1973). Could it just be that it is the human who is the alien after all, living in his/her world? We had to wait for the *Matrix* series to get that answer! Before that, however, it was the turn of the *Star Wars* series which, beginning with the 1977 George Lucas film of that name, changed everything. Special effects, controlled by Lucas with his own Industrial Light and Magic (ILM) studios, set the bar very high and saw the birth of the first sci-fi **blockbuster**. But, sadly, technophilia failed to disguise a very passé indulgence in comic-book adventure-culture and a deep nostalgia for boys-own stuff and, with it, a return to a far more mysoginistic world-view. Bizarrely, with this nostalgic world-view slapped right in the midst of sci-fi imaginings, it is as if we have been returned to the past, and safe middle-America has been conjured back. And (without Lucas possibly knowing it) how prescient this title was of the next decade of middle-America values, sold to the population by President Reagan with his Reaganomics and his stock-piling of high-technology ballistic missiles in readiness for his own brand of Star Wars in which good (USA) would fight evil (the communist bloc).

The more open and critical mood of the early 1970s sci-fi movie had by now long passed and, by the late 1970s, rumblings of nastiness were about. So, by the time we get to Ridley Scott's *Alien*, made in 1979, technology, humans and aliens are now to be feared equally – nay, might even be present in one and the same thing as this film and its three *Alien* sequels (to date) make clear, although in a very specific way. For all its appearance of promoting woman, this *Alien* quadrology ultimately, in a backlash way, addresses the effects of feminism on patriarchy and male **sexuality**. Thus, rather than a political culture feeling under threat (as in the 1950s), it is now (White) male sexual culture that feels threatened. In *Alien*, men give birth to alien babies; by *Alien*³, the only remaining woman is implanted (artificially inseminated) with an alien egg – and kills herself to save humankind. Foolishly, as it transpires. By the time of *Alien Resurrection* (Jeunet, 1997), she is cloned back into life and made human just in time for the aliens to re-commence their dreaded attacks once more. Reproductive technology is here (cloning, artificial insemination). Man has made it, and as such threatens women's reproductive rights, to say nothing of organs. Although this is not the first series of science-fiction films to attract feminist critics to the genre, it sums up why this genre is of interest to them: because it shows the danger of science and technology, explores the underlying social anxieties regarding experiments in reproduction technology and the **ideological** effects of this genre which often construct female sexuality as monstrous (Kuhn and Radstone, 1990: 356). The *Alien* franchise is still rolling on, or should I say backwards, with its prequel *Prometheus* (Ridley Scott, 2012) – a 'who am I, who made me' narrative, 'embodied' in the form of the Android, David; and the sequel to this prequel *Alien: Covenant* (Ridley Scott, 2017) in which Android David is the sole inhabitant of a sinister planet upon which the crew of the spaceship alight ...

By the turn of the century and into the new millennium, sci-fi seems to be solidly embedded in the technics of fear: see, Steven Soderbergh's virus pandemic in *Contagion* (2011), or Christopher Nolan's **CGI** spectacular mind crime, unconscious heist, paranoia inflected sci-fi *Inception* (2010). We are now in an age of genetic engineering, ecological destruction, and formally labelled 'weapons of mass destruction'. We could argue that this climate of fear has been brought about not just by the bombing of the Twin Towers (9/11), but also by President George W. Bush's reaction to these events with both his rhetoric of 'axis of evil' and onslaught on Iraq with his desperate search for weapons of mass destruction that simply were nowhere to be found. How apt, therefore, that the sci-fi genre of the new millennium should produce movies about pre-crime, post-memory and the pre-world. Namely, all that is not quite there. Spielberg's *Minority Report* (2002), and the *Matrix* series come to mind. In some ways it is as if we are back to the paranoia of the 1950s – but then at least the threat to the West was the communist bloc of the East. It was a palpable, geographically located 'other' – even though 'they' could 'look just like us' (as so many US propaganda documentaries of the time declared). Now of course, the enemy is invisible, possibly even virtual. We see 'him' speak in video-recordings we take to be true, but we have no idea where he is, how many followers he has. He is known as the 'axis of evil' or Al-Qaeda or, since 2013, as Isis or Isil or Islamic terror group (and so on) — but none of these entities palpably exist (as an embodied enemy). They exist in name and mediatic terms only, an amorphous unknowable whole. Small surprise, therefore, if the Wachowski brothers' dystopian films *The Matrix* (1999) and its two sequels *The Matrix Reloaded* and *The Matrix Revolutions* (both 2003) are still relevant, speaking as they do to this virtual rhetoric of the current political climate in the West. This film has people imprisoned in a computer-generated world. The world that they perceive is a digitally created one piped into their brains. As if it were not enough to take over female reproductive organs and make man of man (i.e. from technology), now technology has taken over the mind as well! What a surprise: until we consider that the culture of fear that so dominated President Bush's America and which threatened to engulf Europe is, to all intents and purposes, in the world described and inscribed into *The Matrix*. The Matrix is an artificial intelligence that controls the world. But this Matrix is in fact a minotaur (a devourer of human flesh), for the citizens are converted into food and energy to power the Matrix itself. Thus, mankind is preserved, protected and endlessly re-cycled, digitally re-composed, by this mega-computer. But hold on a minute. If we look in the dictionary we learn that matrix presently means a mould for casting type – in other words, it is the original first mould from which stereotypes can be reproduced at will and in any number. We learn, also, that its original (but now obsolete) meaning is the womb, the space of breeding. How clever man is. Since he fears his own obsolescence (as evidenced in the Bush rhetoric about ridding the world of the axis of evil), but cannot see his enemy, what better thing to do than, first, have complete control of the man-making machine and guarantee to have the numbers of bodies to survive all eventualities; and, second, to render the female – womb and all – obsolete because she cannot possibly be counted upon to reproduce at the speed and with the efficiency necessary (she might also refuse!). *The Matrix* and its sequels make a strong statement to the effect that we are the food that megalomaniacs feed *on* and *off* for their own power (World War One was, as we know, a classic and real example).

But, what is also interesting here is how little the mistrust of the female has shifted over time. What, in the final analysis, separates the projection of female barrenness (intellectual and sexual) through the evil robot Maria in *Metropolis* from the drive to rid the world of the need for the womb as exemplified by *The Matrix* and many other films that precede it? We could cite the numerous cross-genetic nasties and womb fantasies made by David Cronenberg (*The Brood*, 1979; *The Fly*, 1986; *Dead Ringers*, 1988) amongst just so many others that wish eternally for the womb to remain absent (*Jurassic Park*, Spielberg, 1993; *Mary Shelley's Frankenstein*, Branagh, 1994). Curiously, too, we have come back to robots – but this time to 'boy' robots (and not just the 'boy' robot Schwartzenegger of the *Terminator* series). We have the boy robot of Spielberg's *A.I.* (2001) who rivals the real boy for the love of his mother. And guess what? For a while he wins. What do we make of a mother who bonds with the robot-child while her own son is temporarily put on ice (literally in the hope that a cure can be found for his congenital disease)? Here the robot exposes just how untrustworthy a mother can be.

This rather makes the point that science fiction is about a projection of man's (*sic*) worst fears in relation to science and the future it holds for us. But, it is also of course about man's fear of his own death – hence the drive to supplant the womb and create life himself (or lifelike robots). The fear is, too, that we cannot control that technology intrinsically for what it is (even as we conveniently forget that we forged it); just as much as we fear those who believe they do have control over that technology (heads of state, scientists); for we do not necessarily perceive them as being the wisest people to have that control. In reality, then, sci-fi is often the expression of a deep malaise we feel about the present, but which we disguise as some sort of future-imperfect or hide under the wrappings of a futuristic imaginary moment or world. And, of course, the way in which we can be made to feel better about this malaise is through the destruction of that futuristic world – whatever its shape (hence the horror felt by

Charlton Heston, at the end of *Planet of the Apes*, when he realizes that the world he thought was alien was in fact his own, his sci-fi trajectory has not brought him relief, quite the opposite).

The science-fiction film, then, is politically **motivated**, but for the most part not in a challenging sense. In general, the genre functions to assert the status quo (destroying the enemy, getting home to safety, etc.). Its ideological effects are mostly (albeit not exclusively) **hegemonic**. Yet, technology *should* be questioned and our attitudes towards outsiders *should* come under scrutiny. But, this is rare, as a quick gloss over the three main categories of films will show. The three types within this genre are: space-flight, alien invaders, futuristic societies. Lang's *Metropolis* is *the* prototype of this last category. But it also set the agenda for a critique of futuristic urban spaces by challenging the 1920s **modernist** belief in technological progress as a source of social change – a challenge still apparent in Jean-Luc Godard's *Alphaville* (1965), Ridley Scott's *Blade Runner* (1982), Luc Besson's *The Fifth Element* (1997), and Alfonso Cuarón's *Children of Men* (2006) – these last two raising ecology issues (see Brereton, 2005). Space-flight films, however, have traditionally devoted more energy to exposing the virtuosities of film technology and as such have functioned as a vehicle for prowess (in real terms for the film industry, and metaphorically for the space industry). Even if there are technological glitches (or indeed man-made mistakes), nonetheless man's ingenuity can overcome them, *The Martian* (Ridley Scott, 2015) being a recent example. Only a handful of space odyssey films truly question man's faith *in* and his assumed superiority *over* technology – Stanley Kubrick's *2001: A Space Odyssey* (1968) is a rare example. Finally, alien invader films (which includes genetic mis-manipulations, viral attacks and infections; see Stacey, 2010), because they are probably the most prolific of the three categories (Nirmod Antal's *Predators*, 2010, being a fairly recent example) and, arguably, the most conservative – in that they point at otherness as threatening to life and/or social mores – represent the most 'worrying' category of all, with their innate potential for misogyny, racism and nationalistic chauvinism (see Cornea, 2007; Nama, 2008).

see also: **genre**

For further reading see Brereton, 2005; Brosnan, 1991; Bukatman, 1993; Cornea, 2007; Featherstone and Burrows, 1995; Hardy *et al.*, 1986; Jancovich, 1996; Johnston, 2011; King and Krzywinska, 2000; Kuhn, 1990, 1999; Nama, 2008; Parrinder, 2001; Rickman, 2004; Sobchack, 1993; Stacey, 2010; Telotte, 1999.

SCOPOPHILIA/SCOPIC DRIVE/VISUAL PLEASURE

Literally, the desire to see. Freud used the term *scopic drive* to refer to the infant's libidinal drive to pleasurable viewing. As such, it is closely attached to the mirror phase and the primal scene. In Lacanian **psychoanalysis**, the **mirror phase** refers to the moment of recognition by the male child of his difference from his mother. And the primal scene, first identified by Freud, refers to the moment when the male child, unseen by his parents, views them copulating. In psychoanalytic film theory (in the 1970s), scopophila was adapted to elucidate the unconscious processes at work when the **spectator** views the screen (see **apparatus**). This spectator–screen analysis revealed that a double phenomenon occurs: first, cinema constructs the spectator as **subject** (the beholder of the **gaze** – that is, at the moment of the mirror phase); second, it establishes the desire to look (the drive to pleasurable viewing – that is, at the moment of the primal scene). Thus, as Metz (1975) stated, at each film viewing there occurs a re-enactment of the unconscious processes involved in the acquisition of sexual difference and, simultaneously, a **voyeuristic** positioning of the spectator (the viewer watches unseen in a darkened room or theatre).

At this juncture (early 1970s), the implications of scopophilia for masculine erotic desire and the male **fetishizing** gaze were never brought into question. This would not occur until the mid-1970s, when the issue of **gendered** spectatorship finally became addressed, first, by Laura Mulvey (1975), then by other feminist critics. They developed a theory of the gaze to show how pleasure is derived from the gaze that is normatively male. They argue that the scopophilic drive is constructed as masculine as an effect of the three dominant points of view implicit within the camera apparatus and its function. First, the camera pointing at the scene is (almost exclusively) operated by a male. Second, the relay of looks within the **mise-en-scène** predominantly favour the male character (who derives pleasure from gazing at the female). Finally, because the camera's eye and the character's gaze within the film are gendered a male, so too is the spectator's. This gaze fixes the woman and in so doing fetishizes her, makes her the object not subject of desire. It fixes her, attributes meanings to her that are derived from another (male) perception or reading of the female bodily text. To this effect the woman has no **agency**.

Cinema functions through its **codes** to construct the way in which woman is to be looked at. This normally starts with the male point of view within the film. The source of pleasure offered by that point of view to the male spectator (through identification) is clear. What, however, Mulvey asks, of the female spectator? Mulvey argues that for her to derive pleasure she must adopt the masculine point of view. Later feminist critics (Doane, 1982) nuance this masculinization of the female spectator, arguing that there are two viewing places: that of the female masochist identifying with the passive female character and that of the transvestite identifying with the active male protagonist or hero. Later still, Bergstrom (1985), Studlar (1985) and Modleski (1988) propose positioning the female spectator bisexually (see **psycho-analysis and the female subject**). In this position, she can identify with the female character's predicament caught within socio-economic and sexual structures that make her 'victim'. But, this identification can then lead to a regendered position that allows for a critique of such structures to take place.

see also: **gaze**

For further discussion see **apparatus, feminist film theory, spectator, suture**.

SEAMLESSNESS – *SEE UNDER* EDITING

SEMIOLOGY/SEMIOTICS/SIGN AND SIGNIFICATION

Semiology was a term coined by the Swiss linguistician Ferdinand de Saussure, in his lecture series on structural linguistics (1907–11), to refer to the study of signs within society; which he believed should be possible thanks to the application of structural linguistics to any sign system. *Semiotics*, coined a little earlier by the American philosopher C. S. Peirce, also refers to the study of signs. However, in general theoretical practice, the term *semiotics* refers more to Saussure's theories than to Peirce's. And since Saussure's theories have had the greater impact, to date, in film theory, we will limit this discussion to his (those interested in the adoption of Peirce's theories should see Wollen, 1972).

Saussure's structural linguistic theories, which were to remain 'unknown' until Roland Barthes brought them into the limelight in the late 1950s (in his book *Mythologies*, 1957), gave birth to a new theoretical system known as **structuralism**. In his *Cours de linguistique générale* (1915), Saussure set out the base paradigm by which all language could be ordered and understood. The base paradigm, *langue/parole*, was intended as a function that could simultaneously address the profound universal structures of language (*langue*) and its manifestation in different cultures, **discourse**/speech (*parole*). Saussure made the vital point that the governing conventions in relation to this sign system are very arbitrary and that there is no necessary correlation between the word (the signifier) and the object or idea being designated (the signified). This arbitrariness is manifest in the differences between languages. It is also this arbitrary relationship between signifier and signified which makes it possible for this linguistic system to function as a general science of signs – meaning that it can address other sign systems, can examine other sign systems as operating like a language. Just to clarify the meaning here: semiotics, in that it studies the social production of meaning through linguistic sign systems, stresses that language as a cultural production is societally not individually bound. Given that there are social or cultural productions *other than language* which produce meanings (e.g. sport, games), that is there are other sign systems, semiotics became a useful tool with which to analyse the process of meaning production in such sign systems as literature, cinema, television and advertising and, ultimately other forms of popular culture (pop songs, dress-codes and so on). Barthes (1957) used semiotics to examine popular cultural artefacts of the 1950s and the language of mass culture – a decade later or so, it entered into film studies.

To explain: Barthes developed Saussure's concept of signification (how signs produce meaning) in his analysis of the way signs work in culture. Within what he terms the semiological system, Barthes identified two orders of signification, **denotation and connotation**, which in turn produce a third – **ideology**. At the first level is denotation: a simple first order of meaning, the surface literal meaning. At the second level, signs operate in two ways: as connotative agents and as mythmakers. This second order of signification occurs when the first order meets the values and **discourses** of the culture (Hartley, 1982: 215). Connotation, as the word implies, means all the associative and eva-luative meanings attributed to the sign by the culture or the person involved in using it – and as such is always sensitive to context. **Myth** is the way in which we are enabled to understand the culture in which we find ourselves. At this connotative level of signification, signs activate myths, provide cultural meaning.

By way of illustration let us take a photograph of Marilyn Monroe. At the denotative level this is a photograph of the movie **star** Marilyn Monroe. At a connotative level we associate this photograph with Marilyn Monroe's star qualities of glamour, **sexuality**, beauty – if this is an early photograph – but also with her depression, drug-taking and untimely death if it is one of her last photographs. At a mythic level we understand this sign as activating the myth of **Hollywood**: the dream factory that produces glamour in the form of the stars it

343

constructs, but also the dream machine that can crush them – all with a view to profit and expediency.

This second order of signification reflects subjective responses, but ones which can only be motivated by the fact that they are shared by the community of a particular culture. This shared **subjectivity** works in two ways and it is in this respect that we can see the third order of signification coming into operation: ideology. This shared subjectivity is culturally determined (Fiske and Hartley, 1978: 46). Thus, on the one hand, our individual response is affected or influenced by the culture in which we find ourselves and, on the other, that response signifies our appertaining to that culture. This dynamic is a prime way in which ideology functions. Ideology inserts itself at the interface between language and political organization and as such is the discourse that invests a culture (a nation) with meaning. In other words, ideology comes to have meaning by subjects colluding with it and by acting according to it because of the reassuring nature of national identity or cultural membership.

To return to our earlier example, the photograph of Marilyn Monroe and its ideological function, the reading we now get is as follows: the film industry as exemplified by Hollywood is a powerful, rich, organized industry, in which one can succeed only by conforming to the pre-ordained role assigned to one. Deviancy (booze, drugs or sexuality) will not be tolerated. In other words, Hollywood is about reproducing the institution, culture or ideology of the White middle-class United States to which all should aspire, or, if they do not, they will perish.

Semiotics in film theory, then, by opening up filmic texts in the way illustrated above, showing how they produce meaning, has served among other things to uncover, make explicit, the **naturalization** process of **realist**, **mainstream cinema**. Latterly, as it became inflected with other theories (**psychoanalysis**, Marxism, feminism) it has broadened its frame of reference, not just to address the filmic text as producer of meaning, but also to examine **spectator**-positioning and the spectator's role in meaning-production. By unravelling how meaning is produced, other questions can be raised, such as the way in which the inscription of sexual difference in the images is 'taken for granted', or how certain ethnic groups are represented or not, and so on. Key, in semiology/semiotics, is 'what do the signs mean?'

see also: **structuralism**

For fuller analyses and greater examination of the evolution of the semiotic debate see Andrew, 1984; Lapsley and Westlake, 1988; Stam, 2000; Stam *et al.*,

1992. In terms of applying the theory see Fiske and Hartley, 1978 (although it addresses television and not film, it is a very clear text for initiates to semiotics); for analyses of representation and sexuality see De Lauretis, 1984; Kuhn, 1985.

SEQUENCE/SEQUENCING

A sequence is normally composed of scenes, all relating to the same logical unit of meaning. For this reason, the length of a sequence is equivalent to the visual and/or **narrative** continuity of an episode within a film. It is useful when studying film to be able to segment out a film into sequences, since this gives the student or **spectator** a sense of the formal structure of the film as well as the relations between the sequences. Since film is (notionally) constructed around the formula of repetition/opposition/variation, to be able to perceive this structurally gives a first reading to the filmic text. On average a ninety-minute film has twenty-three or twenty-four sequences if it is a **mainstream** or **Hollywood** film; European cinema tends towards a lower number (eleven to eighteen). Traditionally, the opening sequence of a film is composed of establishing **shots** to orientate the spectator safely and, in this respect, the beginning of each sequence functions to re-orientate the spectator (alternatively, the last shot or comment in the previous sequence sets up what is to follow). The closing of a sequence is marked by some form of transition: a **fade**, **wipe**, iris or a **cut**. (In an iris the image is phased in or out in imitation of the opening and shutting of the camera lens.) These transitions serve to make the film easy to read, as opposed to **jump cuts** or **unmatched shots** which are two procedures used to counter the safe orientation provided by traditional transition markers. Traditional transitions are like punctuation marks, so they will also be found within sequences. The fade and iris are soft transitions. Wipes and cuts are hard. The former are more readily associated with earlier cinema, although contemporary films do make use of them (sometimes as a homage to the cinema heritage). These soft transition markers can serve to denote a lapse in time, states of mind and the subconscious, so they are less likely to be found within a sequence but rather between sequences. Of the hard transitions, the wipe is hardly ever seen nowadays. Cuts are the most used of all transitions. A cut between sequences can imply a direct link between the two, in either narrative or chronology. Cuts within a sequence serve to give a rhythm (fast or slow, depending on how frequently they are used) and also allow relations of space to become clear to the spectator (so long as the various degree rules are obeyed: see **30-degree rule** and **180-degree rule**). If cuts are not used conventionally within a sequence, they point to the idea of fragmentation or separation.

see also: **editing/Soviet montage**

For more detail on how sequencing functions throughout a film, see **editing**.

SETTING

Part of the total concept of **mise-en-scène**, the setting is literally the location where the action takes place, and it can be artificially constructed (as in studio sets) or natural (what is also termed location shooting). Certain film movements are readily associated with a type of setting: the distorted settings of **German expressionist** films, the dimly lit rain-washed streets and empty cold interiors in **films noir**, the natural settings of Italy's cities and countryside in **Italian neo-realism** films.

SEXUALITY

Cinema is one structure among others that constructs sexuality. Until the impact of **feminist theory** (1970s) this was normally taken to mean White male sexuality. This sexuality was constructed as hetero-normative and active as opposed (in the first instance) to White female passivity. That is, women were perceived or constructed as sex symbols, sex goddesses (objects to be desired, rather than desiring **subjects**). Equally, sexuality was normally taken to refer to heterosexuality and, although this pattern still dominates, a few gaps have opened for representations of otherness (albeit limited). Clearly, sexuality and **gender**, generally speaking, are strongly coded by film **genre**. For example, the sexuality of characters in a **musical** differs from that of characters in a **Western**. At the very least, the hero of the musical is looking to settle down and marry. His sexually desiring body-action is, meantime, displaced into song and dance routines – in duets of course(!). The hero of the Western, however, will satisfy himself with a brief affair and then move on – much of his sexually desiring body-action getting displaced into shootin'-n-fightin'. Needless to say, it is when the coding seems to slip that it becomes really interesting (see *Brokeback Mountain*, Ang Lee, 2005).

Debate around sexuality in film studies came about largely as a result of feminist theorizing on structures which position or construct woman as other in patriarchal society (see **scopophilia** and **psycho-analysis**). Claire Johnston (1976: 209) makes the point that while the earliest stereotyping of woman in the cinema (as vamp or virgin) has changed very little, the image of man has been privileged with greater differentiation. Early silent cinema required fixed **iconography** for audiences to follow the **narrative**, so characters were stereotyped (villain, hero, etc. for men; fallen woman, victim, etc. for women). But, once cinema **codes** became familiar, it was felt that this stereo-typing of the male contravened the notion of character and should be opened up to a broader more complex characterization (ibid.). In this respect, Johnston argues, **Hollywood**'s conventions around sexuality reflect dominant (by which she means patriarchal) **ideology** that ste-reotypes men as active and therefore part of history and women as passive and therefore 'ahistoric and eternal' (ibid.). Thus, within **main-stream cinema**, especially, but not exclusively, stereotyping is not questioned. Masculinity and femininity as constructs were 'taken for granted' and their representation was not questioned – that is, until the 1970s.

Annette Kuhn (1985: 5) acknowledges the usefulness of two French philosophers' thinking on representation: Barthes' (1957) **semiotic** and **structuralist** readings of specific images, and Althusser's (1984) work on ideology (the way it functions to position the subject). However, she also points to their 'gender-blindness', to which we should add colour-blindness. The feminist and Black movements and cultural studies debates of the 1970s and 1980s, as well as the incor-poration of **psychoanalysis** into theory in general and film studies in particular, have meant that the issue of sexuality has broadened from its somewhat narrow (White) male/female binary opposition. Discussions around **spectatorship**, which is not a single entity but composed of so many different types (male, female, Black, Asian, White, lesbian, gay and so on) and **classes**, have elucidated the limitations of this binary con-struct because pleasure in viewing can be derived without reference to this binary paradigm's implicit White heterosexuality. This means that representation is not limited to a reproduction of the patriarchal order – it does that but it does more. It reproduces the dominant ideology but it also reflects those who are inside and those who are outside the culture or **hegemony** as well as the shifting relationships, depending on how close to the centre of the culture they are. For example, in mainstream Hollywood and Western cinema, the White female has more power than the Black female; and, generally speaking, she has more power than the Black male in terms of the **gaze** (imagine the threat that loss of the gaze could pose to White hetero-normativity).

The following comments should serve by way of illustration of how the binary opposition paradigm functions in relation to sexuality within **classical narrative cinema**. Clearly the central positioning of the White male as the site of truth and the natural assumption (or acceptance) of the predominance of the male point of view mean that any other **subjectivity** is occluded. Therefore, White masculinity can be defined as more than just 'his sex'; femininity much less so – and if it is (i.e. more than just her sex), it is usually transgressive or excessive. Woman becomes other or object to the male's subject – she is defined in relation to his centrality, his point of view. As such, she is fixed as an object of his desire, but an object whose sexuality is also perceived by him as dangerous – and therefore to be punished or contained (through death – or its equivalent – or marriage, respectively).

From these early discussions of sexuality and power, the debate on sexuality by the 1990s had evolved and come to be closely identified with gender (including cross-genderization and/or sexual disguise), the representation of sex and desire (heterosexuality, homosexuality lesbianism, transvestism, transsexualism), including its referent (male, female, class, race, age, cross-dressing), the historical and social contexts, and the relationship of the spectator to that representation. This does not mean, however, that there have been great sea-changes in terms of representation in mainstream cinema. The notion of fixity mentioned above also applies to others whose subjectivity is denied by the dominant practice of centring the White male. **Queer** sexuality is one – gays and lesbians on the whole have a hard time being seen or given a space in which to be understood. In this context, the Spanish filmmaker Pedro Almodovar's work (beginning with *Law of Desire*, 1987) has made huge strides for queer sexuality. Black sexuality is another key victim of this foregrounding of the White male sexual imperative. We see very few Black couples, let alone inter-racial ones. Presently, the Black female has no major role in Western mainstream cinema and the Black male, although more readily present (especially since the late 1990s), can hardly be said to be on-screen in a widespread way.

In many mainstream film narratives, racial difference, especially in the person of the Black male, is linked with heightened sexuality and thereby connected to sexual danger, not just for the White female but also for the White male. He is perceived as other, as an object of fascination (with colour or potency), but also of danger. Oddly, however, he is positioned much like the White woman and as such must be contained or punished. The origins of this **fetishization** of the Black male are not, however, the same as those surrounding the White female. They are fixed, first, in colonizing history and then in slave history – what Jane Gaines (1988) refers to as 'racial patriarchy' – a different order of otherness. And it is in relation to those histories that the Black male is punished or contained. Thus, mainstream cinema constructs Black male sexuality against a different set of histories from that of the White male. But these histories are those emanating from White hegemony – the White version of colonial and slave histories. So the Black male is doubly fixed: as other by the White male gaze and as 'less' by White male history. This ideological construct is exemplified by the film industry which, in its **mise-en-scène** of male blackness, pulls on those histories to construct him. D. W. Griffith's *Birth of a Nation* (1915) is the very first film to do this, but Steven Spielberg's *The Color Purple* (1986) also pulls on the **myth** of the bestiality of the lustful Black man. Equally, Sidney Poitier's films of the 1950s and 1960s, which although they address blackness in an 'enlightened' manner, are problematic, nonetheless. It could be argued that Poitier's image of urbane civility does less to counter images of Black male sexual potency and more to point to the civilizing process of American education (read: 'he (Black Sidney Poitier) can be "just like us"'). Nor has that kind of containment disappeared. The depiction of Blacks playing by White rules and losing still persists (e.g. the Eddie Murphy films; *A Soldier's Story*, Norman Jewison, 1984). It is true that certain, more **auteur**-based filmmakers, have provided Black actors with stronger more complex roles and a current star who stands out in this regard is Denzel Washington (from *Philadelphia*, 1993, to *The Manchurian Candidate*, 2004 – both by Jonathan Demme). Furthermore, this mythification and reification of blackness has, since the 1990s, begun to be challenged and countered by **Black cinema** (in the US and the UK). It is the case, though, that the representation of the Black woman and her sexuality has still a long way to *start*! Currently, within the West, it remains fairly stereotyped – if it is present at all. Very few contestatory voices are creeping in. Interestingly, although not that of Black women, there is now a cinema, coming from North Africa, which presents challenging questions about female sexual identity within a very male-dominated Arab world (see Martin, 2011). The Arab female gets to speak of herself in films such as Yamina Benguigui's *Inch'allah dimanche/ Long Live Sunday* (2001), Moufida Tlatli's *Les Silence du palais/Silences of the Palace* (1994) and *La Saison des hommes/The Season of Men* (1999).

Since the late 1990s, within the European context (in terms of production) there have been some challenging insights into White female sexuality within more mainstream cinema. Some have been more positive than others it has to be said. Woman's need for sex, to feel alive, subject matter of Patrice Chéreau's *Intimacy* (2000). While his film foregrounds sex in a graphic and detailed manner (with thirty-five minutes of explicit sex), it is the erotic value of this sex for the woman that we are made aware of in particular (even though in the original text by Hanif Kureshi the focus is far more on the male's mid-life crisis). Catherine Breillat's *Romance* (1999) and *À ma soeur* (2001) expose the traps of conventional heterosexual sexuality and femininity. Brutal though their encounters with sex are, her female protagonists refuse to be victims. Sadly, the same cannot be said for Jane Campion's exploration of female masochism in *In the Cut* (2003, based in New York, but UK/New Zealand produced). And, finally female sado-masochism gets an unhealthy airing in Virginie Depsentes and Coralie Trinh Thi's rape-revenge film *Baise-moi* (2000). Whatever we might feel about these films, they are more than sexploitation, because they open up, more widely than ever before, the concept of the complexity of White female sexuality and **fantasy**. Certain ideological constructs – such as those discussed at the beginning of this entry (wherein female sexuality was overridden in favour of male sexuality) – should now no longer be possible, removed as they so obviously are from the truth of the matter. However, Hollywood regularly persists with fixity. And, if we despair of how long it will take mainstream cinema to give fuller representation to women, imagine how much longer still it is going to take for women of colour. And what of mixed-race relationships? How little we ever see of them. And, finally, what of the representation of still other sexualities that are as yet singularly unvoiced?

see also: **queer**

For further reading see Benshoff and Griffin, 2009; Dyer, 1986; Grosz and Probyn, 1995; Kuhn, 1985; Manatu, 2003; Mellen, 1974; *Screen*, 1988, 1992.

SHOT/REVERSE-ANGLE SHOT

Also known as shot/counter-shot, this is most commonly used for dialogue. Two alternating shots, generally in medium close-up, frame in turn the two speakers. Normally these shots are taken from the point of view of the person listening – as the diagram below should make clear.

In the clearest instances, the shoulder and profile of the listener are just distinguishable in the foreground of the frame and the camera is focused on the face of the speaker. But the **spectator** can assume the presence of both interlocutors even if the listener is not foregrounded because of the series of reverse angles. This type of shot follows visual logic (character A is framed as s/he speaks – cut to character B framed as s/he speaks).

Alternatively, but less usually, the camera can frame the listener (particularly if s/he is under threat). In these two types of reverse-angle shots the position of the spectator shifts. In the first type, the spectator becomes the privileged viewer of the image insofar as the shot permits identification with the position of the listener (the spectator assumes the position of the one being talked to). In the second, the spectator can be far more ambiguously positioned since s/he assumes the position of the speaker and, in this respect, has more power than is possible (after all, the spectator cannot actually speak into the film). The result can be to make the spectator aware of the collusionary role s/he plays as voyeur of the image. This creates a **distancing** effect (see **scopophilia**).

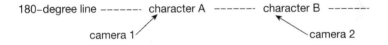

see also: **180-degree rule**, **suture**

SHOTS

There are basically seven types of shots: extreme close-up, close-up, medium close-up, medium shot, medium long shot, long shot, extreme long shot or distance shot. In addition the terms *one-*, *two-* and *three-shots* are used to describe shots framing one, two or three people – usually in medium close-ups or medium shots.

Close-up/extreme close-up (*CU/ECU*) The subject framed by the camera fills the screen. Connotations can be of intimacy, of having access to the mind or thought processes (including the subconscious) of the character. These shots can be used to stress the importance of a particular character at a particular moment in a film or place her or him as central to the **narrative** by singling out the character in CU at the beginning of the film. It can signify the **star** exclusively (as in many **Hollywood** productions of the 1930s and 1940s). CUs often have a symbolic value. For example, the CU of a character looking at their reflection in a mirror or in the water can have connotations of duplicity (what we see is not true) or death (as in the dream or **myth** of Narcissus). CUs can be used on objects and on parts of the body other than the face. In this instance, they can designate imminent action (a hand picking up a knife, for example) and thereby create suspense. Or they can signify that an object will have an important role to play in the development of the narrative. Often these shots have a symbolic value, usually due to their recurrence during the film. How and where they recur is revealing not only of their importance but also of the direction or meaning of the narrative.

Medium close-up (*MCU*) Close-up of one or two (sometimes three) characters, generally framing the shoulders or chest and the head. The term can also be used when the camera frames the characters from the waist up (or down), provided the character is right to the forefront and fills the frame (otherwise this type of shot is a medium shot). An MCU of two or three characters can indicate a coming together, an intimacy, a certain solidarity. Conversely, if there are a series of two and one shots, these MCUs would suggest a complicity between two people against a third who is visually separate in another shot.

Medium shot (*MS*) Generally speaking, this shot frames a character from the waist, hips or knees up (or down). The camera is sufficiently distanced from the body for the character to be seen in relation to their surroundings (in an apartment for example). Typically, characters will occupy half to two-thirds of the frame. This shot is very commonly used in indoor sequences allowing for a visual signification of relationships between characters. Compare a two-shot MS and a series of separate one shots in MS of two people. The former suggests intimacy, the latter distance. The former shot could change in meaning to one of distance, however, if the two characters were separated by an object (a pillar, a table, even a telephone, for example).

Visually, this shot is more complex, more open in terms of its readability than the preceding ones. The characters can be observed in relation to different planes, background, middle ground and foreground, and it is the interrelatedness of these planes that also serves to produce a meaning.

Medium long shot (*MLS*) Halfway between a long and a medium shot. If this shot frames a character then the whole body will be in view towards the middle ground of the shot. A quite open shot in terms of readability, showing considerably more of the surroundings in relation to the character(s).

Long shot (*LS*) Subject or characters are at some distance from the camera; they are seen in full in their surrounding environment.

Extreme long shot (*ELS*) The subject or characters are very much to the background of the shot. Surroundings now have as much if not more importance, especially if the shot is in high angle.

A first way to consider these shots is to say that a shot lends itself to a greater or lesser readability dependent on its type or length. As the camera moves further away from the main subject (whether person or object), the visual field lends itself to an increasingly more complex reading – in terms of the relationship between the main subject and the décor there is more for the **spectator**'s eye to read or decode. This means that the closer up the shot, the more the spectator's eye is directed by the camera to a specified reading. André Bazin (1967: 23ff.), in his discussion of **depth of field**, greatly favoured what he termed the objective **realism** of the **deep focus** shot – generally found in a MLS or LS. Shots, therefore, in and of themselves have a subjective or objective value: the closer the shot, the more subjective its value, the more the meaning is inscribed from within the shot; conversely, the longer the distance of the shot, the more objective its value, the greater the participation of the spectator in the inscription of meaning. To avoid confusion with terms such as *subjective camera* it is better to think and speak of shots as being more or less open (MS to ELS) or closed (MCU to ECU) to a reading. Other factors influence the readability of a shot – primarily the angle of a shot. A high or low camera angle can denaturalize a shot or reinforce its symbolic value. Take, for example, an ELS that is shot at a high angle. This automatically suggests the presence of someone looking; thus, the shot is implicitly a point-of-view shot. In this way, some of the objective value or openness of that shot (which it would retain if angled horizontally at 90 degrees) is taken away, the shot is no longer 'naturally' objective. The shot is still open to a greater reading than a CU however; although the angle imposes a **preferred reading** (someone is looking down from on high). In terms of illustrating what is meant by reinforcing symbolic value, the contrastive examples of a low- and high-angle CU can serve here. The former type of shot will distort the object within the frame, rendering it uglier, more menacing, more derisory; conversely, when a high-angle CU is used, the object can appear more vulnerable, desirable.

These are of course preferred readings or readings that adhere to the **codes and conventions** of traditional cinema. Filmmakers do not necessarily abide by these rules however. And it is in their 'breaking', bending or subverting of cinematic rules regarding filmmaking in general (shots, **editing**, **soundtrack**, etc.) that their films can be said to have their individual hallmarks.

see also: **match cut (cut)**, **jump cuts**, **shot/reverse-angle shot**, **unmatched shots**

353

SOCIAL REALISM

Although it is argued that the advent of **sound**, in 1927, brought about a greater realism in film, the realist tradition was in evidence in cinema's earliest productions, as, for example, in France whose cinematic practices were very much inflected by literary adaptations, especially those of the socio-realist novelist Emile Zola. Social realism in film refers, as it does in literature, to a depiction of social and economic circumstances within which particular echelons of society (usually the working and middle **classes**) find themselves. The earliest examples of this tradition in sound cinema, however, date back to 1930s Britain and John Grierson. It is his work in **documentary** that is generally credited with the introduction of the social-realist aesthetic into **narrative** cinema. Grierson, who was primarily a **producer** and theorist, held that documentary should be in the service of education and propaganda for the greater social good – with an insistence on quality and good taste. Grierson surrounded himself with a group of like-minded filmmakers and organized a loosely formed documentary movement that was to impact on several film movements after World War Two. There were three basic principles to which the group adhered. First, cinema should be taking slice-of-life-reality rather than artificially constructing it. Second, everyday ordinary people should act themselves in real **settings**. Finally, cinema should strive to catch the spontaneous or authentic gesture and uncontrived or natural speech (see Armes, 1974).

Although there are examples, during the 1930s, of individual films that exemplify these principles (such as Jean Renoir's *Toni*, 1934; Carol Reed's *The Stars Look Down*, 1939), it was after the war that actual socio-realist film movements could be discerned. There are three movements in cinema's history that in some way are indebted to this social-realist aesthetic – all of which produced what have been termed social-problem films. First, the **Italian neo-realism** movement of the late 1940s; then, the **Free Cinema Britain** and the **British New Wave** of the late 1950s; and, finally, the loosely formed **cinéma-vérité** group in France during the 1960s. In the UK, filmmakers Stephen Frears, Mike Leigh and Ken Loach have, since the 1980s at least, been most readily associated with this tradition of social realism. Although Lynne Ramsey's work (e.g. *The Ratcatcher*, 1999), as well as that of Pawel Pawlikowski (*Last Resort*, 2000) and Andrea Arnold (*Fish Tank*, 2010), also follow in that tradition.

For further reading see Aitken, 2006; Hallam and Marshment, 2000; Hill, 1986; Lay, 2002.

SOUND/SOUNDTRACK

Before the soundtrack was introduced to cinema **audiences** in 1927, film was accompanied by a musical score played by an orchestra or an organist or pianist (depending on the luxury and means of the cinema theatre; see entry on **music**). Although sound on film dates from 1927, the technology for putting it in place pre-dates the 1920s by at least a decade if not more (depending on which film historian you read). At that time there was no sense of urgency to go to the costly lengths of implementing a sound system, since cinema was proving sufficiently profitable in its silent mode. However, France, Germany and the United States had been competing, almost since the beginnings of the film industry, to synchronize sound and image. The first breakthrough occurred in 1911, when the Frenchman Eugène Lauste, working for the American Edison, demonstrated the first sound-on-film movie. This particular system was greatly improved, in 1918, by German technicians. Systems of sound on disc, synchronized to film, Phonofilm and Vitaphone, were but the latest perfections in the mid-1920s of work started in 1900. Gaumont had been working on a series of processes of synchronized sound since 1902, only to perfect it by 1928. And so on. In the end, however, it would be the American Western Electric and the German Tobis-Klangfilm that, between them, carved up the sound market.

The moment in sound is Alan Crosland's *The Jazz Singer* (starring Al Jolson) produced by Warner Brothers in 1927. Competition and economic exigencies represent a first reason for the launch of sound at this time. Warner Brothers was desperately seeking a way to enter into stronger competition with the then four majors (see **studio system**). The launching of this film shot Warner into the status of a major. In terms of economies of scale, US **audiences** were dropping – because of the impact of the radio and access to other leisure activities – at the very moment that the film industry had invested massively in luxury grand film theatres. Sound was intended to attract the **spectator** back. Sound also made possible a bringing together, into one unit, elements of vaudeville with filmed images which had previously been two disparate entertainment forms in silent cinema spectacles. In the case of **Hollywood**, this produced a new **genre** – the **musical**. However, it also put an end to other generic types, such as the gestural, slapstick **comedy** associated with Chaplin and Keaton. Conversely, it created a new type of comedy: the fast repartee comedy with snappy dialogue (as with the Marx brothers and W. C. Fields) and screwball comedy – usually based on the 'battle between the sexes' with **stars** such as Clark Gable and Cary Grant pitted against the likes of

Claudette Colbert, Katharine Hepburn and Rosalind Russell (as in *It Happened one Night*, Frank Capra, 1934; *Bringing up Baby*; *His Girl Friday*, both by Howard Hawks, 1938 and 1939).

The consequences of sound for cinema were not just generic. It affected the careers of actors. It also impacted on the **narrative**. When the spoken element came in, some actors did not survive because their voice did not match up to their image (this was particularly the case for Hollywood actors) – see *The Artist* (Michael Hazanavicius, 2011) for a recent example of the effects of this transition to sound. Other actors with theatre experience left the boards and ascended onto the silver screen. As for **narrative**, prior to the soundtrack, sound had not been perceived as necessary, or as a crucial element to the registering of authentic reality. Now, sound cinema was touted as being closer to reality. Since there could be dialogue, it was argued, there was greater space for social and psychological reality within the narrative. In the event, all critics (whether for or against sound) had to admit that, once sound was improved (which it was by the early 1930s), it did permit narrative economies – for example, dialogue could move the film's narrative along more speedily than inter-titles. In its earliest days, however, sound was more of a regressive step for cinema because it severely limited camera movement. The new cameras fitted with sound recording systems were heavy, bulky affairs and could not be moved around. Similarly, at first, a single microphone was the only means of recording sound; so, actors could not move around (for an amusing send-up of the beginnings of sound see *Singin' in the Rain*, Stanley Donen, 1952). In both instances, visual **realism** was lost. If this problem was quickly resolved, thanks to technical improvements, sound, as a result of these same improvements, reduced options. Renewed camera mobility and the use of the boom microphone or indeed post-synchronization of the soundtrack gave visual and aural depth to film, but improvised shooting and experimentation decreased. The consequences of sound for the film industry were that it became more labour-intensive (requiring dialoguists and sound engineers): a costly affair that was carefully regimented. The standardization of equipment – due to the cartel on the technology (predominantly Western and Tobis) – meant a standardization in production practices.

Sound technology

From the 1930s until the early 1950s, sound was single-track and was recorded optically. Optical sound is a system whereby light, modulated by sound waves, is recorded onto film, along a strip on one side of the image.

Monophonic optical sound appears to come out of the centre of the image; as such, sound becomes associated with a degree of realism (the dialogue and ambient sounds appear **diegetically** true). However, post-war, a new technology in the form of magnetic tape (a German invention) was introduced. Magnetic tape allowed for more audio channels, was easier to use and produced better sound. It was also a cheaper and more effective method for creating the stereo effect. This shift to tape fitted well with the needs of widescreen cinema: with such a large screen effect, ste-reophonic sound was clearly essential. Thus, in the case of **cinemascope**, the recorded soundtrack (made up of dialogue, sound effects and music) was transferred onto each edge of the film – thus doubling the sound.

In the 1970s, Dolby Stereo replaced the earlier stereophonic system. Dolby used a matrixing system to encode four channels (left/centre/right/surround) into a two-channel soundtrack which was then transferred onto the optical track of the film (the magnetic track could have been placed onto film, but the cost of re-equipping film theatres was too high). This four-channel stereo system is made up of more than fifteen separate tracks that are used to record dialogue, sound effects and music. These tracks are Dolby-Surround, which, as its name implies, is a system whereby sound can be separated out and reproduced through speakers from different parts of the theatre.

The advent of **digital** technology (in the 1990s) has made the pur-suit of fidelity and purity in sound even greater. Dolby-Digital sound is a system whereby sound is stored in a computer (through numbers, so the sound stays clean) and can be re-created in any combination of those numbers. This system was first introduced in 1992 (with *Batman Returns*, Tim Burton). There are 5.1 channels of sound (the additional tenth of a channel '.1' is for low frequency). This 5.1-channel system (known as DSS: digital surround sound) means that there is greater potential for fragmentation; thus, sound can be even more than sur-round. It can be separated out far more clearly, still, and dotted more purely around the cinema theatre. Thus, a single sound (say, of a footstep) can be selected out and played through a speaker directed behind the spectator's head – but in such a way as it feels 'right behind you' and therefore even more scary (for fuller details on this new technology, see Sonnenschein, 2001; Kerins, 2011).

A few key terms

Diegetic sound: the source of sound is visible on-screen (i.e. people speaking; orchestra playing; hi-fi system; cutlery on dinner plates; birds screeching, etc.).

Non-diegetic sound: sound, the source of which is not visible on-screen (the sound is obviously laid on in post-production; the most obvious example is the music track; but sound effects that are off-screen are also non-diegetic if there is no visible source).

ADR: Automatic Dialogue Replacement is a re-recording of original dialogue; commonly used in post-production to obtain a clearer sound or rectify mistakes.

Foley: sound effects matched to action in the picture (e.g. footsteps, rustling of clothes, etc.).

THX: this is not a sound system but is a high-fidelity sound standard for cinema theatres. It refers to the quality of sound therefore. The term *THX* is derived from George Lucas' 1971 film *THX 1138.*

Sound theory

Theoretical writings around the effects of sound have tended to focus on the **naturalizing** effect (Gorbman, 1987). More recently, the focus has been on **ideological** effects (see Altman, 1992; Chion, 1982, 1985, 2009; Lastra, 2000; *Screen*, 1984). Chion, in particular, has focused on the relationship of the voice to the body. This relationship, as we shall see, is at the nub of the theoretical implications of the soundtrack. Let me explain.

Until the development, first, of Dolby and, then, Dolby-Digital/DSS, sound was very closely related to the image. The monophonic optical track made it seem as if sound emanated from the image, and the audience colluded with that relationship. Monophonic optical sound, however, raises several questions around sound and realism. For example, both diegetic and non-diegetic sound will come through the centre of the screen. When non-diegetic sound is a question of music overlay (say, for the purpose of suspense or terror, as in Hitchcock's *Psycho*, 1960), this does not necessarily raise the problematic of realism. We know that this music is an add-on. However, when dialogue or a sound effect is non-diegetic (someone walking and talking off-screen, say), the monophonic soundtrack will still deliver the sound from the centre of the image. The immediate question becomes: what effect does this split have on the concept of the voice and body as a unified being/**subject**? (See the **construction of subjectivity and divided self** in **psychoanalysis** entry.)

Even with Dolby sound, cinema's synchronization of voice and body remains incomplete. The split between body and voice remains, for the following reasons. Most films tend to mix dialogue front and centre with the effect, as Kerins (2011: 258) explains, that voice and body 'are *temporally* synchronized but occupy different *spatial* positions'. The voice emanates from centre screen while the body moves around the image space. However, we accept the pretence that the dialogue spoken by the characters comes straight from their place on-screen. Only if it is not in synch do we take notice of sound drawing attention to itself. In this moment of asynchronism, the dislocation between sound and image points to the fact that what we are seeing up on-screen is an illusion. Among radical filmmakers who have attempted to show the importance of the soundtrack in relation to the image, we can cite Jean-Luc Godard's work during the 1960s (e.g. *Le Mépris*, 1963; *Pierrot le fou*, 1965). In his **deconstruction** of the two elements into two separate entities, he showed the ideological problems inherent in this invisibilization process whereby image and sound are seen as one and as representing reality.

However, with DSS we could well expect a greater realism and that the voices would be placed left, centre, right, front and back, or located with their subject; and that they could also be placed around the theatre (say, for example, if it is a voice off-screen). But, even here, there is a dislocation. And this is because of the simple fact that sound and images are usually **edited** separately. In order to ensure its quality, sound is almost always recorded separately from the image (exceptions being mobile or satellite-phone films, live-broadcast news or **documentaries** on television, or film shoots that deliberately want to use the camera's in-built mike – following a kind of **Dogme** vow of chastity, or a guerrilla filmmaking type of practice). Typically ADR is a very common practice (again to ensure sound quality). So, there is always a rift, something Mike Figgis exposes and exploits in his film *Time-Code* (2000): the image track does one thing, it unravels naturally (a story set in and around a film production company, with four central characters going about their business in a split screen of four separate narratives); but the soundtrack (edited by Figgis in his front room) selects which soundtrack (of the four narratives) will be brought to the forefront at any given time; this has the effect of separating bodies from their voices. Sound is exposed as a construct, therefore, which of course it is (literally, because it is constructed on an editing suite). But the effect of the split is to create a gap; one within which to insert our own perceptions and readings of a film. Chion argues that the split between the body and the voice is a core characteristic of sound cinema and not a 'technological shortcoming' (Kerins, 2011: 261). Less a failing, then, we should think of this rift as a cinematic process that functions to engage us as filmic beings.

For a very full but succinct review of the development of sound technology and film see Konigsberg, 1993: 331ff. For theory see Abel and Altman, 2001; Altman, 1992; Bordwell *et al.*, 1985: 298ff.; Chion, 1985, 1999, 2009; Donnelly, 2005; Gorbman, 1987; Lastra, 2000; Sonnenschein, 2001. On digital sound see especially Kerins, 2011; and the new journal *Soundscape*.

SOVIET CINEMA/SCHOOL

This term refers to a loosely knit group of filmmakers who, after the Bolshevik Revolution of October 1917, experimented with film style and technique. Their work brought the cinema of the Soviet Union to worldwide attention by the mid-1920s. This experimentation did not occur in isolation. The effect of the Revolution was to bring in its wake **experimental** foment in all branches of the arts. The beginnings of this experimentation date back to the Russian futurists (1912), who adopted an experimental and innovatory approach to language. This was to filter through into the post-Revolutionary movement of constructivism. The pre-Revolutionary futurist movement, influenced as it was by the abstract forms of European **modernist** art, believed in technique and the evacuation of fixed meanings. After the Revolution, the constructivists, seeing in technology the huge potential for change, advocated a new order in which art, science and technology in tandem with workers, artists and intellectuals would combine and work together to produce a new vision of society. Art and labour were seen as one. This notion of art as production was eagerly embraced by the newly emergent Soviet cinema of the 1920s and admirably suited the political exigencies of post-Revolutionary Russia, which needed the propagandizing effect of cinema to spread the message that all workers were pulling together to secure the national identity of the new Soviet Republics.

Lenin and Stalin were well aware of cinema's propagandistic and educative value. This was particularly the case with silent film, which was the ideal visual medium to educate the masses, a great proportion of whom were illiterate and spoke in different dialects. The earliest example of this propagandistic move was during the 1915 to 1921 civil war, when film-shows were delivered all around the country on what were called 'agit-trains'. Incidentally, it was in this area of production practices that many of the famous Soviet filmmakers (such as Lev Kuleshov and Dziga Vertov) started their careers. The purpose of the film-shows was to consolidate communist power over the Soviet Republics by telling of the heroic proletarian struggle that made hardship worthwhile and the civil war worth winning for the Revolutionary cause. Trains went out into the country bringing with them **documentary** footage of the goings-on in the major cities, including the activities of the Bolshevik leader Lenin. Filmmakers out in the country on location with these trains took footage of the peasants at work and the rural life in these times of great physical hardship. They then immediately developed this footage and screened it to the assembled **audience** of workers whom they had just filmed.

A second move to secure cinema in its **ideological** function was the nationalizing of the industry in 1919 and the establishment, in that year, of a State Film School headed by Vladimir Gardin. The two most famous nationalized film studios were based in Moscow: Mos-film and Mezhrabpom-Film. But, at first, the effects of nationalizing the industry were disastrous. Many of the previously independent **producers** left the country and took their equipment with them. In fact, the industry did not gain any stability until 1922 when a central coordinating company was established: Gaskino, renamed Sovkino in 1925. By 1929, the industry had become such a tightly centralized structure that it was able to dictate the future trends of Soviet cinema. Indeed, in 1928, an All-Union Party Congress on Film Questions decreed that films must eschew pure formalism and focus on content and **socialist realism**. The experimental wave that had brought Soviet cinema to the aesthetic forefront of world cinema gave way to the edicts of socialist realism; that is, to a representation of life as it *will be*. Congress decreed that Soviet film was to be a medium of communist enlightenment and committed to organizing the masses around social reconstruction. In effect this decree brought a slow end to **Soviet montage** cinema (see below).

The heyday of the Soviet cinema of the silent period (1924–29)

Until 1924, apart from the *agitki* (the films shown on the agit-trains), documentary films and newsreel series (called *kino pravda* – film-truth – beginning in 1922), production was at a very low level indeed, primarily because new film stock was virtually unobtainable (due to an export embargo imposed by the West, but also to the hoarding of raw film stock by private production companies operating in Moscow and Petrograd/St Petersburg which resisted nationalization). The *kino pravda* series was made possible by the effect of Lenin's New Economic Policy (1921) that permitted private companies to operate once more. Production companies released their stock and equipment and a few conventional feature films were also made, as well as the state-endorsed newsreels. The situation was so parlous, with production at a very low level, that in 1922, Lenin sanctioned the importation of foreign films to help raise money for home production. In that year there were 278 foreign and 28 Soviet films. By 1924, however, state production had risen to 69 and by 1926 reached 100; and, in 1930, Soviet products outnumbered foreign imports. This figure lasted until 1933, when the effect of internal **censorship** under Stalin reduced the numbers once more to below the magical 100 figure (this figure was not reached again until 1956, four years after Stalin's death).

By 1924, the state-controlled Sovkino and its regional outlets in the various Soviet States had full monopoly over all aspects of the film industry. During this early period of a nationalized Soviet cinema, new filmmakers emerged, eager to participate in and propagate the new revolutionary culture advocated by Lenin and Stalin. They were determined to produce an ideological cinema for the proletarian **classes** – one which de-individualized the actor (the proletarian classes would be the hero) and which relied upon collective authorship – in this regard Soviet cinema was very advanced theoretically speaking (see **auteur** entry). In 1924, Sergei Eisenstein and Lev Kuleshov established the Association of Revolutionary Cinematography (ARC) which included amongst others Dziga Vertov and (the woman filmmaker) Esfir Shub. Over the years, however, different tendencies and indeed disagreements on what constituted a revolutionary cinema brought about a divergence of groups and practices. The most radical split came with Vertov, who was a major campaigner against the new Soviet cinema fiction film (as produced by Kuleshov and Eisenstein). He left the ARC and established his own *Kinoki* group (the cine-eye group). His films are strongly in the constructivist vein, they are documentaries celebrating industrialization and the worker (see his radical documentary *Man with a Movie Camera*, 1929, which best exemplifies this ethos). Despite divergences, however, what all filmmakers shared in common was a concept of a particular revolutionary film style. A style that is known as Soviet montage (see also under **editing**). How it came about makes for interesting reading.

Soviet montage

The effects of the early hardship in the aftermath of the Revolution brought about this cinematic style that has henceforth been indelibly associated with Soviet cinema: montage cinema. Because film stock was in such short supply, the only way forward was to re-edit old films. Thus, in 1918, the Moscow Film Committee established a special

Re-Editing Department. Although Lev Kuleshov is credited as being the 'inventor' of Soviet montage, it was in fact the head of the State Film School, Vladimir Gardin, who (in 1919) – basing his ideas on this economic necessity of re-editing – advocated montage as a fundamental practice of a new film aesthetics. The use of montage was seen as being in touch with the ideology of the Revolution (rapid and energetic change) and the aesthetics of constructivism (technology and labour as the producer of art). Kuleshov's experiments led the way in this new revolutionary cinema, closely followed by Sergei Eisenstein. **Kuleshov's** principle started from the idea that each **shot** is like a building block (a brick) and that each shot derives its meaning from its context (i.e. the shots placed around it). Thus, if the context of a shot is changed, by placing it in a different sequence, then the whole meaning of the shot and the **sequence** changes. From this principle, Kuleshov developed the idea that juxtaposition must be inherent in all film signs (see **semiotics**). That is, a film shot acquires its meaning in relation to the shots that come before and after it. Shots, like building blocks, acquire meaning when juxtaposed. The famous example taken from Kuleshov's experiments is where he juxtaposes several shots taken from different pieces of film which he then edited into a sequence. These shots comprised a close-up still shot of the actor Ivan Mozzhukhin (Mosjoukine) with three others (a plate of soup, a dead woman in her coffin and a child playing). The effect of the juxtaposition for the **spectator** is that the actor's face changes expression (which in reality it cannot since it is a still shot). In other experiments, Kuleshov created what he terms 'creative geography' by splicing together bits of action taken from other films and re-editing them as one piece of uninterrupted action. In 1920, he assembled five separate bits of action and created an experiment he called *The Created Surface of the Earth* in which a man meets a woman (in Moscow), he points, they look off – we see a shot of the White House (in Washington) – and then the last shot shows them ascending the steps. This creative geography through montage is one that will later influence Vertov's imagined city-scape of *Man with a Movie Camera*.

Eisenstein's view of montage was more radical than Kuleshov's. A committed Marxist, he came into filmmaking from engineering (which, it could be argued, makes him a natural ally with the principles of constructivism). For him, montage is based on the principle of collision and conflict – not just juxtaposition. Conflict occurs within the shot as much as between shots. Shots must collide, creating a shock for the spectator (a montage of attractions was Eisenstein's term for this interaction between screen and spectator). To this effect, Eisenstein's shots were staged for maximum conflict (visually, emotionally and intellectually). Eisenstein was an advocate of intellectual montage. He saw the shot as the raw material which filmmakers *and* the spectator use to construct meaning. For him, montage is a political aesthetics, a visual form of Marx's dialectical materialism. That is, he sees montage as possessing a dynamic of conflict that creates a third meaning whose relevance bears directly on the revolutionary history of Soviet Russia. This third image is the one that is synthesized by the spectator, thus making them as much a producer of meaning as the filmmaker.

Kuleshov's principle of montage had an enormous influence on contemporary filmmakers, the most famous of whom are Sergei Eisenstein, Vsevolod Pudovkin and Alexander Dovzhenko. Some, those who formed the FEK group (the Factory of the Eccentric Actor), went on to develop, from Kuleshov's system of montage, the principle of alienation (more readily associated with Bertolt Brecht). By placing objects or people in unfamiliar contexts, they sought to alienate the spectator and oblige them to reflect on the meaning of the image (see **distanciation**).

Soviet cinema and acting

Kuleshov's other significant contribution to the new Soviet cinema was in the realm of **acting**. He introduced a new style. One that was distinct from theatre acting. Indeed, he discouraged the hiring of theatre-trained actors, preferring to develop a style of acting suitable to the screen. His new model was one that eschewed psychology in favour of a performance based on reflexes and the mechanics of acting. He advocated selecting actors for their type – whose look and performance style would match the role required. He established an acting laboratory to train his actors in the appropriate style. Kuleshov believed in social forces activating performance, not psychology. After all, securing the New Revolutionary Soviet Union was about dealing with social forces, not psychological ones. Thus, in his view, the surface (the exterior, not the interior) of the actor's body was the site of performance, and gesture and movement were primary. The body, then, becomes the site where social forces impacted on the revolutionary hero and it was the reflexes to those forces that constituted the acting.

Again many filmmakers followed this model, but not, significantly, Eisenstein. Eisenstein went for a more radical concept, still, of the protagonist and performance. He would use, in massive numbers, non-actors to create a collective proletarian hero, playing down individualism (see *Battleship Potemkin*, 1925). Pudovkin followed Kuleshov's principles of naturalistic characterization and montage, and produced popular **narrative** films (such as *Mother*, 1926). Pudovkin's characters are individuals with feelings and separate identities. The plotline is, in many ways, indistinct from **Hollywood**'s own 'good' versus 'bad', although this time it is based in Russia's own Revolutionary history. Indeed, it should be recalled that Soviet audiences very much enjoyed Hollywood film products and its **stars** (Mary Pickford, Douglas Fairbanks and Charlie Chaplin were great favourites). Dovzhenko, for his part, also continued in the Kuleshov vein and focused in particular on rural Russia by showing individual idealism and effort overcoming the landed peasantry's resistance to Stalin's collectivizing programme for farms (see *The Earth*, 1930).

Soviet cinema and genre

Kuleshov's impact was less strong in the Soviet cinema's construction of new **genres**, although he did introduce a different kind of detective–action–comedy (a hybrid of Chaplinesque humour with Soviet ideology, see *The Extraordinary Adventures of Mr West in the Land of the Bolsheviks*, 1924). By the mid-1920s, stage–screen hybrids (popular during pre-Revolutionary days) had been to a great extent transcended by the completely new genre – the historical revolutionary **epic** whose greatest exponents were Eisenstein, Dovzhenko and Pudovkin. Within the context of fiction film and epic revolutionary cinema, two basic trends evolved. The first, exemplified by Eisenstein, advocated an intellectual montage cinema – one that was closely aligned with Marx's dialectical materialism (see below); the other, exemplified by Dovzhenko and Pudovkin, was the so-called emotional or lyrical–symbolic montage cinema (a cinema that was heavily based on image-symbols). Another trend – more in the documentary vein – was that exemplified by Vertov and, in a slightly different way, Esfir Shub. Vertov was strongly opposed to fiction film (including stage–screen hybrids, the epic and literary **adaptations**), believing the only true revolutionary cinema was one that subscribed to a cinema of facts. His films aimed at catching life as it was, in a style that can best be described as a cross-fertilization of **cinéma vérité** and montage. Shub's documentary work was based on compilations of earlier footage. In some ways, her work represented the earliest form of new Soviet cinema of making a new film through re-editing footage from old ones. In this way, she compiled three feature length films on contemporary Russian history (1912–28).

Eisenstein and materialist cinema

Eisenstein is the filmmaker most readily associated with this period in Soviet cinema, at least within the Western world, possibly because he obtained international recognition at the time. Although as the above makes clear, he was far from unique (there were many other film-makers around). Nor was he always the pioneer he was made out to be by history – even though, as we saw, he pushed the meaning and function of montage into a new political aesthetics. His film *Strike* (1925) was awarded a prize at the Paris Exhibition that year. In fact, he was much admired and more successful outside the Soviet Union than in it. He lectured all over the Western world: France, Germany and the United States (he also went to Mexico where he made *¡Qué viva México!*, 1932). Doubtless the other contributing factor, over time, is the huge legacy of theoretical writings he left and which were translated into English and other languages. Eisenstein advocated a materialist theory of cinema. He saw cinema as the modality for expressing and representing revolutionary struggle. He believed that a revolutionary country should be given a revolutionary culture (cinema in his case) in order for the masses to obtain a revolutionary consciousness (small wonder Grierson admired Eisenstein's ideological educative fervour). For him, montage meant intellectual montage to make the spectator think. In this light, he is close to Kuleshov's thinking. He believed in the symbolic counterpointing of human beings with objects or other animate forms to create meaning. Thus, in *Strike*, the slaughter of a bull is counterpointed symbolically with that of the strikers. Eisenstein eschewed characterization and went for symbolic ciphers, what he called 'typage'. The actor was but one element in a film. Indeed, the proletariat was the hero of the film, not a particular individual.

Eisenstein's most famous film, *Battleship Potemkin* (1925), was commissioned by the Central Committee. It is exemplary of his radical view of film as an assault on audiences to shock them into political awareness. The film was commissioned to commemorate the unsuccessful Russian Revolution of 1905. Eisenstein focused on one incident, the mutiny on the battleship *Potemkin* and the subsequent slaughter (on the Odessa steps by the Tsarist militia) of the masses cheering and trying to bring food to the mutineers. In 1927, Eisen-stein was again commissioned to make a film, this time in com-memoration of the successful 1917 Revolution. His project, entitled *October*, was to prove the beginning of his falling foul of critics and the state. The film was due to come out in 1927 with other com-missioned projects for the Revolution's Jubilee (which included

Pudovkin's populist-montage film, *Mother*). However, Eisenstein's film had to be massively re-cut because of the expulsion of Trotsky from the party (mainly manoeuvred by Stalin). When the film was finally screened, in 1928, it was criticized for its formalism (although it contained superb ironizing of Kerensky, the provisional head of the Revolutionary government of 1917). In fact, because it had to be so drastically re-cut, the film made little sense to audiences either as an intellectual montage film or as a commemoration of the 1917 Revolution. In any event, by 1928, the state had decreed that the time for montage cinema was over. The need was for morale-lifting and positive post-Revolutionary **discourses** of socialist realism. Stalin's insistence on socialist realism films (utopian narratives; positive heroes working for the socialist cause) sounded the death-knell for Soviet montage cinema. Eisenstein made only two more intellectual montage and formalistically experimental films in the Soviet Union (*The Old and the New/The General Line*, 1928; *Bezhin Meadow*, 1937), after which he was subjected to public humiliation for his use of formalism over content and was obliged (or felt obliged) to denounce his former practices. In 1938, he was commissioned to make the patriotic film, *Alexander Nevsky*. This film is seen as marking the end of Soviet montage (Beumers, 2009). While it was undoubtedly an attempt to bolster Soviet national identity against the imminent threat of fascism and, its brave attempts to sustain a montage approach notwithstanding, it lacked the earlier brilliance of his film techniques even though it was the first of his films to have popular appeal with the Soviet audiences.

For further reading see Beumers, 2009; Christie and Taylor, 1993; Taylor and Christie, 1994a, 1994b; Taylor and Spring, 1993.

SPACE AND TIME/SPATIAL AND TEMPORAL CONTIGUITY

Within **classic narrative cinema** space and time are coherently represented in order to achieve the reality effect. Shots reveal spatial relationships between characters and objects and as such implicate the viewer as spectating **subject**. That is, shots are organized in a specific way so that the **spectator** can make sense of what s/he sees. The way in which space is carved up within a **shot** (size and volume of objects or characters) also provides meaning. Equally, given that **mainstream classic cinema** assumes an unfolding of the traditional **narrative** of order/disorder/order-restored (or enigma and resolution), time is implicitly chronological and so must be seen to run contiguously with space. **Art cinema** has disrupted this notion of temporal and spatial continuity through, for example, **jump cuts**, **unmatched shots**, flash-forwards, looping **images**, and so on. Interestingly, mainstream cinema has adopted many of these techniques, even though they do not serve the same disruptive function, but seem to function more like cinematic jokes which the spectator can enjoy (see, for example, Robert Altman's *The Player*, 1992).

SPECTATOR/SPECTATOR-IDENTIFICATION/ FEMALE SPECTATOR

The issue of spectatorship was first addressed 'theoretically' in the early to mid-1970s as a result of the impact of **semiotics** and **psychoanalysis** on **film theory**. The relationship between cinema and the unconscious is not a new concept however. Cinema as the mediator for unconscious desire, the suitability of the screen as the projection-site for the inner workings of the psyche, had been discussed by earlier theorists in the 1920s and 1930s – as had the similitude between the mechanisms of dreams and the unconscious to those of film. But it was not until the 1970s that full consideration was given to the effect of the cinematic experience upon the spectator.

Spectatorship theory has gone through four stages, to date. In stage one, 1970s film theory, Baudry, Bellour and Metz wrote about cinema as an **apparatus** and an imaginary signifier to explain what happened to the spectator as he (*sic*) sat in the darkened theatre gazing on to the screen. In stage two, post-1975, feminist film theory, the 'natural' assumption, implicit in those first writings, that the masculine was the place from which the spectator looks and the 'natural' acceptance that each viewing was an unproblematic re-enactment of the **Oedipal trajectory** (see under **psychoanalysis**) were strongly contested (in the first instance) by the critic and film-maker Laura Mulvey. In stage three, 1980s, mostly within **feminist film theory**, Mulvey's writings provoked further investigations by theorists who sought to widen the debate by bringing in theoretical approaches other than psychoanalysis. Stage four, audience reception (also known as reception theory), was arguably a natural outcome of the preceding approaches and is one that still prevails today. What follows is a brief synopsis of those four stages and the debates surrounding them.

Stage one

Baudry, Bellour and Metz drew on Freud's analyses of the child's libido drives and Lacan's **mirror stage** to explain how the cinematic apparatus works at the unconscious level. Drawing on the analogy of the screen with the mirror as a way of talking about the spectator–screen relation, these authors state that at each film viewing there is an enactment of the unconscious processes involved in the acquisition of sexual difference, language and autonomous self-hood or **subjectivity**. In other words, each viewing represents a repetition of the **Oedipal trajectory**. This in turn implies that the **subject** of classic narrative cinema is male (Mayne, 1993: 23). (For more details on the **mirror stage** and the **Oedipal trajectory** see **psychoanalysis**.)

According to Baudry (1970), the cinematic apparatus produces an **ideological** position through its system and mechanics of representation (camera, **editing**, projecting, spectator before the screen). The position is ideological because **dominant narrative cinema** practices hide the labour that goes into the manufacturing of the film and the spectator is given the impression of reality. This **seamlessness** gives the spectator a sense of a unitary vision over which he (*sic*) believes he has supremacy. The spectator believes he is the author of the meanings of the filmic text and in this respect colludes with the idealism of the cinematic 'reality-effect'. In fact, argues Baudry, the opposite is true: the spectator is constructed by the meanings of the text. As such, therefore, the cinematic apparatus interpolates the subject as effect of the text. Later, Baudry (1975) moved away from this anti-humanist interpretation of the cinematic apparatus and its ideological connotations and, adopting a more Freudian approach, focused on cinema's ability to embody psychic desire. He also recognized the implicit regressiveness (back to the child) in that particular positioning of the spectator as desiring subject – a point Metz would develop more fully.

Metz and Bellour (both 1975) talked about spectator positioning and the **voyeuristic** aspect of film-viewing whereby the viewer is identified with the look (see **gaze**). Drawing on the analogy of the screen with the mirror, Metz perceived spectator positioning as pre-Oedipal, that is, at the moment of imaginary unity with the self. The spectator then responds in two ways. First, he (*sic*) desires reunification with the mother and his desire is sexually motivated. Second, he denies difference and through that disavowal of difference – because of his own fear of castration – seeks to find the penis in woman (**fetishization**). In cinema, this Oedipal trajectory is re-enacted within both the

narrative *and* the spectator–text relation (again, it was taken for granted, by Metz, that the subject of the gaze is male).

Stage two

Numerous problems arise out of this first stage of theorizing the spectating subject, starting with the assumption that speculation is only a one-way system (spectator to screen), that it is exclusively male in its positioning and that film texts are organized in such a way as to give a **preferred reading**. These issues did not become clear until after the impact of Laura Mulvey's ground-breaking essay ('Visual Pleasure and Narrative Cinema', 1975) which sought to address the issue of female spectatorship within the cinematic apparatus and psychoanalytic frameworks established by the authors discussed above. Mulvey's essay represented a turning point in film theory in that it was the first to introduce emphatically the question of sexual difference as a necessary area for investigation. Indeed, she intended it to act as a catalyst – she readily admits that the essay was intentionally polemical (1989). In her essay, she examined the way in which cinema functions through its **codes and conventions** to construct the way in which woman is to be looked at – a threefold gaze, starting with the man behind the camera, then the male point of view within the film and, subsequently, the spectator who identifies with the male character or protagonist. She describes this process of viewing as **scopophilia** – pleasure in viewing (see also **gaze**).

In her analysis, Mulvey made clear the implications of the dual response, as described by Metz, of the male unconscious (desiring and fetishizing) for both narrative cinema and the spectator–text relation. For this sexualization and objectification of the female form, that the male gaze confers upon it, is not just one of desire, but also one of fear or dread of castration. She demonstrated how, as a first unconscious response to this fear, the camera (and the spectator after it) fetishizes the female form by drawing attention to its beauty, its completeness and perfection. But, in making the female body a fetish object, the camera disavows the possibility of castration and renders it phallus-like and therefore reassuring (since it no longer represents lack). Mulvey demarcated the voyeuristic gaze as the other male unconscious response to this fear. This gaze represents a desire to control, to punish the (perceived) source of the castration anxiety, even to annihilate woman. Mulvey mentioned **film noir** in this context as *the* **genre** that most readily makes these two proclivities, voyeurism and fetishism, visible (but for an extreme example see *Peeping Tom*, Michael Powell, 1960).

Mulvey then went on to ask, given that the narrative of **classical narrative cinema** is preponderantly that of the Oedipal trajectory and, since that trajectory is tightly bound up with male perceptions or fantasies about women (difference, lack, fear of castration and so on), what happens to the female spectator? How does she derive visual pleasure? Mulvey could only conclude that she must either identify with the passive, fetishized position of the female character on-screen (a position of unpleasure, her lack of a penis signifying the threat of castration) or, if she is to derive pleasure, must assume a male positioning (a masculine third person).

Stage three

Mulvey's polemic met with a strong response by feminist critics (as she intended) and the ensuing decades saw extensive work on revising, reworking and extending Mulvey's propositions. In an attempt to refute the phallocentrism of Mulvey's argument, Silberman (1981) and Studlar (1985) described the cinema as an essentially masochistic structure in which the viewer derives pleasure through submission or passivity. Doane (1984), following on from these writings, argued that the female spectator's positioning was twofold. She adopted either a masochistic positioning (identifying with the female passive role) or that of a transvestite (identifying with the male active hero). Mulvey, in her afterthoughts on her earlier essay, warned against this kind of binary thinking (1989). And, indeed, feminists were already con-sidering the possibility that the spectator was not so rigidly positioned in relation to sexual identity, but that it was possible to postulate the bisexuality of the spectator's positioning whereby s/he would alter-nate between the two – suggesting a fluidity and heterogeneity of positioning rather than an 'either/or'. Modleski (1988: 98) made the point most succinctly in relation to the bisexuality of the female spectator. According to psychoanalytic theory, the female spectator is doubly desiring because when going through the mirror phase, the girl child's first love object is the mother, but, in order to achieve 'normal femininity' she must turn away and go towards her father as object of desire. However, the first desire does not go away (there is no castration threat, so she does not have to relinquish it). Thus, the female spectator's bisexual positioning is central to the mother/daughter nexus (see female Oedipal trajectory in **psychoanalysis** entry). The male spectator, much as the male character up on-screen, for the most part suppresses his femininity (often projecting it onto the female and punishing her for it). However, as Modleski (1988:

99) argued, he can find himself bisexually positioned if the male character fluctuates between passive and active modes.

The contiguous question of spectator-as-subject in relation to meaning-production was also broadened. The spectator is no longer a passive interpolated subject of the screen. S/he holds a position of power and makes sense of the images and sounds (in fact, the effect of **sound** renders the screen/mirror analogy somewhat incomplete or unsound). Even though it is a construct of cinema to endow the spectator predominantly with more knowledge than the characters (at least with mainstream narrative cinema), it does not follow that the spectator occupies only one position in relation to those characters (as the apparatus reading would have it). Cowie's (1984) discussion of film as **fantasy** made this clear. In her rethinking or revamping of Laplanche's and Pontalis' three characteristics of fantasy (the primal scene, the seduction fantasy and the fantasies of castration), all of which are a **mise-en-scène** of desire, she made the point that the spectator, as subject *for* and *of* the scenario, can occupy all those positions. As such, s/he is not monolithically placed but can in fact occupy contradictory positions. As an example, take *Fatal Attraction* (Adrian Lyne, 1987) – a film in which it is possible to occupy, at different times within the narrative, the positions of the mistress, the husband and the wife. It should not be forgotten that Glenn Close (who plays the mistress) expressed deep shock and disappointment at the **audience** cheering the end of the film when she is shot dead by the wife. She had assumed (naively) that sympathy or identification with her character would occur.

Stage four

Essentially, these three stages outlined above around spectator-positioning and identification show the gradual shift away from the early monolithic view of the spectator (as subject of the apparatus). This has led to the current, more heterogeneous stage four of the debate. Spectator analysis no longer confines itself to spectator-as-psychic-phenomenon. The debate has become enlarged (thanks, in the main, to cultural studies) and the spectator-as-viewer is an important area of investigation; namely, reception theory and audience reception. Reception theory examines the audience's experience of cinema and how meaning is created through that experience. It deals directly with the audience and seeks empirical evidence, such as audience surveys, to set out its findings. The underlying principle is that context influences the way in which the spectator views and receives the film. Studies of audience reception, initiated in television studies, point to the eclecticism of viewers and acknowledge the difference in readings of the film depending on **class**, age, race, creed, **sexuality**, **gender** and nationality. Thus, historical and empirical models of spectator or viewer analysis have been established. In this respect, spectatorship has been perceived as a matter of historically shifting groups (e.g. differing socio-economic groups over different time periods, such as 1930s working-class women audiences, 1950s teen audiences, etc.). Clearly, the popularity of cinema has shifted over time and has had different effects and been differently affected depending on the make-up of those groups (in terms of economic group, age, gender, race, etc.). Briefly stated, reception theory puts the spectator in his/her context and seeks to unravel all the factors influencing his/her reading of the film. This has meant, then, that spectatorship has also been analysed in relation to **intertextuality**: an examination of all the texts surrounding the actual film text and their impact upon the viewer as reader and receiver. Exhibition – where films are screened and the effect felt by the viewer – is another important consideration, as is audience pleasure in identification.

see also: **apparatus**, **gaze**, **ideology**, **psychoanalysis** (especially **Imaginary/Symbolic**), **scopophilia**, **suture**, **voyeurism/fetishism**

For an extremely thorough, comprehensive and well-written book on spectatorship read Mayne, 1993. On spectator-identification see Ellis, 1982. For specific textual analyses see Modleski, 1988. On female spectatorship see Kaplan, 1983; Pribham, 1988. On reception read Campbell, 2005; Maltby, Stokes and Allen, 2007; Stacey, 1993; Staiger, 2000, 2005 (provides a good overview of reception theory).

STARS/STAR SYSTEM/STAR AS CAPITAL VALUE/ STAR AS CONSTRUCT/STAR AS DEVIANT/STAR AS CULTURAL VALUE: SIGN AND FETISH/ STARGAZING AND PERFORMANCE

A first definition: star as capital value

Even though the French film industry was the first to see the usefulness of stars in promoting its products (especially its **comedy** series and *film d'art* productions, starting in 1908), the star system is generally associated with **Hollywood**, in all its excesses and glory. So what follows most specifically addresses that particular form of stardom (nowadays there are numerous studies on other cinemas where stardom is practised: European, Indian and South East Asian, just to mention the most obvious).

In earliest Hollywood cinema, films were anonymous productions bearing only the name of the studio. It rapidly became evident that certain performers were greater attractions than others. Henceforth, performers were perceived as having capital value. And, by 1919, the star system was established. Although Florence Lawrence, 'the Biograph girl', was the first, named star in the United States (1910), the first 'real' star was Mary Pickford (known as 'little Mary' in her films of that period). Charlie Chaplin shortly followed. But, this capital value of stars was by no means a one-way exchange. Stars made fortunes – that is, as long as they made the **studios**' fortunes.

Before **sound**, both male and female stars were quite archetypal; so, their **iconography** was easily readable. After sound, there was a shift in stereotypes, and roles differentiated. But, as Claire Johnston (1976) has noted, this was predominantly the case for male stars only. Female stars remained, much as before, vamps or virgins or full-scale sex-goddesses whose main purpose was to give the **audience** (and presumably the male star) a 'human sense of beauty and eroticism' (Konigsberg, 1993: 348). Meanwhile, male stars became more complex. No longer just heroes, they could be anti-heroes, rebels-as-heroes, socially aware heroes, and so on.

Hollywood's dominance of the Western film industry since World War One has meant not only that the studios have massively exported their star commodities on celulloid throughout the European continent and the United Kingdom, but also that they have been in a position to offer lucrative enticements to import stars: most famously, arguably, in the silent era, Greta Garbo. For some film stars, 'going to Hollywood' could make them into megastars; for others, it could consign them to oblivion, or – eventually – do both (e.g. the rise and demise of Vivien Leigh and Richard Burton).

Officially, the star system was 'over' by the 1950s, owing to the Hollywood studio system collapse, but, rivalry remained strong in the 1950s between Europe and Hollywood. For example, just on the sex-goddess front, Diana Dors and Shirley Ann Field in the United Kingdom, Brigitte Bardot in France, Gina Lollobrigida and Sophia Loren in Italy were star images served up to counter the US sex-symbols Marilyn Monroe, Ava Gardner and Jayne Mansfield. Rather than 'over' it would be fairer to say that that type of star system went into decline after the 1950s collapse. For stars are still being manufactured. They are of a different order, today. On the one hand, they are closer, perhaps, to celebrities and yet at the same time more prosaic, more instantly recognizable as being 'like us', more ordinary, more accessible. On the other hand, they are established actors (e.g. De Niro, Hoffman, Malkovich, Pacino, Spacey, Streep) who command an aura of greatness (often having also worked in the theatre); they are less ordinary, but they are not as unreachable as the stars of the 1950s (and earlier) appeared to be. Celebrity culture has quite simply democratized glamour, even if it has not yet brought about an abundance of African-American/Black stars (see Regester, 2010).

Stars sell films, but their capital exchange value goes further than that, of course. **Producers** will put up money for films that include the latest top star. Stars can attract financial backing for a film that otherwise might not get off the ground. Film scripts are often written with specific stars in mind (see Robert Altman's *The Player*, 1992, for a satire on Hollywood practices in this respect). And while films are indeed vehicles for stars, allowing them to show a wide range of skills over different **genres**, stars are equally vehicles for film genres (e.g. Fred Astaire and Ginger Rogers, and Gene Kelly are icons of the **musical**; Lauren Bacall, Humphrey Bogart and Edward G. Robinson are closely identified with **film noir** and **gangster films**). Indeed, a need to re-establish a star's commercial viability could be the impetus to disassociate her or him from one type of genre. This was attempted by Anthony Perkins, arguably with some success in *On the Beach* (Stanley Kramer, 1961), but he never really pulled it off. He will always remain Norman Bates of *Psycho* (Alfred Hitchcock, 1960.)

Stars are signs of indigenous cultural codes. Gestures, words, intonations, attitudes, postures – all of these separate one nation's stars from another's, thus affirming the plurality of the cultures. Indeed, it could be argued that the gestural codes, even more so than the **narrative** codes, are deeply rooted in a nation's culture – which is why some stars do not export well. Traditions of performance, then, have national as well as individual resonances and need to be borne in mind when analysing a star's performative style. Gesturality is also tied up with the question of authenticity. We expect certain rituals of performance from our stars. Indeed, the camera colludes with this process of recognition by giving us close-ups of the particular gesture that authenticates the star in question (*the* Garbo smile, *the* Bette Davis wringing of hands, *the* Clint Eastwood side-mouth delivery of the few lines he ever utters, and so on).

A second definition: star as construct

(What follows in this section is largely based on Dyer (1986, re-issued 2004), and Gledhill (1991) – two extremely lucid and useful texts on this subject.)

Stars are constructed by the film industry, but stars (although not all) also have a role in their own construction, participate in their own **myth**-making. Similarly, star status is authenticated by the media (press, fanzines, television and radio, and so on). But, stars also possess markers of their own authenticity and, as such, are involved in their own mythification. Think, for example, of Doris Day, the representative of nice middle-America womanhood; the sexually charged and ambiguous **sexuality** of Marlene Dietrich; the swashbuckling Errol Flynn; the ice-cold maiden Catherine Deneuve, with flawless feminine beauty; the socio-psychologically inept Woody Allen. But, note how today it is more difficult to associate single markers to stars. Indeed, contemporary stars resist this kind of categorization better. Think of the very different types of roles played by Johnny Depp (he can be cool or hyper; menacing or very funny); John Malkovich (sexy, smooth, sinister). And surely Meryl Streep and Glenn Close are two of the hardest Hollywood stars to typify in this way. In fact, it is almost as if things have gone in reverse. Stars who appear to have but a single marker are inclined to be typecast and provide rather predictable performances that make them less interesting as star personas (Harrison Ford, Keanu Reeves and Jack Nicholson come to mind).

Stars are somehow baroque in their image-construction, since it is so predominantly about illusionism, about 'putting there' what in fact isn't there. They *are* appearance in the very diversified meaning of that word: they appear on-screen, but they are not 'really' there – their image on-screen stands in for them so they are *apparence*, a semblance. The look that has been constructed of them, that is up there for all to perceive, is also an appearance, a carefully manufactured appearance (of flawless beauty, of rugged handsomeness, for example). The rest, as Dyer (1986: 2) puts it, is supposedly 'concealed'. Yet we as **spectators** accept this construct as real.

As a way of measuring this sense of reality, let us pick up on Gledhill's comment that stars reach their audience primarily through their bodies (1991: 210). That is, they reach us through their appearance. But, depending on whether it is a male or a female star, this reaching-us-with-their-bodies changes as they age. Not for nothing do so many female stars decry the lack of roles for older, mature, even old women. For male stars, ageing is not (or is less of) an issue where their appearance is concerned. Thus, it is acceptable for a male star to age so long as he is 'healthy', his appearance remains one of good, or reasonable health – read: virile health (e.g. Paul Newman, Clint Eastwood). Even if he grows old unhealthily through body abuse, some types of unhealthiness still do not bring about a rejection of the star-body that is reaching us. In this respect, it is worth comparing the responses to Burton and his facial deterioration through alcohol (described as 'cragged', 'tragic', 'a waste of talent') with the prurient reactions to Rock Hudson, the first star to be openly known to have died of AIDS (even though it was denied for a long time). Certain types of deterioration, such as physical decline from excess in alcohol consumption, are less negatively judged than others, it would appear.

To return to the female star and ageing: the female star has 'trouble' ageing not just for herself (loss of looks equals loss of premier roles), but also in relation to her audience. On the whole, her fans do not like her to age. Curiously, then, the process of ageing matters when it is a woman star – it recalls our own ageing, is too real – not the 'real' we want to see. Just to take a few random examples of stars and ageing, Simone Signoret, whose premature ageing was always said to be a result of heavy drinking and smoking, was severely criticized for losing her looks. She, it would appear, should have exercised the control that no one expected Burton to exercise. Cancer, from which she died at the age of 64, could just as easily have been the cause of her premature ageing as her much-quoted excesses. Rita Hayworth was dismissed at 40 as a drunk, yet she died of Alzheimer's disease. Ageing in a female star is seen as deviancy. Joan Crawford complained of how hard she had to work to look, and stay looking good (Dyer, 1986: 1). Marlene Dietrich spent a fortune on face-lifts. The price of being not-bodily-deviant is high. Brigitte Bardot and Greta Garbo left the screen before age set in – taking the appearance away becoming the other price to pay to 'keep up appearances' (or the only way to escape it). Today, certain female stars embrace their ageing in a far more pragmatic fashion (Glenn Close, Helen Mirren, Meryl Streep).

The star as a construct has three component parts (Gledhill, 1991: 214): first, the real person; second, the 'reel' person/the character s/he plays; third, the star's persona, which exists independently of, but is a combination of, the other two – it is these three parts that create the star as **sign**. The film industry makes the multi-faceted star-image, so does the star, and the audience selects. In this regard, the star-image has four component parts (Dyer, 1986: 3–4): first, what the industry puts out; second, what the media (critics and others) say; third, what the star says and does; fourth, what we (the audience) say, what we can select, even to the point of imitating the star (e.g. James Dean look-alikes) – and each audience will select a different meaning (e.g. Denzel Washington means different things to Black audiences than he does to White ones, or to heterosexuals, or to lesbian and gay audiences).

Star-images, then, are more than just the image. As Dyer (1986: 3–4) makes clear, they are extensive (can extend in meaning, and over the public and private spheres); they are multimedia (photography, film, press, television, and so on); they are **intertextual** (the star's image gets picked up and used by others – a sulking Dean look-alike in a jeans advert); finally they have histories that can and do outlive their lives (especially if they die in tragic circumstances). A star, then, is a cluster of meanings and parts. It is not difficult, therefore, to see that the star phenomenon is profoundly unstable (Dyer, 1986: 6) and extremely paradoxical by nature – as the next three sections will go on to show.

A third definition: star as deviant

In Hollywood, a star's life is controlled by the studio, which means there is very little room for resistance. A few stars have been able to take charge of their meaning construction (e.g. Mary Pickford, Bette Davis, Barbra Streisand, Meryl Streep, Robert De Niro); and this resistance becomes part of their star-image. However, in general, stars collude in the fabrication of themselves as star, participate in the manufacturing of themselves as representative of 'normality'. Why, for example, are there still 'lavender' marriages in Hollywood – marriages of convenience to cover up the fact that one or both partners are gay? Gay stars (whether closeted or 'out') are the most vulnerable in relation to the instability of the star-image because either they must conceal even more than the straight star (if closeted; see, for example, Dirk Bogarde), or (if they are 'out') they must convince through their performance that their appearance is 'really real'; either way their performance is a double masquerade (see Rupert Everett).

It is not difficult to perceive that this collusion in manufacturing a star-image confronts the star with a fragmented rather than a divided self (see **psychoanalysis** and **suture**). As a fragmented self, the star has more than one image and thus too many mirrors reflecting back the multiple self. So, which one is the real image or reflection? The construction of a star, then, is about excess, excess of meaning ascribed to her or him. This excess is mirrored in the star's lifestyle. If it were not excessive (mansions, swimming pools, parties and so on), would we believe in their star status? Occasionally, we accept un-excessive star-images, but they are the exception and that exceptionality is part of their star image. Excess, then, has positive value for studio, star and spectator. But it soon becomes translated into deviancy once it has negative value primarily for the studio. Sexuality and consumption practices are, unsurprisingly, the areas in which stars 'transgress'. Since their sexuality is set up on-screen for us to consume, it is, perversely, through those very sets of comportment that the star (who can no longer cope with this fragmented self) will seek to deny (through excess in sexual practice and consumption abuse) and then expose the masquerade of stardom – through disfigurement or death (on this point, see Shapiro, 2003). James Dean, Heath Ledger and River Phoenix come to mind.

A fourth definition: star as cultural value: sign and fetish

As a sign (see **semiology**) of the indigenous cultural codes, institutional metonymy and site of the **class** war in its national specificity, the signification of the star 'naturally' changes according to the social, economic and political environment. Stars are shifting signifiers, they function as reflectors of the time and as signs to be reflected into society. During the 1950s, when youth emerged as an important class economically and culturally, teenage boys in the United States donned T-shirts, jeans and leather jackets with either Dean or Brando as their icon; in France, teenage girls mimicked the Bardot look – as well as the walk, and so on. Stars have emblematic as well as cultural value in that they 'signify as condensers of moral, social and ideological values' (Gledhill, 1991: 215). Gledhill makes the point that they can also be emblematic of those values being brought into question (e.g. Garland in *A Star is Born*, George Cukor, 1954; Dean in *Rebel Without a Cause*, Nicholas Ray, 1955). We could also question, in this context, the dearth of African-American stars, especially, female stars (see Regester, 2010). Most of those who are of international status are male and well over 40; precious few are under 30 (Anthony Mackie and Gabourey Sidibe are two who have played in Oscar-nominated films respectively in *The Hurt Locker*, Kathryn Bigelow, 2008, and *Precious*, Lee Daniels, 2009). With African-Americans constituting nearly 14 per cent of USA's population, what does this lack of presence say about contemporary America?

The star as sign also functions as mediator between the real and the imaginary and, as such, has spectator expectations transferred onto them. The shifts in the representation of female sexuality, just to take one example, over the past eighty years of cinema show how this process of transference and mutation occurs. In Hollywood, for example, during the 1930s and 1940s, two types of feminine eroticism prevailed: the 'independent just as good as the boys' (Claudette Colbert, Bette Davis, Rosalind Russell, Katharine Hepburn); or the weak, vulnerable type (Vivien Leigh). In the 1950s, the femino-masculine independent type was replaced by the dutiful wife at home supporting her husband (by staying out of the job market); or the self-parodying brunette who eventually 'settles down' (roles played respectively by Doris Day and Jane Russell); the weak type replaced by the dumb blonde (guess who?). By the late 1960s, a new type emerged, embodying a radical–liberal feminist eroticism, which attributes to women the right to decide what they do with their sexuality (Jane Fonda). This woman-in-her-own-right sexuality persisted into late twentieth-century cinema, but has not always sat easily – as if by way of a backlash against feminism. As two contrastive modes of representation, see, on the one hand, Glenn Close in *Fatal Attraction* (Adrian Lyne, 1987) and Jodie Foster in *The Accused* (Jonathan Kaplan, 1988); and, on the other, Linda Fiorentino in *The Last Seduction* (John Dahl, 1994).

These shifts in representation, over time, correspond, first, to different stages in the dominant perception of the American woman's sexuality and, second, to the social, political and economic conditions that prevailed in each of those epochs. Consider also that Fiorentino has not had a major role since that very feisty performance as a woman that no lawman or drug-dealer can catch. Perhaps it was too daring to have a *so-called* sociopathic femme fatale do murder, steal the money and get away with it. Since the new millennium, Hollywood's women have been represented as somewhat one-dimensional, a regressive trend in **gender** politics it has to be said (they are also not that much in evidence in lead roles in Hollywood; the ratio to male lead roles stands at around 1:4). Women leads are either rather unbelievable ass-kicking chicks with or without guns (in the former: Hilary Swank in Eastwood's *Million Dollar Baby*, 2004; Angelina Jolie in the *Lara Croft* series (2001 and 2003) and Uma Thurman in the *Kill Bill* series (2003–4)); side-kicks to male action heroes (the Hollywood remake of *The Girl with the Dragon Tattoo*, David Fincher, 2011); deranged murderers (Cherize Theron, *Monster*, 2003); husband seekers (*Sex in the City* series); bad or good mothers (respectively: Mo'nique in *Precious*; Sandra Bullock in *The Blind Side*, John Lee Hancock, 2009); raunchy and out of control (*Bridesmaids*, Paul Feig, 2011).

Stars are endowed with national iconicity and as such have cultural value. Clearly a star's meaning can shift in the transition from the national to the international level. This is particularly true of the United States' perception of European stars. But, stars also signify on a personal level. They articulate the idea of personhood, which is a fiction for the reproduction of the kind of society we live in (Dyer, 1986: 8). As (national) icon and (individuated) person, the star functions as both extraordinary and ordinary. In the first instance, as extraordinary, s/he is both an object of our speculation and impossible object of our desire. In the latter, as ordinary, 's/he is just like us' – we can identify with the stars – and so the star is a possible object of our desire; s/he is absence made presence. This binary effect functions to fetishize the star – in neither instance is the star **subject**, always object (see **voyeurism/ fetishism**). As holder of the **gaze**, the spectator is positioned voyeur-istically, desiring to look, with all that that connotes in terms of fetishism. But, the absence/presence paradigm also points to the simultaneously impossible and possible nature of that desire, which is also a feature of fetishism (desiring that which cannot be had – what is absent, adulating a fixed object – the star or icon present up on-screen).

The fetish value of a star is strongly underscored by their **mise-en-scène**, starting with the moment of entrance on-screen – awaited with impatience – a use of suspense to give added value to the star. Morphological markers, 'that seem natural or naturally the star's' (such as a certain smile, biting a lip, side-**lighting** eyes), but which privilege us into their emotions, play into the fiction that the spectator or the camera or the eye has caught them unawares (Ellis, 1982: 106). Voyeuristically, we look on: unseen by the star we watch what was once seen-presence but which is now absence – an image standing for star. Even a film itself can obtain fetish status when, for example, a star has died young and/or in tragic circumstances. The film is all that is left of them as movement (e.g. River Phoenix and *My Own Private Idaho*, Gus Van Sant, 1991; Heath Ledger and *The Dark Night*, Christopher Nolan, 2008).

A fifth definition: star gazing: strategies of performance

Two questions will frame this last definition of stardom: who is looking at the star? And what are we looking at? The answer to the first will make clear why strategies of performance inform the answer to the second question. Essentially there are two audiences looking at the star: the diegetic and the extra-diegetic ones (see **diegesis**). That is, those on the inside looking on, and those on the outside looking in – but in both instances also looking *at* the star, if with different effect; with different effect, because the spectator's look is mediated by the diegetic audience. This does not exclude the fact that the spec-tator's gaze is also mediated by the point of view within the film, which is usually that of the star, but we are here discussing who is looking at the star. (The entry on **spectatorship** addresses spectator-positioning more fully.)

Diegetic star-gazing on the female star is one of fairly straightforward fetishization. However, the effect on the male star is twofold. First, if those star-gazers are male, the effect is one of homo-eroticism and a feminizing of the male body (the male body is as much fetishized by the male gaze in this instance as is the female body). This puts an interesting reading on predominantly all-male genres **(Westerns** and crime-**thriller** movies). Second, if the stargazers are female, even if the gaze is now heterosexually charged, the feminizing of the male body still takes place. Women's agencing their gaze onto the male body means they are taking up the privileged male position as holder of the gaze (see **agency** and **gaze**).

The extra-diegetic audience likes to come and see its stars. This implies that the audience has certain expectations of the star. The star is the point of synthesis between representation and identification. S/he represents or re-presents the 'host culture' of which s/he is a part and with which the spectator identifies (King, 1985: 37). S/he also stands for roles s/he has played before. The extra-diegetic star-gazer, then, has come to see what the star is capable of and, depending on the star, expects either a degree of sameness (acting to type or personification) or un-sameness (always changing or impersonation). And, to this effect, strategies of performance are mobilized by both the industry and the star to satisfy this need on the part of the audience. Irrespective of which mode of **acting** is in play (personification or impersonation), these strategies function as markers of authenticity. Thus, a star who plays roles that are consonant with their personality (no matter how constructed that is) will be far more typecast and produce ritualistic performances far in excess of a star who impersonates.

Hollywood tends to prefer the personifying star in the belief that audiences choose films in relation to stars and a knowledge, more or less, of what to expect (e.g. Eastwood, the non-verbal gunman; Jack Nicholson and the leering grin combined with a macho bravura; the Bette Davis flouncing bitchiness; the soulful Barbra Streisand and her songs; the all-American winner and tough guy, John Wayne; Tom Cruise, less of a tough guy, but still an all-American winner; and so on). Stars who impersonate (i.e. who can be true to any conceivable character) are fewer in number and their popularity or success depends to a great degree on how far they go in suppressing the authenticating markers of their real personality or star-image (see Robert De Niro and Al Pacino). While the construction of difference (from the star-image or personality) must be convincing, if the suppression is so total, the audience is likely to reject that performance. In other words, if the impersonation gets to the point where the disguise prevents the signs of the star from being read, so that the star to all intents and purposes 'disappears' (does not appear), the audience feels 'cheated' of the process of spectator recognition, an essential component of the star-image. The audience can no longer select those bits of the star (authenticating markers) which it recognizes or with which it identifies. In this respect, the star Meryl Streep is the one actress who comes to mind because she sails so close to this 'dis-appearance act'. This could explain why she receives such a mixed reaction to her performances, which are not always liked or admired.

see also: **gesturality, studio system**

For further reading see Dyer, 1980, 1993, 2004; Gledhill, 1991; Moseley, 2005; Palmer, 2010; Regester, 2010; Shapiro, 2003.

STRUCTURALISM/POST-STRUCTURALISM

Initially the introduction of structuralism into **film theory** was perceived as a bold move to bring a more rigorous and scientifically based approach to the analysis of film. In its focus on the underlying structures of film, it would also serve (as I explain below) to de-romanticize the filmmaker as **auteur**.

The founding stone of structuralism was structural linguistics (later to become **semiotics**), which dates back to the beginning of the twentieth century, primarily in the form of Ferdinand de Saussure's linguistic theories. However, they remained little known until the theories were brought into the limelight, in France, by the philosopher-semiotician Roland Barthes in the 1950s – especially in his popularizing essays *Mythologies* (1957). Saussure, in his *Cours de linguistique générale*, set out a base paradigm by which all language could be ordered and understood. He distinguished between language as a system (*langue* – an underlying set of rules that is universal as a concept) and language as utterance (*parole* – the speech that can be generated by those rules). The impact of linguistic structuralism in the late 1950s and through the 1960s on other disciplines was quite widespread, affecting anthropology, philosophy and **psychoanalysis** to mention but three that are of immediate importance in the context of film theory. Exemplary of this impact was Claude Lévi-Strauss' anthropological structuralism of the 1960s, which looked at (American) Indian **myths**. Although his thesis was to have a widespread influence, because he was examining **narrative** structures, it was of particular significance in the context of film theory. Lévi-Strauss' thesis was that since all cultures are the products of the human brain, there must be, somewhere, beneath the surface, features common to all. This was an approach that became extremely popular during the 1960s and was adapted in the early 1970s not just by film theoreticians such as Christian Metz, but also by the Marxist philosopher Louis Althusser into his discussions of **ideology** and by Jacques Lacan into psychoanalysis. In terms of Althusser and Lacan's thinking (around ideology and psychoanalysis, respectively), this would not impact fully upon film theory until the mid-1970s as part of the philosophical breakthrough of post-structuralism which advocated a pluralistic approach where theory was concerned (see next section). However, in terms of the concept of the *auteur*, the impact of Roland Barthes' 1967 essay 'Death of the Author', in which he questioned the singularity of the authorial voice, meant that it was no longer sustainable to think of the auteur-filmmaker as the single producer of meaning (see **auteur** entry). As we shall discuss below, the auteur was just one structure amongst many others in relation to the filmic text.

Structuralism affects film theory in that it represents a rethinking of film theory through academically recognized disciplines, those of structural linguistics and semiotics, hence also its appeal to US and British theorists, among others. This pattern would repeat itself in the 1970s with psychoanalysis, philosophy and feminism, and, again in the 1980s, with history. The significance of this trend of essayists and philosophers turning to cinema to apply their theories cannot be underestimated. It is doubtless this work which legitimated film studies as a discipline and brought cinema firmly into the academic arena.

However, structuralism ended up in rigid formalism which removed any discussion of pleasure in the viewing. Symptomatic of this desire for total order in film theory were Christian Metz's endeavours in the mid-1960s to situate cinema within a Saussurian semiology. Metz was the first to set out, in his *Essais sur la signification au cinéma* (1971, 1972), a total-theory approach in the form of his *grande syntagmatique* that could account for all elements of a film's composition. Thus, cinema is a set of syntagmatic relations – that is, of universal rules (much like Saussure's *langue*), a set of relations that could be described as a grammar of film. Syntagmatic relations then relate to the possibility of combination. Each film will be constructed out of a combination of syntagms; but, within these, a specific selection of **shots** will be used (much like Saussure's *parole*).

It is not difficult to see the problematics inherent in Metz's endeavour to impose a total, grand theory on film. First, although structuralist theory purported to reveal the hidden structures behind filmmaking, in its focus on the filmic text per se it simultaneously ignored modes of production, the impact of **stars** on choices and the socio-historical context of production. Fortunately, post-structuralism would make this widening possible. Thus, structuralism, while it might have de-romanticized the auteur (in that s/he is one structure of meaning–production amongst others), nonetheless, continued to focus on the filmmaker and their product and as such was quite limiting. Analysing film this way meant that a critic could scientifically and objectively evaluate a film, determine the style of a particular auteur/filmmaker and indeed determine also if a particular film was consistent with that film-maker's style – hence the term *auteur-structuralism* (see **auteur** entry). The focus, therefore, was on the hidden structures and codes in the text and, in this respect, answers the question of how the text comes to be. Thus, genre comes into focus as well as the notion that **studios** and stars (in fact all the structures of the film industry) are producers of meanings. What gets omitted is the notion of pleasure and **audience** reception.

Post-structuralism

Althusser's discussion of ideology and Derrida's concept of **decon-struction** (understanding, by breaking down the parts of the whole, the ideological effects of structures of meaning) were key elements in terms of the development of post-structuralist theory. This theoretical movement, which does not find an easy definition, sought to ques-tion the structuralist assumption that *knowledge of* the underlying structures was sufficient in and of itself. Post-structuralism argues that the historical and cultural conditions are just as important systems of knowledge as is the *understanding of* the ideological effects of struc-tures. By the mid- to late 1970s post-structuralism, which embraced deconstruction, psychoanalysis, historical and cultural theory, femin-ism (amongst other theories), made it clear that a single grand theory was inadequate and that was what was required was a pluralism of theories that cross-fertilized each other. As its name implies, post-structuralism was born out of a profound mistrust for total theory, and started from the position that all texts are a double articulation of **discourses** and non-discourses (i.e. the said and the non-said). Because post-structuralism looks at all relevant discourses (said or unsaid) revolving around and within the text, many more areas of meaning-production can be identified. Thus, semiotics introduced the theory of the textual **subject** – that is, subject positions within the textual process, including that of the spectator and the auteur – and the text as a series of **signs** producing meanings.

In terms of auteur theory, the effect of post-structuralism was multiple: 'the intervention of semiotics and psychoanalysis' 'shattering' once and for all 'the unity of the auteur' (Caughie, 1981: 200). Having defined the auteur's place within the textual process, auteur theory could now be placed within a theory of textuality. Since there is no such thing as a 'pure' text, the **intertextuality** (effects of different texts upon another) of any film text must be a major consideration, including authorial intertextuality. Thus, the auteur is a figure/text constructed out of their film; for although there exist authorial signs within a film that make it ostensibly that of a certain filmmaker, nonetheless that authorial text is also influenced by those of others (e.g. stars, scriptwriters, cinematographers, costume and set designers).

Psychoanalysis and feminist film theory introduced the theory of the sexual, specular, divided subject (divided by the fact of difference, loss of and separation from the mother (see **psychoanalysis, suture**)). Questions of the subject come into play: who is the subject? The text, the star, the auteur, the **spectator**? These theories also examined the effects of the enunciating text (i.e. the text brought about by the spectator) – this included analysing the two-way ideological effect and the pleasure derived by the spectator as s/he moves in and out of the text (see **spectator–identification**). To speak of text means, too, that the context must also come into play in terms of meaning production: modes of production, the social, political and historical context. Finally and simultaneously, one cannot speak of a text as transparent, natural or innocent, therefore it is to be unpicked, deconstructed so that its modes of representation and ideological effects are fully understood.

Today, this multi-layered approach in film studies is commonplace as a theoretical and analytical model. The positive impact of post-structuralism is easy to see in that it means that film theory is now constantly open to renewal and to the inclusion of new strategies of decoding and new theoretical models.

see also: **apparatus, auteur theory, feminist film theory, film theory, suture**

STUDIO SYSTEM

Normally identified with **Hollywood**, even though the first country to boast a **vertically integrated** studio system was France, which in

1910 had three production companies: the two majors, Gaumont and Pathé, and, on a smaller scale, Éclair. **Vertical integration** means that a studio controls the modes of production, **distribution** and exhibition. The official date for the birth of the studio system is *circa* 1920. However, its earliest prototype in the United States can be found in the pioneering work of Thomas H. Ince, who in 1912 built Inceville in Hollywood, where he both directed and produced films much on the lines adopted by the Hollywood studio system from the 1920s to the early 1950s. Ince set himself up as **director, producer** and manager, and as such supervised all the films being made simultaneously in different studios; it was he who had the final say on everything from the script to the **editing**. From this production practice it was not long before the full-blown Hollywood studio management style emerged. This style was designed along the following lines: a production head to supervise the whole project, a division of labour and the mass production of films (mostly formula films for sure-fire success), which meant among other things shooting films out of **sequence** to save on costs, and the last word on the final cut resting with the director-manager-owner.

Vertical integration was fully realized in the United States in 1917, when Adolph Zukor acquired Paramount Film Corporation – then a distribution company (established in 1914) – and aligned it with his own production company, the Famous Players-Lasky Corporation. This brought him control of both production and distribution. This move had important consequences both for financing films and for exhibition practices. Distribution was the way to finance films, and now that Zukor owned production and distribution he could more or less force cinema theatres to accept block-bookings – to rent and screen films as decreed by exhibitors. There was an attempt to counter this potentially monopolistic putsch. In 1917, an exhibitors' company, First National (originally called the First National Exhibitors' Circuit) was established to fight the block-booking system. It lasted some twelve years and in its heyday – 1921 – owned around 3,500 theatres. By 1922, it had entered into production. Zukor responded by buying up theatres himself, and, by 1920, owned more than a thousand. During this first cycle in the studio system's history (1913–29), four other major production companies consolidated their positions as rivals to Paramount, and full vertical integration for the five majors occurred between 1924 and 1926, the others being Fox Film Corporation (first established in 1913 and fully integrated by 1925); Metro-Goldwyn-Mayer (1924); Warner Brothers (established 1923 and integrated by 1926); RKO (1928). Alongside these five majors there coexisted the 'little three' majors – Universal Pictures (formed 1912), United Artists (1919) and Columbia (1920). They were called 'little' because they were not vertically integrated, but had access to the majors' first-run theatres. (For a brief history of these companies see below.)

During the 1920s, these major companies had a virtual monopoly over the film industry. Profits were enormous, but so too were costs. To counter these increasing costs – due, first, to the effect of vertical integration (an expensive system to finance) and, second, to the advent of **sound** (1927) – studios increasingly came under the control of bankers and businessmen with the effect that not only economic considerations, but also artistic ones became more and more a matter for management-style decisions (see Bordwell *et al.*, 1985: 320–29). Only Warner Brothers, Columbia and Universal escaped direct interference from Wall Street, because of their prudent production practices. The director was but one of many specialists hired by the studio companies who were now organized into different departments. Hollywood meant business, as can be determined by the fact that from 1930 to 1948 the eight majors between them controlled 95 per cent of all films exhibited in the United States and formed a seemingly impenetrable oligopoly (Cook, 1985: 10).

The eighteen-year period of Hollywood's unrivalled studio system (1930–48) can best be summed up as follows. Each studio had a general overseer (usually the vice-president of the company), and its own 'stable' of **stars**, scriptwriters, **directors** and designers (which led to a 'house look'). Hollywood produced some six hundred films a year on an assembly-line process (which led to a standardization of the product but also, more positively, to a greater sophistication of **genres**). Although each company followed similar production practices, they nonetheless tended to specialize in certain types of films and cultivate a distinctive look (see below). Economic exigency meant that films had to follow certain criteria to guarantee box-office success. During the Great Depression (1929–32), in order to give value for money double features became the rule. This meant that the majors and the minor majors, alongside smaller production companies that specialized in low-budget movies (particularly Monogram and Republic), had now to turn their hand to making **B-movies** to supplement the programme. With the exception of Warners, Columbia and United Artists, all majors went bankrupt at some point during the Depression and became subject to direct interference from Wall Street (Bordwell *et al.*, 1985: 400).

In 1948, the majors suffered a reversal in fortune with the Supreme Court-Paramount decision. Litigation had been begun against the studios in 1938, but World War Two put a halt to it, until 1948.

Exhibitors brought an anti-trust action to put an end to the film industry's monopoly over exhibition. On the grounds of unfair practices, the Supreme Court issued decrees that effectively divested the majors of their power as vertically integrated systems. The big five would have to relinquish their theatres, which represented about two-thirds of their capital investment (Cook, 1985: 10); and the little three would, with the big five, have to stop restrictive practices and coercion (block-booking) in the exhibition of their films. This decision opened the doors to **independent film** and, to a lesser degree, to foreign imports. In 1951, several appeals later, the majors had no choice but to comply with the law and enter into fair competition with minor production companies. This was but a first step in the demise of the studio system. Rising costs meant that the double bill and the B-movie with it disappeared. The lower costs of location shooting abroad also impacted upon studio use. Outside the system, other factors contributed to this decline: first, the rise in the popularity of television, and, second, the effect of the House Un-American Activities Committee on Hollywood both in terms of blacklisting certain actors, directors and scriptwriters and in terms of an unspoken or implicit **censorship** whereby certain types of films just would not get made (see **Hollywood blacklist**). Attempts to regain lost **audiences** through new departures in technology – **3-D**, technicolour, **cinemascope** – had only a slight impact.

To stem losses, studios rented out space to television companies and even turned their own hands to making television programmes (in 1957, RKO was bought by Desilu – Lucille Ball's and Desi Arnaz's television production company – solely for making television programmes). Departments closed, land and real estate were sold off. The studio system became a ghost of its former self. Over the 1980s and 1990s, studios were progressively bought up by large conglomerates for whom film production was just one of their practices. The current method of producing films is usually for an independent producer to put a package together and sell it to one or other of the studios (Konigsberg, 1993: 358–59). As of 2007, only five of the original Golden Age studios remain in any position of strength: 20th Century Fox (owned by what is now known as 21st Century Fox which is part of Rupert Murdoch's News Corporation); Paramount (by Viacom as a subsidiary of National Amusements); Columbia (by Sony); Warner Brothers (by Time Warner); Universal (by Comcast/NBC Universal). And Walt Disney has emerged as a new major studio: Buena Vista Motion Pictures Group (initiated 1998).

see also: **Hollywood**, and for a brief history of the studios see this entry in the fourth edition of *Cinema Studies: The Key Concepts*.

For more detail on these studios see Bordwell *et al.*, 1985; Bordwell and Thompson, 1994; Konigsberg, 1993. For an analysis of their history and their political positioning see Cook, 1985.

SUBJECT/SUBJECTIVITY (INCLUDING THE CONCEPT OF 'MISRECOGNITION')

This concept, as it pertains to **film theory**, needs to be viewed within three different, if contiguous, contexts: within the film text itself, as part of theoretical **structuralist/post-structuralist** debate on the subject, and, finally, within **psychoanalytic** theory.

Within the film text

There are subjective points of view, **shots**, as well as **narrative** techniques, that make it clear that one particular character's (subject's) point of view is being privileged within the filmic text. For example, the uses of **flashback** and intra-**diegetic** narrative voice-over (e.g. in **film noir** adaptations of Raymond Chandler's novels) serve as markers to the authenticity of the protagonist's subjectivity. Similarly, point-of-view shots affect the **spectator**–text relation whereby the spectator feels positioned alongside that character's subjectivity and so identifies with that character. **Shot/reverse-angle shots** represent another series of shots that stitch us into the narrative and also into character identification (see **suture**).

As part of the structuralist/post-structuralist debate

The structuralist theory of the subject was based primarily in Marxian-Althusserian thinking (of the 1960s) which perceived the subject as a construct of material structures. Thus, we are subjects of such structures as language, cultural **codes and conventions**, institutions – what Althusser called ideological state apparatuses (ISAs). We are, he argued, interpolated as subject (see **ideology**) by ISAs such as the church, education, police, family and the media. The effect of this somewhat monolithic theory (the subject as effect or construct of institutions) on spectator theory led to the concept that film, as a pre-existing structure, is like all other ISAs in its ideological functioning, and as such interpolates the spectator, thereby constituting her or him as subject. Post-structuralists (Michel Foucault, Jacques Derrida,

Jean-François Lyotard) argued against this totalizing theory and proposed a different vision of the subject as simultaneously constituted and constituting – as both effect and agent of the text (for further discussion see entries on **apparatus, spectator** and **structuralism/post-structuralism**).

Within psychoanalysis (see also psychoanalysis)

According to Jacques Lacan, human subjectivity, the unconscious and language are all interrelated. The unconscious is structured like a language and so is produced in much the same way as the subject, through language. When the child goes through the **mirror phase**, it first perceives itself as a unified being (the ego-ideal); although, in identifying with the reflection, it is in fact identifying with the 'other' (what is there in the mirror) and, in so doing, *misrecognizes* itself. Second, because the child is held up to the mirror by the mother, it then perceives its similitude with, or difference from the mother; as a result of which, it senses absence, loss, separation from the mother and desires reunification with her. The mother becomes the first love-object of the child. However, the child also perceives the mother as lack: lacking the penis. This lack becomes a source of castration anxiety for the boy child as he enters into the Symbolic Order, into language (see **Imaginary/Symbolic** under **psychoanalysis**). The issues around the girl child's entry into the Symbolic are more complex because she simultaneously perceives her mother as her first desired object and sees herself as the same (this point is more fully developed in **feminist film theory** and **psychoanalysis and the female subject** in the **psychoanalysis** entry).

The child's entry into the Symbolic amounts to its entry into and acquisition of language. So, the subject is the speaking subject. However, in order to be part of language and human society, the child must conform to the Law of the Father (the site of language) and reproduce it. To do so, the subject has to appear to be a unified being. Thus, libidinal drives for the mother have to be repressed because according to the Law of the Father they are taboo; he forbids access through the utterance of the patriarchal 'No'. These drives also have to be repressed because to be conscious of them is to be aware that one *is not* a unified being, for the following reasons. These libidinal drives represent a desire to find again the imagined unity with the mother, 'pre-lack' (before the knowledge of lack). However, the child, after entry into the Symbolic, does not leave the Imaginary behind even though it must suppress these particular drives. Part of the child's trajectory is forever trying to return to the Imaginary, but since it may not desire the mother, these particular drives will be repressed into the unconscious (that which is not spoken, but which is inscribed in language as taboo or the patriarchal 'No'). The child will seek an alternative moment of imagined unity to compensate for the lack represented by the mother and will imagine an idealized image of itself as complete (a moment of misrecognition). In other words, it will seek to return to that first stage of the mirror phase when it felt a unified being – the ego-ideal.

Thus the subject is always divided (self/other; unified/not unified). What gets repressed into the unconscious is that which recalls the subject's lack of unity. The unconscious, in this respect, threatens our sense of unity.

It is not difficult to see how this theory of the subject is relevant to film studies. We saw above, considering the structuralist/post-structuralist debate, that the spectating subject is, in a sense, a divided subject (dialectically positioned as constituted *by* or constituting *of*) in relation to the filmic text. Because film projects before us ideal images in the form of **stars** and a **seamless** reality that disguises its illusory unity (see **apparatus** and **suture**), film functions metonymically for this imagined unity of the ego-ideal and as such allows us to identify with that ego-ideal (see **spectator**). But film also does something else. It projects our desires onto the screen; it functions as a release for our repressed unconscious state and our fantasies. Why do so many of us like **thrillers, horror movies, melodramas** and so forth? So film is, simultaneously, the place where the spectator can find imaginary unity *and* the site where the unspoken can be spoken – that is, film constitutes a 'safe' place from which to observe our lack of unity. **Pornographic** and bondage films would be the most extreme in terms of visioning the unconscious, but many a **film noir** replicates our most deep-rooted fantasies and repressed 'hatreds or phobias'.

see also: **apparatus, diegesis, film theory, ideology, psychoanalysis, spectator, suture**

For more depth on this issue see Kaplan, 1983; Kuhn, 1982; Lapsley and Westlake, 1988.

SUBJECTIVE CAMERA

The camera is used in such a way as to suggest the point of view of a particular character. High- or low-angle **shots** indicate where s/he is looking from; a panoramic or panning shot suggests s/he is surveying the scene; a tracking shot or a hand-held camera shot signifies the character in motion. Subjective shots like these also implicate the **spectator** into the **narrative** in that s/he identifies with the point of view.

SURREALISM

A movement that dates back to the 1920s and which impacted upon films of that time but which still has a small influence today – particularly in **horror** films. This movement, much influenced by Freud, strove to embody in art and poetry the irrational forces of dreams and the unconscious. Surrealist films are concerned with depicting the workings of the unconscious (perceived as irrational, excessive, grotesque, libidinal) and with the liberating force of unconscious desires and fantasy that are normally repressed.

see also: **avant-garde, underground cinema**

For more depth see Hammond, 2000; Williams, 1981.

SUTURE

This term means, literally to stitch up (from the medical term for stitching up a cut or wound); subsequently, it was used by Lacan, in the 1960s, in child psychoanalysis. In **film theory** the system of suture has come to mean, in its simplest sense, to stitch the **spectator** into the filmic text. As a critical concept it was introduced into film studies by theorists, starting with Jean-Pierre Oudart (1977).

The most lasting outcome of the debate around suture concerns the **seamless** relationship of the spectator to the screen and the pleasure experienced in cinema's reconstruction within the spectator of an illusory sense of the early-in-life imagined unity. Attendant within this identification process is the separation from the mother and the implicit sexual drives that that separation brings with it. Cinema in this respect becomes a **mise-en-scène** of desire: first, it constructs the spectator as subject and, second, it establishes the desire to look with all that that connotes in terms of **visual pleasure** for the spectator. In its early days, this debate on visual pleasure, which ran concurrently with that on suture, was completely unproblematized in terms of **sexuality** and **scopophilia**. Since then, however, **feminist film**

theory has entered into the debate and widened it to include analyses of masculine erotic desire and the male fetishizing **gaze** as well as female representation and spectatorship (see also **feminist film theory** and **voyeurism/fetishism**).

see also: **audience, gaze, psychoanalysis** (especially sections on **Imaginary/ Symbolic**, and **Oedipal trajectory**), **shot/reverse-angle shot, spectator, subject/subjectivity**

For further reading see Kuhn, 1982; Lapsley and Westlake, 1988; Mast *et al.*, 1992; Rothman, 1976.

THIRD CINEMA

In 1968 a group of radical Argentinian filmmakers, Grupo Cine Liberación, made a three-part, four-and-a-half-hour-long political film, *La hora de los hornos/The Hour of the Furnaces*. It was shot clandestinely and smuggled to Italy for processing. Its importance needs to be measured against the political climate of the times. Argentina's popular president Juan Perón had been deposed in 1955 and since then the country had been ruled by a series of military dictatorships. This film was intended to wake people up and radicalize them against the latest military coup of 1966. Fifty prints were in secret circulation in Argentina over a five-year period, until 1973, when the Peronists won the elections and, however briefly, a less repressive government was in place. This militant film was described by the group as 'a film act' – one that was open to dialogue and designed to be stopped when inter-titles directed questions to the spectator to open up debate (Chanan, 1997: 373).

Following on from the making of this film, two members of the film group, Fernando Solanas and Octavio Getino, wrote a manifesto based on the experience of making the film: 'Towards a Third Cinema' (1969, reprinted in 1983) in which they call for a 'decolonization of culture' through a **counter-cinema** (Chanan, 1997: 373–74). And so the term Third Cinema was coined and as such refers to both theory and practice. The concept Third Cinema was used to distinguish it from First Cinema (**Hollywood**/Eurocentric cinemas) and Second Cinema (European **art cinema** and the cinema of **auteurs**). It was also called Third Cinema because it emanated from countries and continents outside the then two dominant spheres of power: the Western (first world) and the Eastern (second world) superpower blocs (these two blocs now of course no longer exist since the demise of the Soviet Union in 1989). The naming of this Third

Cinema was intentionally playful – a riposte to economists (who had carved the world up in this way) *and* to dominant Western cinemas. Third Cinema was ostensibly political in its conceptualization, since it sought to promote the cause of socialism and to counter what Solanas and Getino perceived as the **ideologically** unsound filmmaking practices of the two other cinemas, especially Hollywood (see **cinema nôvo**).

Thus, Third Cinema challenged First World consumerist cinema and Second World aesthetic auteur cinema. These films were political in terms of making political statements either directly or through allegory in relation to, or about their own country. They were also political stylistically (as a counter-cinema) and as such targeted their own nation's **mainstream cinema** (see below). Finally, they were politicized in their statements (style and content) against dominant film practices outside their country.

This politicization of Third Cinema dates back to the 1960s when liberation struggles and revolutions in these countries became worldwide news and filmmakers made films either advocating or challenging these changes. Since that period also, the cinema of these countries has been fairly consistent in its opposition to the colonial film practices of the Western world, particularly as exemplified by Hollywood. With the exception of India, which has a huge film industry (producing some 900 to 1,000 films per year) and has successfully exported to other continents (especially Africa), American and European products have swamped the screens of these Third World (now known as developing) countries with their pro-capitalist messages. The need was felt, in the 1960s (as it still is now), to project images of the indigenous realities and this was done in a variety of ways depending on the particular country's political culture and the individual filmmakers' vision and working conditions.

Despite major differences amongst the cinemas of the countries constituting Third Cinema, they do have in common a desire to address the effects of colonialism (as in Africa and India) or neo-colonialism (as in Latin America, some African countries and Asia, including the Indian continent), exclusion and oppression (all of these countries or continents). This Third Cinema sets out deliberately to politicize cinema and to create new cinematic **codes and conventions**. Gabriel (1982: 16ff.) discusses the major themes of this Third (politicized) Cinema. This cinema addresses issues of **class**, race, culture, religion, sex and national integrity. Class struggle between the poor and the rich is at the core of this cinema. But, in these films the issue of race is seen within the context of class antagonism (ibid.: 16). The preservation of popular indigenous cultures and the representation of them in opposition to the dominant colonial and imperialist values espoused by the ruling classes constitute an 'aesthetics of liberation' (ibid.: 16) in Third Cinema; as did the foregrounding of contradictions inherent in political struggle within the context of deeply rooted structures of religion and, very occasionally, the struggle for the emancipation of women (see Deepa Metha's *Fire*, 1997, as an example of representation of forbidden desire between two Indian women).

In terms of Third Cinema practice, several nations have had the term ascribed to their work *post facto*. While this is not necessarily a problem, insofar as these cinemas correspond to the ethos of Third Cinema, we do come up against the fact that several of these cinemas owe their existence to either state funding (as is the case for Cuba and to some degree India) or to assistance (in the form of training or finance) from previously colonizing countries (as is the case for some African countries). Thus, in terms of state funding, in 1959, right on the heels of the Cuban Revolution, Fidel Castro set up the Cuban Institute of Cinematographic Art and Industry, and **documentaries** and feature films were soon being produced. Cuba very quickly established itself on the international scene. In the second instance, help from former colonizers, some African countries such as Senegal and the North African countries (Tunisia, Algeria and Morocco) have been assisted in their filmmaking practices, mostly in the form of training (in these cases by France). Similarly, in Ghana the infrastructure of colonial filmmaking (left behind by the British) was used to build the ongoing film industry (see **World Cinemas** for more detail on these countries' film industries; see also Diawara's useful essay (1986: 61–65), and for an in-depth study of African cinema, see Ukadike, 1994).

What is interesting, however, is how so many of these so-called Third World countries came to a similar position in the late 1960s around the need for a third type of cinema even though they may not have evoked the term 'Third Cinema' itself. Thus, in the late 1960s, filmmakers in Africa established independent groups within their own countries and came together to form a Pan-African organizational means for developing cinema as a revolutionary tool. The manifestos written at that time are very similar to those written in Latin America and the intentions were the same (see above). And in 1969, the Fédération Panafricaine des Cinéastes (FEPACI) was established in Algiers 'to use film as a tool for the liberation of the colonized countries and as a step towards the total unity of Africa' (Diawara, 1986: 69). Furthermore, two Film Festivals were launched in the 1960s, committed to the cause and the promotion of the cinema of African and Arab countries: the now annual Carthage Film Festival (first launched in 1966 as a bi-annual event), and the bi-annual Film Festival at Ouagadougou in Burkina Faso established in 1969 – the Festival Panafricaine du cinéma de Ouagadougou (FEPASCO).

Filmmakers from Africa (see **World Cinemas** entry), whose work is clearly politicized and therefore considered as Third Cinema, are not well known in the West, although Ousmane Sembene, Djibril Diop Mambéty and Idrissa Ouedraogo of Senegal, Med Hondo from Mauritania, and Souleymane Cissé from Mali have made the cross-over into Western cinema theatres. Conversely, to take only one example, the Ghanaian independents, active since the late 1970s, are hardly known to us at all. In this context, the Ghanaian independents Kwaw Painstil Ansah and King Ampaw make an interesting comparative study in relation to Third Cinema practice and the need to safeguard creative autonomy. Both claim to have done this, but they have done so at very different prices. For his part, Ansah refused foreign money or partnerships for his films and thus managed with great difficulty to pull off his productions, making two films in seventeen years (*Love Brewed in an African Pot*, 1981, which took him ten years to complete, and *Heritage Africa*, 1988). This story is familiar to other African filmmakers, for example, Mambéty who struggled to finance his few films. The other Ghanaian filmmaker, Ampaw, co-produced his films with foreign companies and foreign funds which allowed him to make two feature films in two years (*Kukurantumi*, 1984, and *Juju*, 1985) (for more detail see Ukadike, 1994: 131–65).

Continuing our survey, Indian cinema has a strong tradition in Third Cinema practice; beginning in 1969, when state-financing made it possible for a new generation of filmmakers to emerge on the scene. Mrinal Sen and Mani Kaul are seen as the originators of this New Indian Cinema. However, the heritage of this contestatory and politicized cinema goes back, first, to the work of the influential communist-backed theatre and film movement, the Indian People's Theatre Association (IPTA) which launched its first film production in 1946 (*Dharti Ke Lal/Children of the Earth*, K. A. Abbas) and, second, to the art cinema made by Satyajit Ray during the 1950s. Mani Kaul's cinema is more evidentially counter-cinematic given its formalist concerns and the debates it raises on cinematic practice (e.g. *Usi Roti/Our Daily Bread*, 1969). But again, Ritwik Ghatak's work of the 1950s and early 1960s pre-dates these concerns, albeit in a slightly different way. Ghatak mixes documentary realism with **myth**, tribal and folk traditions – truly blurring the boundaries between fact and fiction. See, for example, *Nagarik/The Citizen*, 1952, *Ajantrik/The Unmechanical*, 1957. See also his deeply political trilogy about refugee poverty and conditions in Calcutta/Kolkata which is based on his own experience of watching refugees fleeing to Calcutta during the famine of 1943 and the partition of India in 1947 (*Meghe Dhaka Tara/The Cloud-Capped Star*, 1960, *Komal Gandhar*, 1961, *Subarnareka*. 1962). More recently, a new cinema of resistance that appears to follow in Ghatak's tradition – which is not feature film but independent documentary film production – has emerged (see Patwardhan's *We Make History, Father Son and Holy War*, both 1993). (See **Indian cinema** in **world cinema** entry.)

Finally, in this brief overview, we must make mention of Latin American cinema, especially since the term *Third Cinema* emerged from these countries (see Burton, 1986, 1990; Chanan, 1983; King, 1990; King *et al.*, 1993 for more detail). Armed struggle is a theme particularly identified with this Third Cinema. Labels such as *guerilla cinema*, *garbage cinema* and *cannibal-tropicalist cinema* are deliberately and provocatively used by these filmmakers to demarcate their practice from First and Second cinemas – and of course to point to the radical nature of their purpose within their own nation-state. Indeed, indirect and direct social and political criticism of existing regimes are more commonly associated with Latin American Third Cinema films of the 1960s than with any other Third Cinemas of that time. This is particularly the case for Brazil and Argentina. In Brazil this cinema often took the form of an aesthetics of hunger or violence (see **cinema nôvo** entry) – as, for example, in Glauber Rocha's *Terra em Transe* (*Land in Anguish*, 1967). In Argentina, revolutionary cinema took the form of 'avant-garde militant documentary' (Shohat and Stam, 1994: 260) – somewhat in the same light as Pontecorvo's *La Bataille d'Alger/Battle of Algiers* (1965). Exemplary of this style are Getino and Solanas' *La hora de los hornos* and Leopoldo Torre Nilsson's *Piel de verano* (*Summer Skin*, 1961). During this same period, Cuba produced a political cinema that was, it has to be said, closely identified with the socialist programme of the state and to that effect spoke not against the regime but made films that charted the difficulties of implementing the Revolution (thanks to the severity of US sanctions amongst other reasons). Exemplary of this cinema are Tomás Guttiérez Alea's *Memorias del subdesarrollo* (*Memories of Underdevelopment*, 1968) and Humberto Solás' *Lucia*, 1968 (see Chanan (1985) for more details on Cuban cinema).

Third Cinema continues to be an active cinema both within its practice and debates. This entry concludes with a brief overview of these shifting debates (and I am indebted here in what follows to Jacqueline Maingard's lucid synopsis of these debates (1998: 60–93)). In 1982, the concept Third Cinema was elaborated by Teshome

Gabriel in his book *Third Cinema in the Third World: The Aesthetics of Liberation*. The crucial issue raised by Gabriel's book is the relation between the term *Third World* and the concept of Third Cinema as both a concept and a practice. Gabriel's study seems to imply that the two terms *Third Cinema* and *Third World* are easily conflatable. But this conflation is not really sustainable. For example, what do we make of China's cinema? In the 1950s, at the Bandung Conference, China opted for Third World status. However, it is not necessarily practising Third Cinema (given the very heavy **censorship** and state control of the film industry it would be difficult to argue the case). Gabriel's book had the effect, nonetheless, of opening the doors where Third Cinema was concerned. It became a referable concept to other cinemas, not coming from the Third World, but made by filmmakers living in diasporic communities. Thus, a few years later, in 1986, the concept was further elaborated to embrace the cinema of marginalized groups in other parts of the world (residing primarily in the West). In the late 1980s, in Britain, where **Black cinema** had begun to emerge, two conferences were held (one in Edinburgh, 1986, the other in Birmingham, 1988) which in a sense 'officialized' this widened meaning of the term. The debates centred, on a far broader scale than that first considered by Solanas and Getino, on cinematic practices that were developing at that time and their relevance to Third Cinema as a political concept.

Pines and Willemen's book *Questions of Third Cinema* (1989) brought together the Edinburgh conference debates. A special issue of *Framework*, 1989, published those of the Birmingham conference (of which more later). First to be addressed were the developments in cinema practices in Britain and the United States that were taking place outside the White-Euro-American sphere – that is, being made by Black people (see **Black cinema – UK** and **Black cinema – USA**). While not rejecting Gabriel's earlier implicit argument that Third Cinema could refer to non-Third World practitioners, Willemen (1989: 15–17) makes the point that Gabriel's homogenizing Third Cinema (as Third World Cinema) on an internationalist basis disguises the fact that this cinema is profoundly national and regional and must therefore be seen as one of the cinemas making up a nation's cinema. In other words, Third Cinema is a national cinema alongside the mainstream and the auteur-based national cinemas of a nation. It is in this way, in fact, that we can argue for a Black cinema outside the Third World/ developing economies as having the cachet of Third Cinema. Indeed, Gabriel (1989), in his paper, included in Pines and Willemen's book, notes that there can be different types of Third Cinema, depending on the prevailing social conditions in specific places. What is crucial is the relationship between personal memory, identity, history and cinema. Providing that the representations are not of official history but of personal memory, the term *Third Cinema* may be used as a means of identifying, naming and claiming a consciously transformative space for cinemas in parts of the world that, at least geographically, would not be considered as being in the Third World. This challenge to history would, according to Gabriel (1989: 57–59), take a counter-cinematic form: open-ended narrative, multiple points of view, style that grows out of the material of the film, and so on. On these two counts, therefore, it would appear that Third Cinema could be used to define British Black cinema. Willemen (1989: 29) did express the fear – and he was not alone – that Third Cinema might be kidnapped and appropriated into the First World (and indeed even the Second World). But he also makes the point that British Black filmmakers are in a position of being both 'other' and in and of the culture they inhabit. They occupy what he calls an 'in between' position (what Homi Bhabha terms a third space; see **postcolonial**). Thus, it can be argued that the work of Black filmmakers in Britain has both incorporated what can be learned from Third Cinema about 'otherness' and, at the same time, extended and developed already conceived and already received notions of the Third Cinema ethos.

By 1988, in Birmingham, the debates had moved on and broadened to embrace more issues still. At this conference, John Akomfrah made the point that, while Third Cinema had been useful to help place British Black cinema, what was currently needed was 'a re-examination of location and subjectivity' (Akomfrah, 1989: 6). Third Cinema, as a cinema of resistance coming from a third space, raises the two fundamental issues of politics of location and identity politics; namely, where are 'you' shooting from (which nation/location), and who are 'you' and what position are you shooting from (whose **subjectivity** is it)? Coco Fusco made the point that the early Latin American Third Cinema films (see above) were made by men from middle-class and upper-class elites and almost always forgot about **gender** (1989: 9). Crucially, bell hooks (1989: 18) argued that this cinema, wherever it emanates from, must be about 'the struggle of memory against forgetting' – a politics/politicization of memory, therefore.

The Third Cinema debate remains an open one particularly in relation to what counts as 'in'. In general terms, it encompasses politicized and historicized cinemas emanating from what is now referred to as the developing world (formerly known as Third World economies) and the Black and Asian-Indian diasporas. In more purist terms, it can refer to the counter-cinemas of developing countries. For the most part, it is the former reading that dominates, and this should be welcomed on the whole, since it will allow for other diasporic cinemas – such as that of the Native-American, the Asian-American, the Turkish-German, the Arab-French, and so on – to be imagined and viewed in a different way than they presently are. That is, not as ghetto cinemas, but as national cinemas in their own right.

The point is also that Third Cinema should be seen as both national and **transnational** (or even trans-continental). As Gabriel points out, it is a process of becoming – a nomadic cinema even (Chanan, 1997: 382). This latter point is evident if we consider that filmmakers can often be either in exile, but may eventually return to make films, or their films are exiled from their countries but are screened elsewhere in the world. In a sense, Third Cinema asserts difference within its own indigenous cinema, but also dissolves geographical boundaries with, as Michael Chanan so eloquently puts it, 'a virtual geography of its own' (1997: 375). In that it is a combative cinema committed to social liberation and that its aesthetics are an anti-aesthetics, it should also be seen as being capable of emanating from both the collective and the individual filmmaker (ibid.: 382). This means, of course, that individual experimental *auteurs* from Third World continents (Sembene, Cissé, Mambéty, for example) and Europe as well as North America (or indeed collectives: US New Left film group, Sankofa and Black Audio Film Collective in the UK, for example) can be part of this process of Third Cinema-making. As we have seen, Third Cinema is a cinema which possesses a **semiotics** of its own (Guneratne and Dissanayake, 2003: 13). Essentially to figure as Third Cinema, the work must serve to challenge the (capitalist and consumerist) modes of representation inherited from the Hollywood/Eurocentric cinemas. It should challenge these cinemas' erasure of the distinction between history and reality (whereby Hollywood/Eurocentric narratives allow fiction to pass as fact) and place reality (most often in the form of 'what is happening now as it is witnessed') in whatever configuration (political, economic, social, racial, sexual and so on) before our eyes in the form of a dialogue for us to enter into. In summation it should decolonize the mind.

see also: **Black cinema – USA**, **Black cinema – UK**, **cinema nôvo**, **postcolonial theory**, **World Cinemas**

For further reading consult texts cited in this entry. See also Martin's (1995) edited book which contains most of the manifestos of Third Cinemas;

Vieler-Portet's (1991) Third Cinema bibliography; Oshana's (1985) Third World women's filmography; and Bobo's history of Black women's film and video work (1998). See also *Screen* special issue on Third Cinema, 24: 2, 1983; Barnard, 1986; Burton, 1990; Shohat and Stam, 1994; Wayne, 2001. For an excellent summary of the debates see Chanan, 1997; Maingard, 1998. For a rethinking of this cinema see Guneratne and Dissanayake, 2003.

30-DEGREE RULE

A rule applied in the name of continuity which stipulates that, when there is a **cut** to another camera position, the camera should be at least 30 degrees from the previous one. If this rule is not observed and two shots are cut together of the same person or object within the scene, without the camera having moved more than thirty degrees, the effect on the spectator is of a jolt, as if the camera has jumped a bit. Essentially, in terms of spatial logic there is not enough difference between the two **shots** in terms of angle (and, therefore, a clearly understood renewed position on the object) for the transition between the two shots to remain unnoticed. The result is a noticeable jump, what is termed a **jump cut**. The 30-degree rule serves to create an undisturbed **seamlessness** in the film because such a shift does not draw attention to itself and is logically motivated within the **narrative**.

see also: **180-degree rule**

3-D CINEMA/STEREOSCOPIC IMAGERY

The potential for three-dimensional film has been around since the beginning of cinema (1895). Indeed, in photographic terms, stereophonic imaging was first seen in public in 1856 (Rickitt, 2006: 355). Because it is the form of cinema that most readily re-creates our own binocular system of seeing (see below), it is perhaps surprising that it is not the most popular of processes with **audiences**, even though it tends to be revived at times when the film industry most desperately needs to coax audiences back into their cinema theatres. Thus, the two major moments for 3-D are the 1950s and the present period (2000–2010s). It is still a very costly process which is why, quite reasonably, we might expect it to be limited in use to **blockbusters**, **epics** and big spectacular **fantasy** films. Indeed, this has been pretty much the case. However, given the **realism** inherent in the 3-D effect (with its

re-creation of how our eyes actually function), it is perhaps not so sur-
prising that some documentary makers have used 3-D for their purpose.
Thus, recently, a handful of filmmakers have found this technology to
be admirably suited to their **documentary** practice (in particular,
James Cameron, *Aliens of the Deep*, 2005; Werner Herzog, *Cave of
Forgotten Dreams*, 2010; Wim Wenders, *Pina*, 2011).

Three-dimensional film is of course an optical illusion. However,
its principle is based in the very real effect of human binocular
vision. Each of our two eyes (because they are set apart) perceives
whatever is before it from a slightly different perspective. It is the
merging of these two perspectives (point of convergence) that results in
the brain creating the perception of depth (Rickitt, 2006: 355). Thus,
with 3-D cinema, the effect of real depth is created through stereoscopic imagery – basically, two cameras film from two different
perspectives, the two are then merged to simulate binocular vision.
The point at which the two perspectives meet is known as the plane
of **convergence**; objects that are in front of the plane of convergence
appear as if they are in front of the screen (e.g. the Cheshire cat in
Tim Burton's *Alice in Wonderland*, 2010); objects behind the plane
appear at the rear of the screen. In this way the illusion of depth is
complete.

When the two films are projected, however, the effect is murky,
one film image over the other. Thus, the two sets of images have to be
separated out in order for the **spectator** to experience the 3-D effect –
in short, the binocular vision has to be restored to the spectator; and
the way to achieve this is to present each of the two perspectives to
just one of our eyes. This is why audiences have to wear glasses. There
are three major processes (anaglyphic, polarization, and liquid polarization or RealD), and three different types of glasses, therefore, to
ensure this effect. The red-blue/green anaglyphic process, which was
the process used in the 1950s, requires the spectator to wear glasses
with one red and one green lens; each lens obscures the image shown
in its own colour and highlights the image in the opposite colour. To be
clear, the red lens obscures the red image and highlights the green;
meantime, the other lens, the green one does the reverse (obscures
the green and highlights the red). Thus, one eye sees one perspective, the
other another. The brain merges the two perspectives, and binocular
vision provides the 3-D illusion. A second process, polarized light (1950s
to 1980s), requiring polarized glasses, presents each eye with the right
image. This it does through a system of polarizing filters when projecting the two films, with the effect of screening each image
sequentially. Each projector has a filter, one which makes light travel

through horizontally angled slots, the other, through vertical slots. The glasses have similarly horizontal and vertical slotted lenses so that we also view the images from the two films sequentially. Most recently, the polarizing liquid crystal filter process (RealD) can switch polarity 144 times per second as left and right eye images are screened alternately; only one projector is needed, therefore. The liquid crystal glasses react to a beam of infrared light coming from the projector causing them to flicker and give each eye alternate views of the synchronized images on-screen (Rickitt, 2006: 357).

The most extreme form of stereophonic imaging (often referred to as Immersive 3-D) was introduced in the mid-1980s with IMAX 3-D giant-screen cinema projection of *Transitions* (Low and Ianzelo, 1986). At ten times the size of a conventional 35mm film frame, the costs of production of IMAX's 15/70mm format (even in 2-D) tend to limit output to short subject documentaries, although a few fiction and **animation** films have been released or made in this format. Unsurprisingly, not many 3-D IMAX films are made (some fifty in the last thirty years, thirty-eight of which were made since the new millennium).

Until 2010, the yearly release of 3-D films could be counted on one hand. However, with the impact of *Avatar* (Cameron, 2009) and starting with *Alice in Wonderland,* released in March 2010, yearly figures world-wide are reaching the half-century-mark and above (averaging out at fifty-six per year since 2010). These more recent figures indicate something of an upward swing, especially if we consider that, during the first peak period of 3-D (the 1950s), only sixty-one were made (forty-eight in the USA; thirteen worldwide, primarily in former USSR); and that, for a half century in the period 1952 to 2005, a mere 180 3-D films were produced worldwide (fewer than four a year).

For further reading see Rickitt, 2006; Zone, 2007.

THRILLER/PSYCHOLOGICAL THRILLER

A very difficult **genre** to pin down because it covers such a wide range of types of films. Thrillers are films of suspense, so clearly **film noir**, gangster, **science-fiction** or **horror** films are in some respects thrillers, as are political and spy thrillers (e.g. *Clear and Present Danger*, Philip Noyce, 1994; the Bourne trilogy, 2002 to 2007 and its latest itera-tion, *Jason Bourne*, Greengrass, 2016), and detective thrillers (see **gangster films**). Some purists will differentiate terror movies as being distinct from thrillers, since a thriller is supposed to instil terror into the **audience**. I shall ignore that sub-categorizing and focus primarily on the **psychological** thriller, bearing in mind the overlap with the aforementioned genres.

A thriller relies on intricacy of plot to create fear and apprehension in the audience. It plays on our own fears by drawing on our infantile and therefore mostly repressed fantasies that are voyeuristic and sexual in nature. The master of the thriller is Alfred Hitchcock, the greatest creator of anticipation and builder of suspense. Almost unquestionably he is the filmmaker who invented the modern thriller. His secret is of course in the construction of his films. Often at the centre of the **narrative** is a fairly basic theme, usually a struggle around love and/or money, so it is not that which grabs and enthralls the **spectator**. Alfred Hitchcock works through delay. He delays the action which we know is going to occur. We know Marion Crane is going to be murdered (in *Psycho*, 1960), but we do not know when or how. We, like Norman Bates, have been watching her, unseen, as we peep through the holes alongside Norman. When will terror strike? When it finally does, we almost feel relief, certainly a release from all the tension that has been building up through the set of **gazes** that have been conferred on Marion. In this respect, the attacks on women in Alfred Hitchcock's films are clearly sexually motivated. For, even if in some films (such as *The Birds*, 1963) Hitchcock's women do not die, they are assailed by knives, birds or brutally strangled (*Frenzy*, 1972).

Thriller films are, then, sadomasochistic. Indeed, the psychological thriller bases its construction in sadomasochism, madness and **voyeurism**. The killer spies on and ensnares his victim in a series of intricate and sadistic moves, waiting to strike. The killer is most often psychotic and his madness is an explanation for what motivates his actions. He **agences** murderous power through his madness. Such is not usually the luck of the woman. Madness predominantly privileges women-as-victim far more than men. Their madness is a deep-rooted phobia that often has a sexual cause. Marnie's fear of men (in *Marnie*, Hitchcock, 1964) is due to her violent reaction to seeing her mother aggressed by a sailor – which is why Marnie kills him, but she is forever stuck with the neurosis that men equal sexual aggression. She is stuck, that is, until her all-knowing husband cures her. In *Repulsion* (Roman Polanski, 1965), as the title already indicates, the heroine's revulsion at men's sexual advances is the result of the fear and repulsion she experiences when confronted by the primal scene (the parents copulating). Men who get too close to her get murdered.

Voyeurism operates within the film. It is **diegetically** inscribed, but the film also operates to position us as voyeurs. One film that brilliantly exposes this process is Michael Powell's *Peeping Tom* (1960). The film itself foregrounds voyeurism, positions us as voyeur-director and as the victim, and in the closing **shots** makes us voyeur of our 'own' victimness. In this way, we too play out the sadistic scenario and derive pleasure from re-experiencing our primitive and infantile desires. It is noteworthy that many thrillers focus around bad parenting – or that bad parenting is the cause of psychotic behaviour. Norman Bates in *Psycho* and Mark Lewis in *Peeping Tom* both had bad parents: an overbearing mother in the first case, a disapproving father in the second. Sibling rivalry can also cause psychological disorders of a life-threatening kind (as in *Whatever Happened to Baby Jane?*, Robert Aldrich, 1962). But so too can sibling narcissism (as in *Dead Ringers*, David Cronenberg, 1988). The two identical twins, both brilliant gynaecologists, live in perfect harmony with one another until a woman enters their life with an amazing gynaecological problem (a triple cervix!). She disrupts the twins' symbiosis and symbolically castrates them (well, she would with a triple cervix wouldn't she?). Incapable of coping with woman-as-difference and terrified of separation, one of the twins takes to drugs and becomes increasingly hysterical in relation to women. He eventually drags his brother down with him and the two finally succumb to a gruesome double-death.

One final point. Although thrillers are more about **fantasy** than reality, they do fulfil a very real need. Otherwise why would we go to the movies? We do have a psychological fascination with horror, we like being made afraid. For this reason many thrillers have an aura of 'the possible' about them. To achieve this, the **settings** are as ordinary as one's own familiar environment. Hitchcock's *Frenzy* is a good example of this everyday ordinariness in which ordinary women keep getting murdered (the setting is London, more specifically what was formerly Covent Garden, the murderer an ordinary fellow, a fruit-seller). Roman Polanski also combines the fantastic with the ordinary in *Rosemary's Baby* (1966) where he juxtaposes demonic possession and witchcraft with contemporary New York.

see also: **fantasy, film noir, gangster movies, motivation, horror movies, psychoanalysis, science fiction, voyeurism/fetishism**

For further reading see Mason, 2002; Smith, 2004.

TIME-IMAGE/MOVEMENT-IMAGE – *SEE* MOVEMENT-IMAGE/TIME-IMAGE

TRACKING SHOT/TRAVELLING SHOT/ DOLLYING SHOT

Terms used for a **shot** when the camera is being moved by means of wheels: on a dolly (a low wheeled platform on which a film camera is moved) and on tracks (hence tracking shot), in a car or even a train. The movement is normally quite fluid (except perhaps in some of the wilder car chases) and the tracking can be either fast or slow. Depending on the speed, this shot has different **connotations** (e.g. like a dream or trance if excessively slow, or bewildering and frightening if excessively frenetic). A tracking shot can go backwards, forwards, from left to right or right to left, and the way in which a person is framed in that shot has a specific meaning (e.g. if the camera holds a person in the frame but that person is at one extreme or other of the frame, this could suggest a sense of imprisonment).

TRANSNATIONAL CINEMA

Because film is now recognized as a product of so many varied economies (international financing and personnel, cross-cultural influences, and so on) transnational cinema has been developed as a theoretical approach to analyse film in a way that encourages a shift away from the concept of an all-encompassing national cinema. As Andrew Higson noted, 'the concept of national cinema is hardly able to do justice either to the internal diversity of contemporary cultural formations or to the overlaps and interpenetrations between different formations' (2000: 70). Transnational is an attempt, therefore, to acknowledge the changing nature of film production, **distribution** and reception in an increasingly globalized world and offers up an alternative conceptual framework within which to analyse film culture, becoming a 'subtler means of describing cultural and economic formations that are rarely contained by national boundaries' (Higson, 2000: 64).

This approach is not without its perils. For example, Ezra and Rowden suggest that, although 'the transnational can be understood as the global forces that link people or institutions across nations' (2006: 1), nonetheless, the effect is to homogenize. Thus, transnational cinema 'comprises both globalization – in cinematic terms,

Hollywood's domination of world film markets - and the counter **hegemonic** responses of filmmakers from former colonial and third world countries' (2006: 1).

Transnational is not then unproblematic. For this approach suggests that to label all cinema as transnational, from international to marginalized, is to occlude concepts of difference, such as films that challenge **mainstream cinematic narratives** most readily embodied by **Hollywood**. The outcome of this blanket labelling means that marginal cinemas risk being overlooked because they have become subsumed under globalization: a capitalist hegemonic market-model erasing the possibility of engaging with **World Cinemas** as distinct models in and of themselves. Furthermore, as Hjort notes, such an all-encompassing approach 'does little to advance our thinking about important issues if it can mean anything and everything that the occasion would appear to demand' (Hjort, 2009: 15). This raises the question, as Shaw does, would this then mean 'mainstream Hollywood films' are 'transnational as they are distributed throughout the developed world?' (2009: 47) – when in reality they are merely global products.

Hjort offers a potential answer to the above problematic with a detailed typology that links the concept of transnationalism to different models of cinematic production, each motivated by 'specific concerns and designed to achieve particular effects' (2009: 15). Hjort supplies a series of categories to provide a robust framework from which to identify the transnational quality of a film (2009:15):

- epiphanic transnationalism
- affinitive transnationalism
- milieu-building transnationalism
- opportunistic transnationalism
- cosmopolitan transnationalism
- globalizing transnationalism
- auteurist transnationalism
- modernizing transnationalism
- experimental transnationalism

Though Transnational is a wide theoretical model, we can begin to understand how films, actors and directors are transnational yet distinct. For example, the Japanese film *Ringu* (Hideo Nakata, 1998) was remade by Hollywood, redistributed and exhibited in overseas markets. This, in turn, led to Nakata making a sequel for a Hollywood studio. As Lim and Higbee note, in terms of films like *Hero* (Zhang

Yimou, 2002) and *Crouching Tiger, Hidden Dragon* (Ang Lee, 2000), 'from action thrillers to horror films, East Asian cinemas have excited critics who marvel at their ability to beat Hollywood "at its own game"' (2010: 15).

An obvious domain of the Transnational is that of production. Take, for example, the case of a Hollywood **blockbuster**: we expect an Americanization to be prominent throughout the film (a distinctly national product therefore). Ezra and Rowden concur, stating, 'the performance of Americanness is increasingly becoming a universal characteristic in world cinema' (2006: 2). However, this American-ization is itself unstable within productions whose backgrounds are multicultural and multinational. For example, Christopher Nolan's recent *Dark Knight* trilogy (2005, 2008 and 2012) demonstrates how the notion of a national cinema is challenged, even within the notion of Hollywood. The director of the film is British, the majority of the production crew are also British, including the **producer**, **art director** and costume designer. However, the editor (Wally Pfister), scriptwriters and **cinematographers** are American. In terms of **stars**, the ever-present Christian Bale and Michael Caine are British, playing alongside American actors such as Anne Hathaway, Joseph Gordon-Levitt, French actor Marion Cotillard and Australian Heath Ledger.

So is the *Dark Knight* a British or American production? Techni-cally speaking it is a multinational and multicultural product con-stituted from 'cultural and economic formations that are rarely contained by national boundaries' (Higson, 2000: 67). As such it falls into Hjort's category of cosmopolitan transnationalism. But it is also an example of globalizing transnationalism, for, as Higson argues, 'Hollywood of course is one of the longest standing and best orga-nized media institutions with a transnational reach capable of pene-trating even the most heavily policed national spaces' (2000: 67).

In essence then, Transnational allows us to redefine, challenge even, the concept of a national cinema. It makes clear the fact that national cinema has been positioned as an 'imaginary community' (to reference Benedict Anderson), whereas the reality is that we live in a world of fragmented connections. Global communication has eroded traditional borders; **digitization** makes film **distribution** effortless across vast markets. The notion of isolation, of a sense of purity, of a single national identity is undercut in a world defined by fluidity and community. As Higbee and Lim argue, the Transnational is ultimately in dialogue with the national: 'in the study of films, a critical trans-nationalism does not ghettoize transnational film-making in interstitial and marginal spaces but rather interrogates how these film-making activities negotiate with the national on all levels – from cultural policy to financial sources, from the multiculturalism of difference to how it reconfigures the nation's image of itself' (2010: 8).

TRANSPARENCY/TRANSPARENCE

This concept takes both these spelling forms, and refers to the notion that cinema does not provide a window on the world any more than television does. That is, the idea that it offers a one-to-one relationship with reality is a **myth**. Both media can, however, offer a transparence on the world: they can give a reflection *on* the world that surrounds us. Thus, a **war film** such as *All Quiet on the Western Front* (Lewis Milestone, 1930) gives a reflection on the horrors of World War One trench warfare – a reflection that is closer to the truth than the dominant tendency of war films which is to glorify victory and heroize the individual.

see also: **ideology**

UNDERGROUND CINEMA

The underground cinema movement in the 1960s was very important to the growth of US cinema. It was bold, outrageous and scornful of **dominant cinema** practices. It was also known as the New American Cinema Group: this group, formed in 1960, signed a manifesto accusing mainstream or dominant cinema of being morally corrupt. Underground cinema was a name coined by Stan VanDerBeek to qualify this independent filmmaking movement based in New York and San Francisco. This movement grew out of the 1950s Beat Generation and its revolt against conventional artistic practices. VanDerBeek was one of the practitioners of this movement, as were, more famously, Andy Warhol, Stan Brakhage and Kenneth Anger. **Censorship** was still in practice in the US (it was abolished in the late 1960s), hence the term *underground*, because, in subject matter, the films produced by this movement were censorable products. The movement was not a cohesive group, but stood as one in its determination to defy the censorship laws, which it deemed unconstitutional. And, in fact, it was one of the movement's most notorious films, Jack Smith's *Flaming Creatures* (1963) – a **fantasy** film about a transvestite orgy – which was hounded by the New York police and the US Customs but which, in the end, was shown as evidence before the States Supreme Court hearing on the abolition of censorship.

The collective that made up underground cinema were not necessarily filmmakers, but came from different artistic backgrounds and saw in film a new way of self-expression. The heritage of this movement is traced back to Maya Deren's influential experimental film work on the subconscious, most specifically her film *Meshes of the Afternoon* (1943). And she helped to finance projects by other independent filmmakers, particularly Brakhage and Anger. The first so-called underground film, *Pull My Daisy* (1959), was a Beat Generation film made by Robert Frank and the painter Alfred Leslie starring Jack Kerouac as voice-over and Allen Ginsberg as the poet. Kenneth Anger's films explicitly explored homosexual fantasies, rituals and dilemmas (see *Scorpio Rising*, 1963). In *Empire* (1964), Andy Warhol played with reel/real time by setting up his Auricon 16mm camera (famed for its light weight and strong sound range, producing newsreel-style footage) opposite the Empire State building. Supposedly, the filming lasted for just over eight hours and gave the appearance of temporal continuity. In fact, he shot just over six and a half hours at twenty-four frames per second using innumerable canisters of film, but then had it projected at sixteen frames per second – an interesting form of temporal **deconstruction**. He also parodied **Hollywood genres** (e.g. **Westerns** in *Lonesome Cowboys*, 1968). Other filmmakers were more closely associated in their work with the **cinéma-vérité** tradition. Lionel Rigosin's and Shirley Clarke's **documentary** approach produced such politicized films as Rigosin's film on a down-and-out alcoholic in New York, *On the Bowery* (1955), and the clandestinely shot film among Black South Africans, *Come Back Africa* (1959). Clarke's films focused on Black ghetto subculture in Harlem: drugs and jazz (*The Connection*, 1961); adolescent crime and survival (*The Cool World*, 1963); Black male prostitute fantasy (*Portrait of Jason*, 1967).

For further reading see Dixon, 1997; Reeckie, 2007; Sargeant, 2001; Tyler, 1995.

UNMATCHED SHOTS

Cutting from one **shot** to another so that there is no apparent **continuity** in action. This type of editing is typically used in **avant-garde** and **surreal** films as a means of creating a sense of disorientation in time and space. A classic example is Luis Buñuel's *Un chien andalou* (1929).

VERTICAL INTEGRATION

A term used to refer to a film industry practice put in place by **Hollywood** (although there are precursors to Hollywood) whereby the entire system of production, **distribution** and exhibition is controlled by the **studio** making the film product. Thus the studio makes the film, distributes it and controls its exhibition (often in its own theatres).

see also: **studio system**

VOYEURISM/FETISHISM

Voyeurism is the act of viewing the activities of other people unbeknown to them. This often means that the act of looking is illicit or has illicit **connotations**. We pay to go to the movies, but once we are sat before the screen we are positioned as voyeurs, as spectating **subject** watching the goings-on of the people on-screen who are 'unaware' that we are watching them. It is from this positioning that we derive pleasure (known as **scopophilia**, pleasure in viewing). Voyeurism is not limited to the **spectator**, however. The camera that originally filmed the action is also, technically speaking, a 'voyeur'. Often there is a voyeuristic positioning of a character within a film. Alfred Hitchcock is notorious for this (as in *Rear Window*, 1954, and *Psycho*, 1960). A film that admirably foregrounds the complexity of voyeurism and all the subject positionings possible is Michael Powell's *Peeping Tom* (1960).

Fetishism refers to the notion of over-investment in parts of the body, most commonly the female body. Thus, in films, women's breasts or legs are often 'picked out' by the camera and are thereby over-invested with meaning. Similarly dress-codes can be part of this fetishizing process. Thus, a woman might wear a slinky, tight-fitting dress and long black evening gloves. Alternatively, she might be wearing very high heels, stilettos perhaps, and have her fingernails thickly nail-polished (in deep red if it is a film in **colour**).

In **psychoanalytic** terms, *voyeurism* and *fetishism* are two strategies adopted by the male to counter his fear of sexual difference (between himself and the female, sexual other) and the fear of castration, which he feels as a result of that difference (the woman lacks a penis, the male assumes 'she' has been castrated). Thus, adopting the first strategy he fixes the woman with his **gaze**, voyeuristically investigates her body and therefore **sexuality**. She is the object of his investigation and in that way he safely contains her. As the object of his look and surveillance, meaning is ascribed by him to her. Voyeurism, at its most extreme, can lead to sadomasochistic behaviour. The man watches the woman, she may or may not know that he is looking at her, she cannot, however, return the gaze (because it is he who has **agency** over it and thus over her). Ostensibly, she is his victim and he the potential sadist who can violently attack or even kill her. Most **thrillers** and **films noir** depend on this sadomasochistic dynamic for their suspense. *Psycho* is an obvious example, but *The Shining* (Stanley Kubrick, 1950) is another. And by way of a rare reversal of power relations, at least until the bitter end, Kathy Bates in *Misery* (Carl Reiner, 1990) entraps her favourite popular fiction writer who has broken his leg and is therefore 'impotent'; she keeps him under constant surveillance and, when he 'dares' to 'look back' (by refusing to do her bidding and write the novel she wants written!), thinks nothing of brutally attacking him with axes and all sorts of penile or castrating instruments. But all ends well, he gets away – this is after all a comic thriller.

Fetishism is no more kind to the woman. Fetishism is a strategy to disavow difference. The male seeks to find the 'hidden' phallus in the woman. This fetishization takes place by a fragmentation of the body and an over-investment in the part of the body (or a piece of clothing) that has been fragmented off. The purpose of this over-investment is, ultimately, through perceiving them as perfection themselves, to make those parts figure as the missing phallus. The female form is contained this time by a denial of difference. She is phallic, therefore safe – which is why, in the end, the femme fatale of the 1940s film noir is not so dangerous after all! Rita Hayworth, Barbara Stanwyck's femmes get their come-uppance in no uncertain terms.

But things are never that simple and representation can always be read against the grain. Thus, there are always some interesting twists. For example, Marlene Dietrich was a fetishized form, particularly in Von Sternberg's films. However, in these films she often takes on a masculinized female form, which provides spectators with a special frisson. Or again, with Fritz Lang's *Rancho Notorious* (1952), she gets to take over the heroic masculine role. Marilyn Monroe may well have appeared to have been kept sexually safe by over-investment in her breasts and legs; however, she plays the card of the **female masquerade** to the hilt in most of her 1950s films. In the 1980s, many of Kathleen Turner's and Theresa Russell's roles have them (phallically) dressed in tight black dresses, stiletto heels with highly varnished nails and long, sweeping hair – their deep voices just add the finishing touch; however, for the most part, these latter-day phallic women are very successful in eliminating the male.

For fuller discussion see **gaze**, **psychoanalysis**, **scopophilia**, **spectator**, **suture**

WAR FILMS

Given the devastating effects of wars, especially world wars, on the populations of the nations involved, it comes as some surprise that war movies are very much a minority **genre** – both in the West and the East – and that, as far as colonized and formerly colonized countries and nations are concerned, there is even less **transparence**. What transparence there is tends to glorify or put forward the heroics of a particular triumphant nation. Until the 1970s, for the most part, the **myth** of the citizen-army fighting the enemy prevailed, completely over-riding issues of **class** and ethnic diversity. Furthermore, only rarely do these films look at the horrors of war – in some ways they are impossible to represent. Within cinema of the West on the whole, the vanquishing nation or colonizer's moral upper hand in their militaristic endeavours is hardly ever questioned or indeed explained – that is until recently. Finally, the war movie (along with the **Western**) is probably one of the last bastions for the display of heroic masculinity. Recently, several studies have focused on masculinity and **sexuality** in war films (see Donald and MacDonald, 2011; Eberwein, 2007).

The West has known two world wars since the birth of cinema. It has also been involved in various combats with regard to decolonization (particularly France); wars that have been partially the outcome of the Cold War waged between the two superpowers (the United States and the former Soviet Union, e.g. the Korean and Vietnam wars); the more recent wars in Iraq and Bosnia, to say nothing of the very recent civil and ethnic wars in the Middle East. What follows is a synopsis, largely based upon these various periods, of the West's representations of war in movies.

The Great War 1914 to 1918 and its representation in cinema 1914 to 1939

The Great War had been the 'war to end all wars'. The loss of life had been colossal, almost beyond belief – at least 8.5 million servicemen died on the two sides of the combat (the Allies lost 5 million, the Central Powers 3.5) and a further 21 million combatants were wounded. The loss of life on the Eastern front (Germany's Eastern border) was as great as that on the Western front, yet it is the latter front that is the more notorious in film and in history books – perhaps because of the devastating futility of the trench warfare fought out on both sides along the Franco–German border.

In Europe during this period, the propagandist nature of films only lasted for the early part of the hostilities. But the patriotic **melodramas** also did their bit to help enlistment. *England Expects* (1914), *The Fatherland Calls* (*Das Vaterland ruft*, 1914) and *French Mothers* (*Mères françaises*, 1916) are just a sample of the titles that were intended to encourage men into battle and women to support their patriotic sons, lovers and husbands in the war effort. In a similar vein, the British **documentary**, commissioned by the government, *The Battle of the Somme* (1916), with its graphic depiction of trench warfare, was intended as part of the propaganda to muster support for the war effort (it is also, of course, an important historical record that still serves today to shape the way in which we understand that war).

Eventually, **audience** taste waned for these propagandistic films that demonized the enemy, or glorified the sacrificial spirit of the ordinary indigenous people. Preference was felt for the escapist nature of American **comedies** and series. Paradoxically, in terms of patriotic fervour, it would be the United States that would pick up where Europe left off. Until 1917, when the Americans went to war, the United States had adopted an isolationist position in relation to the war, an isolationism that was reflected in the film output. And what few films were made about war were pacifist in nature (e.g. *War Bride*, 1916, urges women to abstain from bearing children until fighting ceases). By 1917, all had changed and films became increasingly militantly pro-war (e.g. *The Kaiser – The Beast of Berlin*, 1918). The change of attitude came about largely as a result of Germany's offensive against the trade embargoes placed upon it and the two other countries of the Central Powers alliance (Austria-Hungary and Italy). To counter the Allies' attempts to deprive it of trading and receiving materials, Germany, in 1915, launched a submarine (U-boat) campaign against the United Kingdom and the mercantile activities of the United States (one famous sinking was of the British liner *Lusitania*, in 1915). Anti-German sentiment, not expressed until this period, at the loss of American lives during this campaign was partly responsible for the United States joining forces with the Allies (France, the Soviet Union and the United Kingdom). Now the German was exposed on film as a ruthless rapist intent on ravishing America's virgins (*The Little United States*, 1917, starring Mary Pickford as the almost hapless victim) or a terrorizing colonialist who would invade America's shores (e.g. *The Sinking of the Lusitania*, 1918). In terms of content, these films did little more than transpose into American culture the jingoistic tone and stereotyping of earlier British and French films (such as, respectively, *The Outrage*, Cecil Hepworth, 1915; *Herr Doktor*, Louis Feuillade, 1917).

Only after the war could a more acerbic eye be turned upon the savagery of that war. But, even so, the number of films produced was minimal. For example, in the immediate aftermath of the war, France produced only one, and it focused on the horrors of war: Abel Gance's *J'accuse* (1919). Not until the tenth anniversary of the Armistice would the French film industry produce another film on the atrocities of that war. If anything, the United States was the more prolific. Capitalizing on the success of Charlie Chaplin's *Shoulder Arms* (1918), **Hollywood** was quick to realize that there was a taste for war movies, and, during the 1920s, several grand-scale reconstruction films of the United States' fighting role in the war were made. *The Four Horsemen of the Apocalypse* (1921), *The Grand Parade* (1925) and *What Price Glory* (1926) are just three examples of films that reconstructed battle scenes (often using veterans as extras). William Wellman's *Wings* (1927) pays homage to the fighter pilots of the war (then in their infancy). His film won the first Oscar ever, for best film.

The film to describe most explicitly the merciless horror of trench warfare was one of the earliest **sound** films to be made, Lewis Milestone's *All Quiet on the Western Front* (1930). The effect of this film was all the greater, since it was the first to bring the sound of war to the images (one of the criticisms levelled at *The Battle of the Somme* was the lack of soundtrack). A strongly pacifist film, it portrays both the Allies and the Germans as victims of war, a senseless war. Jean Renoir's *La Grande illusion* (1937) also picks up on this theme, but by the late 1930s, with war again imminent, the pacifism of his film was met with **censorship**. During the early 1930s, Germany also produced anti-war films, most famously Georg Pabst's *Westfront 1918* (1930). However, given that moment in history and the rise of Nazism, the tendency was for the Germans to pay tribute to their war heroes, particularly those working in the submarines (*Morgenrot/Dawn*, Gustav Uciciky, 1933).

With the advent of World War Two, the Great War (now World War One) sank into oblivion as a film theme until the late 1950s. Stanley Kubrick's *Paths of Glory* (1957) and Joseph Losey's *King and Country* (1964) were just two films among a handful that returned to that 1914 to 1918 period and seriously questioned the practices operated behind the war scenes by officers in power over young conscripts. In both Kubrick's and Losey's films the issue is that of court-martials: three Frenchmen in the former film, a British soldier in the latter. More historically accurate films such as these appear periodically in attempts to put the record straight (showing, for example, the effects of blinding gas in *Aces High*, Jack Gold, 1976) or to put on record war efforts that had been neglected (e.g. the contribution of Australian and New Zealand servicemen to the war in *Gallipoli*, Peter Weir, 1981).

World War Two

If ever proof were needed that wars do not end wars, then perhaps the devastating mortality figures of World War Two will stand as testimony. Over thirty million service people and civilians died in this six-year war (some figures quote fifty million) that left the world divided into two **ideological** parts (at least): the capitalist West and the communist East (of course, geography does not oblige with such a neat schism; for Cuba is in the West and Japan in the East!). The boundaries of traditional warfare had been blown apart by the dropping of the atomic bomb, first, on Hiroshima, then, on Nagasaki (two important Japanese seaports). The savagery of this war can be measured by the fact that almost as many civilians as service people perished (14.7 million civilians, including the systematic annihilation of 5.7 million Jews and an unaccountable number of gypsies and homosexuals; 15.3 million service men and women).

In the United Kingdom, as elsewhere, the **documentary** was perceived as a vital instrument for both morale boosting and propaganda (see **ideology**). Already, in World War One, the documentary had been used to chronicle some parts of the war, that is, once the ban on cameramen was lifted, in 1915, thus permitting them to go to the front. These documentaries included footage of the battle of the Somme (in all its gruesome horror, see above). Documentary was already a strong tradition in the United Kingdom, harking back to work done for the GPO Film Unit by the Grierson Group – a group of documentarists headed up by John Grierson (see **documentary**). This film unit was renamed the Crown Film Unit in 1940. These war-time documentaries focused both on the home front and on hostilities overseas. *London Can Take It* (Harry Watt and Humphrey Jennings, 1940) portrayed life going on as normal in London during the day despite the night raids by German fighter planes. This film was extremely influential in the United States in obtaining funds for Britain's war effort. In the same vein of Britons 'getting on with it' were Jennings' *Heart of Britain* (1941), showing ordinary people coping in the north of England, *Listen to Britain* (1942), about the British facing up to the hardships of wartime, and *Fires Were Started* (1943), about the London fire service. *Target for Tonight* (Watt, 1941) portrayed the RAF bombing raids on Germany, showing what all the home-front hardship was for: victory. (The film was a studio reconstruction, although real

RAF pilots were used.) Nor was the focus uniquely on the confrontation with Germany on European soil. Films from the Service Film Units provided images of campaign victories in North Africa (*Desert Victory* and *Tunisian Victory*, both 1943) and the Far East (*Burma Victory*, 1945).

If the war can be said to have had any positive impact on the filmmaking industry, as far as the United Kingdom and France were concerned, it did free up slots for new talent to emerge. The American film industry in Europe mostly 'went home' (the United States did not join the war until 1941 after the Japanese had bombed its naval base at Pearl Harbor in the Pacific). As for the French presence, certain of the established names, including immigré Germans and Austrians fleeing Nazi Germany, escaped to Hollywood. The new talent emerged from the technician ranks (e.g. assistant camera, etc.) into that of filmmaker: David Lean, Sidney Gilliat, Frank Launder and Charles Frend in the United Kingdom; Robert Bresson, Jacques Becker and Henri-Georges Clouzot in France. In the United Kingdom, many of the films produced were about the RAF, the naval forces and the merchant navy. Exceptionally, with this new generation of filmmakers, the shift in emphasis was away from class, something which was still very much in evidence in other, established filmmakers' work (see Anthony Asquith's *The Way to the Stars*, 1945). Their films exemplified group solidarity dissolving class lines, and they stressed the ordinariness of people fighting the war (see *In Which We Serve*, Lean, 1942; *San Demetrio, London*, Frend, 1943). The importance of women in the war was also signalled (see two 1943 films: *The Gentle Sex*, Leslie Howard, about the women in the Auxiliary Territorial Services, and *Millions Like Us*, Launder and Gilliat, about women working in a munitions factory).

For France, the story was completely the reverse. As an occupied country (1940–44), France could not address the war either as resistant to the Germans or as collaborator. This is why the few films that did appear to have a 'message', commenting on the time, were read by some as resistant and, by others, as collaborationist. A classic example is Clouzot's *Le Corbeau* (1943), a film about a small town riddled with fear as the result of a spate of poison-pen letters. Another example is Jean Grémillon's *Le Ciel est à vous* (1944), about a female aviator who, after successfully completing a transatlantic flight, returns to the bosom of her family and carries on as a good mother and housewife. The former film ran close to the bone in that a significant number of the French did indeed send in letters of denunciation to the German authorities; the latter film was seen to espouse the Vichy ideals of family values. In post-war France very few films indeed reflected the immediate past. Those that did, eulogized the work of the French Resistance (eight films in all immediately after the liberation), most famously perhaps *La Bataille du rail* (René Clément, 1946).

In Germany, propaganda had been underway throughout the Nazi régime since the early 1930s (with Goebbels as Hitler's propaganda minister). The work of Leni Riefenstahl is most often mentioned in this connection (see *Triumph of the Will*, 1934), although during the war she was virtually inactive. The primary message of Germany's propaganda was its Aryan superiority, its victorious war campaigns and its heroism. The most notorious 'documentary' film was Dr Franz Hippler's *The Eternal Jew* (*Der Ewige Jude*, 1940) which purported to document the evils that Jews had wreaked on Germany (including causing Germany the loss of World War One) and showed them as degenerate, even barbaric, in their traditions and culture and as corrupters of German aesthetics. Apart from the documentary propaganda, the German film industry produced a fair number of historical films which, in particular, praised former great leaders of the nation (e.g. *Bismarck*, 1940). Historical films were also produced to target Germany's reviled enemy, Britain. These films attacked Britain as the evil oppressor in Ireland (*The Fox of Glenarvon*, 1940, and *My Life for Ireland*, 1941 – both made by Goebbels' brother-in-law, M. W. Kimmich). Alternatively, Britain was the imperialist creator of concentration camps run by Churchill during the Boer War (*Uncle Kruger*, 1941). This last piece of propaganda was in fact based in truth. During the Boer War the British did set up concentration camps in which some twenty thousand women and children perished.

Both Germany and Britain exploited the historical reconstruction to propagandistic ends: the Germans, to show their courage, their genius and their sense of vision as a nation that was politically and culturally unified; the British, to extol their indomitable spirit against all odds (what is now termed the Dunkirk spirit – oddly since Dunkirk refers to a 'valiant' retreat by the Allies, in 1940, when France was occupied). Bismarck, Schiller, Bach and Diesel were just some of the geniuses Germany paraded before its cinema-going audiences (in films of the same titles). Britain turned to Nelson, exhorting Britain to go to war against Napoleon (*That Hamilton Woman!*, Alexander Korda, 1941); to Disraeli and his defiance of Bismarck (*The Prime Minister*, 1941); and to Henry V and his rallying call to the English for one more effort to overcome the enemy (*Henry V*, Laurence Olivier, 1944).

The war established a documentary tradition for the Soviet Union, United States and Japan. The Soviets often compiled documentaries exemplifying the collective spirit of a united Soviet Republic (see *A Day at War*, 1942, with a hundred contributions from the front and *Berlin*, 1945, with forty contributions capturing the taking of Berlin). The documentary was exploited far less in Japan and on the whole extolled the duty to fight, but not without giving a realistic portrayal of the dangers of war (see Yamamoto's *The War at Sea from Hawaii to Malaya*, 1942, a reconstruction of the bombing of Pearl Harbor). In the United States, documentaries were used to explain why the country had engaged in the war – a necessary procedure given its isolationism and fairly neutral pacifism during the first two-and-a-half years of hostilities. Most exemplary was Frank Capra's documentary series *Why We Fight* (1942–45). The seven documentaries that make up this series document the rise and spread of fascism, the aggression of those fascist nations on others and, finally, the threat of fascism to America. Questioning the merits of engagement does not arise. Indeed, the series was commissioned by the United States War Department. The maverick style in which John Ford's equally propagandistic film *The Battle of Midway* (1942) was made and finally shown to President Roosevelt for approval also points to a committed unquestioning stance. Ford, a lieutenant-commander serving in the Pacific, brought back to the United States actual footage of the Battle of Midway, determined to make a film for the mothers of America so that they would be proud of their sons' bravery in war and be moved to support American engagement (and send more sons to fight). It was made in total secrecy, shown to the president and approved for general distribution. John Ford had become the John Wayne of war documentaries.

Before the United States joined the war, it produced several films, made in Britain, in support of the British. For example, the British film *That Hamilton Woman!* was a United Artists London film. Others showed British courage in the face of German bombing raids (William Wyler's *Mrs Miniver*, 1942). More usually, however, these films took the form of an American serviceman participating in a British campaign (as with *A Yank in the RAF*, Henry King, 1941). These types of film also had the merit of not upsetting the isolationists in the United States who, despite Roosevelt's wish to assist Britain in the war effort, had a strong hold on how the nation conducted itself. Furthermore, these films were muted and were not allowed to be particularly anti-fascist for fear, according to the **studios**, of political and economic reprisals – although why this fear arose is strange, since, by 1940, Hollywood could not export to most of mainland Europe because it was occupied by the Germans, who had imposed a complete ban on the import of American products, including films. This fear may point to the widely acknowledged belief, at the beginning of the war, that the Germans would win the war and that it would be foolish to lose future markets. A simple example will illustrate this fence-sitting attitude. In 1939 (just prior to the war), Warners released Anatole Litvak's *Confessions of a Nazi Spy*, an explicitly anti-Nazi film (starring Conradt Veidt). Germany, which still had a diplomatic presence in the United States, expressed its indignation and Warners were warned off making any such film in the future.

If, until the United States' engagement in the war, Hollywood played a rather minimal and unpartisan role in relation to the war effort, such was not the case once Pearl Harbor brought the United States into the war. Roosevelt put pressure on the studios to participate in the propaganda and morale-boosting necessary to get the United States behind the fight. **Stars** helped either by joining up (Clark Gable, James Stewart), by entertaining troops or getting ordinary Americans to buy war bonds (Bing Crosby, Bob Hope, Rita Hayworth, Bette Davis, Marlene Dietrich). The war film took off: comedies, **musicals** and combat films, films depicting the effects of the war on European citizens – all of these came pouring out of Hollywood, under the strictest of government guidelines. In the period 1942 to 1945, Hollywood produced some 500 war movies out of a total output of 1,700 films. The earliest films obeyed the governmental criteria of patriotism against fascism (see two 1942 films, *Yankee Doodle Dandy*, a musical, and *Remember Pearl Harbor*, a war film with a clear call to arms). A different form of patriotism, joining the Resistance, is advocated in Jean Renoir's (American produced) *This Land is Mine* (1943). What makes it unusual is that the central protagonist, played by Charles Laughton, declaims on two occasions in the film the right to freedom of speech, life, liberty and democracy based on the founding principles of socialism: equal rights for all. Given that leftist tinge, it is surprising it slipped through unnoticed; especially when one considers that the war was at one of its most critical moments (the defeat of the Germans at Stalingrad and El Alamein). But then, even though Renoir was in exile in the USA, this still didn't prevent him from getting his personal, socialist message out.

On the whole, the stereotyping in the war films reveals a curious mixture of jingoism, ambivalence and naivety. A jingoistic attitude prevailed in Hollywood's representation of the Japanese. They were the evil, sadistic torturers who would go to any lengths to win (as in *Across the Pacific* and *Wake Island*, both 1942, and the fiercely anti-Japanese *Purple Heart*, Lewis Milestone, 1943). As far as the representation of the Germans was concerned, they were either the evil

Nazi (*Hitler's Children*, 1942) or the good German (*The North Star*, 1943). They could in fact be a blend of the two as in Conrad Veidt's Nazi in *Casablanca* (Michael Curtiz, 1942). Veidt, it will be recalled, was *the* fetish star of the **German expressionist** films (so not a little irony here, since Hitler held the Jews responsible for the decadence of expressionism! And doubly ironic, since Veidt had fled his native Germany in the face of the rise of Hitler). The ambivalence in these particular films can be understood in the light of the large numbers of German immigrants and second-generation Germans residing in the United States. The open hostility to the Japanese, however, resides in their otherness and purported inscrutability.

But, in terms of stereotypes, by far the oddest response was to the Soviets. In Hollywood films such as *Mission to Moscow, North Star* and *Song of Russia* (all 1943), Soviets were cast as ordinary people just like the 'folks back home'. Ideologically, there was little to separate the two 'great nations'. The Soviet Union was a virtual reflection of the United States: singing, dancing and uncomplicated. Stalin was Uncle Jo, and his repression of dissidents a necessary step for national and international security in the time of war (let it not be forgotten that the United States had incarcerated thousands of Japanese-Americans in California, under the same pretext of national security). This whitewashing by the USA of a precarious ally – after all, the Soviet Union had signed a non-aggression pact with Hitler which broke down only when the Germans decided to invade the Soviet Union in June 1941 – is, however, not astonishing in the light of war. Beyond the strategic need for fighting to take place on Germany's Eastern front (thus dispersing German resources and weakening the enemy), there was doubtless a more hidden agenda that explains this naive representation of the Soviets. The Soviet armed forces were needed if public support for the war was to be maintained 'back home'. Presidential popularity, therefore security of office, is and always has been notoriously tied – in times of combat – to the number of 'body bags' sent home. Eleven million Soviet combatants died in this war and seven million civilians (over half the total deaths in this war). American casualties were not light, but in relation to those figures they are certainly less awesome (292,131 combatants and 6,000 civilians).

The idea that the United States was fighting a just war and that sacrifices were necessary was not a mood that prevailed, however. By 1943, doubtless because returning servicemen were bringing the message home that the war was not being won, several films had begun to reflect a greater reality in sharp contrast to the heroization and fervent patriotism expressed in the general run of war movies.

Several films reflected the setbacks and defeats suffered by American troops against the Japanese. *Bataan* (Tay Garnett, 1943) ends with the massacre of an American patrol. *Air Force* (Howard Hawks, 1943) and *Thirty Seconds over Tokyo* (Mervyn LeRoy, 1944) showed the gruesome reality of air combat. *The Purple Heart* depicted the torture of American prisoners of war at the hands of the Japanese.

Immediately after the war, several American war movies began, if not to question, then certainly to expose the futility of war, its horrors and the atrocious conditions under which it is fought (as in *The Story of GI Joe*, William Wellman, and *They Were Expendable*, John Ford, both 1945). But, by the late 1940s, Hollywood was back to its more jingoistic practices, undoubtedly as a result of the Cold War and the activities of the House Un-American Activities Committee (HUAC). An exemplary film in this context is *The Sands of Iwo Jima* (1949), subtitled *The Marines' Greatest Hour*, and starring John Wayne. A notable exception is William Welland's *Battleground* (1949) – a film about the unglamorous nature of war and which would not have got made but for the persistence of MGM's production chief Dore Schary (unusually, for that time within the industry, a man of the left).

War-wearied Britain dropped the genre only to return to it with grand-scale heroization of the RAF in *The Dam Busters* (Michael Anderson, 1955). This jingoism and heroization was sharply contrasted with the sense of loss and defeat apparent in the few films made by the losing nations, Germany and Japan. It is revealing that they were not post-war films as such, but products of reflection, coming some ten years after the end of hostilities. Kon Ichikawa's two films on the devastation and dehumanizing effects of war, *The Burmese Harp* (1956) and *Fires of the Plain* (1959), reveal the full horror to which Japanese troops were exposed. In the first film, a former army scout becomes a Buddhist monk who roams across Japan burying the war dead; in the second, which is set towards the end of the war, starving troops are reduced to cannibalism. The desperate lengths to which Germany would go in the face of the inevitable loss of the war are virulently described in *The Bridge* (Bernhard Wicki, 1959). Short of manpower, young adolescents are conscripted to defend a bridge, futilely, since they get blown up.

As with the **Western**, the war movie, at least until this period, had a fairly unchanging **iconography**. Combat is either on a grand scale (military manoeuvres, tanks and so on) or on a small, even individual one (as with fighter pilots). Quite frequently there is a target to be obtained (a hill, a bridge). There is an ensemble within the corps of servicemen with whom we identify (see **spectator-identification**) and who display different types of courage. Comradeship is paramount. The enemy is absent, except as an impersonal other (and therefore bad).

There were, of course, some exceptions to this uncritical heroic representation of war. Class conflict destroying prisoner of war morale is central to David Lean's *The Bridge on the River Kwai* (1957), and the corruption of officers and their indifference to the fate of their men is exposed in Stanley Kubrick's film (based in World War One) *Paths of Glory*. As with other genres in the 1950s, **psychology** was being introduced as a mainspring to character **motivation**. Thus, a certain number of films which attempted to counter the dominant trend tried to examine the psychological effects of warfare – as in Lewis Milestone's *Halls of Montezuma* (1950), about combat fatigue; Fred Zinnemann's *The Men* (1950), starring Marlon Brando, which shows the devastating realities faced by war-veteran paraplegics who return home from the war, wounded and psychologically broken; and Robert Aldrich's *Attack!* (1956), which looks at officers' cowardice and the fear of fighting.

But then again, in the UK, in the late 1960s and 1970s, there were odd switches back to the glory of the war heroics – primarily in the star-studded blockbusters *Battle of Britain* (Guy Hamilton, 1969) and *A Bridge Too Far* (Richard Attenborough, 1977). So there isn't necessarily a forward evolution of the genre towards a greater truth in representation or more realistic portrayal of men at war – although there is great play for 'authenticity' through extremely mobile camera-work, blurred images of combat and special effects. This lack of change is made evident by the fact that, even though more recently, in the 1990s and the new millenium, there have been films showing local heroism within the magnitude and horror of war, where the gore of war is matched by the unheralded heroism of an individual who stands for humanity, nonetheless, there can be startlingly contrasting versions of this representation. Steven Spielberg's *Saving Private Ryan* (1998) and Terrence Malick's *The Thin Red Line* (1998) are exemplary in this context. Spielberg's film remains an utterly straightforward American take on World War Two – an overly simplistic narrative reduced to small-time heroics that have no real bearing in history and based in sentimentalism – despite the gory and realistic first thirty minutes of the landing on Omaha beach (and, typically, the ending is a bloody defending of a bridge). Malick's film completely contrasts with Spielberg's film about individual heroics and takes a deep look into military behaviour and the nature of evil. In his film, there are no all-American heroes. Rather, Malick's film shows – in complete contradistinction with Spielberg's – how war erodes and undermines personal identity and humanity.

The true ghastliness of war can probably never be represented (at least in feature films) – very few films come close. Spielberg's *Saving Private Ryan* only sustains it for half an hour; his controversial *Schindler's List* (1993) still does not escape the heroization of an individual and has (in my view) an unforgivable sentimental edge. Similarly, albeit in a different register, Roberto Benigni's *Life is Beautiful* (1997) sanitizes the atrocities of the Holocaust away. Nor, with time, does the truth come any closer/easier. *Pearl Harbor* (Michael Bay, 2001) is nothing short of a distortion or evacuation of history. More of a video-game full of beautiful men and pyrotechnics and fireball extravaganzas, it is as thin as the lack of characterization it skates on. It asks no questions and tells us nothing of the true nature of soldiering and combat. Compared to Zinnemann's *From Here to Eternity* (1953) with which it arguably shares some similarities – a love story set in the Pearl Harbor moment – it lacks Zinnemann's sense of what the endurance of war and the horribleness of being in the army meant.

Exceptions to this overwhelming trend of sanitizing and **naturalizing** the misery of war are very rare, and mention must be made of the Soviet filmmaker Elem Klimov's *Come See* (1985). This account of an adolescent's experience during the German occupation of Belarus, in 1943, shows the unbearable. Based in Klimov's personal experience (as well as Adamovich's novel *The Story of Khatyn*), it feels deeply rooted in the real. The adolescent has already witnessed a massacre in his own village. When he manages to struggle on to another, he sees the SS German Commandos arriving and doing exactly the same: taking food from the villagers then rounding them up into a church and setting fire to the building. We, like the boy, watch the grotesque reality unfurl (apparently 628 Belarussian villages were destroyed in this way). The cycle of violence is unending in this film, as we are obliged to 'come see' (Wrathall, 2004: 28–30).

The 'truth' about the war – with one or two brave exceptions (usually censored) – rarely comes out until some decent amount of time has elapsed and the nation's psyche has had time to recover. Interestingly, this was not the case with Japan. After 1952, when the occupation of Japan by the American Allies was over, Japan made several post-Holocaust films about the atomic bombing of Hiroshima and Nagasaki that had brought the country to an abrupt cessation of hostilities with the Allies. Until that date, Japan was not permitted to broach the subject from a critical or realistic point of view. Once the ban was lifted, a variety of films on the subject of the effects of the atomic Holocaust were made. The horror of the Holocaust was represented in Kaneto Shindo's *Children of the Atom Bomb* (1952), Heideo Sekigawa's

Hiroshima, Hiroshima (1953) and Akira Kurosawa's *Record of a Human Being* (1955). The effects of the atomic fall-out, such as producing monsters and mutants, is the subject of Ishiro Honda's **horror** movie *Godzilla* (1954). Conversely and more typically, in the West, issues raised by the atomic bombing – such as the kind of reasoning that makes such attacks possible – did not get raised until the mid-1960s, some twenty years after the event. In 1964, Stanley Kubrick launched a virulent satire on those in charge and capable of unleashing atomic warfare (*Dr Strangelove*) and, in 1965, Peter Watkins made a politically uncompromising film that examined the effects of a nuclear attack on Britain (*The War Game*).

In general, vanquishing nations tend not to look too closely at the ambiguities of war. This is also true of film. Questions can be asked only if there is doubt, and victory is less conducive to doubt than defeat. And it is worth noting that, as far as the United States was concerned, only when the ignominy of defeat became undeniable and questions had to be asked – as they were over Vietnam – did an 'unglorious' look at war become more commonplace. But before that came the Cold War.

The Cold War and Vietnam

The term *Cold War* refers to the hostilities between the two superpowers (the USA and the former USSR) and their allies following World War Two. The fear of nuclear war (as exemplified by the effects of dropping atomic bombs on Hiroshima and Nagasaki) proscribed military confrontation (even though both powers stockpiled nuclear arms). So war was conducted on economic, political and ideological fronts. This was the epoch for the spy, counter-espionage, paranoia about the spread of communism or capitalism and, finally, the age of intervention into the political arena of countries too small to prevent the encroachment of the two superpowers that annexed them as satellites.

The Cold War produced anti-communist films from Hollywood (such as *The Red Menace*, *The Red Danube*, both 1949; *I Was a Communist for the FBI*, 1951; *Big Jim McClain* and *My Son John*, both 1952). These were virulent anti-communist **melodramas** where protagonists either wake up to the dangers of communism and sniff it out, or die for their mistake in believing that communism was a good thing. Alternatively, the Red Menace could take an alien form, as in *Red Planet Mars* (1952) and *Invasion of the Body Snatchers* (1956). Paranoia was also felt at the risk of nuclear war. This mood generated a series of films either in the apocalyptic mode (*The Beginning or the End?*,

1947; *White Heat*, 1949) or in the post-holocaust one (*Five*, 1951; *The World, the Flesh and the Devil*, 1959). Unsurprisingly, the Soviets produced their own anti-American films. Mostly these focused on the imputed evil-doings of the CIA (e.g. *Secret Mission* and *Conspiracy of the Doomed*, both 1950).

However, perhaps the filmmaker most associated with Cold War movies is the American Samuel Fuller. He made three films based on US intervention during the hostilities between North and South Korea: *The Steel Helmet, Fixed Bayonets* (both 1951) and *Hell and High Water* (1954). They are all extremely violent films. Perhaps as **B-movies**, they suffered less interference from the censors. But, his representation of violence set a precedence for movies to come, particularly in the 1960s and 1970s films of Arthur Penn and Sam Peckinpah (e.g. *Bonnie and Clyde*, 1967, and *The Wild Bunch*, 1969, respectively). Fuller's influence extended beyond the depiction of violence however. His **editing** style, which **deconstructed** the **seamlessness** of traditional Hollywood practices, considerably influenced Jean-Luc Godard and, later, certain filmmakers of the **New German Cinema** (Rainer Werner Fassbinder and Wim Wenders), and later still Martin Scorsese. Fuller's modernity or prescience is (arguably) evidenced by the fact that he was the first to portray the Vietnam War as an issue for the United States, long before it became officially engaged in the war. His 1958 film, *China Gate*, tells the story of an American legionnaire, fighting for the French in Vietnam. As opposed to the traditional role of a legionnaire as detached from any patriotic or personal motivation, his fighting of the communist enemy is personalized. He sees the defeat of the Vietcong as the imperative that will allow him to take his son (the progeny of his marriage to a Eurasian woman) back to the United States.

With regard to Vietnam and the truth about the war – although of course there were the usual range of jingoistic efforts, for example, John Wayne (*Green Berets*, John Wayne/Ray Kellogg, 1968) and Sylvester Stallone (*Rambo: First Blood, Part II*, George P. Cosmatos, 1985) – Hollywood was, perhaps surprisingly, not so slow to produce films that attempted to view critically the impact of that war on the American mentality, particularly that of the American GI. But, even as early as 1969, Robert Altman's film *M*A*S*H*, despite being set in a surgical unit during the Korean war, was readily being understood as a metaphor for the carnage of Vietnam.

The Vietnam war was officially over by 1976. Martin Scorsese made *Taxi Driver* in the same year. Then, in 1978 and 1979, came Michael Cimino's *The Deer Hunter* and Francis Ford Coppola's

Apocalypse Now. These three films focus on the effect of the war on the individual and in that light can be seen as progressive. They do not, however, question America's legitimacy in fighting that war. In Scorsese's film, the neglected and despised Vietnam veteran becomes a self-appointed vigilante of urban New York and finally wins acclaim as a hero. In the other two films, the real issue of why the war was being fought is again side-stepped and, although the protagonists are clearly severely disturbed by what has happened to them in Vietnam, there is no mistaking that the cause for the action in both films is the sadism of the enemy, the unknown other. The only film of the period that came close to a committed questioning of the United States' involvement in Vietnam was Hal Ashby's *Coming Home* (1978), starring Jon Voigt as the disabled veteran and Jane Fonda (who, in real life, had been politically active against the war) as the woman who falls in love with him. Unfairly perhaps, some critics slated the film as sentimental, worse still as letting America off the hook in terms of guilt about the war. Rather, the film, while it does centre the Vietnam issue in one person, raises issues about why American troops were sent there and why they were so devalorized when they came home alive or half alive (in some ways reminiscent of *The Men*, see above). It does, therefore, put America's warmongers on the stand. Ten years later, using a similar narrative, Oliver Stone's *Born on the Fourth of July* (1989) is in a position to take this questioning a whole lot further – condemning the war and exposing the lack of compassion and proper care made available to veteran victims of the war. In the late 1980s and early 1990s, a smattering of films addressed the Vietnam war more realistically, with portrayals of American brutality, the horror of the actual fighting, the racism suffered by Black Americans from their own compatriots – and so on (e.g. *Platoon*, Oliver Stone, 1986; *Hamburger Hill*, John Irvin, 1987; *Full Metal Jacket*, Stanley Kubrick, 1987).

More recent conflagrations: Bosnia and the two Iraq wars

While this entry has limited its points of reference to the major world wars of the twentieth century, it is true that other wars have found their expression in film. In the Hollywood context, obviously there is the American Civil War (often the subject of Westerns). It is worth mentioning how far representation of this war has shifted from the first film on the subject, *The Birth of a Nation* (D. W. Griffith, 1915), and a more recent one, *Glory* (Edward Zwick, 1989). In the first, Griffith is unapologetically nostalgic for the good old days of

Southern wealth (based on cotton plantations) and his film remains deeply racist (as indeed it was then, with, amongst other things, a glorification of the Ku Klux Klan, a stereotyping of blacks and a normalization of their general mistreatment, including lynching). In the second film, Zwick marks the bravery of the war's first Black fighting unit.

With regard to more contemporary conflicts, for example, the Gulf war of 1991 (George Bush Snr's so-called smart war against Iraq), there exist parlous few films – *Courage under Fire* (Zwick, 1996) and *Three Kings* (David O'Russell, 1999) are the ones that come to mind, and both in different ways sanitize the awfulness of that war. In the former, investigation of the truth behind a fellow officer's courage is quickly reduced to a matter of personal redemption. In the latter, the heroes of a non-existent war of liberation function allegorically for the political **discourse** surrounding that war: blatant self-interest passed off as humanitarian concern.

The Bosnian war (1992–95) has been the subject of a significant number of European-made films focusing almost exclusively on the unjust nature of the war. During and in the immediate aftermath of the war, twenty-two films were made, two Bosnian (*MGM Sarajevo: Man God and the Monster*, Ismet Arnautlic, 1994; *The Perfect Circle*, Ademir Kenovic, 1997), four Serbian (including the controversial *Pretty Village, Pretty Flame*, Srjdan Dragojevic, 1996, which attempts to put the Serbian army's point of view and redress the negative press the Serbs received in the media), ten French (most famously Jean-Luc Godard's *Forever Mozart*, 1996), two British (the best known being Michael Winterbottom's *Welcome to Sarajevo*, 1997). Since the new millennium some eleven films have been made (the most important of which has to be *No Man's Land*, Danis Tanovic, 2001, which totally encapsulates the folly, horror, stupidity and individual hypocrisy of the war).

In total, these thirty-three films about the Bosnian conflict tell us something quite significant in terms of both an international reaction to this hideous one-sided conflict and a willingness to address the issues. This becomes especially clear when we consider that – after the devastation of 9/11 (the attacks on New York and Washington, 11 September 2001), which in turn led to the (second) Iraq War (2003–11) – only some twenty-six films, that in some way refer to the war, have been made by the US film industry, most of them since 2005. If there is a disinclination to address the Iraq War in numerical terms, nonetheless, what is interesting is how diversified is the representation of it, to say nothing of the message contained in these films – even before Bush Jnr stood down as president (2009). A number of these films show distressed soldiers returning home, or the impact of their deaths on their families back home (*The Messenger*, Oren Moverman, 2009); others question the validity of the war (*In the Valley of Elah*, Paul Haggis, 2007; *Fair Game*, Doug Liman, 2010) and the USA's treatment of prisoners of war or suspected terrorists (*Redacted*, Brian de Palma, and *Lions for Lambs*, Robert Redford, both 2007); still others reveal the individual heroism of the American GI (*Grace is Gone*, James C. Strouse, 2007; *The Hurt Locker*, Kathryn Bigelow, 2008) or CIA agent (*Body of Lies*, Ridley Scott, 2008) (see Barker (2011) for a full study of these films). Could it be that, finally, in terms of modern conflicts and wars, the new communications technology of satellite and mobile phones, the internet and many other forms of social networking, make it impossible for there to be simple, simplified renditions on-screen of the complexities of mankind's warmongering? Everything can be shown with immediacy, including the unrelenting nature of the terror of war.

A coda on Syria: And then there are the wars that have yet to generate any such films. Of the most recent, and most terrible civil war (and possibly a displaced neo-Cold War between Russia and the USA), what is occurring in Syria, with half a million deaths (civilian and military) as this book goes to press, defies narrative. There is a documentary diary (released on Vimeo every Friday) being maintained, since 2011, by a film collective called *Abounaddara/The Man with the Glasses* (made up mostly of women filmmakers). It blends **art cinema** with news (a sort of art-cinéma-vérité). Committed to express *karameh*/dignity (a keyword for Syrian protestors), its short films are both lyrical and ironic in tone. There have been a few documentaries that have been smuggled out successfully (see entry on **Syrian cinema** under **world cinema**).

see also: **genre**

For further reading see Aldgate, 2007; Barker, 2011; Chapman, 2008; Donald and MacDonald, 2011; Eberwein, 2007; King, 2000; Lipschutz, 2001; Russell, 2002; Shapiro, 2002; Shaw, 2001; Tasker, 2011.

WESTERNS

Also known as the Horse Opera or Oater, the Western became a **genre** that was incorporated very early into the film industry's repertoire. The first, official, Western was by the American filmmaker Edwin S. Porter, *The Great Train Robbery* (1903). Although the Western is considered an exclusively American genre, this is not the case. The French, for example, were making Westerns and exporting them successfully to the United States at least until World War One – most famously the *Arizona Bill* series, starring Joë Hammond (1912–14). And, of course, later on in the history of this genre the Italians turned to making the so-called spaghetti Westerns (1965–75).

In a sense, the silent Westerns (though of course they were accompanied by **music**) were simply carrying on where reality had left off. The 'civilizing' of the West was virtually completed when cinema was born, and the cowboy's life as a herder had more or less come to an end as a result of the land-rush and subsequent homesteading. The effect of this great migration west was to close off the open range. The land-rush to all intents and purposes made the cowboy defunct. Given the mythic value of the cowboy as far as Westerns are concerned, it comes as some surprise that, as herders, cowboys only existed fully for a brief period (1865–80) at which point the beef boom foundered. Homesteading was complete, the new towns and cities were established and there was no more need for driving the cattle west to feed the people. These factors – civilization and the open range or wilderness – are two first keys to the typology of this genre. The hero (*sic*) is constantly operating at the point of conjuncture of these two opposing values. He never really wants to accept civilization, as embodied by the woman (who brings with her from the East Coast the notion of community family, and so on). Rather, he is always desiring to be on the move in the Wild West. The cowboy with his restless energy and rugged, dogged individualism is the embodiment of American frontiersmanship, or at least the **myth** of that frontiersmanship. However, the fact that the cowboy or gunman is always represented as being caught between the two values points to the **ideological** contradictions inherent in the myth of that frontiersmanship. The hero's actual ambivalence reveals the nation's own ambiguous attitude towards the West. Civilizing the West meant giving up the freedom it represented, including of course freedom of the individual – a high price for Americans to pay for national unity. However, the duration of the genre – possibly the longest lasting one of all – points to America's fascination with the frontier as a site of hope for something new and better.

The tradition of the cowboy as mythic hero dates back to the Western dime novels published from the 1860s. These novels dramatized lives that were both real and fictional and elevated the cowboy to mythic status. In the early days of cinema, at least, these novels were the primary sources for the Western movie, which is a part explanation for the highly ritualized nature of this genre. These novels both heroized outlaws (Jesse James being a favourite) and lawmen. And as we shall see, the heroization of the outlaw also became a typology of this genre. In fact, real-live outlaws and cowboys – especially cowboys who had been rodeo riders – came into the film industry up until as late as the 1930s and 1940s (Gene Autry and Roy Rogers are two well-known names). Buffalo Bill starred in his own film *The Adventures of Buffalo Bill* (1913). A reformed bank robber, Al Jennings, starred in several early Westerns. However, his films did not glamorize the West; rather, they told the truth about the sordid money-grabbing practices that were so prevalent (as in *The Lady in the Dugout*, 1918). These were not the images the public wanted to see, so his career soon ended.

Audience expectation, then, is a second factor explaining the ritualistic and formulaic nature of the Western. This ritualization needs to be discussed before continuing with the history of this genre. The dime novels tried to explain 'how the West was won', even though of course it was not won. It was taken away from the Indians by the 'few' property speculators, and what was left over from the good gold-mining terrain and profitable land, which they kept, was sold to the beleaguered pioneers who had come so far for so little. Dime novels could not tell this story, any more than the films. Audiences wanted to see the West as it should have been, that is, as myth. The ritualistic narratives of the Western do, however, reveal the ideological contradictions of this myth. Rituals are about the fear of loss of control, of mastery. Thus, the eternal repetition, as represented by rituals and the formulaic construction of the genre as well as the audience's own ritual in going repeatedly to see these films, reflects the desire to reassert that control and mastery (we know this is not the truth, it is myth, but we keep going back to see it because we want it to be so). The narrative rituals of robbery, chase and retribution, of lawlessness and restoration of law, are **iconographically** inscribed in the Western, right down to the very last detail and gesture. Attacks are repeated in different ways. The stagecoach chase is replaced by the wagon-train attack, the train robbery, the cavalry charge or the Indians swooping down on 'innocent' homesteaders. Cattle drives, gold prospecting and railroad building are other standard markers saluting the glory of going West. The ritual of the gunfight (in or out of the saloon), the pushing through the saloon swing-doors and swaggering up to the bar – all are images that we immediately associate with the genre. All, of course, constitute a massive cover-up of how the West was colonized in the name of capitalism. That story would be told, but only rarely, and Al Jennings was one of the first to tell it so. However, back to history.

The first Western hero was one of his own making, Gilbert M. Anderson. He persuaded Thomas H. Ince to let him star in *The Great Train Robbery*. Just as importantly it was he who took the Western out West in the name of authenticity. He formed his own production company, Essanay, and made a large number of films starring himself as Bronco Billy. The Bronco Billy series lasted from 1910 to 1918 (e.g. *Bronco Billy's Redemption*, 1910; *The Making of Bronco Billy*, 1913). He was quickly followed by William S. Hart, who made his début in 1914. He too strove for authenticity and worked first for Ince, then for Paramount. Hart's films were quite pessimistic and bleak. He played the same role of the baddie who is really good deep down inside and who gets redeemed by the end of the film. His most accomplished film is *Tumbleweeds* (1925), which he produced and in which he starred. It contains extraordinarily realistic footage, including the settlers' land-rush sequence composed of three hundred wagons and at least a thousand men, women and horses.

By the late 1910s, the Western, by now a great favourite, spawned five big Western **stars**, whose careers went well into the 1920s – some lasting as long as into the 1930s (i.e. into **sound**). The five 'greats' were, first, Tom Mix, who wore highly stylized outfits, the first to do so, a tradition that carried on through into the fringed shirts, soft leather gloves and gaily painted leather boots worn by Roy Rogers. More macho in image and in action were Buck Jones and Tim McCoy, great stuntmen who had, like Mix, started out their careers in rodeo and Wild-West shows. The last two, Hoot Gibson and Ken Maynard, were often paired in films. Between them, they significantly developed the iconography of this genre: Mix's costumes have already been mentioned; the horse became a focal point, almost a second hero; finally, cowboys started to sing.

The first Western **epic** is James Cruze's *The Covered Wagon* (1923), closely followed by John Ford's *The Iron Horse* (1924). What is exceptional about Cruze's film, apart from the mammoth undertaking of attempting to put into film the enormity of the migration west, was that it was shot, not in the studios, but on location, and was therefore a reconstruction of the migration as it had been experienced. Thus, there were river crossings, Indian attacks and struggles through arduous weather conditions, all of which worked to give the film a **realism** that no other Western to that date had produced. Lasting two hours, the film convincingly evoked the two-thousand-mile trajectory undertaken by the pioneers.

The other contemporaneous epic, *The Iron Horse*, tells the end-part of the pioneering American spirit, the building of the railroads west. In this respect, this film and Cruze's are the bookends of the history of that epoch, at least the mythic version of it. Clearly, in this epic context, the mythical value of these films has nationalistic overtones. Indeed, Ford, the son of an immigrant family from Ireland, makes no attempt to disguise his commitment to the concept of America as the land of opportunity and to the Lincolnian belief in America as one nation (he dedicated his film to Abraham Lincoln). The overriding message of this film is a belief in progress (the iron horse replaces the horse). However, not at any price: unity among men, not individualism, is the only way of achieving it.

John Ford is arguably the greatest Western filmmaker of all time, although Howard Hawks is a strong rival. Ford started his career making Westerns for Universal, the largest producers of the genre until the early 1920s (see **studio system**). In 1920, after three years with Universal, he went over to Fox. His film career spans over forty years (*The Man Who Shot Liberty Valance*, 1962, is a late example of his work in this genre alone). It is often said that, because of his own immigrant past and his desire to belong, he was obsessed with American history and with the notion of the family. Whatever the case, it is certain that the notion that unity creates stability and a sense of community is central to his films, including the Western. In this respect, his vision seems to go counter to the ideology inherent in the Western of the wandering cowboy or gun-hand who must restlessly move on. However, this first disposition of Ford's in fact enhances the tension in his film between the opposing values of *wilderness* and civilization precisely because, for the most part, his heroes do not settle down but live out and with this contradiction (as in *My Darling Clementine*, 1946, and, in a more complex way, *The Searchers*, 1956). His fetish star was John Wayne who, when he first worked with Ford, almost got himself thrown out of the studio for being insubordinate.

Back to the history of this genre. The advent of sound brought about a big drop in the production of the Western, at least as an A-movie. The drop occurred largely because there was so little dialogue. The audience was now used to 'talkies' and the Western did not adapt well at first. As an action-packed film, before sound, it had little need for much talk. Clint Eastwood's almost silent movies of the 1980s and 1990s merely carry on this tradition (although he is not that heavy on action either!). Interestingly, however, during the 1930s, Westerns continued to be produced as **B-movies** and were very popular. As a B-movie, a Western was a low-budget product that could be quickly and cheaply produced to fill the double-bill requirement (a practice introduced during the Depression years to attract audiences by giving two films for the price of one). The smaller studios, Monogram and

Republic in particular, were largely responsible for this output although, among the majors, Warners was also a significant producer. It was the B-Westerns that launched the singing cowboy – starting with John Wayne in 1933 (*Riders of Destiny*) and closely followed by Gene Autry (*Tumbling Tumbleweeds*, 1935) and Roy Rogers. As a type, the B-Western was iconographically simplistic and ideologically populist. The goodies and the baddies were easily identifiable. The former wore white, the latter black, and unquestionably the goodies would win. No room here for redemption – bad is bad. By the mid-1950s, the B-Western (and the B-movie in general) had disappeared after the Supreme Court's decision, in the Paramount case of 1948, finally took effect by breaking up the major studios' cartel (see **studio system**). But it did not go out with a whimper. In 1952 and 1954, Republic won best director Oscars for, respectively Ford's *The Quiet Man* and Nicholas Ray's *Johnny Guitar*.

Briefly, in the late 1930s, there was a big surge in production of A-feature Westerns. A first cause was the United States' isolationism in the face of the war in Europe. The revival of the genre reflects an inward-looking nationalism that is simultaneously nostalgic, having regard for things American but things of the past, in this instance, the nation's heroic and civilizing expansion into the west. By curious coincidence John Wayne, *the* true-grit American as we now know him, finally attained star status, in this brief period of production upswing, when he starred in Ford's *Stagecoach* (1939). Pioneers were celebrated (as in *The Westerner*, 1940, with squeaky-clean Gary Cooper). Often the **narrative** depicted the individual fighting against giant corporations (railroad companies, banks, etc.). Certain outlaws were also celebrated. A particular favourite was Billy the Kid (see *Billy the Kid*, 1941, and Howard Hughes' *The Outlaw*, 1943, but not released until 1946 – see below). This heroization of outlaws, as already mentioned, was part of the mythologizing of the west started by the Western dime novels of the 1860s. Because the west was largely monopolized by land-grabbing companies, to take the law into one's own hands was perceived as a legitimate practice. An outlaw in these circumstances came to represent freedom in much the same way as the cowboy. The outlaw asserted individual 'rights' over the big bosses. Similarly, the lonesome lawman was a hero in his standing up to the baddies who threaten to disrupt the community. (For an in-depth study of the political implications of Ford and Hughes' Westerns, see Pippin, 2010.)

There was, however, the burgeoning of another type of Western: one that was more socially critical and which set a trend that would be more fully developed in the 1950s. William A. Wellman is credited with being the progenitor of this so-called 'modern Western', which, because it deals with social issues, is also described as the psychological Western. In the first of these films, *The Ox-bow Incident* (1943), Wellman polemicizes against the lynch law. The rough justice meted out in Western folklore is severely criticized, but not through a goodies-versus-baddies confrontation. Collusion and passivity on the part of 'decent, ordinary folk' are as much responsible for the lynching of the innocent men as those baying for their blood. In this uncompromising film, Wellman takes to task the ideological functioning of the traditional Western: nostalgic escapism at the service of corporate capitalism. He repeated this in his 1944 film criticizing the White colonization of the West, *Buffalo Bill*.

The introduction of **colour** on a bigger scale in the mid- to late 1940s meant that violence now appeared more real. This was greeted with considerable consternation by the censors. But, far more to their consternation were the implications for sex on-screen. Sex did not come onto the screen in the Western until the late 1940s and even so it came in with great difficulty. Howard Hughes' *The Outlaw* was made in 1943 and was a vehicle for his new star, Jane Russell. However, the league of decency (see **censorship**) created a furore over its premiere, complaining that the over-exposure of Jane Russell's breasts was indecent. The film was withdrawn and re-released with a few cuts in 1940. Jane Russell was the first of a number of actors to play the role of a 'smouldering', sexy décolletée Mexican woman. Sex was launched, but it had to be had with stereotypes. Plenty of hot-blooded foreign womanhood but not 'nice, nice Ms American pie' – she had to be kept virginal at all costs. Until this eruption of sex, the characterization of women was fairly peripheral. The Western is a man's movie. A man with a horse; a man in action; a loner who leaves the woman behind rather than staying. His lust for adventure far outweighs his lust for women. As a genre, the Western is the antithesis to the **melodrama** and domesticity. The Western stands out in its refusal to complete the **Oedipal trajectory** (see under **psychoanalysis**). It is very rare for the hero, having once rescued the abducted, but pure woman, to go on to marry her. The hero's job is to make the West safe for the virgins to come out and reproduce, but not with him, that is the job for the rest of the community. He has to 'move on out'.

In the Western very few exceptions exist to the misrepresentation of the frontierswomen. Women are either floozies in the saloon, who are to be driven out of town (not until after good use however) or shot, or pure as the driven snow and totally vulnerable to marauding men and, of course, abducting Indians. In truth, cowgirls did exist, gun-toting just like the men, and dressed in men's clothes. Indeed, *The Ballad of Little Jo* (Maggie Greenwald, 1993) is based on a real woman whose **gender** was discovered only after her death. During the 1930s, only a handful of films paid homage to the role of women in the West. *Annie Oakley* (1935) was a first, starring Barbara Stanwyck, followed by *Plainsman* (1936) with Jean Arthur in the role of Calamity Jane. And two films starring Mae West, *Klondike Annie* (1936) and *My Little Chickadee* (1940), complete the list. The 1950s did not see any great improvement on this tally. Again, only a handful come to mind. Wellman's quite authentic film about frontierswomen, *Westward Women* (1951), and their dangerous and stressful drive out west to find husbands is one. So too is Ray's *Johnny Guitar*, starring Joan Crawford as the gun-slinging cross-dressed Vienna who, once she has cleared the town of the threat of a lynch mob and their leader (another woman, Emma, played by Mercedes McCambridge), is able to don feminine clothes again (in fact, in the dramatic concluding sequences to the film, she switches back and forth with the greatest of ease between male and female attire). In all these films, women cross-dressing occurs and represents **diegetically** an embodiment of power and independence. And, as far as the female **spectator** is concerned, despite the fact that in some of the films the woman gives up her clothes and gets her man, there is nonetheless a pleasurable identification with that empowerment. Not that those in feminine attire necessarily lack force. Barbara Stanwyck had several strong roles to play – most brilliantly in *Forty Guns* (Samuel Fuller, 1957), where she is a ranch boss with forty hired guns. Finally, Marlene Dietrich (playing true to type) was the star in *Rancho Notorious* (Fritz Lang, 1952). Cross-dressed passing women in Westerns are extremely thin on the ground and seem doomed to remain a lesbian fantasy. Jo in *The Ballad of Little Jo is* the one who comes closest – although as R. Ruby Rich argues there is no true 'play' with her **sexuality**, so her cross-dressing offers limited pleasures to a lesbian audience (see Rich's useful article in *Sight and Sound*, November 1993, vol. 3, issue 11, 18–22). Cowgirls, it would appear, never look like becoming a good idea in movies (see Loy, 2004, for further discussion of women in Westerns).

If you can count female Westerns on two fingers, you can count Black Westerns on just about one hand (if you include Black presence in a major role). Unsurprisingly, the major 'spurt' of Black Westerns occurred in the early 1970s, coming in the wake, or on the back of, the successful **Blaxploitation** movies. One such film that is guilty of exploiting the Blaxploitation moment is Anthony Dawson's *Take a Hard Ride* (1975), with its crude 'rushing for the bounty' narrative that attempts to marry the Italian spaghetti Western with the anti-movie. *El Condor* (John Guillerman, 1970) just pre-dates the Blaxploitation moment by one year and follows more in the trend of the newly violent Western *à la* Peckinpah. This flashily violent film features among its main protagonists a Black chain-gang fugitive and an Apache Indian hunting down buried treasure. *Boss Nigger* (aka *The Black Bounty Killer*, Jack Arnold, 1974) stands out among this generation of Black Westerns because of its intentional parody of the genre through its play with cliché and violence. In a different vein, Sidney Poitier's *Buck and the Preacher* (1971) examines the struggles of Black wagoners (freed slaves) trying to head out west. The Black cowboy reappears briefly in *Silverado* (Lawrence Kasdan, 1985). And that is about it, until Mario Van Peebles' *Posse* (1993) and the rather silly *Wild Wild West* (Barry Sonnenfeld, 1999). Apart from these few forays, the Western remains an essentially all-White male affair. So let us return to its history.

By the 1950s, the Western's hero had become more complex, more psychologically motivated (see **motivation**). He had a past. The introduction of **psychoanalysis** into this genre is credited to Wellman (as mentioned above), but it took off in a big way in the 1950s in part owing to the influence of the **film noir**. The broody, introspective, angst-ridden film noir protagonist reappears with spurs. Something in his past has deeply scarred his persona. He still rides in and out of the wilderness as before, but now that wilderness is also part of his temperament and embedded in his psyche. The other exemplary filmmaker of this new type of Western was Anthony Mann, who worked with James Stewart as his fetish star. Before turning to the Western, Mann had made several films noir (such as *T-Men*, 1947, and *Raw Deal*, 1948) so the cross-over of mood is quite visible in his films. He gave an uncompromising vision of the West. His heroes are often solitary, mentally and morally divided personae (as was their film noir prototype), bent on revenge and yet wanting to find peace of mind and thereby rest from their avenging souls (see *Winchester '73*, 1950; *Bend of the River*, 1952; *The Naked Spur*, 1953 – all Stewart vehicles). Mann's Westerns are intentionally violent – a tradition followed by Arthur Penn (as in *The Left-Handed Gun*, 1958) and Sam Peckinpah (*The Wild Bunch*, 1969).

The demise of the studios, in the early 1950s, led to location shooting, and this, coupled with the implementation of **cinemascope** and colour, gave the Western increased visual **realism** alongside the greater psychological realism (discussed above). Although, on the whole, the Western, then as before, was seen as an escapist genre, nonetheless certain films, especially those made during the first half of the 1950s, can be read as commentaries on the contemporary political climate of McCarthyism as well as reflections of the political uncertainties of the Cold War. *High Noon* (Fred Zinnemann, 1952) and *Johnny Guitar* are the two that are most often cited as allegories of McCarthyism and the fear and mistrust brought about by the Cold War. The former film was scripted by Carl Foreman, a communist who was blacklisted (see **Hollywood blacklist**), and he clearly meant his loose adaptation of the novel *The Tin Star* (by John W. Cunningham) to act as an indictment of US justice and society. In the film the hero (played by Gary Cooper) is the lone marshal who has to gun down an ex-convict and his gang bent on revenge. The marshal tries to drum up support but no one will come to his assistance. A similar instance of community cowardice and a refusal to get involved is at the core of *Johnny Guitar* (which was shot in Spain in 1954 while Ray was in self-imposed exile, and also free of the constraints of Hollywood). In this film, the community hide behind the law to rid themselves of 'outsiders', 'aliens', people coming from outside and 'who don't belong' – even though, in the end, Vienna and Johnny put a stop to it.

High Noon certainly re-established the reputation of the Western, and the 1950s produced many great Westerns. Indeed, the traditions of this epoch of films are partly a progenitor to Clint Eastwood's 1980s and 1990s Westerns. Alan Ladd's portrayal of nervous heroism in *Shane* (George Stevens, 1953), Gregory Peck's unsuccessful attempts to outrun his past as the fastest gun in the West in *Gunfighter* (George King, 1950) and the restless, drifting hero coming into town and then leaving having resolved a problem of a community in crisis – these are all hallmarks of Eastwood's performance as exemplified in two films also directed by him, *Pale Rider* (1985) and *Unforgiven* (1992).

Until the 1950s, Indians on the whole were represented as killers, abductors and pyromaniacs – hardly ever as individuals, certainly not with any attempt to understand or reflect their side of history. John Ford's *The Searchers* is a perplexing and difficult film in this context. In one respect, it appears to advocate (by the end of the film) greater tolerance of difference. However, it is not difficult to read the entire narrative – with its expressed anxiety about rape, miscegenation and the genetic determination of race (an anxiety embodied incidentally by the ruthless Ethan Edwards, played by John Wayne) – as a metaphor for concern about the growth, in the 1950s, of the Civil Rights movement. Furthermore, no attempt is made to 'explain' the Indian side of the story (see Pippin, 2010). There were, however, one or two exceptions to this a-historical approach to Indian Western history. In these rare films, there is a new respect for the Indian (*Broken Arrow*, Delmer Daves, 1950) and a bitter condemnation of the exploitation of the Indian by the White man (*Devil's Doorway*, Mann, 1950). Kevin Costner's *Dances with Wolves* (1990) is but another in a short line of this attempt to redress the history of the West. (For further discussion of Indians in Westerns, see Buscombe, 2006 and French, 2005.)

By the 1960s, in an attempt to attract audiences back into the cinemas, the Western went super-epic. The psychological realism was dropped in favour of bulk value for money: **widescreen** productions filled with as many stars as possible, such as John Sturges' *The Magnificent Seven*, 1960, with seven stars (and reworked three times). The community had gone, and with it the notion of service. Group solidarity was in, but only among the gang. Alternatively, the protagonist was motivated by revenge, but contrary to the complex Western of the 1950s, there was no visible reason or moral point of view that explained this motivation (see Henry Hathaway's *Nevada Smith*, 1966). What also prevailed was an aesthetics of violence not seen heretofore, primarily in Penn and Peckinpah's films (e.g. Peckinpah's *Straw Dogs*, 1971). One explanation for this violence could be the abolition of film **censorship** in the United States, since this new, even excessive, violence characterizes many films of that decade and the next (notably Arthur Penn's *Bonnie and Clyde*, 1967). Another could be that the old-established generation of filmmakers (particularly Ford and Hawks) were coming to the end of their careers and a new way had to be found of telling what is intrinsically the same story. The Western had become as action-packed as in its early silent days, but on the whole it lacked inventiveness, bar a few smash hits (such as *Butch Cassidy and the Sundance Kid*, George Roy Hill, 1969). A third reason might be that it was a genre out of touch with the climate of the times. The United States had proved to itself that it was still a violent and corrupt country (the Watergate scandal, the assassinations of President Kennedy, his brother Robert Kennedy and Martin Luther King), so the myth of pioneering spirits, frontiersmanship and a united nation – with all that it denotes of optimism, wholesomeness and integrity – did not sit easily with reality.

By the 1960s, the Western, perhaps the longest-lasting genre, looked set to die out, even though Peckinpah was still making them. See, for example, his *Pat Garrett and Billy the Kid* (1973), an answer perhaps to the revisionist *Chisum* made in 1970 by Andrew McLaglen and starring the ubiquitous Western iconic star John Wayne. But, its fortunes were revived, largely thanks to its moving to Europe into the form of the so-called spaghetti Westerns (made by Italian directors and so-called in the belief that they were shot in Italy; in fact they were, for the most part, shot in Spain). These films challenged the Hollywood model by its shift in emphasis from reality to parody. They politicized the genre in a way Hollywood never did – they were often anti-clerical and the outsider did not instinctively fight for the poor, but might well help revolutionaries in their cause. The true success of the genre came about as a result of a fortunate meeting in 1964 between the Italian filmmaker Sergio Leone and a fairly unknown American actor Clint Eastwood. The quiet, almost static aloofness of the 'man with no name', as Eastwood was known in his first film, *A Fistful of Dollars* (1964), in combination with Leone's ironic treatment of the Western proved to be unbeatable. And if the genre has been revitalized on the American front, then its regeneration is in large part due to the parodying it underwent under Leone's direction. The genre itself was called into question. Leone's films provided a criticism of the ideological operations at work in Hollywood's mythic construction of the West. The footage was not all action-packed, the pace was slowed down. Eastwood hardly spoke and barely moved. Eastwood claims that he deliberately cut out most of the dialogue to facilitate direction since he and Leone had no common language. This first film was such a success that Eastwood went on to make three more. Other American actors went to Europe to work with Leone (Henry Fonda, Charles Bronson and Rod Steiger). And the whole series of spaghetti Westerns lasted a decade. But, the Western was changed forever, away from the prevailing optimism, puritanism and nationalism it had displayed before. The genre had been **deconstructed**, it could now go back West. Certainly Quentin Tarantino has recently shown his admiration for this tradition in his two spaghetti-styled homages to Leone – *Django Unchained*, 2012, and *The Hateful Eight*, 2015 – both with Black lead actors (Jamie Foxx and Samuel L. Jackson respectively), and both with the participation of Ennio Morricone (a song in the former, complete score in the latter). (For further reading on spaghetti Westerns see Staig and Williams, 1975; Frayling, 1998, 2005.)

The success of the spaghetti Westerns is their difference. Their caricatural nature pokes fun at the iconography of the Western. The baddies are not only bad, they are ugly and dirty. The films themselves are cynical in tone. Sleaziness and dishonesty are the order of the day.

Only one man, Eastwood, can clean it all up and even then not for long if the first sequel to *A Fistful of Dollars, For a Few Dollars More* (1966), is anything to go by. Following the success of these films, Eastwood returned to the United States, since when he has been directing and producing and starring in his films (e.g. *The Outlaw Josey Wales*, 1976). He has become the icon of the contemporary Western to the point that he is almost solely identified with it.

The Western still remains with us today. Not as popular a genre in terms of numbers as it used to be – and arguably replaced by the **blockbuster** film – but certainly a box-office hit when its epic nature provides the appropriate mix in its appeal to American audiences' nostalgic take on the past; namely, the wide, ever-expanding horizons of the frontiers, the interaction with the American-Indian, the challenging of corrupt settlers, and so on. In this context, see Kevin Costner's *Dances with Wolves* (1990), or even more interestingly Costner's lengthy homage to Western film history in general and Ford in particular in his film *Open Range* (2003). Curiously, however, inter-racial sex still seems a problem, albeit not in Costner's films. Indeed, Costner's *Dances with Wolves* argues for tolerance. But another film, Ron Howard's *Missing* (2003), shows that it is still not something that rests easy with the American psyche – particularly if it is a white woman whose sexuality is at stake.

see also: **genre**

For further reading see Blake, 2003; Bold, 1987; Buscombe, 1988, 2006; Frayling, 1998, 2005; French, 2005; Loy, 2004; McGee, 2007; Pippin, 2010; Ramirez-Berg, 2002; Saunders, 2001; Stanfield, 2001; Studlar, 2001; Tompkin, 1992; Tuska, 1976; Walker, 2001; Wright, 1975.

WIDESCREEN

Experimentation with widescreen has been around since at least the 1920s. However, none of the various systems really took off until the 1950s with the introduction of **Cinemascope**, thanks to the **anamorphic lens**. In the late 1920s, several **Hollywood** companies experimented with different gauge widths – from 56 to 70mm – but, in general, because of the costs incurred, especially by cinema theatres, thanks to the advent of **sound** very few were in a position to afford the expense of new widescreen equipment on top of that needed for sound. The early 1950s use of the anamorphic lens gave an aspect ratio of 2.35:1 (by first squeezing the image onto a 35mm print and then un-squeezing it by projecting the film through an anamorphic lens) – up until that time the standard aspect ratio was 1.33:1. By the late 1950s, technology for widescreen had moved forward and managed to compress the image and then un-squeeze it onto a 70mm print – thereby dispensing with the anamorphic lens. Yet another system used to create the widescreen effect was to shoot a film on 65mm and then print onto 70mm. When projected, the effect was widescreen with an aspect ratio of 2.2:1 (now the standard widescreen projection ratio for 70mm). More recently (before the **digital** age), for the widescreen effect, films were shot on 35mm (via an anamorphic lens – Panavision is standard) and then transferred to 70mm. However, when 35mm films are projected in widescreen, the aspect ratio diminishes somewhat to 1.85:1 in USA and 1.66:1 in Europe. Now, in the digital age, the current widescreen cinema standard is 2.39:1. Digital CCD cameras (charged-coupled device: that converts light into electrons), with their built-in widescreen applications, mean that the shooting format can be flicked with a switch from standard 4:3 to 16:9 widescreen shooting format. The Red 4k digital cinema camera is presently the most popular prototype.

see also: **anamorphic lens** and **cinemascope**

For further details on this technology and its effect see Belton, 1992; on widescreen systems in the digital age see Belton, Hall and Neale, 2010.

WIPE

A transition between two **shots** whereby the earlier one appears to be pushed aside by the latter, creating the effect of wiping off a scene and replacing it with another.

WOMEN'S FILMS *SEE* MELODRAMA

WORLD CINEMAS/WORLD CINEMA/THIRD WORLD CINEMAS

Preamble – contextualizing terminologies

It is impossible to discuss the term *World Cinema* without first putting in place the concept that predates it: Third World Cinemas. Indeed, when the first edition of *Cinema Studies: The Key Concepts* was published in 1996, the term *World Cinema*, as a theoretical or nominative concept, held little to no currency. In fact, at the time of that first edition, the term *World Cinema* – in that it was merely a convenience label for all foreign films on sale in video stores – would have seemed inadequate, even inaccurate, to refer to a whole swathe of cinemas, many of which were all but ignored by Film Studies programmes (in the West). However, feedback from Film Studies lecturers on the third edition of this book argued that Third World Cinemas was *passé* (even patronizing) and that the appropriate term was *World* or *International Cinema*. I struggled, in amending the fourth edition, to know what to do with updating the existing section on Third World Cinemas. I was very clear that it was not in the remit of this kind of book to lay out all of World Cinema (an impossible task). Furthermore, in the second and third editions, I had deliberately given a great deal of space to Third World Cinemas, precisely to claim a place, in Film Studies programmes in Western academes, for these cinemas emanating from developing countries. To abandon them seemed irresponsible, therefore. The problem, as this section and the next two will go on to explain, is that by moving from Third World Cinemas to World Cinema, there is a strong possibility that this, ultimately, vaguer term will lead us to overlook certain cinemas of the margins, for example, the cinema of nations that do not have a fully fledged film industry themselves, but who nonetheless in collaboration with other (perhaps neighbouring countries, such as the case for North African nations) manage to produce a number of films on a yearly basis. And that, conversely, cinemas emanating from nations that have a vibrant enough industry (China, **East Asian cinemas** and India) will become a predominant feature of World Cinema Film Studies programmes. Thus, it is for these reasons that I feel that, at the very least, we must argue for a pluralization of the term, World Cinemas (this argument is developed further in the section entitled **World Cinema**).

As to the idea that this concept is 'passé', I ask, to whom?, in much the same vein as many years ago a young South African student challenged my use of **postcolonial** cinema as a term to identify his nation's new, post-Apartheid cinema. He asked, 'postcolonial for whom?' Indeed, in the late 1990s – at least from a Black perspective – that nation was not yet postcolonial.

Historically speaking, the term *Third World Cinema* as a concept derives in part from the flurry of the late 1960s debates around **Third Cinema** – a term first coined by radical Latin American filmmakers as an ironic comment on the way in which the spheres of economic influence had been carved up post-war (by the West). Before venturing any further, what first needs clarifying is what is meant by these two terms (*Third* and *Third World Cinema*). As explained in the entry on Third Cinema, these two terms are not co-terminous, even though both types of film production emanate, primarily, from (what were then deemed) economically speaking underdeveloped countries. Third Cinema, however, is specifically a politicized cinema (and, as the separate entry makes clear, it is not necessarily dependent on geographical location); Third World Cinema refers to the national productions as a whole coming from the Third World economic sphere (see discussion below).

By the mid-1980s, Third World Cinema was firmly established as a concept, and lively discussions ensued as to how First World theory should or should not be applied to its practice (see Grant and Kuhn, 2006: 3–5). By the late 1980s and early 1990s, as a direct response to the impact of the growing theoretical field of postcolonial studies on film studies, the concept had gained considerable momentum, and was used to refer to cinemas emanating from Third World economies. In that regard, the desire was to draw attention to the fact that, up until this time, film scholarship, by placing the primary focus on **Hollywood** cinema and European cinemas, was in fact 'guilty' of omission. The idea was to bring these missing cinemas to the forefront; namely, African cinemas, Latin American cinemas, the cinemas of China, India and Pakistan, and, finally, Middle Eastern cinemas. In the 1990s, all of these cinemas (with the exception of Israel) emanated from Third World economies. By the new millennium, the economic landscape had apparently changed. At least according to Goldman Sachs who determined, in 2001, that certain nations (Brazil, Russia, India, China) that had recently become industrialized countries, or whose economy (i.e. Russia's) was on a par, were the 'hot' newly emerging markets: BRIC. In 2010, South Africa joined the club, renamed BRICS. However, by 2015, the BRICS were either in slowdown mode (China, South Africa), or struggling with economic reforms (India), or in deep recession (Brazil, Russia). So much so, that Goldman Sachs closed down its BRICS fund (moving to 'hot' emerging markets elsewhere). Thus, for our purposes, it makes sense to see these countries as emerging economies and not part of a first or second order economy (for clarification on this terminology see next paragraph). However, in terms of our own labelling, because the former Soviet Union was considered a second order economy, Russian cinema has always been considered as part of European cinema, and therefore never came under the label of Third World Cinemas.

Third World Cinema as a concept, then, came into being by association with world order spheres of influence – namely, First, Second and Third World, terms used to determine specific countries and continents in relation to their global economic, social, political and cultural spheres of influence (I explain below how this concept then became pluralized, that is, 'Cinemas'). The term *Third World* was coined in 1952, at the height of the Cold War, to refer to countries that were not aligned with either of the two superpowers (the USA and the former Soviet Union). At that time, the term *First World* designated the dominant economies of the West, and *Second World* those of the Soviet Union and its satellites. By the 1980s, the terms *First* and *Second World economies* were rather loosely applied to the economies of North America, much of Europe, Australia, New Zealand and some countries in the Middle East. *Third World* applied, as an economic term, to all other continents and countries – excluding those countries that became known, after World War Two, as the Western Pacific Rim (a global economic term used to refer to Japan, South Korea, Taiwan, Singapore, Thailand and Malaysia); that is, countries until recently considered as constituting an important economy in their own right (the so-called Tiger economies – a term no longer invoked since their demise in the late 1990s). Some would say the Pacific Rim was an artificial economic sphere established by the Americans to ensure a Western, Eurocentric, economic ethos to counter the perceived communist threat (of China and the former Soviet Union). By analogy with the term *Third World*, Third World Cinema has, until very recently, been used to refer to the cinemas of the African continent, the Middle Eastern territories, the Indian continent, China and Asian territories, and Latin America. As we can see, the concept is again used rather loosely, since not all the cinemas included under this broad umbrella are necessarily Third World economies (a prime example being Israel). Clearly, not all countries of the Middle East are poor, but what they singularly are not is Eurocentric.

However, just as the term *Third World* itself is not unproblematic, so too the concept Third World Cinema. Some thirty years ago, Homi Bhabha (1989: 112–13) made the point that, although Third World was one we were obliged to use, it remained hugely problematic because of its pejorative connotations and its assumptions about a geopolitical worldview. Thus, by the late 1990s, Third World was superseded by the expression 'developing countries'; still later, in the 2000s, by 'advanced and secondary emerging economies' and also the BRICS economies (see above). Unfortunately, for cinema, the way forward has been to appropriate the rather imprecise term *World Cinema*. But, before moving

on to a discussion of the merits and pitfalls of this term, let us first consider the original concept: Third World Cinema – or more appropriately, the plural form, Third World Cinemas.

Shifting terminologies – concept one: Third World Cinemas – issues and debates

Curiously, the issues raised here are ones that still prevail with the
new labelling, World Cinema (see next section, below). In fact, if anything they are more pronounced, for reasons that become clearer
below. The first paradox to emerge in relation to the term Third
World Cinema is that the very fact of talking of this cinema as one
entity (a unified whole) is already problematic. Clearly, Third World
Cinema constitutes a very diverse set of cinemas – far more so than
those emanating from the USA and even Europe – hence the need to
use the term in the plural: Third World Cinemas. A second paradox
is that if we were to take all these cinemas as a whole (as we do with
Europe, in our definition of it as Second cinema), then it is this
cinema that makes up most of cinema (in terms of output and audiences). Yet, this cinema is treated as if it were the subaltern, the
shadow cinema of the 'real' cinema of North America and Europe.
Furthermore, until fairly recently, the Western world had a very poor
idea of what these Third World Cinemas were and seemed far from
curious to import them and find out. But, by the 1980s, as theory
began to embrace a more cultural studies-based approach to film,
attitudes towards Third World Cinemas began to evolve. As the
Western nations continued to become more aware of their own
multiculturalism, and as studies in postcolonial theory and practice
became more widespread, so too, by the 1990s, the teaching of Third
World Cinemas became more prevalent (in Film Studies programmes
in Western academe). Furthermore, as the technology for the culture
of consumption developed (through access to movies on the internet,
video and DVD sales), so, too, cinemas from all over the world
became available to the globalized consumers. For example, Birmingham and Bradford Asian communities in the UK are big consumers of
Indian and Pakistani cinemas.

In terms of how to approach Third World Cinemas, how to teach
and write about it in the West, Ella Shohat and Robert Stam's book
Unthinking Eurocentrism: Multiculturalism and the Media (1994) was and
still is a key text for helping those of us in the Western world avoid
falling into what Appiah (1992) calls the pseudo-universalism of
Eurocentric theories and their applications to all cinemas. In other

words, we must not imagine the Third World Cinemas through (our) Western, Eurocentric eyes, mentalities and theoretical frameworks. To take an evident example, it is clear that constructions of **gender** will differ according to the placing of femininity and masculinity within a nation's cultural traditions. Nor must we imagine that Third World Cinemas are without their own traditions and theories. Nor must we imagine that these cinemas 'occurred' only recently in the post-colonial moment or in some cases the post-revolutionary, or *coup d'état* and post-*coup d'état* moments. Indeed not. Third World Cinemas, in many cases, are cinemas that were in place as early as, or shortly after the emergence of cinemas in Europe and North America. For example, the Lumière brothers travelled the world with their *cinématographe*, thereby encouraging imperialist nations to take their own images of their colonies. By the early 1900s, many colonizing nations had established their Colonial Film Units and, in some cases, were actively encouraging indigenous filmmakers to create their own films to entertain local audiences. In other countries, where colonialism was not about cultural assimilation, as in the case of India, indigenous traders financed filmmaking companies as early as the 1900s. In fact, to cite India again, it is as early as 1896 that we can speak of it as having its 'own' cinema. India's tremendous theatre tradition (the Parsee/Pharsi theatre is perhaps the tradition best known to Westerners) meant that there were 'ready-made' venues for the screening of these early short films as attractions at the end of performances.

A further thought we need to bear in mind is that Third World Cinemas have established their own theoretical **discourses** around film. Again, to take the example of India, we can point to an emergence of **film theory** as early as 1948 (at least) with the writings of Satyajit Ray and Chidananda Das Gupta on the importance of a post-independence cinema that would function culturally as a national integrating force. Their writings and those, a bit later, of Ritwik Chatak and Kobita Sarkar (in the 1960s and 1970s) have provided a central core of theoretical debates on **realism** versus **modernism**, modernism versus **avant-garde**, nationalist cinema versus regional cinema, and so on. But, in relation to all these issues, we could equally look to Bangladeshi, Bhojpuri, North Korean, Sri Lankan, Tamil and Vietnamese, cinemas about which, currently, very little is known/written except for those rare films that make it to Film Festivals.

Nor must 'our' (i.e. the Western film critics/academe) awareness of such concepts as Third World Cinemas blind us to the fact that there are also what Shohat and Stam (1994: 32) call the Fourth World cinemas. As Shohat and Stam explain, when we speak of Fourth

World we are referring to peoples who are 'the still-residing descendants of the original inhabitants of territories taken over or circumscribed by alien conquest or settlement' (ibid.), for example, Native-Americans in the USA, Native-Indians in Latin American countries, Maoris in New Zealand, Aborigines in Australia, Palestinians in Israel-Palestine – all of whom have produced cinemas of their own. What of the Caribbean cinemas (French and English) and the occasional films that make a big hit internationally (e.g. *The Harder they Come*, Perry Henzell, 1972)? Where do we place these? And the cinemas of Peru, Chile and Bolivia? These distinctions between Third and Fourth Worlds are therefore extremely helpful when talking about non-Eurocentric cinemas. They prevent a homogenization, by us in the West, of cinemas that we barely know, let alone understand. They also make it clear that when we think about cinemas and their cultural traditions – wherever they are located – we should be mindful of the fact that belief in Western domination (whether in terms of domination of a market or cultural **hegemony**) is often a little closer to fiction than fact. Finally, they lay open the possibility of a concept of a Fifth Cinema – which could refer to cinemas with very poor production values because of lack of investment in the film industry – either by default (little funding available – for example, Vietnamese cinema, Caribbean cinemas, the smaller Latin American cinemas) or by design (a nation wishing to control and contain its cinematic production – for example, North Korean cinema).

It is because of these very precise distinctions (plurality of cinemas; Third and Fourth cinemas, even Fifth cinemas) and the notion of the vital importance of contexts of production and **distribution**, that the new term, *World Cinema*, that has come to replace the concept Third World Cinemas, needs to be considered critically. Thus, what follows below is an explanation of the new term, but also the setting out of a polemical debate as to the term's limitations. It is also important to note the distinction I have made all along between the word *concept*, which I use in relation to Third World Cinemas, and *term*, which I apply to World Cinema. Concept means a broad, abstract, evolving idea of how cultures behave and are perceived; and term is a word used to mean something more delimiting and homogenizing.

Shifting terminologies – concept two: World Cinema – World Cinemas

In this part of the entry, I am using the term *World Cinema* in the singular, since that is the term most often employed in current studies.

However, as I shall go on to argue, the singular is not satisfactory and the next section of this entry will shift to a plural form: World Cinemas.

Since the mid-2000s, there has been a turning away from the concept *Third World Cinemas* – almost as if it is no longer 'politically correct' to refer to emerging economies as Third World economies and therefore, by analogy, to refer to their cinemas as Third World Cinemas. Furthermore, several of the former Third economy nations have emerged into first order economies: Brazil, Russia, India, China and South Africa (known as the BRICS economies). Thus, economic labelling would seem to dictate that it is no longer appropriate to speak of those particular cinemas as Third World Cinemas, even if some of these nations are still, in reality, what we term developing or emerging economies and are no longer endorsed by Goldman Sachs. China may be the second fastest-growing economy, nonetheless a huge proportion of its citizens live in poverty; similarly with India, which currently ranks seventh. Moreover, investment in film production, in all these BRICS nations, still remains far lower than the USA. So the question becomes, is the term *World Cinema* (or even *International Cinema*) adequate enough? For, the term *World Cinema* is used, depending on the scholarship you read, to refer to either all cinemas except Hollywood and Europe, or all cinemas except Hollywood, or all cinemas (including Hollywood). Is it all-embracing? Perhaps, but it sets in place the notion of binaries (i.e. Hollywood/rest of the world), something Third World Cinemas managed to avoid; or it implies the concept of a globalized cinema (everything is included), which is far from the truth (if only from the point of view of distribution and exhibition practices). Third World Cinemas – as opposed to World Cinema – does not define itself against or in opposition to **mainstream cinema**. For, indeed, which mainstream are we talking about? After all, each of these cinemas produces popular (mainstream) films as well as the more radical challenging film. Each of these cinemas is constituted by a cinematic industry in its own right emanating from a geo-economic sphere that specifies its own industrial practices even if investment in production is far less than in cinemas of the first and second order economies.

Writing in 1996, Ella Shohat spoke of the need for the concept of Third World Cinema. Shohat warns us of a post-Third-Worldist culture when she says: 'Third-Worldist euphoria has given way to the collapse of communism and the indefinite postponement of the devoutly wished "tri-continental revolution"' (reprinted, 2006: 42). It is almost as if she is saying, the excitement felt (by the West, in the 1980s and 1990s) at discovering new cinemas from economically underdeveloped countries (and which we then called Third World

Cinemas) was bound to be short-lived and that, in its stead, given the economic changes brought about by the collapse of communism and the spread of global capitalism, scholarly interest would follow the areas of fiscal growth, in particular the two areas with the greatest industrial output: India and Asia (with, combined, some 1,625 films per annum, compared with North America and Europe together at 1,550 (Toby Miller, in Badley *et al.*, 2006: xi–xiii)). Shohat's words were prophetic. The most significant impact of this new nomenclature (World Cinema) has been the rise in academic research into and teaching of Indian (primarily **Bollywood**) and Asian cinemas (East and South), including Japan, Taiwan, Hong Kong (see Ciecko, 2006, as just one example). While this research development within the discipline of Film Studies is entirely to be welcomed in one way, the fact remains that *none* of these Asian countries are third order economies, nor are their cinemas (see **East Asian Cinema** entry). This growing attention, then, has been at the expense of other, more peripheral cinemas, those emanating from underdeveloped economies. As Grant and Kuhn point out (2006: 5), World Cinema as a term has emerged out of an alignment with world systems approach (itself an effect of globalization). They go on to state: 'the decline in the usage of terms like Third World and Third Cinema is revealing in this context; as, relatedly, is the rather greater attention given in recent studies of world cinema to Asian, especially Chinese, cinemas as against those of, say, Latin America and Africa' (ibid.).

It is useful to consider, first, how this term, *World Cinema*, came to be in vogue. The reasons are twofold. The first is motivated by a desire to move away from binaries (Hollywood/Rest of the World) and to be all-embracing. This approach finds its roots in **postmodernism**, which argues for pluralism. While it seems anodyne enough, if we are not alert, this all-inclusive approach dilutes concepts of difference and distinctiveness. It has the potential, as we can see from the discussion in the entry on postmodernism, of a-historicism. We can literally hop from one film archetype to another; be familiar with, but lack deep knowledge of these cinemas – that is, have *connaissance* but not *savoir*. Furthermore, as I pointed out above, this approach risks re-imposing binaries and as Hill and Church-Gibson note, 'some have adopted World Cinema as if it is not a fraught term and take it to mean non-Hollywood cinema' (2000: xiv–xv). The fact that it is used so consistently in the singular should also give us pause for thought – it becomes almost impossibly meaningless: how can there be a single world cinema?

The second reason for the emergence of this term is a marketing one. As Grant and Kuhn (2006: 1) in their lucid discussion of World

Cinema explain, the term seems to cover more or less the same territory as that 'embraced in the widespread coinage "world music"'.
Rather than talk, say, of a Mali film or a Mali singer, the product is
placed on the shelves of World Cinema or World Music. Dennison
and Lim (2006: 1) make a similar point to Grant and Kuhn in their
thoughtful study when they say, 'world cinema is analogous to
"world music" and "world literature" in that they are categories created
in the Western world to refer to cultural products and practices that are
mainly non-western'. Dennison and Lim also clarify the problematics
of this approach when they argue that, in a sense, this labelling is a
continuation of 'the effects of colonialism in an age of globalization'
(ibid.: 2). Specificity is lost at this most basic level. We see the effects of
these market forces and labelling when we consider that several academic publishers have joined this bandwagon with their 'World
Cinema Series'. In a survey I have just conducted on publications since
the third edition of this book in 2006, some hundred new books have
appeared with 'World Cinema' in their title, many of which encourage
us to see World Cinema as an all-embracing phenomenon. Intellect
Press, Bristol, for example, has a *Directory of World Cinema* series which
seems to cover nearly everything, but in such a catch-all way that it
makes no distinction between economies of scale or different typologies (e.g. countries with major industries versus those with small ones;
mainstream versus counter-cinema, and so on). Thus, its series includes
books on large nations, such as the USA, small countries such as Scot-
land. Furthermore, it sections off parts of a nation's cinema such as Hollywood (calling it *Directory of World Cinema: Hollywood*), and again with
American Independent cinema (*Directory of World Cinema: American
Independent*). Soon, one suspects, **genres** themselves will be World
Cinema. Everything is World. How does this help, I ask myself?

Thus, we have to be aware that this all-encompassing term *World
Cinema*, though it has its advantages, is also not without its drawbacks.
It simplifies and homogenizes the artefacts as if they are of a similar
nature, which of course they are not. In so doing, this labelling runs
the risk of losing the contextual specificities – modes of production,
legal prescriptions, **myths** and artefacts of a nation's social psyche
(etc.), what I would term multicultural specificities. When using
Third World Cinemas as a concept, the intention was to show
the extent and diversity of cinemas with their separate industrial
practices. The focus was their difference, the pluralism of film cultures
(what Shohat and Stam refer to as 'polycentric multiculturalism',
1994: 28). And there is a danger that this political specificity will get
lost both by the lumping of all cinemas together under a universal

title and by the approach adopted in studies on World Cinema; namely, looking for the interconnectedness of cinematic practices and cultures in the age of globalization (Dennison and Lim, 2006: 6) at the expense of their differences and divergences. Both must be present, clearly (interconnectedness and difference). Grant and Kuhn are correct when they state that the impact of world systems and global capitalism have had a deleterious effect on certain world cinemas. What we get to see and what gets talked about has diminished. As Grant and Kuhn write: 'It is surely no coincidence that those areas of the world most prominently involved in transformations in the global cultural economy are precisely the ones ... that figure so prominently in current studies of world cinema', namely, India and China (2006: 5), to which we must add East Asian cinemas. And the major outcome of this squeeze is a diminishing of the political discursive frame (ibid.: 5) and a greater homogenization. And a related problematic to this is the delimiting effect of the concentration on genre in scholarship and teaching of world cinema – doubtless a further outcome of the focus on the newly emerging economies (India and China). As Grant and Kuhn (ibid.: 6), perhaps a little contentiously, this approach has had the unfortunate consequence of reducing world cinema to two dominant film genres: the action picture (especially Hong Kong martial arts films) and the (Indian) melodrama. These objects of study are of course very merit-worthy. Both address, in entirely different ways, questions of national identity and the impact of modernization and globalization. But, as we can observe, the consequence of focusing on dominant genres is limiting and it again tilts the axis of interest away from the other World Cinemas (see, for example, Gamm and Clark, 2004).

One of the potentially useful theoretical models that has been invoked to discuss World Cinema has been the concept of **transnationalism** (see entry on **transnational cinema**). Sami Chaudhuri (2005: 2) explains that because cinema is a multinational system it is 'part of the digital **convergence** with other media' and thus inherently transnational in its practice; as a result, 'it increasingly makes sense to think in terms of "world cinema"'. But here too there are problems. In the first instance, we could argue that cinema has always already been a transnational affair at least in terms of exchanges and border crossings (e.g. French film industry outlets all over the world at the turn of the nineteenth century; European émigré personnel travelling to work in Hollywood from the 1920s onwards; the rise in co-productions post-World War Two; cross-fertilization between **art, auteur** and **mainstream cinema**, and so on). Second, this, approach, in that it presupposes an interconnectedness between cinema practices across the world as a natural outcome of globalization, risks failing to recognize the nuances of difference (see Hunt and Wing-fai, 2008). Finally, how does it embrace the fact that certain filmmakers (particularly in Latin American and African nations) have elected to make films in an intrinsic way (i.e. deliberately chosen not to be transnational in terms of financing, practice and **narrative**)?

Thankfully, critical film theory is not unaware of the shortfalls of transnationalism as an approach. As Dennison and Lim argue, we must remain aware of crucial issues such as relations of power, the political resonances of diasporic movements within cinematic practice – what Hamid Naficy (2001) usefully terms 'accented cinema'. Transnationalism, as an approach, must be polycentric, adopt what Shohat and Stam refer to as 'polycentric multiculturalism'. The advantage of polycentric multiculturalism is that it refers to a practice (and is suggestive of myriad cross-fertilization possibilities), whereas transnationalism as a stand-alone term is more an effect (of globalization in this instance).

Indeed, certain theorists make clear that transnationalism cannot be left (on its own) to bear the brunt of representation as a model for World Cinema. Some propose a matrix of approaches as follows: national, transnational, diasporic cinemas and diachronic realism (for details on all these adapted approaches, see Nagib et al., 2012). Other film theorists have sought to qualify the term (see Higbee, 2007; Higbee and Lim, 2010). Thus, we read of utopian transnationalism (a nostalgia for the periphery, the marginal cinema); adversarial transnationalism (a separation of the term from its associations with globalization/global capitalism); critical transnationalism (investigating relations of power). Hjort (2009) usefully proposes a detailed typology that links transnationalism with different models of cinematic production, such as cosmopolitan transnationalism, globalizing transnationalism (these two would readily apply to large exporting film industries, Hollywood and Bollywood, for example), auteurist transnationalism, modernizing transnationalism (more readily ascribable perhaps to African, European, Latin American and Middle Eastern cinemas) (see **Transnational Cinema** entry).

These hyphenations suggest that the concept of transnational on its own is not enough, and should give us pause for thought. It suggests to me at least that, in a similar vein (and based on arguments presented above), World Cinema is not the right term either. So, for the sake of the entries below, in that there is a logic for their inclusion, I am going to opt for a pluralization of 'World Cinemas', with the qualifier (in parenthesis) of either 'emerging' or 'developing economies'. For example, India and China are World Cinemas of 'emerging economies'; those of the Maghreb are 'developing economies'.

Please be aware that what follows in this entry is merely an *overview* of those World Cinemas coming from these new emerging and developing economies only. It is *modest* and inevitably schematic, but its intention is to 'point the way'. It is impossible to take on every single cinema, many of which have plenty of space elsewhere, some of which still await major scholarship (North Korea and Vietnam, for example). What is proposed here is a brief description of each continental or territorialized Emerging or Developing Economy World Cinema, highlighting some of the major issues and providing useful bibliographical references for readers who wish to investigate further.

The cinemas of the African continent

Status: all countries in the African continent are developing economies, except for South Africa, which is considered an emerging economy (and is currently part of the BRICS group).

It is far from straightforward to talk about African cinema as a concept. Not only are there broad distinctions such as that which can be drawn between Northern African cinemas and Sub-Saharan ones, there are also other distinctions that can be drawn *intra*-nationally – what Ukadike (1994: 12) terms the co-existence of ethnic subcultures. For example, the Ife and Nok cultures in Nigeria are quite distinct, as are the local languages of that nation. Furthermore, much of its cinema is based on literary adaptations and is heavily influenced by the Yoruba travelling theatre tradition. Thus, while most of the films may be based on the Yoruba language, other films that are based on different indigenous cultures are shot in the relevant language (e.g. Igbo in *Amadi*, Ola Balogan, 1974; Hausa in *Kanta of Kebbi*, Adamu Halilu, 1984).

These disparities notwithstanding, it is crucial to note that, although most African nations are hard pressed to produce films (Nigeria and South Africa being, perhaps, the two exceptions), the African continent hosts two major Film Festivals: Festival Panafricaine du cinéma de Ouagadougou in Burkina Faso, and Journées cinématographiques de Carthage in Tunisia (see below); and, since 2005, has held its own Academy Awards ceremony (Africa Movie Academy Awards). All of which serve to promote the visibility of African cinemas worldwide. To facilitate clarity, this entry comes in two parts: Sub-Saharan African cinema and North African cinemas.

For further reading consult Bisschoff and Murphy, 2013; Dyssanayake, 1994.

Sub-Saharan cinemas

In the colonial period, Sub-Saharan Africa was divided up between Britain, Belgium, France, Portugal and the Netherlands. This has produced three main linguistic spheres of reference when talking about the cinemas that make up this part of Africa's continent: Francophone, Anglophone and Lusophone (the latter refers to former Portuguese colonies). In the Netherlands' case there has been no such distinct linguistic or cinematic 'legacy', since, although there is an Afrikaner cinema that emanates from South Africa, it has nothing to do with the former Dutch colonialists. Afrikaners were Dutch settlers who, early in Dutch colonialism (over 270 years ago), separated themselves from the Dutch and established their own language and culture. Afrikaans is a dialect of Dutch that exists in its own right. One does not, therefore, speak of a 'Netherlandophone' cinema. Presently, much of Sub-Saharan Africa is at a neo-colonialist stage, by which I mean that most countries have not yet reached full democratic status, primarily because of the indirect domination by Europe or the United States (in the form of military oligarchies or dictatorships) and/or by the economic hi-jacking of these countries to whom huge loans have been made by the World Bank and the International Monetary Fund but which no country is in a state to repay (most African nations' GNP goes towards paying off the interest only).

Cultural colonialism is another great problem encountered by African cinemas. Hollywood monopolizes the cinema theatres of most Sub-Saharan African countries, although there is also a strong presence of Indian musicals and Hong Kong Kung-Fu films. Either African audiences do not get much occasion to view their cinema, or the attractions of the 'other' cinemas are so great that they neglect their indigenous product. Another form of cultural colonialism is of course the presence (albeit still not huge) of television. South Africa has the largest presence in terms of TV consumption, but most of what it shows is not indigenously produced and, since MNET satellite and cable have taken hold, there is a proliferation of foreign products and in particular foreign (mostly American) films. The television in other African nations is state-controlled in most instances and is a tool of control and propaganda.

Cinema arrived in Sub-Saharan Africa at different periods in its colonial history. As a source of entertainment for indigenous peoples, we can locate its presence as early as 1896 in South Africa and the early 1900s in Senegal. Elsewhere, missionary zeal may have led to its use but not much more before the early 1920s. Where cinema did have a more marked presence, however, was as an investigative tool of the indigenous people. Under the guise of **ethnographic filming**, or filming solely for the purposes of entertainment, the Black African body and culture were exoticized for consumption by intrigued audiences 'back home' in the West. This cinema soon began to influence and cross over into narrative cinema produced for the most part in studios in Europe and the USA. Black people were represented either as submissive workers for the colonialist master (and mistress) or as savage or cannibalistic. Films made by Westerners exploited the exotic otherness of Africans basically to show their undeniable inferiority to the White people. A few titles will suffice to make the point: *The Wooing and Wedding of a Coon* (1905), *Kings of the Cannibal Islands* (1909), *Voodoo Vengeance* (1913). Nor did this fascination dissipate. In the 1930s, both **documentary** and feature films, claiming to offer true images of Darkest Africa, showed us the Black person as barbaric and untamed (e.g. in the anthropological-based *Congorilla*, 1932) or as the noble savage (e.g. in the feature film *King Solomon's Mines*, 1937).

Sub-Saharan cinema as an African cinema has its beginnings in the mid-1950s. It first emerged in the form of short films. The very first film is credited to Paulin Soumano Vieyra and his *Afrique sur Seine* (1955), followed not very shortly by Ousmane Sembène's *Borom Sarret* in 1963. Both filmmakers are Senegalese and both are seen as important trail-blazers in the field of filmmaking and film history. Vieyra is perhaps best known for his didactic documentaries (e.g. *Mol*, 1957, *En résidence surveillée/Under House Arrest*, 1981). He is also the author of two important books on African cinema (Vieyra, 1975, 1983) which have pioneered 'a' writing of Africa's film history from within. In African film contexts, Sembène is considered the most significant pioneer of African Francophone cinema. Senegal has maintained a leading role in Sub-Saharan African cinema. The first Black African feature film is Sembène's *La Noire de* ... (1966, poorly translated as *Black Girl*, since it means *The Black Woman from* ...). And Senegal also produced the first Black African woman's film *Kaddu Beykatt* (*Letter from My Village*, Safi Faye, 1975). Senegal's leadership has inspired the development of cinemas in other Francophone countries: Burkina Faso, Niger, Cameroon, Mali and Mauritania. And, although we are only talking in terms of small numbers of films, Francophone cinema is, compared to Anglophone and Lusophone cinemas, an extremely vibrant one, producing as it does 80 per cent of the Sub-Saharan cinema.

The crucial problem for all Sub-Saharan cinemas is the lack of a strong infrastructure that could provide training for filmmakers, to say nothing of funding and help at the distribution level. Sub-Saharan cinemas emerged after independence and, apart from the Ghanaian Film School in Accra and a few university-based film departments where filmmaking is taught, African filmmakers are dependent on film-training abroad. Since becoming a democracy, South Africa has put money into film-training, but television acts as the main venue for gaining experience. And that about sums up what is available, which is very little indeed. The fact of having to go abroad is not in itself the problem; what matters is the lack of independence of these cinemas to fully underwrite their products.

African Lusophone cinema: Since the independence of the five countries that constitute the former Portuguese colonial empire in Africa, apart from Mozambique (with forty films since 1975), the other nations (Angola, Cape Verde, Guinea-Bissau, Sao Tomé) have managed a very small output indeed — at best five films since independence in the mid-1970s. Due of course to poor financial conditions, the lack of any industrial infrastructure, let alone any film schools. However, Angolan cinema's *O Heroí/The Hero* (Zézé Gambo, 2004), a co-production with France and Portugal, was a breakthrough film winning the Sundance World Dramatic Cinema Jury Grand Prize at the Sundance Film Festival in 2005.

Traditionally, *African Francophone cinemas* have received more support than Anglophone or Lusophone cinemas. All cinemas receive some form of state support, but a more significant contributor to the establishing of African Francophone cinemas on the international front has, undoubtedly, been the support they have received both directly and indirectly from their previous colonizers, particularly the French. French governments through their successive Ministries of Culture (which date from the 1960s) have provided financial support for African Francophone cinemas. They have also helped in terms of distribution outside of Africa, most especially in France and other Francophone countries, but also in countries where they have an active cultural attaché and Institute (e.g. South Africa, the UK and Canada). This practice of French aid continues today, with various funding bodies (ADCSud 2000–2003; Fonds Images Afrique initiated 2004) sponsoring African productions and facilitating festival screenings (including Cannes) and exhibition in Parisian art cinemas (Armes, 2006: 148). Many of the first wave of filmmakers (born in the 1930s) had the opportunity to study in French film schools: Balogun, Cissé, Faye, Hondo, Mambéty, Sembène. But that was not their only experience. Some also went to Moscow to study the **Soviet school of cinema** (Cissé and Sembène). Yet others went to Rome to train.

This tradition has continued for the newer generation of filmmakers, those born in the 1960s: Sissako (in Moscow), Kpaï (Munich), Kouyaté (Paris). But, as Armes (2006: 145) points out, the lack of a true cinematic industry infrastucture in the Francophone African countries has led many of these 'new millennium' African filmmakers to set up a collective production base in Paris where a range of funding is available, primarily, European, but some African. Their diasporic status notwithstanding, Africa remains their concern. Thus, from Mali, Aderrahmane Sissako's *Bamako* (2006) attacks the effects of globalization on the Malian citizens, and Cissé's *Dis-moi qui tu es* (2009) tackles the question of polygamy. From Senegal, Sembène's *Moolaadé* (2004) explores the difficult issue of female circumcision in Africa, and Moussa Touré's *La Pirogue* (2012) follows the desperate plight of boat people endeavouring to get to mainland Europe. From Burkina Faso, Pierre Yaméogo's *Bayiri, la patrie* (2011) explores the effects of the civil war in the Ivory Coast on Burkina Faso migrants, reduced to refugee status and victims to the whims of the rebellious troops; and Fanta Régina Nacro's *La Nuit de la vérité/The Night of Truth* (2005) shows the festering wounds, left by ten years of inter-ethnic war, as both sides struggle to bring about peace and reconciliation. From Chad, Serge Coelo's *Daresalam* (2000) and *Ndjamena City* (2009) trace the effects of civil war. Sadly, as we can see, most of these films confront the very thing that prevents a vibrant film industry from taking off in their countries (to say nothing of democratic well-being), namely, 'wars that have wracked the continent since independence' (Armes, 2006: 150).

As for *Anglophone African cinemas*, although in some instances (particularly Ghana and Nigeria), they were better equipped than the Francophone countries, nonetheless, they failed to capitalize fully on the legacy left them by the colonizing nations. Broadly speaking, the legacy was twofold. First, the Bantu Film Projects (mostly educational and health films). These were founded, in 1935, by Major L. A. Notcutt and sponsored by the Colonial Office of the British Film Institute. Second, the Colonial Film Unit (CFU), which was set up by the British, in 1939. During this period, Africans were trained to do much of the routine work, but the products made were almost entirely for the purposes of propagating the superiority of British ways and, a bit later, to persuade Africans to fight in World War Two. Further to this, in 1949, the CFU established a film school in Accra, the capital city of Ghana. The effect of this legacy meant that, after independence, Ghana and Nigeria were left with sophisticated film studios. But, they were also left with colonialist practices where the structures of film production were concerned. Thus, although President Nkrumah of Ghana greatly developed the film industry's infra-structure, the people who took over the infrastructure itself were not always progressive in their **ideologies** and continued practices estab-lished by their former colonizers. If we take the example of Ghana and Nigeria, those indigenous filmmakers who were fully trained remained neo-colonialist and the types of films they produced reflected coloni-alist 'aesthetics' (slow-paced films with elementary narratives) (for more detail, see Diawara, 1986). A further complication for Anglophone cinemas since the early independence years is that the nations' econo-mies have suffered terribly under the militaristic rule to which (until recently, in the case of Ghana and Nigeria) they have been subjected. Thus, it is hardly surprising that poor planning strategies, lack of finance, to say nothing of a lack of a government policy, have meant that Ghana and Nigeria have been far from strong in terms of the number of film products made. For example, Ghana made six full feature films during the 1980s. Kwaw Painstil Ansah, Ghana's most famous award-winning filmmaker, was only able to make two films in that entire decade despite the international acclaim of his first film, *Love Brewed in the African Pot* (1980). His second film, *Heritage Africa* (1989), was equally acclaimed. But the struggle to make these films was so debilitating, he has gone on to making documentaries and TV series.

Things changed dramatically for both countries by the early 1990s when cheaper new technologies made it possible for filmmakers to switch from the huge expense of celluloid film to video-filmmaking (subsequently DV) for production. Nigeria has set itself up as one of the world's top five producers of films with its cheap budget movies that get released on video and DVD (rather than film theatre screening). This very profitable side of the Nigerian film industry is purely commercial and has successfully capitalized on the effects of globalization combined with new cheap **digital technology**. Known as Nollywood, this video-tape and DVD-based industry churns out between 500 and 800 films per year – these sell well within Nigeria and as exports. The films' narratives are local-based stories, **comedies**, romantic comedies, **thrillers**, happy family stories (all very imitative of Hollywood narrative structures but embedded in the local). Since the 2000s, under a more liberal and progressive government, more controversial subjects have been treated: prostitution, AIDS, incest, witchcraft, honour-killing of widows (and so on) – for some exam-ples see *Hit the Street* (Chico Ejira, 2004) and *Claws of the Lion* (Francis Onwocki, 2006). Since the late 2000s a New Nigerian Cinema has emerged, a return to cinema-release movies with high production values (digital film, strong narratives, literary **adaptations**, and so on). The lead film in this context is *The Figurine: Araromire* (Kunle Afolayan, 2009), a psychological thriller. Filmmakers included in this group are Tunde Kelani (mostly **social-realist** films and literary adaptations, see his *Dazzling Mirage*, 2014, about a sickle-cell sufferer), Tade Odigan (*Family on Fire*, 2011, about the drugs trade), and Robert Peters (whose *30 Days in Atlanta*, 2014, a romantic comedy, is listed as Nigeria's top-grossing film of all time).

Although not on the same scale, Ghana has also managed to increase its DV film production (69 films in 2009; 160 in 2010). And, even though there is a lack of distribution and exhibition channels, filmmakers are managing to get some of their films into cinema theatres before they are released on DVD.

In a different light, there is a growing, if still small, South African film industry post-Apartheid – now being referred to as the New South African Cinema – which deals very much with the contemporary. So far this cinema has been seen outside Africa on the festival circuit or in special programmes only. For example, in May 2001, the National Film Theatre in London launched a programme of new South African films as part of the Celebrate South Africa Festival (films included *Chikin Biznis ... The Whole Story*, Luruli; *Hijack Stories*, Schmitz; and *Pure Blood*, Kenneth Kaplan – all 2001). And Ramadan Sideman's exposure of the fissures that still exist in post-Apartheid South Africa, *Zulu Love Letter* (2004), at least made it as far as the Carthage film festival Journées cinématographiques de Carthage (JCC) – where it won the Silver Tanit Prize. Currently, some twenty-five films are produced annually, of which, on average, six or seven are South African releases.

On the whole, the picture remains rather bleak where Sub-Saharan cinemas are concerned. It is an extraordinary feat that, despite the absence of material resources, there has been any cinema produced at all. Extraordinary, too, are the implications of this lack of resources. For, even though it takes filmmakers many years to complete a project, nonetheless, it will still get done. They are prepared to wait lengths of time that might shock and deter filmmakers in the West from pursuing the project. It is not uncommon for a project (even as a co-production) to take anything from seven to ten years. Mambéty of Senegal, Hondo of Mauritania, Ansah of Ghana, Ogundipe of Nigeria and Ecaré of the Ivory Coast have all known exceedingly long waits. Ecaré's controversial film *Visage de femmes/Faces of Women* (1985) with its explicit eroticism (a taboo in African cinema) took twelve years to make. In recent film history, it is possible to point to only one 'success' story in terms of volume of production. Ola

Balogun, a Nigerian filmmaker trained in France, set up his own production company in 1973 (Afrocult Foundation Limited) and proceeded to make on average one film per year – some in the Igbo language and others (most predominantly) in Yoruba. The secret to his success was his collaboration with theatre practitioners with whom he fully exploited the rich vein of the Yoruba travelling theatre tradition. Each of his Yoruba-based productions has met with huge audience response, which then allowed him to recoup expenses and go on to produce the next film. Only when he has stepped out of this format and attempted a more politically **motivated** cinema has he been unsuccessful – as was the case for his film on the Mau Mau struggle, *Cry Freedom*, 1981 (not to be confused with Richard Attenborough's film of the same title released in 1987, and dealing with Apartheid South Africa).

Emanating from these African nations there is also a cinema that is one of national consciousness, one that denounces the effects of colonialism, and one that questions modernity versus tradition (a most recent example is Sissako's *Bamako*, 2006, set in Mali which puts the World Bank and the IMF in the dock, literally, and finds them guilty of exploiting the country). This radical cinema looks to tradition and modernity which it then questions or valorizes; it is a cinema that may seek to entrench certain traditions and scrutinize others, just as it reveals the plusses and minuses of modernity (for an illustration of this, see below for a discussion of Mambéty's film work). It is a revolutionary and resisting cinema therefore and one that is identified with Third Cinema (see **Third Cinema** for further details). Initially, in the late 1960s and during the 1970s, much of the thinking that went into its practice was inspired by the writings of Frantz Fanon (see **postcolonial theory**) and to some extent by Marxist writers (particularly Louis Althusser and his thinking on **ideology**). In this regard, the presence of numerous Black African filmmakers in Paris during that period meant that when they returned to their African nations, they could bring with them their knowledge of these radical writings. In the manifestos emanating from Black African filmmakers (see **Third Cinema** entry) there is a clearly stated ethos that African cinemas must unite in their opposition to escapist Western cinemas and remain committed to the undoing or counterposing – through full representation of African identities – of the image given to the Black African by White Western filmmakers.

But, the other key factor that must be mentioned, before discussing further the nature of this cinema, is the crucial formation, in 1969, of the Fédération Panafricaine des cinéastes (FEPACI) and the equally crucial launching, in that same year, of the Festival Panafricaine du cinéma de Ouagadougou (FESPACO), a bi-annual festival of African cinema (in Burkina Faso) – in fact, the biggest Film Festival in the world. The other important Film Festival from FESPACO is the Journées ciné-matographiques de Carthage (JCC). All three (FEPACI, FESPACO, JCC) have been central to the process of identifying what is the Africanness of the continent's cinemas. It is crucial to recall that FEPACI is a pan-African federation and so includes North African countries. Thus, this question of what is pan-African cinema and what must its function be concerns North African cinemas just as much as the Sub-Saharan ones. Indeed, we must recall that the Charter of the African Cinéaste was drawn up and signed by the union of African filmmakers (FEPACI) in Algiers, in 1975; and that of the two Film Festivals, one is held in North Africa, Tunisia (JCC), the other in Sub-Saharan Africa, Burkina Faso.

What follows here, therefore, in relation to 'What is pan-African cinema?' applies equally to all African cinemas.

What is Pan-African Cinema? What must its function be?

There are three main answers. First, this cinema must narrate the nations' histories and cultures. Second, it must focus on the socio-political contradictions apparent in contemporary Africa. And, third, it must produce a film aesthetics of decolonization. In terms of what actually gets produced, obviously the intention is that all three of these practices overlap. So let us develop them a bit further. The African tradition of history is mostly an oral tradition and as such it is well suited to cinema. This process of history-telling is part of the raising of a national consciousness which the philosopher Frantz Fanon speaks of when, in his writings on the cultural lives and psychological sufferings of the colonized Algerians, he talks of the poet's duty in pioneering the raising of a national consciousness (see *Black Skin, White Masks*, 1967, and *Wretched of the Earth*, 1968). Thus, cinema must denounce colonization, but it must not do it in a simplistic (binary) way. It must revivify the lost heritage and identity of its African nation and in so doing lead the nation to a revolutionary consciousness that will build the future. The poet filmmaker must not speak *for* his or her nation, but through film give him or herself over to the process of national consciousness – that is, speak from *within* but not *for* the nation.

Clearly this consciousness will manifest itself differently amongst nations. But in a simplified way we could say that, where North African and especially Maghreb (Algerian, Moroccan and Tunisian) cinemas are concerned, the poet filmmaker addresses socio-political questions and the postcolonial condition mostly from a micro-political point of view, often in order to avoid **censorship** (see below); whereas the sub-Saharan poet filmmaker tends to follow the earlier oral traditions of narration (which is a multi-layered and pluri-historical affair). This form of narrating demands a syncretic style – by which is meant a collection of art forms, a multi-layering of narratives, **intertexts** and artefacts/traditions. Djibril Diop Mambéty's film *Hyenas* (Senegal, 1992) is exemplary of this function. Through this allegorical tale about hope, greed and deception at a local (village) level where magic is an everyday reality and the exchange of oral narratives is central to the community's spiritual economy, Mambéty exposes the terrible poverty to which, first, colonialism and subsequently the World Bank have reduced the Senegalese people. But this film also shows how the indigenous people have not resisted and chosen to go down the false path of consumerism stretched out before them by the West. Denouncing colonization takes other forms, such as the denunciation of the effects of Christianity and Islam on African spirituality (see Sembene's *Xala*, 1974). The conflict between the old and new world orders is often at the heart of these films as well. The clash between Western political economies and the social economies of African society is highlighted in Mambéty's earlier film *Touki-Bouki/The Hyena's Journey* (1973), a wonderfully constructed satire on the conflict between tradition and modernity.

What is surprising and not a little disconcerting is that more recent examples of this cinema, which has become more directly political, are having difficulty being distributed outside Africa. It seems as if 'African tradition' films, with their magic realism and use of symbols (including music and song) and language as a way of perpetuating memory, is the kind of authenticity the West is prepared to see. But, when it comes to a cinema that points the mirror outwards to the West and exposes, in a far more politically obvious way, the effects of colonialism, then distribution outside is almost impossible, or the films are sharply criticized as giving inadequate or improper representation. Thus, the trajectory of the Burkina Faso filmmaker Idrissa Ouedraogo is a good case to cite. His early films – very much set in the 'African tradition' – *Yaaba* (1957), *Tilaï* (1990) were extremely well received (*Tilaï* received the Grand Prix at Cannes). But, his *Samba Traoré* (1992) which endeavoured to transpose the American Western into an African context was not liked by Western critics; and his socio-realist *Le Cri du coeur* (1995), set in France, was liked even less. The formerly so in-vogue Senegalese director Sembène's film *Guelwaar*

(1992), which denounces institutional charity, was hardly distributed at all, any more than the Mali director Cissé's *Waati* (1995). The Ethiopian director Haile Gerima's *Sankofa* (1992), about slavery, got no distribution at all. A deeply politicized filmmaker, he claims no national affiliation at all – but sees himself rather as a modern-day oral historian/artist, a transnational griot.

As for the aesthetics of decolonization, the film style of Pan-African cinema is one that 'escapes' Eurocentric interpretation and resists readings that threaten to 'domesticate the subversive elements of [the films'] cultural traditions' (Ukadike, 1994: 2). The syncretism and intertextuality of the film narrative are matched by the synergistic use of time and space in these films (time moves at many speeds and the representations of time and space are incredibly dense). It is a style that mixes fiction with documentary, **fantasy**, allegory and myth. The style is also marked by a certain hybridity. Since so many filmmakers trained outside of Africa, it is not unusual for them to play with tropes from Western cinema, or indeed other cinemas with which they are familiar (e.g. Cuban, Indian and Egyptian). For example, Sissako, who claims Mambéty as an important influence, cleverly weaves politics, melodrama, satire and comedy in his internationally successful *Bamako*. Often, films are structured around mythological patterns, not generic **codes and conventions**. The play in this pan-African aesthetics is with form not with **genre** (which has no function or meaning). An ethnographic approach to the memories of ancestors is also part of the experimental mode of representation and exploration of identity. Film language deliberately challenges its audiences not only with images that are innovative but also with images that repel (e.g. the end of *Hyenas*). As Ukadike, in his marvellously comprehensive book on African cinema, says, here is a cinema that cannot be reduced to simple economic determinism (1994: 12).

For further reading on Sub-Saharan cinemas consult Appiah, 1992; Armes, 2006; Bakari and Chaim, 1996; Diawara, 1986; Fanon, 1967, 1968; Maingard, 2007; Martin, 1995; Givanni, 2000; Shiri, 1993; Tomaselli, 1988, Ukadike, 1994, 1995. For journals consult *Ecrans d'Afrique, Screen Africa*. (We note that there are still very few major studies of Sub-Saharan African cinema published in the West in the twenty years that have elapsed since the first edition of this book.)

North African cinemas

As was made clear above, the North African cinemas are also members of FEPACI; the filmmakers are equally committed to the Charter of the African Cinéaste and their role in raising national conscious-ness. Their cinemas of the postcolonial era, therefore, also address questions of identity, political and social instability. They also address, in a few rarefied instances, the place and condition of women within what, for the most part, are strongly patriarchal regimes.

North African cinemas consist of Egypt and a major grouping of nations, the Maghreb (Algeria, Morocco and Tunisia). While Libya is also seen as part of the Maghreb, during the dictatorship under Colonel Gaddafi (1969–2011) there was no cinema to speak of and this trend continues today (for reasons of censorship under Gaddafi and now the civil unrest, and Jihadi presence). Since 2010, two of the cinema nations of North Africa, Egypt and Tunisia, have been majorly affected by the revolutionary movement of the Arab Spring and its aftermath. Indeed, Tunisia spearheaded a series of citizens' uprisings when the street vendor Mohammed Bouazzi (a victim of the continued humiliating harassment by government officials) set himself on fire on 17 December 2010. His act caught the mood and became the catalyst for the Tunisian revolution and the wider Arab Spring that brought dictators and their oppressive regimes throughout countries of the Arab League (Egypt, Iraq, Libya) to their knees. Insurgencies and civil wars also broke out in Syria and the Yemen.

Since 2012, however, repressive regimes have reasserted them-selves (supposedly to defend the afflicted nations against the 'drea-ded' enemy be it the Muslim brotherhood, or ISIS or ISIL, whichever is the considered threat). Nonetheless, there was a brief window when a new cinema popped its head above the parapet and a handful of films were made that referred directly to those moments of citizen uprisings (see below). In those heady days, there was a hope that a new cinema would emerge, free from censorship as soon as political stability, in the form of new democracies, was established. Sadly, the old order very quickly re-established itself, to differing degrees of repression: Egypt in particular (and of course Syria with dreadful consequences). But, before coming to these present situations, first, a bit of cinema history.

Once again the ubiquitous presence of the Lumière brothers and their *cinématographe* can be traced to these countries. The year 1896 is again recorded as the date of its first screening exhibitions. Exhibition practices in these early days were fairly similar to those practised in India (see below). At first, it was only elite audiences (mostly ex-patriot colo-nialists in the case of the Maghreb countries) who were privy to these screenings. A little later (1908), screenings were provided for a wider, more popular indigenous audience and a tiny handful of indigenous films were made during the 1920s by Egypt. Indeed, Egypt was the first, in the 1930s, to establish a film industry which successfully produced a cinema with wide appeal, primarily in the form of the Egyptian **musical**. Other countries in Northern Africa were much later in coming to any such level of production. Thus, Egyptian cinema 'dominated' the Arab world. It was in fact the only cinema and exported its products to other Arab countries. It is unsurprising, therefore, that the impact of this early domination is still felt in other Arab nations and their cinemas in terms of production and consumption. Thus, when other Arab nations came to establish their own cinemas, their own filmmaking was very much influenced by the mechanisms, standards and practices introduced by Egyptian cinema. Furthermore, most other Arab countries have consistently experienced great difficulty in sustaining a viable indigenous cinema for a number of complex factors. First, due to the lack of a strong economic infrastructure, their film industry is unable to make enough films to meet national demand. Second, lack of movie theatres means that not enough revenue can be generated to finance new products. Finally, imports (from Egypt, India and the USA) fill the gaps and are cheaper to hire.

Egypt: Egypt made on average ten or so films a year in the 1930s, peaking at twenty-five films a year by the mid-1940s. The foundations for the film industry were laid when Misr Bank established Studio Misr, in 1935. Interestingly there were one or two women filmmakers practising during the 1930s (e.g. Bahiga Hafiz, *Leyla the Bedouin*, 1937), setting a small tradition that has been perpetuated in one or two rare instances in other Arab countries. By 1948, six further studios had been built and production increased proportionally. By the 1950s, film production in Egypt rose to fifty films per year, making the film industry the most profitable industrial sector after textiles. In the 1980s, Egyptian cinema experienced a New Wave of sorts which helped the average to rise to seventy films per year. These films offered a more muted social criticism than that put in place by the politicized filmmakers of the 1950s and 1960s (see below). By the late 1980s, production rates declined by half due to poor investment in the industry and the concomitant rise in consumption of electronic entertainment (TV, videos, etc.). And now the trend is ever-downwards with production around twelve or so films per year.

Egypt's increase in production, during the 1940s and 1950s, led to a broader generic output. Beyond the earlier Egyptian musical, genres now included social dramas, **melodramas**, farces, police films, **epics** (especially historical epics) and rural dramas. Although Egyptian narrative traditions and traditions of performance (song and dance) predominated, by the 1950s and early 1960s (the period known as the Golden Age of Egyptian cinema), its cinema was happily pulling on elements of Hollywood cinema to enhance its own indigenous products. But, realist literature also played a decisive role in establishing a strand of cinema known as Egyptian Realism (about 10 per cent of production). This cinema owes a great deal to the influence of Egyptian novelist Naguib Mahfouz. Egyptian Realism used the melodrama aspects of the commercial genre, but the films emphasized the evils of poverty brought about by unscrupulous businessmen, corrupt nouveaux riches and unbridled commercialism. Three filmmakers dominated the scene in the 1950s: Salah Abou-Seif (known primarily for studio melodramas with a political edge, he worked in close collaboration with Mahfouz; see *Beginning and End*, 1960, and *Cairo 30*, 1966); Youssef Chahine (whose name now is readily associated with the epic style, as with *Adieu Bonaparte/Goodbye Bonaparte*, 1985, but whose work at that time covered all genres); and Tewfik Salah (whose socially committed work aligns him with the practitioners of **Third Cinema**, see *La Ruelle des fous/The Backstreets of the Madmen*, 1955).

In 1961, the Egyptian film industry came under the control of the state-sponsored Central Organization of Egyptian Cinema. To all intents and purposes the industry was nationalized. This had a restricting effect on independent producers and the work of some of the established filmmakers, as a result of which some went to Syria – Tewfik Salah went, in 1971, and made *Les Dupes/The Deceived*, one of the best films on the Palestinian situation. Others, such as Youssef Chahine (born 1927), who studied filmmaking in the USA, briefly left to work in the Lebanon and then returned shortly after to make his homage to Nasser, *Saladin*, 1963. Chahine's work oscillates between the introspectively autobiographical and historical and social criticism. His films have consistently been politically motivated, whether attempting to describe the schizophrenic state of the Arab consciousness that finds itself trapped between greatness and impotence (full of pride in Arab nationalism and despondency at the successive defeats and demagogy of its leaders) as in *Le Moineau/The Sparrow* (1974), which traces the disastrous effects on Egypt and Nasser of the Six Day War with Israel, or addressing religious fundamentalism, violence and intolerance as in *Le Destin/Fate* (1997) and *L'Autre/The Other* (1999).

One lasting and positive effect of the industry's nationalization, however, was the establishing of a film school to train indigenous filmmakers (the Higher Institute of Cinema in Cairo, established in 1959). Egypt is the only Arab country to boast a film school still in existence. This nationalization of the film industry lasted until 1971, when it was partially re-privatized by president Sadat. Under Sadat's regime filmmakers in exile were able to return and/or continue to work with greater freedom once more, even though financing projects had become increasingly difficult. As a result of the economic constraints, filmmakers established their own production companies (e.g. Chahine and his Misr International Films) and turned to making co-productions, first, with other Arab states, and later with Western countries (such as France in the case of Chahine).

Given the poverty of film production in Egypt, it is not surprising that the more commercially based production companies are disinclined to invest profits into the industry. This means that the more serious projects struggle to get off the ground. The case of Asmá a El-Bakri is a good case in point. El-Bakri is one of the few Egyptian women filmmakers who got to make feature length films, three in her lifetime. Her pioneering work engages with social and political issues. She began as an assistant (amongst others to Chahine) in the 1970s, and then turned her hand to documentary work until she managed to garner the finance to direct her first feature film, *Mendiants et orgueilleux/ The Proud and the Beggars* (1990) – a film set in Cairo in 1945 relating the murder of a young prostitute by a university professor. Her second feature, about the love of a lowly Egyptian civil servant for a European concert violinist, *Concerto Darb Saada* (1998), failed commercially. Her last film, *La Violence et la dérision/Violence and Laughter* (2003), shifts away from **class** and cross-cultural relationships and takes on a far more hard-hitting subject, albeit with a light touch. The film revolves around the attempt to dethrone the tyrannical ruler of a Mediterranean city. Two strategies are employed to achieve this: violence and humour. El-Bakri makes it clear that violence is the weapon of the weak and, in this film, it is the humour that ends up winning the day. In a web interview about this film, El-Bakri tells us that the tyrant is a symbol for the USA and the Arab regimes that comply with him (El-Assyouti, 2003).

In the first decade of the new millennium, production steadily increased from some ten or so films per year to around forty. Interestingly, in the light of the Arab Spring Revolution (which had yet to come), there was a renaissance, in the early 2000s, amongst young filmmakers of a socially conscious and politically aware type of cinema (see Shafik (2007) for further details). Alef Hetata's first feature film, *Les Portes fermées/Closed Doors* (1998), is a story about the Gulf crisis and the rise of Islamic fundamentalism. Daoud Abdel Sayed's *A Citizen, an Inspector and a Thief* (2001) interweaves tales of a thief and his victim set in modern-day Egypt. Marwen Hamed's *L'Immeuble*

Yacoubian/The Yacoubian Building (2006) investigates Egypt's gradual descent from a modern, open-minded society into an increasingly intolerant one. In Yousri Nasrallah's *Femmes du Caire/Scheherazade Tell Me a Story* (2009), a young talk-show host, under pressure to stop being so politically motivated in her TV programme, decides to do a series of interviews with women from all classes. The outcome is a political minefield in its own right with women talking openly about sexual, religious and social repression. Finally and most controversially, Hanif Khatifa's *Sleepless Nights* (2003) provides a frank portrayal of marriage, **sexuality** and adultery amongst the middle-classes, and *Awkat Faragh/Free Times* (Mohammed Moustafa, 2006) follows the difficulties of young people in present-day Egypt (both films were box-office sensations).

Clearly, since the revolution of 25 January 2011, with the removal of Mubarak as head of state and, subsequently in 2013, the ousting of President Morsi during the coup d'état led by the Chief of the Egyptian Armed Forces, Abdel Fattah el-Sisi, who is now the current president (more or less bringing the military back into power), the film industry has undergone numerous uncertainties. However, in the immediate aftermath of the 2011 revolution, a number of documentaries and/or reconstructed stories were made on the events themselves. Thus, *18 jours/Eighteen Days* (a series of ten films made by a film collective headed by Marwen Hamed) was presented at Cannes in 2011; and the fiction film *Tahrir (Place de la Révolution)/Tahrir (Revolution Square)*, by Stefano Savona (2011), follows the commitment of three young revolutionaries committed to the overthrow of Mubarak's regime. While Morsi was in power, the industry went virtually into close-down mode. However, over the past two years, it would seem it is picking up again with a yearly output of twelve films or so, predominantly comedies (they are for the most part of fairly poor quality, particularly those directed or produced by the El Sokby brothers). There are, nonetheless, a few exceptions to this trend. A small but new generation of filmmakers is coming on board. Some are funded by small productions companies such as Rahala (mostly financing shorts; see Naji Ismail's *Om Amira/Amira's Mother*, 2014), Zero Production (see Tamer El-Saïd's *Akher Ayam el Madina/In the Last Days of the City*, 2016). Some are crowd-funding and screening their films online (see *Fathy La Yaaish Hena Baad El-An/Fathy No Longer Lives Here*, Maged Nader, 2016). Furthermore, a handful of films made by established directors are unafraid to speak to recent events and the crisis of political polarization. Two 2016 releases stand out in particular: *Eshtebak/Clash* (Mohammed Diab) about factionalism and civil unrest after Morsi was deposed; *Harem El-Gasad/Sins of the Flesh* (Khaled El-Hagar) about the misuse and abuse of power during a revolution. This latter film was produced by Chahine's company Misr International Film. Indeed, it is heartening that even after his death (2008), Chahine's spirit of defiance and integrity lives on. Moreover, a subsidiary within his company (Zawya, promoting *Cinéma d'art et essai*/**experimental** and **art cinema**) was established in 2014 to help promote a new generation of socially conscious filmmakers.

The Maghreb: Tunisia and Morocco gained independence in 1956, Algeria in 1962. The foundations for cinema in the Maghreb countries were laid in the struggle for liberation from colonialist rule (1950s and 1960s). This is particularly true for Algeria. During the war of liberation, Algeria had a resistant **underground cinema** that it established in 1957 (the Tebessan Film Unit, Groupe Farid, which was annexed to the provisional Algerian government based in Tunis, Tunisia).

Since the 1960s, if we take their cinema as a whole, these three Maghrebi countries are, with Egypt, the other most 'prolific' film-producers of the North African countries (with around twenty to twenty-five films per year). Unlike Egypt, however, their films do not enjoy the same popular acclaim within their own countries and are more readily seen outside of the Maghreb, in Film Festivals. Thanks, historically, to the French colonial presence in the Maghreb, there is a stronger tradition for filmmaking than in most other Arab countries – although, after withdrawal, the French, for the most part, removed the studios they had established in the three countries (these studios had been created by the French for propaganda purposes to make Arab-language films to counter the Egyptian products). The lack of infrastructure, therefore, post-independence, meant that the first films to be produced in the mid- to late 1960s were very much in the documentary–naturalist–realist tradition associated with **Italian neorealism**. Equally, this lack of infrastructure, which still exists today, means that filmmakers are either self-taught or tend to be trained abroad (mostly in France) – although Algeria briefly boasted a film school of its own (the Institut National du Cinéma d'Alger, 1964–67). In more recent years, filmmakers have also come into film from television.

Of the three countries, it is Algeria (paradoxically) that is the most structured in terms of organizational bodies and their tutelage of the film industry. As a country, however, it produces a very small number of films (three to four, yearly). The industry's modest infrastructure means that it lacks technicians and production management, still, today. In 1968, the government established a state-funding system for films (FDATIC). Still in existence, funding is hard to come by, however. Its first central organization body, the Office National pour le Commerce et l'Industrie Cinématographique (ONCIC), was established in 1969 with two branches (ENAPROC for production and ENADEC for distribution). Since then this body has known several different forms until its most recent one, established in 1987, when there was a major reorganization of the industry with the setting up of the Centre Algérien pour l'Art et l'Industrie Cinématographiques (CAAIC).

Algerian cinema was state-controlled until the mid-1980s. This meant that state policy tended to guide production. Thus, the early years of liberation (mid-1960s to mid-1970s) saw a spate of anti-imperialist films, made by filmmakers who had been involved in the struggle and had often been members of the FLN (Front de Libération Nationale). These films celebrated the revolutionary liberation struggle. Arguably, Gilles Pontecorvo's *La Bataille d'Alger/Battle of Algiers* (1965, an Algerian-Italian co-production) was a reference film for this cinema. But, more significant still, was the crucial input, during the struggle years, of the French documentarist René Vautier, an FLN sympathizer who worked with the FLN freedom-fighters and (according to some accounts) led the Tebessan Film Unit. His two documentary films, *Afrique 50* (1955) and *Algérie en flammes/Algeria in Flames* (1958), which were banned in France, were the precursors to the documentary-realist tradition so much in evidence in the indigenous cinema of the first ten years of independence. Mohamed Lakhdar-Hamina's two films that span this period, *Le Vent des Aurès/The Wind from the Aurès* (1966) and *Chronique des années de braise/Chronicle of the Years of Embers* (1975), are exemplary of this tradition. By the 1970s, issues of rural reform were of primary concern, and feature films were produced to support the agrarian revolution introduced by President Boumedienne. These films exposed the poverty of rural life, and spoke out against traditional taboos and unjust property conditions that were based on native feudalism. As such, they were as much about the class and the rural struggle. They also touched upon female emancipation. Abdeleziz Tobi's *Noua* (1972) is exemplary in addressing all three of these issues. The tradition of maraboutism (magic practised by holy men) and sexual segregation also came under attack in this cinema. These aspects of traditional culture and religion are represented as obstacles to progress (see, for example, Mohamed Slim Riad's *Vent du sud/Wind from the South*, 1975).

This first decade of Algerian cinema is marked, as Viola Shafik in her excellent study of Arab cinema makes clear (1998: 175–76), by a monumentalization – first, of the Algerian resistance hero and, subsequently, the peasant. Films at this stage were busily engaged in selling an Algerian national identity that was unified and not diverse. By the late 1970s, however, just prior to its dissolution as a state-controlled industry, a more diversified cinema had emerged that talked about the poor social conditions experienced by most Algerians, and represented the contradictions inherent in Algerian society (as a hybrid culture), including the oppression of women. During this period, the only Algerian woman filmmaker, Assia Djebar, made two films looking at the role of women during colonial occupation and the struggle for independence (*La Nouba des femmes du mont Chenoua/ The Nouba of the Women of Mount Chenoua*, 1978, and *La Zerda ou les chants de l'oubli/The Zerda and the Songs of Forgetfulness*, 1980). The 1970s were also marked by a close collaboration with the state television service (Radio Telévision Arabe, RTA). Djebar's films were co-produced by RTA. And, by the 1980s, television-trained directors turned to filmmaking. From 1983 until the early 1990s, when the new military regime came into full force, Algerian cinema continued in this same vein, but it also took a new, ironic look at its own history (*Les Années folles du twist/Mad Years of the Twist*, Mahmoud Zemmouri, 1983), and issues of multiculturalism (*Histoire d'une rencontre/Story of an Encounter*, Ibrahim Tsaki, 1983).

The 1990s were known as the *Décennie noir/Dark Decade*, during which period a civil war broke out between the government, in the form of a military junta anxious to prevent the Islamic Salvation Front from coming to power, and various groups of Islamist insurgents. President Abdelaziz Bouteflika, who was elected in 1999 (and is now in his fourth term), brought this war to an end. In the light of the Arab Spring, which produced civil unrest in Algeria, he lifted the Emergency Rule (February 2011) which had been in place since 1992. The effect of the civil war on the film industry was profound. Production came to a virtual standstill. **Censorship** extended to cinema theatres which diminished in number from 400 to a mere 100 nation-wide; although, according to some there are far fewer, alternatively citing ten or twenty theatres. It is difficult to be precise, since, during the Dark Decade, many cinemas were smashed up by fundamentalists. Of those that remain, most have been turned into men-only zones, under the orders of local Islamic rulers (although mobile cinemas are travelling country-wide, aided by AARC, the state-run organization that develops and promotes Algerian culture, and many films are presently accessible on YouTube).

Also during the Dark Decade, several Algerian filmmakers were sentenced to death and went into exile. Merzak Allouache was one such filmmaker; although in recent years he has been able to return to Algeria and make a number of films: *Harragas* (2010) about clandestine Algerians trying to escape by a small boat to Europe; *Normal!* (2011), a biting drama about the role of cinema in Algeria today; *Le Repenti* (2012) about peace and reconciliation post the civil war; and *Les Terrasses* (2013), which examines the fall-out of the Dark Decade. Allouache has always been sensitive to the contradictions in Algerian society (a post-colonial nation beset by fundamentalist intolerance, a modern nation governed directly or indirectly by a strongly censorious army, etc.). Thus, when in exile in France, he made his 'trilogy' on this sense of exile and mood of fundamentalist intolerance: *Bab El-Oued City* (1994), set shortly after the bloody war of 1988, foretells the rise of Islamic fundamentalism in Algeria which would ultimately lead to the civil war of the mid- to late 1990s (this film won the Cannes International Critics Prize in 1996); *Salut cousin!/Hey Cousin* (1996) evokes the feeling for those Algerians who (for political or economic reasons) will never return to their homeland, but who equally feel they will never be at home in France; *Algiers/Beyrouth: pour mémoire/Algiers/Beirut: A Souvenir* (1997) traces the encounter between a self-exiled Lebanese journalist who returns to war-ravaged Beirut and an old colleague she meets there, who is now a fugitive from the violence of his Algerian homeland. The shared experience is less one of a souvenir and more one of terror. Another outspoken film on Islamist fundamentalism, this time made by a film director not yet in exile, is Yamina Bachir-Chouikh's *Rachida* (2002). This courageous film is set during the darkest days of Algeria's fight against Islamic fundamentalism. Rachida, a young schoolteacher, refuses to plant a bomb in her school. She is shot, but miraculously survives and runs away to her home village where she begins teaching again, only to befriend a former student whose father is a terrorist.

In 2003, there was a slight relaxation of censorship, since when, on average, some ten films per years have been made. In terms of production, one-third of films are documentaries; the rest are features of different generic types of which a small number address the difficulties of the Dark Decade and its legacy. Documentaries represent the more direct voice of the poet-filmmaker Fanon speaks of, and in this context Habiba Djahnine's work should be cited, especially her *Lettre à ma soeur/Letter to my Sister* (2006) which recounts the murder of her sister, in 1993, by Islamist fundamentalists. Djahnine speaks of the need for documentaries to be made, no matter the difficulty in obtaining funding and the even greater difficulty in being distributed (TV channels refuse to screen documentaries, theatres are non-existent, online is the only method). In this light, we note Nassima Guessoum's recent documentary, *10949 femmes/10949 Women* (2014), about a woman's struggle for Algeria's independence and her subsequent questioning in today's climate of 'what price freedom?' Of the feature films that echo this view of a need for a voice from within, there are also a few women filmmakers of note. Djamila Sahraoui addresses the effects of the Dark Decade on Algerian citizens in *Barakat!/Enough!* (2006) and *Yema/Ouardia Had Two Children* (2012). Fatma Zohra Zamoum depicts the violence experienced in Algiers in *Z'har* (2009). Amongst the contesting films made by men, the plight of and difficulties encountered by Algerian women in the restricted climate of Algeria's political culture is at the heart of Nadir Moknèche's trilogy *Viva Laldjérie/Viva Algeria* (2004), *Délice Paloma* (2007) and *Goodbye Morocco* (2013). Cultural anomalies of contemporary Algeria are present in *Bled Number One/Number One Village*, Rabah Ameur-Zaïmeche, 2006, and *Mascarades*, Lyès Salem, 2008. A further two films look at the tragedies encountered by the Algerian poor (*La Maison jaune/The Yellow House*, Amor Hakkar, 2008; *Harragas*, Allouache). (For further reading see Armes, 1996, 2006; Dines, 1994; Hadj-Moussa, 1994; Shafik, 1998.)

Moroccan and Tunisian cinemas do not enjoy the same industrial infrastructure that Algeria does. Although Morocco has around 250 cinema theatres, the theatres are almost entirely dominated by foreign imports. Tunisia has only about seventy-five film theatres. So, in the case of both countries (albeit for differing reasons), there is little resourcing for indigenous products. Film production is, therefore, a far more individualistic affair. Yet, despite these restrictions, Morocco produces, on average, twelve to sixteen films annually, and Tunisia, five to six. Strict Islamic laws and severe censorship in the Maghreb countries mean that women filmmakers are extremely thin on the ground. Tunisia has the lead with ten (Raja Amari, Selma Baccar, Kaouter Ben Hania, Néjia Ben Mabrouk, Férial Ben Mahmoud, Kalthoum Bornaz, Leyla Bouzid, Sonia Chamkhi, Nadia El Fani, Moufida Tatli). For reasons of financing, only five have managed to make two or more feature films (and these have been far from plain-sailing); the other five have made maybe one feature and otherwise shorts and/or documentaries. Baccar's *Fatma 75* (1975) was banned for several years because of the scenes about sex education; her other two films, while dealing with hot or controversial topics, nonetheless, were given release: *Habiba M'sika: La Danse du feu/The Fire Dance* (1995), based on the last years of the charismatic singer-dancer (and 'It' girl) Habiba Msika who was incinerated by a jealous lover in 1930 (she was only 27 years old); *Khochkhach/Flower of Forgetfulness* (2005), about a young woman's drug addiction and subsequent recovery, it is set in the 1940s, a difficult period for Tunisia as a triply-occupied country during World War Two (Vichy France, Germans and the Allied Forces). El Fani's two films, the very wry comedy-satire *Bédouin Hacker* (2003), in which a female hacker hijacks the airwaves in North Africa to expose state surveillance and disinformation, and the self-explanatory *Ni Allah, Ni Maître/Laïcité, inch'Allah/Neither God nor Master* (2011) were subject to censorship in Tunisia and screened only at international venues. El Fani lives in exile. Amari's first two films *Satin Rouge/Red Satin* (2002) and *Dowaha/Buried Secrets* (2009) are about female self-empowerment in that they address women's traditional roles and the possibility of self-expression in contemporary Tunisia; her third film *Printemps Tunisien/Tunisian Spring* (2014) gives a direct voice to young Tunisians during the events of Tunisia's Spring Revolution. Bornaz (who died in 2016, as a result of a gas explosion in her apartment) made two films, both relating to the conditions of women (arranged marriage, rape, inheritance): *Keswa, le fil perdu/The Lost Thread* (1998) and a sequel ten years later *L'Autre motié du ciel/The Other Half of the Sky* (2008). Finally, Moufida Tatli, whose work investigates issues of class, gender and sexuality through the prism of marital life (see *Les Silences du Palais/Silences of the Palace*, 1994; *La Saison des hommes*, 2001; and *Nadia and Sarra*, 2004).

Filmmakers are either self-taught or have trained outside the country. They do, however, have studios to work in, in their native country. But, financing remains the key issue. Many work collaboratively helping each other out on their films, as is the case, in Tunisia, for Nouri Bouzid, Férid Boughedir and Moufida Tlatli. Interestingly, Bouzid and Boughedir's first films, *Man of Ashes* (1986) and *Halfaouine* (1990), are both concerned with the troubling dynamics or difficult relationships between father figures and sons, whereas Tlatli's focus (in *Silences of the Palace* and *La Saison des hommes*) – while also on the micropolitics of everyday life – is on the unwritten story of female sexuality. Martin Stollery (2001) writes illuminatingly on these overlaps and differences. Bouzid exposes the conflict between hegemonic masculinities and male inter-generational relationships but nevertheless offers a message of cultural openness that can exist between Arab and Jew (ibid.: 55). Boughedir explores in a far more light-hearted fashion the young adolescent boy Noura's negotiation with male hierarchies of power and his own entry into manhood (ibid.: 57). Tlatli's films reveal how, beneath the woman's exterior appearance that all is alright, there lies a secret pain which she holds in silence: that of the abuse and repression imposed by the dominant patriarchal ideologies upon female sexuality (ibid.: 60).

In the post-revolutionary period, immediately after the Arab Spring, a cluster of documentary films appeared, all screened in 2011, all focusing on the events surrounding the revolution. First, a 90-second animated film, *La Révolution du jasmin/The Jasmine Revolution* (Nassar Ayad); second, *Plus jamais peur/No More Fear* (Mourad Ben Cheikh); third, *Tunisie année zéro/Freedom* (Fériel Ben Mahmoud). Although Tunisia is currently under secular rule (since 2014 with President Essebsi), nonetheless, the voice and violence of Islamist forces are ominipresent and riots have broken out over films deemed anti-Islam. So too have a number of Jihadi-led attacks and assassinations. Moreover, the failure of consecutive governments since the revolution to consolidate the economy of the country and provide social stability has led to further unrest and protests, including a mass suicide attempt by unemployed graduate students at Kasserine (2016). Thus the signs do not bode well presently for an openness of representation, even though Ridha Behi's 2016 film, *Fleur d'Alep/Flower of Aleppo*, shows the intent to address ISIS ideology and the way in which the Jihadi recruits young disenchanted teenagers. And Mohamed Ben Attia's *Inhebbek Hedi/Hedi* (2016) shows a young man prepared at last to take on board a life more committed to the ideals of the revolution and less to his parents' bourgeois values.

Morocco's situation is somewhat different, since there has been no revolutionary uprising – this is not to say that there will not be an impact, given the nation's geographical location and political status with an executive monarchy. Two fairly recent Moroccan films, *Ruses de Femmes/Women's Wiles* (Farida Benlyazid, 1999) and *A Casablanca les anges ne volent pas/In Casablanca Angels Don't Fly* (Mohamed Asli, 2003, winner of The Tanit d'Or), in different ways again take on the micro-political issues of the place men and women can or cannot hope to occupy. In Benlyazid's film, which pits the wit of the woman against that of the man, we are offered a feminist take on the Scheherazade myth. Far more darkly, in Asli's film, we see the effects of chronic poverty on a Berber family as the father of the home is forced to travel to Casablanca to work in a desperate effort to support his wife and children (it ends badly with the wife dying).

More recently, Morocco's cinema has become more clearly politicized (at least in relation to its past), as can be seen by a handful of films (starting with Ahmed Boulane's *Ali, Rabiaa et les autres/Ali, Rabiaa and the Others*, 2000) dealing with the 1970s years of political repression – the so-called 'années de plomb/dark years'. The torture, rape and hunger strike of a young woman is the theme of *Jawhara/ Pearl* (Saad Chraïbi, 2004); torture, this time of a man is at the core of *La Chambre noire/The Black Room* (Hassan Benjelloun, 2004); memory or the refusal of memory to recall these dreadful events is central to a cluster of films – *Mona Saber* (Abdelhaï Laraki, 2001), *Mille mois/A Thousand Months* (Faouzi Bensaïdi, 2003), *Face à face/Face to Face* (Abdelkader Lagtâa, 2003) and *Mémoire en détention/Memory on Hold* (Jilali Ferhati, 2006).

Contemporary social issues are also forefronted in a number of films made by a slightly younger generation of filmmakers. These mostly present stories of the unemployed (*Road to Kabul*, Brahim Chkiri, 2012), street kids (*Ali Zaoua*, Nabil Ayouch, 2012), women forced into prostitution (*Zine Li Fik/Much Loved*, Nabil Ayouch, 2015, a film banned in Morocco), petty thieves (*Casanegra*, Anas El Baz, 2008; *Mort à vendre/Death for Sale*, Bensaïdi, 2011), individuals in short for whom all routes to a decent life are closed off.

Although Morocco had established a state-sponsored Centre Cinématographique (CMM) as early as 1944, the CMM did not really take on an active role in funding until the late 1970s at which point production rose from a meagre average of one film every two years to an average three to four indigenous films per year. But the CMM only helps finance projects to a degree; in much the same way as Tunisia's now defunct SATPEC (Société Anonyme Tunisienne de Production et d'Expansion Cinématographique, 1957–94) could only finance a small percentage of the cost of production. This lack of finance has three effects. First, Morocco and Tunisia have had to seek finance for their films through co-productions. Second, filmmakers often only get to make one film per decade. Finally, both countries have opened their studios to Western filmmakers in an effort to boost their own industry. French filmmakers in particular take advantage of the cheaper labour costs offered by these countries. Tunisia, for its part, has also successfully pre-sold film rights to European television companies (French Arte and Channel Four in particular). In this way, it has financed several international successes, in particular the films of Férid Boughedir (*Halfaouine*, and *Un été à La Goulette*, 1995). Tunisia also has a major standing as one of the most important festival venues for African and Arab cinema. The country hosts the annual film festival (the JCC). In the meantime, Morocco has expanded its studio facilities in the southern region. Studios Atlas (established in the 1980s) has now been joined by Studios Kanzaman (2004) and CLA

Studios is in development – all with a view to attracting international film crews.

Bearing the above overview in mind, there is a case to be made for a **transnational** approach to Maghrebi cinemas; at least insofar as production practices are concerned, but also, to a limited degree, in terms of themes (the socio-political nature of some of the films points to a culture of resistance).

For further reading see Andrea Khalil (2015) for an overview of North African cinema, Viola Shafik on Arab cinemas (1998) and the dictionary of North African cinemas by Roy Armes (1996) and his more recent study on African filmmaking (2006). For the various manifestos see Bakari and Chaim (1996). For a useful discussion of African filmmakers see Armes (2008). For a comprehensive study of Maghrebi women filmmakers see Florence Martin (2011).

The cinemas of China

Status: China is considered to be an emerging economy.

Preamble: our view of Chinese cinemas from the West is, currently, a fairly limited one; one that is the result of both a highly selective distribution system (in the West) and the influential outcomes of international film festivals (Beus, 2008: 312). Thus, we are aware of a handful of filmmakers and a limited generic knowledge of these cinemas (e.g. Hong Kong martial arts films). However, numerous cinemas make up China's cinema history. There are the three regions – China, Taiwan and Hong Kong (for the latter two, see **East Asian Cinema** entry). But, there are other smaller cinemas, lumped together as East Asian and Southeast Asian cinemas, the diasporic Chinese cinemas in the US and Canada (what Shohat and Stam would have usefully termed Fourth Cinemas). It is clear also that, since the impact of globalization, to say nothing of the return of Hong Kong to mainland China in 1997, all of these cinemas have become evermore transnationally accented (at least in terms of financing, production and distribution) (see Sheldon Lu (1997) for a full discussion of this). Indeed, there is considerable ongoing debate about definitions of Chinese cinema(s) and the question of identity; after all, the three regions are more distinct than they are unified linguistically (and even then, Mandarin is the official language for China, but Cantonese is used in Hong Kong). Nor are Hong Kong and Taiwan part of a consensual Chinese culture (see Beus, 2008). Intertwined histories, yes; geo-politically different, definitely (ibid.: 311). **Action films** emanating from these two countries should doubtless be considered in the light of their ambivalent relationship to the mainland. Beus (ibid.: 310) usefully sums up the impact of China's complex political history on its cinemas by stating that they have to be perceived from two perspectives (both sides of the Taiwan Strait) and 'as a living, paradoxical rhizome that stretches into multiple levels of existence and meaning'.

Indeed, economically and politically, both Taiwan and Hong Kong are very distinct from China. Taiwan (officially, the Republic of China, ROC) is an advanced industrial economy even if its political status is a contentious issue. It was originally given to Japan in 1895 by China. But, ever since it was ceded back to China after World War Two, the People's Republic of China (PRC, i.e. mainland China) has never controlled Taiwan, despite its claims that the island belongs to them. Taiwan's ROC government continues to view itself as a sovereign state. Needless to say, cross-strait relations are complex. As for Hong Kong, sovereignty was transferred back to PRC in 1997. However, Hong Kong governs its political system and it remains a major global financial centre. It is also the third largest film industry in the world (after the US and India).

Since neither Taiwan nor Hong Kong were Third World economies at the time of their indigenous cinema's development, and since the focus of World Cinemas in this entry is on emerging and developing economies, the entry below is limited to the cinemas of mainland China only. The reasoning behind keeping China in this entry is that, even though it is now listed as an emerging economy (an effect of its joining the World Trade Organization in 2001), it was, until very recently, registered as a third order economy and, given its level of poverty, still remains an emerging economy (albeit a member of BRICS).

Mainland China: to give a sense of China's cinema history, it is perhaps helpful to divide its history into two epochs. The first starts at the earliest presence of cinema in China in 1896 and lasts until the establishment of the People's Republic in 1949 (PRC). The second stretches from 1949 to the present day. These two epochs, however, subdivide into different periods producing, in turn, different or assimilated or recuperated cinemas (as I will explain below).

1896 to 1949

The beginnings of cinema in China are not dissimilar from those of India. The first *cinématographe* screening took place on 11 August 1890 in Shanghai and, shortly thereafter, in other cities and provinces. By

1905, Chinese camera operators were filming local Chinese opera and by the 1920s China was producing melodrama and comedies. The first Chinese film was *Dingjun Mountain* (1905), a filming of Beijing opera performed by the renowned actor Tan Xinpei. Even at this time, though, this popular cinema displayed a resistance to Western Imperialism, and for the following reasons. During this first period, Chinese cinema was not a thriving industry, companies quickly folded, and in terms of cultural capital, the dominant presence in Chinese cinema venues was Western cinema. Chris Berry (1996: 409) quotes the figures of dominance as 90 per cent foreign, almost all of which was American. This dominance lasted until 1949. In the period 1910 to 1930, what little Chinese cinema there was found its sources in and drew its narratives primarily from the popular Mandarin Duck-and-Butterfly literary tradition. Although these were escapist films that narrated melodramatic and sentimental tales, they were films that warned against the effects of Westernization which was already considerably in evidence in major Chinese cities, particularly Shanghai. Curiously, therefore, this populist cinema was both assimilated to its culture and resistant to it (it was escapist but challenging of Western ideology).

Shortly after this first period of populist filmmaking, during the 1930s, China witnessed the emergence of a second type of cinema, this time far more directly politicized: that of a nationalistic leftist cinema that would eventually become identified with the Communist Party in its fight to liberate China from Japanese Imperialism (which lasted throughout the 1930s). The catalyst for this new cinema was the invasion of China by Japan in 1931. Intellectuals of the left infiltrated the film industry and some established communist cells. These leftist intellectuals were responsible for producing what are known as leftist films, a product which has come to exemplify the first golden age of Chinese cinema. However, the point needs to be made that these leftist films were directly inspired by the nationalistic May Fourth Movement (1919), a crucial factor that would lead Chairman Mao to advocate their rejection in the new Revolutionary China (see below). The May Fourth Movement was a protest movement headed by intellectuals and students and led against the Chinese government for their pro-Western and pro-Japan policies. The movement also protested against the stifling nature of Chinese tradition and culture and advocated a new China that could be both patriotic and open to new and foreign ideas. The cinema produced by leftist intellectuals was based on the literary work produced by that May Fourth Movement and, while it was certainly politicized, it nonetheless remained populist in its appeal as entertainment. During this entire fifty-year span, Shanghai remained the film centre of China. Only after the revolution would more studios be established in Beijing (including a Film Academy) and Changchun. If, in 1949, this leftist cinema was rejected by Chairman Mao, it was because of political self-interest. Accusing this cinema of being Westernized (primarily because it was based in Shanghai, a melting pot of many cultures, including those of the West), he sought to impose his own cultural apparatchiks who had been trained in Yen'an. By 1953, the Shanghai studios were nationalized, thereby effectively putting a stop to the production of films that were not considered consonant with the Maoist line, a form of total recuperation that would last on and off for thirty years.

Just before the People's Republic of China (PCR) came into being, China experienced what is referred to as its second golden age of production. During just three years, 1946 to 1949 (after the war with Japan and World War Two ended), leftist filmmakers re-established themselves in Shanghai and produced social realist films which documented the civil war between the ruling bodies of that period and the communists as they fought to come to power. (See Zhang (2004) for more details.)

1949 to 2010s

There are six waves to this epoch of China's cinema. The first wave, 1949 to 1966, was something of a paradox. It began with the Social Realist worker–peasant–soldier cinema which was heavily influenced by Soviet cinema. This cinema served to propagate the idea of a revolutionary nation and a classical revolutionary cinema. During this period, China set up an integrated national film industry whereby the state controlled all aspects of production including, of course, censorship; in this context, Hollywood films all but disappeared from China (Sheldon Lu, 1997: 6). By 1950, it was decided that cinema needed to change direction and should look to China's history rather than to its present. The new directive was to produce a revolutionary realism and a revolutionary romanticism: films had to depict the revolutionary struggle and achieve a new film aesthetic. To this effect, curiously, filmmakers were able to return to the literary tradition of the May Fourth Movement as well as to the operatic tradition. In other words, cinema was allowed to revert to a previously disavowed or at least denounced practice. This relaxation of the pressure to make politically motivated cinema stemmed from Chairman Mao's famous policy of a Hundred Flowers (Let a Hundred Flowers Bloom and a Hundred Schools of Thought Contend). Restrictions on the creative process of filmmaking were lifted. Filmmakers were able to visit

European Film Festival venues, and foreign films were allowed into China – but only those from European and other Third World cinemas. Films that openly criticized the bureaucracy of government were allowed to pass uncensored. And it was at this time that studios were opened up in Beijing and Changchun; Shanghai opened three more studios. This spirit of openness was an up and down affair. In 1957, 1958 and again in 1964, the Anti-Rightist movement accused certain films of bourgeois tendencies and effectively had them censored.

This movement did not die away but was to re-emerge in 1966 as part of the Cultural Revolution. Indeed, its leader, Kang Shen, became one of the Gang of Four who, along with Madame Mao, formed the uncompromising leaders of revolutionary taste during the terrible years of the Cultural Revolution. From 1966 to 1972 – the second wave of China's cinema and the period of the Cultural Revolution – there was virtually no cinema at all. Only ten films were made. All of them had to adhere to the very strict rules and filmic guidelines imposed by Madame Mao. Strongly didactic and stylized, these films (which were revolutionary model-operas) propagated the myth of the perfect proletarian class hero and heroine. During this period, the Film Academy in Beijing was closed, many filmmakers were sent to prison or to work-camps – many perished under those conditions.

From 1972 to 1984 (the third wave) feature film slowly reprised and, from 1977 to 1984, a genre of films called 'scar' or 'wound' films emerged exposing the unjustified persecution that took place during the Cultural Revolution. A fourth wave occurred, in the mid-1980s, thanks to a new relationship between the state and the film industry which saw a relaxation of controls imposed upon film practice. First, the industry was no longer obliged to make films closely associated with Chinese operatic theatre. Second, film could now investigate the aesthetics of films and not be tied to the revolutionary propaganda cause (the so-called revolutionary realism). Finally, the state agreed both to the principle and to the financing of a cinema that was audience-based, which meant that entertainment films could now replace the earlier practice of didactic cinema. The effect, beyond entertainment films, was some ground-breaking experimental work produced by a 'movement' of young filmmakers, graduates of the Beijing Film Academy (which had reopened in 1978). They were known as the Fifth Generation. Their films were considered elliptical and were accused of elitism, and they were not successful with audiences. They remain, however, as a testimony to a moment of film language experimentation and modernization. A few Fifth Generation filmmakers went on to produce more 'accessible' films, some of which were financed by foreign money (Taiwan, Hong Kong, UK/ Germany). Of all the filmmakers of that generation it is Zhang Yimou and Chen Kaige who have successfully managed to combine experimentation with popular narration. And, from that generation, it is their work that Western audiences get to see. Yimou's films have been highly acclaimed in the West. His *Red Sorghum* (1987) won the Berlin Golden Bear in 1988. *The Story of Qui Ju* (1992) won the Venice Golden Lion. And two other films, *Raise the Red Lantern* (1991, banned in China) and *Shanghai Triad* (1995), have met with audience acclaim outside China. Chen Kaige's breakthrough film *Yellow Earth* (1984) helped to put the Fifth Generation and China on the world film map and his *Farewell My Concubine* (1993) won the 1993 Cannes Palme d'Or. Incidentally, *Yellow Earth* was shot by Yimou and he is co-credited with the making of the film along with the designer He Qun.

The fifth phase of China's cinemas stretches from the late 1980s to the late 1990s, with films expressing different messages but in which it is not difficult to read a disenchantment with the government. The Tiananmen Square massacre of 1989 only brought further repression and censorship to filmmakers other than those making historic films or action movies (although paradoxically given the climate, in 1995, restrictions on the quota of Hollywood films were lifted). Chen Kaige and Zhang Yimou now enjoy a sufficiently strong international reputation that they can obtain outside financing for their projects and post-produce outside China, which effectively puts their films out of China's censorship net.

Younger filmmakers were not so lucky (the Sixth Generation). Either their projects were censored and shelved or they had to go underground and attempt to get their films released outside China – in particular the blacklisted filmmakers Zhang Yuan and Ning Dai. This self-nominated Sixth Generation of filmmakers has succeeded in obtaining international recognition with films such as Wang Xiaoshuai's *The Days* (1993) and Zhang Yuan's *Mama* (1990, but only released in China two years later). His gay film – China's first (if we except *Farewell My Concubine* which is more **queer** than gay) – *East Palace, West Palace*, completed in 1996 and screened in Western film festival venues, has yet to be released in China. Sixth Generation filmmakers are committed to a new vision of truth and, unlike the previous generation's work, which was concerned with traditional culture, the rural and allegory, their work focuses on the urban and the uncertain situation of everyday life. For example, Wang's *So Close* *to Paradise* (1998) investigates prostitution; his later film *Beijing Bicycle* (2001) looks at the rapidly changing cityscape. Some filmmakers take a critical look at the Cultural Revolution, three of which, interestingly, are made by women filmmakers: Dai Sijie's *China, My Sorrow* (1989) and *Little Chinese Seamstress* (2002); and Joan Chen's *Xiu Xiu: The Sent Down Girl* (1998).

The sixth wave coincides with the new era of what is termed *post-socialist China*; namely, the new millennium decades (which began when China joined the WTO). These years have witnessed an expansion of consumerism and the spread of popular culture. This is reflected to a degree in the generic types of films being produced. What dominate are historical films (often mixed with comedy, action or romance), action films, comedy and romance. In narrative terms, the films address similar questions as above. On the one hand, there are films about contemporary China including, in a serious vein, urbanization and disaffection with society (see Lou Ye's *Suzhou River*, 2002, and *Summer Palace*, 2006), strife in marriage and child bullying (respectively, Zhang Yuan's *I Love You*, 2002, and *Little Red Flowers*, 2006); or in a more comic tone, how to juggle personal and private lives (see Xu Jinglei's *Go Lala Go!*, 2010). On the other hand, period dramas still abound, but often act as allegories for the nation's psyche (Zhang Yimou's *Hero*, 2002, and *House of Flying Daggers*, 2004). Currently there is a growing number of post-Sixth Generation filmmakers, an independent film movement known as the dGeneration (sic), making films with extremely low budgets and using digital technology. For the most part these films are only seen on the international film circuit, not only because they are made outside of the Chinese film industrial complex, but also because they hold up an uncomfortable image of contemporary Chinese life (see Ying Liang, *Taking Father Home*, 2005, *The Other Half*, 2006; Liu Jiayin, *Oxhide*, 2004, *Oxhide II*, 2010). Also emerging are documentaries, known under the label of the New Documentary Movement (NDM). As opposed to what one might expect, these films are mostly in the **cinema-vérité** style and personal testimonies. Co-productions between mainland China and Hong Kong and Taiwan are becoming a more regular feature since 2010. A greater relaxation has also taken place in regard to studios, not all of which are state-owned any longer (see Y. Zhang, 2010).

For further reading see Berry, 1991; Browne *et al.*, 1994; Clark, 1987; Cui, 2003; Eder and Rossell, 1993; Rayns and Meek, 1980; Sheldon Lu, 1997 and 2010; Yau, 1996; Xu, 2007; Y. Zhang, 2004, 2010; Y. Zhang and Xiao, 1998; X. Zhang, 1998, 2007.

Indian cinemas

Status: India is an emerging economy; Pakistan and Bangladesh are developing economies.

Preamble: although India's cinema industry is the most developed and the largest producer of film, there are several other cinemas of the Indian continent which evolved either post-Partition (Pakistan, 1947) or post-independence (Bangladesh, which was part of India, then part of Pakistan before its independence in 1971). It is well worth taking a look at the map of the Indian subcontinent to form an idea of the geographical and political complexities of its various nations.

Quantitatively, Pakistan ranks amongst the top ten film-producing countries, and for that reason there is a separate entry on Pakistan cinema (see below). Bangladeshi cinema produces some fifty to eighty films per year, which puts it on a par with UK cinema production. However, I will briefly address this cinema here, because there are complex issues when discussing it, most of which emanate from the effects of post-independence on the financial strength of its film industry, and which prevent it from falling into any easy category. For example, three of Bangladesh's most famous filmmakers – Satyajit Ray, Mrinal Sen and Ritwik Ghatak – have more readily been identified with Indian cinema and have exerted considerable influence over its film aesthetics and politics (see below). Thus, even though Ray insisted that his films be spoken in Bengali, his films (pre-independence) were Indian-produced (e.g. *Aparajito*, 1956; *The Philosopher's Stone*, 1958; *Devi*, 1960); and apart from his Calcutta trilogy (1970–75), which are Bengali productions, virtually all of his work, post-independence, was Indian-produced, some in the Hindi/Urdu language (e.g. *The Chess Players*, 1977), but most, still, in Bengali (e.g. *Kingdom of Diamonds*, 1980; *The Guest*, 1991). The same is true for Sen and Ghatak. A newer generation of Bangladeshi filmmakers has emerged, but they are small in number at present and, for the most part, independents (**auteur**-type filmmakers) and not part of the mainstream production of Bangladesh which, in the main, relies either on rather low-quality melodramas or crude sex-and-violence films – neither of which enjoy great audience appeal. Mainstream Bangladesh cinema does not sit easily under any rubric, although we might use the concept of Fifth Cinema because it is seriously under-developed in terms of production values. This cinema is struggling to remain commercially viable; its audience figures are constantly on the decrease, losing out to foreign imports and satellite TV. That of the independents, however, can readily be associated with Third Cinema (many of their films deal with the

Liberation war of Bangladesh of 1971; see the work of Humayun Ahmed, Morshedul Islam, Tareque Masud).

Indian cinema

India produces more films than any other nation, around 1,000 per year and at least twelve regional cinemas make up the cinemas of India (compared to USA's 400 to 600 films per year, usually in one language). **Bollywood** accounts for one-fifth of the output (at around 200 films per year). Indian cinema rivals Hollywood in terms of films and audiences, but not in terms of revenues. In that respect Hollywood cannot be rivalled, precisely because it has the infrastructure for world distribution and exhibition which Indian cinema, as yet, does not possess to the same degree (Joshri, 2001: 54), although this scenario is evolving. Indian cinema is big business in India and as a cultural force it outstrips the USA cinema market in terms of consumption within its own cinema theatres and venues alone. More Indians (12 million go to the cinema every day) watch their indigenous products than Americans do theirs (bear in mind though that India's population is almost twice that of the USA). Indian cinema is big business also in relation to its **stars**. Stars have a major influence and standing and often play an active role in politics.

Indian cinema is still a very popular form of entertainment especially for young male audiences. It is, however, the case that the increasing popularity of television, since the 1990s, has affected audiences (primarily in the major cities). Nowadays, of the yearly products, only 1 per cent will be a huge box-office success (Kabir, 2003: 6–7). Thus, much of this current cinema has now become the mainstay of television programming (Gokulsing and Dissanayake, 2003: 123). The dominant popular **genres** are mythologicals, melodramas, musicals, romance, adventure films – often these are all rolled into one and labelled as song-dance-action films and, since the 1980s have become known as **Bollywood** films. Their popularity has to do with the tremendous legacy of India's theatre which has heavily influenced the generic tradition of mainstream Indian cinema. Another contributing factor is that, with their seamless mix of Hindi and Urdu, they are immediately accessible to half of India's population. But, beyond this extremely popular mainstream cinema there exist other cinemas – regional cinemas, art cinema, that are often state-subsidized, and avant-garde cinema which is made by independents and is not necessarily state-subsidized.

Although the birth of the Indian film industry dates from 1913, film made its entry into India on 7 July 1896. Maurice Sestier, an envoy of the Lumière brothers, started *cinématographe* exhibitions in Bombay, now Mumbai. By the 1900s, itinerant showmen took film beyond the cities of Bombay/Mumbai, Calcutta/Kolkata and Madras/Chennai and set up tent shows which at times would house as many as 10,000 spectators. The making of the first Indian feature film is credited to Dhundiraj Govind Palke with his mythological *Harishchandra* (the date given varies as either 1913 or 1914). Palke is credited with introducing the mythologicals, which were extremely popular with 'ordinary people' (i.e. not the educated elite) – what **postcolonial theory** would term the subaltern classes. The narratives of these early silent films, where gods did battle with demons, borrowed heavily from Hindi epic tiles from the *Mahabharata* and from the *Ramayan* (Kabir, 2003: 6). These mythologicals, then, developed in the mid-1920s into devotional or religious and allegorical films. However, if we are to be true to history, Hiralal Sen is really India's first filmmaker. He established the Royal Bioscope Company in Calcutta/Kolkata and filmed plays from the major theatres in that city. A first film of his (dating from 1903), *Alibaba and the Forty Thieves*, not only marks Sen out as the first filmmaker in India, but, interestingly, also pre-dates by four years France's version of the same story (Pathé's *Ali Baba*, 1907).

The 1920s can be taken as the period when India truly established a film industry. At that time, Hollywood was a reference point for the structuring of the industry and remained as such until state intervention in the early 1960s changed the nature of industrial practice (see below). The mid-1920s saw the founding of the major studios first in Bombay/ Mumbai and Calcutta/Kolkata and then in Poona/Pune and later still in Madras/Chennai (1930s). But the economic management and practice of these studios were a far cry from the seamless vertically integrated system of Hollywood. The financing for films was extremely difficult and dependent on the country's trader-industrialists (mostly mercantile traders) and if that failed, then, recourse had to be made to usurers. With the advent of sound, Indian cinema had to compete with foreign products (particularly American films). It created its own indigenous sound film that included songs and dance. These routines were often extra-**diegetic**, but they were a great success and so guaranteed the popularity of any particular film in which they featured. They also, of course, perpetuated and extended the star system to include not just theatre actors or dancers as stars but now singers too. If we could speak of an integrated cinema industry at that time, then, it would be in terms of a cinema run by families and friends and financed by the lower rungs of capitalist entrepreneurship and speculators. This made the industry a fairly precarious affair, to say the least; so it is not surprising if, after World War Two, the studio system collapsed. Freelancing became the primary production practice, beginning in the 1950s – interestingly the decade that is known as the Golden Age of Indian cinema. Currently, this system still prevails, albeit with an increased corporatisation. This has led the Indian government to grant the Indian cinema industry-status, which gives it access to banking facilities and insurance cover (Gokulsing and Dissanayake, 2003: 111 and 121). The effect has been to give the industry 'a more organized look than ever before' (ibid.: 121).

The Bombay Talkies and musicals of the 1930s are considered the true precursor of today's mainstream Indian cinema. Bombay Talkies refers to a studio established in 1934 that made mostly rural melodramas – although it also made social films, a strand that would get perpetuated in the New Indian Cinema of the late 1960s. Bombay musicals is a loose term used to refer to the song–dance–action movies. This heritage won the Bombay studios the epithet of Bollywood (which is now used freely to refer to the films themselves). The three largest studios are the Kohinoor Film Company, the Ranjit Movietone studio and the Imperial Film Company (all established in the 1920s). Imperial produced India's first sound film, *Alam Ara* (1931). These studios produced Hindu mythologicals, melodramas, song–dance–action films. They also produced some realist films which transposed orientalist narratives into period movies so that they appeared to be allegories or mythologicals. In fact, they were a thinly disguised criticism of the colonial–nationalist conflict. Bombay/Mumbai, however, was not the only geographical site of the film industry and we need to be conscious of the important work being produced at that time by other studios dotted over the country: the Prabhat studios in Poona/Pune, the New Theatre studios in Calcutta/Kolkata and the United Artists Corporation in Madras/Chennai. Nor should we forget the small Punjabi-based studios in Lahore (which of course is now part of Pakistan) that, prior to the Partition of 1947, produced **fantasy** films. After Partition, many of these studios and film practitioners moved to India and their products became integrated into Indian cinema. These became known in the 1970s and 1980s as the Hindi 'masala' movies – namely, a song-and-dance film that mixed genres.

Someswar Bhowmik (1995), in his very useful overview of Indian cinema, provides us with the following survey of pre-Independence cinema of the 1930s. Globally speaking it was made up of the following categories. Sixty per cent were romance and love-affair films. This broad category includes many of the musicals, romance-melodramas, mythologicals and allegories associated with Indian cinema. Thirty per

489

cent of film production was about problems facing Indian families (in-laws, marital maladjustments, and so on). This category also includes films that are known as reform socials, films that reflected the state-reform programme that called for widows to remarry and other programmes dealing with the condition of women. These films are the precursor to Indian melodramas of the post-independence cinema. The third category makes up 10 per cent of production and are films that reflect the growing awareness of a society influx as it faces the almost insuperable conflicts of orthodoxy with modernity. Much of India's cinema, pre- and post-independence, makes allusions (however indirectly) to the struggle between traditional authenticity and capitalist modernity. And, in this context, it is worth citing one filmmaker whose work straddles these two periods, Mehboob Khan and his fetish female star Nargis (who often embodied these tensions in her performances). Mehboob used the costume drama as his forum for his **mise-en-scène** of these conflicts (see *Humayun*, 1945, *Romeo and Juliet*, 1947, and *Andaz*, 1949).

The Golden Age of Indian cinema covers a fifteen-year span (1950–65). Budgets were low and filmmakers could afford to experiment. Mehboob Khan, Bimal Roy, Raj Kapoor and Guru Dutt are the four names that still hold importance today because they 'transformed the film song into an art form' by mastering the use of film music and choreography (Kabir, 2003: 7). In all areas of film practice – cinematography, set design, editing – they re-invigorated Indian cinema. In terms of narrative and characterization, they gave depth where, before, stereotype had predominated. It was also the golden age for stars; the galaxy was dominated by four major names – Dilip Kumar, Dev Anand, actor-director Raj Kapoor and Nargis (the major female vehicle for Khan and Kapoor). The benchmark film was Kapoor's *Awaara* (1951), which broke box-office records and was an international hit in the East (from USSR/Russia to the Middle East). This film set the precedent for Indian popular cinema of this era. Narratives were a blend of social realism and popular cinema. Lyrics came from leftist poets (Shailendra, Sahir Ludhianivi). Roy's *Devdas* (1955), Mehboob's *Mother India* (1957) and Dutt's *Pyaasa* (1957) are classics of this Golden Age cinema with their social concerns embedded in effective use of song, dance and music to heighten feeling.

Contrary to Eurocentric cinemas, whose fortunes waned in the late 1970s, India's boom in the industry in terms of production occurred in 1979 and continues today. Pre-independence, India produced between 100 and 170 films per year. Post-independence, India made 200. This number subsequently grew to 400 films per year in the

1970s. By 1979 production soared to 700 and up to 948 depending on the year. Lack of mass consumption of television sets is a part explanation of this extraordinary increase in film production, but so too is the shift in the conceptualization of the industry which only post-independence was properly geared to the reproduction of capital (Bhowmik, 1995: 38). Two other reasons are contributory causes. The first was the introduction of a series of state measures to aid the industry, starting in 1960, with the Film Finance Corporation (FFC), an independent but state-established body. By the mid-1950s, most of the studios were in a parlous state and had either closed down or attempted to break into the mainstream Bombay-Bollywood type of production. The FFC's objective was twofold: first, to promote and assist mainstream cinema and, second, to develop film as an instrument of national culture. In this latter respect, the FFC made it possible for a whole new generation of filmmakers to get into production. This, in effect, was the launching-pad of the New Indian Cinema (see below, and **Third Cinema** entry for more details of this cinema). In 1980, the FFC subsequently became the NFDC (the National Film Development Corporation), a quasi(state)-monopoly for financing, distributing and exhibiting films. The second reason for the extraordinary upswing in film production was the withdrawal, in 1974, of the Motion Picture Export Association of America (MPEAA) from the Indian market, which allowed India, in the form of the FFC, to import films for local distribution and make a tidy profit in the process and further finance its own production.

There are three major trends in Indian cinema dating from the 1960s: the Hindi movie which embraces many different types including the social film, but which predominantly refers to the dance–song–action movie (see entry on **Bollywood**); the art cinema (best exemplified for Westerners by Satyajit Ray); and, finally, the avant-garde/formalist or **counter-cinema** more closely identified with Third Cinema practices. The Hindi film follows much in the tradition of genres that were established pre-independence (for further details see Chakravarti, 1993). There is considerable overlap between the other two cinemas (art and counter-cinema) although the latter cinema is closely identified with the earlier work of the Indian People's Theatre Association (ITPA), a communist-backed theatre and film movement. The art cinema, so associated with Ray's work – although we should not overlook his important contemporary Ritwik Ghatak (see below) – is one that looks to a way of representing history within the framework of post-independence discourses of the nationalist enterprise. Ray's cinema is a cinema of realism but the content is often located in the past. It is also a regionalist cinema rather than a nationalist cinema – which in a sense reinforces the very point that Third Cinema makes, namely, that a national cinema is made up of many national cinemas. Ashish Rajadhyaksha, one of the leading experts on the history of Indian cinema, puts it well when he describes Ray's realism 'as a vantage point from where to restage "the past": to re-present memory in a land that could now, so to speak, celebrate the arrival of history' (1996: 682). This practice of returning to history to make history is a key to understanding Ray's films. In a different way, but also in a regionalist vein, Ray's contemporary, Mrinal Sen, also seeks to represent India and its history, but does so through a realism grounded in the present. Indeed, his 1969 film *Bhuvan Shome* is a good example of this desire to stress differences in regional cultures, languages and customs (Kabir, 2001: 4). Sen's film is credited with launching India's New Cinema. Themes that preoccupied filmmakers of this New Cinema of the 1970s were based in the everyday reality of India: questions of caste, exploitation of workers, bad landlords, political corruption, and so on. As Kabir (2001: 4) notes, this is a far cry from popular cinema's preoccupation with romance. This New Cinema, also labelled anti-establishment cinema, necessitated a more realistic and natural acting style so producing a new type of actor on-screen, the most well known in Western eyes being Om Puri.

In 'purely' political terms, India's post-1947 history falls into three phases: 1947 to 1969, the period of secular nationalism advocated by Nehru and which was based on a politics of integration; 1970 to 2004 which witnessed the increasing importance of Hindu nationalism as exemplified by the rise in popularity of the BJP (the Bahratiya Janata Party) and its electoral success in 1998; the most recent, 2004 to the present, with the demise of the BJP and accession to power of the social democratic Congress Party.

What of the film industry? Partition divided the film industry and, in the early years of Partition, India was the country to gain in terms of studios and personnel. A few years later, however, some filmmakers returned to their now native Pakistan (see below). Indian films about the traumas of the Partition were, however, very thin on the ground. Indeed, films that addressed the recent history of India tended to continue the earlier trend of pre-independence films about the struggle for freedom and they were few in terms of numbers (twenty or so over a thirty-year period, 1925 to 1957). Ritwik Ghatak's 1960s trilogy on refugee poverty and conditions in Calcutta/Kolkata was the first to show the effects of Partition on ordinary people (*Meghe Dhaka Tara/The Cloud-Capped Star*, 1960, *Komal Ghandar*, 1961, *Subarnareka*,

1962). But the first film to impact hugely on audiences was *Garam Hava/Hot Winds* (M. S. Sathyu, 1973), a film which focused on the plight of a Muslim family in North India. Since then, a handful of films have been made on this topic from a sympathetic viewpoint (a more recent example of which is Pamela Rooks' *Train to Pakistan*, 1997). Another film of the 1970s with a similar impact to *Garam Hava* was *Sholay/Flames* (Ramesh Sippy, 1975), only this time the reference was not Pakistan but contemporary India and its civil unrest (Prime Minister Indira Ghandi declared a state of emergency in the same year).

The 1990s witnessed the emergence of films that addressed India's contemporary political condition. In terms of the early 1990s, Mani Rathnam's *Roja* (1992) and *Bombay* (1994) are extraordinary given the political upheavals of those times. Extraordinary, because *Roja* met with wide audience appeal, suggesting that Indians do want a political cinema. Extraordinary, because *Bombay* got through censorship. *Roja is* about the nationalist struggle between Kashmiri separatists and India. *Bombay* is a love story between a Muslim and a Hindu set against the backdrop of the Hindu–Muslim conflict (see Gokulsing, 1999).

However, once the BJP came to political power (1998), there was a move away from radical themes and a shift to the production of an increasing number of films with national and political agendas, reflecting, this time, the party's determination to develop a particular notion of Indian-ness and get even with history (Gokulsing and Dissanayake, 2003: 110). This included a cinema promoting Indian cultural values; the Bollywood musical was a primary vehicle in this regard (for an interesting take on this see the Bollywood musical-sports film *Lagaan*, Ashutosh Gowariker, 2001, set in the Victorian British Raj period) and also a cinema that no longer held back from hitting out against Pakistan. In this latter context, two films need mentioning: Anil Sharma's *Gadar – Ek Prem Katha/Uprising, A Love Story* (2001) and *The Hero* (2003). In these formulaic films, the hero takes on the enemy nation (Pakistan) and defeats or outwits them. Although, intriguingly, a couple of 2004 films appear not to have towed the BJP line: *Main Hoon Na* (Farah Khan) and *Veer Zaara* (Yash Chopra), both of which adopt a sympathetic approach to the conflict (see Dudrah, 2012: 15–27).

In 2004, the BJP lost the elections and the reins of power passed to the social democrat Congress Party. Indian cinema then saw some important changes during the ten-year period of Congress rule, 2004 to 2014 (after which the BJP returned to power; see below). First, the shift in narratives away from the former propagandistic masala films, heavily endorsed by the former ruling BJP party (with their retro-gressive message of a return to the motherland and family values).

Films were now set in the contemporary and dealt with realistic situations (ranging from venal small town politics, to people in emotional difficulties). Romantic comedies continued to be popular – often in the form of Bollywood musicals – even incidentally to the extent of a queer musical, *Dostana* (Tarun Mansukhani, 2008), in which two men become friends and pretend to be gay so they can share a flat with a beautiful woman (see Dudrah, 2010: 43–61). Second, the industry became better organized, multiplexes were on the increase, the boom in multiplexes in the major cities produced even greater demand for films, which explains why production continues to run at around 1,000 films a year. Third, greater openness led to an expanding market overseas. With an eye to export markets, some Indian films were made in English (e.g. Homi Adajania's *Being Cyrus*, 2006), others in a mixture of Hindi and English (e.g. Rakeysh Omprakash Mehra's *Rang de Basanti*, 2006), or Hindi and Indian English (e.g. Sanjay Leela Bhansali's *Black*, 2005). Finally, the emergence of a new generation of filmmakers and stars who are not part of the dynasty of the film industry's great family of filmmakers and stars (such as the Bachchans and Kapoors), served to re-energize India's production (for filmmakers see, for example, Bhansali's *Black*; Adajania's *Being Cyrus*; Padrip Sarkar's *Parineeta*, 2005; Rajkumar Hirani,'s *Munna Bhai*, 2006; Mehra's *Rang de Basanti*. For new male stars see Aamir Kahn and Hrithik Roshan; female: Madhuri Dixit and Aishwarya Rai).

This ten-year period also witnessed a greater openness within the internal market, thanks to the impact of globalization. Thus, the ideology of consumption found a ready reflection in the modern-style Bollywood products (fashion, food and cars have a strong presence). Diasporic filmmakers also had an impact. Deepa Metha, Gurinder Chadha and Mira Nair – all women filmmakers – have all helped to 'bring India' to Western audiences. A new kind of cross-fertilization occurred: namely, India influencing Western products, as well as Western products having an impact on those of India. In this context, *Devdas* (Bhansali, 2002), starring India's current top male star, Sharukh Khan, is a good example. Exported to Western countries, this film has done extremely well. Or, as another example, films made with Indian financing, shot by Indian personnel, with Indian stars, but set in the Indian diaspora (e.g. *Jhoom Barabar Jhoom/Dance Baby Dance*, Shaad Ali Sahgal, 2007, set in Southall, West London, known as Little India). In a reverse sense, Chadha has gone to India and made *Bride and Prejudice* (2004). A further interesting case of cross-cultural exchange is another British film, *Slumdog Millionaire* (Danny Boyle,

2008) – based on an Indian novel, set in India, and co-directed in Indian by Loveleen Tandan.

In 2014, the BJP was returned to power and, while it has committed to establish an art and culture cell devoted exclusively to developing and promoting films themed on Indian tradition (including family values), nonetheless, for the most part it has (to all present appearances) not begun to interfere with current trends. Thus, even if there is an upsurge in religious nationalism under the Modi government, which has brought about the banning of certain films such as *Unfreedom* (Raj Amit Kumar, 2015, about lesbianism) and *Papilio Buddha* (Jayan K. Cherian, 2013), about the discrimination against the Dalit minority community (finally certified for release after cuts were made), it is still to be hoped that the/a climate of openness will prevail.

For further reading on Indian cinema see first Rajadhyaksha and Willemen (1994) *Encyclopedia of Indian Cinema* (now updated to 2014). This is an important reference book on Indian cinema. For histories of Indian cinema see Bhowmik, 1995; Sarkar, 2009. For representation in popular Indian cinema see Ahmed, 2015; Chakravarti, 1993; Dudrah, 2006, 2012; Dudrah and Desai, 2008; Dwyer, 2006; Dwyer and Pinto, 2011; Gokulsing and Dissanayake, 1998, 2003; Gopalan, 2002; Saari, 2011; Sarkar, 2009; Raheja and Kothari, 2004. For a recent study of Indian new independent cinema see Devasundaram, 2016. And the journals *Bioscope: South Asian Screen Studies*; *Cinemaya: Asian Film Quarterly* (which also includes articles on Arab diaspora cinemas); *South Asian Film and Media*.

Pakistan cinema

Although it mostly caters to the local market, Pakistan's film industry, with an average of eighty films per year, ranks amongst the top-ten film production countries (Gazdar, 1997: 1). Little is known of this cinema outside of its own country, with the exception of diasporas (e.g. Birmingham and Bradford in the UK) where DVD club rentals make these films available. Nor is there much written about this cinema, at least in the West. However, readers seeking to find out more would find that Mushtaq Gazdar's (1997) comprehensive study provides an informative picture of Pakistan's production; and on the representation of women see Dönmez-Colin (2004).

The first era of Pakistan's film industry is, of course, pre-Partition (1947). United Players was the first studio to be established in Lahore in the 1920s and, in fact, one of its early filmmakers was the first Indian woman filmmaker, Fatima Begum, who made *Bulbule-Pakistan* (1926). In terms of production, the industry was not competitive enough to fight against the Bombay/Mumbai silent movies. Only the advent of sound brought about some success for films emanating from the Punjab. The 1947 Partition had a considerable impact upon existing studios in the new Pakistan. Kamla Movietone (established 1924), later known as Shorey Studios, moved to Bombay/Mumbai after Partition. The founder of Pancholi Art Pictures (established late 1930s), Dalsukh Pancholi, fled to Bombay/Mumbai. In 1948, these studios were taken over by Agha G. A. Gul, who had already established his own Evernew Studios in 1937. Gul's dominant position meant that he became a major pioneer of Pakistan cinema after Partition. During the early Partition days there was some collaboration between India and Pakistan. And, two years after Partition, there was some reverse in migration from Bombay/Mumbai to Lahore and some filmmakers returned to their native city. One famous example is Nazir (born in Lahore), who returned in 1949 and became an actor, director and producer in Pakistan and worked in a successful partnership with his actress wife, Swaranlata (see *Pheray*, 1949, *Sachthai*, 1949, *Anokhi Dastan*, 1950). The first Pakistan film was *Teri Yaad* (Daud Chand, 1948), but the first film made by an indigenous Pakistan filmmaker was *Do Ansoo* (Anwar Kanal Pasha, 1949). At this stage, however, the Pakistan film industry was too small to meet audience demand. Consequently, cinema theatres relied mostly on Indian film imports.

Gul was the major producer of the 1950s. But quick to follow on his heels was J. C. Anand, whose first big hit was *Sassi* (Chand, 1954). By the mid-1950s, quota restrictions imposed on Indian imports greatly helped the Pakistan film industry to grow. And by the 1960s, Lahore had become the Hollywood of Pakistan – Lollywood. While the state did little to help the industry, it did establish a very strict code of censorship. This meant that the cinema of the 1950s and 1960s was predominantly a-political (on both social and political issues). What dominate during this period are comedies, folk tales and musicals; although films on the history of Pakistan were deemed acceptable and represent a small exception to mainstream cinema of this time. Thus, Saifudin Saif made *Kartar Singh* (1959) about the effects of Partition; Khahil Qaiser made a film on the anti-colonial struggle, *Shaheed* (1962); and Raza Mir made a film based on the effects of Partition on Hindu-Muslim relations, *Lakhon Mein Eik* (1967).

In the late 1960s and early 1970s, the ascendancy of television began to take its toll on the film industry, as indeed did the political upheavals that led to the secession of Bangladesh from Pakistan. In order to assist the ailing industry, the Bhutto government, in 1973, established the National Film Development Corporation (NAFDEC, quite similar to India's NFDC), which was an autonomous body under the tutelage of the Ministry of Culture. Box-office receipts on foreign imports went to NAFDEC (which was responsible for importing foreign films). These revenues went forward to finance indigenous products and the tendency was to finance big budget movies and stars. The net effect was a boom in film production during the 1970s (averaging 100 films per year).

Then of course, in 1977, came the military coup of General Zia-ul-Haq, who got rid of Bhutto (by execution in 1979), imposed martial law and established a dictatorship (the Zia junta) in the name of Islam. Zia's junta fought the Afghan war on behalf of its Western allies. It also governed on a policy of divide and rule by supporting sectarian and ethnic groups and leaving them to fight among each other. The effects on cinema (particularly that of the 1980s) was an increase in films glamorizing violence (e.g. Yunus Malik's *Jeera Sain*, 1977). Two social–realist films of the period stand out as exceptions to this trend. *Muthi Bhar Chawal*, made by the woman filmmaker Sangeeta (1978), is a film about village family life and the struggle of a family to survive once the mother becomes widowed. This social film, on the condition and status of women in contemporary Pakistan, pre-dates tougher censorship laws (introduced a year later) which might have got it banned. Even so, after the new laws, Sangeeta continued to be the prolific filmmaker she had been, throughout the 1970s, making up to three films a year (as she did in 1979). The other film is *Maula Jat*, directed by Yunus Malik (1979), which deals with the indifference of officials to the plight of ordinary people. This film was banned, in 1981, under the pretext that it was too violent, but, clearly, its reference was too close to the Bhutto story to be acceptable to the junta – or the new censorship laws (the Motion Pictures Ordinance, 1979). These new laws represented a heavy clamp-down, imposing moral and religious values which were, in fact, a barely disguised form of political censorship. This censorship included the closing down of the majority of cinemas, banning the work of certain filmmakers (e.g. Jamil Dehlavi who fled to the UK). The effect was a major decline in the film industry's output. It went from 100 films per year to 61, in 1980, and then balanced out at around 80 per year.

The first half of the 1980s was a disastrous period for Pakistan cinema. Poor products (due to the all-pervasive censorship laws) met with declining audiences (especially among the elite classes). Cinema complexes were turned into shopping centres (especially in Karachi). The majority audience was now composed of rural and urban working-class male audiences and they were provided with a diet of comedies, musicals and above all violent films. By the late 1980s, rising costs and the decline in the film industry's fortunes had led to an increase in co-productions with South Asian and Far Eastern countries (and not with India because of political tensions). This brought new talent into the industry, particularly in the form of stars (e.g. Sabita from Sri Lanka and Shiva from Nepal). In the 1990s, the effects of media globalization led increasingly to commercially orientated films, imitating Hollywood and Bollywood, targeting youth audiences (e.g. see Sangeeta's violent and sexually explosive film *Khilona*, 1996, which is based on contemporary Hollywood psychopath thrillers). Production rose to almost 100 films per year.

However, in the new millennium, Lollywood still remains the poor relation to Bollywood. Poor equipment (some dating from the 1960s), poorly produced films, stuck to predictable formulas, have served to alienate a diversified audience as has, in a more significant way, the complex political situation which includes suicide bombings and attacks on film theatres (amongst other venues) by the Taliban in reprisal for military operations taken against them. Moreover, there has been a fall in production from some 100 films per year to around 30 (but sometimes as few as 12, as in 2010). Ironically, the one factor that previously had helped it to survive, the forty-year ban on Indian imports, was lifted in 2005 in a move to put a stop to the further decline in the number of cinema theatres. Presently, production seems limited to horror or crime films or musicals (the latter very derivative of Bollywood); with a few more politically inflected films about terrorism such as Jarrar Rizvi's *Son of Pakistan* (2011) and Bilal Lashari's *Waar* (2012); and a mere handful of independent filmmakers producing a political cinema (see *Bhai Log*, Syed Faisal Bukhari, 2011, about Karachi's underworld; *Kaptaan*, Faisal Aman Khan, 2012, about Imran Khan's rise in politics).

For further reading see Gazdar, 1997; Dönmez-Colin, 2004.

Latin American cinemas

Status: Argentina, Brazil and Mexico are all emerging economies; Cuba is listed as a developing economy.

Between 1896, when the Lumière brothers' *cinématographe* first penetrated Latin America, and 1911, almost all the countries of this continent had established exhibition venues for the screening of short films made either by indigenous filmmakers or imported from Europe. Audiences were mainly the elite classes who were privy to an exoticization of their country through the documentary images brought to them. We have seen how a similar exoticization occurred in countries of the African context, the major difference being that the images taken there were for the entertainment of the privileged colonizing classes and for export to the Motherland. In Latin America's case there was, however, a form of colonization brought about by Hollywood's forceful distribution practices which soon penetrated the countries of central and southern America and, by the 1920s, had garnered 80 per cent of the indigenous markets (Mexico, in particular, has a very complex relationship with the USA that dates back, at least, to the Mexican Revolution, 1910 to 1917).

Knowledge of the early years of Latin American cinema is still somewhat scant. Only now are film historians engaged in uncovering the hidden pre-1930s cinemas (see Lopez, 2000). What is known is that in the first decades (1900–30), only Mexico, Argentina and Brazil had anything like an indigenous film production infrastructure. In Brazil, where films were made in regional centres, production by the 1910s had reached 100 films per year. These were mostly cowboy and rural dramas, a genre that was also extremely successful in Argentina. Mexican cinema, in these early years, focused on traditional narratives but also made controversial films (at least in the eyes of its northern neighbours in the USA) about the conditions of Mexican workers in Northern America.

The advent of sound in Latin American countries was a slow affair because of the enormous financial burden of equipping cinema theatres. However, it did have the advantage of promoting national cultures in a more specific way and it brought, in its wake, the musical genre. In Argentina it was the *tanguera* (tango melodramas, based as the name suggests on Argentina's indigenous dance form, the tango). In Brazil it was the *chanchada* (a hybrid form of Hollywood musicals and the Brazilian samba dance, carnival and comic theatre traditions). In Mexico it was the *ranchada* (a cowboy musical) and the *cabareteras* (cabaret melodramas). The Mexican cowboy musical is a hybridization of the American genre with Mexican rural traditions, whereas the cabaret melodramas are more a hybrid of the Mexican street/city genre and the Hollywood cabaret or backstage musical. Within this notion of hybridity, Brazilian and Mexican filmmaking has tended to merge the practices or genres of other cinemas with their own indigenous cultural traditions and film style. The overall effect of this hybridization is a deep textual and textural layering of meanings – what is known as syncretism (a syncretic style). Brazil mimicked the Hollywood action movies (especially Westerns) by transposing them into their own context and environment and Mexico's singing cowboy films came immediately upon the heels (spurs?) of the Hollywood prototype of the mid-1930s (first exemplified by John Wayne and shortly followed by Gene Autry and Roy Rogers).

The Mexican film industry was the first to be formed in Latin America, in the mid-1930s, and it enjoyed a golden age of cinema through until the 1950s (particularly the decade 1943 to 1953). This period is marked, primarily, by the distinguished collaboration between the filmmaker Emilio Fernandez and the cinematographer Gabriel Figueroa. Figueroa trained in Hollywood under Gregg Toland (the cinematographic genius behind Welles' *Citizen Kane*, 1941). An early film Fernandez and Figueroa made together, *María Candelaria* (1943), won the Palme d'Or at Cannes in 1946. Figueroa also worked with Buñuel when he was in exile in Mexico and made *Los olvidados* (1950) with him. Another, earlier formative influence on Mexican cinema was Eisenstein, who visited Mexico in 1930 to 1932 (where he shot *¡Qué viva Mexico!*, 1931).

During Mexico's cinematic golden age, the Argentinian cinema went through a decline (partly due to its pro-fascist but supposedly neutral political stance during World War Two which led to the USA withholding vital film stock). In 1946, the ailing Argentinian film industry was given a boost by the newly established Peronist government. But the cinema produced, due to tremendous pressure and censorship, mainly safe and uncritical bourgeois melodramas. Only one voice spoke out against the Peronist oligarchy: Leopoldo Torre Nilsson, whose film *La mano en la trampa/The Hand in the Tray* (1961) won the International Press Prize at Cannes.

What all these cinemas had in common was a similarity of cultural references and an artisanal style that did in fact constitute a heritage for the later radical cinema of the 1960s and the still later cinema of the 1980s and 1990s. The Latin American cinemas drew on their landscapes, costumes, customs and traditions including their oral narrative traditions and their music. This local and culturally syncretic structure of their films was matched by an equally hybrid cinematic style that was both industrial and artisanal. What distinguishes the cinemas of that period (pre-1960s) from the later cinemas is the apparent lack of political **motivation** within the cinematic practice. What also marks this cinema of the 1940s and 1950s was the degree of cross-fertilization and the migration of talent. Europeans and Americans came to work in the Latin American continent; Latin American filmmakers went to Europe; Cubans contributed to Mexican and Argentinian cinemas; Argentinians went to Brazil and Venezuela. This migrancy has also left an important heritage, one which is mirrored by the present trend of transnationalism (especially in the form of co-productions) in Latin American cinemas and one which, because of the dynamics of exchange, has come to be termed transculturation.

The late 1950s saw a new cinema emerging, one which was to last through until the early 1970s across the Latin American continent. This cinema was a militant, revolutionary, counter-cinema. It was one which denounced poverty and celebrated protest. This new cinema was started by filmmakers whose products often, ironically enough, were financed by the very state machineries against which they sought to militate. A film made in Bolivia is an interesting example of these paradoxes and yet shows how militant and effective some of this cinema could be. *The Blood of the Condor* (1969), made by a Bolivian film collective (Ukamau), exposed the forced sterilization of Quechua Indian women by the American Peace Corps. The effect was the Peace Corps' expulsion by the Bolivian government. The year 1959 can count as the watershed year in which this radicalization of cinema came into practice, starting with the Documentary Film School of Santa Fe in Argentina, the cinema nôvo in Brazil and the Film Institute in Cuba (founded in that year, after the Cuban Revolution). These groupings produced an ethnographic and social–realist cinema showing the poverty of their countries. They also made a cinema termed the Tropicalist style (see **cinema nôvo** for more detail). This was a syncretic and stylized cinema that fused Catholic religion with indigenous mysticism, allegory with legend and semi-pagan religion, cult with African-Latin American ritual, producing a more surreal cinema (see the works of Glauber Rocha, especially *Antonio das Mortes*, 1969). And the impact of these groupings was such that it grew into a movement that embraced all Latin American countries producing a resisting cinema. This movement became known as the New Latin American Cinema. At the same time, debates on representation and identity were taking place in film journals. The impact of this wave of change was enormous and had worldwide repercussions, best exemplified by the huge influence of the Third Cinema Manifesto (written by the Argentinian filmmakers Fernando Solanas and Octavio Getino in 1969) and the international impact of the Argentinian collective film *La hora de los hornos* (*The hour of the Furnaces*, Grupo Cine Liberación, 1968) (see **Third Cinema**).

The Cuban Institute of Film Art controlled the film industry between 1960 and the late 1980s (when the economy collapsed due to the demise of Soviet Russia). It was a model of socialist filmmaking. With a yearly output of six to ten feature films and forty or more documentaries, production was small but consistent, and always experimental. Santiago Alvarez was a leading light in the documentary tradition and Tomás Gutiérrez Alea was a major figure in feature film. Both domains cultivated a deliberate counter-cinema, a cinema that is improvised, social–realist, allegorical – deeply experimental and deliberately rough-edged. An intentionally Imperfect Cinema, as Julio Garcia Espinosa puts it (see Chanan, 1996: 743–45).

The 1960s and early 1970s, therefore, produced an extremely vibrant cinema throughout Latin America, even though (with the exception of Cuba which seemed to tolerate criticism) some films were banned and in certain countries, where military dictatorships had already taken hold, filmmakers were persecuted. This revolutionary cinema worked outside of genre and more in the vein of syncretic cinema (see **cinema nôvo**). In Brazil, one form of this syncretic cinema that espoused the aesthetics of garbage (a cinema working with scavenged and scarce resources) was Tropicalism. This was a cinema based on Afro-Brazilian or Afro-Caribbean culture, allegory and mythology (see above and Shohat and Stam (1994: 310) for more detail). By the mid-1970s everything worsened, with military coups occurring over the entire Latin American continent forcing filmmakers underground or into exile from where they made a cinema of exile. Persecution meant death, not just the force of censorship. A diasporic film culture grew outside the Latin American countries (in North America and France in particular). Militant filmmakers such as the Chilean Raúl Ruiz eventually ended up in France where he went on to make what we can certainly call radical and experimental films, but films which would be considered more auteur-based than revolutionary (see *La Ville des pirates/The City of Pirates*, 1983, or his 1998 film adaptation of Proust's *A la recherche du temps perdu*).

In some regards, there has been a shift in cinematic practices, since the 1980s, towards an international art cinema. At least, that is one of the major trends. A primary reason for this shift has been the growing importance of television as a consumer commodity for the reasonably affluent middle classes (who make up most of the cinema-going audiences) as well as its presence as a shared commodity in shanty-towns (*favelas*). In a sense, cinema has re-become an elitist cultural artefact (as it was in its earliest days). Thus, it has had to pitch towards a more international audience if it is to remain viable. A film that well exemplifies this tendency is Brazil's Oscar contender *Central do Brazil/ Central Station* (Walter Salles, 1998), a multi-co-production (Brazil/ France/Spain/Japan) which enjoyed enormous success outside Brazil (winning the Berlin Golden Bear, 1998). A road movie, scored by indigenous (Brazilian) music, it focuses on two protagonists (young and old) whose individual quests for identity act as an allegory for contemporary Brazil. Past and present inflect this travel towards the unknown future. The protagonists' poverty is matched by the pain of deprivation and insecurity experienced by the great majority of rural and metropolitan Brazilians. Religion and myth intersect to countermand belief in rational chronology (a concept which the two protagonists profoundly mistrust anyway).

But there was also the emergence of another new type of cinema – or, rather, new movements in cinema. The 1980s and 1990s saw the emergence of a woman's cinema, a gay cinema and the native residents' cinema (what Shohat and Stam, 1994, refer to as Fourth Cinema – see above). Often, working in video and super-8, but not exclusively, this cinema continued the tradition of the resisting counter-cinema of the 1960s. But it produced a new type of representation of national identity, a more complex and less homogeneous one than that imaged in the 1960s by the militant New Latin American Cinema movement (see above), which pitted the true inheritors of the earth (i.e. the subalterns: the disenfranchised Indians, peasants and workers) against the elites. This cinema breaks free from an evocation of the dependency culture to which the elites had subjugated the Latin American nations. Geographically and spiritually this cinema is a more fragmented one, very much a regional cinema that represents rural and metropolitan Latin America in its many manifestations. Indians film themselves (e.g. the Kayapo Indians in Brazil and the Nambiquara Indians of the Amazon Basin). Women relate their stories across generations of women (e.g. Suzana Amaral's *A hora da estrela/The Hour of the Star*, 1985). And gays get a very rare voice (e.g. Jaime Humberto Hermosillo's *Doña Herlinda y su hijo/Dona Herlinda and Her Son*, 1986). This fragmentation can be read (and probably should) as a positive sign and not as one of miserabilism. In other words, it can be read as if the national consciousness that was required of the earlier militant cinema of the 1960s is now surpassed and is no longer a necessary driving force of contemporary Latin American cinemas.

Currently in the new millennium there has been something of a renaissance of Latin American cinemas – particularly where Argentina, Brazil and Mexico are concerned – but not, regrettably, for Cuban cinema, which is only managing to produce a film every two to three years (*Memories of Overdevelopment*, Miguel Coyula, 2010, is the most recent international release, and has been well received in Film Festivals). As we shall see, different financing and structural practices have helped bring about this new wave of production, but, interestingly, there is a common transnational thread in that, often, these films seek out the truth about their nations' troubled past, or expose, unwaveringly, the difficult social conditions experienced by these nations' poorest inhabitants.

Argentina's official film school, INCAA, has set up a subsidy plan to foster new talent – it has some 10,000 film students and film production is subsidized by a 10 per cent levy on cinema tickets and video sales. New talent includes Lucrecia Martel (*Nina santa/The Holy Girl*, 2004), Fabián Bielinsky (*Nine Queens*, 2001), Leonardo di Cesare (*Buena vida Delivery*, 2004), Juan José Campanella (*Luna de Avallaneda*, 2004) and Alejo Daube (*Uno de dos/One or the Other*, 2003). The New Argentine Cinema, that emerged in 1999 in the wake of the economic crisis, and which is formed of this new generation of filmmakers, addresses the nation's politico-economic issues and their impact on ordinary people's lives (e.g. Mario Santos' collective production *Mala época/Bad Times*, 1998; Fabián Bielinsky's *Nine Queens*, 2001; Ariel Rotter's *Sólo por hoy/Only for Today*, 2001; Israel Caetano's *Un oso roso/Red Bear*, 2002; Alejo Daube's *Uno de dos/One or the Other*, 2003; Martin Rejtman's *Los guantes mágicos/Magic Gloves*, 2003). The corrupt past of the 1970s dictatorship also comes under scrutiny in Juan José Campanella's Oscar-winning *El secreto de sus ojos/The Secret in Their Eyes* (2010). Ironically, given that Argentina has suffered decades of economic malaise, and that it is still caught in a somewhat volatile political situation and besieged by terrible social problems, nonetheless, its film industry has to count as one of the successful ones in today's world (producing around 120 to 150 films per year, a quarter of which are made by Argentinian filmmakers). Since 2005, there has been space for more personal, quite dark existential films (see *El Aura/The Aura*, Bielinsky, 2005; *La mujer sin cabeza/The Headless Woman*, Martel, 2008; *Leonera/The Lioness' Den*, Pablo Trapero, 2008). Furthermore, this New Argentinian Cinema continues to thrive at home and on the international festival scene. Still more new filmmakers join this loosely formed group of cineastes (e.g. Milagros Mumenthaler, Laura Citarella, Santiago Mitre, Pablo Giorgelli, Gustavo Taretto and Hermes Paralluelo). (For a really useful article on this latest collective of filmmakers see Mar Diestro-Dópido's 'The New Argentine Cinema', http://www.bfi.org.uk/news-opinion/sight-sound-magazine/comment/festivals/lff-2011-new-new-argentine-cinema.)

Brazil is experiencing a revival, not seen since the early 1980s, thanks it could be argued to the enormous success of Walter Salles' *Central Station* (see above) – but also thanks to the introduction in the early 1990s, by the state, of incentive laws (the so-called *retomada*, a funding of films from companies in exchange for tax relief). Salles' success can be singled out as a turning point because it brought in its wake serious international co-funding which made possible, amongst others, two further Salles international hits, *Behind the Sun* (Brazil/ Switzerland/France: 2001) – a tale of bloody feuding between two neighbouring sugar-cane growing families – and *The Motorcycle Diaries* (UK/USA/France: 2004) – the memoirs of the Argentinian Che Guevarra's early travels through the poverty-ridden Western nations of Latin America (Chile, Peru and on to Venezuela). In all three of these films, although the initial impulse is the quest for identity, the personal quickly becomes the political and in each case the dreadful conditions of labour (be it rural, metropolitan, farming or mining) are quickly exposed for the unjust practices that they are. In a slightly different way, the enormously successful *Cidade de Deus/City of God* (2002), by the equally socially conscious younger generation of Brazilian filmmakers Fernando Meirelles and Katia Lund, also exposes the scandalous poverty of those living in shanty-towns. In their quasi-documentary about the street gangs of the desperately poor youth class, they not only portray the terrible brutality of this life, they also propose a way out of the trap through their central character Rocket who chooses the camera over the gun. Incidentally, this rescue culture was also exemplified by the way the young actors were selected. None of them were actors, but were auditioned from the shanty-towns and trained up. Life in the *favelas* continues to be a recurrent theme (*Cidade dos Homens/City of Men*, Paulo Morelli, 2007; *Elite da Tropa/ The Elite Squad*, José Padilha, 2007). More directly political films addressing the former years of dictatorship is an ongoing thematic: *O Que É Isso, Companheiro?/Four Days in September* (Bruno Barreto, 1997) being an early example; as indeed are films that deal with social issues – Sérgio Bianchi being a leader where this trend is concerned (see, for example, *Cronicamente Inviável/Chronically Unfeasible*, 2000; *Quanto Vale ou É por Quilo?/What Is It Worth?*, 2005).

Nor should veteran Hector Babenco (1946–2016) be forgotten in this consideration of Brazil's revival. A filmmaker who has been at the hard edge of social and political commentary since the late 1970s (see his *Pixote*, 1981, which depicts the plight of Brazil's abandoned street children, or *Kiss of the Spiderwoman*, 1984, about the brutal repression of revolutionaries and gays). His film *Carandiru* (2004) recounts the lives of several of the prison inmates before the entire community (all 111 of them) was brutally massacred by the riot-police. His last film, *Meu amigo hindu/My Hindu Friend* (2016), presciently recounts the story of a film director dying of cancer.

Finally, *Mexico*. Despite recurring hardship and a decline in state funding since the notoriously corrupt Institutional Revolutionary Parry (PRI) seventy-year rule came to an end in 2000, Mexican cinema (albeit small at ten to seventeen films or so per year) is doing extremely well nationally and internationally. While in power (2000-12), the new rightist government (National Action Party, PAN) has cut funding to the film institute IMCINE with the effect of a reduced investment in production, but private money was found to produce a small but vibrant cinema. This cinema has become known as the New Mexican Cinema (spanning from the 1990s to the present). The first internationally acclaimed film from this new era of cinema was Alfonso Arau's *Como agua para chocolate/Like Water for Chocolate* (1992), a magic–realist film about passion and repression set against the background of the Mexican Revolution. *Amores perros/Love's a Bitch*, González Iñárritu (2000), *Y tu mamá también/And Your Mother Too*, Alfonso Cuarón (2002), *El crimen de padre Amaro/The Crime of Father Amaro*, Carlos Carrera (2002), *El laberinto del fauno/Pan's Labyrinth*, Guillermo del Toro (2006) have all been huge box-office hits in Mexico before making it big internationally. In general terms, this cinema is not the cinema of denunciation of the 1980s and 1990s which exposed poverty and exploitation among the under-classes. In this context see, for example, *Los motivos de luz/Light Motives*, Felipe Gonzales, 1985 and *La ley de Herodes/Herod's Law*, Luis Estrada, 1999 (this latter a particularly hard-hitting film exposing the corruption practices of the PRI). Overall, this new cinema is more based in humour, often the middle classes are the focus. This is not to say that that these films are without their political edge, however. *El laberinto del fauno* is a hard-hitting dark fantasy film that combines a sinister fairy-tale ambience with a real-time period in post-civil war Spain to reveal the grim brutalities of war (early summer 1944, with Franco's falangists hunting down the Spanish maquis/resistors) – it is hard not to read, in this film, an indictment of fascism (wherever it rears its ugly head). Many of the ambient images in *Y tu mamá también* (a road movie about identity, that of the characters as much as about the country itself) present us with the oppression of the less fortunate. The gender politics of this film are also quite challenging in that the female character exposes the homo-eroticism latent in Mexican machismo. *Amores perros* for its part indirectly criticizes the lack of freedom of expression under the former ruling party, the PRI, and makes plain the legacy of its long rule. It also reveals a city (Mexico city) where the huge chasm between rich and poor is ever growing and crime, as a means of survival, is rife. Such was the worldwide success of these three films that their filmmakers have moved to Hollywood and now direct on an international scale (i.e. Cuarón, *Harry Potter and the Prisoner of Azkaban*, 2001, *Children of Men*, 2006, and *Gravity*, 2013; Del Toro, *Hellboy II: The Golden Army*, 2008; Iñárritu, *Babel*, 2006). But that has not led to a drain on indigenous talent, of which there appears to be a continuous supply; and Iñárritu returned home to shoot *Biutiful* (2010). Newly emerging talent (coming through film school, some with a documentary training) includes Enrique Begné, Ernesto Contreras, Patricia Riggen (who has now moved to the USA), Juan Carlos Rulfo.

Since the return, in 2012, of the PRI to power, albeit not with a legislative majority, government incentives, educational centres and private investment have seen Mexican film production on the rise again. Thanks to financial incentives for foreign film companies, Mexico has produced 130 films (foreign and indigenous; and including the following categories: animation, made for television, documentary and feature), a huge number given that their own indigenous product of feature films stands at around 45 films post-2012 (i.e. about ten per year). Independent cinema production is making itself visible again. See, for example, *Post Tenebras Lux/Light after Darkness*, Carlos Reygadas and 2010, *Heli*, Amat Escalante, 2013 (both winners at Cannes Film Festival). The Mexican film industry is conscious also of its neighbouring USA ready-made market of Hispanic audiences which it can target with its commercial products (via its US-based Pantelion distribution company). Independent filmmakers, for their part, have a number of independent film production companies to foster their work. Two stand-out companies worth mentioning are Jaime Romandía's Mantarray Films (which produced Reygadas and Escalante's prize-winning films, above) and Canana Films (with an impressive list of twenty films produced since 2006), formed by the Mexican actors Gael García Berna, Pablo Cruz, Diego Luna, Elena Fortes.

For further reading see Barnard and Rist, 1996; Burton, 1986; Burton-Carjaval, 1996; Chanan, 1985, 1996, 2004; Elena and Lopez, 2004; Hart, 2004; Hernandez-Rodriguez, 2010; Johnson and Stam, 1982; King, 1990; Mora, 2006; Noble, 2004; Page, 2009; Pick, 1993; Shaw and Dennison, 2007; Shohat and Stam, 1994; Wood, 2006. See also *Screen* special issue on Latin American cinema, 38: 4, 1997.

Middle Eastern cinemas

Status: all Middle Eastern countries are listed as developing economies except Palestine (which has no listing at all), Turkey which is listed as an emerging economy, and Israel which is an advanced economy.

Iranian, Iraqi, Israeli, Kuwait, Lebanese, Palestinian, Sudanese, Syrian and Turkish cinemas come under this rather loose denomination. Let us begin with the Eastern Arab states, leaving aside Palestine for the moment. Syria, the Lebanon, Kuwait, the Sudan and Iraq have yet to produce a national cinema that competes with Egypt or the Maghreb. Some countries (Syria, Lebanon and Iraq) established governing bodies called the General Organization for Cinema (GOC) whose purpose it is to implement policies for filmmaking (quotas and the fostering of new filmmaking talent). In this context of the Eastern Arab states, only Syria and Lebanon have managed to produce a regular if small amount of films per year; and so I'll address these two cinemas briefly here.

Syrian cinema

In 2012, when updating the fourth edition of this book, I wrote that it was unlikely, given the climate in Syria of civil war (2011 and ongoing), that any film other than mini-documentaries filmed on mobile or satellite phones and then posted on YouTube (relayed from Beirut) could reflect what was occurring (the internet was, and still is, completely under government control, although activists are continuing to find ways to bypass this censorship). At the time of going to press with this fifth edition (2016), the situation in Syria, as we all know, has worsened (half a million dead, five million refugees). Since 2012, somehow, two feature films have emerged. The first, Najdat Anzour's *King of the Sands* (2012/13) was screened in the Syrian Opera House, Damascus (and possibly in Latakia and Tartous). As for the second film, *Ladder to Damascus* (Mohamed Malas, 2013), I have been unable to determine if it has been screened within Syria (certainly it was screened in Qatar and Lebanon and at the 2013 Toronto Film Festival). Anzour has made his reputation as a film and television filmmaker of historical epics, and his *King of the Sands* follows this tradition in that it is a biopic of Ibn Saud, the founder of present-day Saudi-Arabia. Set in the 1920s to 1930s, it is an exemplary exposition of a leader's single-minded ruthlessness to establish a nation in his name. The Royal House of Saudi have protested against the film; but the President of Syria, Bashar Al-Assad, not at all. One might think a lack of self-reflexivity is at work here until one learns that Anzour supports the current President and his regime. As for Malas, although his films have consistently been banned in Syria, he is nonetheless considered as one of Syria's first **auteur** filmmakers. *Ladder to Damascus* is a love story set against the beginnings of the tumultuous events in Syria.

Three full-length documentaries, all relating to this terrible civil war, have also managed to be made and screened outside of Syria: Talal Derki's *Return to Homs* (2013); Ossama Mohammed and Wiam Simav Bedirxan's *Eau argentée, Syrie auto-portrait/Silver Water, Syria Self-Portrait* (2014); and the French war correspondents Sophie Nivelle-Cardinale and Etienne Huver's *Disparus, la guerre invisible de Syrie/The Disappeared: The Invisible Syrian War* (2015). Derki's film documents the struggles of daily life in the bombed-out city of Homs; Mohammed and Bedirxan's film combines eye-witnesses accounts and edited phone-footage shot during the siege of Homs; testimonies from survivors or exiled Syrians is at the heart of Nivelle-Cardinale and Huver's film about the 'disappeared' civilians who have been arrested, tortured and killed (Nivelle-Cardinale also made *Au coeur de la bataille d'Alep/In the Heart of the Battle of Aleppo*, 2013). Finally, the short animation film *Raqqa: An Inside Story* (Abu Ibrahim al-Raqqawi – a pseudonym, 2015) on the destruction of Raqqa first by Assad then by ISIS makes for compelling viewing on the internet.

Before these years of civil war and destruction, Syria had a film industry of sorts which I shall briefly consider here. Syria's film production has always been small in terms of feature films (on average two to three films per year), and virtually all films deal with the various conflicts surrounding the nation, be it the successive military coups Syria experienced in the 1950s (*Dreams of a City*, Mohamed Malas, 1984), or the Arab–Israeli conflict (*The Night*, Malas, 1992; *Two Moons and an Olive*, Abdellatif Abdelhamid, 2001). Given the difficulties between Syria and Palestine, it is worth mentioning the thoughtful film by Syrian filmmaker Raymond Bustros, *Refuge* (1997), which is about the 1948 to 1949 deportation of Palestinians to Syria after the formation of Israel. Mention must also be made of Malas' courageous film, *Passion* (2005), which is very critical of the patriarchal oppression of women in traditional Islamic society (it is banned in Syria).

Rather than feature films, what has dominated in terms of production since the 1960s, when Syria's GOC took control, are documentaries (eight to twelve annually). Some are state-financed, others privately funded. The former promote the government's advances in health, agriculture and transportation – see Omar Amiralay's 1970 *Film Essay on the Euphrates*, which sings the praises of the government's dam-building programme – an uncritical position Amiralay was quick to renounce. Very soon after this film, Amiralay began a series of documentaries exposing the humiliating existence of the dispossessed (*Everyday Life in a Syrian Village*, 1974) and has since become the undisputed pioneer of contemporary Syrian documentary. Those documentaries that are privately funded are counter-ideological (see, for example, Joude Gorani's *Before Vanishing*, 2005, about the pollution of Damascus' Barada river).

The Lebanese film industry, until civil war (1975–91) broke out in Lebanon and suffered the Israeli raids and Syrian occupation, produced twenty to twenty-five films per year. Under strict censorship, production was resumed in the late 1980s with about ten films per year. But, for the most part, Lebanese cinema is a diasporic one with filmmakers in exile making documentary–fiction films that treat the war-torn Beirut they have left behind or to which they return to film at great personal risk. Maroun Baghdadi (killed in Beirut in 1993) made *Hors la vie/Out of Life* (1990, a French-Lebanese co-production). Shooting in extremely dangerous conditions, Heiny Srour took seven years to make her *Layla and the Wolves* (1984), a film about the participation of Palestinian women in the fight for independence. In the 1990s, a younger generation of Lebanese filmmakers emerged and made films on the same nation-shattering topic (see, for example, Samir Habshi, *Vortex*, 1992; Jean-Claude Kodsi, *Histoire d'un retour/Story of a Return*, 1994; Layla Assaf, *The Gang of Freedom*, 1994). This concern is one that refuses to go away as the films of the late 1990s to the present (the late 2010s) testify. Ziad Doueiri's *West Beirut* (1998) is set in 1975 and narrates the Lebanese civil war as experienced by three teenage Muslims as they move around in the war-torn city. Set in the opening days of the civil war, *The Stray Bullet* (Georges Hachem, 2010) mixes the personal with the political as the young woman Noha is forced to choose between love and her family's wishes. So too with Habshi's *Beyrouth, ville ouverte/Beirut, Open City* (2007), showing the shortcomings of post-independence. The personal becomes the starting point of the political in Eliane Raheb's *So Near Yet So Far* (2001) in which the killing of a young child leads to an investigation of the effects of the Palestinian cause on Arab peoples. The effects of the civil war are central to Raheb's *Nuits sans sommeil/Sleepless Nights* (2011). The loss of direction of the post-war generation is the central thrust of Ghassan Salhab's sexually daring *Terra Incognita* (2002) with its focus on the young people of Beirut – a generation suspended in time, hanging in the present not daring to look to the past or to the uncertain future. The impact of this extended civil war (lasting fifteen years) on Beirut's blue-collar workers is at the heart of Simon el Habre's *Gate No. 5* (2012). Less political in nature, the role of women in a number of guises is addressed in Nadine Labaki's two films: *Caramel* (2007), a comedy in which five women exchange their everyday problems (forbidden love, repressed sexuality, lesbianism, tradition, ageing); in *Where Do We Go*

Now? (2011), a fantasy film, women in a remote Lebanese village endeavour by all means fair and foul to maintain peace between the Christian and Muslim residents. The darker side of Islamic (or pre-Islamic) tradition in the form of 'honour killing' is the subject of Kodsi's film, *A Man of Honor* (2012), in which he shows how the supremacy of the community squashes the rights of the individual. Since 2012 (with fourteen film releases), there has been a severe decline in production with only ten or so films being released between 2013 and 2016. And these are either romantic comedies, adventure or action films. Not much in the way of the politically conscious work of before, therefore. Those voices have moved over to making shorts it seems (e.g. *Submarine*, Mounia Akl, 2016). Although Vatche Boulghourjian's full feature *Tramontane* (2016) remains a rare exception to this trend with its story of a blind man in search of his real identity (a metaphor for a nation incapable of relating to its history); and Salhab's *La Vallée/The Valley* (2016) which also asks questions about the Lebanon of today.

Economic conditions, civil strife or political censorship make it difficult for any of the Eastern Arab states to boast of a national cinema (even if their films regularly get accepted for major Film Festivals). It is the case, however, that since 2000, there has been a rise in production in terms of Lebanese films (fifty-five films in the 2000s; and in the period 2010 to 2016, thirty-eight films have been released). About two-thirds are feature films, with shorts and documentaries sharing the other one-third pretty evenly. On the whole, though, it is much more the case of individual filmmakers making a breakthrough or having to leave and work in other countries, migrating to other Arab or Middle Eastern countries or to the West. Where national film products are concerned, it is almost impossible to recover costs of a film from indigenous audiences, so filmmakers are obliged to turn to other solutions: either making shorts or documentaries or seeking out international co-productions.

For further reading on Middle East cinemas see Dönmez-Colin, 2007; Khatib, 2006, 2008 (on Lebanese cinema).

Palestinian cinema

If it is hard to talk about the above nations as having a film industry, there is even greater difficulty in talking about a Palestinian cinema – at least since 1948, when Palestine became an occupied territory. Palestine has in fact always been an occupied country. The Jews believe that it is their promised land and that they have the right to live there, but so too do the Palestinian Arabs. The present occupation of the territory came about, in 1947, when the then Palestine was divided into a Jewish state (which officially became Israel in 1948) and an Arab state that was shared between Egypt (the Gaza strip) and Jordan (the West Bank). Both these Arab territories were reclaimed by Israel in the Six-Day War of 1967. And, since then, the territories have been continuously contested by Israelis and Arabs, including the Palestinian Arabs who quite clearly feel totally dispossessed. Until 2012, the Palestinian Arabs remained without an official state of their own, even though they possessed a national identity and lived in two areas of what were called the Palestinian Territories (the West Bank, in a walled-off area, and the Gaza Strip). According to Shohat and Stam's categories (see above), film products made by Palestinian Arabs could arguably be considered as Fourth World cinema – for they are certainly diasporic. Since becoming a state, however, things have not greatly improved (see below).

First, some background. The historic area of Palestine was a popular 'site' for early cinematographers. During the late 1890s to early 1900s, the Lumière brothers and Edison made travelogue-documentary films of Jerusalem and the 'Holy Land'. However, *Palestinian cinema* itself emerged out of the resistance that was established after the defeat of the Six-Day War in 1967, when Egypt, Syria and Jordan were defeated by the Israelis. Most of its cinema is diasporic, created outside of 'Palestine' by Palestinian exiles (in Iraq, Jordan and Lebanon). A small group of filmmakers founded a resistance film unit in Jordan that was directly annexed to the al-Fatah/PLO movement (led by Yasser Arafat). After the Black September Massacre of 1971 (the Jordanian massacre of Palestinian refugees and freedom-fighters), the unit moved to Beirut (in Lebanon). Subsequent to Israel's invasion of Beirut, in 1982, this unit, as well as other Palestinian filmmakers based in that city, left and settled in Tunis (Tunisia). A major trend in Palestinian cinema is the documentary one (for obvious reasons of economy) and in this context, mention must be made of May Masri, the first Palestinian woman to make films (documentaries) co-directed with the Lebanese filmmaker Jean Chamoun. This documentary trend is one which sits well both with the Palestinian need to make a political cinema and with the Palestinian oral tradition.

A major Palestinian filmmaker is Michel Khleifi, an Israel–Palestinian citizen who has lived in Belgium since the mid-1970s. His feature films and documentaries are strongly politicized and address – among other issues – the lack of female emancipation within Palestinian political culture and Palestinian dispossession in the face of the Israelis (see his documentary *Al Dhikrayat al Kasibah (al-Djakira alkhisba)/Fertile Memories,*

1980). Similarly, he addresses the double occupation experienced by Palestinian women who suffer oppression from both their own patriarchal society and the Israeli occupation (*Urs fil Jalil/Marriage in Galilee*, 1987). In *Canticle of the Stones* (1990), two Palestinian lovers are parted, in the 1960s, when the man resists Israeli occupation. They come together eighteen years later in Palestine only to observe how much worse things have become. Khleifi's *Tale of the Three Jewels* (1995) mixes documentary style with fiction: against the backdrop of the Palestinian–Israeli conflict, a young man seeks the three missing jewels that will permit him to win the love of the young woman of his dreams.

In a similar vein, Rachid Masharawi mixes documentary and allegory in his film about Palestinian refugees packed into Gaza refugee camps (*Curfew*, 1993, *Haifa*, 1995). Elia Suleiman's two films of the 1990s (*Homage by Assassination*, 1990, and *Chronicle of a Disappearance*, 1996) are remarkable reflections on the psychological effects of dispossession and occupation – themes which he has pursued in his black humour film *Divine Intervention* (2002), a not thinly veiled reaction to the ruins in which the Oslo agreements have fallen. Other recent occupation films include *Ranu's Wedding* (Hany Abu-Assad, 2000) where life in Jerusalem under Israeli occupation makes the task of trying to arrange her wedding a virtual impossibility for a beleaguered Ranu. Hanna Elias' *The Olive Harvest* (2003) tells the tale of two brothers in love with the same woman set against the backdrop of tensions between Palestinian farmers and Israeli settlers.

Unsurprisingly, in this cinema of Palestine, what dominates is the brutality of military occupation and its scarring effects on the Palestinian psyche. Intriguingly, in 2006, there was a surge in documentary films dealing with many of the issues Palestinians confront on an everyday basis. *The Color of Olives* (Carolina Rivas, 2006) records the impact on a Palestinian family of the building of the Wall separating Israel from the West Bank; life in a refugee camp is at the core of *First Picture* (Akram Al-Ashqar, 2006); *The Iron Wall* (Mohamed Al-Atar, 2006) focuses on the Israeli settlements in the West Bank and their effects on the peace process. In terms of fiction film, the most remarkable film in recent years – because of the way in which it speaks to the desperation of a disenfranchised nation – has to be *Paradise Now* (Hany Abu-Assad, 2005) in which two Palestinians plan a suicide bombing attack on Tel Aviv.

I had hoped that by the time of updating this book to its fifth edition (in late 2016) things would be different for Palestine: that the peace process would have moved forward. It hasn't really. The Israeli government and army are in part responsible for the continued conflict; but so too is the division within Palestine itself of its political groupings, Hamas and Fatah. Even though, in 1993, the Oslo Accords allowed for Palestinian administrative institutions within the Palestinian states, nonetheless, the two factions (Hamas and Fatah) were unable to unite and, instead, fought over who should govern. As a result of the inter-Palestinian conflict (which came to an end of sorts in 2006), Hamas got to rule over the Gaza Strip and Fatah the West Bank. Since 2012, Palestine has been recognized as a sovereign state and is ruled by a Unity Government (supposedly a consensual government between Hamas and Fatah, but which continues to be a conflict situation). Palestinian cinema has suffered as a consequence; particularly in the Gaza Strip because of Hamas' strict Islamic rules. But even the West Bank is suffering. In 2004, the Goethe and French Institutes built a Cultural Centre in Ramallah specifically to host the newly inaugurated Ramallah International Festival in July 2004. While the centre still exists and continues in its purpose to promote a space for Palestinian culture, nonetheless, no subsequent festival has been held. In the period 2004 to 2016, approximately seventeen films have been made (mostly outside of Palestine) and released in some venue (if not in Palestine then in international film festivals or neighbouring countries sympathetic to Palestine's cause). There are six recent releases I'd like to mention, for the diversity of their approach to the one main problem: a country riven by political instability. Annemarie Jacir's *When I First Saw You* (2012) about the Palestine refugee crisis in 1967 when tens of thousands of Palestinians fled to Jordan; Masharawi's *Palestine Stereo* (2013) a subtle satire about the life of a wedding singer and his brother living in the war zone and political minefield that is Palestine today; Najwa Najjar's *Eyes of a Thief* (2014), set in 2011, shows what happens to ordinary people as the occupation of the Palestinian territories continues; Mai Nasri's *3000 Nights* (2015) tells the story of a Palestinian woman falsely accused of terrorism and held in an Israeli jail where she gives birth to her son and is subject to all sorts of threats (both from the Israeli captors and some of the other Palestinian inmates who want to revolt); Hany Abu-Assad's *The Idol* (2015), perhaps the only upbeat optimistic film of this group, relates the (true) story of a wedding singer who escapes to Egypt from a refugee camp in Gaza and goes on to win the 2013 Arab Idol competition; and, finally, the comic satire by the Nasser brothers *Dégradé/Degraded* (2015); set in a hair salon, women gripe about the political situation when all of a sudden a lion appears in the square outside which sparks a violent conflict between the ruling government, Hamas, who want the lion back, and a local influential family who 'took' the lion from the local zoo funded by Hamas.

For further reading see Dabashi, 2006; Gertz and Khleifi, 2008.

Israeli cinema

The sad predicament in which Palestine finds itself is one that Elia Suleiman qualifies (speaking in an interview about his film *Divine Intervention*, 2002) as 'the paralysis that comes from the conscious or unconscious acknowledgment that the dominant force that rules over you can't be shaken' (quoted in *Journal of Palestinian Studies*, 2003: 70). He was referring to Israel of course, as a nation whose force totally crushes Palestinians – and it is the desperation felt by this powerlessness that much of Palestine's cinema reveals. Israeli cinema, for its part, continuously articulates two recurrent themes: siege mentality and entrapment. But, while it is an advanced economy (which makes it difficult to justify its inclusion in this overview), because much of its cinema (though obviously not all) can be usefully read as being in some kind of dialogue with Palestinian cinema, it feels necessary to make space, here, for a brief discussion of it.

Since 1948, Israeli cinema is, in many cases, nationalist and full of ethnic rhetoric vaunting its superiority over Arab nationalists (see Eli Cohen's *Ricochets*, 1986), even though, during the 1980s, Israeli cinema produced a different representation of the Israeli–Arab conflict, one which was sympathetic to and acknowledged a Palestinian entity. These films which gave 'progressive images of the conflict' (Shohat, 1989: 240) showed the Palestinians as victim. These films, made by Israeli filmmakers, were known as the Palestinian Wave films. They were not liked by the Israeli Right (who labelled them Leftist), nor were they appreciated by the Palestinians (who viewed them with suspicion). For the most part, these Palestinian Wave films sought to represent the conflict and the attempt to transcend it through a love affair between a mixed couple – mostly an Israeli woman and Palestinian man (see *Hamsin*, Daniel Wachsman, 1982, although *A Very Narrow Bridge*, Nissim Dayan, 1985, controversially reverses the order).

Conversely, in the predominantly heroic–nationalist films, gender and sexuality are very differently represented. Often, the female body is the site upon which many of the nationalist ideals get played out. Thus, women are represented as persons who, unlike their Arab counterparts, have egalitarian status and wield weapons and work the land. The Israeli woman sacrifices herself for the nation, bears arms and suffers unconditionally for her supposed privilege of equality. The reality is of course more complex. Many different Jews make up the Israeli state, some of whom have greater equal status than others. There are European/Ashkenazi Jews and Oriental/Arab Jews. The Oriental Jews are either Palestinian Jews or Sephardi-Mizrahi Jews. These Jews are considered ethnically inferior to the European Jew. What is noteworthy (as Shohat and Stam point out, 1994: 315) is that Israel's 'conflictual syncretisms' have given birth to an indigenous genre, the Bourekas genre (which takes the form of either a comedy or melodrama), in which the tensions between the two ethnic Jewish groupings are played out and in which the woman frequently figures as the Sephardi Jew.

Outside of Israel, Amos Gitaï is arguably one of the better-known filmmakers. His films are politically courageous, often perceived as didactic and, thereby, controversial (several of his documentary films have been banned from Israeli television). His early work consisted of documentaries on the Israeli–Palestinian conflict; he then went to France, in the 1980s, to begin his career in fiction films, returning to Israel, in 1993, where he has made a trilogy of films, each one based in separate Israeli cities and in separate orthodoxies. Thus, *Devarin/Things* (1995) is set in Tel Aviv amongst the first generation of Israelis to be born in their new state. He then made *Yom Yom/Day after Day* (1998) where he investigates an Arab–Jewish marriage against the backdrop of Haifa. In *Kadosh/Sacred* (1999) it is Jerusalem that he portrays and the structures of orthodox Jewish life as they affect the marriage between two Hasidic Jews.

The psychology of siege and the claustrophobic sense of confinement are key elements of Israeli films of the new millennium. In particular, several 'anti-war' films articulate the horrors of war and the traumas experienced by the soldiers who carry out the orders of warmongers. Gitaï's *Kippur* (2000) – which revisits the Yom Kippur War of 1973 – has at its core the Israeli mentality of siege and entrapment. A rescue unit is detailed to airlift dead and wounded soldiers after their arrogant officer has led them into a heavy bombardment. In the end, all but one of his troops perishes as the rescue unit struggles through the mud, under fire, trying in vain to get these men onto the helicopter. Scenes shot in the cockpit add to the feeling of claustrophobia: men squeezed in together, breathing is tough. The same theme is present in Samuel Maoz's *Lebanon* (2009). Shot entirely from within the tank's hull, with views to the outside combat area through the driver's hatch and the gun turret's optical periscope, the four-men crew (and subsequent prisoner) sweat in this space of confinement and claustrophobia as they attempt to follow orders to search and destroy any enemy in a bombed-out town somewhere in Lebanon. The Lebanese war of 1982 is also the subject of Ari Folman's animated docu-fiction/ reconstruction film *Waltz with Bashir* (2008), which depicts the halluci-nated half-memories of an Israeli soldier (Folman's) of the Sabra and Shatila massacre. His troops let off flares to illuminate the Palestinian refugee camp, thus allowing the subsequent carnage perpetrated by the Lebanese Christian phalange militia. In the end, he acknowledges he is as guilty of the massacre as those who carried it out.

Also in the new millennium, the earlier tradition of the 1990s anti-occupation documentaries (e.g. Eyal Sivan, *Izkor: Slaves of Memory*, 1991; David Benchetrit, *Through the Veil of Exile*, 1992) is perpetuated in the work and campaigning of several Israeli filmmakers. The Israeli-Arab filmmaker Mohamed Barki's *Jenin, Jenin* (2002) is about the Israeli armed invasion and subsequent purported massacre of Palestinian civilians in Jenin. It was banned from screening in Israel on the basis that it was libellous, a ruling subsequently overturned. See also the Israeli Sivan and Palestinian Khleifi's collaborative documentary *Route 181, Fragments of a Journey in Palestine-Israel* (2003). Funded by European money, the film records the effects of the borders on those that live close by them and examines the ideological intention behind them. It was banned from a screening in France, one of the funding countries. In 2000, the Israeli filmmaker-producer Osnat Trabelsi initiated the first International Human Rights Film Festival in Israel/ Palestine. She founded Trabelsi Productions with the specific remit of promoting documentaries that are politically engaged with the injustices being perpetrated against the Palestinians (e.g. Danniel Danniel and Julian Mer-Khamis' *Arna's Children*, 2004; Eyal Sivan's *Jaffa, The Orange's Clockwork*, 2010).

For further reading see Shohat, 1989, 2010; Kronish, 1996; Loshitzky, 2001; Tolman and Peleg, 2011; Yosef, 2011.

Turkish cinema

Turkey was the first country amongst these Middle Eastern nations to produce an indigenous cinema, primarily in the form of documentaries (e.g. the 1914 documentary *The Demolition of the Russian Monument at St Stephen*). The early period of feature film production did not get underway until the 1920s. A small number of films were made and (like Indian and Chinese cinemas) the main source of reference was the Turkish theatre. During this first period of Turkish cinema, which lasted through until 1940, there was only one production company (Ipek) and one filmmaker Mushim Ertugrul who worked in close association with the Municipal Theatre in Istanbul. This period was also one in which Turkey was very orientated towards the West; thus, Western film styles strongly influenced what few products were made (particularly French and German vaudevilles and melodramas). The second period, that of the 1940s, saw the establishing of a second production company (Ha-Ka Film) which broke the previous monopoly and made it possible for new talent to emerge and different types of films to be made that had more in common with Turkish national culture. The beginning of the boom years coincided with the coming of a multi-party system, in 1950. By the late 1950s, production had risen to a range of 150 to 200 films per year (on a par therefore with, or even exceeding, France's output). Generic types were quite broad: melodramas, rural dramas and city-based dramas, action films and urban comedies. This decade also saw the birth of the star system and the establishing of a mainstream popular film industry: Yesilçam (Turkey's Hollywood). Yesilçam developed a particular visual style, highly saturated colour and minimal camera movement, and produced fairly stereotypical melodramas (of redemption and sacrifice).

The military coup of 1960 changed the direction of Turkish cinema and it veered towards a more inward-looking (as opposed to Western-looking) cinema that would draw on Turkish visual culture and tradition in an effort to establish a national cinema. An indication of the difficulties involved in producing a national cinema is exemplified by the presence, during the 1960s, of two completely opposing national film movements. The first movement was based on the belief that Turkish national cinema had to address the fundamental conflict, embodied by the nation itself, between modern Western values and Islamic traditional values. The second was based on Islamic ideology only.

By the late 1960s to early 1970s, repression under military rule and the effects of a sustained civil war led to a peculiar type of censorship whereby semi-pornographic films were not banned, but the social–realist films of committed nationalist filmmakers were. A major victim of this repression was Yilmaz Güney who, after years in prison, spent the last few years of his short life in exile (in France). When in prison, he wrote scripts that were produced. He scripted *Yol/The Way*, made in 1982 by Serif Gören, which won the Palme d'Or at Cannes in 1983. Güney's films of the early 1970s (e.g. *The Hope*, 1970; *The Elegy*, *The Sorrow*, both 1971), based as they were in themes of rural poverty and oppression, did not endear him to the authorities but they set a trend in Turkish cinema which became known as the New Turkish Cinema, an art cinema which still perdures today (see below).

During the 1970s, which was a period of stiff competition on the exhibition front (against Hollywood majors primarily), production soared to an average of almost 300 films per year. This hugely inflated number is mostly due to the inclusion of uncensored soft-porn (and even hard-core porn) movies which made up half the total number of films, and the 'cheapie' karate films being made at the time. The more traditional arabesque (musical) genre also figures, but in a fairly minor way when compared to the porn movies. The effect, however, was a diminution of audience figures which led to a crisis, in the 1980s, and the eventual collapse of Yesilçam. Production slumped to seventy films per year, until 1986, when the Ministry of Culture intervened to protect Turkish cinema from competition (both from television and the American majors). The result was a rise in production – not to former levels but to an average of 185 films per year. This is a remarkable achievement if one considers that the 1980s was a difficult period of censorship thanks to the new military regime which came in on the back of the 1980 military coup. But, the post-coup Republic/military dictatorship endorsed a mixed culture of economic liberalism and apoliticization of its citizens (thus porn films continued to be made, but political cinema was censored).

The cinema of the late 1980s and through the 1990s is one that draws once more on Turkish tradition and saw a resurgence of the type of socio-realist national cinema first advocated in the 1960s (one that addresses the tensions inherent in Turkish society and which also reflects Turkish narrative traditions). And it is noteworthy, in this context, that the prime mover behind the nationalist cinema of the 1960s, Halit Refig, was back on the scene making films (*The Lady*, 1988, *Two Strangers*, 1990). Production decreased greatly in the early 1990s (to around four films per year) due to competition for financing and the effects of television. Some 90 per cent of the cinema market was dominated by American products. And television's rapacious demand for film products meant that channels went for cheap imports rather than for the more expensive indigenous product. On a more positive note, however, the state put in place a system of aid which meant that, henceforth, Turkey could access Euro-Images for assistance on the production and distribution side of the industry. And, by the mid-1990s, Turkish cinema was on the resurgence again (production rising to some forty films per year by the new millennium). Furthermore, the 1990s witnessed the emergence of a new generation of filmmakers, including a very healthy proportion of women directors (Mahinur Ergun,

Canan Gerede, Tomris Giritlioglu, Furuzan, Biket Ilhan, Hanan Ipekçi Isil Özgentürk, Yesim Ustaoglu and Seçkin Yasar).

Several factors have combined to bring about a revival in Turkish popular cinema since the mid-1990s, culminating in the spectacular success of several recent films: *G.O.R.A.* (Ömar Faruk Sorak, 2004), a science-fiction comedy film, garnering an audience of four million; followed by a sequel *O.R.A.G.* (2008); Faruk Aksoy's deeply nationalistic historic epic *Fetih 1453* (2012), Turkey's most expensive and most successful film ever with over five million spectators. Two key films, *The Bandit* (Yavuz Turgul, 1996), a romantic-action film and *Vizontele* (Yilman Erdogan and Sorak, 2001), a comedy, were instrumental in bringing about the renaissance of Yesilçam. Audience response was huge (two and a half and three million respectively). These successes were followed by further investment in Turkish film. Arguably, what dominates in this new popular cinema is a cinema of nostalgia, primarily in the form of an idealized representation of the past, or memories of a familial home as a felicitous space (Suner, 2010: 16). Even so, popular films with a political edge have made it in a big way: *My Father and My Son* (Çagan Irmak, 2005) is about a family torn apart by the 1980 military coup; *The Valley of the Wolves* (Serdar Akar, 2006), set during the occupation of Iraq, portrays the gruesome aftermath of the arrest of allied Turkish soldiers by the US army and their subsequent hooding (a real-life incident).

Throughout all this politically difficult time, New Turkish Cinema, while small in output, has never disappeared. Intriguingly, therefore, its life span is over forty years and still ongoing. Keywords to its practice show how distinct it is from most of the Yesiçlam in-house studio style: credibility, naturalness, shooting with sound (as opposed to dubbed sound in post-production), psychological types (as opposed to stereotypes), representations of the changing role of women since the 1980s (as opposed to fixed constructions), masculinity in crisis. Some of this cinema is directly political and critically confronts the traumatic events of the past (Suner, 2010: 17). This includes the persecution of the Kurds by the Turks (*Journey to the Sun*, Yesim Ustaoglu, 1999), police torture (*In Nowhere Land*, Tayfun Pirselimoglu, 2002), religious and ethnic discrimination (*Waiting for the Clouds*, Ustaoglu, 2003). Elsewhere there is the work of two fiercely independent filmmakers, both of whom, in completely different tones, make intimist films (i.e. told from within the characters' psychic space) which are deeply questioning and moral in their approach to the issue of belonging. The first, quite violent in his imaging and themes, is the work of Zeki Demirkubuz (*Innocence*, 1997; *Fate*, 2001; *Confession*,

2001; *Destiny*, 2005; *Envy*, 2009). The second, more interior, more aesthetically polished, but no less provocative is the work of Nuri Bilge Ceylan (see his trilogy: *The Small Town*, 1998; *Clouds of May*, 2000; *Distant*, 2003; or his more recent *Climates*, 2006, and *Winter Sleep*, 2014).

Since the election of President Recep Tayyip Erdogan in 2014, film production has maintained its high output at over 100 films per year (mostly comedies, some horror, a few thrillers and a healthy amount of action movies). Even though Erdogan's reputation for extreme authoritarianism (to say nothing of the current state of emergency imposed in 2016) might lead us to fear the worst for Turkish cinema, nonetheless, censorship appears not be affecting the more edgy films that have been released and gone to international festivals and exhibitions. I think especially of *Mustang* (Denise Gamze Ergüven, 2015) which tells the tale of five sisters who are orphaned and brought up by their very traditional grandmother and her son, a decidedly patriarchal and controlling uncle (who also rapes several of the sisters). Forced marriage is imposed on one sister, another runs away with her beloved boyfriend, the youngest finally makes her escape (by now, her uncle has them under lock and key) and rejoins her teacher in the city (one hopes she goes on to live a free life). Fatih Akin's *The Cut* (2014) finally addresses the taboo subject of the brutality meted out to the Armenians in World War One by the Turks. In December 2016, a film portraying the life of Erdogan from his early days in poverty to his ascendancy to Major of Istanbul in 1999 was released, *Reis/Chief* (Hüdaverdi Yavuz), but was already rated in October (before its release) as the number one top-ranking film by IMDb Turkish cinema listings (need I say more).

For further reading see Basutçu, 1996; Ozguc, 1988; Woodhead, 1989; Erdogan and Göktürk, 2001; Suner, 2010.

Iranian cinema

Iranian cinema (formerly Persian until the Revolution of 1978) began in the 1900s with documentary films commissioned by the Shah. These were, as one might expect given their source, spectacles of Royal ceremonies and attractions (weddings, births, the Royal zoo) and were made for an elite consumption, that is, the Shah and his Royal entourage. This state sponsorship of documentary still prevails today. Iran's first feature films appeared in the 1930s. First came a silent film, *Abi and Rabi* (Avanes Ghanian, 1930), then Iran's first sound film,

The Lost Girl, which was directed in India by Ardeshir Irani (1933). It took a long time for Iran to set up its own film studios. Pars Film Studio, established in the late 1940s, was the first and was owned by Esma'il Kushan, who directed the two first sound films produced in Iran (*The Tempest of Life*, 1948, and *Prisoner of the Emir*, 1949). Films of this era were based on the Iranian traditions of folklore and epics. This tradition was to return and remain, albeit in a slightly different guise, in post-Revolutionary Iran (1979 onwards). Thus, what dominate, currently, are films filled with religious (e.g. *With Naked Feet in Heaven*, Bahram Tavakoli, 1997) and national motifs (often celebrating the 1979 Revolution or treating the Iran–Iraq war; see *In the Name of the Father*, by female director Golshifteh Farahani, 2005; *M Like Mother*, Rasou Mollaqolipour, 2007), comedies and romantic melodramas.

In some ways, the 1950s is the most socially interesting period where Iranian cinema is concerned, especially in terms of the representation of women. It is as if woman becomes, particularly in the family melodramas, the site and embodiment of the permanent political tension between the Shah's Pahlavi state and the religious Shi'a establishment. These films often pitted the modern woman versus the traditional one; some films encouraged the emergence of the new woman, others ridiculed her (Sadr, 2006: 79). The 1950s saw a number of measures put in place by the government (endorsed by the Shah) to increase the role of women in society (these included: the compulsory unveiling of women; enrolment of women into physical education; opening of the civil service to women; more university places for women; teacher training college producing women teachers for girls' schools, etc.). These measures culminated with the right to vote being granted to women in 1963. Despite these liberal measures, the Shah's increasing autocracy (in most other domains) led to his overthrow, in 1979, by a campaign of civil resistance led by the Ayatollah Khomeini and other political factions. The outcome was the establishment of an Islamic Republic. Since that time women's rights have been severely reversed.

In the 1960s, the state took control over the film industry, which until then had been a mixed economy of private sector film production and state-subsidized films. The move was political and motivated by the USA's concerns about the spread of communism into Islamic states. The Shah was perceived as a natural ally to (and controlled some might say by) the United States. Films of the late 1950s and early 1960s had expressed concern over the increased presence of Western values and their seeming erosion of traditional Iranian ones. Thus, the state take-over was intended to redress this negative view and to foster a more pro-Western cinema. Production for a while was quite mediocre which, of course, sent audiences off to other cinema venues (to watch Western products). The indigenous types of films being produced were comedies, melodramas and action-hero movies (the latter did not attract as much as their 'superior' American prototype). However, in 1969, two films launched what became known as the Iranian New Wave. *Qaisar* by Mas'ud Kimai was an action-hero film with a difference, thus recasting the poorer Iranian prototype. The film shows the negative effects of American Westernization on the Iranian people (the action-hero rescues the Iranian damsel in Western distress). The other film, *The Cow,* directed by Dariush Mehrju'i, was a rural film filmed in the social–realist vein. Although this was not the dominant cinema of the 1970s (indeed, it had great trouble getting its products financed), this New Wave lasted and informed film practices through until the Revolution of 1979.

During the first year of the Revolution, cinema was proscribed. It was banished as corrupt and redolent with Western cultural imperialism. Cinema theatres were burnt down (in 1979 there were 470, now there are only 270). Almost all indigenous products were banned and, once production got underway again, only a quarter of new products were passed by censorship and, therefore, got made. Strict imposition of Islamic law meant that women virtually disappeared off the screen. Many filmmakers sought exile, from where they have continued to make a diasporic cinema of Iran. In 1983, the Ministry of Culture established the Farabi Cinema Foundation, a body whose function was to overview film practice and to ensure high-quality products. By 1987, women were allowed back on the screen, but were shot according to strict criteria for modesty. Women filmmakers also began to appear (around six in all).

Censorship remains unabated, however. Iranian filmmakers have to negotiate not just delicate taboo issues (such as the proscription of sex and any physical contact between opposite sexes, unless they are related in real life), but also the equally difficult issue of political taboos. There are five levels of censorship – all have to be passed before a film can be exhibited in the country. Thus, even films that have been made can subsequently be banned. The Islamist freedom-fighter and filmmaker (who fought against the Shah) Mohsen Makhmalbaf has had his work banned by the censor board of Iran (*Gabbeh*, 1994, for being subversive, *A Moment of Innocence*, 1996, for being anti-revolutionary). However, his popular reputation in Iran has protected him. Furthermore, Makhmalbaf has established his own production company and co-produces with France. In 1997, he co-produced his daughter's, Samirah Makhmalbaf, first feature film (*The Apple*), which passed through the levels of censorship. Since 2009, however, he has lived in exile and yet he still continues to make films which criticize political intolerance and dictatorship of any order (see *The Gardener*, 2012, and *The President*, 2014). His work is banned in Iran and pressure can be brought on neighbouring countries not to show his work (e.g. the Lebanese Film Festival was obliged to withdraw *The President* from its screening programme).

The strict laws in Iran can produce other anomalies such as the filmmaker Abbas Kiarostami who has managed to escape censorship, but who is more widely applauded internationally than he is nationally. His films are not commercially successful in Iran but they are with Western audiences (see his Iranian films *The White Balloon*, 1995, *Through the Olive Trees*, 1996, *A Taste of Cherry*, 1997, which won the Cannes Palme d'Or). Recently, Kiarostami has turned his hand to a European co-production with his French-Italian-Iranian-produced film *Copie conforme/Certified Copy* (2010), starring Juliette Binoche (but which Iran banned on the premise of Binoche's dress-code).

Where Iranian cinema is presently concerned, therefore, it would be fair to say that, while the infrastructure for production has been put in place ensuring quality films, and that the levy on cinema tickets ensures a ploughing of resources back into the industry, nonetheless, distribution and exhibition systems are in a parlous state (partly because of the burning down of so many theatres and partly due to lack of available funding to remedy those specific problems). Lack of film products means that the television market (often illegally accessed by satellite) and video black-markets are taking care of audience needs. Undoubtedly, however, censorship is the most severe obstacle filmmakers have to overcome to get their work seen – and the latest new wave of cinema, called New Iranian Cinema, is remarkable in this respect. Babak Payami, now living in exile, had to smuggle his film *Silence Between Two Thoughts* (2003) out of Iran on DV. The negative was confiscated because the film was deemed too controversial. Payami's film tells how, in accordance with the village's reading of Islamic law, a young woman is sentenced to death for not being a virgin. The executioner's hand is stayed at the last minute: she is a virgin, after all; however, he is such a zealot he is persuaded to marry and deflower her so he can carry out the sentence. Jafar Panahi still lives in Iran and, despite the board of censors giving him a very difficult time, managed, until very recently, to get his films made and distributed outside his country. His films *The Circle* (2000) and *Crimson Gold* (2003) have not been seen in Iran – and the filmmaker refuses to make cuts that would allow their exhibition. However, since then, in 2010, Panahi has been sentenced to six years imprisonment. He was placed under house arrest for pro-democracy activity, subjected to a twenty-year ban on filmmaking, forbidden interviews or to leave his country during this period. Amazingly, he managed to smuggle out (on a USB memory stick) a seventy-five-minute DV documentary entitled *This Is Not a Film* (2011, screened at Cannes Film Festival). Since 2013, and a change in presidential leader (from Mahmoud Ahmadinejad to Hassan Rouhani), Panahi has been allowed to move around Iran, but not to leave the country. The twenty-year ban on filmmaking is still in force (as is his prison sentence which has yet to be enforced fully). Despite this, Panahi has managed to make two films: *Closed Curtain* (2013) and *Taxi* (2015), both of which were screened at the Berlin Film Festival and both of which received awards. Tenacious courage indeed. Certain political prisoners have been released. It is to be hoped that the current international pressure will eventually favour Panahi's release also.

Until 2009, Samirah Makhmalbaf continued in the wake of her early success, *The Apple*, to make internationally acclaimed films (*Blackboards*, 2000; *At 5 in the Afternoon*, 2003) – all her films address in different ways the theme of women's rights. Since 2009, however, she has not released another film: *The Two-Legged Horse* appears to be her last film.

The Iranian Culture ministry finds itself in a very paradoxical situation with its internationally successful filmmakers. It celebrates these filmmakers' worldwide renown and yet it may well refuse their products any kind of release in Iran. These films get made thanks to two different sets of circumstances. On the one hand, many of them get international funding (which guarantees their international release). On the other hand, the authorities (since the mid-1990s) have 'softened' the censorship laws so that, now, films get the go-ahead for shooting based on a short synopsis. However, they can step in at the last stage and refuse a screening licence. The intention behind this softening was to foster self-censorship, which is clearly not working where the above filmmakers are concerned.

Much has been made of the influence of **Italian neo-realism** on this New Iranian Cinema. Filmmakers use primarily non-professional actors, the stories are grounded in the real and bear a strong relationship to contemporary Iranian social reality. In this context see Asghar Farhadi's highly acclaimed social realist films, *About Elly* (2009) and *A Separation* (2011). Alternatively, the narrations may be told in allegorical form, which in itself gestures to the limits of what can be shown (see *The*

Apple; *The White Balloon*, Panahi, 1995). The trajectories are often circular, the spaces disconnected, children feature largely (often one suspects because of the difficulty of casting women, see above), but there is nearly always a quest (to leave the city, *The Circle*; to escape patriarchal imprisonment, *The Apple*; to help a friend, *Where is the Friend's House?*, Kiarostami, 1987; to challenge the division caused by boundaries, *Blackboards*; a woman's return to her homeland to try to locate her sister in *Kandahar*, Mohsen Makhmalbaf, 2001). This quest suggests the psychological disconnectedness felt by the characters, both men and women, in this nation that presently so rigidly asserts a single reality.

For further reading see Dabashi, 2007; Issa and Whitaker, 1999; Jahed, 2012; Naficy, 1979, 1992, 1993; Tapper, 2002; Mirbakhtyar, 2006.

see also: **Black cinema – USA, Black cinema – UK, cinema nôvo, postcolonial theory, Third Cinema**

ZOOM

The zoom lens was developed in the 1950s, constituting another technological attraction for audiences, as did the introduction of colour and cinemascope in the same decade. A zoom shot is one that is taken with the use of a variable focal length lens (known as a zoom lens). A zoom-forward normally ends in a close-up, a zoom-back in a general shot. Both types of shot imply a rapid movement in time and space, and as such create the illusion of displacement in time and space. A zoom-in picks out and isolates a person or object, a zoom-out places that person or object in a wider context. A zoom shot can be seen, therefore, as **voyeurism** at its most desirably perfect.

BIBLIOGRAPHY

Aaron, M. (2004) *New Queer Cinema: A Critical Reader*, New Jersey, Rutgers University Press

——(2007) *Spectatorship: The Power of Looking*, London and New York, Wallflower Press

Abbott, S. and Jermyn, D. (eds) (2009) *Falling in Love Again: Romantic Comedy in Contemporary Cinema*, London and New York, I. B. Tauris

Abel, R. (1984) *French Cinema: The First Wave, 1915–1929*, Princeton, NJ, Princeton University Press

——(1994) *The Ciné Goes to Town: French Cinema 1896–1914*, Berkeley, New York and London, University of California Press

Abel, R. and Altman, R. (eds) (2001) *The Sounds of Early Cinema*, Bloomington, IN, Indiana University Press

Ahmad, A. (1996) 'The Politics of Literary Postcoloniality', in: Mongia, P. (ed.) *Contemporary Postcolonial Theory: A Reader*, London, New York, Sydney and Auckland, Arnold

Ahmed, O. (2015) *Indian Cinema*, Leighton Buzzard, Auteur Publishing

Aitken, I. (ed.) (2005) *Encyclopedia of the Documentary Film*, New York and London, Routledge

——(ed.) (2006) *Realist Film: Theory and Cinema*, Manchester, Manchester University Press

Akomfrah, J. (1989) 'Introduction to the Morning Session', Birmingham Third Space Section of the 1988 Birmingham Film and Television Film Festival, *Framework*, vol. 36

Aldgate, A. (2001) *Censorship and the British Society: British Cinema and Theatre 1955–1965*, Oxford, Clarendon Press

——(2007) *Britain Can Take It: British Cinema in the Second World War*, new edition, London and New York, I. B. Tauris

Alexander, K. (1988) *Ethnic Notions: Towards a Cinema of Cultural Diversity*, London, British Film Institute Publishing

Alexenberg, M. (2011) *The Future of Art in a Postdigital Age*, Bristol, Intellect

Althusser, L. (1984) *Essays in Ideology*, London, Verso

Altman, R. (1989) *The American Film Musical*, Bloomington, IN, Indiana University Press

——(ed.) (1992) *Sound Theory and Sound Practice*, New York and London, Routledge and American Film Institute

——(1999) *Film/Genre*, London, British Film Institute Publishing

——(2008) *A Theory of Narrative*, New York, Columbia University Press

Alton, J. (1995) *Painting with Light* (with an introduction by Todd McCarthy), Berkeley and London, University of California Press

Anderson, L. (1954) 'Only Connect!', *Sight and Sound*, vol. 23, no. 4, April/June

Andrew, D. (1984) *Concepts in Film Theory*, New York and Oxford, Oxford University Press

——(1995) *Mists of Regret: French Poetic Realism*, Princeton, NJ, Princeton University Press

Antonio, S. D. (2002) *Contemporary African American Cinema*, New York and Oxford, Peter Lang

Appiah, K. A. (1992) *In My Father's House: Africa in the Philosophy of Culture*, Oxford, Oxford University Press

Armes, R. (1974) *Film and Reality: An Historical Survey*, Harmondsworth, Pelican

——(1996) *Dictionnaire des cinéastes du Maghreb/Dictionary of North African Filmmakers*, Paris, Editions des Trois Mondes

——(2006) *African Filmmaking: North and South of the Sahara*, Edinburgh, Edinburgh University Press

——(2008) *Dictionary of African Filmmakers*, Bloomington, Indiana University Press

Armstrong, R. (2005) *Understanding Realism*, London, British Film Institute Publishing

Arthur, P. (2005) *A Line of Light: American Avant-Garde Film since 1965*, Minneapolis and London, University of Minneapolis Press

Ascher, S. A. and Pincus, E. (2007) *The Filmmaker's Handbook*, 3rd edition, London, Penguin Books

Ashcroft, B., Griffiths, G. and Tiffin, H. (1995) *The Post-Colonial Studies Reader*, London and New York, Routledge

——(1998) *Key Concepts in Post-Colonial Studies*, London and New York, Routledge

Astruc, A. (1948) 'Naissance d'une nouvelle avant-garde', *Le Film*, no. 144

Attile, M. and Blackwood, M. (1986) 'Black Women and Representation', in: Brunsdon, C. (ed.) *Films For Women*, London, British Film Institute Publishing

Backman-Rodgers, A. (2015) *American Independent Cinema*, Edinburgh, Edinburgh University Press

Bad Object-Choices (1991) *How Do I Look?: Queer Film and Video*, Seattle, Bay Press

Badley, L., Barton-Palmer, R. and Schneider, S. J. (2006) *Traditions in World Cinema*, Edinburgh, Edinburgh University Press

Baird, R. and Rosenbaum, S. (eds) (1991) *Pornography*, Buffalo, Prometheus Books

Bakari, I. (1993) 'Le Facteur X du nouveau cinéma afro-américain', *Ecrans d'Afrique*, no. 4

Bakari, I. and Chaim, M. (eds) (1996) *African Experiences of Cinema*, London, British Film Institute Publishing

Baker, M. (2006) *Documentary in the Digital Age*, Amsterdam, Boston and Heidelberg, Focal Press

Balmain, C. (2017) *Introduction to Japanese Horror Film*, Edinburgh, Edinburgh University Press

Banaji, S. (2006) *Reading Bollywood: The Young Audience and Hindi Films*, Basingstoke, Palgrave Macmillan

Barefoot, G. (2001) *Gaslight Melodrama: From Victorian London to 1940 Hollywood*, London and New York, Continuum

Barker, M. (2011) *A 'Toxic' Genre: The Iraq War Films*, London, Pluto Press

Barnard, T. (ed.) (1986) *Argentine Cinema*, Toronto, Nightwood Editions

Barnard, T. and Rist, P. (eds) (1996) *South-American Cinema: A Critical Filmography 1915–1994*, New York, Garland

Barsam, R. M. (1992) *Non-Fiction Film: A Critical History*, Bloomington, IN, Indiana University Press, revised edition

Barthes, R. (1957) *Mythologies*, Paris, Editions du Seuil (also available in English translation: A. Layers (trans.) London, Paladin, 1989)

——(1967) 'Death of the Author', *Aspen Magazine,* nos 5/6

——(1973) *Le Plaisir du texte*, Paris, Editions du Seuil

Baschiera, R. and Hunter, R. (eds) (2016) *Italian Horror Film*, Edinburgh, Edinburgh University Press

Basutçu, M. (ed.) (1996) *Le Cinéma Turc*, Paris, Editions Centre Georges Pompidou

Baudry, J.-L. (1970) 'Cinéma: effets idéologiques produits par l'appareil de base', *Cinéthique*, Nos 7–8, translated as 'Ideological Effects of the Basic Cinematic Apparatus', in: Rosen P. (ed.) (1986) *Narrative, Apparatus, Ideology*, New York, Columbia University Press

——(1975) 'Le Dispositif', *Communications*, no. 23, translated as 'The Apparatus: Metaphysical Approaches to Ideology', in: Rosen, E. (ed.) (1986) *Narrative, Apparatus, Ideology*, New York, Columbia University Press

Bazin, A. (1967) *What Is Cinema?* vol. I (essays selected and translated by H. Gray), Berkeley, University of California Press

——(2011) *André Bazin and Italian Neo-realism* (edited by P. Cardullo), New York, Continuum

Bellin, J. D. (2005) *Framing Monsters: Fantasy Film and Social Alienation*, Carbondale, IL, Southern Illinois Press

Bellour, R. (1975) 'Le blocage symbolique', *Communications*, no. 23

Belton, J. (1992) *Widescreen Cinema*, Cambridge, MA and London, Harvard University Press

Belton, J., Hall, S. and Neale, S. (eds) (2010) *Widescreen Worldwide*, New Barnet, Herts, John Libbey

Bendazzi, G. (1994) *Cartoons: One Hundred Years of Cinema Animation*, (trans. A. Taraboletti), London, Paris and Rome, John Libbey

Benshoff, H. M. and Griffin, S. (eds) (2004) *Queer Cinema: the Film Reader*, New York, London, Routledge

——(2009) *America on Film: Representing Race, Class, Gender and Sexuality at the Movies*, 2nd edition, Malden, MA and Oxford, Blackwell

Benvenuto, B. and Kennedy, R. (1986) *The Works of Jacques Lacan: An Introduction*, New York, St. Martin's Press

Bergstrom, J. (1985) 'Sexuality at a Loss: The Films of F. W. Murnau', *Poetics Today*, vol. 6, nos 1–2

Bernardi, D. (ed.) (1996) *The Birth of Whiteness: Race and the Emergence of US Cinema*, New Jersey, Rutgers University Press

Bernstein, M. and Studlar, G. (eds) (1997) *Visions of the East: Orientalism in Film*, London and New York, I. B. Tauris

Berry, C. (ed.) (1991) *Perspectives on Chinese Cinema*, London, British Film Institute Publishing

——(1996) 'China before 1949', in: Nowell-Smith, G. (ed.) *The Oxford History of World Cinema*, Oxford and New York, Oxford University Press

Beumers, B. (2009) *A History of Russian Cinema*, Oxford, Berg

Beus, Y. (2008) 'Far Away, So Close? Nation, Global Chinese Cinema and the Question of Identity', *Quarterly Review of Film and Video*, vol. 25, no. 6, 306–14

Bhabha, H. (1989) 'The Commitment to Theory', in: Pines, J. and Willemen, P. (eds) *Questions of Third Cinema*, London, British Film Institute

——(1994) *The Location of Culture*, London, Routledge

Bhowmik, S. (1995) *Indian Cinema: Colonial Contours*, Calcutta, Papyrus

Bisschoff, L. and Murphy, D. (eds) (2013) *New Histories of African Cinema*, Oxford, Legenda Books

Black, G. D. (1994) *Hollywood Censored: Morality Codes, Catholics, and the Movies*, Cambridge, Cambridge University Press

Blake, M. F. (2003) *Code of Honour: The Making of Three Great American Westerns, High Noon, Shane and The Searchers*, Lanham, MD, New York and Oxford, Taylor Trade Publishing

Bluestone, G. (1971) *Novels into Film*, Los Angeles, University of California Press

Bobo, J. (ed.) (1998) *Black Women Film and Video Artists*, London and New York, Routledge

Bodnar, J. (2003) *Blue Collar Hollywood: Liberation, Democracy, and Working People in American Film*, Baltimore, MD, and London, Johns Hopkins University Press

Boggs, C. (2003) *A World in Chaos: Social Crisis and the Rise of Postmodern Cinema*, Lanham, MD, Boulder, CO, New York and Oxford, Rowman and Littlefield

Bogle, D. (1988) *Blacks in American Film and Television: An Encyclopedia*, New York and London, Garland Publishing Company

——(1994) *Coons, Mulattoes, Marries and Bucks: An Interpretative History of Blacks in American Films*, 3rd edition, Oxford, Roundhouse Publishing Company

Bold, C. (1987) *Selling the Wild West: Popular Western Fiction 1860–1960*, Bloomington, IN, Indiana University Press

Booker, M. K. (2007) *Postmodern Hollywood: What's New in Film and Why it Makes us Feel so Strange*, Westport, CT, and London, Praeger

Bordwell, D. (1986) *Narration in the Fictional Film*, New York and London, Routledge

——(2008) *Poetics of Cinema*, New York and London, Routledge

Bordwell, D. and Thompson, K. (1980) *Film Art: An Introduction*, Reading, MA, Addison-Wesley Publishing Company (4th edition 1993, New York, McGraw-Hill)

——(1994) *Film History: An Introduction*, New York, McGraw Hill

Bordwell, D., Staiger, J. and Thompson, K. (1985) *The Classical Hollywood Cinema: Film Style and Production to 1960*, London, Routledge and Kegan Paul

Bose, D. (2006) *Brand Bollywood: A New Global Entertainment Order*, New Delhi and London, Sage Publications

Bottomore, T. (1984) *The Frankfurt School*, London and New York, Tavistock Publications

Bourgault du Coudray, C. (2006) *The Curse of the Werewolf: Fantasy, Horror and the Beast within*, London and New York, I. B. Tauris

Bourne, S. (2001) *Black in the British Frame: The Black Experience in British Film and Television*, London and New York, Continuum

Bowser, P. and Spence, L. (1996) 'Identity and Betrayal: *The Symbol of the Unconquered* and Oscar Micheaux's "Biographical Legend" ', in: Bernardi, D. (ed.) *The Birth of Whiteness: Race and Emergence of US Cinema*, New Jersey, Rutgers University Press

Boyd, B., Carroll, J. and Gottschall, J. (eds) (2010) *Evolution, Literature and Film: A Reader*, New York, Columbia University Press

Brakage, S. (1992) *Film at Wit's End: Eight Avant-Garde Filmmakers*, Kingston, NY, Documentext, McPherson and Company

Branigan, E. (1992) *Narrative and the Comprehension of Film*, London and New York, Routledge

Bratton, J., Cook, J. and Gledhill C. (eds) (1994) *Stage, Picture, Screen*, London, British Film Institute Publishing

Braudy, L. (1992) 'From the World in a Frame', in: Mast, G., Cohen, M. and Braudy, L. (eds) *Film Theory and Criticism*, New York and Oxford, Oxford University Press

Brereton, S. (2005) *Hollywood Utopia: Ecology in Contemporary American Cinema*, Bristol and Portland, OR, Intellect

Bristow, J. (1997) *Sexuality*, London and New York, Routledge

Brooks, P. (1976) *The Melodramatic Imagination: Balzac, Henry James, Melodrama and the Mode of Excess*, New Haven, CT, Yale University Press

Brosnan, J. (1991) *The Primal Screen: A History of Science Fiction Film*, London and Sydney, Orbit Books

Brown, S. and Street, S. (eds) (2012) *Colour and the Moving Image: History, Theory, Aesthetics, Archive*, New York and London, Routledge

Browne, N., Pickowicz, P. G., Sobchack, V. and Yau, E. (1994) *New Chinese Cinemas: Forms, Identities, Politics*, Cambridge, Cambridge University Press

Brunette, P. (1987) *Roberto Rosellini*, Oxford, Oxford University Press

Bruno, G. (1987) 'Ramble City: Postmodernism and *Blade Runner*', October, no. 41

Brunovska Karnick, K. and Jenkins, H. (eds) (1995) *Classical Hollywood Comedy*, New York and London, Routledge

Brunsdon, C. (ed.) (1986) *Films for Women*, London, British Film Institute Publishing

Bruzzi, S. (1997) *Undressing Cinema: Clothing and Identity in the Movies*, London and New York, Routledge

——(2000) *New Documentary: A Critical Introduction*, London and New York, Routledge

——(2006) *New Documentary: A Critical Introduction*, 2nd edition, London and New York, Routledge

Buchanan, I. and Swiboda, M. (2004) *Deleuze and Music*, Edinburgh, Edinburgh University Press

Bukatman, S. (1993) *Terminal Identity: The Virtual Subject in Postmodern Science Fiction*, Durham, NC, and London, Duke University Press

Burch, N. (1973) *Theory of Film Practice*, New York, Praeger

Burgoyne, R. (1990) *Life to Those Shadows*, trans. and ed. B. Brewster, London, British Film Institute Publishing

——(ed.) (2009) *The Epic Film in World Culture*, New York and London, Routledge

Burns, E. (1983) *Introduction to Marxism*, ninth reprint, London, Lawrence and Wishart

Burston, P. and Richardson, C. (eds) (1995) *A Queer Romance: Lesbians, Gay Men and Popular Culture*, London and New York, Routledge

Burt, G. (1994) *The Art of Film Music*, Boston, MA, Northeastern University Press

Burton, J. (ed.) (1986) *Cinema and Social Change in Latin America: Conversations with Filmmakers*, Austin, University of Texas Press

——(1990) *The Social Documentary in Latin America*, Pittsburgh, University of Pittsburgh Press

Burton-Carjaval, J. (1996) 'South American Cinema', in: Hill, J. and Church Gibson, P. (eds) *The Oxford Guide to Film Studies*, Oxford, Oxford University Press

Buscombe, E. (ed.) (1988) *The BFI Companion to the Western*, London, André Deutsch/British Film Institute Publishing

——(2006) *Injuns! Native Americans in the Movies*, London, Reaktion

Butler, D. (2009) *Fantasy Cinema: Impossible Worlds on Screen*, London and New York, Wallflower Press

Butler, J. (1990) *Gender Trouble*, New York and London, Routledge

——(1993) *Bodies that Matter*, London and New York, Routledge

Cameron, I. (ed.) (1992) *The Movie Book of Film Noir*, London, Studio Vista

Campbell, J. (2005) *Film and Cinema Spectatorship: Melodrama and Mimesis*, Cambridge, Polity Press

Carolyn, A. (2008) *It Lives again! Horror Movies in the New Millenium*, Surrey, Telos

Cartmell, D. and Whelehan, I. (1999) *Adaptations: From Text to Screen*, London and New York, Routledge

Cascone, K. (2000) 'The Aesthetics of Failure: "Post-Digital" Tendencies in Contemporary Computer Music', *Computer Music Journal*, vol. 24, no. 4, 12–18

Caughie, J. (ed.) (1981) *Theories of Authorship*, London, Routledge and Kegan Paul

Cawelti, J. G. (1992) '*Chinatown* and Generic Transformation in Recent American Films', in: Mast, G., Cohen, M. and Braudy, L. (eds) *Film Theory and Criticism*, 4th edition, Oxford, Oxford University Press

Chakravarti, S. S. (1993) *National Identity in Indian Popular Cinema 1947–87*, Austin, University of Texas Press

Chambers, I. and Curti, L. (1996) *The Post-Colonial Question*, London and New York, Routledge

Chanan, M. (ed.) (1983) *Twenty-Five Years of the New Latin American Cinema*, London, British Film Institute Publishing

——(1985) *The Cuban Experience*, London, British Film Institute Publishing

——(1996) 'Cinema in Latin America', in: Nowell-Smith, G. (ed.) *The Oxford History of World Cinema*, Oxford, Oxford University Press

——(1997) 'The Changing Geography of Third Cinema', *Screen*, no. 38, vol. 4, 372–88

——(2004) *Cuban Cinema*, Minneapolis and London, University of Minnesota Press

——(2007) *The Politics of Documentary*, London, British Film Institute Publishing

Chapman, James (2008) *War and Film*, London, Reaktion

Chapman, Jane (2009) *Issues in Contemporary Documentary*, Cambridge and Malden, MA, Polity Press

Chaudhuri, S. (2005) *Contemporary World Cinema: Europe, the Middle East and South Asia*, Edinburgh, Edinburgh University Press

——(2006) *Feminist Film Theorists: Laura Mulvey, Kaja Silverman, Teresa de Lauretis, Barbara Creed*, London and New York, Routledge

Chibnall, S. (2007) *Quota Quickies: The Birth of the British 'B' Film*, London, British Film Institute Publishing

Chibnall, S. and Petley, J. (eds) (2002) *British Horror Cinema*, London and New York, Routledge

Childs, P. and Williams, P. (1997) *An Introduction to Post-Colonial Theory*, London and New York, Prentice Hall/Harvest Wheatsheaf

Chion, M. (1982) *La Voix au cinéma*, Paris, Cahiers du Cinéma, Editions de L'Etoile

——(1985) *Le Son au cinéma*, Paris, Cahiers du Cinéma, Editions de L'Etoile

——(1994) *Audio-vision; Sound on Screen*, ed. and trans. C. Gorbman, New York, Columbia University Press

——(1999) *The Voice in Cinema*, ed. and trans. C. Gorbman, New York, Columbia University Press

——(2009) *Film: A Sound Art*, trans. C. Gorbman, New York, Columbia University Press

Chow, R. (1995) *Primitive Passions: Visibility, Ethnography, and Contemporary Chinese Style*, New York, Columbia University Press

Christie, I. and Taylor, R. (eds) (1993) *Eisenstein Rediscovered*, London and New York, Routledge

Church-Gibson, P. (ed) (2004) *More Dirty Looks: Gender, Pornography and Power*, 2nd edition, London, British Film Institute Publishing

Ciecko, A. T. (ed.) (2006) *Contemporary Asian Cinema: Popular Culture in a Global Frame*, Oxford and New York, Berg

Clark, L. (2002) quoted in James Mottram's article 'Daddy Cool', *Sight and Sound*, vol. 12, issue 3, 24–26

Clark, P. (1987) *Chinese Cinema: Culture and Politics since 1949*, Cambridge, Cambridge University Press

Coates, P. (1991) *The Gorgon's Gaze: German Cinema, Expressionism and the Image of Horror*, Cambridge, Cambridge University Press

——(2010) *Cinema and Colour: The Saturated Image*, London, British Film Institute Publishing

Codell, J. F. (2007) *Genre, Gender, Race and World Cinema*, Malden, MA, Oxford and Victoria, Blackwell

Cohan, S. (ed.) (2002) *Hollywood Musicals: The Film Reader*, London, Routledge

——(2005) *Incongruous Entertainment: Camp Cultural Value and the MGM Musical*, Durham, NC, and London, Duke University Press

Cohan, S. and Hark, I. R. (eds) (1997) *The Road Movie Book*, London and New York, Routledge

Colebrook, C. (2002) *Understanding Deleuze*, Hammersmith, Allen and Unwin

Colman, F. (2011) *Deleuze and Cinema: The Film Concepts*, Oxford and New York, Berg

Comolli, J.-L. and Narboni, J. (1969/1977) 'Cinéma/Idéologie/Critique', *Cahiers du cinéma* (Oct–Nov 1969); English translation in: *Screen Reader: Cinema/Ideology/Politics*, London, Society for Education in Film and Television

Conard, M. Y. (2006) *The Philosophy of Film Noir*, Lexington, KY, The University Press of Kentucky

Cook, P. (1980) 'Duplicity in *Mildred Pierce*', in: Kaplan, E. A. (ed.) *Women in Film Noir*, revised edition, London, British Film Institute Publishing

——(ed.) (1985) *The Cinema Book*, London, British Film Institute Publishing

——(1996) *Fashioning the Nation: Costume and Identity in British Cinema*, London, British Film Institute Publishing

Cook, P. and Dodd, P. (eds) (1993) *Women and Film: A Sight and Sound Reader*, London, British Film Institute Publishing

Cooke, M. (2008) *A History of Film Music*, Cambridge, Cambridge University Press

Copjec, J. (ed.) (1993) *Shades of Film Noir*, London and New York, Verso

Cornea, C. (2007) *Science Fiction Cinema: between Fantasy and Reality*, Edinburgh, Edinburgh University Press

Corrigan, T. (1983) *New German Film: The Displaced Image*, Austin, Texas University Press

Courthion, P. (1968) 'Introduction', in: Ragon, M. (ed.) *Expressionism*, London, Heron Books

Cowie, E. (1984) 'Fantasia', *m/f*, no. 9

Coyle, R. (2010) *Drawn to Sound: Animation Film Music and Sonicity*, London and Oakville, Equinox

Creed, B. (1993) *The Monstrous Feminine: Film, Feminism and Psychoanalysis*, New York and London, Routledge

Creekmur, C. K. and Dory, A. (1995) *Out in Culture: Gay, Lesbian and Queer Essays on Popular Culture*, London, Cassell

Cripps, T. (1977) *Slow Fade to Black: The Negro in American Film 1900–1942*, Oxford and New York, Oxford University Press

——(1978) *Black Film as Genre*, Bloomington and London, Indiana University Press

——(1982) 'New Black Cinema and Uses of the Past', in: Yearwood, G. (ed.) *Black Cinema Aesthetics: Issues in Black Filmmaking*, Ohio, Ohio University Papers on Afro-American, African and Caribbean Studies

——(1993) *Making Movies Black: The Hollywood Message Movies from World War Two to the Civil Rights Era*, Oxford and New York, Oxford University Press

Crisp, C. (1993) *The Classic French Cinema 1930–60*, Bloomington, Indiana University Press

Cubitt, S. (2005) 'Distribution and Media Flows', *Cultural Politics*, vol. 1, no. 2

Cui, S. (2003) *Women through the Lens: Gender and Nation in a Century of Chinese Cinema*, Honolulu, University of Hawaï

Culham, S. (1988) *Animation From the Script to the Screen*, London, Columbus Books

Dabashi, H. (ed.) (2006) *Dreams of a Nation: On Palestinian Cinema*, New York and London, Verso

——(2007) *Masters and Masterpieces of Iranian Cinema*, Waldorf, MD, Mage Publishers

Dalle-Vache, A. and Price, B. (eds) (2006) *Colour: The Film Reader*, New York and London, Routledge

Dave, P. (2006) *Visions of England: Class and Culture in Contemporary Cinema*, Oxford and New York, Berg

Davies, K., Dickey, J. and Stratford, T. (eds) (1987) *Out of Focus: Writings on Women and the Media*, London, The Women's Press

Davis, A. (1981) *Women, Race and Class*, New York, Random House

Davison, A. (2004) *Hollywood Theory: Non-Hollywood Practice, Cinema Soundtrack in the 1980s and 1990s*, Aldershot, Ashgate

Dayan, D. (1974) 'The Tudor Code of Classical Cinema', *Film Quarterly*, vol. 28, no. 1

De Lauretis, T. (1984) *Alice Doesn't: Feminism, Semiotics, Cinema*, Bloomington, Indiana University Press

——(1985) 'Oedipus Interruptus', *Wide-Angle*, vol. 7, nos 1–2

——(1989) *Technologies of Gender: Essays on Theory, Film and Fiction*, London, Macmillan

——(2005) *Figures of Resistance: Essays in Feminist Theory*, Urbana, IL, and Chicago, University of Illinois Press

De Lauretis, T. and Heath, S. (eds) (1980) *The Cinematic Apparatus*, New York, St Martin's Press

Deleuze, G. (1986) *Cinema I: The Mouvement-Image*, trans. Tomlinson, H. and Habberjam, B., Minneapolis, University of Minnesota Press

——(1989) *Cinema II: The Time-Image*, trans. Tomlinson, H. and Habberjam, B., Minneapolis, University of Minnesota Press

Dennison, S. and Lim, S. H. (eds) (2006) *Remapping World Cinema: Identity, Culture and Politics in Film*, London and New York, Wallflower Press

Denzin, N. K. (1991) *Images of Postmodern Society: Social Theory and Contemporary Cinema*, London, Sage

Deren, M. (1946) 'Cinema as an Art Form', *1913, A Journal of Forms,* issue 2, copyright @2005 by 1913 Press

Derrida, J. (1979) 'Living on Borderlines', In: Bloom, H., De Man, P., Derrida, J., Hartman, G. H. and Hillis-Miller, J. (eds) *Deconstruction and Criticism*, London, Routledge and Kegan Paul

Desai, J. (2004) *Beyond Bollywood: The Cultural Politics of South Asian Diasporic Film*, London and New York, Routledge

Devasundaram, A. I. (2016) *India's New Independent Cinema*, New York and London, Routledge

Dever, S. (2003) *Celluloid Nationalism and other Melodrama: From Post-Revolutionary Mexico to fin de siècle Mexamerica*, Albany, NY, State University Press

Diawara, M. (1986) 'Sub-Saharan African Film Production: Technological Paternalism', *Jump Cut*, vol. 32

——(ed.) (1993) *Black American Cinema: Aesthetics and Spectatorship*, New York and London, Routledge

Dickinson, K. (ed.) (2003) *Movie Music: The Film Reader*, London and New York, Routledge

Dickos, A. (2002) *Street with No Name: A History of the Classic American Film Noir*, Lexington, University Press of Kentucky

Dimendberg, E. (2004) *Film Noir and the Spaces of Modernity*, Cambridge, MA, and London, Harvard University Press

Dines, G. and Hurnez, J. (eds) (1995) *Gender, Race and Class in the Media*, London, Sage

Dines, G., Jensen, R. and Russo, A. (1998) *Pornography: The Production and Consumption of Inequality*, London and New York, Routledge

Dines, P. (1994) *Images of the Algerian War: French Fiction and Film 1954–1992*, Oxford, Clarendon Press

Dixon, W. W. (1997) *The Exploding Eye: A Re-Visionary History of 1960s American Experimental Cinema*, Albany, NY, State University of New York Press

Doane, M. A. (1982) 'Film and the Masquerade: Theorising the Female Spectator', *Screen*, no. 23, vols 3–4

——(1984) 'The Woman's Film: Possession and Address', in: Doane, M. A., Mellencamp, P. and Williams, L. (eds) *Re-vision: Essays in Feminist Film Criticism*, Frederick, MD, The American Film Institute/University Publications of America

——(1987) *The Desire to Desire: The Woman's Film of the 1940s*, Bloomington, Indiana University Press

——(1992) *Femmes Fatales: Feminism, Film Studies and Psychoanalysis*, New York and London, Routledge

Doane, M. A., Mellencamp, P. and Williams, L. (eds) (1984) *Re-vision: Essays in Feminist Film Criticism*, Frederick, MD, The American Film Institute/University Publications of America

Doherty, T. (1988) *Teenagers and Teenpics: The Juvenilization of American Movies in the 1950s*, Boston, Unwin

——(2002) *Teenagers and Teenpics: The Juvenilization of American Movies in the 1950s*, new edition, Philadelphia, PA, Temple University Press

Donald, J. (1989) *Fantasy and the Cinema*, London, British Film Institute Publishing

Donald, R. and MacDonald, K. (2011) *Reel Men at War: Masculinity and the American War Film*, Lanham, MD, Toronto and Plymouth, UK, The Scarecrow Press Inc.

Donaldson, M. (2003) *Black Directors in Hollywood*, Texas, University of Texas Press

Donnelly, K. J. (ed.) (2001) *Film Music: Critical Approaches*, Edinburgh, Edinburgh University Press

——(2005) *The Spectre of Sound: Music in Film and Television*, London, British Film Institute Publishing

Dönmez-Colin, G. (2004) *Women, Islam and Cinema*, London, Reaktion

——(2007) *The Cinema of North Africa and the Middle East*, London and New York, Wallflower Press

Dorenkamp, M. and Henke, R. (1995) *Negotiating Lesbian and Gay Subjects*, New York and London, Routledge

Downing, L. and Saxton, L. (2010) *Film and Ethics: Foreclosed Encounters*, London and New York, Routledge

Doy, G. (2000) *Black Visual Culture, Modernity and Postmodernity*, London and New York, I. B. Tauris

Dudrah, R. (2006) *Bollywood: Sociology Goes to the Movies*, New Delhi, Thousand Oaks, CA, and London, Sage

——(2012) *Bollywood Travels: Culture, Diaspora and Border Crossings in Popular Hindi Cinema*, London and New York, Routledge

Dudrah, R. and Desai, J. (eds) (2008) *The Bollywood Reader*, Maidenhead, McGraw Hill, Open University Press

Dworkin, A. (1991) *Pornography: Men Possessing Women*, London, Women's Press

Dwyer, R. (2006) *Filming the Gods: Religion and Indian Cinema*, London and New York, Routledge

Dwyer, R. and Pinto, J. (eds) (2011) *Beyond the Boundaries of Bollywood: The Many Forms of Hindi Cinema*, New Delhi, Oxford University Press

Dyer, R. (1977a) 'Entertainment and Utopia', *Movie*, 24 (no pages)

——(1977b) *Gays and Film*, London, British Institute Publishing

——(1980) *Stars*, London, British Film Institute Publishing

——(1986) *Heavenly Bodies: Film Stars and Society*, London, Cinema British Film Institute Series, Macmillan

——(1990) *Now You See It: Studies in Lesbian and Gay Film*, London and New York, Routledge

——(1993a) 'Dracula and Desire', *Sight and Sound*, vol. 3, no. 1

——(1993b) *The Matter of Images: Essays on Representation*, London and New York, Routledge

——(1997) *White*, London and New York, Routledge

——(2002) *The Culture of Queers*, London and New York, Routledge

——(2004) 'The Talented Mr Rota', *Sight and Sound*, vol. 14, no. 9

——(2007) *Pastiche*, London and New York, Routledge

Dyssanayake, W. (ed.) (1994) *Colonialism and Nationalism in Asian Cinema*, Bloomington, Indiana University Press

Easton, S. (1994) *The Problem of Pornography*, London and New York, Routledge

Eberwein, R. T. (2007) *Armed Forces: Masculinity and Sexuality in the American War Film*, New Brunswick, NJ, and London, Rutgers University Press

Eder, K. and Rossell, D. (eds) (1993) *New Chinese Cinema*, London, National Film Theatre, British Film Institute Publishing

Eisner, L. (1969) *The Haunted Screen: Expressionism and the German Cinema*, London, Thames and Hudson

El-Assyouti, M. (2003) 'Asma El-Bakri: Freudian Slips', *Al-Ahram Weekly on line*, no. 619: http://weekly.ahram.org.eg/2003/619/profile.htm (accessed 07.04.05)

Elena, A. and Lopez, M. D. (eds) (2004) *The Cinema of Latin America*, London, Wallflower Press

Elley, D. (1984) *The Epic Film: Myth and History*, New York and London, Routledge

Elliot, A. (2014) *The Return of the Epic Film: Genre, Aesthetics and History*, Edinburgh, Edinburgh University Press

Ellis, J. (1982) *Visible Fictions*, London and New York, Routledge and Kegan Paul

——(2011) *Documentary: Witness and Self-Relevation*, London and New York, Routledge

Ellis, J. C. and McLane, B. A. (2005) *A New History of Documentary Film*, New York, Continuum International

Elsaesser, T. (1987) 'Tales of Sound and Fury: Observations on the Family Melodrama', in: Gledhill, C. (ed.) *Home Is Where the Heart Is: Studies in Melodrama and the Woman's Film*, London, British Film Institute Publishing

——(1989) *New German Cinema: A History*, London, British Film Institute Publishing

——(1996) 'Germany: The Weimar Years', in: Nowell-Smith, G. (ed.) *The Oxford History of World Cinema*, Oxford and New York, Oxford University Press

——(2000) *Weimar Cinema and After: Germany's Historical Imaginary*, London and New York, Routledge

Elsaesser, T. and Hagener, M. (eds) (2009) *Film Theory: An Introduction through the Senses*, London and New York, Routledge

Elsaesser, T., Horwath, A. and King, N. (eds) (2004) *The Last Great American Picture Show: New Hollywood Cinema in the 1970s*, Amsterdam, Amsterdam University Press

Erdogan, N. and Göktürk, D. (2001) 'Turkish Cinema', in: Leaman, O. (ed.) *Companion Encyclopedia of Middle Eastern and North African Film*, London and New York, Routledge, 537–39

Everett, A. (2004) 'Click This: From Analog Dreams to Digital Realities', *Cinema Journal*, 43, no. 3

Everett, W. (ed) (2007) *Questions of Colour in Cinema: From Paintbrush to Pixel*, Oxford, Bern and Berlin, Peter Lang

Ezra, E. (ed.) (2004) *European Cinema*, Oxford, Oxford University Press

Ezra, E. and Rowden, T. (2006) 'General Introduction: What is Transnational Cinema?', In: Ezra, E. and Rowden, T. (eds) *Transnational Cinema: The Film Reader*, London, Routledge

Faber, L. and Walters, H. (2004) *Animation Unlimited: Innovative Short Films since 1940*, London, Laurence King Publications

Fanon, F. (1967) *Black Skin, White Masks*, first published 1952, New York, Grove Press

——(1968) *The Wretched of the Earth*, first published 1961, New York, Grove Press

Fay, J. and Nielan, J. (2010) *Film Noir: Hard Boiled Modernity and the Culture of Globalisation*, London and New York, Routledge

Featherstone, M. and Burrows, R. (eds) (1995) *Cyberspace/Cyberbodies/Cyberpunk*, London, Sage

Ferncase, R. (1995) *Film and Video Lighting: Terms and Concepts*, Newton, MA, Focal Press, Butterworth-Heinemann

Feuer, J. (1982) *The Hollywood Musical*, London, Macmillan

Figgis, M. (2007) *Digital Film-making*, London, Faber and Faber

Finney, A. (1996) *The State of European Cinema*, London and New York, Cassell

Fischer, L. (1989) *Shot/Countershot: Film Tradition and Woman's Cinema*, Princeton, NJ, Princeton University Press, and London, British Film Institute/Macmillan Education

Fiske, J. and Hartley, J. (1978) *Reading Television*, London and New York, Methuen

Flitterman-Lewis, S. (1990) *To Desire Differently: Feminism and the French Cinema*, Urbana, and Chicago, IL, University of Illinois Press

Flory, D. (2008) *Philosophy, Black Film, Film Noir*, University Park, PA, Pennsylvania State University Press

Forbes, J. and Street, S. (2000) *European Cinema: An Introduction*, Basingstoke, Palgrave

Foucault, M. (1969) 'Qu'est-ce qu'un auteur?', *Bulletin de la Société française de philosophie* no.3, trans. R. Hurley et al., 'What is an Author?', In: Faubion, J. P. (ed.) (1998) *The Essential Works of Foucault Volume II*, New York, New York University Press

——(1977) *Discipline and Punish: The Birth of the Prison*, trans. A. Sheridan, New York, Pantheon

——(1978) *The History of Sexuality*, vol. 1, trans. R. Hurley, New York, Pantheon

Frampton, D. (2006) *Filmosophy*, London and New York, Wallflower Press

Frayling, C. (1998) *Spaghetti Westerns: Cowboys and Europeans from Karl May to Sergio Leone*, London, I. B. Taurus

——(2005) *Sergio Leone: Once upon a Time in Italy*, London, Thames and Hudson

French, P. (2005) *Westerns*, Manchester, Carcanet

Freud, S. (1931) 'Female Sexuality', reprinted in *The Standard Edition of the Complete Works of Sigmund Freud*, trans. J. Strachey, London, Hogarth Press, 1953–74, vol. 21, pp. 64–145

Frieden, S., McCormick, R. W., Petersen, V. R. and Vogelsang, L. M. (eds) (1993) *Gender and German Cinema: Feminist Interventions*, vols I and II, Providence, RI, and Oxford, Berg Publishers

Friedman, L. (ed.) (1993) *British Cinema and Thatcherism*, London, University College London Press

Fuery, P. (2004) *Madness and Cinema: Psychoanalysis, Spectatorship and Culture*, Basingstoke and New York, Palgrave Macmillan

Furby, J. and Hines, C. (2012) *Fantasy*, London and New York, Routledge

Furniss, M. (1998) *Art in Motion: Animation Aesthetics*, London, Paris and Rome, John Libbey

Furstenau, M. (ed.) (2010) *Film Theory Reader: Debates and Arguments*, London and New York, Routledge

Fusco, C. (1989) 'About Locating Ourselves and Our Representations', Birmingham Third Space Section of the 1988 Birmingham Film and Television Film Festival, *Framework*, vol. 36

Fuss, D. (ed.) (1992) *Inside/Out: Lesbian Theories, Gay Theories*, New York and London, Routledge

Gabbard, K. (2004) *Black Magic: White Hollywood and African-American Culture*, New Brunswick, NJ, and London, Rutgers University Press

Gabbard, K. and Luhr, T. (eds) (2008) *Screening Genders*, New Brunswick, NJ, and London, Rutgers University Press

Gabriel, T. (1982) *Third Cinema in the Third World: The Aesthetics of Liberation*, Ann Arbor, Michigan University Press

——(1989) 'Third Cinema as Guardian of Popular Memory: Towards a Third Aesthetics', in: Pines, J. and Willemen, P. (eds) *Questions of Third Cinema*, London, British Film Institute Publishing

Gaines, J. (1988) 'White Privilege and Looking Relations: Race and Gender in Feminist Film Theory', *Screen*, vol. 29, no. 4

Galloway, P. (2006) *Asia Shock: Horror and Dark Cinema from Japan, Korea, Hong Kong and Thailand*, Berkeley, CA, Stone Bridge Press

Galt, R. (2006) *The New European Cinema: Redrawing the Map*, New York, Columbia University Press

Gamm, K. with Clark, V. (2004) *Teaching World Cinema*, London, British Film Institute Education

Garrett, R. (2007) *Postmodern Chick Flicks: the Return of the Woman's Film*, Basingstoke and New York, Palgrave Macmillan

Garwood, I. (2015) *The Sense of Film Narration*, Edinburgh, Edinburgh University Press

Gaunt, J. T. J. (2011) *Adaptation in a Post-Digital Age: Aesthetics and Methodological Approaches to Reviving Texts of the Past*, unpublished thesis, University of Exeter.

Gazdar, M. (1997) *Pakistan Cinema: 1947–1997*, Karachi, New York, Oxford and Delhi, Oxford University Press

Geiger, J. (2011) *American Documentary Film: Projecting the Nation*, Edinburgh, Edinburgh University Press

Genette, G. (1980) *Narrative Discourse*, trans. J. E. Lewin, Oxford, Blackwell

Geraghty, C. (2000) 'Re-examining Stardom: Questions of Texts, Bodies and Performance', In: Gledhill, C. and Williams, L. (eds) *Reinventing Film Studies*, London, Arnold

——(2008) *Now a Major Motion Picture: Film Adaptations of Literature and Drama*, Lanham, MD, Boulder, CO, New York and Toronto, Rowman and Littlefield

Gertz, N. and Khleifi, G. (2008) *Palestinian Cinema: Landscape, Memory, Trauma*, Edinburgh, Edinburgh University Press

Gever, M., Parmar, P. and Greyson, J. (eds) (1993) *Queer Looks*, New York and London, Routledge

Ghanian, T. A. and Phillips, M. E. (1996) *Digital Filmmaking: The Changing Art and Craft of Making Motion Pictures*, Washington, DC, Focal Press, Butterworth-Heinemann

Gibbs, J. (2002) *Mise-en-scène: Film Style and Interpretation*, London and New York, Wallflower Press

Gidal, P. (1989) *Materialist Film*, London and New York, Routledge

Gill, J. (1995) *Queer Noises*, London, Cassell

Gillett, P. (2003) *British Working Class in Postwar Film*, Manchester, Manchester University Press

Gilroy, P. (1993) *The Black Atlantic: Modernity and National Consciousness*, reprinted 1995, London and New York, Verso

Givanni, J. (1992) *Black Film and Video List*, London, British Film Institute Publishing

——(2000) (ed.) *Symbolic Narratives/African Cinema: Audiences, Theory and the Moving Image*, London, British Film Institute Publishing

Givanni, J. and Reynaud, B. (1993) 'Images de femmes noires', *CinémAction*, no. 67

Gledhill, C. (1980) '*Klute* 1: A Contemporary Film Noir and Feminist Criticism', in: Kaplan, E. A. (ed.) *Women in Film Noir*, revised edition, London, British Film Institute Publishing

——(ed.) (1987) *Home Is Where the Heart Is: Studies in Melodrama and the Woman's Film*, London, British Film Institute Publishing

——(1991) *Stardom: The Industry of Desire*, London and New York, Routledge

Glitre, K. (2006) *Hollywood Romantic Comedy: States of the Union 1934–65*, Manchester and New York, Manchester University Press

Godard, J.-L. (1980) *Introduction à une véritable histoire du cinéma*, Paris, Albatross

Gokulsing, K. M. (1999) 'Fatal Attraction? Nationalist and Patriotic Themes in Indian Films', unpublished paper

Gokulsing, K. M. and Dissanayake, W. (1998) *Indian Popular Cinema: A Narrative of Cultural Change*, Staffordshire, Trentham Books

——(2003) *Indian Popular Cinema*, new revised edition, Stoke-on-Trent, UK, and Sterling, USA, Trentham Books

Gomery, D. (2009) *The Hollywood Studio System: A History*, London, British Film Institute Publishing

Gopalan, L. (2002) *Cinema of Interruptions: Action Genres in Contemporary Indian Cinema*, London, British Film Institute Publishing

Gorbman, C. (1987) *Unheard Melodies: Narrative Film Music*, London, British Film Institute Publishing; Bloomington, IN, Indiana University Press

Grant, B. K. (ed.) (1986) *Film Genre Reader*, Austin, University of Texas Press

——(1995) *Film Genre Reader II*, 2nd edition, Austin, University of Texas Press

——(2003) *Film Genre Reader III*, 3rd edition, Austin, University of Texas Press

——(2004) 'Diversity of Dilution? Thoughts on Film Studies and the SCMS.', *Cinema Journal*, no. 43

——(2007) *Film Genre: From Iconography to Ideology*, London and New York, Wallflower Press

——(2012) *The Hollywood Film Musical*, Chichester, Wiley-Blackwell

Grant, C. and Kuhn, A. (eds) (2006) *Screening World Cinema*, London and New York, Routledge

Grant, J. (1987) *Encyclopedia of Walt Disney's Animated Characters*, New York, Harper and Row

——(2001) *Masters of Animation*, London, B. T. Batsford

Grant, P. S. (2004) *Blockbusters and Trade Wars: Popular Culture in a Globalized World*, Vancouver and Toronto, Douglas and McIntyre

Grant IV, W. R. (2004) *Post-Soul Black Cinema: Discontinuities, Innovation and Breakpoints 1970–1995*, New York and London, Routledge

Griffin, S. (1988) *Pornography and Silence*, London, The Women's Press.

Griffith, J. (1997) *Adaptations as Limitations*, Cranbury, University of Delaware Press

Grimshaw, A. (2002) *The Ethnographer's Eye: Ways of Seeing Anthropology*, Cambridge, Cambridge University Press

Grindon, L. (2011) *The Hollywood Romantic Comedy: Conventions, History, Controversies*, Chichester, Wiley-Blackwell

Grodal, T. (1997) *Moving Pictures: A New Theory of Genres, Feelings, and Cognition*, Oxford, Clarendon Press

——(2009) *Embodied Visions: Evolution, Emotion, Culture and Film*, Oxford, Oxford University Press

Grossman, A. (ed.) (2000) *Queer Asian Cinema: Shadows in the Dark*, New York, London and Oxford, Harrington Park Press

Grosz, E. (1990) *Jacques Lacan: A Feminist Introduction*, London and New York, Routledge

Grosz, E. and Probyn, E. (eds) (1995) *Sexy Bodies: The Strange Carnalities of Feminism*, London and New York, Routledge

Guerrero, E. (1993) *Framing Blackness: The African American Image in Film*, Philadelphia, PA, Temple University Press

——(1994) 'Framing Blackness: The African-American Image in the Cinema of the Nineties', *Cineaste*, vol. 20, no. 2

Guha, R. (ed.) (1982) *Subaltern Studies 1: Writings on South Asian History and Society*, 7 vols, Delhi, Oxford University Press

Guneratne, A. R. and Dissanayake, W. (2003) *Rethinking Third Cinema*, New York and London, Routledge

Gunning, T. (1986) 'The Cinema of Attraction, Early Film, Its Spectator and the Avant-garde', *Wide-Angle*, vol. 8, nos 3–4

Haaland, T. (2014) *Italian Neo-Realist Cinema*, Edinburgh, Edinburgh University Press

Hadj-Moussa, R. (1994) *Le Corps, L'Histoire, Le Territoire: Les Rapports de genre dans le cinéma d'Algérie*, Montreal and Paris, Les Editions de Balzac

Hake, S. (2002) *German National Cinema*, London and New York, Routledge

Hall, S. (1996) 'When was "The Post-Colonial"? Thinking at the Limit', in: Chambers, I. and Curti, L. *The Post-Colonial Question*, London and New York, Routledge

Hall, S. and Neale, S. (2010) *Epics, Spectacles and Blockbusters: A Hollywood History*, Detroit, MI, Wayne State University Press

Hallam, J. and Marshment, M. (2000) *Realism and Popular Cinema*, Manchester, Manchester University Press

Hammond, P. (2000) *The Shadow and Its Shadows: Surrealist Writings on the Cinema*, 3rd edition, San Francisco, CA, City Lights Books

Hampton, H. (2001) 'Whatever you Desire: Notes on Movieland and Pornotopia', *Film Comment*, vol. 37, no. 4, 36–45

Hanson, E. (ed.) (1999) *Out Takes: Essays on Queer Theory and Film*, Durham, NC, and London, Duke University Press

Hardy, P., Milne, T. and Willemen, P. (eds) (1986) *The Aurum Encyclopedia of Horror*, New York, Harper and Row

Hare, W. (2003) *Early Film Noir: Greed, Lust and Murder Hollywood Style*, Jefferson, NC, and London, McFarland

——(2004) *LA Noir: Nine Dark Visions of the City of Angels*, Jefferson, NC, and London, McFarland

Harper, G. and Mendik, X. (eds) (2000) *Unruly Pleasures: The Cult Film and Its Critics*, Guilford, FAB Press

Harper, J. (2004) *Legacy of Blood: A Comprehensive Guide to Slasher Movies*, Manchester, Headpress/Critical Vision

Harper, S. (1987) 'Historical Pleasures: Gainsborough Costume Melodrama', in: Gledhill, C. (ed.) *Home Is Where the Heart Is: Studies in Melodrama and Women's Film*, London, British Film Institute Publishing

——(1994) *Picturing the Past: The Rise and Fall of the Costume Drama*, London, British Film Institute Publishing

Hart, J. (1999) *The Art of the Storyboard: Storyboarding for Film, TV and Animation*, Woburn, MA, Butterworth-Heinemann

Hart, S. M. (2004) *A Companion to Latin American Film*, Rochester, NY, Boydell and Brewer

Hartley, J. (1982) *Understanding News*, London, Edward Arnold

Haskell, M. (1974) *From Reverence to Rape: The Treatment of Women in the Movies*, Harmondsworth, Penguin Books

Hawthorn, J. (1992) *A Concise Glossary of Contemporary Literary Theory*, London, Edward Arnold

Hayward, S. (1992) 'A history of French Cinema: 1895–1991 – Pioneering Filmmakers (Guy, Dulac, Varda) and Their Heritage', *Paragraph*, vol. 15, no. 1

——(2005) *French National Cinema*, London and New York, Routledge (with contributions from Will Higbee)

——(2006) *Cinema Studies: The Key Concepts*, 3rd edition, London and New York, Routledge

——(2010) *French Costume Drama of the 1950s: Fashioning Politics in Film*, Bristol, Intellect

Heath, S. (1978) 'Difference', *Screen*, vol. 19, no. 3

——(1981) *Questions of Cinema*, London, Macmillan

Hebdige, D. (1988) *Hiding in the Light*, London and New York, Routledge

Heffelfinger, E. (2011) *Visual Difference: Postcolonial Studies and Intercultural Cinema*, New York and Oxford, Peter Lang

Hernandez-Rodriguez, R. (2010) *Splendors of Latin Cinema*, Santa Barbara, CA, Denver, CO, and Oxford, Praeger

Higbee, W. E. (2007) 'Beyond the (Trans)national: Towards a Cinema of Transvergence in Postcolonial and Diasporic Francophone Cinema(s)', *Studies in French Cinema*, vol. 7, no. 2, 79–91

Higbee, W. E. and Lim, S. H. (2010) 'Concepts of Transnational Cinema: Towards a Critical Transnationalism in Film Studies', *Transnational Cinemas*, vol. 1, no. 1, 7–21

Higson, A. (1986) 'Film Acting and Independent Cinema', *Screen*, vol. 27, nos 3–4

——(1993) 'Re-presenting the National Past: Nostalgia and Pastiche in the Heritage Film', in: Friedman, L. (ed.) *British Cinema and Thatcherism*, London, University College London Press

——(2000) 'The Limiting Imagination of National Cinema', in: Hjort, M. and Mackenzie, S. (eds) *Cinema and Nation*, London, Routledge

Higson, A. and Maltby, R. (1999) *Film Europe and Film America: Cinema, Commerce and Cultural Exchange 1920–1939*, Exeter, Exeter University Press

Hill, J. (1986) *Sex, Class and Realism: British Cinema 1956–63*, London, British Film Institute Publishing

Hill, J. and Church-Gibson, P. (2000) *World Cinema: Critical Approaches*, Oxford, Oxford University Press

Hillier, J. (2001) *American Independent Cinema: A Sight and Sound Reader*, London, British Film Institute Publishing

Hjort, M. (2009) 'On the Plurality of Cinematic Transnationalism', in: Durovicova, N. and Newman, K. (eds) *World Cinemas, Transnational Perspectives*, Abingdon, Routledge

Hjort, M. and Mackenzie, S. (eds) (2000) *Cinema and Nation*, London, Routledge

——(2003) *Purity and Provocation*, London, British Film Institute Publishing

Ho, S. (ed.) (2002) *Planet Eros: New Japanese Independent Cinema*, Hong Kong, Hong Kong Arts Centre, Hong Kong Arts Development Centre

Hoffer, T. J. (1981) *Animation Reference Guide*, Westport, CN, Greenwood Press

Hogarth, D. (2006) *Realer than Reel: Global Directions in Documentary*, Austin, University of Texas Press

Holmlund, C. and Wyatt, J. (2005) *Contemporary American Independent Films*, London and New York, Routledge

hooks, b. (1981) *Ain't I a Woman: Black Women and Feminism*, Boston, MA, Long Haul Press

——(1989) 'Choosing the Margin as a Space of Radical Openness', Birmingham Third Space Section of the 1988 Birmingham Film and Television Film Festival, *Framework*, vol. 36

——(1992) *Black Looks: Race and Representation*, Boston, MA, South End Press

Hopkins, I. (2005) *Screening the Gothic*, Austin, University of Texas Press

Horne, P. and Lewis, R. (eds) (1996) *Outlooks: Lesbian and Gay Sexualities and Visual Cultures*, London and New York, Routledge

Horton, A. and Magretta, J. (1981) *Modern European Filmmakers and the Art of Adaptation*, New York, Frederick Ungar Publishing

Hull, G., Scott, P. B. and Smith, B. (eds) (1982) *All the Women Are White, All the Blacks Are Men, But Some of Us Are Brave*, New York, The Feminist Press

Humphries, R. (2002) *The American Horror Film: An Introduction*, Edinburgh, Edinburgh University Press

Hunt, L. and Wing-Fai, L. (2008a) *East Asian Cinemas: Exploring Transnational Connections in Films*, London and New York, I. B. Tauris

——(2008b) 'Introduction', In: Hunt, L. and Wing-Fai, L. (eds) *East Asian Cinemas: Exploring Transnational Connections on Film,* London and New York, I. B. Tauris

Huss, N. and Silverstein, R. (1968) *The Film Experience: Elements of Motion Picture Art,* New York, Dell Publishing

Hutcheon, L. (2006) *A Theory of Adaptation,* New York and London, Routledge

Huyssen, A. (1986) *After the Great Divide: Modernism, Mass Culture and Postmodernism,* London, Macmillan Press

——(1990) 'Mapping the Postmodern', in: Nicholson, L. (ed.) *Feminism/Postmodernism,* New York and London, Routledge

Indick, W. (2004) *Movies of the Mind: Theories of the Great Psychoanalysts Applied to Film,* Jefferson, NC, London, McFarland

Inglis, I. (ed.) (2003) *Popular Music and Film,* London, Wallflower Press

Issa, R. and Whitaker, S. (eds) (1999) *Life and Art: The New Iranian Cinema,* London, British Film Institute, National Film Theatre Publishing

Itzin, C. (1992) *Pornography: Women, Violence and Civil Liberties,* Oxford, Oxford University Press

Jäckel, A. (2003) *European Film Industries,* London, British Film Institute Publishing

Jackson, C. and Tapp, P. (1997) *The Bent Lens: A World Guide to Gay and Lesbian Film,* St Kilda, Victoria, Australian Catalogue Company

Jahed, P. (2012) *Directory of World Cinema: Iran,* Bristol, Intellect Press

Jameson, E. (1983) 'Postmodernism and Consumer Society', in: Foster, H. (ed.) *Postmodern Culture,* London, Pluto Press

Jancovich, M. (1992) *Horror,* London, B. T. Batsford

——(1996) *Rational Fears: American Horror in the 1950s,* Manchester and New York, Manchester University Press

——(2002) *Horror: The Film Reader,* London and New York, Routledge

Jeffers MacDonald, T. (2007) *Romantic Comedy: Boy Meets Girl Meets Genre,* London, Wallflower Press

Jenkins, H. (1992) *Textual Poachers: Television Fans and Participatory Culture,* New York and London, Routledge

——(2006) *Convergence Cultures: Where Old and New Media Collide,* New York, New York University Press

Johnson, R. and Stam, R. (eds) (1982/1995) *Brazilian Cinema,* Toronto, Associated University Presses

Johnston, C. (1973) *Notes on Women's Cinema,* Screen Pamphlet, London, Society for Education in Film and Television

——(1976) 'Women's Cinema as Counter-cinema', in: Nicholls, B. (ed.) *Movies and Methods,* Berkeley, University of California Press

Johnston, K. M. (2011) *Science Fiction Film: A Critical Introduction,* Oxford and New York, Berg

Jones, J. (1991) 'The New Ghetto Aesthetic', *Wide Angle,* vol. 13, nos 3 and 4

Jones, K. (2001) 'Bay Watch: Bigger, Faster, Louder', *Film Comment,* vol. 37, no. 4, 27–29

Joshri, L. M. (2001) *Bollywood: Popular Indian Cinema,* London, Dakini Books

Julius, M. (1996) *Action! The Action Movie A–Z,* London, B. T. Batsford

Kabir, N. M. (2001) *Bollywood: The Indian Cinema Story,* Kent, Chatham Press

——(2003) 'A Way of Life: An Introduction to Indian Cinema', in: Torgovnik, J. (ed.) *Bollywood Dreams*, London and New York, Phaidon Press

Kaes, A. (1996) 'The New German Cinema', in: Nowell-Smith, G. (ed.) *The Oxford History of World Cinema*, Oxford and New York, Oxford University Press

Kalinak, K. M. (1992) *Settling the Score: Music and the Classical Hollywood Film*, Madison, Madison University Press

Kaplan, E. A. (ed.) (1980) *Women in Film Noir*, revised edition, London, British Film Institute

——(1983) *Women and Film: Both Sides of the Camera*, New York and London, Methuen

——(ed.) (1990) *Psychoanalysis and Cinema*, New York and London, Routledge

——(1992) *Motherhood and Representation: The Mother in Popular Culture and Melodrama*, London and New York, Routledge

——(1997) *Looking for the Other: Feminism, Film, and the Imperial Gaze*, London and New York, Routledge

Kassabian, A. (2000) *Hearing Film: Tracking Identifications in Contemporary Hollywood Film Music*, London and New York, Routledge

Kaur, R. and Sinha, A. J. (eds) (2005) *Bollyworld: Popular Indian Cinema Through a Transnational Lens*, New Delhi, Thousand Oaks, CA, and London, Sage

Kawin, B. F. (1995) 'Children of the Light', in: Grant, B. K. (ed.) *Film Genre Reader*, Austin, University of Texas Press, pp. 309–29

Keesey, D. (2001) 'They Kill for Love: Defining the Erotic Thriller as a Film Genre', *CinéAction*, no. 58, 44–53

Kelly, R. (2000) *The Name of the Book is Dogme*, London, Faber and Faber

Kennedy, B. M. (2002) *Deleuze and Cinema: The Aesthetics of Sensation*, Edinburgh, Edinburgh University Press.

Kennedy, L. (1993) 'Is Malcolm X the Right Thing?', *Sight and Sound*, vol. 3, 2

Kerins, M. (2011) *Beyond Dolby (Stereo): Cinema in the Digital Sound Age*, Bloomington, IN, Indiana University Press

Khalil, A. (2015) *North African Cinema in the Global Context*, London and New York, Routledge

Khatib, L. (2006) *Filming the Modern Middle East: Politics in the Cinema of Hollywood and the Arab World*, New York and London, I. B. Tauris

——(2008) *Lebanese Cinema: Imagining the Civil War and beyond*, New York and London, I. B. Tauris

Kim, K. H. (2004) *The Remasculinization of Korean Cinema*, Durham, NC, and London, Duke University Press

King, B. (1985) 'Articulating Stardom', *Screen*, vol. 26, no. 5

——(1987) 'The Star and the Commodity: Notes Towards a Performance Theory of Stardom', *Cultural Studies*, vol. 1, no. 2

King, G. (2000) *Spectacular Narratives: Hollywood in the Age of the Blockbuster*, London and New York, I. B. Tauris

——(2002) *New Hollywood Cinema: An Introduction*, London and New York, I. B. Tauris

King, G. and Krzywinska, T. (2000) *Science Fiction Cinema*, London, Wallflower Press

King, J. (1990) *Magical Reels: A History of Cinema in Latin America*, London, Verso

King, J., Lopez, A. and Alvarado, M. (eds) (1993) *Mediating Two Worlds: Cinematic Encounters in the Americas*, London, British Film Institute Publishing

Kinsey, W. (2007) *Hammer Films: The Elstree Years*, Sheffield, Tomohawk Press

——(2010) *Hammer Films: The Unsung Heroes: The Team behind the Legend*, Sheffield, Tomohawk Press

Kirkham, P. and Thumin, J. (eds) (1995) *Me Jane: Masculinity, Movies and Women*, London, Lawrence and Wishart

Kline, T. J. (1992) *Screening the Text: Intertextuality in New Wave French Cinema*, Baltimore, MD, and London, Johns Hopkins University Press

Knight, A. (2002) *Disintegrating the Musical: Black Performance and American Musical Film*, Durham, NC, and London, Duke University Press

Knight, J. (1992) *Women and the New German Cinema*, London and New York, Verso

Konigsberg, I. (1993) *The Complete Film Dictionary*, London, Bloomsbury

Kracauer, S. (1992) 'From Caligari to Hitler', in: Mast, G., Cohen, M. and Braudy, L. (eds) *Film Theory and Criticism: Introductory Readings*, 4th edition, New York and Oxford, Oxford University Press

Kronish, A. (1996) *World Cinema: Israel*, Flicker Books, Madison, Farleigh Dickinson University Press

Krutnik, E. (1991) *In a Lonely Street: Film Noir, Genre, Masculinity*, London and New York, Routledge

Kuhn, A. (1982) *Women's Pictures: Feminism and Cinema*, London, and Boston, MA, Routledge and Kegan Paul

——(1985) *The Power of the Image: Essays on Representation and Sexuality*, London and New York, Routledge and Kegan Paul

——(1988) *Cinema, Censorship and Sexuality 1909–25*, London and New York, Routledge

——(1990) *Alien Zone*, London and New York, Verso

——(ed.) (1999) *Alien Zone II: The Spaces of Science Fiction Cinema*, London, Verso

Kuhn, A. (ed.) with Radstone, S. (1990) *The Women's Companion to International Film*, London, Virago

Kuzniar, A. (2000) *The Queer German Cinema*, Stanford, CA, Stanford University Press

Lacan, J. (1977) *Ecrits: A Selection*, trans. A. Sheridan, London, Tavistock Publications

Langford, B. (2005) *Film Genre: Hollywood and Beyond*, Edinburgh, Edinburgh University Press

Lapsley, R. and Westlake, M. (1988, reprinted in 1992) *Film Theory: An Introduction*, Manchester, Manchester University Press

Lassiter, J. and Davy S. (1995) *Toy Story: The Art and Making of the Animated Film*, New York, Hyperion

Lastra, J. (2000) *Sound Technology and the American Cinema: Perception, Representation, Modernity*, New York and Chichester, Columbia University Press

Lawrence, N. (2008) *Blaxploitation Films of the 1970s: Blackness and Genre*, New York and London, Routledge

Lay, S. (2002) *British Social Realism*, London and New York, Wallflower Press

Lázaro-Reboll, A. (2012) *Spanish Horror Film*, Edinburgh, Edinburgh University Press

Lebeau, V. (1994) *Lost Angels: Psychoanalysis and the Cinema*, London and New York, Routledge

——(2001) *Psychoanalysis and the Cinema: The Play of Shadows*, London and New York, Wallflower Press

Lee, V. P.-Y. (2011) *East Asian Cinemas: Regional Flows and Global Transformations*, New York, Palgrave Macmillan

Le Grice, M. (2006) *Experimental Cinema in the Digital Age*, London, British Film Institute Publishing

Lehman, P. (2006) *Pornography: Film and Culture*, New Brunswick, NJ, and London, Rutgers University Press

Lehman, P. and Luhr, W. (2003) *Thinking About Movies: Watching, Questioning, Enjoying*, Oxford, Blackwell

Leonard, D. J. (2006) *Screens Fade to Black: Contemporary African American Cinema*, Westport, CT, and London, Praeger

Lesage, J. (1974) 'Feminist Film Criticism: Theory and Practice', *Women and Film*, vol. 1, nos 5–6

Lichtenfeld, E. (2007) *Action Speaks Louder: Violence, Spectacle and the American Action Movie*, Middleton, CT, Weslyan University Press

Lim, S. G.-L., and Dissanayake, W. (1999). 'Introduction', in: Lim, S. G.-L., Smith, L. E. and Dissanayake, W. (eds) *Transnational Asia Pacific: Gender, Culture, and the Public Sphere*, Urbana, Illinois University Press

Lipschutz, R. D. (2001) *Cold War Fantasies: Film, Fiction and Foreign Policy*, Lanham, MD, Boulder, CO, New York and Oxford, Rowman and Littlefield Publishers

Littleton, D. (2006) *Black Comedians on Black Comedy: How African Americans Taught Us to Laugh*, New York, Applause Theatre and Cinema Books

Lobarto, R. and Ryan, M. D. (2010) 'Rethinking Genre Studies through Distribution Analysis Issues in International Horror Movie Circuits', *New Review of Film and Television Studies*, vol. 9, no. 2

Lopez, A. M. (2000) 'Early Cinema and Modernity in Latin America', *Cinema Journal*, vol. 40, no. 1, 48–78

Lord, P. and Sibley, B. (1998) *Creating 3-D Animation: The Aardman Book of Filmmaking*, New York, Harry N. Abrams

Loshitzky, Y. (2001) *Identity Politics on the Israeli Screen*, Austin, University of Texas Press

Lovell, A. and Hillier, J. (1972) *Studies in Documentary*, London, Secker and Warburg

Low, G. C.-L. (1996) *White Skins, Black Masks: Representation and Colonialism*, London and New York, Routledge

Loy, R. P. (2004) *Westerns in Changing America 1955–2000*, Jefferson, NC, and London, McFarland

Luhr, W. (2012) *Film Noir: New Approaches to Film Genre*, Chichester and Oxford, Wiley-Blackwell

Luhrmann, B. (2001) 'Strictly Red: Baz Luhrmann Interview by Graham Fuller', *Sight and Sound*, vol. 11, no. 6, 14–16

Lupack, B. T. (2002) *Literary Adaptations in Black American Cinema: From Micheaux to Morrison*, Rochester, NY, University of Rochester Press

Lurie, S. (1980) 'Pornography and the Dread of Women', in: Lederer, L. (ed.) *Take Back the Night*, New York, William Morrow

MacDonald, S. (1993) *Avant-Garde Film: Motion Studies*, Cambridge, Cambridge University Press

Macdonell, D. (1986) *Theories of Discourse: An Introduction*, Oxford, Blackwell

McCabe, J. (2004) *Feminist Film Studies: Writing the Woman into Cinema*, London and New York, Wallflower Press

McClean, S. T. M. (2007) *Digital Storytelling: The Narrative Power of Digital Effects in Film*, Cambridge, MA, and London, The MIT Press

McClintock, A. (1995) *Imperial Leather: Race, Gender and Sexuality in the Colonial Context*, London and New York, Routledge

McDonald, P. (1998) 'Film Acting', In: Hill, J. and Church-Gibson, P. (eds.) *The Oxford Guide to Film Studies*, Oxford, Oxford University Press

McFarlane, B. (1996) *Novel to Film: An Introduction to the Theory of Adaptation*, New York and Oxford, Clarendon Press

McGee, P. (2007) *From Shane to Kill Bill: Rethinking the Western*, Malden, MA, Oxford, and Victoria, Berg

McGowan, T. (2004) *Lacan and Contemporary Film*, New York, Other Press

McKernan, B. (2005) *Digital Cinema: The Revolution in Cinematography, Post-production and Distribution*, New York, The McGraw-Hill Companies

McMahon, B. and Quin, R. (1986) *Reel Images: Film and Television*, South Melbourne, Australia, Macmillan

McNair, B. (1996) *Mediated Sex*, London, Arnold

——(2002) *Striptease Culture: Sex, Media and the Democratisation of Desire*, London and New York, Routledge

McRoy, J. (ed.) (2005) *Japanese Horror Cinema*, Edinburgh, Edinburgh University Press

Maingard, J. (1998) *Strategies of Representation in South African Anti-Apartheid Documentary Film and Video from 1976–1995*, unpublished PhD thesis, University of the Witwatersrand

——(2007) *South African National Cinema*, London and New York, Routledge

Malik, K. (1996) *The Meaning of Race: Race, History and Culture in Western Society*, New York, New York University Press

Malkiewicz, K. (1986) *Film Lighting*, New York, Prentice Hall

Maltby, R. (2003) *Hollywood Cinema*, 2nd edition, Malden, MA, and Oxford, Blackwell

Maltby, R., Stokes, M. and Allen, R. C. (2007) *Going to the Movies: Hollywood and the Social Experience of Cinema*, Exeter, University of Exeter Press

Manatu, N. (2003) *African American Women and Sexuality in the Cinema*, Jefferson, NC, and London, MacFarland and Co. Publishers

Manovich, L. (1999) 'What is Digital Cinema?' In: Lunefield, P. (ed.) *The Digital Dialectic: New Essays on New Media*, Cambridge, The Massachussetts Institute of Technology Press

——(2001) *The Language of New Media*, Cambridge, MA, The MIT Press

——(2005) *Soft Cinema: Navigating the Database*, Cambridge, MA, The MIT Press

Manuell, R. and Fraenkel, H. (1971) *The German Cinema*, London, J. M. Dent and Sons

Marcus, F. (ed.) (1971) *Film and Literature: Contrasts in the Media*, New York, Chandler Publishing

Marcus, M. (1987) *Film in the Light of Neo Realism*, Princeton, NJ, Princeton University Press

——(1993) *Filmmaking by the Book: Italian Cinema and Literary Adaptation*, Baltimore, MD, Johns Hopkins University Press

Marie, M. (2003) *The French New Wave: An Artistic School*, Oxford, Blackwell

Marks, L. (2000) *The Skin of Film: International Cinema, Embodiment, and the Senses*, Durham, NC, and London, Duke University Press

Marshall, B. and Stilwell, R. (eds) (2000) *Musicals: Hollywood and Beyond*, Exeter, UK and Portland, OR, Intellect Books

Martin, F. (2011) *Screens and Veils: Magrebhi Womens Cinema*, Bloomington, IN, Indiana University Press

Martin, M. T. (ed.) (1995) *Cinemas in the Black Diaspora: Diversity, Dependence and Oppositionality*, Detroit, Wayne State University Press

Martin-Jones, D. (2006) *Deleuze, Cinema and National Identity: Narrative Time in National Contexts*, Edinburgh, Edinburgh University Press

Mason, F. (2002) *American Gangster Cinema: From Little Caesar to Pulp Fiction*, Basingstoke and New York, Palgrave Macmillan

Masoud, P. (2003) *African American Urban Experiences in Film*, Philadelphia, PA, Temple University Press

Mast, G., Cohen, M. and Braudy, L. (eds) (1992) *Film Theory and Criticism*, 4th edition, Oxford, Oxford University Press

Mathijs, E. and Mendik, X. (2008) *The Cult Film Reader*, Maidenhead, McGraw Hill, Open University Press

——(2011) *100 Cult Films*, Basingstoke and London, British Film Institute Publishing, Palgrave Macmillan

Matthews, T. D. (1994) *Censored*, London, Chatto and Windus

Mayne, J. (1984) 'Women at the Keyhole: Women's Cinema and Feminist Criticism', in: Doane, M. A., Mellencamp, P. and Williams, L. (eds) *Revision: Essays in Feminist Film Criticism*, Frederick, MD, The American Film Institute/University Publications of America

——(1993) *Cinema and Spectatorship*, London and New York, Routledge

Medhurst, A. (2007) *A National Joke: Popular Comedy and English Cultural Identities*, London and New York, Routledge

Medovoi, L. (1998) 'Theorizing Historicity, or the Many Meanings of *Blacula*', *Screen*, vol. 39, no. 1

Mellen, J. (1974) *Women and Their Sexuality in the New Film*, New York, Dell

Mellencamp, P. (1995) *A Fine Romance: Five Ages of Film Feminism*, Philadelphia, PA, Temple University Press

Mell-Metereau, R. (1993) *Hollywood Androgyny*, New York, Columbia University Press

Mercer, K. (ed.) (1988) *Black Film: British Cinema*, ICA document no. 7, London, British Film Institute/ICA Publishing

——(1990) 'Diaspora Culture and the Dialogic Imagination: The Aesthetics of Black Independent Film in Britain', in: Alvarado, M. and Thompson, J. O. (eds) *The Media Reader*, London, British Film Institute Publishing

Mercer, J. and Shingler, M. (2001) *Melodrama: Genre, Style, Sensibility*, London and New York, Wallflower Press

Merquior, J. G. (1985) *Foucault*, London, Collins

Merton, P. (2007) *Silent Comedy*, London, Random House

Metz, C. (1971) *Essais sur la signification au cinéma, Tome I*, Paris, Editions Klincksieck

——(1972) *Essais sur la signification au cinéma, Tome II*, Paris, Editions Klincksieck; both volumes trans. M. Taylor (1974) as *Film Language: A Semiotics of the Cinema*, New York, Oxford University Press

——(1975) 'The Imaginary Signifier', *Screen*, vol. 16, no. 3

Meyer, S. C. (2017) *Music in Epic Film*, London and New York, Routledge

Meyers, R. (2001) *Great Martial Arts Movies: From Bruce Lee to Jackie Chan and More*, New York, Citadel Press

Millicent, M. (1987) *Film in the Light of Neo Realism*, Princeton, NJ, Princeton University Press

Milner, A. and Johnson, D., (2002) 'The Idea of Asia', https://digitalcollections.anu.edu.au/bitstream/1885/41891/1/idea.html (accessed 27 June 2016)

Minh-ha, T. T. (1989) 'Outside In Inside Out', in: Pines, J. and Willemen, P. (eds) *Questions of Third Cinema*, London, British Film Institute Publishing.

Mirbakhtyar, S. (2006) *Iranian Cinema and the Islamic Revolution*, Jefferson, NC, McFarland

Misek, R. (2010) *Chromatic Cinema: A History of Screen Colour*, Malden, MA, and Oxford, Wiley-Blackwell

Mishra, V. (2002) *Bollywood Cinema Temple of Desire*, London and New York, Routledge

Modleski, T. (1982) 'Never To Be Thirty-Six Years Old: *Rebecca* as Female Oedipal Drama', *Wide Angle*, vol. 5, no. 1

——(1988) *The Women Who Knew Too Much: Hitchcock and Feminist Theory*, New York and London, Methuen

——(1992) 'Time and Desire in the Woman's Film', in: Mast, G., Cohen, M. and Braudy, L. (eds) *Film Theory and Criticism*, 4th edition, Oxford, Oxford University Press

Moi, T. (1985) *Sexual/Textual Politics: Feminist Literary Theory*, London and New York, Routledge

Mongia, P. (ed.) (1996) *Contemporary Postcolonial Theory: A Reader*, London, New York, Sidney and Auckland, Arnold

Monk, C. (1996) 'Review of *Sense and Sensibility*', *Sight and Sound*, vol. 6, no. 3

Mora, S. de la (2006) *Cinemachismo: Masculinities and Sexuality in Mexican Cinema*, Austin, University of Texas Press

Moraga, C. and Anzaldua, G. (eds) (1981) *This Bridge Called My Back*, New York, Persephone Press

Morrissette, B. (1985) *Novel and Film: Essays in Two Genres*, Chicago, IL, Chicago University Press

Moseley, R. (ed.) (2005) *Fashioning Film Stars: Dress, Culture, Identity*, London, British Film Institute Publishing

Mudimbe, Y. V. (1988) *The Invention of Africa: Gnosis, Philosophy and the Order of Knowledge*, London, James Currey

——(1992) *The Surreptitious Speech: Présence Africaine and the Politics of Otherness, 1947–1987*, Chicago, IL, University of Chicago Press

——(1994) *The Idea of Africa*, Bloomington, Indiana University Press

Muir, J. K. (2005) *Singing a New Tune: The Rebirth of the Modern Film Musical, from Evita to De-Lovely and Beyond*, New York, Applause Theatre and Cinema Books

Mulvey, L. (1975) 'Visual Pleasure and Narrative Cinema', *Screen*, vol. 16, no. 3

——(1977) 'Notes on Sirk and Melodrama', *Movie*, no. 25

——(1987) 'Notes on Sirk and Melodrama' (updated), in: Gledhill, C. (ed.) *Home Is Where the Heart Is: Studies in Melodrama and Woman's Film*, London, British Film Institute Publishing

——(1989) *Visual and Other Pleasures*, London, Macmillan

——(2006) *Death 24x a Second: Stillness and the Moving Image*, London, Reaktion Books

Murray, B. (1990) *Film and the German Left in the Weimar Republic: From Caligari to Kuhle Wampe*, Austin, University of Texas Press

Naficy, H. (1979) 'Iranian Feature Films: A Brief Critical History', *Quarterly Review of Film Studies*, vol. 4

——(1992) 'Islamizing Cinema in Iran', in: Farsoun, S. K. and Mehrdad Mashayeki (eds) *Iran: Political Culture in the Islamic Republic*, London and New York, Routledge

——(1993) *The Making of Exile Cultures: Iranian Television in Los Angeles*, Minneapolis, University of Minnesota

——(2001) *An Accented Cinema: Exilic and Diasporic Filmmaking*, Princeton, NJ, Princeton University Press

Naficy, H. and Gabriel, T. (eds) (1993) *Otherness and the Media: The Ethnography of the Imagined and the Imaged*, Chur, Switzerland, Harwood Academic Publishers

Nagib, L. (2011) *World Cinema and the Ethics of Realism*, New York, Continuum International Publishing

Nagib, L., Perriam, C. and Dudrah, R. (eds) (2012) *Theorizing World Cinema*, London and New York, I. B. Tauris

Nama, A. (2008) *Black Space: Imagining Race in Science Fiction Film*, Austin, University of Texas Press

Napier, S. J. (2005) *Anime from Akira to Howl's Moving Castle: Experiencing Contemporary Japanese Animation*, New York, Palgrave

Naremore, J. (1988) *Acting in the Cinema*, Berkeley, University of California Press

Natoli, J. (2001) *Postmodern Journeys: Film and Culture 1996–1998*, New York, State University of New York Press

Neale, S. (1980) *Genre*, London, British Film Institute Publishing

——(1985) *Cinema and Technology: Image, Sound and Colour*, London, Macmillan/British Film Institute Publishing

——(1990) 'Questions of Genre', *Screen*, vol. 31, no. 1

——(2000) *Genre and Hollywood*, London and New York, Routledge

Neale, S. and Smith, M. (1998) *Contemporary Hollywood Cinema*, London and New York, Routledge

Nelmes, J. (2007) 'Women and Film', in: Nelmes, J. (ed.) *An Introduction to Film Studies*, Abingdon, Oxon, Routledge

Neupert, R. (1995) *The End: Narration and Closure in the Cinema*, Detroit, Wayne State University Press

Nichols, B. (1991) *Representing Reality: Issues and Concepts in Documentary*, Bloomington, Indiana University Press

——(2001) *Introduction to the Documentary*, Bloomington, Indiana University Press

Nicholson, L. (ed.) (1990) *Feminism/Postmodernism*, New York and London, Routledge

Noble, A. (2004) *Mexican National Cinema*, London and New York, Routledge

Novak, M. (2002) 'Speciation, Transvergence, Allogenesis: Notes on the Production of the Alien', *Architectural Design*, vol. 72, no. 3, 64–71

Nowell-Smith, A. (1987) 'Minnelli and Melodrama', in: Gledhill, C. (ed.) *Home Is Where the Heart Is: Studies in Melodrama and Woman's Film*, London, British Film Institute

Orr, J. (1993) *Cinema and Modernity*, Cambridge, Polity Press

Oshana, M. (1985) *Women of Colour: A Filmography of Minority and Third Would Women*, New York and London, Garland Publishing

O'Sullivan, T., Hartley, J., Saunders, D. and Fiske, J. (1992) *Key Concepts in Communication*, sixth reprint, London and New York, Routledge

Oudart, J.-P (1977) 'Cinema and Suture', *Screen*, vol. 18, no. 1

Ozguc, A. (1988) *A Chronological History of the Turkish Cinema: 1914–1988*, Istanbul, Ministry of Tourism

Page, J. (2009) *Crisis in Capitalism in Contemporary Argentinian Cinema*, Durham, NC, and London, Duke University Press

Palfrey, J. and Gasser, U. (2008) *Born Digital. Understanding the First Generation of Digital Natives*, New York, Basic Books

Palmer, R. B. (ed.) (2010) *Larger than Life: Movie Stars of the 1950s*, New Brunswick, NJ, and London, Rutgers University Press

Parrinder, P. (ed.) (2001) *Learning from Other Worlds: Estrangement, Cognition and the Politics of Science Fiction and Utopia*, Durham, NC, and London, Duke University Press

Paul, W. (1994) *Laughing Screaming: Modern Hollywood Horror and Comedy*, New York, Columbia University Press

Peacock, S. (2010) *Colour*, Manchester and New York, Manchester University Press

Pearson, R. (1992) *Eloquent Gestures: The Transformation of Performance Style in the Griffith Biograph Films*, Berkeley, University of California Press

Penley, C. (1985) 'Feminism, Film Theory and the Bachelor Machines', *m/f*, no. 10

——(1988) *Feminism and Film Theory*, New York, Routledge, and London, British Film Institute Publishing

——(1989) *The Future of an Illusion: Film, Feminism and Psychoanalysis*, New York and London, Routledge

Pepperell, R. and Punt, M. (2000) *The Postdigital Membrane: Imagination, Technology and Desire*, Bristol, Intellect Books

Petrie, D. (1996) *The British Cinematographer*, London, British Film Institute Publishing

——(2005) *Contemporary Scottish Fictions: Film, Television and the Novel*, Edinburgh, Edinburgh University Press; New York, Columbia University Press

Pettey, H. and Palmer, B. (2014a) *Film Noir*, Edinburgh, Edinburgh University Press

——(2014b) *International Noir*, Edinburgh, Edinburgh University Press

——(2014c) *Film Noir (Traditions in World Cinema)*, Edinburgh, Edinburgh University Press

Phillips, G. D. (2000) *Creatures of Darkness, Detective Fiction and Film Noir*, Lexington, University Press of Kentucky

Phillips, J. (2006) *Transgender on Screen*, Basingstoke and New York, Palgrave Press

Pick, S. (1993) *The New Latin American Cinema: A Continental Project*, Austin, University of Texas Press

Pierse, A. and Martin, D. (eds) (2013) *Korean Horror Film*, Edinburgh, Edinburgh University Press

Pillig, J. (ed.) (1992) *Women and Animation: A Compendium*, London, British Film Institute Publishing

——(1997) *A Reader in Animation Studies*, London, Paris, and Rome, John Libbey

Pines, J. and Willemen, P. (eds) (1989) *Questions of Third Cinema*, London, British Film Institute Publishing

Pippin, R. B. (2010) *Hollywood Westerns and American Myth: The Importance of Howard Hawkes and John Ford for Political Philosophy*, New Haven, CT, and London, Yale University Press

Place, J. (1980) 'Women in Film Noir', in: Kaplan, E. A. (ed.) *Women in Film Noir*, revised edition, London, British Film Institute

Porfirio, R., Silver, A. and Ursini, J. (eds) (2002) *Film Noir Reader 3: Interviews with Filmmakers of the Classic Noir Period*, New York, Limelight Editions

Powell, A. (2005) *Deleuze and Horror Film*, Edinburgh, Edinburgh University Press

Powrie, P. and Stilwell, R. (eds) (2005) *Changing Tunes: The Use of Pre-existing Music in Films*, Aldershot, Ashgate

Powrie, P., Davies, A. and Babington, B. (eds) (2004) *The Trouble with Men: Masculinities in European and Hollywood Cinema*, London and New York, Wallflower Press

Pribham, D. (ed.) (1988) *Female Spectators*, London and New York, Verso

Price, D. A. (2008) *The Pixar Touch: The Making of a Company*, New York, Alfred A. Knopf

Radner, H. and Stringer, R. (eds) (2011) *Feminism at the Movies: Understanding Gender in Contemporary Popular Film*, Abingdon, Oxon, Routledge

Raheja, D. and Kothari, J. (2004) *Indian Cinema: The Bollywood Saga*, London, Arum

Rajadhyaksha, A. (1996) 'India: Filming the Nation', in: Nowell-Smith, G. (ed.) *The Oxford History of World Cinema*, Oxford, Oxford University Press
——(2009) *Indian Cinema in the Time of Celluloid: from Bollywood to the Emergency*, Bloomington, IN, Indiana University Press

Rajadhyaksha, A. and Willemen, P. (1994) *Encyclopedia of Indian Film*, New Delhi and London, British Film Institute Publishing and Oxford University Press

Ramanathan, G. (2006) *Feminist Auteurs: Reading Women's Films*, London and New York, Wallflower Press

Ramirez-Berg, C. (2002) *Latino Images in Film: Stereotypes, Subversion, Resistance*, Austin, University of Texas Press

Rayns, T. and Meek, S. (eds) (1980) *Electric Shadows: Forty-five Years of Chinese Cinema*, London, British Film Institute Publishing

Reay, P. (2004) *Music in Film: Soundtracks and Synergy*, London and New York, Wallflower Press

Redner, G. (2010) *Deleuze and Film Music*, Chicago, IL, Chicago University Press

Reeckie, D. (2007) *Subversion: The Definitive History of Underground Cinema*, London and New York, Wallflower Press

Rees, A. L. (1997) 'Avant-Garde Film: The Second Wave', in: Nowell-Smith, G. (ed.) *The Oxford History of World Cinema*, Oxford, Oxford University Press

Regester, C. (2010) *African American Actresses and the Struggle for Visibility 1900–1960*, Bloomington, IN, Indiana University Press

Reid, M. A. (1993) *Redefining Black Film*, Berkeley, Los Angeles and Oxford, University of California Press
——(2005) *Black Lenses, Black Voices: African American Film now*, Lanham, MD, Boulder, CO, New York, Toronto and Oxford, Rowman and Littlefield Publishers

Renov, M. (ed.) (1993) *Theorizing Documentary*, New York and London, Routledge
——(2004) *The Subject of Documentary*, Minneapolis, Minnesota University Press

Rentschler, E. (1988) *West German Filmmakers on Film: Visions and Voices*, New York and London, Holmes and Meier

Rheudan, J. (1993) 'The Marriage of Maria Braun: History, Melodrama, Ideology', in: Friedan, S., McCormick, R. W., Petersen, V. R. and Vogelsang, L. M. (eds) *Gender and German Cinema, Feminist Interventions*, Oxford, Berg Publishers

Rich, B. R. (1992) 'New Queer Cinema', *Sight and Sound*, vol. 2, no. 15, 30–34

Rickitt, R. (2006) *Special Effects: The History and Technique*, London, Arum Press

Rickman, G. (ed.) (2001) *Film Comedy Reader*, New York, Limelight Editions
——(2004) *The Science Fiction Film Reader*, New York, Limelight Editions

Robe, C. (2010) *Left of Hollywood: Cinema and Modernism, and the Emergence of US Radical Film Culture*, Austin, University of Texas Press

Roberts, I. (2008) *German Expressionist Cinema: The World of Light and Shadow*, London and New York, Wallflower Press

Rocchio, V. F. (2000) *Reel Racism: Confronting Hollywood's Construction of Afro-American Culture*, Boulder, CO, and Oxford, Westview Press

Rodgerson, G. and Wilson, E. (eds) (1991) *Pornography and Feminism: The Case Against Censorship*, London, Lawrence and Wishart

Rodowick, D. N. (ed.) (2010) *Afterimages of Gilles Deleuze's Film Philosophy*, Minneapolis and London, University of Minnesota Press

Rombes, N. D. (2009) *Cinema in the Digital Age*, London and New York, Wallflower Press

Rose, Jacqueline (1986) *Sexuality in the Field of Vision*, London, Verso

Rose, Jane (2009) *Beyond Hammer: British Horror since 1970*, Leighton Buzzard, Auteur

Rosen, M. (1973) *Popcorn Venus: Women, Movies and the American Dream*, New York, Coward McCann and Geoghegan

Ross, K. (1996) *Black and White Media: Black Images in Popuhu Film and Television*, Cambridge, Polity Press

Rothman, G. (1976) 'Against "The System of the Suture" ', in: Nicholls, B. (ed.) *Movies and Methods: An Anthology*, Berkeley, University of California Press

Rowbotham, S. and Benyon, H. (eds) (2001) *Looking at Class: Film, Television and the Working Class in Britain*, London, Rivers Oram Press

Rozik, E. (2002) 'Acting: The Quintessence of Theatricality', *SubStance* vol. 31, nos 2/3, Special Issue: Theatricality

Russell, C. (1999) *Experimental Ethnography*, Durham, NC, and London, Duke University Press.

——(2000) 'Parallax Historiography: The Flâneuse as Cyberfeminist', *Scope On-Line Journal of Film Studies*, http://www.nottingham.ac.uk/film/journal (accessed 12 August 2016)

Russell, J. (2002) *The Pocket Essential Vietnam War Movie*, Harpenden, Hertfordshire, Pocket Essentials

Russo, V. (1981) *The Celluloid Closet: Homosexuality in the Movies*, New York, Harper and Row

——(1987) *The Celluloid Closet: Homosexuality in the Movies*, 2nd edition, New York, Harper and Row

Saari, A. (2011) *Indian Cinema: The Faces behind the Masks*, Oxford, Oxford University Press

Sadr, H. R. (2006) *Iranian Cinema: A Political History*, New York and London, I. B. Tauris

Saïd, E. (1978) *Orientalism*, New York, Pantheon

Salt, B. (1977) 'Film Style and Technology in the 1940s', *Film Quarterly*, Fall

——(1983) *Film Style and Technology: History and Analysis*, London, Starword

Sandler, K. S. (1998) (ed.) *Reading the Rabbit: Explorations in Warner Brothers Animation*, Brunswick, NJ, Rutgers University Press

Sargeant, J. (2001) *The Naked Lens: Beat Cinema*, updates and expanded edition, London, Creation

Sarkar, B. (2009) *Mourning the Nation: Indian Cinema in the Wake of Partition*, Durham, NC, and London, Duke University Press

Saunders, J. (2001) *The Western Genre: From Lordsburg to Big Whiskey*, London and New York, Wallflower Press

Schaefer, E. (1999) *'Bold! Daring! Shocking! True!': A History of Exploitation Films, 1919–1959*, Durham, NC, and London, Duke University Press

Schatz, T. (1981) *Hollywood Genres*, New York, Random House

Scheunemann, D. (ed.) (2003) *Expressionist Film: New Perspectives*, Rochester, NY, and Woodbridge (Suffolk), Camden House

Schneider, S. J. (2003) *Fear without Frontiers: Horror Cinema across the Globe*, Godalming, Surrey, FAB Press

——(ed.) (2004) *Horror Film and Psychoanalysis: Freud's Worst Nightmare*, Cambridge, Cambridge University Press

Schofield Clark, L. (2003) *From Angels to Aliens: Teenagers, the Media and the Supernatural*, Oxford and New York, Oxford University Press

Schoonover, K. (2012) *Brutal Vision: The Neorealist Body in Postwar Italian Cinema*, Minnesota, University of Minnesota Press

Schoonover, K. and Galt, R. (2016) *Queer Cinema in the World*, Durham, NC, Duke University Press

Schwartz, R. (2001) *Noir, Now and Then: Film Noir Originals and Remakes (1944–1999)*, Santa Barbara, CA, Greenwood Press

Schweinitz, J. (2011) *Film and Stereotype: A Challenge for Cinema and Theory*, trans. Laura Schleussner, New York, Columbia University Press

Screen (1984) 'Special Issue on the Soundtrack', vol. 25, no. 3

——(1988) 'Special Issue on Race', vol. 29, no. 4

——(1992) *Sexing the Subject: A Screen Reader in Sexuality*, London and New York, Routledge

Segal, L. and McIntosh, M. (eds) (1992) *Sex Exposed: Sexuality and the Pornography Debate*, London, Virago

Shafik, V. (1998) *Arab Cinema: History and Cultural Identity*, Cairo, American University in Cairo Press

——(2007) *Popular Egyptian Cinema: Gender, Class and Nation*, Cairo, American University in Cairo Press

Shapiro, H. (2003) *Shooting Stars: Drugs, Hollywood and the Movies*, London, Serpent's Tail

Shapiro, J. (2002) *Atomic Bomb Cinema: The Apocalyptic Imagination on Film*, New York and London, Routledge

Shary, T. (2009) *Teen Movies: American Youth on Screen*, New York and Chichester, UK, Columbia University Press (Wallflower Short Cuts Series)

Shaviro, S. (1993) *The Cinematic Body*, Minneapolis, University of Minnesota Press

Shaw, D. (2013) 'Deconstructing and Reconstructing "Transnational Cinema"', in: Dennison, S. (ed.) *Contemporary Hispanic Cinema: Interrogating Transnationalism in Spanish and Latin American Film*, Woodbridge, Tamesis

Shaw, L. and Dennison, S. (2007) *Brazilian National Cinema*, London and New York, Routledge

Shaw, T. (2001) *The British Cinema and the Cold War Film*, London and New York, I. B. Tauris

Sheldon Lu (ed.) (1997) *Transnational Chinese Cinemas: Identity, Nationhood, Gender*, Honolulu, University of Hawaï Press

Sheldon Lu and Mi, J. (2009) *Chinese Ecocinema: In the Age of Environmental Challenge*, Hong Kong, Hong Kong University Press

Shiel, M. (2006) *Italian Neo-Realism: Rebuilding the Cinematic City*, London and New York, Wallflower Press

Shiri, K. (ed.) (1993) *Africa at the Pictures*, British Film Institute Dossier no. 10, London, National Film Theatre Publication

Shohat, E. (1989) *Israeli Cinema: East/West and the Politics of Representation*, Austin, University of Texas Press

——(1996) 'Post-Third-Worldist Culture: Gender, Nation and the Cinema', in: Alexander, J. and Moharty, C. T. (eds) *Feminist Genealogies, Colonial Legacies, Democratic Futures*, London and New York, Routledge

——(2003) *Multiculturalism, Postcoloniality and Transnational Media*, New Brunswick, NJ, and London, Rutgers University Press

——(2006) 'Post-Third-Worldist-Culture', in: Ezra, E. and Rowden, T. (eds) *Transnational Cinema: The Film Reader*, London and New York, Routledge, 39–56

——(2010) *Israeli Cinema: East/West and the Politics of Representation*, new edition, New York and London, I. B. Tauris

Shohat, E. and Stam, R. (1994) *Unthinking Eurocentrism: Multiculturalism and the Media*, New York and London, Routledge

Showalter, E. (ed.) (1989) *Speaking of Gender*, New York and London, Routledge

Silberman, K. (1981) 'Masochism and Subjectivity', *Framework*, no. 12

Silberman, M. (1996) 'What is German in the German Cinema?', *Film History*, vol. 8

Singer, B. (2001) *Melodrama and Modernity: Early Sensational Cinema and its Contexts*, New York, Columbia University Press

Sitney, P. A. (1974) *Visionary Film: The American Avant-Garde*, New York, Oxford University Press

——(1978) *The Avant-Garde Film: A Reader of Theory and Criticism*, New York, New York University Press

Slobin, M. (ed.) (2008) *Global Sound Tracks: Worlds of Film Music*, Middleton, CT, Wesleyan University Press

Slocum, D. J. (2001) *Violence and American Cinema*, New York and London, Routledge

Smith, J. (2004) *Gangster Films*, London, Virgin

Smith, M. (1998) 'Modernism and the Avant-Gardes', in: Hill, J. and Church-Gibson, P. (eds) *The Oxford Guide to Film Studies*, Oxford, Oxford University Press

Smith, S. (2005) *The Musical: Race, Gender and Performance*, London and New York, Wallflower Press

Snead, J., MacCabe, C. and West, C. (eds) (1994) *White Screen, Black Images: Hollywood from the Dark Side*, New York and London, Routledge

Sobchack, V. (1992) *The Address of the Eye: A Phenomenology of Film Experience*, Princeton, NJ, Princeton University Press

——(1993) *Screening Space: The American Science Fiction Film*, New York, New York University Press

Soderbergh, S. (1999) 'The Flash-back Kid: Interview with Steven Soderbergh, by Sheila Johnston', *Sight and Sound*, no. 9, vol. 11, 12–14

Solanas, F. and Getino, O. (1983) 'Towards a Third Cinema', in: Chanan, M. (ed.) *Twenty-Five Years of the New Latin American Cinema*, London, British Film Institute Publishing

Solomon, C. (ed.) (1987) *The Art of the Animated Image*, Los Angeles, American Film Institute

——(1994) *History of Animation*, New York, Wings Books, Random House

Sonnenschein, D. (2001) *Sound Design: The Expressive Power of Music, Voice and Sound*, Studio City, CA, Michael Wise Productions

Sorlin, E. (1991) *European Cinemas, European Societies 1939–1990*, New York and London, Routledge

Spicer, A. (2002) *Film Noir*, Harlow (Essex), Pearson Education

Spivak, G. C. (1985) 'Can the Subaltern Speak? Speculations on Widow Sacrifice', *Wedge*, vol. 7, no. 8

——(1987) *In Other Worlds: Essays on Cultural Politics*, New York, Methuen

Stacey, J. (1993) *Star Gazing: Hollywood Cinema and Female Spectatorship*, London and New York, Routledge

——(2010) *The Cinematic Life of a Gene*, Durham, NC, and London, Duke University Press

Stacey, J. and Street, S. (eds) (2007) *Queer Screen: A Screen Reader*, London and New York, Routledge

Staig, L. and Williams, T. (1975) *The Italian Western: The Opera of Violence*, London, Lorrimer

Staiger, J. (2000) *Perverse Spectators: The Practices of Film Reception*, New York and London, University of New York Press

——(2005) *Media Reception Studies*, New York and London, New York University Press

Stam, R. (2000) *Film Theory: An Introduction*, London and New York, Blackwell

——(2005) *Literature through Film: Realism, Magic and the Art of Adaptation*, Malden, MA, and Oxford, Blackwell Publishing

Stam, R., Burgoyne, R. and Flitterman-Lewis, S. (1992) *New Vocabularies in Film Semiotics: Structuralism, Post-Structuralism and Beyond*, New York and London, Routledge

Stanfield, P. (2001) *Hollywood, Westerns and the 1930s: The Lost Trail*, Exeter, Exeter University Press

Stead, P. (1989) *Film and Working Class*, London and New York, Routledge

Stephens, M. L. (1995) *Film Noir: A Comprehensive Illustrated Reference to Movies, Terms and Persons*, North Carolina and London, McFarland Publishers

Stevenson, J. (ed.) (2000) *Fleshpot: Cinema's Sexual Myth and Taboo Breakers*, Manchester, Head Press

——(2003) *Dogme Uncut: Lars Von Trier, Thomas Vinterberg and the Gang that Took on Hollywood*, Santa Monica, CA, Santa Monica Press

Stollery, M. (2001) 'Masculinities, Generations, and Cultural Transformation in Contemporary Tunisian Cinema', *Screen*, vol. 42, no. 1, 48–63

Street, S. (2001) *Costume and Cinema: Dress Codes in Popular Film*, London and New York, Wallflower Press

Stringer, J. (ed.) (2003) *Movie Blockbusters*, London and New York, Routledge

Strong, J. (1999) *Six Novels Adapted for Cinema*, unpublished PhD thesis, Stirling University

Studlar, G. (1985) 'Masochism and the Perverse Pleasures of the Cinema', in: Nicholls, B. (ed.) *Movies and Methods*, vol. 2, Berkeley, University of California Press

——(ed.) (2001) *John Ford Made Westerns: Filming the Legend in the Sound Era*, Bloomington, IN, Indiana University Press

Suleri, S. (1992) 'Woman Skin Deep: Feminism and the Postcolonial Condition', *Critical Inquiry*, no. 18, vol. 4

Suner, A. (2010) *New Turkish Cinema: Belonging, Identity and Memory*, London and New York, I. B. Tauris

Tapper, R. (ed.) (2002) *The New Iranian Cinema: Politics, Representation and Identity*, London, I. B. Tauris

Tarr, C. (2005) *Reframing Difference: Beur and Banlieue Film-Making in France*, Manchester, Manchester University Press

Tasker, Y. (1993) *Spectacular Bodies: Gender, Genre and the Action Cinema*, Comedia Series, New York and London, Routledge

——(2011) *'Soldiers' Stories: Military Women in Cinema and Television since World War II*, Durham, NC, and London, Duke University Press

Tasker, Y. and Negra, D. (eds) (2007) *Interpreting Postfeminism: Gender and the Politics of Popular Culture*, Durham, NC, and London, Duke University Press

Taylor, C. (1986) 'The L.A. Rebellion: New Spirit in American Film', *Black Film Review*, vol. 2, no. 2

——(1996a) *The Encyclopedia of Animation Techniques*, Oxford, Boston, Johannesburg, Melbourne, New Delhi and Singapore, Focal Press

——(1996b) 'The Re-birth of the Aesthetic in Cinema', in: Bernardi, D. (ed.) *The Birth of Whiteness: Race and the Emergence of US Cinema*, New Jersey, Rutgers University Press

Taylor, R. and Christie, I. (eds) (1994a) *The Film Factory: Russian and Soviet Cinema in Documents 1896–1939*, London and New York, Routledge

——(1994b) *Inside the Film Factory: New Approaches to Russian and Soviet Cinema*, London and New York, Routledge

Taylor, R. and Spring, D. (eds) (1993) *Stalinism and Soviet Cinema*, London and New York, Routledge

Telotte, J. P. (ed.) (1991) *The Film Cult Experience: Beyond all Reason*, Austin, University of Texas Press

——(1999) *A Distant Technology: Science Fiction and the Machine Age*, New England, Wesleyan University Press of New England

Teo, S. (2008) 'Promise and Perhaps Love: Pan-Asian Production and the Hong Kong–China Interrelationship', in: *Inter-Asia Cultural Studies*, vol. 9, no. 3, London, Routledge

Thomas, D. (2000) *Beyond Genre: Melodrama, Comedy and Romance in Hollywood Films*, Moffat, Dumfrieshire, Cameron and Hollis

Tolman, M. and Peleg, Y. (eds) (2011) *Israeli Cinema: Identities in Motion*, Austin, University of Texas Press

Tomaselli, K. (1988) *The Cinema of Apartheid*, New York, Smyrna Press

Tompkin, J. (1992) *West of Everything: The Inner Life of Westerns*, New York, Oxford University Press

Torgovnik, J. (2003) *Bollywood Dreams*, London and New York, Phaidon Press

Trifonova, T. (ed.) (2009) *European Film Theory*, New York and London, Routledge

Tryon, C. (2009) *Reinventing Cinema: Movies in the Age of Media Convergence*, New Brunswick, NJ, and London, Rutgers University Press

Tudor, A. (1989) *Monsters and Mad Scientists: A Cultural History of the Horror Movie*, Oxford, Blackwell

Turim, M. (1989) *Flashbacks in Film: Memory and History*, New York and London, Routledge

Turner, G. (1988) *Film as Social Practice*, London and New York, Routledge

Tuska, J. (1976) *The Films of the West*, New York, Doubleday and Co

Tyler, P. (1995) *Underground Film: A Critical History*, reprinted, New York, Da Capo

Tzioumakis, Y. (2006) *American Independent Cinema*, Edinburgh, Edinburgh University Press

——(2013) *Hollywood's Indies*, Edinburgh, Edinburgh University Press

Ukadike, N. F. (1994) *Black African Cinema*, Berkeley, Los Angeles and London, University of California

——(ed.) (1995) *New Discourses of African Cinema*, Special Issue of *Iris*, no. 18

Van Sant, G. (2004) quoted in S. F. Saïd's article 'Shock Corridors', *Sight and Sound*, vol. 14, no. 2, 16–18

Vasey, R. (1997) *The World According to Hollywood: 1918–1939*, Exeter, Exeter University Press

Verhoeven, D. (1997) 'The Sexual Terrain of the Australian Feature Film: Putting the Outback into the Ocker', in: Jackson, C. and Tapp, P. (eds) *The Bent Lens: A World Guide to Gay and Lesbian Film*, St Kilda, Victoria, Australian Catalogue Company

Vieler-Portet, C. (1991) *Black and Third World Cinema: Film and Television Bibliography*, London, British Film Institute Publishing

Viera, J. D. and Viera, M. (2005) *Lighting for Film and Digital Cinematography*, Independence, KY, Wadsworth

Vieyra, P. S. (1975) *Le Cinéma Africain des origines à 1973*, Paris, Présence Africaine

——(1983) *Le Cinéma au Sénégal*, Brussels and Paris, OCIC/L Harmattan

Vincendeau, G. (ed.) (1995) *Encyclopedia of European Cinema*, New York, Facts on File

——(2001) *Film/Literature/Heritage, A Sight and Sound Reader*, London, British Film Institute Publishing

Von Gunden, K. (2001) *Flights of Fancy: The Great Fantasy Films*, Jefferson, NC, London, McFarland

Wagner, G. (1975) *The Novel and the Cinema*, New York, Associated University Presses

Wagstaff, C. (2007) *Italian Neo-Realist Cinema*, Toronto, Toronto Italian Studies

Walker, J. (ed.) (2001) *Westerns: Films through History*, New York and London, Routledge

——(2015) *Contemporary British Horror*, Edinburgh, Edinburgh University Press

Walters, J. (2011) *Fantasy Film: A Critical Introduction*, Oxford and New York, Berg

Washburn, D. (2001) *Word and Image in Japanese Cinema*, Cambridge and New York, Cambridge University Press

Watkins, S. C. (1998) *Representing Hip-Hop Culture and the Production of Black Cinema*, Chicago and London, University of Chicago Press

Wayne, M. (2001) *Political Film: The Dialectics of Third Cinema*, London and Sterling, VA, Pluto Press

Weishar, P. (2004) *Moving Pixels: Blockbuster Animation and 3D Modelling Today*, London, Thames and Hudson

Weiss, A. (1990) *Vampires and Violets: Lesbian Representation in the Cinema*, London, Pandora Press

Weisser, T. (1997) *Asian Cult Cinema*, New York, Boulevard Books

Wells, P. (1998) *Understanding Animation*, London, Routledge

——(2002a) *Animation and America*, Edinburgh, Edinburgh University Press

——(2002b) *Animation: Genre and Authorship*, London, Wallflower Press

——(2008) *Re-Imagining Animation: The Changing Face of Moving Images*, Lausanne, AVA

Whelelan, T. (2000) *Overloaded: Popular Culture and the Future of Feminism*, Ebbw Vale, The Women's Press

Whisman, V. (1995) *Queer by Choice: Lesbians and Gayness and the Politics of Identity*, New York, Routledge

Wilderson III, F. B. (2010) *Red, White and Black: Cinema and the Structure of U.S. Antagonisms*, Durham, NC, and London, Duke University Press

Wilkins, M. (1989) 'I'm Gonna Git You Sucka: A Glance at the Blaxploitation Era', *Black Face*, no. 1

Willemen, P. (1989) 'The Third Cinema Question: Notes and Reflections', in: Pines, J. and Willemen, P. (eds) *Questions of Third Cinema*, London, British Film Institute Publishing

——(1994) *Looks and Frictions: Essays in Cultural Studies and Film Theory*, London, British Film Institute Publishing

Williams, C. (ed.) (1980) *Realism in the Cinema*, London and Henley, Routledge and Kegan Paul

Williams, L. (1981) *Figures of Desire: A Theory and Analysis of Surrealist Film*, Urbana, Chicago and London, University of Illinois Press

——(1984) 'When the Woman Looks', in: Doane, M. A., Mellencamp, P. and Williams, L. (eds) *Re-vision: Essays in Feminist Film Criticism*, Frederick, MD, The American Film Institute/University Publications of America

——(2002) *Playing the Race Card: Melodramas of Black and White from Uncle Tom to O. J. Simpson*, Princeton, NJ, Princeton University Press

——(2004) *Porn Studies*, Durham, NC, and London, Duke University Press

Williams, L. R. (2005) *The Erotic Thriller in Contemporary Cinema*, Edinburgh, Edinburgh University Press

Willis, H. (2005) *New Digital Cinema: Re-inventing the Moving Image*, London and New York, Wallflower Press

Wilson, A. (2002) *24 Hour Party People: What the Sleeve Notes never Tell You*, London, Channel 4 Books

Winston, B. (1995) *Claiming the Real: The Documentary Film Revisited*, London, British Film Institute Publishing

Wojcik, P. R. and Knight, A. (eds) (2001) *Soundtrack Available: Essays on Film and Popular Music*, Durham, NC, Duke University Press

Wollen, P. (1972) *Signs and Meaning in the Cinema*, London, Secker and Warburg

——(1982) *Semiotic Counter-Strategies: Readings and Writings*, London, Verso

Wood, J. (2006) *The Faber Book of Mexican Cinema*, London, Faber and Faber

Wood, R. (1979) 'Introduction', in: Wood, R. and Lippe, R. (eds) *The American Nightmare: Essays on the Horror Film*, Toronto, Festivals of Festivals

——(1992) 'Ideology, Genre, Auteur', in: Mast, G., Cohen, M. and Braudy, L. (eds) *Film Theory and Criticism*, Oxford, Oxford University Press

Woodhead, C. (ed.) (1989) *Turkish Cinema: An Introduction*, London, Centre for Near and Middle-Eastern Studies, Occasional Paper 5

Worley, A. (2005) *Empires of the Imagination: A Critical Survey of Fantasy Cinema from Georges Méliès to The Lord of the Rings*, Jefferson, NC, and London, McFarland

Wrathall, J. (2004) 'Excursion to Hell', *Sight and Sound*, vol. 14, no. 2, 28–30

Wright, W. (1975) *Six Guns and Society: A Structural Study of the Western*, Berkeley, Los Angeles and London, University of California Press

Xavier, I. (1997) 'The Humiliation of the Father: Melodrama and Cinema Nôvo's Critique of Conservative Modernization', *Screen*, no. 38, 4

Xu, G. G. (2007) *Sinscape: Contemporary Chinese Cinema*, Lanham, MD, Boulder, CO, New York and Toronto, Rowman and Littlefield

Yau, E. (1996) 'China after the Revolution', in: Nowell-Smith, G. (ed.), *The Oxford History of World Cinema*, Oxford and New York, Oxford University Press

Yosef, R. C. (2011) *The Politics of Loss and Trauma in Contemporary Israeli Cinema*, London, Routledge

Young, L. (1996) *Fear of the Dark: 'Race', Gender and Sexuality in the Cinema*, London and New York, Routledge

Zhang, X. (1998) *Chinese Modernism in the Era of Reform*, Durham, NC, Duke University Press

Zhang, Y. (2004) *Chinese National Cinema*, London and New York, Routledge

——(2010) *Cinema, Space, and Polylocality in a Globalizing China*, Honolulu, University of Hawaï Press

Zhang, Y. and Xiao, Z. (eds) (1998) *Encyclopedia of Chinese Film*, London and New York, Routledge

Zhang, Z. (ed.) (2007) *The Urban Generation: Chinese Cinema and Society at the Turn of the Twenty-First Century*, Durham, NC, and London, Duke University Press

Zizek, S. (1999) *The Fright of Real Tears: The Uses and Misuses of Lacan in Film Theory*, London, British Film Institute Publishing

——(2010) *Everything You always Wanted to Know about Lacan (but Were Afraid to Ask Hitchcock)*, updated edition, London and New York, Verso

Zone, R. (2007) *Stereoscopic Cinema and the Origins of 3-D Film 1838–1952*, Lexington, The University Press of Kentucky

INDEX OF FILMS

Note: **Bold** page numbers indicate tables

4 little girls 58
12 Years a Slave 47, 243
13ᵗʰ 62
18 jours (*Eighteen Days*) 470
23 Quai du Commerce 41–2
25th Hour 59
28 Days Later 223
30 Days in Atlanta 461
Les 400 Coups 182
2001: A Space Odyssey 202, 336, 340
3000 Nights 514
10949 femmes (*10949 Women*) 475

À Casablanca les anges ne volent pas (*In Casablanca Angels Don't Fly*) 477
À ma soeur (*For my Sister*) 291, 350
À nous la liberté (*Freedom for Us*) 31
Abi and Rabi 521
About Elly 525
The Accused 380
Aces High 416, 476
Across the Pacific 421
Adieu Bonaparte (*Goodbye Bonaparte*) 468
The Adventures of Buffalo Bill 432, 436
Adventures of Priscilla, Queen of the Desert 76, 275, 327, 333
The Adventures of Robin Hood 8
The African Queen 97
Afrique 50 472
Afrique sur Seine 457
The Age of Innocence 13, 100
The Age of Stupid 99
Aguirre, Wrath of God 213
A.I. 339
Aileen Wuornos: Life and Death of a Serial Killer 127

Air Force 423
Ajantrik (*The Unmechanical*) 397
Akher Ayam el Madina (*In the Last Days of the City*) 470
Al Dhikrayat al Kasibah (*al-Djakira alkhisba*) (*Fertile Memories*) 512–13
Alam Ara 72
Alexander 140
Alexander Nevsky 367
Algérie en flammes (*Algeria in Flames*) 472
Algiers/Beyrouth: pour mémoire (*Algiers/ Beirut: A Souvenir*) 474
Ali Baba 488
Ali, Rabiaa et les autres (*Ali, Rabiaa and the Others*) 477–8
Ali Zaoua 478
Alibaba and the Forty Thieves 488
Alice in Wonderland 403
Alien 3 151, 223, 337
Alien Resurrection 337
Alien trilogy 11, 151, 223, 337
Aliens of the Deep 403
All Quiet on the Western Front 410, 416
All that Heaven Allows 246, 249, 255
Alphaville 340
Alum Ara 489
Amadi 455
Ama's Children 517
Amateur 231
An American in Paris 273, 277
Amores perros (*Love's a Bitch*) 506
Amy 47
Anatomy of Hell 291
Andaz 490

Annabelle series 224
L'Année dernière à Marienbad 138, 265
Les Années folles du twist (Mad Years of the Twist) 473
Annie Oakley 437
Anokhi Dastan 496
Antonio das Mortes 79, 500, 501
Antz 23
Aparajito 486
Apocalypse Now 231, 427–8
The Apple 523–4, 525–6
Arizona Bill 431
Armageddon 10
Arroseur arrosé 97
The Artist 356
Ascenseur pour l'échafaud (Lift to the Scaffold) 267
L'Assassinat du duc de Guise 172
At 5 in the Afternoon 525
Attack! 424
Attila 139
Au coeur de la bataille d'Alep (In the Heart of the Battle of Aleppo) 509
El Aura (The Aura) 504
Austin Powers 98
L'Autre (The Other) 468
L'Autre motié du ciel (The Other Half of the Sky) 476
Avatar 10, **64**, 65, 78, 99, 115, 117, 403
The Avengers **64**, 65
The Aviator 202
Awaara 490
Awkat Faragh (Free Times) 470

Bab El-Oued City 474
Babel 507
Babes in Arms 272
Babes on Broadway 272
Backwards Birth of a Nation 145
Badlands 333
Baise-moi 291–2, 350
Baldwin's Nigger 43
The Ballad of Little Jo 437
Bamako 459, 462
Bamboozled 130
Bande à part 305
The Bandit 520
Bangkok Dangerous 7
Barakat! (Enough!) 475

Barb Wire 12
The Barkleys of Broadway 277
Basic Instinct 291
The Bat 109
Bataan 423
La Bataille d'Alger (Battle of Algiers) 398, 472
La Bataille du rail 419
Batman Returns 357
Battle of Britain 424
The Battle of Midway 420
Battle for the Planet of the Apes 336
The Battle of the Somme 415, 416
Battleground 423
Battleship Potemkin 137, 261, 365, 366–7
Bayiri, la patrie 459
The Beast from 20,000 Fathoms 221
Le Beau Serge 182
Bédouin Hacker 476
Before Vanishing 510
Beginning and End 468
The Beginning or the End? 426–7
Behind the Green Door 290
Behind the Sun 505
Beijing Bicycle 485
Being Cyrus 494
Being John Malkovich 328
Belle 46
La Belle et la Bête 225–6, 268
La Belle équipe 184
Beloved 13
Ben Hur 138
Bend it Like Beckham 47
Bend of the River 438
Beneath the Planet of the Apes 336
Beowulf 78
Berlin 420
A Better Tomorrow 7
Beyrouth, ville ouverte (Beirut, Open City) 510
Bezhin Meadow 367
Bhai Log 498
Bhaji on the Beach 46
The Big Boss 7
Big Jim McClain 426
The Big Lebowski 103
Big Timers 50
Bigger than Life 248
Billy the Kid 435

The Birds 405
The Birth of a Nation 48, 50, 139, 145, 349, 428
Birth of a Race 50
Bismarck 419
Biutiful 507
Black 494
Black Joy 279
Black Narcissus 269
Black Skin, White Masks 463
The Blackboard Jungle 146
Blackboards 525, 526
Blacula 55, 56, 57
Blade Runner 340
Blair Witch Project 130
Blazing Saddles 199
Bled Number One (Number One Village) 475
The Blind Side 380
The Blob 221
Blood Feast 218
The Blood of the Condor 500
Blue Collar 231
Blue Denim 147
Blue Velvet 231
The Body Beautiful 46
Body of Evidence 291
Body of Lies 99, 430
Bombay 493
Bond movies 6, 10
Bonnie and Clyde 427, 440
Boogie Nights 231, 290
Born in Flames 326
Born on the Fourth of July 428
Borome Sarret 457
Boss Nigger (The Black Bounty Killer) 55, 438
Bound 328
Bourne Identity 9
Bourne Supremacy 9
Bourne Trilogy 9, 66
Bourne Ultimatum 9
À bout de souffle (Breathless) 4, 103, 104, 182, 237, 243
Bowling for Columbine 128
Boys Don't Cry 328
Boyz n the Hood 61, 227
Brick 171
Bride and Prejudice 47, 72, 494
Bridesmaids 380

The Bridge 423
The Bridge on the River Kwai 424
A Bridge Too Far 424
Bridget Jones 98
Bringing up Baby 356
The Broadway Melody 270
Brokeback Mountain 76, 326, 329, 346
Broken Arrow 199, 440
Bronco Billy's Redemption 433
The Brood 222, 268, 339
The Brute 51
Bruxelles 42
Bubble 119
Buck and the Preacher 438
Buena vida Delivery 504
Buffalo Bill 436
Bulbule-Pakistan 495
Bullet Boy 46
Bully 149
Burma Victory 418
The Burmese Harp 423
Burning an Illusion 44
Butch Cassidy and the Sundance Kid 75, 201, 440
Butterfly Kiss 329

Cabaret 280
Cabin in the Sky 273, 278
The Cabinet of Dr Caligari 107, 207, 208–9, 219
Cairo 30 468
Canticle of the Stones 513
Capitalism: A Love Story 128
Captain Blood 8
Caramel 510
Carandiru 505
Carefree 271
Carry On movies 98
Casablanca 103, 118, 422
Casanova 268
Casenegra 478
Cat People 68, 220
Cave of Forgotten Dreams 128, 403
Central do Brazil (Central Station) 502, 504
Le Chagrin et la pitié 126
La Chambre noire (The Black Room) 478
Le Chant d'amour 324
Chariots of Fire 100

Charlie's Angels 11
The Chess Players 486
Chicago 275
Chicken Ranch 127
Chicken Run 24
Un chien andalou 41, 138, 411
Chikin Biznis ... The Whole Story 461
Children of Men 340, 507
Children of the Atom Bomb 425
China Gate 427
China, My Sorrow 485
Chinatown 199
La Chinoise 41
Chisum 441
Christopher Strong 249
Chronicle of a Disappearance 513
Chronique des années de braise (*Chronicle of the Years of Embers*) 472
Chronique d'un été 126
Cidade de Deus (*City of God*) 505
Le Ciel est à vous 418
The Circle 524, 526
A Citizen, an Inspector and a Thief 469
Citizen Kane 108, 109, 110, 500
City of Hope 232
Clash of the Titans 10
Claws of the Lion 460
Clean Pastures 21
Clear and Present Danger 404
Cleopatra 64, 138, 140
Cleopatra Jones 56
Clerks 231
Climates 521
Close Encounters of the Third Kind 336
Closed Curtain 525
Clouds of May 521
Coal Black and De Sebben Dwarves 21
Coalface 125
Cobra 66
The Cobweb 248
Coffy 56
Collateral 6, 10, 66, 67
Collateral Damage 8
The Color of Money 75
The Color of Olives 513
The Color Purple 13, 349
The Colossus of New York 221
Colossus of Rhodes 139
Come Back Africa 411
Come See 425

Coming Home 428
Como agua para chocolate (*Like Water for Chocolate*) 506
Complusion 325
Concerto Darb Saada 469
Confession 520–1
Confessions of a Nazi Spy 421
Congorilla 457
Conjuring 224
The Connection 411
Conquest of the Planet of the Apes 336
Conspiracy of the Doomed 427
Contagion 337
The Conversation 231
The Cool and the Crazy 145
The Cool World 52, 411
Copie conforme (*Certified Copy*) 524
La Coquille et Ie clergyman 41, 262
Le Coubeau 418
Courage under Fire 429
Covenant 337
The Covered Wagon 433
The Cow 523
The Created Surface of the Earth 363
Le Cri du coeur 464
Le Crime de M. Lange 184
Crime in the Streets 146
El crimen de padre Amaro (*The Crime of Father Amaro*) 506
Crimson Gold 524
Cronicamente Inviável (*Chronically Unfeasible*) 505
Crouching Tiger, Hidden Dragon 7, 408–9
The Crow 9
Cry Freedom 462
The Crying Game 194
Curfew 513
The Cut 521
Cyrano de Bergerac 142

Dam 21
The Dam Busters 179–80, 423
Dancer in the Dark 275, 282
Dances with Wolves 440, 442
Dancing Darkies 49
The Dancing Nig 49
A Dangerous Method 268
Daresalam 459
Dark Knight trilogy 409

The Dark Night 381
Daughters of the Dust 54
A Day at War 420
The Day the Earth Caught Fire 335
The Days 484
Dazzling Mirage 461
Dead End 109
Dead Man 232
Dead Ringers 151, 202, 268, 339, 406
Death in Venice 266
Death Wish series 11
Deep Throat 103, 290
The Deer Hunter 427
Dégradé (Degraded) 514
Délice Paloma 475
Les Demoiselles de Rochefon 275
Demolition Man 11
The Demolition of the Russian
    Monument at St Stephen 517
Derek 46
Desert Hearts 326
Desert Victory 418
Le Destin (Fate) 468
Destiny 209, 521
Deuses e os Morios (The Gods and the
    Dead) 80
Devarin (Things) 516
Devdas 69, 72, 490
Devi 486
Devil's Doorway 440
Dharti Ke Lal (Children of the
    Earth) 397
Die Hard series 6, 11
Dingjun Mountain 481
Dirty Gertie from Harlem 50
Dis-moi qui tu es 459
Disparus, la guerre invisible de Syrie (The
    Disappeared: The Invisible Syrian
    War) 509
Distant 521
The Divine Horsemen 141
Divine Intervention 513
Django Unchained 441
Do Ansoo 496
Do the Right Thing 58
Dogville 130
The Dolly Sisters 272
Doña Herlinda y su hijo (Dona Herlinda
    and Her Son) 503
Dostana 71, 494

Double Indemnity 169
Dowaha (Buried Secrets) 476
Dr Jekyll and Mr Hyde 219, 222
Dr Mabuse, the Gambler 206, 209
Dr Strangelove: or, How I Learned to
    Stop Worrying and Love the Bomb
    335, 426
Dracula (1931) 218
Dracula (1992) 220, 224
Dragstrip Girl 146
Dragstrip Riot 146
Dreaming Rivers 46
Dreams of a City 509
The Driller Killer 218
Drive 171
Drop Zone 11
Drugstore Cowboy 232
Les Dupes (The Deceived) 468

The Earth 365
East Palace (West Palace) 329, 484
Easy Rider 75, 91, 231, 280, 333
Eau argentée, Syrie auto-portrait (Silver
    Water, Syria Self-Portrait) 509
Edward II 325
The Elegy 518
Elephant 232
Elite da Tropa (The Elite Squad) 505
Emmanuelle 103
Empire 144, 262, 411
En résidence surveillée (Under House
    Arrest) 457
Enemies of the People 128
Engineman 180
England Expects 415
Entr'acte 105, 261
Envy 521
Equal Wages for Men and Women 214
Eraserhead 103, 231
Eshtebak (Clash) 470–1
E.T. 336
Et Dieu créa la femme 181
Un été à La Goulette 478
The Eternal Jew (Der Ewige Jude) 419
Even Cowgirls Get the Blues 325
Every Day Except Christmas 180
Everyday Life in a Syrian Village 509
Evita 275
The Exorcist 222–3, 225
Expresso Bongo 274

The Extraordinary Adventures of Mr West in the Land of the Bolsheviks 365
Eyes of a Thief 514

Face à face (Face to Face) 478
Face/Off 7
Fahrenheit 9/11 128
Fair Game 430
The Fall Guy 50
Fame 275
Family on Fire 461
Fantasmagorie 19
Fantômas 185
Far from Heaven 203
Farewell My Concubine 329, 484
Fatal Attraction 151, 290, 372, 380
Fate 520
Father Son and Holy War 398
The Fatherland Calls (Das Vaterland ruft) 415
Fathy La Yaaish Hena Baad El-An (Fathy No Longer Lives Here) 470
Faust 208
Fear Eats the Soul 213, 325
Felix the Cat 19
Femmes du Caire (Scheherazade Tell Me a Story) 470
Festen 116, 117
Festen, Mifune 130
Fetih 1453 520
The Fifth Element 340
The Figurine: Araromire 461
Film Essay on the Euphrates 509
Final Analysis 291
Finding Forrester 232
Fires of the Plain 423
Fires Were Started 417
First Picture 513
Fish Tank 354
Fist Fight 142
Fist of Fury 7
A Fistful of Dollars 441, 442
Fixed Bayonets 427
Flaming Creatures 410–11
Flash Gordon 335
Fleur d'Alep (Flower of Aleppo) 477
Flirt 231
The Fly 151, 339
Flying Down to Rio 270
Follow the Fleet 271

For a Few Dollars More 442
For Massa's Sake 49
Forrest Gump 306
Forty Guns 437
Four Eyed Monsters 99
The Four Horsemen of the Apocalypse 416
The Fox of Glenarvon 419
Foxy Brown 56
Frankenstein 151, 218, 220, 221, 328
Frantz Fanon: Black Skin White Mask 45
The French Connection 199
The French Lieutenant's Woman 254
French Mothers (Mères françaises) 415
Frenzy 406
Fresh Kill 326
Friday the 13th 225
From Here to Eternity 254, 425
Frozen **64**, 65
Full Contact 7
Full Metal Jacket 428
Funny Girl 274
Funny Lady 275

Gabbeh 523
Gadar – Ek Prem Katha (Uprising, A Love Story) 493
Gallipoli 417
The Gang of Freedom 510
Garam Hava (Hot Winds) 493
Garden State 148
The Gardener 524
Gaslight 252
Gate No. 5 510
Genesis 21
The Gentle Sex 418
Gentlemen Prefer Blondes 97
Germany in Autumn 213
Gerry 232
Gertie the Dinosaur 19
Get Carter 232
Ghost World 148
GI Blues 147
The Giant 248, 255
Gidget 147
Gigi 277
Gilda 170
Girl Crazy 272
The Girl with the Dragon Tattoo 380

Gladiator 140
The Glass Shield 54
Glenn Miller Story 273
Glory 428
Go Fish! 325–6, 327
Go Lala Go! 485
The Godfather 268, 304
Gods and Monsters 328
Godspell 274
Godzilla 133, 134, 222, 426
Gold Diggers 272
Gone too Far! 46
Gone With the Wind 88, 93
Good Will Hunting 232
Goodbye Morocco 475
G.O.R.A. 520
Gorgo 221
Grace is Gone 430
The Grand Parade 416
La Grande illusion 103, 416
Gravity 507
Grease 274
The Great Gatsby 13
The Great Train Robbery 430, 433
Green Berets 427
The Green Pastures 50, 278
Gridlock'd 60
Los guantes mágicos (*Magic Gloves*) 504
Guelwaar 464–5
The Guest 486
Gueule d'amour 184
Gunfighter 439

Habiba M'sika: La Danse du feu (*The Fire Dance*) 475–6
Haifa 513
Hair 274
Halfaouine 476, 478
Hallelujah 278
Halloween 225
Halls of Montezuma 424
Hamburger Hill 428
Hamsim 515
The Hand 21
Handsworth Songs 45
Happy Birthday Türke! 215
Happy Together 329
Hard Candy 148
A Hard Day's Night 274
Hardcore 290

The Harder They Come 274, 449
Harem El-Gasad (*Sins of the Flesh*) 471
Harishchandra 488
Harlan County 126
Harragas 474, 475
Harry Potter and the Deathly Hallows Pt 2 **64**, 78
Harry Potter and the Prisoner of Azkaban 507
Harry Potter series 65, 202
The Hateful Eight 441
Heart of Britain 417
Heaven's Gate 64
Heavenly Creatures 328
Heimat 211–12
Hell and High Water 427
Hellboy II: The Golden Army 507
Hello Dolly 275
Help! 274
Henry V 419
Hercules 139
Heritage Africa 397, 460
Hero 7, 408, 485
The Hero 493
Herr Doktor 415
Hidden Dragon 7
High Art 328
High Noon 112, 439
High School Confidential 147
Hijack Stories 461
Hiroshima, Hiroshima 425–6
Hiroshima mon amour 136, 182
His Girl Friday 356
Histoire d'A 127
Histoire d'un crime 177
Histoire d'une rencontre (*Story of an Encounter*) 473
Histoire d'un retour (*Story of a Return*) 510
Hit the Street 460
Hitler's Children 422
Homage by Assassination 513
Home Away from Home 46
Home from the Hill 248–9
The Homesteader 51
The Hope 518
A hora da estrela (*The Hour of the Star*) 503
La hora de los hornos (*The Hour of the Furnaces*) 126, 394, 398, 501

Hors la vie (Out of Life) 510
Hotel 130
The House Behind the Cedars 51
House of Flying Daggers 485
Howards End 142
Humayun 490
Hunger 305
The Hunger 220
Hunger Games 32
The Hurt Locker 379, 430
Hyenas 464, 465

I Love You 485
I Walked with a Zombie 220
I Was a Communist for the FBI 426
The Idiots 129, 130
The Idol 514
I'll Cry Tomorrow 272
I'm Gonna Git You Sucka 57
Imitation of Life 247, 249
L'Immeuble Yacoubian (The Yacoubian
    Building) 469–70
In the Cut 350
In the Heat of he Night 52
In the Name of the Father 522
In Nowhere Land 520
In the Valley of Elah 430
In Which We Serve 418
Incendiary Blonde 272
Inception 337
Inch'allah dimanche (Long Live Sunday)
    349
An Inconvenient Truth 128
The Incredibles 23
Indiana Jones series 11
Industrial Britain 125
Inhebbek Hedi (Hedi) 477
Inland Empire 114, 130, 231
Innocence 520
Inside Man 59
Inside Out 23
The Insider 67
Insidious 224
Interview with the Vampire 220, 307
Intimacy 349–50
Into the Abyss: A Tale of Death, a Tale
    of Life 127–8
Invaders from Mars 335
Invasion of the Body Snatchers 426
The Iron Horse 433–4

The Iron Lady 154
The Iron Wall 513
It Came from Outer Space 335
It Conquered the World 335
It Happened One Night 356
It's All About Love 130
I've Heard the Mermaids Singing 326
Izkor: Slaves of Memory 517

J'accuse 416
Jackie Brown 56
Jaffa, The Orange's Clockwork 517
Jailhouse Rock 147, 274
Jason and the Argonauts 21
Jason Bourne 404
Jawhara (Pearl) 478
Jaws 137
The Jazz Singer 270, 355
Jeanne Dielman 41
Jedda 141
Jeera Sain 497
Jemima and Johnny 43
Jenin, Jenin 517
Jesus Christ Superstar 274
Jhoom Barabar Jhoom (Dance Baby
    Dance) 494
Johnny Guitar 327, 435, 437, 439
Jollies 326
Le Jour se lève 110, 168, 184
Journey to the Sun 520
Juice 60
Juju 394
Julien Donkey-Boy 130
Juno 148
Jurassic Park 23, 78, 153, 307, 339
Just Another Girl on the IRT 61

Kaddu Beykatt (Letter from My
    Village) 457
Kadosh (Sacred) 516
The Kaiser – The Beast of Berlin 415
Kameradschaft 210
Kandahar 526
Kanta of Kebbi 455
Kaptaan 498
Kartar Singh 496
Keep Punching 50
Ken Park 148
Keswa, le fil perdu (The Lost
    Thread) 476

Khilona 498
Khochkhach (Flower of Forgetfulness) 476
Khush 326
Kill Bill 380
Killer of Sheep 54
Kind of Loving, A 74
King and Country 416
The King and I 274
King Arthur 6, 140
King Kong 19, 221
King of the Sands 508
King Solomon's Mines (1937) 278, 457
Kingdom of Diamonds 486
Kings of the Cannibal Islands 457
Kippur 516
Kiss Me Deadly 170, 305
The Kiss of the Spiderwoman 196,
    325, 505
Kitchen 262
Klondike Annie 437
Komal Gandhar 398, 492
Kukurantumi 397

LA Confidential 172
El laberinto del fauno (Pan's
    Labyrinth) 506
Ladder to Damascus 508
Ladri di bicicletti (Bicycle Thieves) 235
The Lady 519
The Lady in the Dugout 432
Lady Sings the Blues 272
Ladybird, Ladybird! 288
Lakhon Mein Eik 496
Lara Croft series 380
Lara Croft: Tomb Raider 12, 65
Last Days 232
The Last Laugh 208
The Last Movie 231
Last Resort 354
The Last Seduction 155, 380
Last Tango in Paris 290
The Last Temptation of Christ 76
Laura 269, 285
Law of Desire 348
Lawrence of Arabia 139
Layla and the Wolves 510
Lebanon 516
The Left-Handed Gun 438
The Legend of Nigger Charlie 56
Leonera (The Lioness' Den) 504

Lethal Weapon series 6, 11
Letter from an Unknown Woman 251
Lettre à ma soeur (Letter to my
    Sister) 474
La ley de Herodes (Herod's Law) 506
Leyla the Bedouin 467
Life is All You Get 214
Life is Beautiful 425
Lillian Russell 272
The Limey 232
Lions for Lambs 430
Listen to Britain 417
Little Caesar 169, 185, 186
Little Chinese Seamstress 485
Little Red Flowers 485
The Little United States 415
Living Dead series 223
London Can Take It 417
Lone Star 232
The Loneliness of the Long Distance
    Runner 74
Lonesome Cowboys 411
The Long Goodbye 199
Long Road to Mazatlan 45
Longtime Companion 76
Look Back in Anger 73, 180, 181
Look at Britain 180
Looking for Langston 45
The Lord of the Rings 65, 78, 115
Losing Ground 63
The Lost Girl 520–1
Lost Highway 231
Lost in Translation 233, 305
Love Brewed in an African Pot 397, 460
Love is the Devil 328
Love Me Tender 147
A Love Story 493
The Lovers 130
Luna de Avallaneda 504

M. Butterfly 268
M Like Mother 522
Machorka-Muff 213
The Magnificent Seven 133, 440
Magnolia 231
Main Hoon Na 493
La Maison jaune (The Yellow House)
    475
The Making of Bronco Billy 433
Mala época (Bad Times) 504

Malcolm X 58, 62
The Maltese Falcon 167, 168
Maly Western 21
Mama 484
Mamma Mia! 275
Man of Ashes 476
A Man of Honor 511
Man on Wire 128
The Man Who Fell to Earth 336
The Man Who Shot Liberty Valance 434
The Man Who Wasn't There 171, 203, 232
Man with a Movie Camera 362, 363
The Manchurian Candidate 349
La Mano en la trampa (The Hand in the Trap) 500
Manon des sources 142
March of the Penguins 128
María Candelaria 500
Marie-Antoinette 233, 305
Marnie 161, 249, 253, 405
Marriage in Galilee 299
The Marriage of Maria Braun 325
The Martian 340
Mary Shelley's Frankenstein 307, 339
Mascarades 475
M★A★S★H 427
The Matrix 78, 118, 336, 338–9
Matrix Reloaded 338–9
Matrix Revolutions 338–9
Maula Jat 497
Maurice 100
Mean Streets 231
Meet Me in St Louis 273, 278
Meghe Dhaka Tara (The Cloud-Capped Star) 398, 492
Mémoire en détention (Memory on Hold) 478
Memorias del subdesarrollo (Memories of Underdevelopment) 398
Memories of Overdevelopment 503
The Men 424, 428
Menace II Society 60, 61
Mendiants et orgueilleux (The Proud and the Beggars) 469
Le Mépris 28, 81, 359
Merrie Melodies 20
Meshes of the Afternoon 41, 144, 262, 411
The Messenger 430

Metropolis 206, 208, 210, 335, 339, 340
Meu amigo hindu (My Hindu Friend) 505
MGM Sarajevo: Man God and the Monster 429
Mildred Pierce 112, 247, 253
Miles Ahead 61
Milk 232, 329
Mille mois (A Thousand Months) 478
Million Dollar Baby 380
Millions Like Us 418
Minority Report 338
The Mirror Image of Dorian Gray in the Yellow Press 214
Misery 413
Miss Queencake 46
Missing 442
Mission Impossible II 7
Mission to Moscow 422
Mississippi Marsala 48, 63
Moana 124
Le Moineau (The Sparrow) 468
Mol 457
A Moment of Innocence 523
Momma Don't Allow 178, 180
Mona Saber 478
Monsoon Wedding 72
Monster 380
Moolaadé 459
Moonrise Kingdom 232
Morgenrot (Dawn) 416
Mort à vendre (Death for Sale) 478
Mother 365, 367
Mother India 490
Los motivos de luz (Light Motives) 506
The Motorcycle Diaries 505
Motorcycle Gang 146
Moulin Rouge! 67, 266, 275, 281
The Movie 271, 279
Mr Magoo series 20
Mrs Miniver 420
La mujer sin cabeza (The Headless Woman) 504
Mulholland Drive 203, 231
Munna Bhai 494
Murder My Sweet 169
Mustang 521
Muthi Bhar Chawal 497

Mutiny on the Bounty 8
My Beautiful Launderette 327
My Darling Clementine 434
My Fair Lady 274
My Father and My Son 520
My Life for Ireland 419
My Little Chickadee 437
My Own Private Idaho 232, 325, 381
My Son John 426
My Summer of Love 328
My Week with Marilyn 154
Mystery Train 232

Nadia and Sarra 476
Nagarik (The Citizen) 397
The Naked Spur 438
Nanook of the North 124, 125, 141
Nashville 280
Naughty Marietta 270
Ndjamena City 459
Negro Dancers 49
Nevada Smith 440
New Jack City 11, 59, 227
New Moon 270
Ni Allah, Ni Maître (Laïcité, inch'Allah) (Neither God nor Master) 476
Nice Time 180
The Night 509
Night Cries: A Rural Tragedy 141
Night and Day 272
The Night of the Living Dead 222
Night Mail 125
Night Shapes 214
Nightfall 305
Nightjohn 54
A Nightmare on Elm Street 225
Nihon no Yoru to Kiri (Night and Fog) 144
Nikita 12
Nina santa (The Holy Girl) 504
The Nine Muses 45
Nine Queens 504
Ninotchka 277
No Man's Land 429
La Noire de … 457
Normal! 474
The North Star 422
Nosferatu 209, 219
Notting Hill 98

La Nouba des femmes du mont Chenoua (The Nouba of the Women of Mount Chenoua) 473
Now Voyager 161, 249, 253
La Nuit Américaine (Day for Night) 106, 240, 254
La Nuit de la vérité (The Night of Truth) 459
Nuits sans sommeil (Sleepless Nights) 510

O Dreamland 178
O Heroí (The Hero) 458
O Que É Isso, Companheiro? (Four Days in September) 505
October 366
Oklahoma 274, 278
Old Boy 7
The Old and the New (The General Line) 367
The Olive Harvest 513
Los Olvidados 500
Om Amira (Amira's Mother) 470
On the Beach 375
On the Bowery 411
On a Clear Day You Can See Forever 275
On the Town 273
On the Waterfront 254
One Hundred Men and a Girl 272
One Night Stand 242
One Potato, Two Potato 52
Ong-Bak 132
Open Range 442
O.R.A.G. 520
Un oso roso (Red Bear) 504
Ossessione (Obsession) 234
The Other Half 485
Out of the Inkwell series 19
The Outlaw 435, 436
The Outlaw Josey Wales 442
The Outrage 415
The Ox-bow Incident 436
Oxhide (II) 485

Pale Rider 227, 439
Palestine Stereo 514
Pan's Labyrinth 506
Papilio Buddha 495
Paradise Now 513

Paradiso Omeros 46
Paragraph 218 214
Paranoid Park 232
Les Parapluies de Cherbourg 275
Parineeta 494
Paris is Burning 326
Paris, Texas 91, 333
Passion 509
The Passion of Remembrance 46
Pat Garrett and Billy the Kid 440–1
Paths of Glory 416, 424
Pearl Harbor 10, 425
Peeping Tom 220, 254, 269, 370,
     406, 412
Pépé le Moko 184
Peppermint Candy 7
The Perfect Circle 429
Perfect Image? 46
Phantom of the Opera 275
Phat Girlz 63
Pheray 496
Philadelphia 326, 329, 349
Philadelphia Story 97
The Philosopher's Stone 486
Philosophy of a Knife 76
Photogénies 261
Pickanninies 49
Piel de verano (Summer Skin) 398
Pierrot le fou 81, 359
Pina 128, 403
The Pirate 273
La Pirogue 459
Pixote 505
Plainsman 437
Planet of the Apes 151, 336, 340
Platoon 428
The Player 303–4, 368, 375
Playtime 45
Plus jamais peur (No More
     Fear) 477
La Pointe courte 182
Polar Express 20
Police Story 7
Ponyo 22
Popeye the Sailor series 19–20
Porgy and Bess 278
Les Portes fermées (Closed Doors) 469
Portrait of Jason 411
Portrait of a Lady 13
Posse 438

Possessed 253
Post Tenebras Lux (Light after
     Darkness) 507
The Postman always Rings Twice 235
The Power of Men is the Patience of
     Women 214
Precious 379, 380
Predator 66
Predators 340
The President 524
Pressure 43
Pretty Village, Pretty Flame 429
Pride and Prejudice 12
The Prime Minister 419
Princess Monoke 22
Printemps Tunisien (Tunisian
     Spring) 476
Prisoner of the Emir 522
Prometheus 337
Psycho 89, 151, 159, 220, 232, 266,
     358, 375, 405, 406, 412, 413
The Public Enemy 185, 186
Pull My Daisy 411
Pulp Fiction 305
Pure Blood 461
The Purple Heart 421
Pyaasa 490

Qaisar 523
Quai des brumes 184
Quanto Vale ou É por Quilo? (What Is
     It Worth?) 505
¡Qué viva México! 366, 500
Querelle 325
The Quiet Man 435
Quo Vadis 139

Rabid 222
Rachida 474
The Railroad Porter 50
Raise the Red Lantern 484
Rambo 6, 66, 427
Rancho Notorious 413, 437
Rang de Basanti 494
Ranu's Wedding 513
Raqqa: An Inside Story 509
The Ratcatcher 354
Raw Deal 438
Rear Window 412
Rebecca 112, 161, 252

Rebel Without a Cause 146, 152, 248, 249, 379
Record of a Human Being 426
The Red Danube 426
Red Ensign 330
The Red Menace 426
Red Planet Mars 426
The Red Shoes 269
Red Sorghum 484
Redacted 99, 430
Refuge England 180
Reggae 43
La Règle du jeu 184
Reis (*Chief*) 521
Remember Pearl Harbor 421
Le Repenti 474
Repulsion 405
Reservoir Dogs 187, 304
Return to Homs 509
La Révolution du jasmin (*The Jasmine Revolution*) 477
Rhapsody in Blue 272
Ricochet 11
Ricochets 515
Riders of Destiny 435
The Ring 133
Ringu 408
Road to Kabul 478
Road to Perdition 203
Road Runner series 21
The Robe 18, 139
Rock 6
Rock around the Clock 147
The Rocky Horror Picture Show 103
Roger and Me 128
Roja 493
Roma città aperta (*Rome Open City*) 234, 235–6
Roman Scandals 272
Romance 291, 350
Romeo and Juliet (1947) 490
Romeo and Juliet (1996) 13
Room at the Top 74
A Room with a View 16, 142
Rope 114, 325
The Rose 272
Rosemary's Baby 223
Le Rouge aux lèvres 220
Route 181, Fragments of a Journey in Palestine-Israel 517

The Royal Tenenbaums 232
La Ruelle des fous (*The Backstreets of the Madmen*) 468
Run Lola Run 65
Ruses de Femmes (*Women's Wiles*) 477

Sachthai 496
La Saison des hommes (*The Season of Men*) 349, 476
Saladin 468
Salut cousin! (*Hey cousin!*) 474
Samba Traoré 464
San Demetrio, London 418
Sanders of the River 278
The Sands of Iwo Jima 423
Le Sang d'un poète 324
Sankofa 465
Sans toit ni loi 42
Sassi 496
Satin Rouge (*Red Satin*) 476
Saturday Night Fever 274
Saturday Night and Sunday Morning 74, 181
Satyricon 268
Saving Private Ryan 65, 424, 425
Saw series 224
Scarface 185
Schindler's List 76, 425
The School of Rock 148
Scorpio Rising 145, 411
The Searchers 49, 434, 439
Second Coming 46
Secret Mission 427
Selma 62
Senna 47
Sense and Sensibility 15, 100
A Separation 525
Serbian Film, A 76
Seven Brides for Seven Brothers 278
The Seven Samurai 133
Seven Songs for Malcolm X 43
The Seven Year Itch 97
The Seventh Victim 220–1
Sex in the City series 380
Shadows 231
Shaft 55, 58, 280
Shaheed 496
Shame 292, 305
Shane 439
Shanghai Triad 484

She's Gotta Have It 58, 62
The Shining 413
Shivers 222
Sholay (Flames) 71, 493
Shoulder Arms 416
Showboat 278
Sicko 99, 128
Sight and Sound 304, 305, 325, 437
Silence Between Two Thoughts 524
The Silence of the Lambs 226
Silences of the Palace 299, 349, 476
Silk Stockings 277
Singin' in the Rain 254, 270, 303, 356
A Single Man 329
The Sinking of the Lusitania 415
Sleep 144
Sleepless Nights 470
Slumdog Millionaire 494–5
The Small Town 521
Smoker 291
The Snake Pit 253
Snow White and the Seven Dwarfs 19
So Close to Paradise 484–5
So Near Yet So Far 510
Solaris 336
A Soldier's Story 349
Sólo por hoy (Only for Today) 504
Some Like it Hot 97, 195
Somewhere 233
Son of Pakistan 498
Sonatine 7
Song 55
Song of Russia 422
The Sorrow 518
The Soul of Nigger Charlie 56
The Sound of Music 275
La Souriante Mme Beudet 40
South Pacific 274
Spare Time 125
Spartacus 140
Speak Like a Child 45
Spellbound 249
Spirited Away 22
The St. Valentine's Day Massacre 304
Stagecoach 435
A Star is Born 93, 272, 273, 379
Star Wars Episode I: The Phantom
    Menace 113, 117
Star Wars Episode II: Attack of the
    Clones 117

Star Wars: The Force Awakens 64, 65,
    123, 303
Star Wars series 64, 78, 336–7
The Stars Look Down 354
Staying Alive 275
Steamboat Willie 19
The Steel Helmet 427
Stella Dallas 247
Still a Brother: Inside the Negro Middle
    Class 52
The Sting 75
The Story of GI Joe 423
The Story of Qui Ju 484
Straight Out of Brooklyn 61
The Straight Story 333
Straw Dogs 440
The Stray Bullet 510
A Streetcar Named Desire 254
Strictly Ballroom 275, 280
Strike 137, 261, 366
Strike Up the Band 272
Strongman Ferdinand 213
The Stuart Hall Project 45
Subarnareka 398, 492
Summer Holiday 274
Summer of Sam 59
Summer Palace 485
Summer Place 147
Sunset Boulevard 303
Sunshine State 232
Superfly 55, 280
Supersize Me 127
Suspicious Minds 128
Suzhou River 485
Sweeney Todd: The Demon Barber of
    Fleet Street 329
Sweet Charity 280
Sweet Sweetback's Baadasssss Song 54
Swoon 325
The Symbol of the Unconquered 51, 52

T-Men 438
Tahrir (Place de la Révolution) (Tahrir
    (Revolution Square)) 470
Take a Hard Ride 438
Taking Father Home 485
Tale of the Three Jewels 513
The Talented Mr Ripley 328
Target for Tonight 417
A Taste of Cherry 524

A Taste of Honey 74
Taxi 525
Taxi Driver 231, 304, 427
The Tempest of Life 522
Ten Bob in Winter 43
The Ten Commandments 138
Ten Minutes to Live 52
Ten Thousand Waves 46
Teri Yaad 496
Terminator series 78, 339
Terra Incognita 510
Terra em Transe (Land in Anguish)
  79, 398
La Terra trema (The Earth Trembles)
  235
Les Terrasses 474
Il tetto (The Roof) 236
The Texas Chainsaw Massacre 218,
  220, 225
Thank God it's Friday 279
That Hamilton Woman! 419, 420
Thelma and Louise 76, 286, 333
They Were Expendable 423
Thief 67
The Thin Blue Line 127
The Thin Red Line 424
The Thing 223
Things to Come 335
Thirteen 148
Thirty Seconds over Tokyo 423
This Is Not a Film 525
This Land is Mine 421
This Sporting Life 74, 181
Three Kings 429
Thriller 102
Through the Olive Trees 524
Through the Veil of Exile 517
Tilaï 464
Till the Clouds Roll By 272, 273
Time-Code 116, 130, 359
The Tin Star 439
Titanic 64
To Sleep with Anger 54
Together 180
Tom and Jerry series 21
Tom Jones 74, 75
Toni 234, 354
Tootsie 195, 196
Top Hat 271
Total Recall 78

Touching the Void 128
Touki-Bouki (The Hyena's Journey) 464
Toy Story 23, 78
Tracking down Maggie 127
Train to Pakistan 493
Trainspotting 12
Tramontane 511
Transamerica 329, 333
Transitions 403
Trapped 61
Triumph of the Will 419
Trouble I've Seen 63
The Trouble with Love 214
Troy 6, 8, 140
Trust 231
Tumbleweeds 433
Tumbling Tumbleweeds 435
Tunisian Victory 418
Tunisie année zéro (Freedom) 477
Twilight Saga series 220
The Two-Legged Horse 525
Two Moons and an Olive 509
Two Strangers 519

Uncle Kruger 419
Underworld series 220
Unforgiven 227, 439
Unfreedom 495
Uno de dos (One or the Other) 504
Urs fil Jalil (Marriage in Galilee) 513
Usi Roti (Our Daily Bread) 397

Vagabondia 45
La Vallée (The Valley) 511
The Valley of the Wolves 520
Vampire in Brooklyn 57
Vampire Lovers 220
Les Vampires 219
The Vampyre 218
Veer Zaara 493
Velvet Goldmine 232
Le Vent des Aurès (The Wind from the
  Aurès) 472
Vent du sud (Wind from the South) 472
Vertigo 221
A Very Narrow Bridge 515
Victor/Victoria 196
Vidas Secas (Barren Lives) 79
La vie d'Adèle (Blue is the Warmest
  Colour) 328

La Vie de Christ 12
La Vie est à nous 184
La Vie et passion de Jésus Christ 12
La Ville des pirates (*The City of Pirates*) 502
La Violence et la dérision (*Violence and Laughter*) 469
Virgin Suicides 233
Visage de femmes (*Faces of Women*) 461
Viva Laldjérie (*Viva Algeria*) 475
Vizontele 520
Voodoo Vengeance 457
Vortex 510
Voyage à la lune 19

Waar 498
Waiting for the Clouds 520
Wake Island 421
Wallace and Gromit 24
Waltz with Bashir 517
The War at Sea from Hawaii to Malaya 420
War Bride 415
The War Game 426
War of the Worlds 335
Warrior 47
Way of Life 46
The Way to the Stars 418
The Way We Were 275
Wayne's World 97, 147
We are the Lambeth Boys 180
We Make History 398
Weekend 41
Welcome to Sarajevo 429
Welcome II the Terrordome 46
West Beirut 510
West Side Story 274, 275, 282
The Westerner 435
Westfront 416
Westward Women 437
What Price Glory 416
What We Have Against It 214
Whatever Happened to Baby Jane? 406
When I First Saw You 514
When Night is Falling 326
Where Do We Go Now? 510–11
Where is the Friend's House? 526
The White Balloon 524, 525–6

White Heat 427
White Ribbon 115
Who Framed Roger Rabbit 19
Why We Fight 420
The Wild Angels 147
The Wild Bunch 427, 438
Wild Wild West 438
William Shakespeare's Romeo and Juliet 280–1
Winchester '73 438
Wings 416
Winter Sleep 521
With Naked Feet in Heaven 522
The Wizard of Oz 272
Woman in the Window 170
Wonderland 130
Woodstock 274
The Wooing and Wedding of a Coon 457
Words and Music 272
The World, the Flesh and the Devil 427
Wretched of the Earth 463
Written on the Wind 249

Xala 464
Xiu Xiu: The Send Down Girl 485

Y tu mamá también (*And Your Mother Too*) 506
Yaaba 464
A Yank in the RAF 420
Yankee Doodle Dandy 272, 421
Years of Hunger 214
Yellow Earth 484
Yema (*Ouardia Had Two Children*) 475
Yesterday Girl 213
Yol (*The Way*) 518
Yom Yom (*Day after Day*) 516
Young Mr Lincoln 229
Young Soul Rebels 45
Young Törless 213

La Zerda ou les chants de l'oubli (*The Zerda and the Songs of Forgetfulness*) 473
Z'har 475
Zine Li Fik (*Much Loved*) 478
Zulu Love Letter 461

NAME INDEX

Note: **Bold** page numbers indicate tables

Abbas, K.A. 397, 524
Abbott, 304
Abdelhamid, Abdellatif 509
Abdul Sayed, Daoud 469
Abel, Richard 19
Abou-Seif, Salah 468
Abrams, J. J. **64**, 303
Abu-Assad, Hany 513
Adajania, Homi 494
Adam, Ken 6, 10
Adamovich, A. 425
Afolayan, Kunle 461
Ahmed, Humayun 487
Akar, Serdar 520
Akerman, Chantal 28, 40–1, 122, 324
Akin, Fatih 521
Akl, Mounia 511
Akomfrah, John 44–5, 400
Aksoy, Faruk 520
Aldrich, Robert 170, 305, 406, 424
Alea, Tomás Gutiérrez 502
Allégret, Yves 183
Allen, Woody 376
Allouache, Merzak 473–4, 475
Almodovar, Pedro 348
Althusser, Louis 37–8, 83, 84–5,
    156–7, 228, 347, 384, 385, 462
Altman, Robert 199, 272, 276–7,
    278, 279, 280, 303–4, 368,
    375, 427
Alvarez, Santiago 502
Amaral, Suzana 503
Amari, Raja 475, 476
Ameur-Zaïmeche, Rabah 475
Amiralay, Omar 509
Ampaw, King 397

Anand, Dev 70, 490
Anand, J. C. 496
Anderson, Benedict 409
Anderson, Gilbert M. 433
Anderson, Lindsay 73, 124, 178, 179,
    180, 181
Anderson, Michael 179–80, 423
Anderson, Pamela 12
Anderson, Paul Thomas 231, 290
Anderson, Wes 232
Andreotti, Giulio 236
Andrew, Dudley 41
Anger, Kenneth 145, 410, 411
Ansah, Kwaw Painstil 397, 460, 461
Antal, Nirmod 340
Antonioni, Michelangelo 236
Anzour, Najdat 508
Apichatpong Weerasethakul 132
Appiah, Kwame 294, 447
Araki, Gregg 325
Arau, Alfonso 506
Arbuckle, Fatty 77, 97
Armes, R. 459
Armstrong, Franny 99
Armstrong, Louis 21
Arnautlic, Ismet 429
Arnold, Andrea 354
Arnold, Jack 55, 147, 438
Aronofsky, Darren 231
Arthur, Jean 437
Arzner, Dorothy 249, 250
Asante, Amma 46
Ashby, Hal 428
Ashcroft, B. 293
Al-Ashqar, Akram 513
Asli, Mohamed 477

Asquith, Anthony 418
Assaf, Layla 510
Astaire, Fred 270, 271, 272, 273–4, 279, 375
Astruc, Alexandre 33, 173
Al-Atar, Mohamed 513
Attenborough, Richard 74, 424, 462
Attile, Martine 46
Auric, George 267–8
Austen, Jane 15
Autant-Lara, Claude 18
Autry, Gene 432, 435
Avery, Tex 20
Ayad, Nassar 477
Ayouch, Nabil 478

Babenco, Hector 196, 325, 505
Bacall, Lauren 375
Baccar, Selma 475
Bachchan, Amitabh 71
Bachir-Chouikh, Yamina 474
Badham, John 11, 220
Baghdadi, Maroun 510
Baker, Roy Ward 220
El-Bakri, Asma 469
Bakshi, Ralph 78
Balász, Z. 173
Bale, Christian 409
Balogun, Ola 455, 458, 461–2
Bank, Misr 467
Bardot, Brigitte 28, 181, 374, 377
Barker, M. 430
Barki, Mohamed 517
Barr, Jean-Marc 130
Barreto, Bruno 505
Barry, John 268
Barthes, Roland 35, 38, 283, 284, 342, 343, 347, 383, 384
Bates, Alan 73, 74
Baudrillard, Jean 306–7
Baudry, Jean-Louis 24, 322, 368, 369
Bay, Michael 6, 10, 425
El Baz, Anas 478
Bazin, André 12, 33, 109–10, 136, 173, 197, 353
Beatles, The 274
Beaumont, Harry 270
Becker, Jacques 418
Becker, Wolfgang 215

Beckett, Samuel 256, 303
Bedirxan, Wiam Simav 509
Beer, Robert 24
Begné, Enrique 507
Begum, Fatima 495
Behi, Ridha 477
Belafonte, Harry 56
Bellour, Raymond 25, 189, 322, 368, 369
Belmont, Charles 127
Ben Attia, Mohamed 477
Ben Cheikh, Mourad 477
Ben Hania, Kaouter 475
Ben Mabrouk, Néjia 475, 476
Ben Mahmoud, Férial 475, 477
Benchetrit, David 517
Bendazzi, G. 21–2
Benguigui, Yamina 349
Benigni, Roberto 425
Benjelloun, Hassan 478
Benlyazid, Farida 477
Benning, Sadie 326
Bensaïdi, Faouzi 478
Bentham, Jeremy 256
Bergman, Ingmar 29
Bergstrom, J. 342
Berkeley, Busby 271–2, 279
Berlin, Irving 271, 278
Bernardi, Daniel 48
Bernhardt, Curtis 253
Berri, Claude 142
Berry, Chris 481
Bertolucci, Bernado 290
Besson, Luc 12, 340
Bhabha, Homi 294, 298, 400
Bhansali, Sanjay Leela 494
Bhowmik, Someswar 489
Bhutto, Z. A. 496, 497
Bianchi, Sérgio 505
Bielensky, Fabían 504
Bigelow, Kathryn 379, 430
Binoche, Juliette 524
Björk 282, 283
Blackwood, Maureen 46
Bogarde, Dirk 378
Bogart, Humphrey 167, 171, 375
Bonham-Carter, Helena 12
Borden, Lizzie 326
Bordwell, David 88, 89, 90, 109, 135, 241, 263, 287

Bornaz, Kalthoum 475, 476
Borowczyk, Walerian 21
Boughedir, Férid 478
Boulane, Ahmed 477–8
Boulghourjian, Vatche 511
Bouzid, Leyla 475
Bouzid, Nouri 476
Boyle, Danny 223, 494–5
Bradley, David 146
Braff, Zach 148
Braine, John 74
Brakhage, Stan 410, 411
Brambilla, Marco 11
Branagh, Kenneth 307, 339
Branch, William 52
Brando, Marlon 202, 254, 424
Braque, Georges 258
Braudy, Leo 199
Brecht, Bertolt 41, 121–2, 280, 364
Breer, Robert 144
Breillat, Catherine 291, 350
Bresson, Robert 122, 418
Broccoli, Albert 'Cubby' and
    Barbara 6
Bronson, Charles 10–11, 441
Brooks, Mel 199
Brooks, Peter 243, 244
Brooks, Richard 146
Broomfield, Nick 127
Brown, Jim 56
Browning, Tod 218
Bruckner, Jutta 214
Brunsdon, Charlotte 244
Buck, Christopher **64**
Buice, Susan 99
Bukhari, Syed Faisal 498
Bullock, Sandra 380
Buñuel, Luis 41, 138, 411
Burch, Noel 107
Burnett, Charles 54, 60, 62
Burton, Richard 73, 74, 374, 377
Burton, Tim 357, 403
Bush, George Jnr 338, 429
Bush, George Snr 429
Bustros, Raymond 509

Caetano, Israel 504
Cain, James M. 235
Caine, Michael 73, 409
Calloway, Cab 21

Calm, Edward 146
Cameron, James 10, **64**, 78, 99, 115,
    117, 120, 403, 404
Campanella, Juan José 504
Campion, Jane 13, 350
Canudo, Ricciotto 172–3
Capra, Frank 355, 420
Carlyle, Robert 12
Carné, Marcel 112, 168, 180, 183,
    184, 185
Carpenter, John 223, 225
Carrera, Carlos 506
Cascone, Kim 115
Cassavates, John 231
Castro, Fidel 396
Catmull, Ed 23
Cavani, Liliani 28
Césaire, Aimé 295
Ceylan, Nuri Bilge 521
Chabrol, Claude 182
Chadha, Gurinder 46–7, 72, 494
Chaffey, Don 21
Chahine, Youssef 468, 469, 471
Chamkhi, Sonia 475
Chamoun, Jean 512
Chan, Jackie 7
Chanan, Michael 401
Chand, Daud 496
Chandler, Raymond 390
Chang-Dong, Lee 7
Chaplin, Charlie 4, 97, 365, 374, 415
Chapman, Jane 124
Charisse, Cyd 273, 274, 277
Chatak, Ritwik 448
Chaudhuri, S. 133, 134, 166, 453
Chauvel, Charles 141
Cheadle, Don 61
Cheang, Shu Lea 326
Chen, Joan 485
Chen Kaige 329, 484
Chéreau, Patrice 349–50
Cherian, Jayan K. 495
Chibnall, Steve 329–30, 331
Chion, M. 266, 358
Chkiri, Brahim 478
Cholodenko, Lisa 328
Chopra, Yash 493
Chow, Rey 166
Chow, Yun-Fat 7
Chraïbi, Saad 478

Chrétien, Henri 17
Church-Gibson, P. 451
Churchill, Winston 419
Cimino, Michael 64, 427
Cissé, Souleymane 397, 401, 459, 465
Citarella, Laura 504
Clair, René 31, 40, 105, 261
Clampett, Bob 20, 21
Clark, Larry 38, 148, 149
Clarke, Shirley 52, 410
Clayton, Jack 13, 74
Clein, John 50
Clément, René 419
Cleopatra 140
Clift, Montgomery 254
Close, Glenn 372, 376, 377, 380
Clouzot, Henri-Georges 418
Cocteau, Jean 180, 225–6, 268, 323
Coelo, Serge 459
Coen Brothers 103, 203, 232
Coen, Joel 171
Cohen, Eli 515
Cohl, Émile 19
Colbert, Claudette 356, 379
Collins, Kathleen 63
Comolli, J.-L. 230
Condon, Bill 328
Connelly, Marc 278
Connery, Sean 10, 11, 253
Contreras, Ernesto 507
Cook, Pam 156, 225, 244
Cooper, Gary 112, 435, 439
Cooper-Hewitt, Peter 237
Coppola, Francis Ford 87, 220, 224, 231, 268, 304, 427–8
Coppola, Sofia 233, 305
Corman, Roger 147, 304
Cosmatos, George P. 66, 427
Costello, 304
Costner, Kevin 440, 442
Cotillard, Marion 409
Cowie, E. 372
Coyula, Miguel 503
Crain, William 55
Craven, Wes 57, 225
Crawford, Joan 253, 327, 377, 437
Cripps, Thomas 49
Cronenberg, David 151, 202, 222, 268, 269, 339, 406

Crosby, Bing 274, 421
Crosland, Alan 270, 355
Cruise, Tom 11, 67, 75, 382
Crumley, Arin 99
Cruz, Pablo 507
Cruze, James 433–4
Cuarón, Alfonso 340, 506, 507
Cuba, Larry 78
Cubitt, S. 122–3
Cukor, George 93, 97, 248, 252, 379
Cunningham, John W. 225, 439
Curtis, Simon 154
Curtis, Tony 195
Curtis-Hall, Vondie 60
Curtiz, Michael 8, 103, 112, 170, 247
Cushing, Peter 219

Dahl, John 155, 380
Dai Sijie 485
Damiano, Gerard 103, 290
Damon, Matt 9
Daniels, Lee 57, 379
Danniel, Danniel 517
Das Gupta, Chidananda 448
Dash, Julie 54, 60, 62
Daube, Alejo 504
Daves, Delmer 147, 199, 440
Davis, Andrew 8
Davis, Bette 375, 378, 379, 382, 421
Davis, Miles 61, 267
Dawson, Anthony 438
Day, Doris 95, 376, 380
Dayan, Nissim 515
De Bont, Jan 65
De Lauretis, Dino 139
De Lauretis, Teresa 160–1, 163, 164–6
De Mille, Cecil B. 139
De Niro, Robert 3, 202, 375, 378, 382
De Palma, Brian 99, 430
Dean, James 77, 146, 152, 202, 246, 248, 254, 379
Dee, Sandra 147
Dehlavi, Jamil 497
Deitch, Donna 326
Del Toro, Guillermo 506, 507
Delaney, Shelagh 74
Deleuze, Giles 264–5
Delluc, Louis 40, 107, 261

Demirkubuz, Zeki 520–1
Demme, Jonathan 13, 226, 326, 329, 349
Demy, Jacques 275
Deneuve, Catherine 282, 376
Denis, Claire 223
Dennison, S. 452, 454
Depp, Johnny 376
Depsentes, Virginie 350
Deren, Maya 41, 107, 141, 144, 262, 411
Derki, Talal 509
Derrida, Jacques 106–7, 108, 174, 385, 390–1
Despentes, Virginie 291
di Cesare, Leonardo 504
Diab, Mohammed 470–1
Diawara, M. 396
Dibb, Saul 46
Dickerson, Ernest R. 60
Diestro-Dópido, Mar 504
Dietrich, Marlene 376, 377, 413, 421, 437
Disney, Walt 93
Disraeli, Benjamin 419
Dissanayake, W. 132
Dixit, Madhuri 71, 494
Djahnine, Habiba 474
Djebar, Assia 473
Dmytryk, Edward 169
Doane, M. A. 163, 244, 250, 251, 252, 253, 371
Dobson, Tamara 56
Donen, Stanley 254, 270, 278, 356
Dönmez-Colin, G. 495
Dörrie, Doris 214, 215
Dors, Diana 374
dos Santos, Nelson Pereira 79
Doueiri, Ziad 510
Douglas, Gordon 222
Dovnikovi, Birovoi 24
Dovzhenko, Alexander 364, 365
Dragojevic, Srjdan 429
Dresen, Andreas 215
Driessen, Paul 24
Duke, Vernon 278
Dulac, Germaine 40, 41, 262
Dunne, Philip 147
Dupont, E. A. 281
Duras, Marguerite 42, 305

Durbin, Deanna 272
Dutt, Guru 70, 490
DuVernay, Ava 62, 243
Duvivier, Julien 168, 183, 184
Dworkin, Andrea 292
Dyer, Richard 224, 241–2, 271, 276, 279, 375, 376, 378

Easdale, Brian 269
Eastwood, Clint 10, 11, 91, 136, 227, 375, 376, 382, 434, 439, 441
Ecaré, D. 461
Eckhard, Sabine 214
Eddy, Nelson 270, 272
Edel, U. 291
Edeson, Arthur 109
Edwards, Blake 196
Eisenstein, Sergei 41, 110, 134, 137, 173, 261, 362, 363–5, 366–7, 500
Ejira, Chico 460
Ekaragha, Destiny 46
Elias, Hanna 513
Ellington, Duke 273
Elliott, Stephan 76, 275, 327, 333
Elsaesser, Thomas 140, 206, 214, 244, 249–50
Epstein, Jean 40, 261
Erdogan, Recep Tayyip 521
Erdogan, Yilman 520
Ergun, Mahinur 519–20
Ergüven, Denise Gamze 521
Ertugrul, Mushim 518
Escalante, Amat 507
Espinosa, Julio Garcia 502
Estrada, Luis 506
Eustache, Jean 83
Everett, Anna 119
Everett, Francine 50
Everett, Rupert 378
Ezra, E. 407, 409

Fairbanks, Douglas 8, 365
El Fani, Nadia 475, 476
Fanon, Frantz 293–4, 462, 463, 474
Farahani, Golshifteh 522
Farhadi, Asghar 525
Fassbinder, Rainer Werner 34, 211, 212, 213, 324, 427
Faye, Safi 457, 458
Feig, Paul 380

Fellini, Federico 236, 268, 280
Ferhati, Jilali 478
Fernandez, Emilio 500
Ferrara, Abel 218
Fetchit, Stepin 21
Feuillade, Louis 172, 185, 219, 415
Field, Shirley Ann 374
Fields, W. C. 97, 355
Figgis, Mike 116, 130, 242, 359
Figueroa, Gabriel 500
Fincher, David 113, 151, 223, 380
Finney, Albert 73, 74
Fiorentino, Linda 155, 380
Firth, Colin 12, 98
Fischer, Lucy 251
Fischinger, Oskar 24
Fiske, J. 345
Fitzgerald, Scott 13
Flaherty, Robert 124, 125, 141, 180
Fleischer, Dave and Max 19–20
Fleischer, Richard 325
Fleming, Victor 88, 93, 272
Flower, Gene 147
Flynn, Errol 8, 376
Folman, Ali 517
Fonda, Henry 441
Fonda, Jane 380, 428
Fonda, Peter 147
Forbes, Bryan 74
Ford, Harrison 11, 376
Ford, John 33, 34, 49, 180, 229, 420, 423, 433, 434, 435, 439
Ford, Tom 329
Foreman, Carl 439
Formby, George 330–1
Forster, E. M. 15, 100
Fortes, Elena 507
Fosse, Bob 280
Foster, Bill 49, 50
Foster, Jodie 380
Foucault, Michel 38, 162–3, 164, 329, 390–1
Foxworth, Heather 63
Foxx, Jamie 67, 441
Fraenkel, H. 206, 209
Frampton, D. 176, 287
Francisci, Pietro 139
Franju, Georges 126
Frank, Robert 411
Frears, Stephen 327, 354

Freed, Arthur 270, 273
Freleng, Fritz 21
Frend, Charles 418
Freud, Sigmund 25, 152, 154, 188, 312–14, 315, 318–19, 321, 322, 323, 341, 369
Friedkin, William 199, 222, 225
Fuller, Samuel 33, 34, 427
Fuqua, Antoine 6, 140
Furuzan 520
Fusco, Coco 400

Gabin, Jean 184
Gable, Clark 8, 355, 421
Gabriel, Teshome 395, 398–400, 401
Gaines, Jane 349
Gambo, Zézé 458
Gance, Abel 416
Gandhi, Indira 71
Garbo, Greta 374, 375, 377
García Bernal, Gael 507
Gardin, Vladimir 361, 363
Gardner, Ava 374
Garland, Judy 77, 146, 272, 273, 274, 379
Garnett, Tay 423
Gasser, U. 117
Gazdar, Mushtaq 495
Genet, Jean 324, 325
Geraghty, C. 3
Gerede, Canan 520
Gerima, Hailé 54, 465
Gershwin, George 271, 273, 278
Gershwin, Ira 271
Getino, Octavio 80, 126, 394, 395, 398, 501
Ghanian, Avanes 521
Ghatak, Ritwik 397–8, 486, 491, 492
Gibson, Hoot 433
Gibson, Mel 11
Gidal, Peter 83
Giersz, Witold 21
Gilliat, Sidney 418
Ginsberg, Allen 411
Giorgelli, Pablo 504
Giritlioglu, Tomris 520
Giroud, Françoise 181
Gitaï, Amos 516
Gledhill, Ruth 200, 244, 245, 250, 375, 376, 379

Glover, Danny 11
Godard, Jean-Luc 4, 28, 34, 41, 81, 83, 102, 104, 111, 122, 182, 237, 262, 263, 305, 340, 359, 427, 429
Goebbels, Josef 419
Gold, Jack 416
Goliath 140
Gomery, D. 123
Gonzalez, Felipe 506
Gorani, Joude 510
Gorbman, C. 266
Gordon-Levitt, Joseph 409
Gore, Al 128
Gören, Serif 518
Goretta, Claude 180
Gosling, Ryan 171
Gowariker, Ashutosh 493
Gramsci, Antonio 83, 84, 216, 296
Grant, Cary 355
Grant, Catherine 451–2, 453
Grant, Hugh 98
Grant, P. S. 119
Greaves, William 52
Greenaway, Peter 267
Greengrass, Paul 404
Greenwald, Maggie 437
Grémillon, Jean 180, 184, 418
Grier, Pam 56
Grierson, John 124, 125, 354, 366, 417
Griffith, D. W. 48–9, 50, 139, 145, 349, 428–9
Grisby, Robert 180
Grodal, Torben 176–7
Guazzoni, Enrico 139
Guérin, François 83
Guerra, Ruy 79, 80
Guerrero, Ed 49, 59, 60
Guessoum, Nassima 475
Guest, Val 335
Guevarra, Che 505
Guggenheim, David 128
Guillerman, John 438
Guillotine, Dr 256
Gul, Agha G. A. 496
Güney, Yilmaz 518–19
Gunning, Tom 79
Guttiérez, Tomás 398
Guy, Alice 12

El Habre, Simon 510
Habshi, Samir 510
Hachem, Georges 510
Hafiz, Bahiga 467
El-Hagar, Khaled 471
Haggis, Paul 430
Hake, Sabine 214
Hakkar, Amor 475
Haley, Bill 147
Halilu, Adamu 455
Hall, Stuart 45, 294
Hamed, Marwen 469–70
Hamilton, Guy 424
Hammer, Mike 305
Hammerstein, Oscar 271
Hammett, Dashiel 167, 171
Hammond, Joë 431
Hampton, Howard 290
Hancock, John Lee 380
Haneke, Michael 34, 115
Hanks, Tom 20
Hanson, Curtis 172
Haq, Ziaul 497
Hardwicke, Catherine 148
Harris, Julie 254
Harris, Leslie 61
Harryhausen, Ray 21
Hart, John 18–19
Hart, Lorenz 271
Hart, William H. 433
Hartley, Hal 231
Hartley, J. 345
Haskell, Molly 156, 158
Hathaway, Anne 409
Hathaway, Henry 440
Hawks, Howard 33, 34, 97, 356, 423, 434
Hayes, Isaac 55
Haynes, Todd 203, 232, 325
Hays, William H. 77
Hayworth, Rita 95, 377, 413, 421
Hazanavicius, Michael 356
He Qun 484
Hebdige, Dick 283
Heidegger, Martin 106
Henry V 419
Hepburn, Katherine 97, 356, 379
Hepworth, Cecil 415
Hermosillo, Jaime Humberto 503
Herrmann, Bernard 269

Herzog, Werner 34, 127–8, 212, 213, 403
Heston, Charlton 339–40
Hetata, Alef 469
Higbee, W. E. 297, 408–10
Higson, Andrew 15, 267, 407
Hill, George Roy 75, 201, 440
Hill, J. 451
Hippler, Franz 419
Hirani, Rajkumar 494
Hitchcock, Alfred 33, 34, 89, 112, 114, 151, 155, 159, 161, 220, 221, 249, 252, 266, 267, 269, 325, 375, 405, 406, 412
Hitler, Adolf 419, 422
Hjort, M. 408, 409, 454
Hoffman, Dustin 375
Hogan, David 12
Holiday, Amanda 46
Honda, Ishiro 133, 222, 397, 426
Hondo, Med 458, 461
Honegger, Arthur 267
hooks, bell 52
Hooper, Tobe 218, 220
Hope, Bob 421
Hopper, Dennis 75, 91, 231, 280, 333
Hopper, Edward 305
Howard, Leslie 418
Howard, Ron 442
Hudlin, Warrington 62
Hudson, Hugh 100
Hudson, Rock 246, 377
Hughes, Albert 60
Hughes, Allen 60
Hughes, Howard 435, 436
Hughes, Langston 45
Huillet, Danièle 212, 213
Hunt, L. 133
Hunter, Holly 12
Huston, John 167, 168, 281
Huver, Etienne 509

Ichikawa, Kon 423
Ilhan, Biket 520
Iñárritu, González 506, 507
Ince, Thomas H. 387, 433
Irani, Ardeshir 522
Irmak, Çagan 520
Irvin, John 428

Iskanov, Andrey 76
Islam, Morshedal 487
Ismail, Naji 470
Issartel, Marielle 127
Ivens, Joris 83
Ivory, James 16

Jacir, Annemarie 513
Jackson, Michael 156
Jackson, Peter 65, 115, 120, 328
Jackson, Samuel L. 441
Jacquet, Luc 128
James, Henry 13
James, Jesse 431
Jameson, Fredric 301
Janni, Joseph 74
Jannings, Emil 205, 208
Janowitz, Hans 209
Jarman, Derek 46, 325
Jarmusch, Jim 232
Jaubert, Maurice 267
Jenkins, H. 32, 118
Jennings, Al 432
Jennings, Humphrey 125, 179, 180, 417
Jeunet, J.-P. 337
Jewison, Norman 53, 349
Jiayin, Liu 485
Jimbo, Matsue 22
Joanou, P. 291
Jobs, Steve 23
Johnson, D. 132
Johnson, George 49
Johnson, Noble 49
Johnson, Rian 171
Johnston, Claire 107, 157, 164, 175, 189, 347, 374
Jolie, Angelina 380
Jolson, Al 355
Jones, Buck 433
Jones, Chuck 20, 21
Jones, Jacqui 59
Jones, Kent 10
Jonze, Spike 328
Jordan, Neil 194, 220, 307
Julien, Isaac 45–6, 325, 327
Julius, Marshall 5

Kabir, N. M. 72
Kaes, A. 213

Kahn, Aamir 494
Kajol (Mukherjee) 73
Kalin, Tom 325
Kalmus, Natalie 93, 94
Kandinsky, Wassily 204
Kang Shen 483
Kaplan, E. Ann 190, 244, 250
Kaplan, Jonathan 380
Kaplan, Kenneth 461
Kaplan, Nelly 28
Kapoor, Kareena 73
Kapoor, Karisma 73
Kapoor, Raj 70, 490
KarWar, Wong 329
Kasdan, Lawrence 438
Kasper, Barbara 214
Kaul, Mani 397
Kawin, Bruce 218
Kazan, Elia 254
Keaton, Buster 97
Kechiche, Abdellatif 328
Keesey, Douglas 291
Keighley, William 278
Kelani, Tunde 461
Kellogg, Ray 427
Kelly, Gene 273, 276, 277, 303, 375
Kennedy, John F. 140, 440
Kenovic, Ademir 429
Kerensky, A. F. 367
Kerins, M. 358–9
Kermode, Mark 225
Kern, Jerome 271, 278
Kerouac, Jack 411
Kerr, Deborah 95
Khan, Faisal Aman 498
Khan, Farah 493
Khan, Imran 498
Khan, Mehboob 490
Khan, Shahrukh 72, 494
Khatifa, Hanif 470
Khleifi, Michel 512–13, 517
Khomeini, Ayatollah 522
Kiarostami, Abbas 524, 526
Kidman, Nicole 12, 281–2
Kimai, Mas'ud 523
Kimmich, M. W. 419
King, B. 3, 4, 6, 7, 65–6, 67
King, George William 329, 439
King, Henry 420
King, Martin Luther 45, 53, 440

Kinski, Klaus 212
Kitano, Takeshi 7
Klane, Robert 279
Kleifi, Michel 299
Klein, Melanie 152
Klimov, Elem 425
Klimt, Gustav 204
Kluge, Alexander 212, 213
Knight, Julia 214, 215
Kodsi, Jean-Claude 510, 511
Kooning, Willem de 309
Kopple, Barbara 126
Korda, Alexander 278, 419
Korine, Harmony 130
Kosma, Joseph 184
Koster, Henry 18, 139
Kouyaté, S. 459
Kpaï, I. M. 459
Kracauer, S. 173
Kragh-Jacobsen, Soren 130
Kramer, Stanley 375
Krauss, Werner 205
Kristeva, Julia 96
Kubrick, Stanley 140, 202, 335, 336,
    340, 413, 416, 424, 426, 428
Kuhn, Annette 131, 156, 191, 195–6,
    229, 244, 347, 451–2, 453
Kuleshov, Lev 137, 360, 362, 363,
    364, 365, 366
Kumar, Dilip 70, 490
Kumar, Raj Amit 495
Kumel, Harry 220
Kureshi, Hanif 350
Kurosawa, Akira 133, 426
Kushan, Esma'il 522
Kyung Hyun Kim 166

Labaki, Nadine 510–11
Lacan, Jacques 25–6, 154, 161, 188,
    191, 307, 312, 314–18, 319, 321,
    323, 341, 384, 391
Ladd, Alan 439
Lagtâa, Abdelkader 478
Lakhdar-Hamina, Mohamed 472
Lam, Ringo 7
Lane, Charles 62
Lanfield, Sidney 281
Lang, Fritz 168, 170, 206, 208, 209,
    210, 335, 413, 437
Laplanche, J. 372

Lapsley, R. 26
Laraki, Abdelhaï 478
Larraz, José 220
Lashari, Bilal 498
Lassally, Walter 180
Lasseter, John 78
Laughton, Charles 8, 421
Launder, Frank 418
Lauste, Eugène 355
Lawrence, Florence 374
Le Corbusier 259
Le Fanu, Sheridan 219
Lean, David 139, 418, 424
Ledger, Heath 379, 381, 409
Lee, Ang 7, 15, 76, 100, 326, 329, 346, 409
Lee, Brandon 9
Lee, Bruce 7
Lee, Christopher 219
Lee, Jennifer **64**
Lee, Spike 57, 58–9, 62, 63, 130
Lee, V. P-Y. 133
Lehman, P. 123
Leigh, Mike 354
Leigh, Vivien 374, 380
Lemkin, Rob 128
Lemmon, Jack 195
Lenica, Jan 21
Lenin, Vladimir 360, 361–2
Leone, Sergio 139, 268, 441
LeRoy, Mervyn 169, 185, 423
LeSage, J. 244
Leslie, Alfred 411
Leterrier, Louis 9
LeVeques, Les 145
Lévi-Strauss, Claude 36, 283–4, 285, 288, 383–4
Lewis, H. G. 218
Lewton, Val 68, 220
Likké, Nnegest 63
Lim, S. G.-L. 132
Lim, S. H. 408–10, 452, 454
Liman, Doug 430
Linklater, Richard 148
Litvak, Anatole 253, 421
Livingstone, Jennie 325
Lloyd, Frank 8
Lloyd, Phyllida 154, 275
Lo Wei 7
Loach, Ken 288, 354

Lobarto, R. 122
Lollobrigida, Gina 374
Lord, Peter 24
Loren, Sophia 374
Losey, Joseph 416
Lou Ye 485
Lourié, Eugene 221
Lovelace, Linda 290
Lubitsch, Ernst 210
Lucas, George 23, 64, 78, 113, 117, 336–7, 358
Luessenhop, John 225
Luhrmann, Baz 13, 67, 266, 275, 280–2
Lumet, Sydney 34
Lumière brothers 12, 97, 124, 466, 487–8, 512
Luna, Diego 507
Lund, Katia 505
Lurr, W. 123
Luruli, N. W. 461
Lye, Len 24
Lynch, David 34, 103, 114, 130, 203, 231, 333
Lynd, Laurie 325
Lyne, Adrian 151, 291, 372, 380
Lyotard, Jean-François 390–1

MacDonald, Jeannette 270, 272
MacDonald, Kevin 128
MacDonald, Peter 66
Mackie, Anthony 379
Magnani, Anna 235
Mahfouz, Naguib 468
Mahler, Gustav 266
Maingard, Jacqueline 397
Makhmalbaf, Mohsen 523–4, 526
Makhmalbaf, Samirah 524, 525
Malas, Mohamed 508, 509
Malick, Terrence 333, 424
Malik, Yunus 497
Malkovich, John 328, 375, 376
Malle, Louis 267
Maltby, R. 4
Mambéty, Djibril Diop 397, 401, 458, 461, 462, 464, 465
Mamoulian, Rouben 277
Mankiewicz, Joseph 64
Mann, Anthony 438
Mann, Michael 6, 10, 66, 67

Manovich, L. 118
Mansfield, Jayne 374
Mansukhani, Tarun 71, 494
Manuell, R. 206, 209
Mao, Chairman 481, 482
Mao, Madame 483
Maoz, Samuel 516–17
March, James 128
Marcus, M. 14
Marcuse, Herbert 83, 84, 85
Marglova, Jan 21
Marker, Chris 83
Marks, Laura 176
Marshall, Rob 275
Martel, Lucrecia 504
Marx, Karl 83–4, 85, 227–8, 364, 365
Marx brothers 97, 355
Masharawi, Rachid 513
Mason, James 273
Masri, May 512, 513
Masud, Tareque 487
Maybury, J. 328
Mayer, Carl 209
Mayer, Louis B. 270
Maynard, Ken 433
Mazzett, Lorenza 178, 180
McCambridge, Mercedes 437
McCarthy, Joseph R. 139, 217, 335
McCay, Winsor 19
McCoy, Tim 433
McDonald, P. 3
McG 11
McGregor, Ewan 12, 282
McKernan, B. 117, 118
McLagen, Andrew 441
McNair, Brian 292
McQueen, Steve 47, 243, 292, 305
McTiernan, John 66
Medovoi, Leerom 56, 60
Medvedkin, Alexander 126
Mehra, Rakeysh Omprakash 494
Mehrju'i, Dariush 523
Meirelles, Fernando 505
Méliès, Georges 19, 334
Mellencamp, John 244
Mendes, Sam 203
Menzies, William 335
Mer-Khamis, Julian 517
Merleau-Ponty, M. 176

Messmer, Otto 19
Metha, Deepa 396, 494
Metz, Christian 25, 36–7, 174, 189, 200, 322–3, 341, 368, 369–70, 384–5
Micheaux, Oscar 49, 51–2
Milestone, Lewis 410, 416, 421, 424
Milhaud, Darius 267
Miller, Glenn 273
Miller, Max 330–1
Milner, A. 132
Mineo, Sal 152
Minghella, Anthony 328
Minnelli, Vincente 248, 273, 277, 278
Mir, Raza 496
Mirren, Helen 377
Mishra, V. 72
Mitchell, Roger 98
Mitchell Bros 290
Mitre, Santiago 504
Mix, Tom 433
Miyazaki, Hayao 22
Modleski, T. 155, 160–1, 250, 342, 371–2
Moffatt, Tracey 141
Mohammed, Ossama 509
Moknèche, Nadir 475
Mollaqolipour, Rasou 522
Mongia, Padmini 293, 294
Mo'nique 380
Monk, C. 14
Monroe, Marilyn 77, 97, 202, 343–4, 374, 413
Moore, Michael 99, 128
Morelli, Paulo 505
Morin, Edgar 126
Morricone, Ennio 268, 441
Morris, Errol 127
Morrison, Toni 13
Moustafa, Mohammed 470
Moverman, Oren 430
Mozzhukhin, Ivan (Mosjoukine) 363
Msika, Habiba 475–6
Mudimbe, V. Y. 294
Mulcahy, Russell 11
Mulvey, Laura 27, 156, 157, 158, 175, 189, 190, 244, 246, 323, 341–2, 368, 370–1
Mumenthaler, Milagros 504

Munch, Edvard 204
Münsterberg, Hugo 173
Murdoch, Rupert 389
Murnau, Friedrich 208, 209, 219
Murphy, Eddie 57, 58, 349
Musidora 219
Mussolini, Benito 234
Myles, Linda 157
Myrick, Daniel 130

Nacro, Fanta Régina 459
Nader, Maged 470
Naficy, Hamid 454
Nair, Mira 48, 63, 72, 494
Najjar, Najwa 513
Nakata, Hideo 134, 408
Narboni, J. 230
Naremore, J. 3
Nargis 70, 490
Nasrallah, Yousri 470
Nasser, Gamal Abdel 468
Nasser brothers 513–14
Nazir, Ahmed Khan 496
Neale, Steve 95–6, 195, 197, 198,
    201, 219
Nehru 492
Nelson, Lord 419
Newman, Paul 75, 376
Ngakane, Lionel 43
Nicholson, Jack 4, 376, 382
Nilsson, Leopoldo Torre 398, 500
Ning Dai 484
Nivelle-Cardinale, Sophie 509
Noiret, Philippe 182
Nolan, Christopher 120, 337,
    381, 409
Notcutt, L. A. 459
Novak, M. 296–7
Nowell-Smith, Geoffrey 244, 250
Noyce, Philip 404
Nyman, Michael 267

Oberon, Merle 240
Odigan, Tate 461
Ogundipe, M. 461
Olivier, Lawrence 419
Olmi, Emmanuel 235
O'Neal, Ron 56
Onwocki, Francis 460
Onwurah, Ngozi 46

Ophuls, Marcel 126
Ophuls, Max 168, 248, 251
Orr, John 260, 306
O'Russell, David 429
Osborne, John 73, 74, 178, 181
Oshima, Nagisa 144
Ottinger, Ulrike 214, 324
Oudart, Jean-Pierre 393
Ouedraogo, Idrissa 397, 464
Ové, Horace 43
Özgentürk, Ipekçi Isil 520

Pabst, Georg 210, 416
Pacino, Al 3, 375, 382
Padilha, José 505
Pagnol, Marcel 15
Pakula, Alan 38
Palfrey, J. 117
Palke, Dhundiraj Govind 488
Panahi, Jafar 524–5, 526
Pancholi, Dalsukh 496
Pang brothers 7
Panijel, Jacques 83
Paralluelo, Hermes 504
Park, Nick 24
Park Chan-Wook 7
Parker, Alan 275
Parks, Gordon 53–4
Parmar, Pratibha 324, 326
Pasha, Anwar Kanal 496
Patwardham, A. 398
Pawlikowksi, Pawel 328, 354
Payami, Babak 524
Pearson, George 330
Peck, Gregory 439
Peckinpah, Sam 427, 438, 440
Peerce, Larry 52
Peirce, C. S. 328, 342
Pen-ek Ratanaruang 132
Penn, Arthur 427, 438, 440
Perincioli, Cristina 214
Perkins, Anthony 375
Peters, Robert 461
Peterson, Wolfgang 6, 140
Pfister, Wally 409
Philipe, Gérard 181
Phoenix, River 77, 379, 381
Picasso, Pablo 258
Pickford, Mary 365, 374, 378, 415
Pietrangeli, Antonio 234

Pines, J. 399
Pirselimoglu, Tayfun 520
Pitt, Brad 202
Place, Janey 169, 171
Poitier, Sidney 52–3, 55, 56, 349, 438
Polanski, Roman 199, 223, 405, 406
Polidori, Dr 218
Pollack, Sydney 195
Pollard, Bud 50
Pollock, Jackson 258, 309
Pommer, Erich 207, 209
Pontalis, J. B. 372
Pontecorvo, Gilles 472
Porter, Cole 271
Porter, Dawn 61
Porter, Edwin C. 430
Post, Ted 336
Postlethwaite, Pete 99
Potter, Sally 100, 102, 145
Powell, Michael 220, 254, 269, 330, 370, 406, 412
Preminger, Otto 168, 269, 278, 285
Presley, Elvis 274
Prévert, Jacques 185
Propp, Vladimir 200, 285
Proyas, Alex 9
Pudovkin, Vsevolod 173, 364, 365, 366–7
Puri, Om 492

Qaiser, Khahil 496
Quay brothers 24

Raheb, Eliane 510
Rai, Aishwarya 73, 494
Rajadhyaksha, Ashish 492
Raksin, David 269
Ramsey, Lynne 354
Rappeneau, Jean-Paul 142
Rapper, Irving 161, 249
al-Raqqawi, Abu Ibrahim 509
Rathnam, Mani 493
Ray, Aldo 305
Ray, Nicholas 146, 152, 248, 327, 379, 435, 437
Ray, Satyajit 70, 236, 397, 448, 486, 491, 492
Reagan, Ronald 66
Reckord, Lloyd 43

Redford, Robert 75, 430
Reed, Carol 354
Reeves, Keanu 376
Refig, Halit 519
Refn, Nicholas Winding 171
Reichenbach, François 83
Reiman, Walter 209
Reiner, Carl 413
Reinhardt, Max 205
Reisz, Karel 73, 178, 179, 180, 181, 254
Reitman, Jason 148
Reitz, Edgar 178
Rejtman, Martin 504
René, Norman 76
Renoir, Jean 34, 103, 108, 168, 180, 183, 184, 234, 354, 416, 421
Resnais, Alain 29, 122, 126, 136, 138, 182, 265, 305
Reygadas, Carlos 507
Riad, Mohamed Slim 472
Rich, B. Ruby 325, 437
Rich, Matty 61
Richard, Cliff 274
Richardson, Tony 73, 74, 178, 179, 180, 181
Riefenstahl, Leni 419
Riggen, Patricia 507
Rigosin, Lionel 410
Rivas, Carolina 513
Rivette, Jacques 182
Rizvi, Jarrar 498
Robbe-Grillet, Alain 305
Roberts, Julia 98
Roberts, Rachel 73
Robertson, John 222
Robeson, Paul 278–9
Robinson, Bill 'Bojangles' 21
Robinson, Edward G. 169, 375
Robson, Mark 220–1
Rocha, Glauber 79, 398, 501
Rocker, Veronica 291
Rodgers, Richard 271
Roeg, Nicholas 336
Rogers, Ginger 270, 271, 272, 375
Rogers, Roy 432, 433, 435
Rohmer, Eric 182
Röhrig, Walter 209
Romandía, Jaime 507
Rombes, N. D. 79, 114–15

Romero, George 222, 223
Rooks, Pamela 493
Rooney, Mickey 146, 272
Roosevelt, Franklin D. 187, 230, 420, 421
Roshan, Hrithik 494
Ross, Karen 42
Rossellini, Roberto 234, 236
Rota, Nino 268
Rotter, Ariel 504
Rouch, Jean 82, 83, 126, 141
Rowden, T. 409
Rowntree, Richard 56
Roy, Bimal 490
Rozema, Patricia 326
Rozik, E. 4, 5
Ruiz, Raúl 502
Rulfo, Juan Carlos 507
Ruspoli, Mario 83
Russell, Catherine 118–19
Russell, Jane 380, 436
Russell, Ken 126
Russell, Rosalind 355, 379
Russell, Theresa 413
Ryan, M. D. 122

Sabita 498
Sadat, Anwar 469
Sade, Marquis de 256
Sahgal, Shaad Ali 494
Sahhab, Ghassan 510
Sahraoui, Djamila 475
Saïd, Edward 293, 294, 295
El-Saïd, Tamer 470
Saif, Saifudin 496
Saint-Saëns 267
Salah, Tewfik 468
Salem, Lyès 475
Salhab, G. 511
Salles, Walter 502, 504–5
Sambath, Thet 128
Sánchez, Eduardo 130
Sander, Helke 214
Sanders-Brahms, Helma 214
Sangeeta 497, 498
Santos, Mario 504
Sarkar, Kobita 448
Sarkar, Padrip 494
Sarris, Andrew 35
Sathyu, M. S. 493

Saussure, Ferdinand de 35, 85, 342–3, 383
Savona, Stefano 470
Schaffner, Franklin 151, 336
Schiele, Egon 204
Schlesinger, John 75
Schlöndorff, Volker 212, 213
Schmitz, O. 461
Schneeman, Carolee 262
Schoedask, Ernest B. 19
Schrader, Paul 231, 290
Schumacher, Joel 275
Schwarzenegger, Arnold 8–9, 11, 65, 339
Schygulla, Hanna 212
Scorsese, Martin 13, 34, 75, 76, 87, 100, 120, 202, 231, 304, 427
Scott, Emmett J. 49, 50
Scott, Ridley 76, 99, 140, 286, 333, 337, 340, 430
Scott, Tony 220
Sears, Fred 147
Sédar, Léopold 295
Seif, Salah Abou 468
Sekigawa, Heideo 425–6
Sembène, Ousmane 397, 401, 457, 458, 459, 464–5
Sen, Hiralal 488
Sen, Mrinal 70, 397, 486, 492
Senghor, Leopold Sedar 295
Sennett, Mack 97
Sestier, Maurice 487–8
Shabazz, Menelik 44
Shakespeare, William 13
Shakur, Tupac 60
Sharma, Anil 493
Sharman, Jim 103
Shaviro, Steven 175–6
Shaw, D. 408
Shelley, Mary Wollstonecraft 151, 218
Shindo, Kaneto 425
Shiva 498
Shohat, Ella 447, 448–9, 450, 451, 452, 454, 512
Shore, Howard 268, 269
Shostakovitch, Dmitri 267
Shub, Esfir 362, 365
Sica, Vittorio de 180, 234, 235, 236
Sideman, Ramadan 461

Sidibe, Gabourey 379
Siegel, Don 146
Siffredi, Rocco 291
Signoret, Simone 377
Silberman, Marc 207, 208, 371
Sillitoe, Alan 74
Simmons, Anthony 279
Sinatra, Frank 274
Sinatra, Nancy 147
Singleton, John 61, 63, 226, 227
Siodmak, Robert 168
Sippy, Ramesh 493
Sirk, Douglas 168, 246, 248,
    249, 255
Sissako, Aderrahmane 459,
    462, 465
Sivan, Eyal 517
Slade, David 148
Smith, Jack 410–11
Smith, Kevin 231
Smith, M. 143
Snipes, Wesley 11
Soderburgh, Steven 119, 145,
    232, 337
El Sokby brothers 470
Solanas, Fernando 80, 126, 394, 395,
    398, 501
Solás, Humberto 398
Sonnenfeld, Barry 438
Sorak, Ömar Faruk 520
Soutine, Chaïm 204
Spacey, Kevin 375
Spasjevic, Srdan 76
Spheeris, Penelope 147
Spielberg, Steven 13, 23, 65, 76, 78,
    120, 137, 153, 307, 336, 338, 339,
    349, 424, 425
Spivak, Gayatri 294
Sproxton, David 24
Spurlock, Morgan 127
Srour, Henri 510
Stahl, John 247, 249
Stalin, Josef 360, 362, 367, 422
Stallone, Sylvester 3, 11, 65, 427
Stam, R. 79, 447, 448–9, 452, 454,
    512
Stanislavsky, Konstantin 254
Stanwyck, Barbara 413, 437
Starrett, Jack 56
Steiger, Rod 254, 441

Sternberg, Josef von 168, 413
Stevens, George 255, 439
Stevenson, R. 278
Stewart, James 421, 438
Stoker, Bram 219
Stokowski, Leopold 272
Stollery, Martin 476
Stone, Oliver 140, 428
Storey, David 74
Straub, Jean-Marie 212, 213
Streep, Meryl 3, 154, 375, 376, 377,
    378, 383
Streisand, Barbra 274–5,
    378, 382
Strong, J. 16, 17
Strouse, James C. 430
Studlar, G. 342, 371
Sturges, John 134, 440
Sucksdorff, Arne 180
Suleiman, Elia 513, 515
Surjik, Stephen 147
Svankmajer, Jan 24
Swank, Hilary 380
Swaranlata 496

Takahata, Isao 22
Tan Xinepei 481
Tandin, Loveleen 495
Tanner, Alain 180
Tanovic, Danis 429
Tarantino, Quentin 34, 120, 187,
    232, 304, 305, 441
Taretto, Gustavo 504
Tarkovsky, A. 336
Tarr, Belá 232
Tatli, Moufida 475, 476
Taurog, Norman 147
Tavakoli, Bahram 522
Taylor, Clyde 48, 49
Taylor, Elizabeth 140
Teo, S. 133
Thatcher, Margaret 100, 154
Theron, Charlize 380
Thompson, Emma 12, 15
Thompson, J. L. 336
Thompson, K. 241
Thorpe, Richard 147
Thurman, Uma 380
Tlatli, Moufida 299, 349, 476–7
Tobi, Abdeleziz 472

Toland, Gregg 109, 136, 500
Touraine, Alain 85
Touré, Moussa 459
Tourneur, Jacques 220, 305
Trabelsi, Osnat 517
Tracey, Spencer 97
Trapero, Pablo 504
Trauner, Alexander 184
Travolta, John 275, 276
Trinh Tri, Coralie 291–2, 350
Trnka, Jiri 21
Troche, Rose 325–6
Trotsky, Leon 367
Truffaut, François 33, 34, 106, 182,
    240, 254
Tsaki, Ibrahim 473
Tucker, Duncan 329, 333
tucker green, debbie 46
Turgul, Yavuz 520
Turim, Maureen 177
Turner, Kathleen 413
Tushingham, Rita 73
Tykwer, Tom 65

Uciciky, Gustav 416
Ukadike, N. F. 396, 465
Ustaoglu, Yesim 520

Vadim, Roger 181
Van Damme, Claude 11, 65
Van Dyke, Woody 270
Van Gogh, Vincent 204
Van Peebles, Mario 11, 59, 61, 63,
    227, 438
Van Peebles, Melvin 53–4, 55
Van Sant, Gus 145, 149, 232, 325,
    329, 381
VanDerBeek, Stan 410
Varda, Agnès 28, 34, 42, 102, 126,
    182, 263
Vas, Robert 180
Vautier, René 472
Veidt, Conrad 205, 208–9,
    421, 422
Verbinski, Gore 134
Verhoeven, Paul 78, 291
Verne, Jules 334
Vertov, Dziga 82, 125–6, 141, 360,
    362, 365
Vidor, Charles 170

Vidor, King 247, 278
Vieyra, Paulin Soumano 457
Vigo, Jean 34, 180
Vintenberg, Thomas 116, 117,
    129, 130
Visconti, Luchino 234, 235, 236
Voigt, Jon 428
Von Trier, Lars 116, 129, 130–1,
    145, 275, 282–3
von Trotta, Margarethe 34,
    214, 263

Wachowski, Larry and Andy 78,
    328, 338
Wachsman, Daniel 515
Walker, Alice 13
Waller, Fats 21
Walters, Charles 277
Wan, James 224
Wang, Wayne 48
Wang Xiaoshuai 484–5
Warhol, Andy 114, 134, 144, 262,
    410, 411
Warm, Hermann 209
Washington, Denzel 11, 349, 377
Watkins, Peter 426
Watt, Harry 417
Wayne, John 3, 91, 136, 382, 423,
    427, 434, 435, 439, 441
Wayne, Keenan Ivory 57
Weaver, Sigourney 11
Wegener, Paul 209
Weir, Peter 417
Welland, William 423
Welles, Orson 34, 87, 108, 500
Wellman, William 185, 416,
    423, 436
Wells, H. G. 334, 335
Welsh, Irvine 16
Wenders, Wim 34, 91, 212, 333,
    403, 427
Wendkos, Paul 147
West, Mae 437
West, Simon 12
Westlake, M. 26
Whale, James 218, 278, 328
Wharton, Edith 13
Whedon, Joss **64**, 65
Wicki, Bernhard 423
Wiene, Robert 107, 208, 219

Wilder, Billy 97, 168, 169, 171, 195, 303
Willemen, P. 399, 400
Williams, Linda 190, 244
Williams, Raymond 310
Williams, Robbie 326
Williams, Spencer D. 50
Williamson, Fred 55–6
Willis, Bruce 11
Willis, H. 77–8
Winterbottom, Michael 130, 329, 429
Wise, Robert 275
Witney, William 147
Wollen, Peter 41
Wong Kar-Wai 329
Woo, John 7
Wood, Natalie 152
Wood, Robin 198, 225
Wright, W. 200
Wuornos, Aileen 127
Wyler, William 109

Xavier, Ismail 80
Xu Jinglei 485

Yamamoto, Kajiro 420
Yaméogo, Pierre 459
Yasar, Seçkin 520
Yates, David **64**, 78
Yavuz, Hüdaverdi 521
Yearworth Jnr, Irvin 221
Ying Liang 485
Young, Lola 44

Zecca, Ferdinand 177
Zellweger, Renée 98
Zemeckis, Robert 19, 306
Zemmouri, Mahmoud 473
Zhang Yimou 7, 408–9, 484, 485
Zhang Yuan 329, 484, 485
Zia-ul-Haq, General 497
Zinnemann, Fred 112, 254, 278, 424, 425, 439
Zinta, Preity 73
Zola, Emile 354
Zukor, Adolph 387
Zwick, Edward 428, 429
Zwigoff, Terry 148

SUBJECT INDEX

Note: *italicised* page numbers indicate illustrations

3-D cinema 10, 65, 113, 389, 402–4
30-degree rule 104, 345–6, 402
180-degree rule 17–18, 81, 135, 289, 345–6

Aardman Animation group 24
ABC 179, 180
Abounaddara/The Man with the Glasses 430
absence/presence 3, 26, 321, 323, 331, 381
acting: method 254; and performance 3–5
action movies 5–12; blockbusters 66–7; Bollywood 70; East Asian 479–80; frontier myth 66–7
Actors Studio 254
adaptation 12–17, 33, 74, 100, 219
ADR (Automatic Dialogue Replacement) 358, 359
African cinemas 82, 355–479; documentary 126, 128, 457, 465, 469, 470, 471, 472, 474, 475, 477; Maghreb 396, 455, 463–4, 471–9; North Africa 444, 465–79; Pan-African 463–5; postcolonial theory 293, 294; Sub-Saharan 456–63; women filmmakers 467, 469, 473, 474–7; women in 466, 472, 473, 476–7
African-American cinema *see* Black cinema, African-American
Afrocult Foundation Limited 462
agency 17, 31, 299, 309, 413; and women 96, 102, 175, 190, 252, 291, 341

Agfa 94
Algeria 396, 463–4, 466, 471–5
American Dream 90, 148, 167, 186, 277, 283, 284
anamorphic lens 17–18, 81, 442–3
Anglophone Africa 456, 457, 459–63
Angola 458
Animal Logic 282
animation 18–24, 65, 78, 93
Animatrix videos 118
apparatus 24–7; and ideology 24–5, 85, 163, 229, 311, 369
Arab Spring 128, 229, 466, 469, 470, 473, 477
Argentina 80, 126, 394, 398, 499, 500, 501, 503, 504
ARRAY 62
art cinema 27–9, 101, 105, 142, 143, 368; Black British 44–5; classic canons 91; East Asia 133; France 27–8, 32, 183; Indian cinemas 491–2; Latin America 502; Middle East 430, 519; North Africa 464
aspect ratio 18, 30
Association of Revolutionary Cinematography (ARC) 362
asynchronization of sound 31
audience 31–2, 163; and adaptations 15, 16; and agency 17, 31; and Bollywood 70, 72; diegetic 111–12, 381, 382; and distanciation 122; reception theory 31, 368, 372–3; semiotics and 37; *see also* spectator
Australia 28, 141, 446, 449

auteur/auteur theory 32–9, *36*, 113, 119–20, 173–4, 175, 197, 211; East Asian Cinema 132; and genre 197, 200, 201; Indian cinema 69; Middle Eastern cinemas 508; and mise-en-scène 255; and (post-)structuralism 35–7, 384, 385; Third Cinema 401; time-image 264, 265
Autorenfilm (author's film) 32–3
avant-garde 39–42, 101, 198, 241; American 41, 262; and CGI 79; and distanciation 122; editing 40, 134, 411; French 28, 40, 261, 262; Indian 491; and modernism 257, 258, 261–2; montage cuts 105; music 267; postmodernism 303; queer cinema 324

B-movies 16, 68, 167, 220, 304, 329, 388, 389, 427, 434–5
back-lighting 238, 239, 240, 241, 242
back-stage musical 270
Bangladesh 448, 486–7, 496
Bantu Film Projects 459
Beaver Films 74
Betty Boop 19
BFF (Black Filmmakers Foundation) 62
BFI (British Film Institute) 43, 44, 180
Bioskop 207
'The Birth of the Sixth Art' 172–3
Black Audio Film Collective 43, 45, 401
Black cinema, African-American 44, 47–63, 280, 349, 399; adaptations 14; Black aesthetic 52, 54, 59, 60; Blaxploitation 11, 54–8, 60, 203, 437–8; comedy 61; documentary 58, 61, 62, 63; gangsta-chic 59–60, 61; ghettocentric 52, 56, 57, 58, 59–60, 63; hip-hop-rap films 58; and Hollywood 53–5, 56–7, 59, 61, 62; 'hood films 59–61; mainstream 57–61; musicals 273, 278–9; sexuality in 53, 55, 56; Westerns 437–8; women in 50, 52, 54, 56, 57, 58, 60–1, 63
Black cinema, British 42–7, 349, 399, 400; Asian Indian 42, 46–7, 48;

documentaries 42, 43, 44, 45, 46, 47; women in 46–7
Black cinema, French 47, 183
Black Lives Matter 62
Black Power movement 53, 57, 229
Black Skin, White Masks 293
Blaxploitation cinema 11, 54–8, 60, 203, 437–8
blockbusters 63–8, 71, 78, 123, 128, 133, 140–1, 336
Board for the New German Cinema 210, 212
body theory 175–6, 287, 311
Bolivia 449, 501
Bollywood 68–73, 487, 489, 493, 494
Bombay Talkies 489
Bosnia 429
Bourekas genre 516
boy-meets-girl 17, 69, 271
Brazil 79–80, 325, 398, 445, 450, 499, 500, 502–3, 504–5
bricolage 99, 117, 305
British cinema 6, 92, 100, 101, 142, 144, 166; animation 24; comedy 98; documentary 125; Free Cinema 73, 124, 178–81, 210, 354; horror movies 218; New Wave 16, 17, 73–5, 180–1, 212, 236, 332, 354; war films 415, 417–18, 423, 424, 429; *see also* Black cinema, British
British International Pictures 330
British Lion 74, 75
Broadway 270, 271
Bryanston Films 74
buddy films 75–6
Buena Vista Motion Pictures Group 389
Burkina Faso 397, 457, 459, 464

Cahiers du cinéma 32–9, 81, 129, 181, 182, 230, 255
Cambodia 128
camera: digital 82, 94, 113–14, 443; lightweight 126, 129, 183
Camera Obscura 158
Cameroon 457
Camflex cameras 129
Canada 82, 83

Canana Films 507
Cannes 45, 458, 464, 470, 500, 507, 524
Cape Verde 458
capitalism 198–9, 243–4, 245, 248, 276, 280, 283, 301, 307, 308, 408, 432, 453
Caribbean cinemas 449; Cuba 396, 398, 500, 501–2, 503; Haïti 141
Carthage Film Festival 396–7
castration 154, 159, 250, 314, 318, 321, 369, 370, 371, 372, 391, 406, 412
censorship 7, 28, 76–7, 96, 187, 206, 213, 290, 389, 410–11, 436, 440; African cinemas 464, 466, 473, 474, 475, 476; China 399, 483, 484; Latin America 500, 502; and melodrama 249–50; Middle Eastern cinemas 508, 510, 511, 518, 519, 521, 523–5; Pakistan 496, 497; Soviet 362; war films 416
CGI (Computer Graphic Imaging) 22–3, 65, 77–9, 115, 154, 202, 225, 305, 337
Chad 459
chiaroscuro lighting 205, 207
Chile 449
China 6, 7, 132, 133, 399, 444, 445, 446, 450, 453, 455, 479–85, 488
ciné-train 126
Cinecittà studios 234
Cinema 16 144
Cinema Action 144
cinema nôvo 79–80, 501
cinéma-vérité 82–3, 126, 127, 141, 354, 365, 411, 485
cinemascope 18, 30, 64, 80–1, 93, 139, 202, 260, 357, 438, 442
The Cinematic Body (Theory out of Bounds) 175–6
Cinematograph Films Act (1927) 330, 331
cinematographer 82
Civil Rights (USA) 49, 53, 439–40
Civil War (USA) 230, 428–9
class 83–7; and costume dramas 100; and feminist film theory 161–2; Free Cinema 178, 179–80; French

poetic realism 183; gangster films 186, 187; and gender issues 83, 85–6; and hegemony 216; and horror movies 224; and ideology 227–8; and independent cinema 231; and Italian neo-realism 235; and melodrama 243–4, 245; and naturalizing 288; and Third Cinema 395; in war films 418, 424
classical Hollywood (narrative) cinema 88–91, 264–5; agency 17; and asynchronization 31; and class analysis 87; denotation/connotation 111; and editing 90, 135, 137; and female spectator 158; and lighting 240; and myth 283–4; and Oedipal trajectory 314, 320, 322, 324, 371; and sexuality 89, 169, 348–50
'Click This: From Analog Dreams to Digital Realities' 119
close-up shots (CU) 90, 91, 105, 351–2
codes and conventions 91–2, 96, 158, 263, 353; action movies 9–11; art cinema 29; avant-garde 41; Bollywood 69; in counter-cinema 101; and deconstruction 106–7; and gaze 370; and genre 198, 199, 200, 201; horror movies 219; in melodrama 247–50; and narrative 284, 287; Pan-African Cinema 465; road movies 333; and scopophilia 341–2; and sexuality 346, 347; and subject 390; Third Cinema 395; Westerns 346
Cold War 139, 167, 203, 211, 217, 221, 248, 309, 335, 423, 426–7, 439, 446
collision editing 134
Colonial Film Unit (CFU) 459
colonialism 395, 448, 462, 464
colour 19, 80–1, 82, 92–6, 101; blockbusters 64; British New Wave 74; and gender 195; Indian cinema 70; and lighting 239; musicals 274
Columbia 232, 387–8, 389
Comédie Française 28

comedy 97–8, 240; and Black cinema 46, 47, 57, 61; and class analysis 85, 86; cross-dressing 196; screwball 355–6; teen 147–8

compilation shots 105

connotation/denotation 110–11, 157, 343, 412

constructivism 39, 360, 362, 363

consumption 118–19, 197, 244; *see also* convergence

Contemporary Postcolonial Theory: A Reader 293

continuity cuts 104

continuity editing 4, 31, 134–5, 150, 411

convergence 98–100, 113, 117, 118; *see also* digital technology

costume dramas (heritage) 13, 15, 93, 100–1, 490

counter-cinema (oppositional) 4, 101–2, 163–4, 261; and avant-garde 40, 41; and classic canons 91; and colour 96; and deconstruction 106–7; and distanciation 122; and extra-diegetic sounds 111; and French New Wave 182; and Indian cinema 491–2; Latin America 501, 502; and Third Cinema 394, 400–1

Cours de linguistique générale 35, 342, 385

cross-cutting 90, 102, 105, 136

cross-dressing 194, 195–6, 268, 318, 327, 348, 437

Crown Film Unit 417

Cuba 396, 398, 465, 500, 501–2, 503

cult cinema 103, 118, 152, 199

cultural studies 35, 162, 166, 175, 310

cut 78–9, 94, 103–6, 345–6, 402; continuity 104; cross-cutting 90, 102, 105, 136; cutaways 105; eyeline 90, 105; jump 101, 104, 122, 236–7, 345, 368, 402; match 90, 104–5; montage 105; rough 106

Czech School 21

day/night for night 106, 240–1

Decla (-Bioskop) 207, 209

deconstruction *36*, 38, 106–8, 157, 174–5, 232, 254, 263, 305, 385, 386, 411, 427; and Black cinema 62–3; feminist film theory 107, 157, 323–4; and gender 193–4; and montage 105, 126, 138; and narrative 107, 261, 285; and sound 111, 359; and Westerns 441

deep focus 6, 81, 108–10, 134, 136, 137–8, 332, 353

Denmark 130

denotation/connotation 110–11, 157, 343, 412

depth of field 81, 108–10, 353

Desilu 389

dGeneration 485

diegesis 40, 111–12, 122, 129, 152, 170, 184, 190, 263, 285, 286, 357–8

diegetic audiences 111–12, 381, 382

diegetic sound 111, 129, 357

digital cameras 82, 94, 113–14, 443

digital cinema 113–17, 239

Digital Domain 78

digital technology 8, 64–5, 98–100, 114, 115, 116, 117–19; and colour 94; and consumption 118–19; and distribution 123, 409; and documentary 127; and Dogme *95* 129, 130; experimental cinema 144; and lighting 242–3; and sound 357; Sub-Saharan cinemas 460; widescreen 443; *see also* CGI; internet

digitization 78, 117–19, 409

direct cinema *see cinéma-vérité*

director 119–20; and auteurs 33–4, 35; Dogme *95* 129

director of photography (DOP) 82

director's cut 106, 119

Directory of World Cinema series 452

discourse 120–1, 227, 288; and auteurism 37; and avant-garde 40; and colour 95, 96; and deconstruction 107; and feminist film theory 158, 161, 162, 164, 165; and film noir 170; and gaze/look 189, 190; and genre 197, 199; and post-structuralism 38–9, 385; postcolonial 294, 295, 298, 299;

postmodern 305, 306; and semiology 342–3, 345; and sexuality 164–5; World Cinemas 448, 491

Disney Productions 19, 20, 22, 23, 389

dissolve 112, 121, 135

distanciation 41, 104, 121–2, 182, 364

distribution 98–9, 113, 122–3, 144, 213, 387; African cinemas 464–5, 474–5; and digitization 117, 118

divided self 322–4

documentary 92, 124–8, 198; and 3-D cinema 402–3; African cinemas 126, 128, 457, 465, 469, 470, 471, 472, 474, 475, 477; avant-garde 40; Black African-American cinema 58, 61, 62, 63; Black British 42, 43, 44, 45, 46, 47; British New Wave 73; China 485; *cinéma direct* 82; cinema nôvo 79; ethnographic 457; European 143; exploitation movies 149; Free Cinema 178, 179, 180; Latin America 126, 499, 501, 502; Middle Eastern cinemas 128, 508, 509–10, 512, 513, 517, 521, 525; and musicals 274; New German cinema 213; and social realism 354; and Soviet cinema 361, 362; and war films 415, 417, 419–20

Dogme 95 116, 117, 129–31, 282, 359

Dolby Stereo/Surround/Digital 357, 358

dollying shot 407

dominant/mainstream cinema 3, 40, 57–61, 106–7, 120, 131, 135, 137; and Black cinema 47, 49, 57–61; and Dogme 95 130; and experimental cinema 145; the female body 96; the gaze 190; and identification 26, 87; and myth 283–4; and postmodernism 303–4, 305–6; and psychoanalysis 320; and Third Cinema 395; and World Cinema 450; *see also* classical Hollywood (narrative) cinema

DreamWorks 20, 23

Dreamz Unlimited 72

DSLR technology 113

DSS (digital surround sound) 158, 357, 359

DVDs 64, 103, 123, 460, 461, 495

Dynamation 21

Dziga-Vertov group 83

Ealing Comedies 98

East Asian Cinemas 131–4, 408–9, 444, 451, 453; China 6, 7, 132, 133, 399, 444, 445, 446, 450, 453, 455, 479–85, 488; Hong Kong 6–7, 132, 133, 451, 453, 456, 479–80, 485; Japan 6–7, 22, 28, 94, 126, 132, 133–4, 408, 420, 425–6, 446, 451; North Korea 448, 449, 455; South Korea 6–7, 132, 133, 166, 446; Taiwan 6–7, 132, 133, 446, 451, 479–80, 485; Thailand 132; Vietnam 448, 449, 455

Eastman-Kodak 93

Eastmancolor 94

Éclair 387

écriture 41

Edison 30, 49, 92, 355, 512

editing 3, 134–8; of adaptations 14; avant-garde 40, 134, 411; *cinéma-vérité* 82, 83; and classical Hollywood (narrative) cinema 90, 135, 137; collision 134; continuity 4, 31, 134–5, 150, 411; deep focus 6, 81, 108–10, 134, 136, 137–8, 332, 353; Free Cinema 180; and French New Wave 182; parallel 102, 136; *see also* cut

Egypt 466–71

Egyptian Realism 468

ellipsis 483–4

Embodied Visions 176–7

Empire Marketing Board 125

Enlightenment 256, 257, 258, 260, 296

Enter the Matrix (video game) 118

epics 138–41, 199; in Bollywood 69; colour 94; Hollywood's racism 48–9; Soviet cinema 364; Westerns 433–4, 440

eroticism 28, 251, 374, 379, 380, 461

Essais sur la signification au cinéma
37, 384
Essanay 433
Ethiopia 465
ethnographic film 82, 141, 457, 465
Eurimages 143
EUROPA CINEMAS 143
European cinema and financing
142–3
Evernew Studios (Pakistan) 496
'Evolution of the Language of
Cinema' 109
evolutionary theory 176–7
experimental film 27, 40, 45, 101,
103, 109, 137, 143–5, 173, 262;
animation 22, 24; China 483–4;
and digital technology 130, 144;
Latin America 501–2; Third World
401, 464, 471; *see also*
expressionism, German
Experimental Film Fund (BFI) 180
exploitation movies 145–50
L'Express 181
expressionism, German 28, 40, 107,
109, 168, 183, 204–10, 219, 239,
255, 346
extra-diegetic audience 112,
381, 382
extra-diegetic routines, Indian
cinema 488
extra-diegetic sounds 111
extreme close-up shots (ECU)
351, 353
extreme long shots (ELS) 352, 353
eyeline cuts 90, 105
eyeline matching 150

fade 135, 150–1, 345
fairy tales 151, 285
Famous Players-Lasky
Corporation 387
fantasy 151–3, 274, 312, 350,
372, 489
FEK (Factory of the Eccentric Actor)
group 364
female child 313, 314, 318–20, 391
female masquerade 154–5, 169–70
female spectator 156, 158, 160, 161,
163, 189, 190, 246, 251, 252, 342,
370, 371, 394, 437

female stars 11–12, 95, 195, 242,
343–4, 374, 376, 377, 379–80,
382, 436, 437
femininity 154, 155, 156, 163, 192,
249, 348, 350, 448
feminism 15, 107, 140, 155, 165–6,
191–2, 311, 380; in African
cinemas 477; auteur theory *36*, 38;
avant-garde 41–2; and Black
American cinema 58; documentary
126–7; Germany 214–15; North
African cinemas 477; and
postcolonial theory 298–9; and
postmodernism 306, 310; and
psychoanalysis 318–20, 321; and
science fiction 337; and sexuality
346–7; and spectatorship 341, 342,
368, 371, 394–5; and stars 380
feminist film theory 95, 155–67, 175,
326, 368, 393–4; and class 160,
162; codes and conventions 91,
158; and counter-cinema 102, 157;
and deconstruction 107, 157, 324;
female Oedipal trajectory 160–1,
318; on film noir 159, 311, 370;
Foucauldian theory 162–4; horror
movies 159; melodrama 159–60,
230, 244, 311; and psychoanalysis
323, 386, 391; and race 166; and
sexuality 326; and spectator 156,
158, 160, 189, 311, 368; World
Cinemas 166
femme fatale 154, 155, 169, 171, 227,
318, 320, 323, 380, 413
FEPACI (Fédération Panafricaine des
cinéastes) 396, 462, 463, 465
FESPACO (Festival Panafricaine du
cinéma de Ouagadougou) 397, 463
fetishism 318, 321, 323, 341, 348–9,
370, 381, 382, 412–13
FFC (Film Finance Corporation) 491
Fifth Cinema 449, 486
fill lighting 239, 240, 241
Film d'Art 32, 33, 172, 373
Le Film esthétique 172
Film Finance Corporation (FCC) 491
film noir 154, 159, 167–72, 203, 210,
320, 332, 392; and music 268–9;
and narrative 284–5; setting 240,
346; and Westerns 438; and

women 159, 311, 318, 320, 323, 370
Film Studies 48, 155–6, 384, 444, 447
Film Subsidy Law 212
film theory 172–7; *see also individual theories*
finance: African cinemas 458, 459, 460, 461, 469, 472, 475, 478; China 479, 484; crowd-funding 99; East Asian Cinema 479; European cinema 142–3; experimental cinema 143–4; Free Cinema 180; independent cinema 232, 233; Indian cinemas 487, 488–9, 491; Italian 236; Latin American cinemas 501–2, 503, 504–5, 506, 507; Middle Eastern cinemas 509–10, 517, 519, 524; New German cinema 212–13; and quota quickies 329, 330; stars and 375; studio system 387, 388, 389; Third Cinema 396, 397, 398, 448; World Cinemas 449, 450, 454
First Cinema 394, 395, 398
First National 387
flashback 112, 121, 135, 144, 170–1, 177–8, 249, 390
Flashbacks in Film: Memory and History 177–8
floodlight 239
Foley sound effects 358
folk musicals 278
Ford of Dagenham 180
foregrounding 3, 144, 157, 159, 170, 195, 219, 231, 244, 261, 348, 349–50, 406, 412
Foster Photoplay Company 50
Fourth World cinemas 448–9, 479, 503, 512
Fox Film Corporation (20th Century Fox) 387, 389
Fox studios 18, 434
framing 81, 207, 254, 351, 352
France 18, 98, 100, 101, 142, 143, 172, 256–7, 261; animation 18, 19; art cinema 27–8, 32, 33, 172; and auteur 33–5; avant-garde 28, 40, 261, 262; Black cinema 47, 458, 459, 462; and cult/counter-cinema 102, 103; film noir 167, 168; gangster films 185; horror movies 334; melodrama 247–8; New Wave (*Nouvelle Vague*) 27–8, 33, 81, 181–3, 212, 236, 332; poetic realism 168, 183–5, 234–5, 267; pornography 290, 291; postmodernism 302; and realism 82, 332; studio system 386–7; war films 418–19, 429; Westerns 431
Francophone Africa 456, 457, 458–9
Frankfurt School 308–9
Frauen and Film 214
Free Cinema (Britain) 73, 124, 178–81, 210, 354
From Reverence to Rape: The Treatment of Women in the Movies 156
Fujicolor 94
Fujifilm 94

Gakken 22
gangsta-chic 59–60
gangster films 136, 185–8, 226, 227, 247
Gaskino 361
GATT 142
Gaumont 183, 355, 387
gay culture 16, 76, 127, 145, 275, 348; World Cinemas 484, 503, 505; *see also* queer cinema
gaze/look 188–91; and 180-degree rule 289; and Black body 49; and counter-cinema 102; and digitization 114; ethnographic 141; eyeline matching 90, 150; female 190, 382; and hegemony 347; male 40, 102, 154–5, 190, 321, 341, 370, 382, 394, 412; and melodrama 252, 253; and modernism 260, 261; and musicals 272; and postmodernism 310; and queer cinema 325, 327–8; and scopophilia 341; and shame 26–7; and voyeurism 321
gender 87, 191–7, 268, 301, 380, 400; and adaptation 16–17; and Black cinema 44; and class 83, 85–6, 87; in comedy 97; and costume dramas 100; and epics 139; and genre 156, 158, 159, 175,

198, 333, 337, 346, 382; and ideology 87, 161, 165, 193, 194–5, 198, 276, 288; and lighting 195, 242; and melodrama 245–7, 248, 249, 250–1; and musicals 276–7, 281; postmodernism 301, 306, 309, 310; power relations 165–6; and spectator 156, 160, 175, 195, 341; stereotypes 97, 333, 347; technology of 164–5; and World Cinemas 448, 476, 506, 515; *see also* feminist film theory

genre 37, 197–203, 279–80, 281, 324–5, 334, 388; and avant-garde 40; and Black cinema 50, 52, 54–5; and class analysis 85; codes and conventions 91, 94, 198, 199–200, 219, 247, 263, 279–80, 385; East Asian Cinemas 132; and gender 156, 158, 159, 175, 198, 333, 337, 346, 382; and iconography 226–7, 432, 433; and ideology 198–9, 203, 229, 276, 337; and music 268; postmodernism 305; and Soviet cinema 365; and stars 70, 202, 375, 382; sub-genre 54–5, 76, 85, 167, 188, 198, 203, 218, 247, 270, 333–4; and World Cinema 452, 453, 465, 467, 499, 502, 516

Germany 32–3, 76, 94, 107, 142; expressionism 28, 40, 107, 109, 168, 183, 204–10, 219, 239, 255, 346; New German cinema 27–8, 210–15, 332, 427; war films 416, 419

gesture 5, 23, 97, 111, 154, 155, 185, 195, 208, 355, 364, 375, 432

Gevacolor 94

Ghana 396, 397, 458, 459–60, 461

Ghibli studios 22, 23

globalization 117–19, 128, 129, 301, 308, 329, 407–8, 409, 447, 450, 451, 452, 453–4, 459, 460, 479, 494, 498

GOC (General Organization for Cinema) 508, 509

Gothic woman's film 252, 257

GPO 125, 417

Grierson Group 417

Grupo Cine Liberación 394

Guinea-Bissau 458

Gulf war 8, 9, 469

Haïti 141

Hammer Productions 218, 219

Harlem Renaissance Movement 45, 50, 295

Hays Code 28, 77, 142, 187–8, 215–16

hegemony 63–4, 76, 87, 102, 120, 143, 164, 198, 216, 297, 327, 340, 349; and World Cinema 408, 449, 476

Heimat (TV series) 212

heritage cinema *see* costume dramas (heritage)

heterosexuality, dominance of 75, 87, 89, 111, 121, 131, 151, 189, 196, 229, 346, 347

hip-hop-rap films 57, 58, 60

The History of Sexuality 164

Hollywood 54, 142, 216–17, 263–4; action movies 6, 7–8; adaptations 13, 14, 16; and African cinemas 456, 460, 468; and art cinema 28–9; and auteurism 33–4, 35, 37; B-movies 68; and Black cinema 47, 48–9, 50, 53–9, 61–2; blacklist 217, 389, 439; and Bollywood 69; and Brazilian cinema 79, 80; and British New Wave 74–5; and censorship 77, 389; and China 482, 484; and class 87; and colour 92, 93, 94–5; and counter-cinema 102; cut 105, 106; dominance of heterosexuality 89, 97, 151, 189, 196, 229, 286, 347; editing 135, 136; epics 138, 139, 140, 199; and European cinema 142; exploitation movies 145–9; and feminist film theory 156, 160, 163; and film noir 168, 169, 171–2, 210; and finance 68, 74, 123, 138; and horror movies 218, 219; and independents 131, 231, 232–3; and Indian cinemas 487, 488, 496, 498; and Latin America 499–500, 506–7; and lighting 238, 239, 240, 241, 242; and melodrama 248, 249, 252; musicals 269–83, 355; and

myth 283, 343–4; and
pornography 290–1; producer 311;
and queer cinema 326, 328; racism
48–9, 51, 347–8; science-fiction
335–6; stars 77, 216, 272, 273–5,
343–4, 373–83; studio system 70,
75, 131, 216–17, 311, 374,
386–90, 412; and transnationalism
134, 407–9, 454; war films 89,
416, 420–1, 422–3, 424, 426–8;
and World Cinema 450, 451, 452,
453, 456, 468, 482, 484, 487; *see
also* classical Hollywood (narrative)
cinema; dominant/mainstream
cinema
homosexuality 45, 73, 145, 194, 196,
219, 220, 268, 327; *see also* queer
cinema
Hong Kong 6–7, 132, 133, 451,
453, 456, 479, 485
'hood films 59–61
horror movies 103, 151, 159,
218–26, 426; body horror 220,
221; Gothic horror 218, 219, 247;
Hammer Horror 218, 219; lighting
240; psychological 220, 224–6,
405–6; 'unnatural' 220, 221–4;
vampire horror 218, 219–20,
223, 328
House of Un-American Activities
Committee (HUAC) 139, 217,
335, 389, 423
hybridity 19, 297, 298, 364,
499–500

iconography 87, 155, 157, 187, 195,
202, 203, 226–7, 279, 423; and
genre 226–7, 432, 433
identification *see* spectator-
identification
ideology 9, 34, 66, 88, 89, 120, 121,
122, 131, 142, 151, 216, 227–30,
233, 257, 331, 417; and apparatus
24–5, 85, 163, 229, 311, 369; and
auteurism 34, *36*, 37–8; and
avant-garde 41; and Black cinema
53, 58; Bollywood 69, 72, 494;
and *cinéma-vérité* 83; and class 84–5,
87, 91, 227–8, 362; and colour 93,
95; and continuity editing 135; and

costume dramas 100, 101; and
deconstruction 107, 157; and deep
focus 108, 109, 110, 136, 137; and
documentary 124, 417; and epics
139, 140; European cinema 142,
211, 214; frontier myth 66–7; and
gangster films 186, 187; and gender
87, 91, 95, 165, 175, 191, 192,
193–6, 229; and genre 175, 198–9,
229; and horror movies 225; and
lighting 195, 227, 241–3; and
mainstream cinema 131; and
melodrama 230, 245–6, 251; and
modernism 257, 260, 263; and
musical 271, 276, 278; and
myth 111, 171, 230, 283; and
naturalizing 288; and
(post-)structuralism 175, 384, 385,
390; and postcolonial theory 295;
and postmodernism 301, 302, 306,
307, 308, 310; and science fiction
337, 340; and semiology 343, 344;
and sexuality 111, 121, 347, 349,
350; and sound 358, 359; and
Soviet cinema 360–1, 362, 363,
365, 366; and spectatorship 39,
175, 228, 246, 310, 369, 386; and
stars 379; and subjectivity 344; and
textual analysis 158; war films 422,
426; and Westerns 91, 227, 431–2,
434, 435, 436, 441; and women
95, 156–7, 158, 162, 165, 170,
171, 230, 242, 251, 337, 350,
476–7; World Cinemas 460,
476–7, 481, 509–10; *see also* ISA
(ideological state apparatuses);
patriarchy
Imaginary Order 25–6, 151, 189,
192, 307, 315, 316, 322, 323,
391–2
IMAX 3-D 404
Imperial Film Company 489
independent cinema (American)
230–3
Indian cinemas 123, 395, 396,
397–8, 444, 445, 446, 448, 450,
451, 453, 454–5, 486–95; art
cinema 28, 491; Bangladesh 448,
486–7, 496; finance 487, 488–9,
491; Pakistan 445, 486, 489, 492,

495–8; Sri Lanka 448; stars 487, 488, 490; Tamil 448; women filmmakers 494, 495; *see also* Bollywood
Indian People's Theatre Association (ITPA) 397
Industrial Light and Magic (ILM) 23
internet 32, 98, 99, 113, 117, 123, 128, 148–9, 292, 308, 430, 447, 508, 509
intertextuality 39, 108, 175, 198, 202, 219, 233–4, 263–4, 266, 281, 303, 304–5, 373, 378, 386; Pan-African Cinema 464, 465
intra-diegetic sound 112, 390
Iran 508, 521–6
Iraq 466; cinema 508, 512; wars 8, 9, 128, 140, 338, 429–30, 520, 522
iris 345
ISA (ideological state apparatuses) 38, 84–5, 390
Israel 445, 446, 449, 468, 507, 508, 515–17
Italy: epics 139; neo-realism 79, 234–6, 332, 346, 354, 525; Westerns 431, 441
Ivory Coast 461

Japan 6–7, 22, 28, 94, 126, 132, 133–4, 446, 451; war films 408, 420, 425–6
JCC (Journées cinématographiques de Carthage) 455, 461, 463, 478
jouissance 251, 316, 322
jump cuts 101, 104, 122, 236–7, 345, 368, 402

Kamla Movietone (Pakistan) 496
Key Concepts in Post-Colonial Studies 293
key lighting 168, 239, 240, 241
kick-light 240
Kickstarter 144
The Kingdom TV miniseries 131
Kino-Pravda 82, 125–6
Klieg lights 238, 242
Kodachrome 93
Kohinoor Film Company 489
Kuwait 508

langue/parole 35, 36, 37, 342, 384
lap-dissolve 121
Latin American cinemas 28, 48, 295, 451, 454, 498–507; Argentina 80, 126, 394, 398, 499, 500, 501, 503, 504; Bolivia 449, 501; Brazil 79–80, 325, 398, 445, 450, 499, 500, 502–3, 504–5; Chile 449; Cuba 396, 398, 465, 500, 501–2, 503; documentary 126, 499, 501, 502; Fifth Cinema 449; Mexico 247, 366, 499, 500, 503, 506–7; Third Cinema 80, 231, 398, 400, 444–5, 446; women in 503
Law of the Father 26, 317, 319, 391
Lebanon 468, 508, 510–11, 512
lesbian filmmakers 127, 309, 325–6, 328
Libya 466
lighting 90, 114, 237–43; and avant-garde 40; back-lighting 238, 239, 240, 241, 242; British New Wave 73; *chiaroscuro* 205, 207; and class 86; and connotation 110–11; day/night for night 106, 240–1; Dogme 95 129; and feminist film theory 157; fill 239, 240, 241; and film noir 168–9, 227, 240, 311; floodlight 239; French poetic realism 184, 185; and gender 157, 195; and German expressionism 205, 207, 208, 219, 239; hair 240, 242; high/low key 168, 239, 240; and ideology 195, 227, 241–3; key 241; and motivation 263; practice 239–41; and race 242–3; separation 239; side-lighting 185, 241, 381; three-point 91, 238; and women 157, 195
The Listener 179
Lollywood 496, 498
London Film Festival 62
long shots (LS) 90, 105, 332, 352, 353
Look Back in Anger 178, 181
low-angle 239, 392
low-key lighting 168, 239, 240
Lusophone Africa 456, 457, 458

Maghreb cinemas 455, 463–4, 466, 471–9; Algeria 396, 463–4, 466, 471–5; Libya 466; Mauritania 397, 457, 461; Morocco 396, 463–4, 466, 471, 475, 477–9; Tunisia 396, 463–4, 466, 471, 475–7, 478
mainstream cinema *see* dominant/ mainstream cinema
Mali 397, 457, 459, 462, 465
manga 22, 132
Mantarray Films 507
martial arts films 6–7, 65, 479
Marxism 83–5, 125, 192, 193, 227–8, 244
Masala films 71
mash-ups 99–100
Mass Observation Unit 125
massacre movies 218, 224–6
match cuts 90, 104–5
materialist cinema 41, 366–7
Mauritania 397, 457, 461
Max Reinhardt theatre 205
MEDIA programmes 143
medium close-up shots (MCU) 352, 353
medium long shots (MLS) 352, 353
medium shots (MS) 352
Méliès, Georges 19, 92, 334
melodrama 40, 154, 175, 243–53; in Bollywood 69; China 481; and class 84, 85, 86, 243–4, 245; codes and conventions 247–50; and gender 245–7, 248, 249, 250–1; and ideology 230, 245–6; Italian 234; and masochism 247, 250, 251–2; mise-en-scène 244, 246, 249, 250, 251, 255; paranoia 245, 248, 250, 252; and psychoanalysis 224, 244, 247, 248–9, 250, 251, 321; and war films 415, 426; and women 156, 158, 159–60, 245–6, 248; and women's films 250–3
merchandising 64
Merchant-Ivory 100, 142
method acting 254
Metro-Goldwyn-Mayer (MGM) 20, 21, 270, 272, 273, 387, 423
Mexico 247, 366, 499, 500, 503, 506–7

Middle Eastern cinemas 48, 445, 446, 454, 507–26; art cinema 519; censorship 518, 519, 521, 523–5; documentary 128, 509–10, 512, 513, 517, 521, 525; Iran 508, 521–6; Iraq 508, 512; Israel 445, 446, 449, 507, 508, 515–17; Kuwait 508; Lebanon 468, 508, 510–11, 512; Palestine 299, 449, 507, 508, 511–15; Sudan 508; Syria 430, 466, 468, 508, 509; Turkey 507, 508, 517–21; women filmmakers 430, 519–20, 523, 525; women in 509, 510–11, 512–13, 515–16, 522, 523, 526
Miramax 98, 232
mirror stage 25–6, 188, 313, 315, 316, 321, 322, 341, 369, 371, 391, 392
mise-en-abîme 14, 254, 281, 304
mise-en-scène 81, 82, 101, 153, 219, 254–5, 346, 372; in adaptations 14; and auteur 33; and depth of field 109; East Asian Cinema 133; French poetic realism 183, 184; and gender 195; and German expressionism 205, 207, 208; and lighting 241; in melodrama 244, 246, 249, 250, 251, 255; and mise-en-abîme 254; in musicals 281; and race 349; and scopophilia 341; and stars 381
Misr International Film 469, 471
misrecognition 316, 391, 392
mobile phones 32, 99, 113, 430, 508
Mocap/Motion Capture 115
modernism 113, 243, 244–5, 250, 255–63; and avant-garde 257, 258, 261–2; and cinema 260–3; and ideology 259; music 267; and postcolonial theory 296; and postmodernism 300, 301, 310; and psychoanalysis 258; and realism 257, 258, 263
Monogram 68, 388, 434–5
montage 6, 7, 41, 81, 105, 109–10, 137–8, 208, 305; *see also* Soviet Union: montage
Morocco 396, 463–4, 466, 471, 475, 477–9

motion capture 78
motivation 88, 143, 236, 250–1, 263–4, 284, 287, 340, 424, 438, 500
movement image 264–6
Movie (journal) 35, 37
Mozambique 458
MPAA (Motion Picture Association of America) 77, 215
MPEAA (Motion Picture Export Association of America) 77
MPPDA (Motion Picture Producers and Distributors of America) 77
music 266–9; *see also* sound/soundtrack
musical 67, 147, 154, 269–83, 305, 355; Black American 50, 273, 278–9, 280; Bollywood 69, 70, 71, 72, 487, 489, 493, 494; codes and conventions 247, 263, 270, 275–83; colour 93, 94, 274; cross-dressing 195–6; and diegetic audiences 112; Egypt 467; folk 278; Latin America 499; lighting 240; Pakistan 496, 497–8; queer 275, 328, 494; rock 274–5, 279–80; sexuality 272, 274, 276–7, 278, 279, 281, 346; stars 270, 271, 272, 273–5, 375; war films 421
myth 91, 140, 171, 271, 283–4, 383; American Dream 90, 148, 167, 186, 277, 283, 284; cinema nôvo 79, 80; and denotation/connotation 110, 343; of the frontier 66–7; Indian cinemas 488, 489; and race 46, 59, 349; and stars 343–4, 376; and war films 414; and Westerns 320, 431–2, 441; of women 198; *see also* castration; Oedipal complex
Mythologies 35, 283, 385

NAFDEC (National Film Development Corporation) 496–7
narrative 4, 91, 122, 131, 152, 198, 263–4, 284–8, 390; adaptation 14, 15; African cinemas 457, 460–1, 463, 464, 465, 467; and animation 19, 24; art cinema 27, 29; avant-garde 40, 41; and

blockbusters 65–6, 67; Bollywood 69, 70, 71; and *Cahiers du cinéma* 81; and censorship 77; and CGI 78; cinema nôvo 80; and cinemascope 81; and costume dramas 100, 101; and counter-cinema 101; and cuts 104, 105, 237, 345; and deconstruction 107, 261, 285; and diegesis 111, 112; and editing 134–5, 136; and experimental cinema 143, 144, 145; and exploitation movies 145, 146, 147, 148–9; and film noir 168, 170, 284–5; and flashback 112, 177; and gangster films 185, 187; and genre 199, 200–1, 202; and horror 219, 220, 223; Indian cinema 488, 489, 490, 493; and lighting 237, 241, 285; melodrama 246, 248, 250, 252; and modernism 258, 259; and movement-image 264–5; and music 266; musical 271, 272, 273, 279, 282; postmodern 310; and psychoanalysis 312, 314, 320, 321; queer cinema 328–9; and realism 258, 331; science-fiction 334, 336, 337; sexuality 347, 348, 370–1; and sound 356; Soviet cinema 365; and structuralism 36, 383; war films 424, 428, 430; Westerns 432, 435, 438, 439; and women 145, 146, 147, 190, 246, 252, 284–5, 291, 322, 324, 348, 370–1; World Cinemas 400, 481, 484, 485, 499, 500, 519; *see also* classical Hollywood (narrative) cinema
naturalism 40, 110, 173, 238, 263, 273, 288, 365
naturalizing 86, 263, 273, 283, 285, 288, 331, 344, 425; class 87, 228; of gaze 190; of gender/sexuality 89, 191, 196; ideology 228, 229
neo-colonialism 395, 456, 460
neo-realism, Italian 79, 234–6, 346, 354, 471, 525
Netflix 32, 62, 113, 123
New American Cinema Group 410
New Argentine Cinema 504
New Deal (Roosevelt) 37, 230

New Documentary Movement (NDM) 485
New German cinema 27–8, 210–15, 332, 427
New Indian Cinema 489, 491, 492
New Latin American Cinema 501, 503
New Nigerian Cinema 460–1
New Scottish cinema 16, 17
New South African Cinema 461
New Theatre studios (India) 489
New Turkish Cinema 519, 520
New Wave 129, 264; British 16, 17, 180–1, 236, 332, 354; French (*Nouvelle Vague*) 27–8, 33, 81, 181–3, 210, 212, 236, 332; German 27–8, 210–15, 332, 427; Iranian 523, 524
New Zealand 350, 446, 449
Niger 457
Nigeria 459–62
night/day for night 106, 240–1
Nollywood 460
non-diegetic sound 111, 112, 129, 358
North African cinemas 128, 396, 444, 455, 463, 465–79; Algeria 396, 463, 466, 471–5; Egypt 466–71; Morocco 396, 463–4, 466, 471, 475, 477–9; Tunisia 396, 463, 466, 471, 475–7, 478; women in 349
North Korea 448, 449, 455
North Vietnam 126
Notes on Women's Cinema 157

Oberhausen Manifesto 210
Obie light 240
Oedipal complex 25, 312–14, 315, 316, 317, 319
Oedipal trajectory 89, 131, 153, 157, 158–9, 189, 225, 247, 286, 314, 320–2, 324; female 160–1, 318–20, 321–2, 324; and spectatorship theory 368, 369–70, 371
Of Grammatology 106
oppositional cinema *see* counter-cinema (oppositional)
optical sound 356–7
Orientalism 293, 295
Oscars 19, 23, 47, 55, 128, 232, 329, 379, 416, 435, 502, 504

Pakistan 445, 486, 489, 492, 495–8
Palestinian Wave films 515
Pan-African Cinema 463–5
Pantelion distribution 507
'Parallax historiography: The Flâneuse as Cyberfeminist' 118–19
parallel editing 102, 136
parallel sequencing 135
Paramount 19, 330, 387, 388–9, 433, 435
parody 57, 97, 117, 155, 187, 199, 200, 203, 303–4, 305, 333, 411, 441
parole/langue 35, 36, 37, 342, 384
Pars Film Studio 522
pastiche 303–4, 305, 306
Pathé Frères 92, 183, 387
patriarchy 61, 91, 95, 169, 191, 243; and class analysis 86, 87; and classical narrative cinema 89, 190; and female masquerade 154, 155, 214; and feminist film theory 156, 159–62, 164, 310, 346–7; and melodrama 159, 230, 246, 252, 253; and pornography 291, 292; and postmodernism 310; and psychoanalysis 189, 192–3, 313, 317–18, 321, 324, 391, 392; and science fiction 337; World Cinemas 80, 466, 476–7, 509, 513, 521
Peru 449
phallic woman 154, 159, 161, 224, 250, 253, 318, 321, 413
phallocentrism 75–6, 102, 154, 323, 324, 371
philosophy and film theory 36, 176, 177
Phonofilm 355
piracy 99–100
Pixar 23, 78
poetic realist films 168, 183–5, 234–5, 267
Poland 21
political cinema 182, 262–3, 398, 493, 498, 512, 519
politique des auteurs 28, 32–9, *36*
pornography 27, 28, 96, 103, 145, 289–93, 328, 392, 518, 519

The Post-Colonial Studies Reader 293
postcolonial theory 175, 293–300,
    445, 488
post-digital cinema 113, 115–17
postmodernism 113, 225, 255–6, 257,
    300–11, 451; and musicals 281,
    282; queer theory 326–9
post-structuralism 13, 174–5, 257,
    298, 300–1, 302, 384, 385–6; and
    auteur theory *36*, 38–9; and class
    83, 85; and subject 390–1
Prabhat studios 489
preferred reading 4, 169, 195,
    201, 266, 311, 323, 331, 332,
    353, 370
presence/absence 3, 26, 323,
    331, 381
producer 119, 311–12
production: for adaptations 16; and
    convergence 99–100; and
    digitization 113–14, 116, 117;
    and independent cinema 231,
    389; and transnationalism 133,
    408, 409
projector 18, 24, 123, 188, 322,
    403, 404
psychoanalysis 40, 177, 312–24, 347,
    438; auteurism 36, *36*, 38, 39, 386;
    and feminist film theory 163, 164,
    323, 386, 391; gaze/look 188, 190,
    191; and gender 192, 193; and
    German expressionism 204; and
    melodrama 224, 244, 247, 248–9,
    250, 251; and modernism 258; and
    patriarchy 189, 192–3, 313,
    317–18, 321, 324, 391, 392; and
    (post)-structuralism 384, 385, 386;
    and subject 192, 193, 391–2; and
    Westerns 438; *see also* castration;
    mirror stage; Oedipal trajectory;
    unconscious, the
psychological horror/thriller 220,
    224–6, 405–6
pure cinema 40, 262

queer cinema 45–6, 232, 268, 324–9,
    348; music 268; *see also* gay culture;
    homosexuality
Questions of Third Cinema 399
quota quickies 329–30

race films 49–50, 55
racism 145, 213, 222, 340, 348–9,
    457; in animations 20–1; and Black
    cinema 43, 46, 48, 50–1, 52–3, 55;
    and documentary 127, 457; and
    post-colonial theory 293; and
    science fiction 336, 340; in war
    films 428–9
Ranjit Movietone studio 489
Rank Organisation 179
rap culture 57, 58, 60, 62
realism 4, 90, 135, 173, 260, 331–2;
    and 3-D cinema 402–3; African
    cinema(s) 464, 468, 471, 472; and
    animations 19, 20, 23; art cinema
    28, 29–30; and Black cinema 52,
    62–3; British New Wave 16, 73,
    332; and CGI 78; China 482, 483;
    and cinemascope 81; and colour
    94, 95, 96, 239, 331–2; and
    comedy 97; and deep focus 109,
    136, 332, 353; and digitization
    114, 115, 118; gangster films 186,
    187; Indian cinemas 397, 448,
    491–2; and lighting 91, 238, 239,
    241, 331–2; and melodrama 250;
    and modernism 250, 257, 258,
    263, 448; and musicals 274, 275,
    282; New German cinema 213;
    and sound 356, 357, 358, 359; and
    transnationalism 454; and Westerns
    433, 438, 440; *see also* neo-realism,
    Italian; poetic realist films; social
    realism
reception theory 31, 368, 372–3
Red One 113
Red Seal studio 19
Republic 68, 388, 434–5
reverse-angle shot 90, 150, 289,
    350–1, 390
RK Films 70
RKO (Radio Pictures Incorporated)
    68, 220, 270, 387, 389
road movies 91, 275, 280, 333,
    502–3
rock musicals 279–80
rom-coms 98
rotoscope process 20
rough cut 106
Routledge 108

Royal Bioscope Company 488
RTA (Radio Telévision Arabe) 473
Russia 76, 445, 450; *see also* Soviet Union

Sankofa Collective 43, 45, 46, 401
Sao Tomé 458
SATPEC (Société Anonyme Tunisienne de Production et d'Expansion Cinématographique) 478
science-fiction 22, 91, 103, 151, 202, 218, 284, 333–40
scopophilia 67, 95, 158, 341–2, 370, 412
Scottish films 16, 17
Screen (journal) 38
seamlessness 101, 135–6, 229, 241, 260, 323, 331, 332, 369, 402
Second Cinema 394, 395, 398, 447
semiotics (semiology) 35–7, *36*, 39, 40, 85, 174, 207, 342–5, 363, 368, 383–4, 385–6; denotation/connotation 110–11, 343; and feminist film theory 157; myth 283–4, 343; and Third Cinema 401
Senegal 396, 397, 456, 457, 459, 461, 464–5
separation lighting 239
Sequence (film review) 179
sequence/sequencing 121, 345–6, 363
Serbia 429
setting 207, 263, 346, 406
sexual difference 159–60, 161, 165, 189, 191, 196, 246, 250, 319, 321, 322, 369, 412
sexual identity 127, 151, 159, 169, 194, 319, 326, 349, 371
sexuality 164–5, 169, 191, 193, 198, 204, 223, 276, 286, 313, 327, 346–50, 414; Black 45, 53, 55, 63, 248–9, 288; Bollywood 70; and costume 30; exploitation movies 145, 149; and gender 191–2, 194, 281, 327, 348; and music 268, 269; and stars 376, 378–80; war films 414; *see also* heterosexuality, dominance of; queer cinema

sexuality, female 164–5, 169, 170, 196, 291, 310, 313, 318, 325–6, 328, 337, 379, 380, 412, 437, 442; World Cinemas 349, 476–7, 510–11
Shanghai 481–2, 483
Shorey Studios (Pakistan) 496
shorts 21, 43, 44, 45, 46, 178, 180, 214, 330, 470, 475, 511
shots 40, 90–1, 351–3, 367, 390, 402; close-up (CU) 90, 91, 105, 351–2; compilation 105; and cuts 105; and digitization 114; extreme close-up (ECU) 351, 353; extreme long (EL) 352, 353; and intertextuality 234; long (LS) 90, 105, 332, 352, 353; medium (MS) 352; medium close-up (MCU) 352, 353; medium long (ML) 352, 353; in musicals 271, 272; reverse-angle 90, 150, 289, 350–1, 390; and Soviet montage 363–4; spliced 104; and subjective cinema 392–3; tracking 272, 279, 333, 407; travelling 407; unmatched 40, 122, 345, 368, 411
side-lighting 185, 241, 381
signs *see* semiotics (semiology)
silent movies 30, 31, 97, 109, 122, 196, 219, 267, 330, 334, 347, 355, 360, 361–2, 374, 375, 431, 434, 488, 521
SimulCam 115
The Skin of the Film 176
slasher movies 224–5
social networking 98, 99, 128, 430
social realism 29, 34, 40, 85, 187, 236, 354, 356, 490, 501, 518, 519, 525
socialist realism 361, 367
soft transition 121
sound/soundtrack 4, 19, 81, 106, 173, 355; diegetic 111, 129, 357; extra-diegetic 111; gangster films 185, 186; intra-diegetic 112, 390; non-diegetic 111, 129, 358; technology 356–7; theory 358–60; *see also* music
South Africa 445, 456, 458, 461
South Korea 6–7, 132, 133, 166, 446

Soviet Union 105, 122, 173, 261, 360–7, 419–20, 425; and China 482; documentary 62, 125–6, 361, 365, 419, 420; montage 40, 105, 109, 126, 137, 261, 361, 362–4, 365, 366, 367; and Sub-Saharan filmmakers 458, 459
Sovkino 361, 362
spaghetti Westerns 431, 441–2
Spain 142
spatial/temporal contiguity 367–8
special effects 7, 8, 64–5, 82, 115; see also CGI
spectator 108, 119–20, 347, 351, *351*, 368–73; action movies 5, 10; and agency 17, 27, 41; auteur theory *36*, 38, 386; and counter-cinema 101–2; and digitization 114, 118–19; female 156, 158, 160, 161, 163, 189, 190, 246, 251, 252, 342, 370, 371, 394, 437; and horror movies 226; male 27, 163, 246, 251, 341, 370; and meaning 5, 27, 108, 110, 137–8, 255, 287, 344, 353, 364; as subject 25, 26, 31, 175, 188, 322, 323, 324, 341, 372, 390, 393; see also gaze/look; voyeurism
spectator-identification 26, 39, 87, 152, 182, 186, 188, 189, 368–73, 386, 423–4
spectator-screen relationship 25, 29, 37–8, 40, 41, 158, 173, 188, 266, 322, 323, 324, 341, 363–4, 369–70, 393
spectator-text relations 37, 85, 108, 201, 228, 285–6, 287, 288, 310, 312, 369–70, 390
spliced shots 104
spotlight 239
Sri Lanka 448
stars 3, 120, 174, 215, 234, 239, 264, 373–83; acting/performance 4, 5, 375, 382–3; adaptation 14, 16; and auteur theory 37, 38; Black 55, 56, 58, 309, 349, 375, 378, 379; Bollywood 70, 71, 72–3, 487, 488, 490, 494; British New Wave 73; as capital (exchange) value 86–7,

373–5; as construct 375–8; as cultural value 379–81; deviant 378–9; and diegetic audiences 111–12; and epics 138; female 11–12, 95, 195, 242, 343–4, 374, 376, 377, 379–80, 382, 436, 437; and genre 70, 202, 375, 382; Hollywood 77, 216, 343–4, 351, 373–5, 382, 388; musical 270, 271, 272, 273–5, 375; New German cinema 212; sexuality 376, 378–80; and structuralism 385; transnational cinema 409; and war films 421; Westerns 424, 433, 434, 435, 436, 437, 438, 440–1; World Cinemas 498, 518
State Film School (Soviet Cinema) 361, 363
stereotypes 102; Black 49, 50, 54, 56, 61; gender 68, 74, 97, 347, 349, 436; sexuality 327, 349, 436; of Soviets 422; World Cinemas 490
structuralism 13, 35–7, *36*, 85, 173, 174, 200–1, 259, 283–4, 300, 312, 342, 383–6, 390; and narrative 285, 287, 288
Studio Misr 467
studio system 202, 215–16, 374, 386–90, 412; Bollywood 70; China 482, 483, 485; France 386–7; India 488, 489
Studios Atlas 478
Studios Kanzaman 478–9
sub-genre 54–5, 76, 85, 167, 188, 198, 203, 218, 247, 270, 333–4
Sub-Saharan film industry 456–63; Anglophone 456, 457, 459–63; Angola 458; Burkina Faso 397, 457, 459, 464; Cameroon 457; Chad 459; Ethiopia 465; Francophone 456, 457, 458–9; Ghana 458, 459–60, 461; Guinea-Bissau 458; Ivory Coast 461; Lusophone 456, 457, 458; Mali 397, 457, 459, 462, 465; Mauritania 397, 457, 461; Mozambique 458; Niger 457; Nigeria 459–62; Sao Tomé 458; Senegal 396, 397, 456, 457, 459,

461, 464–5; South Africa 445, 456, 458, 461
subject 175, 390–2; in Black cinema 61–3; spectator as 25, 26, 31, 175, 188, 322, 323, 324, 341, 372, 390, 393; women as 96, 102
subjective cinema 40, 392–3
subjectivity 26, 29, 112, 114, 175, 344, 369, 390–2, 400; avant-garde 40, 41; female 102, 107, 155, 157, 158, 160, 170–1, 251, 252–3, 261, 318, 319; gendered 162, 164, 175, 189, 191, 192–4; male 159, 169, 224, 319–20, 321, 348; and music 268; and postcolonial theory 297, 299; and postmodernism 307, 309, 310; and psychoanalysis 192–4, 307, 312, 313, 315, 321, 322–4; and sexuality 348
Sudan 508
surrealism 39, 40, 107, 125, 144, 393, 411
surrealist cinema 41, 261–2
suture 90, 111, 331–2, 393–4
Sweden 130
Symbolic Order 25–6, 170, 189, 192, 193, 307, 315, 316, 317, 318, 319, 322, 323, 391
syncretism 298, 502
Syria 430, 466, 468, 508, 509

Taiwan 6–7, 132, 133, 446, 451, 479–80, 485
Tamil cinemas 448
Tebessan Film Unit 471, 472
technicolour 92–3
Technicolor Motion Pictures Corporation 92–3
'Technology of Gender' 164–5
teen pics 145–50
television 57, 95, 113, 120, 123; and adaptation 12; African cinema(s) 456, 458, 471; and documentary 126; Indian cinemas 487, 491, 496; Latin America 502, 507; Middle Eastern cinemas 516, 519, 524; threat to cinema 30, 92, 119, 126, 139, 146, 211, 212, 217, 389, 487, 496, 502, 519, 524
Thailand 132, 446

Third Cinema 43, 46, 80, 231, 394–402, 444–5, 451, 462, 486–7, 492; see also World Cinema(s)
Third Cinema in the Third World: The Aesthetics of Liberation 398–9
Third World Cinema(s) 48, 80, 299, 395, 396, 399, 401, 408, 443, 444–9, 450–1; see also World Cinema(s)
three-point lighting 91, 238
thrillers 136, 240, 404–6
THX sound standard 358
time image 264–6
Tobis-Klangfilm 355, 356
Toei 22
total theory 173, 174
Trabelsi Productions 517
tracking shot 272, 279, 333, 407
transculturalism 298
transitions 40, 103–4, 105, 121, 135, 150, 237, 345, 402, 443
transnational cinema 130, 133–4, 401, 407–10, 453–4, 479, 500–1, 503–4; and musicals 275, 282
transparency/transparence 173, 179, 276, 410, 414
transvergence 296–7, 299
travelling shot 407
Tributes cyber community 32
Tropicalism 80, 501, 502
Tunisia 396, 463–4, 466, 471, 475–7, 478
Turkey 507, 508, 517–21
Turner Prize 45

UCLA Film School 52, 53–4
UFA (Universum-Film Aktiengesellschaft) 207
unconscious, the 151, 152, 190, 225, 239, 261–2, 267–8, 341, 368, 370; and psychoanalysis 312, 313, 315–16, 318, 322, 323
underground cinema 28, 145, 261, 324, 410–11
United Artists (USA) 74–5, 387–8, 420
United Artists Corporation (India) 489
United Kingdom see British cinema
United Players (Pakistan) 495

United Productions of America (UPA) 20
Universal Pictures 98, 272, 387–8, 389, 434
unmatched shots 40, 122, 345, 368, 411
'unnatural' horror movies 220, 221–4
Unthinking Eurocentrism: Multiculturalism and the Media 447

vampire horror 218, 219–20, 223, 328
Venice Film Festival 234
vertical integration 386–7, 388, 389, 412
Vic Films 74
Vietnam war 8, 75, 89, 126, 336, 427–8
Vietnamese cinema 448, 449, 455
Vimeo 99, 113, 144, 430
violence: action movies 7, 8, 10; Black cinema 46, 56, 60, 61, 63, 227; Brazil 79, 398; and censorship 76; and comedy 97; domestic 159–60, 214, 246; East Asian Cinemas 132; gangster films 159–60, 186, 187, 188, 215–16, 225, 304; Indian cinemas 71, 486, 496–7; teen pics 146; war films 425, 427; Westerns 436, 438, 440
'Visual Pleasure and Narrative Cinema' 158, 190
Vitaphone 355
voice-over 112, 135, 390
voyeurism 26–7, 40, 154, 159, 189, 190, 202, 254, 321, 322–3, 341, 369, 370, 381, 405–6, 412–13, 526

war films 6, 88–9, 198, 284, 414–30; American Civil War 428–9; blockbusters 65; Bosnia 429; Cold War 414, 423, 426–7; frontier myth 66; Iraq 414, 429–30; Syria 430; Vietnam 414, 427–8; Yom Kippur 516–17; *see also* World War One; World War Two
war technology and cinema 8, 9
Warner Brothers 8, 20, 23, 62, 179, 186–7, 272, 355, 387, 388, 389, 421, 435
Weimar studios 211
Western Electric 355, 356

Westerns 49, 66, 76, 91, 112, 136, 158–9, 175, 199, 200–1, 202–3, 430–42; Black 437–8; iconography 226–7; and ideology 91, 227, 431–2, 434, 435, 436, 441; and music 268; and myth 431–2, 441; and psychoanalysis 320, 438; sex and sexuality 436, 437, 442; spaghetti 431, 441–2; stars 424, 433, 434, 435, 436, 437, 438, 440–1; and women 436–7, 442; World Cinemas 71, 464, 499–500
White 241–2
widescreen 18, 30, 64, 202, 440, 442–3
wipe 345, 443
women: in Black American cinema 50, 52, 54, 56, 57, 58, 60–1, 63; in Black British cinema 44, 46; in British New Wave 73–4; and colour films 92, 95–6; female masquerade 154–5; and film noir 159, 168, 169, 311, 318, 320, 323, 370; and iconography 227; and melodrama 156, 158, 159–60, 245–7, 248, 249, 250–3; Middle Eastern cinemas 509, 510–11, 512–13, 515–16, 522, 523, 526; in science fiction 339, 340; in Westerns 436–7, 442; *see also* patriarchy
Women and Film 158
women filmmakers 28, 41–2, 102, 155, 214–15, 233; African cinemas 467, 469, 473, 474–7; Black 46, 63, 233, 309; Indian cinemas 494, 495; Middle Eastern cinemas 430, 519–20, 523, 525; World Cinemas 485, 497
'Women's Cinema as Countercinema' 107, 157
Woodfall Films 74, 181
World Bank 456, 464
World Cinema(s) 48, 132, 408, 443–526; syncretism 298, 464, 465, 499, 500, 501, 502, 516; terminology 443–55; transnationalism 408, 453–4, 465, 479, 500–1, 503; *see also* African cinemas; East Asian Cinemas; Indian cinemas; Latin American

cinemas; Middle Eastern cinemas;
Third Cinema
World Cinemas, women filmmakers
485, 497
World War One 17, 302, 339, 410,
414–17, 419, 521
World War Two 33, 65, 89, 167, 171,
229–30, 235, 302, 417–26, 459, 500
The Wretched of the Earth 293, 294

Yemen 466
Yesilçam 518, 519, 520
Young Mr Lincoln debate 37
YouTube 99, 113, 123, 144,
473, 508

Zagreb School 22
zombies 222
zoom 526